FINAL REPORT OF THE TRUTH AND RECONCILIATION COMMISSION OF CANADA

VOLUME ONE: SUMMARY

Honouring the Truth, Reconciling for the Future

Honouring the Truth, Reconciling for the Future

Summary of the Final Report of the Truth and Reconciliation Commission of Canada

LORIMER

JAMES LORIMER & COMPANY LTD., PUBLISHERS
TORONTO

Note to readers:
This second printing includes includes a preface and appendices added to the report by the Commission in July-August 2015. It is otherwise identical to the first printing of this edition of the report.

Truth and Reconciliation Commission of Canada, 2015
1500–360 Main Street
Winnipeg, Manitoba
R3C 3Z3
Telephone: (204) 984-5885
Toll Free: 1-888-872-5554 (1-888-TRC-5554)
Fax: (204) 984-5915
E-mail: info@trc.ca
Website: www.trc.ca

James Lorimer & Company Ltd., Publishers acknowledges the support of the Ontario Arts Council. We acknowledge the support of the Canada Council for the Arts which last year invested $24.3 million in writing and publishing throughout Canada. We acknowledge the Government of Ontario through the Ontario Media Development Corporation's Ontario Book Initiative.

Canada Council for the Arts
Conseil des Arts du Canada

Cover Design: Tyler Cleroux
Cover images: The General Synod Archives, Anglican Church of Canada, P9314-470; Library and Archives Canada (PA-010634, PA-123243); From Truth to Reconciliation: Transforming the Legacy of Residential Schools by Aboriginal Healing Foundation.

Library and Archives Canada Cataloguing

Truth and Reconciliation Commission of Canada
[Honouring the truth, reconciling for the future]
Final report of the Truth and Reconciliation Commission of Canada. Volume one : summary : honouring the truth, reconciling for the future.

Contains: Honouring the truth, reconciling for the future summary of the final report of the Truth and Reconciliation Commission of Canada.
Includes bibliographical references and index.
Issued in print and electronic formats.
ISBN 978-1-4594-1068-8 (bound).--ISBN 978-1-4594-1067-1 (paperback).--
ISBN 978-1-4594-1069-5 (epub)

1. Native peoples--Canada--Residential schools. 2. Native peoples--Canada--History. 3. Native peoples--Canada--Social conditions. 4. Native peoples--Canada--Government relations. 5. Truth and Reconciliation Commission of Canada. 6. Truth commissions--Canada. I. Title.

E96.5.T782 2015 971.004'97 C2015-904676-9
C2015-904677-7

James Lorimer & Company Ltd., Publishers
317 Adelaide Street West, Suite 1002
Toronto, ON, Canada
M5V 1P9
www.lorimer.ca

Printed and bound in Canada

Contents

Preface

Canada's residential school system for Aboriginal children was an education system in name only for much of its existence. These residential schools were created for the purpose of separating Aboriginal children from their families, in order to minimize and weaken family ties and cultural linkages, and to indoctrinate children into a new culture—the culture of the legally dominant Euro-Christian Canadian society, led by Canada's first prime minister, Sir John A. Macdonald. The schools were in existence for well over 100 years, and many successive generations of children from the same communities and families endured the experience of them. That experience was hidden for most of Canada's history, until Survivors of the system were finally able to find the strength, courage, and support to bring their experiences to light in several thousand court cases that ultimately led to the largest class-action lawsuit in Canada's history.

The Truth and Reconciliation Commission of Canada was a commission like no other in Canada. Constituted and created by the Indian Residential Schools Settlement Agreement, which settled the class actions, the Commission spent six years travelling to all parts of Canada to hear from the Aboriginal people who had been taken from their families as children, forcibly if necessary, and placed for much of their childhoods in residential schools.

This volume is a summary of the discussion and findings contained in the Commission's final multi-volume report. The Final Report discusses what the Commission did and how it went about its work, as well as what it heard, read, and concluded about the schools and afterwards, based on all the evidence available to it. This summary must be read in conjunction with the Final Report.

The Commission heard from more than 6,000 witnesses, most of whom survived the experience of living in the schools as students. The stories of that experience are sometimes difficult to accept as something that could have happened in a country such as Canada, which has long prided itself on being a bastion of democracy, peace, and kindness throughout the world. Children were abused, physically and sexually, and they died in the schools in numbers that would not have been tolerated in any school system anywhere in the country, or in the world.

But, shaming and pointing out wrongdoing were not the purpose of the Commission's mandate. Ultimately, the Commission's focus on truth determination was intended to lay the foundation for the important question of reconciliation. Now that we know about residential schools and their legacy, what do we do about it?

Getting to the truth was hard, but getting to reconciliation will be harder. It requires that the paternalistic and racist foundations of the residential school system be rejected as the basis for an ongoing relationship. Reconciliation requires that a new vision, based on a commitment to mutual respect, be developed. It also requires an understanding that the most harmful impacts of residential schools have been the loss of pride and self-respect of Aboriginal people, and the lack of respect that non-Aboriginal people have been raised to have for their Aboriginal neighbours. Reconciliation is not an Aboriginal problem; it is a Canadian one. Virtually all aspects of Canadian society may need to be reconsidered. This summary is intended to be the initial reference point in that important discussion. Reconciliation will take some time.

Introduction

For over a century, the central goals of Canada's Aboriginal policy were to eliminate Aboriginal governments; ignore Aboriginal rights; terminate the Treaties; and, through a process of assimilation, cause Aboriginal peoples to cease to exist as distinct legal, social, cultural, religious, and racial entities in Canada. The establishment and operation of residential schools were a central element of this policy, which can best be described as "cultural genocide."

Physical genocide is the mass killing of the members of a targeted group, and *biological genocide* is the destruction of the group's reproductive capacity. *Cultural genocide* is the destruction of those structures and practices that allow the group to continue as a group. States that engage in cultural genocide set out to destroy the political and social institutions of the targeted group. Land is seized, and populations are forcibly transferred and their movement is restricted. Languages are banned. Spiritual leaders are persecuted, spiritual practices are forbidden, and objects of spiritual value are confiscated and destroyed. And, most significantly to the issue at hand, families are disrupted to prevent the transmission of cultural values and identity from one generation to the next.

In its dealing with Aboriginal people, Canada did all these things.

Canada asserted control over Aboriginal land. In some locations, Canada negotiated Treaties with First Nations; in others, the land was simply occupied or seized. The negotiation of Treaties, while seemingly honourable and legal, was often marked by fraud and coercion, and Canada was, and remains, slow to implement their provisions and intent.[1]

On occasion, Canada forced First Nations to relocate their reserves from agriculturally valuable or resource-rich land onto remote and economically marginal reserves.[2]

Without legal authority or foundation, in the 1880s Canada instituted a "pass system" that was intended to confine First Nations people to their reserves.[3]

Canada replaced existing forms of Aboriginal government with relatively powerless band councils whose decisions it could override and whose leaders it could depose.[4] In the process, it disempowered Aboriginal women, who had held significant

Alert Bay, British Columbia, school, 1885. The federal government has estimated that over 150,000 students attended Canada's residential schools. Library and Archives Canada, George Dawson, PA-037934.

influence and powerful roles in many First Nations, including the Mohawks, the Carrier, and Tlingit.[5]

Canada denied the right to participate fully in Canadian political, economic, and social life to those Aboriginal people who refused to abandon their Aboriginal identity.[6]

Canada outlawed Aboriginal spiritual practices, jailed Aboriginal spiritual leaders, and confiscated sacred objects.[7]

And, Canada separated children from their parents, sending them to residential schools. This was done not to educate them, but primarily to break their link to their culture and identity. In justifying the government's residential school policy, Canada's first prime minister, Sir John A. Macdonald, told the House of Commons in 1883:

> When the school is on the reserve the child lives with its parents, who are savages; he is surrounded by savages, and though he may learn to read and write his habits, and training and mode of thought are Indian. He is simply a savage who can read and write. It has been strongly pressed on myself, as the head of the Department, that Indian children should be withdrawn as much as possible from the parental influence, and the only way to do that would be to put them in central training industrial schools where they will acquire the habits and modes of thought of white men.[8]

These measures were part of a coherent policy to eliminate Aboriginal people as distinct peoples and to assimilate them into the Canadian mainstream against their will. Deputy Minister of Indian Affairs Duncan Campbell Scott outlined the goals of that policy in 1920, when he told a parliamentary committee that "our object is to continue until there is not a single Indian in Canada that has not been absorbed into the body politic."[9] These goals were reiterated in 1969 in the federal government's *Statement on Indian Policy* (more often referred to as the "White Paper"), which sought to end Indian status and terminate the Treaties that the federal government had negotiated with First Nations.[10]

The Canadian government pursued this policy of cultural genocide because it wished to divest itself of its legal and financial obligations to Aboriginal people and gain control over their land and resources. If every Aboriginal person had been "absorbed into the body politic," there would be no reserves, no Treaties, and no Aboriginal rights.

Residential schooling quickly became a central element in the federal government's Aboriginal policy. When Canada was created as a country in 1867, Canadian churches were already operating a small number of boarding schools for Aboriginal people. As settlement moved westward in the 1870s, Roman Catholic and Protestant missionaries established missions and small boarding schools across the Prairies, in the North, and in British Columbia. Most of these schools received small, per-student grants from the federal government. In 1883, the federal government moved to establish three, large, residential schools for First Nation children in western Canada. In the following years, the system grew dramatically. According to the Indian Affairs annual report for 1930, there were eighty residential schools in operation across the country.[11] The Indian Residential Schools Settlement Agreement provided compensation to students who attended 139 residential schools and residences.[12] The federal government has estimated that at least 150,000 First Nation, Métis, and Inuit students passed through the system.[13]

Roman Catholic, Anglican, United, Methodist, and Presbyterian churches were the major denominations involved in the administration of the residential school system. The government's partnership with the churches remained in place until 1969, and, although most of the schools had closed by the 1980s, the last federally supported residential schools remained in operation until the late 1990s.

For children, life in these schools was lonely and alien. Buildings were poorly located, poorly built, and poorly maintained. The staff was limited in numbers, often poorly trained, and not adequately supervised. Many schools were poorly heated and poorly ventilated, and the diet was meagre and of poor quality. Discipline was harsh, and daily life was highly regimented. Aboriginal languages and cultures were denigrated and suppressed. The educational goals of the schools were limited and confused, and usually reflected a low regard for the intellectual capabilities of Aboriginal

The Mission, British Columbia, school opened in the early 1860s and remained in operation until 1984. Mission Community Archives.

people. For the students, education and technical training too often gave way to the drudgery of doing the chores necessary to make the schools self-sustaining. Child neglect was institutionalized, and the lack of supervision created situations where students were prey to sexual and physical abusers.

In establishing residential schools, the Canadian government essentially declared Aboriginal people to be unfit parents. Aboriginal parents were labelled as being indifferent to the future of their children—a judgment contradicted by the fact that parents often kept their children out of schools because they saw those schools, quite accurately, as dangerous and harsh institutions that sought to raise their children in alien ways. Once in the schools, brothers and sisters were kept apart, and the government and churches even arranged marriages for students after they finished their education.

The residential school system was based on an assumption that European civilization and Christian religions were superior to Aboriginal culture, which was seen as being savage and brutal. Government officials also were insistent that children be discouraged—and often prohibited—from speaking their own languages. The missionaries who ran the schools played prominent roles in the church-led campaigns to ban Aboriginal spiritual practices such as the Potlatch and the Sun Dance (more properly called the "Thirst Dance"), and to end traditional Aboriginal marriage practices. Although, in most of their official pronouncements, government and church

The goal of residential schooling was to separate children from their families, culture, and identity. Saskatchewan Archives Board, R-A2690.

officials took the position that Aboriginal people could be civilized, it is clear that many believed that Aboriginal culture was inherently inferior.

This hostility to Aboriginal cultural and spiritual practice continued well into the twentieth century. In 1942, John House, the principal of the Anglican school in Gleichen, Alberta, became involved in a campaign to have two Blackfoot chiefs deposed, in part because of their support for traditional dance ceremonies.[14] In 1947, Roman Catholic official J. O. Plourde told a federal parliamentary committee that since Canada was a Christian nation that was committed to having "all its citizens belonging to one or other of the Christian churches," he could see no reason why the residential schools "should foster aboriginal beliefs."[15] United Church official George Dorey told the same committee that he questioned whether there was such a thing as "native religion."[16]

Into the 1950s and 1960s, the prime mission of residential schools was the cultural transformation of Aboriginal children. In 1953, J. E. Andrews, the principal of the Presbyterian school in Kenora, Ontario, wrote that "we must face realistically the fact that the only hope for the Canadian Indian is eventual assimilation into the white race."[17] In 1957, the principal of the Gordon's Reserve school in Saskatchewan, Albert Southard, wrote that he believed that the goal of residential schooling was to "change the philosophy of the Indian child. In other words since they must work and live with 'whites' then they must begin to think as 'whites.'" Southard said that the Gordon's school could never have a student council, since "in so far as the Indian understands the department's policy, he is against it."[18] In a 1958 article on residential schools, senior Oblate Andre Renaud echoed the words of John A. Macdonald, arguing that when students at day schools went back to their "homes at the end of the school day and for the weekend, the pupils are re-exposed to their native culture, however diluted, from which the school is trying to separate them." A residential school, on the other hand, could "surround its pupils almost twenty-four hours a day with non-Indian Canadian culture through radio, television, public address system, movies, books, newspapers, group activities, etc."[19]

Despite the coercive measures that the government adopted, it failed to achieve its policy goals. Although Aboriginal peoples and cultures have been badly damaged, they continue to exist. Aboriginal people have refused to surrender their identity. It was the former students, the Survivors of Canada's residential schools, who placed the residential school issue on the public agenda. Their efforts led to the negotiation of the Indian Residential Schools Settlement Agreement that mandated the establishment of a residential school Truth and Reconciliation Commission of Canada (TRC).

The Survivors acted with courage and determination. We should do no less. It is time to commit to a process of reconciliation. By establishing a new and respectful relationship, we restore what must be restored, repair what must be repaired, and return what must be returned.

Reconciliation at the crossroads

To some people, *reconciliation* is the re-establishment of a conciliatory state. However, this is a state that many Aboriginal people assert never has existed between Aboriginal and non-Aboriginal people. To others, reconciliation, in the context of Indian residential schools, is similar to dealing with a situation of family violence. It's about coming to terms with events of the past in a manner that overcomes conflict and establishes a respectful and healthy relationship among people, going forward. It is in the latter context that the Truth and Reconciliation Commission of Canada has approached the question of reconciliation.

To the Commission, reconciliation is about establishing and maintaining a mutually respectful relationship between Aboriginal and non-Aboriginal peoples in this country. In order for that to happen, there has to be awareness of the past,

Survivors' Sharing Circle at Truth and Reconciliation Commission Manitoba National Event, June 2010.

acknowledgement of the harm that has been inflicted, atonement for the causes, and action to change behaviour.

We are not there yet. The relationship between Aboriginal and non-Aboriginal peoples is not a mutually respectful one. But, we believe we can get there, and we believe we can maintain it. Our ambition is to show how we can do that.

In 1996, the *Report of the Royal Commission on Aboriginal Peoples* urged Canadians to begin a national process of reconciliation that would have set the country on a bold new path, fundamentally changing the very foundations of Canada's relationship with Aboriginal peoples. Much of what the Royal Commission had to say has been ignored by government; a majority of its recommendations were never implemented. But the report and its findings opened people's eyes and changed the conversation about the reality for Aboriginal people in this country.

In 2015, as the Truth and Reconciliation Commission of Canada wraps up its work, the country has a rare second chance to seize a lost opportunity for reconciliation. We live in a twenty-first-century global world. At stake is Canada's place as a prosperous, just, and inclusive democracy within that global world. At the TRC's first National Event in Winnipeg, Manitoba, in 2010, residential school Survivor Alma Mann Scott said,

> The healing is happening—the reconciliation.... I feel that there's some hope for us not just as Canadians, but for the world, because I know I'm not the only one. I know that Anishinaabe people across Canada, First Nations, are not the only ones. My brothers and sisters in New Zealand, Australia, Ireland—there's differ-

ent areas of the world where this type of stuff happened.... I don't see it happening in a year, but we can start making changes to laws and to education systems ... so that we can move forward.[20]

Reconciliation must support Aboriginal peoples as they heal from the destructive legacies of colonization that have wreaked such havoc in their lives. But it must do even more. Reconciliation must inspire Aboriginal and non-Aboriginal peoples to transform Canadian society so that our children and grandchildren can live together in dignity, peace, and prosperity on these lands we now share.

The urgent need for reconciliation runs deep in Canada. Expanding public dialogue and action on reconciliation beyond residential schools will be critical in the coming years. Although some progress has been made, significant barriers to reconciliation remain. The relationship between the federal government and Aboriginal peoples is deteriorating. Instead of moving towards reconciliation, there have been divisive conflicts over Aboriginal education, child welfare, and justice.[21] The daily news has been filled with reports of controversial issues ranging from the call for a national inquiry on violence towards Aboriginal women and girls to the impact of the economic development of lands and resources on Treaties and Aboriginal title and rights.[22] The courts continue to hear Aboriginal rights cases, and new litigation has been filed by Survivors of day schools not covered under the Indian Residential Schools Settlement Agreement, as well as by victims of the "Sixties Scoop," which was a child-welfare policy that removed Aboriginal children from their homes and placed them with non-Aboriginal families.[23] The promise of reconciliation, which seemed so imminent back in 2008 when the prime minister, on behalf of all Canadians, apologized to Survivors, has faded.

Too many Canadians know little or nothing about the deep historical roots of these conflicts. This lack of historical knowledge has serious consequences for First Nations, Inuit, and Métis peoples, and for Canada as a whole. In government circles, it makes for poor public policy decisions. In the public realm, it reinforces racist attitudes and fuels civic distrust between Aboriginal peoples and other Canadians.[24] Too many Canadians still do not know the history of Aboriginal peoples' contributions to Canada, or understand that by virtue of the historical and modern Treaties negotiated by our government, we are all Treaty people. History plays an important role in reconciliation; to build for the future, Canadians must look to, and learn from, the past.

As Commissioners, we understood from the start that although reconciliation could not be achieved during the TRC's lifetime, the country could and must take ongoing positive and concrete steps forward. While the Commission has been a catalyst for deepening our national awareness of the meaning and potential of reconciliation, it will take many heads, hands, and hearts, working together, at all levels of society to maintain momentum in the years ahead. It will also take sustained political will at all levels of government and concerted material resources.

The thousands of Survivors who publicly shared their residential school experiences at TRC events in every region of this country have launched a much-needed dialogue about what is necessary to heal themselves, their families, communities, and the nation. Canadians have much to benefit from listening to the voices, experiences, and wisdom of Survivors, Elders, and Traditional Knowledge Keepers—and much more to learn about reconciliation. Aboriginal peoples have an important contribution to make to reconciliation. Their knowledge systems, oral histories, laws, and connections to the land have vitally informed the reconciliation process to date, and are essential to its ongoing progress.

At a Traditional Knowledge Keepers Forum sponsored by the TRC, Anishinaabe Elder Mary Deleary spoke about the responsibility for reconciliation that both Aboriginal and non-Aboriginal people carry. She emphasized that the work of reconciliation must continue in ways that honour the ancestors, respect the land, and rebalance relationships. She said,

> I'm so filled with belief and hope because when I hear your voices at the table, I hear and know that the responsibilities that our ancestors carried ... are still being carried ... even through all of the struggles, even through all of what has been disrupted ... we can still hear the voice of the land. We can hear the care and love for the children. We can hear about our law. We can hear about our stories, our governance, our feasts, [and] our medicines.... We have work to do. That work we are [already] doing as [Aboriginal] peoples. Our relatives who have come from across the water [non-Aboriginal people], you still have work to do on your road.... The land is made up of the dust of our ancestors' bones. And so to reconcile with this land and everything that has happened, there is much work to be done ... in order to create balance.[25]

At the Victoria Regional Event in 2012, Survivor Archie Little said,

> [For] me reconciliation is righting a wrong. And how do we do that? All these people in this room, a lot of non-Aboriginals, a lot of Aboriginals that probably didn't go to residential school; we need to work together.... My mother had a high standing in our cultural ways. We lost that. It was taken away.... And I think it's time for you non-Aboriginals ... to go to your politicians and tell them that we have to take responsibility for what happened. We have to work together.[26]

The Reverend Stan McKay of the United Church, who is also a Survivor, believes that reconciliation can happen only when everyone accepts responsibility for healing in ways that foster respect. He said,

> [There must be] a change in perspective about the way in which Aboriginal peoples would be engaged with Canadian society in the quest for reconciliation.... [We cannot] perpetuate the paternalistic concept that only Aboriginal peoples are in need of healing.... The perpetrators are wounded and marked by history in

Aboriginal and non-Aboriginal representatives from 4Rs Youth Movement present the 4Rs drum made by Nisga'a artist Mike Dangeli, as an expression of reconciliation at the Truth and Reconciliation Commission Alberta National Event, March 2014.

> ways that are different from the victims, but both groups require healing.... How can a conversation about reconciliation take place if all involved do not adopt an attitude of humility and respect? ... We all have stories to tell and in order to grow in tolerance and understanding we must listen to the stories of others.[27]

Over the past five years, the Truth and Reconciliation Commission of Canada urged Canadians not to wait until our final report was issued before contributing to the reconciliation process. We have been encouraged to see that across the country, many people have been answering that call.

The youth of this country are taking up the challenge of reconciliation. Aboriginal and non-Aboriginal youth who attended TRC National Events made powerful statements about why reconciliation matters to them. At the Alberta National Event in Edmonton in March 2014, an Indigenous youth spoke on behalf of a national Indigenous and non-Indigenous collaboration known as the "4Rs Youth Movement." Jessica Bolduc said,

> We have re-examined our thoughts and beliefs around colonialism, and have made a commitment to unpack our own baggage, and to enter into a new relationship with each other, using this momentum, to move our country forward, in light of the 150th anniversary of the Confederation of Canada in 2017.

Truth and Reconciliation Commission Traditional Knowledge Keepers Forum, June 2014. University of Manitoba, Adam Dolman.

> At this point in time, we ask ourselves, "What does that anniversary mean for us, as Indigenous youth and non-Indigenous youth, and how do we arrive at that day with something we can celebrate together?"... Our hope is that, one day, we will live together, as recognized nations, within a country we can all be proud of.[28]

In 2013, at the British Columbia National Event in Vancouver, where over 5,000 elementary and secondary school students attended Education Day, several non-Aboriginal youth talked about what they had learned. Matthew Meneses said, "I'll never forget this day. This is the first day they ever told us about residential schools. If I were to see someone who's Aboriginal, I'd ask them if they can speak their language because I think speaking their language is a pretty cool thing." Antonio Jordao said, "It makes me sad for those kids. They took them away from their homes—it was torture, it's not fair. They took them away from their homes. I don't agree with that. It's really wrong. That's one of the worst things that Canada did." Cassidy Morris said, "It's good that we're finally learning about what happened." Jacqulyn Byers told us, "I hope that events like this are able to bring closure to the horrible things that happened, and that a whole lot of people now recognize that the crime happened and that we need to make amends for it."[29]

At the same National Event, TRC Honorary Witness Patsy George paid tribute to the strength of Aboriginal women and their contributions to the reconciliation process despite the oppression and violence they have experienced. She said,

> Women have always been a beacon of hope for me. Mothers and grandmothers in the lives of our children, and in the survival of our communities, must be recognized and supported. The justified rage we all feel and share today must be turned into instruments of transformation of our hearts and our souls, clearing the ground for respect, love, honesty, humility, wisdom and truth. We owe it to all those who suffered, and we owe it to the children of today and tomorrow. May this day and the days ahead bring us peace and justice.[30]

Aboriginal and non-Aboriginal Canadians from all walks of life spoke to us about the importance of reaching out to one another in ways that create hope for a better future. Whether one is First Nations, Inuit, Métis, a descendant of European settlers, a member of a minority group that suffered historical discrimination in Canada, or a new Canadian, we all inherit both the benefits and obligations of Canada. We are all Treaty people who share responsibility for taking action on reconciliation.

Without truth, justice, and healing, there can be no genuine reconciliation. Reconciliation is not about "closing a sad chapter of Canada's past," but about opening new healing pathways of reconciliation that are forged in truth and justice. We are mindful that knowing the truth about what happened in residential schools in and of itself does not necessarily lead to reconciliation. Yet, the importance of truth telling in its own right should not be underestimated; it restores the human dignity of victims of violence and calls governments and citizens to account. Without truth, justice is not served, healing cannot happen, and there can be no genuine reconciliation between Aboriginal and non-Aboriginal peoples in Canada. Speaking to us at the Traditional Knowledge Keepers Forum in June of 2014, Elder Dave Courchene posed a critical question: "When you talk about truth, whose truth are you talking about?"[31]

The Commission's answer to Elder Courchene's question is that by *truth,* we mean not only the truth revealed in government and church residential school documents, but also the truth of lived experiences as told to us by Survivors and others in their statements to this Commission. Together, these public testimonies constitute a new oral history record, one based on Indigenous legal traditions and the practice of witnessing.[32] As people gathered at various TRC National Events and Community Hearings, they shared the experiences of truth telling and of offering expressions of reconciliation.

Over the course of its work, the Commission inducted a growing circle of TRC Honorary Witnesses. Their role has been to bear official witness to the testimonies of Survivors and their families, former school staff and their descendants, government and church officials, and any others whose lives have been affected by the residential schools. Beyond the work of the TRC, the Honorary Witnesses have pledged their commitment to the ongoing work of reconciliation between Aboriginal and non-Aboriginal peoples. We also encouraged everyone who attended TRC National Events or Community Hearings to see themselves as witnesses also, with an obligation to find ways of making reconciliation a concrete reality in their own lives, communities, schools, and workplaces.

As Elder Jim Dumont explained at the Traditional Knowledge Keepers Forum in June 2014, "in Ojibwe thinking, to speak the truth is to actually speak from the heart."[33] At the Community Hearing in Key First Nation, Saskatchewan, in 2012, Survivor Wilfred Whitehawk told us he was glad that he disclosed his abuse.

> I don't regret it because it taught me something. It taught me to talk about truth, about me, to be honest about who I am.... I am very proud of who I am today. It took me a long time, but I'm there. And what I have, my values and belief systems are mine and no one is going to impose theirs on me. And no one today is going to take advantage of me, man or woman, the government or the RCMP, because I have a voice today. I can speak for me and no one can take that away.[34]

Survivor and the child of Survivors Vitaline Elsie Jenner said, "I'm quite happy to be able to share my story.... I want the people of Canada to hear, to listen, for it is the truth.... I also want my grandchildren to learn, to learn from me that, yes, it did happen."[35]

Another descendant of Survivors, Daniel Elliot, told the Commission,

> I think all Canadians need to stop and take a look and not look away. Yeah, it's embarrassing, yeah, it's an ugly part of our history. We don't want to know about it. What I want to see from the Commission is to rewrite the history books so that other generations will understand and not go through the same thing that we're going through now, like it never happened.[36]

President of the Métis National Council Clement Chartier spoke to the Commission about the importance of truth to justice and reconciliation. At the Saskatchewan National Event, he said,

> The truth is important. So I'll try to address the truth and a bit of reconciliation as well. The truth is that the Métis Nation, represented by the Métis National Council, is not a party to the Indian Residential Schools Settlement Agreement.... And the truth is that the exclusion of the Métis Nation or the Métis as a people is reflected throughout this whole period not only in the Indian Residential Schools Settlement Agreement but in the apology made by Canada as well....
>
> We are, however, the products ... of the same assimilationist policy that the federal government foisted upon the Treaty Indian kids. So there ought to be some solution.... The Métis boarding schools, residential schools, are excluded. And we need to ensure that everyone was aware of that and hopefully some point down the road, you will help advocate and get, you know, the governments or whoever

> is responsible to accept responsibility and to move forward on a path to reconciliation, because reconciliation should be for all Aboriginal peoples and not only some Aboriginal peoples.[37]

At the British Columbia National Event, the former lieutenant-governor of British Columbia, the Honourable Steven Point, said,

> And so many of you have said today, so many of the witnesses that came forward said, "I cannot forgive. I'm not ready to forgive." And I wondered why. Reconciliation is about hearing the truth, that's for sure. It's also about acknowledging that truth. Acknowledging that what you've said is true. Accepting responsibility for your pain and putting those children back in the place they would have been, had they not been taken from their homes....
>
> What are the blockages to reconciliation? The continuing poverty in our communities and the failure of our government to recognize that "Yes, we own the land." Stop the destruction of our territories and for God's sake, stop the deaths of so many of our women on highways across this country.... I'm going to continue to talk about reconciliation, but just as important, I'm going to foster healing in our own people, so that our children can avoid this pain, can avoid this destruction and finally, take our rightful place in this "Our Canada."[38]

When former residential school staff attended public TRC events, some thought it was most important to hear directly from Survivors, even if their own perspectives and memories of the schools might differ from those of the Survivors. At a Community Hearing in Thunder Bay, Ontario, Merle Nisley, who worked at the Poplar Hill residential school in the early 1970s, said,

> I think it would be valuable for people who have been involved in the schools to hear stories personally. And I also think it would be valuable, when it's appropriate ... [for] former students who are on the healing path to ... hear some of our stories, or to hear some of our perspectives. But I know that's a very difficult thing to do.... Certainly this is not the time to try to ask all those former students to sit and listen to the rationale of the former staff because there's just too much emotion there ... and there's too little trust ... you can't do things like that when there's low levels of trust. So I think really a very important thing is for former staff to hear the stories and to be courageous enough just to hear them.... Where wrongs were done, where abuses happened, where punishment was over the top, and wherever sexual abuse happened, somehow we need to courageously sit and talk about that, and apologize. I don't know how that will happen.[39]

Nisley's reflections highlight one of the difficulties the Commission faced in trying to create a space for respectful dialogue between former residential school students and staff. While, in most cases, this was possible, in other instances, Survivors and their family members found it very difficult to listen to former staff, particularly if they perceived the speaker to be an apologist for the schools.

At the TRC Victoria Regional Event, Brother Tom Cavanaugh, the district superior of the Oblates of Mary Immaculate for British Columbia and the Yukon, spoke about his time as a supervisor at the Christie residential school.

> What I experienced over the six years I was at Christie residential school was a staff, Native and non-Native alike, working together to provide as much as possible, a safe loving environment for the children attending Christie school. Was it a perfect situation? No, it wasn't a perfect situation ... but again, there didn't seem to be, at that time, any other viable alternative in providing a good education for so many children who lived in relatively small and isolated communities.

Survivors and family members who were present in the audience spoke out, saying, "Truth, tell the truth." Brother Cavanaugh replied, "If you give me a chance, I will tell you the truth." When TRC Chair Justice Murray Sinclair intervened to ask the audience to allow Brother Cavanaugh to finish his statement, he was able to do so without further interruption. Visibly shaken, Cavanaugh then went on to acknowledge that children had also been abused in the schools, and he condemned such actions, expressing his sorrow and regret for this breach of trust.

> I can honestly say that our men are hurting too because of the abuse scandal and the rift that this has created between First Nations and church representatives. Many of our men who are still working with First Nations have attended various truth and reconciliation sessions as well as Returning to Spirit sessions, hoping to bring about healing for all concerned. The Oblates desire healing for the abused and for all touched by the past breach of trust. It is our hope that together we can continue to build a better society.[40]

Later that same day, Ina Seitcher, who attended the Christie residential school, painted a very different picture of the school from what Brother Cavanaugh had described.

> I went to Christie residential school. This morning I heard a priest talking about his Christie residential school. I want to tell him [about] my Christie residential school. I went there for ten months. Ten months that impacted my life for fifty years. I am just now on my healing journey.... I need to do this, I need to speak out. I need to speak for my mom and dad who went to residential school, for my aunts, my uncles, all that are beyond now.... All the pain of our people, the hurt, the anger.... That priest that talked about how loving that Christie residential school was—it was not. That priest was most likely in his office not knowing what was going on down in the dorms or in the lunchroom.... There were things that happened at Christie residential school, and like I said, I'm just starting my healing journey. There are doors that I don't even want to open. I don't even want to open those doors because I don't know what it would do to me.[41]

These two, seemingly irreconcilable, truths are a stark reminder that there are no easy shortcuts to reconciliation. The fact that there were few direct exchanges at TRC events between Survivors and former school staff indicates that for many, the time for reconciliation had not yet arrived. Indeed, for some, it may never arrive. At the Manitoba National Event in 2010, Survivor Evelyn Brockwood talked about why it is important to ensure that there is adequate time for healing to occur in the truth and reconciliation process. She said,

> When this came out at the beginning, I believe it was 1990, about residential schools, people coming out with their stories, and ... I thought the term, the words they were using, were truth, healing and reconciliation. But somehow it seems like we are going from truth telling to reconciliation, to reconcile with our white brothers and sisters. My brothers and sisters, we have a lot of work to do in the middle. We should really lift up the word healing.... Go slow, we are going too fast, too fast.... We have many tears to shed before we even get to the word reconciliation.[42]

To determine the truth and to tell the full and complete story of residential schools in this country, the TRC needed to hear from Survivors and their families, former staff, government and church officials, and all those affected by residential schools. Canada's national history in the future must be based on the truth about what happened in the residential schools. One hundred years from now, our children's children and their children must know and still remember this history, because they will inherit from us the responsibility of ensuring that it never happens again.

What is reconciliation?

During the course of the Commission's work, it has become clear that the concept of reconciliation means different things to different people, communities, institutions, and organizations. The TRC mandate describes reconciliation as "an ongoing individual and collective process, and will require commitment from all those affected including First Nations, Inuit and Métis former Indian Residential School (IRS) students, their families, communities, religious entities, former school employees, government and the people of Canada. Reconciliation may occur between any of the above groups."[43]

The Commission defines *reconciliation* as an ongoing process of establishing and maintaining respectful relationships. A critical part of this process involves repairing damaged trust by making apologies, providing individual and collective reparations, and following through with concrete actions that demonstrate real societal change. Establishing respectful relationships also requires the revitalization of Indigenous law and legal traditions. It is important that all Canadians understand how traditional

First Nations, Inuit, and Métis approaches to resolving conflict, repairing harm, and restoring relationships can inform the reconciliation process.

Traditional Knowledge Keepers and Elders have long dealt with conflicts and harms using spiritual ceremonies and peacemaking practices, and by retelling oral history stories that reveal how their ancestors restored harmony to families and communities. These traditions and practices are the foundation of Indigenous law; they contain wisdom and practical guidance for moving towards reconciliation across this land.[44]

As First Nations, Inuit, and Métis communities access and revitalize their spirituality, cultures, languages, laws, and governance systems, and as non-Aboriginal Canadians increasingly come to understand Indigenous history within Canada, and to recognize and respect Indigenous approaches to establishing and maintaining respectful relationships, Canadians can work together to forge a new covenant of reconciliation.

Despite the ravages of colonialism, every Indigenous nation across the country, each with its own distinctive culture and language, has kept its legal traditions and peacemaking practices alive in its communities. While Elders and Knowledge Keepers across the land have told us that there is no specific word for "reconciliation" in their own languages, there are many words, stories, and songs, as well as sacred objects such as wampum belts, peace pipes, eagle down, cedar boughs, drums, and regalia, that are used to establish relationships, repair conflicts, restore harmony, and make peace. The ceremonies and protocols of Indigenous law are still remembered and practised in many Aboriginal communities.

At the TRC Traditional Knowledge Keepers Forum in June 2014, TRC Survivor Committee member and Elder Barney Williams told us that

> from sea to sea, we hear words that allude to ... what is reconciliation? What does healing or forgiveness mean? And how there's parallels to all those words that the Creator gave to all the nations.... When I listen and reflect on the voices of the ancestors, your ancestors, I hear my ancestor alluding to the same thing with a different dialect.... My understanding [of reconciliation] comes from a place and time when there was no English spoken ... from my grandmother who was born in the 1800s.... I really feel privileged to have been chosen by my grandmother to be the keeper of our knowledge.... What do we need to do? ... We need to go back to ceremony and embrace ceremony as part of moving forward. We need to understand the laws of our people.[45]

At the same Forum, Elder Stephen Augustine explained the roles of silence and negotiation in Mi'kmaq law. He said silence is a concept, and can be used as a consequence for a wrong action or to teach a lesson. Silence is employed according to proper procedures, and ends at a particular time too. Elder Augustine suggested that there is both a place for talking about reconciliation and a need for quiet reflection.

Reconciliation cannot occur without listening, contemplation, meditation, and deeper internal deliberation. Silence in the face of residential school harms is an appropriate response for many Indigenous peoples. We must enlarge the space for respectful silence in journeying towards reconciliation, particularly for Survivors who regard this as key to healing. There is a place for discussion and negotiation for those who want to move beyond silence. Dialogue and mutual adjustment are significant components of Mi'kmaq law. Elder Augustine suggested that other dimensions of human experience—our relationships with the earth and all living beings—are also relevant in working towards reconciliation. This profound insight is an Indigenous law, which could be applied more generally.[46]

Elder Reg Crowshoe told the Commission that Indigenous peoples' world views, oral history traditions, and practices have much to teach us about how to establish respectful relationships among peoples and with the land and all living things. Learning how to live together in a good way happens through sharing stories and practising reconciliation in our everyday lives.

> When we talk about the concept of reconciliation, I think about some of the stories that I've heard in our culture and stories are important.... These stories are so important as theories but at the same time stories are important to oral cultures. So when we talk about stories, we talk about defining our environment and how we look at authorities that come from the land and how that land, when we talk about our relationship with the land, how we look at forgiveness and reconciliation is so important when we look at it historically.
>
> We have stories in our culture about our superheroes, how we treat each other, stories about how animals and plants give us authorities and privileges to use plants as healing, but we also have stories about practices. How would we practise reconciliation? How would we practise getting together to talk about reconciliation in an oral perspective? And those practices are so important.[47]

As Elder Crowshoe explained further, reconciliation requires talking, but our conversations must be broader than Canada's conventional approaches. Reconciliation between Aboriginal and non-Aboriginal Canadians, from an Aboriginal perspective, also requires reconciliation with the natural world. If human beings resolve problems between themselves but continue to destroy the natural world, then reconciliation remains incomplete. This is a perspective that we as Commissioners have repeatedly heard: that reconciliation will never occur unless we are also reconciled with the earth. Mi'kmaq and other Indigenous laws stress that humans must journey through life in conversation and negotiation with all creation. Reciprocity and mutual respect help sustain our survival. It is this kind of healing and survival that is needed in moving forward from the residential school experience.

Over the course of its work, the Commission created space for exploring the meanings and concepts of reconciliation. In public Sharing Circles at National Events and

Truth and Reconciliation Commission Northern National Event, Inuvik, Northwest Territories, June 2011.

Community Hearings, we bore witness to powerful moments of truth sharing and humbling acts of reconciliation. Many Survivors had never been able to tell their own families the whole truth of what happened to them in the schools. At hearings in Regina, Saskatchewan, Elder Kirby Littletent said, "I never told, I just told my children, my grandchildren I went to boarding school, that's all. I never shared my experiences."[48]

Many spoke to honour the memory of relatives who have passed on. Simone, an Inuk Survivor from Chesterfield Inlet, Nunavut, said,

> I'm here for my parents—'Did you miss me when I went away?' 'Did you cry for me?'—and I'm here for my brother, who was a victim, and my niece at the age of five who suffered a head injury and never came home, and her parents never had closure. To this day, they have not found the grave in Winnipeg. And I'm here for them first, and that's why I'm making a public statement.[49]

Others talked about the importance of reconciling with family members, and cautioned that this process is just beginning. Patrick Etherington, a Survivor from St. Anne's residential school in Fort Albany, Ontario, walked with his son and others from Cochrane, Ontario, to the National Event in Winnipeg. He said that the walk helped him to reconnect with his son, and that he "just wanted to be here because I feel this process that we are starting, we got a long ways to go."[50]

We saw the children and grandchildren of Survivors who, in searching for their own identity and place in the world, found compassion and gained new respect for their relatives who went to the schools, once they heard about and began to understand their experiences. At the Northern National Event in Inuvik, Northwest Territories, Maxine Lacorne said,

> As a youth, a young lady, I talk with people my age because I have a good understanding. I talk to people who are residential school Survivors because I like to hear their stories, you know, and it gives me more understanding of my parents.... It is an honour to be here, to sit here among you guys, Survivors. Wow. You guys are strong people, you guys survived everything. And we're still going to be here. They tried to take us away. They tried to take our language away. You guys are still here, we're still here. I'm still here.[51]

We heard about children whose small acts of everyday resistance in the face of rampant abuse, neglect, and bullying in the schools were quite simply heroic. At the TRC British Columbia National Event, Elder Barney Williams said that "many of us, through our pain and suffering, managed to hold our heads up ... we were brave children."[52] We saw old bonds of childhood friendship renewed as people gathered and found each other at TRC-sponsored events. Together, they remembered the horrors they had endured even as they recalled with pride long-forgotten accomplishments in various school sports teams, music, or art activities. We heard from resilient, courageous Survivors who, despite their traumatic childhood experiences, went on to become influential leaders in their communities and in all walks of Canadian life, including politics, government, law, education, medicine, the corporate world, and the arts.

We heard from officials representing the federal government that administered the schools. In a Sharing Circle at the Manitoba National Event, the Honourable Chuck Strahl (then minister of Indian Affairs and Northern Development Canada) said,

> Governments like to write ... policy, and they like to write legislation, and they like to codify things and so on. And Aboriginal people want to talk about restoration, reconciliation, forgiveness, about healing ... about truth. And those things are all things of the heart and of relationship, and not of government policy. Governments do a bad job of that.[53]

Church representatives spoke about their struggles to right the relationship with Aboriginal peoples. In Inuvik, Anglican Archbishop Fred Hiltz told us that

> as a Church, we are renewing our commitment to work with the Assembly of First Nations in addressing long-standing, Indigenous justice issues. As a Church, we are requiring anyone who serves the Church at a national level to go through anti-racism training.... We have a lot to do in our Church to make sure that racism is eliminated.[54]

Educators told us about their growing awareness of the inadequate role that post-secondary institutions played in training the teachers who taught in the schools. They have pledged to change educational practices and curriculum to be more inclusive of Aboriginal knowledge and history. Artists shared their ideas and feelings about truth and reconciliation through songs, paintings, dance, film, and other media. Corporations provided resources to bring Survivors to events, and, in some cases, some of their own staff and managers.

For non-Aboriginal Canadians who came to bear witness to Survivors' life stories, the experience was powerful. One woman said simply, "By listening to your story, my story can change. By listening to your story, I can change."[55]

Reconciliation as relationship

In its 2012 *Interim Report*, the TRC recommended that federal, provincial, and territorial governments, and all parties to the Settlement Agreement, undertake to meet and explore the *United Nations Declaration on the Rights of Indigenous Peoples*, as a framework for reconciliation in Canada. We remain convinced that the *United Nations Declaration* provides the necessary principles, norms, and standards for reconciliation to flourish in twenty-first-century Canada.

A reconciliation framework is one in which Canada's political and legal systems, educational and religious institutions, the corporate sector and civic society function in ways that are consistent with the principles set out in the *United Nations Declaration on the Rights of Indigenous Peoples*, which Canada has endorsed. Together, Canadians must do more than just *talk* about reconciliation; we must learn how to *practise* reconciliation in our everyday lives—within ourselves and our families, and in our communities, governments, places of worship, schools, and workplaces. To do so constructively, Canadians must remain committed to the ongoing work of establishing and maintaining respectful relationships.

For many Survivors and their families, this commitment is foremost about healing themselves, their communities, and nations, in ways that revitalize individuals as well as Indigenous cultures, languages, spirituality, laws, and governance systems. For governments, building a respectful relationship involves dismantling a centuries-old political and bureaucratic culture in which, all too often, policies and programs are still based on failed notions of assimilation. For churches, demonstrating long-term commitment requires atoning for actions within the residential schools, respecting Indigenous spirituality, and supporting Indigenous peoples' struggles for justice and equity. Schools must teach history in ways that foster mutual respect, empathy, and engagement. All Canadian children and youth deserve to know Canada's honest history, including what happened in the residential schools, and to appreciate the rich history and knowledge of Indigenous nations who continue to make such a strong contribution to Canada, including our very name and collective identity as a country. For Canadians from all walks of life, reconciliation offers a new way of living together.

Commission activities

The Truth and Reconciliation Commission of Canada was established in 2008 under the terms of the Indian Residential Schools Settlement Agreement. The Commission was mandated to

- reveal to Canadians the complex truth about the history and the ongoing legacy of the church-run residential schools, in a manner that fully documents the individual and collective harms perpetrated against Aboriginal peoples, and honours the resilience and courage of former students, their families, and communities; and
- guide and inspire a process of truth and healing, leading toward reconciliation within Aboriginal families, and between Aboriginal peoples and non-Aboriginal communities, churches, governments, and Canadians generally. The process was to work to renew relationships on a basis of inclusion, mutual understanding, and respect.

More specifically, the Commission was required to hold seven National Events; to gather documents and statements about residential schools and their legacy; to fund truth and reconciliation events at the community level; to recommend commemoration initiatives to the federal government for funding; to set up a research centre that will permanently house the Commission's records and documents, which the parties were obligated to provide to the Commission, thereby establishing a living legacy of the Commission's work; and to issue a report with recommendations.

Three Commissioners were appointed in 2008: the Honourable Justice Harry Laforme as Chair, and Jane Brewin-Morley and Claudette Dumont-Smith. They resigned shortly after being appointed and new Commissioners were appointed. The current Commissioners, the Honourable Justice Murray Sinclair as Chair, and Chief Wilton Littlechild and Dr. Marie Wilson, were appointed to replace them in 2009 by the parties to the Settlement Agreement.

An Indian Residential School Survivor Committee (IRSSC) provided advice and support to the Commission. Its members included John Banksland, Inuvialuit from the Northwest Territories; John Morriseau, Métis from Grand Rapids, Manitoba; Eugene

The Indian Residential School Survivor Committee. Left to right, starting in the back: John Morrisseau, Terri Brown, Eugene Arcand, Doris Young, Lottie May Johnson, John Banksland. Seated: Rebekah Uqi Williams, Barney Williams, Gordon Williams, Commissioner Chief Wilton Littlechild, Madeleine Basile.

Arcand, Cree from Muskeg Lake First Nation, Saskatchewan; Madeleine Basile, a member of the Atikamekw Nation from Wemotaci, Québec; Lottie May Johnson, Mi'kmaq from Eskasoni, Nova Scotia; Rebekah Uqi Williams, Inuk from Nunavut; Doris Young, Cree from The Pas, Manitoba; Barney Williams Jr. (Taa-eee-sim-chilth), Nuu-chah-nulth from the Tla-o-qui-aht First Nations on Meares Island, British Columbia; Gordon Williams, from the Peguis First Nation in Manitoba, now residing in Ontario; and Kukdookaa Terri Brown, from the Tahltan Nation in British Columbia. Raymond Arcand, a former chief of the Alexander First Nation near Edmonton, Alberta, served on the Survivors Committee until his death in November 2009.

The Commission received continuing support throughout its mandate from the parties to the Settlement Agreement. Regular All Parties Meetings were held to discuss opportunities and challenges that arose in fulfilling the Commission's goals. The Commission worked with the parties to address topics such as document collection, communications, public education, and Survivor travel support for completion of the Commission's work. Representatives of the parties also took part in working groups at the national and local levels to support the Commission in planning and implementing its National and Regional Events.

The Commission established its head office in Winnipeg, Manitoba, retained a small Ottawa office, and opened satellite offices in Vancouver, British Columbia; Hobbema, Alberta; and Yellowknife, Northwest Territories.

In recognition of the unique cultures of the Inuit, and of their experiences and the impacts of residential schools on them, the Commission also established an Inuit Sub-Commission. Seven regional liaison officers were hired with advice from the IRSSC and were assigned responsibility to work in the following regions: Québec and Atlantic Canada, Ontario, Manitoba, Saskatchewan, Alberta, British Columbia, and Yukon and the Northwest Territories.

Meeting from coast to coast

During the six years of its operation, the Commission held events in all parts of the country. The largest and most visible of these were the National Events held in Winnipeg, Inuvik, Halifax, Saskatoon, Montreal, Vancouver, and Edmonton between June 2010 and March 2014. The Commission estimates there were as many as 155,000 visits to the seven National Events; over 9,000 residential school Survivors registered to attend them (while many others attended but did not register).[1] To augment its statement-gathering activities and to help build public interest and participation in its National Events, the TRC organized Regional Events in Victoria and Whitehorse. It also held 238 days of local hearings in seventy-seven communities across the country.

The Commission also sponsored "town halls" on reconciliation at its Victoria Regional Event in April 2012 and at subsequent National Events as a means to draw a greater number of visitors into conversation with the TRC about healing and reconciliation. Members of the general public were invited to come forward at the town halls to share information about what they are already doing to support reconciliation and to describe their ideas about what more needs to be done.

Statement gathering

Until the Commission was established, the voices of those who were most directly affected by the residential school experience, particularly the former students, had largely been missing from the historical record. The Commission made a commitment to offer everyone involved with the residential school system the opportunity to speak about their experience. The Commission received over 6,750 statements from Survivors of residential schools, members of their families, and other individuals who wished to share their knowledge of the residential school system and its legacy.

The Kuujjuaq community hearing, Nunavik, March 2011. Photo credit: Piita Irniq.

Statements were gathered at public Sharing Panels and Sharing Circles at National, Regional, and Community Events and at Commission hearings. They were also collected through private conversations with statement gatherers. The Commission also gathered statements in correctional institutions in Kenora, Ontario, and Yellowknife, Northwest Territories, recognizing the high rates of incarceration of Aboriginal peoples and how the experience of residential schools has contributed to the kinds of personal struggles that may lead to incarceration. Health-support workers, cultural support workers, and/or professional therapists were present everywhere the Commission gathered statements to provide support and counselling as needed.

In an effort to understand all aspects of the residential school experience, the Commission also made a concerted effort to gather statements from former staff of residential schools. With the assistance of the church parties to the Settlement Agreement, the Commission conducted ninety-six separate interviews with former staff and the children of former staff. In addition, the Commission received statements from former staff and their family members at its National and Regional Events and Community Hearings. The statements gathered will form part of a permanent collection of documents relating to residential schools.

Under the terms of the Settlement Agreement, the federal government and the churches were obliged to turn over relevant documents in their possession to the Commission. The Commission has had to overcome some significant challenges to completing this task, and has had to seek court direction to resolve disputes with the parties about the handing over of documents. Once the Commission's document-collection processes began, it became increasingly apparent that Canada would not produce numerous documents that appeared to be relevant to the Commission's work.[2]

First, the federal government declined to produce all relevant documents held in its national archives, Library and Archives Canada. Library and Archives Canada took a position that it was not required to organize and produce to the Commission up to five million documents in its possession that were directly relevant to residential schools. Library and Archives Canada maintained that the Settlement Agreement required it to provide the Commission only with access to its archives. A lengthy process, which included the filing of written arguments, affidavit evidence, and court-ordered mediation between Canada and the Commission, culminated in a hearing before the Honourable Justice Stephen Goudge of the Ontario Court of Appeal (sitting as an Ontario Superior Court Justice) on December 20 and 21, 2012. By judgment dated January 30, 2013, Justice Goudge ruled in favour of the Commission's position, that the terms of the Settlement Agreement provided that all relevant documents held by the Government of Canada, wherever they may be held, must be produced to the Commission.[3] Following the ruling, the Government of Canada began producing documents from Library and Archives Canada to the Commission.

Less than a year later, the Commission once again was required to go to court for judicial guidance respecting Canada's document-production obligations. At issue were records in the possession of the Government of Canada from the investigation of the Ontario Provincial Police (OPP) into abuse at the Fort Albany, Ontario, residential school in Ontario (also known as the St. Anne's school). The Commission had attempted to obtain the OPP documents from both the OPP and the federal government. Although the OPP did not respond to the Commission's overtures, it later took the position that it required judicial authorization to produce the records to the Commission, but it did not oppose disclosure. The Government of Canada, however, opposed production of the documents to both the Commission and to the lawyers for residential school Survivors. The government took the position that it was barred from producing the documents because they obtained the documents from the OPP subject to an undertaking that it would not, in turn, disclose the documents to any third party.[4] The Government of Canada further argued that it was not obliged to seek documents from third parties for disclosure to the Commission and that any disclosure to the Commission of the St. Anne's records would amount to burdening the Government of Canada with this obligation.[5]

On October 18, 2013, the Commission filed a Request for Directions as to whether the Government of Canada was obliged to disclose the records of the OPP investigation of St. Anne's. After argument before the Honourable Justice Paul Perell of the Ontario Superior Court of Justice on December 17 and 18, 2013, the court ordered Canada to produce its documents to the Commission.[6] Recognizing that Canada had only a subset of the OPP investigation documents, the court went one step further and ordered that the OPP produce all the investigation records in its possession to the Commission.[7]

Less than a year after Justice Perell rendered his decision in the St. Anne's case, the Commission was faced with yet another document-collection issue that called for court guidance. The documents at issue were records from the Independent Assessment Process (IAP). The IAP is one of the components of the Settlement Agreement. The IAP is an adjudicative process for financial compensation to residential school Survivors who suffered serious abuse at residential schools. Consequently, the body that administers the IAP process, the Indian Residential Schools Adjudication Secretariat (IRSAS), is in possession of a wealth of documents relevant to the legacy of Indian residential schools.

The Residential Schools Settlement Agreement provides that Survivors who go through the IAP can give their consent to have their statements and testimony archived with the archive created by the National Centre for Truth and Reconciliation for future research. The intention was apparently to eliminate the need for a Survivor to have to testify before an IAP adjudicator, and then have to repeat the same story to the TRC. From mid-2010 to early 2012, the Commission engaged in negotiations with IRSAS to archive and preserve those documents. The parties' discussions focused on the development of a consent form for IAP claimants to sign during the IAP process. The consent form would explain to IAP Survivors how their information would be shared with the Commission and it would allow them to provide written consent to the sharing of their stories. The Commission had discovered that the IAP staff and adjudicators had repeatedly failed to inform Survivors of their right to have their statements delivered to the TRC's archive, and, instead, had required an undertaking of strict confidentiality of all parties to the IAP hearings, including the Survivors themselves. In June 2014, the chief adjudicator of IAP publicly announced that he supported the immediate destruction of all documents related to the adjudication of claims by residential school Survivors.

The Commission emphasized that the requirement of strict confidentiality imposed by IRSAS was incompatible with the terms of the Settlement Agreement. Furthermore, the Commission stated that the destruction of some IAP documents would constitute a major loss for future generations of Canadians. The Commission and IRSAS were unable to come to an agreement as to the mechanisms for allowing the Commission to access the documents, and the matter was brought before Justice Perell for direction.

In the hearing held from July 14 to 16, 2014, the Commission advanced the position that a notice program should be ordered by the court, which would allow IAP claimants to be notified that they may share their IAP testimony with the Commission should they so desire. The Commission narrowed the categories of documents it sought to preserve in recognition of the legitimate privacy interests of IAP Survivors. The Commission argued that it sought only to archive the IAP applications, transcripts, and audio recordings from IAP hearings and IAP adjudicator decisions.

On August 6, 2014, Justice Perell delivered reasons in which he held that the IAP documents would be subject to a fifteen-year retention period, during which a notice program to Survivors would be administered by the Commission or the National Centre for Truth and Reconciliation.[8] The precise parameters of the notice program would be decided by the court in a subsequent hearing. Importantly, Justice Perell ruled that every copy of the IAP documents, no matter who possesses them, must be destroyed after the conclusion of the retention period if the IAP claimants do not consent to having the documents archived.

Justice Perell also directed that the Commission commence a further Request for Direction and return to court for a determination of the issue of the parameters of a notice program to inform Survivors about their option to archive their IAP applications, the transcripts and audio recordings of their hearings, and the decisions with the Commission. The Commission (along with the National Centre for Truth and Reconciliation) has been entrusted to commence further proceedings to determine how to engage claimants in the exercise of ensuring informed consent on the issue of the fate of their records.

Justice Perell's ruling is the subject of appeal.[9] The Commission feels strongly that any steps taken to ensure that the informed consent of Survivors is obtained must be robust, culturally appropriate, and sensitive to the challenges of contacting Survivors, some of whom cannot read, have problems speaking English or French, and reside in remote locations. The Commission believes that it is not enough that a notice simply be mailed to the last known address of Survivors. A multi-faceted and personal approach that actively engages Survivors is required.

The Commission strongly believes that Survivors' stories must be preserved. The loss of these documents would be a blow to Canada's national memory of a significant historic injustice, could contribute to the possibility that future generations would never know of the abuses in residential schools, and could contribute to the argument of those who would assert that this never happened. The Commission intends to vigorously advance a position to prevent the destruction of the IAP documents without the informed consent of individual Survivors.

Concert showcasing local Aboriginal talent, Atlantic National Event, Halifax, 2011.

The National Events

The four-day National Events served as important milestones over the course of the Commission's six-year mandate. As well as offering a forum for Survivors and their families, the National Events raised public awareness of the history and legacy of residential schools. They also built momentum for the collective journey towards national healing and reconciliation—a journey that will need to continue well beyond the Commission's closing ceremony.

Traditional knowledge and practice guided much of the Commission's work. The Seven Sacred Teachings of the Anishinaabe—Respect, Courage, Love, Truth, Humility, Honesty, and Wisdom—served as the themes for the seven National Events, and ceremony and traditional observance played an important part in the National Events. Sacred fires were lit at the beginning of each National Event and every day's proceedings began with ceremony. As much as possible, the observances followed the cultural protocols, customs, and traditions of the Aboriginal peoples in whose territories the Commission was a guest. Similar ceremonies were held at Regional and Community Events.

Education was a key part of the Commission's mandate. Although students were involved in all the National Events, beginning at the third National Event in Halifax, and at all subsequent National Events, local schools were invited to send students to

Her Excellency, the Honorable Michaëlle Jean at the Winnipeg National Event, June 2010.

take part in a day of learning. These Education Days were also part of Regional Events on Vancouver Island and in Yukon, and a stand-alone event was organized in Toronto for students from the surrounding area. In all, more than 15,000 students participated by attending presentations and cultural performances, observing and taking part in panel discussions and workshops, and visiting displays in the Learning Places.

The Commission organized activities to help teachers prepare their students for the National Event Education Days and consider follow-up activities in the classroom. In addition, the Commission worked with universities, educators, and Traditional Knowledge Keepers to hold academic conferences and panel discussions at its National Events on a number of topics related to the legacy of colonialism and residential schools, and on healing and reconciliation.

Cultural performances were also key elements of each National Event. Through concerts and talent shows, thousands of people experienced some of the richness of Aboriginal culture, language, and artistic expression—cultural forms that residential schools sought to destroy.

The Commission was able to share its work with Canadians everywhere, and with a worldwide audience, through live streaming of the National Events on the internet and additional postings on the Commission's website and social-media platforms. There were over 93,350 views of its webcast during the National Events from at least sixty-two different countries.

Witnessing and expressions of reconciliation

One of the goals of the Commission's public outreach activities was to encourage Canadians from all backgrounds to learn more about the legacy of residential schools and take part in the work of reconciliation by witnessing Commission events.

Inviting respected guests to represent all witnesses at an event or the conduct of business gives the event import and legitimacy and is in keeping with the traditions of many Aboriginal cultures. To this end, the Commission appointed Honorary Witnesses to be present at its major events. Her Excellency, the Right Honourable Michaëlle Jean, who served as governor general of Canada at the start of the Commission's mandate, agreed to be the Commission's first Honorary Witness. She began her role as a witness by hosting a special event called Witnessing the Future at Rideau Hall in Ottawa on October 15, 2009. In the following years, the current governor general of Canada, His Excellency the Right Honourable David Johnston; two former prime ministers, the Right Honourable Joe Clark and the Right Honourable Paul Martin; two former national Aboriginal leaders, Chief Phil Fontaine of the Assembly of First Nations and former Ambassador Mary Simon, Past President of Inuit Tapiriit Kanatami; and a host of other distinguished individuals have all agreed to serve as Honorary Witnesses.

The Commission also invited Canadians to make expressions of reconciliation at its National and Regional Events. The Commission received more than 180 expressions from individuals, organizations, and the parties to the Settlement Agreement who wished to publicly state their commitment to the journey of healing and reconciliation and speak to the ways in which they are contributing to that journey. Documents and items related to each expression of reconciliation were placed in ceremony in the beautiful Bentwood Box created by Coast Salish carver Luke Marston. The box will become part of the permanent legacy of the TRC housed in the National Centre for Truth and Reconciliation.

Education and outreach

The Commission worked throughout its mandate to educate the public about the legacy of residential schools and to invite and encourage public participation in its events and activities. The Commission took part in nearly 900 separate events. These included a number of special events that the TRC organized with various partners to engage with Survivors' organizations and other Aboriginal groups, youth, women, faith communities, the philanthropic community, and new Canadians. The Commission also accepted invitations to share information about its work internationally through the United Nations, the International Centre for Transitional Justice, and a number of university law faculties.[10]

In the final year of its mandate, the Commission organized two events to gather additional information for its report. It held a Traditional Knowledge Keepers Forum to learn how traditional Aboriginal knowledge can contribute to reconciliation. It also organized, with the support of Égale Canada Human Rights Trust, a forum with members of the Two Spirit community to discuss the impacts of residential schools and what needs to be done to support reconciliation and healing in that community.

Commemoration and community events funding

The Settlement Agreement allocated $20 million for commemoration initiatives. These were defined as initiatives that would honour, educate, remember, memorialize, and pay tribute to former residential school students, their families, and their communities. The Commission issued two separate calls for commemoration project proposals. The maximum funding award for a project advanced by a single group was $50,000. Up to ten communities could collaborate on a submission for a maximum contribution of $500,000, and a commemoration project of national scope was eligible for a contribution of up to $2 million. The Commission recommended 152 projects to the federal Department of Aboriginal Affairs and Northern Development for funding, and 143 projects were approved.[11]

It is important to note that the Commission's work inspired others to undertake commemorative projects using their own resources. One example is the Government of Canada's decision to memorialize the legacy of Indian residential schools through the permanent installation of a stained-glass window in the Centre Block of Parliament Hill. The design selected for the window was created by Aboriginal artist Christi Belcourt and is entitled *Giniigaaniimenaaning* or *Looking Ahead.*

The Commission issued a separate call for proposals for community events and allocated funding to approved projects up to a maximum of $15,000 per event. The TRC supported seventy-five community events, which were designed to promote healing and reconciliation by developing collective community narratives about the impact of the residential school system on former students, families, and communities.

Interim report

In February 2012, as part of its mandate, the Commission issued an *Interim Report* with findings and recommendations, along with a short history of residential schools, entitled *They Came for the Children.* Because recommendations in the *Interim Report* dealt with gaps in school curricula, the Commission made it a priority to meet with provincial and territorial education ministers to advocate for the development of

Tens of thousands participate in the Walk for Reconciliation through downtown Vancouver, September 2013.

curriculum on the legacy of residential schools and the mandatory adoption of that curriculum in all jurisdictions.

National Centre for Truth and Reconciliation

The Commission was mandated to create a national research centre, which would hold all the material created and received as part of its work. The centre is intended to be accessible to Survivors, their families, and communities, as well as to the general public. The Commission held a forum in March 2011 to consult with national and international experts on establishing such a centre. This informed the Commission's subsequent call for proposals to house the centre.

The Commission reviewed a number of proposals for housing the research centre and, in June 2013, announced that the University of Manitoba had been selected to become the permanent host of the National Centre for Truth and Reconciliation (NCTR). The NCTR is governed by a Trust Deed and Administrative Agreement signed by the Commission and the university. A Governing Circle and Survivors Circle play important roles in ensuring the promises undertaken to Survivors are honoured.

The NCTR also works in direct partnership with a growing number of universities, colleges, and other organizations across the country, including: the University of

British Columbia, the University of Winnipeg, l'Université de St. Boniface, Carleton University, the University of Regina, Lakehead University, University College of the North, Algoma University, Red River College, the Archives of Manitoba, the Canadian Museum for Human Rights, the National Association of Friendship Centres, the Legacy of Hope Foundation, and le Centre du patrimoine. The goal is to create the broadest possible network from coast to coast to coast.

Officially opening in the summer of 2015, the NCTR will be the permanent home for all statements, documents, and other materials gathered by the Commission. In future, it will house other Indigenous collections. The NCTR will encourage and engage in respectful dialogue on many issues that hinder or foster reconciliation. It will ensure that:

- Survivors and their families have access to their own history;
- educators can share the residential school history with new generations of students;
- researchers can delve more deeply into the residential school experience and legacy;
- the public can access historical records and other materials to help foster reconciliation and healing; and
- the history and legacy of the residential school system are never forgotten.

The search to understand the truth about Indian residential schools has taken the Truth and Reconciliation Commission to all parts of Canada. The Commission has listened to thousands of Survivors give their accounts of the residential school experience and how that experience has shaped their lives. The Commission has explored what the legacy of the residential school system has meant to Aboriginal people in particular and to Canada as a whole. This journey led the Commission to chart some of the pathways described in this report that may lead eventually to reconciliation within this country.

The history

A group of students and parents from the Saddle Lake Reserve, en route to the Methodist-operated school in Red Deer, Alberta. Woodruff, Library and Archives Canada, PA-040715.

It can start with a knock on the door one morning. It is the local Indian agent, or the parish priest, or, perhaps, a Mounted Police officer. The bus for residential school leaves that morning. It is a day the parents have long been dreading. Even if the children have been warned in advance, the morning's events are still a shock. The officials have arrived and the children must go.

For tens of thousands of Aboriginal children for over a century, this was the beginning of their residential schooling. They were torn from their parents, who often surrendered them only under threat of prosecution. Then, they were hurled into a strange and frightening place, one in which their parents and culture would be demeaned and oppressed.

For Frederick Ernest Koe, it started when the Anglican minister and the Mounted Police arrived with a message that he had to leave his parents' home in Aklavik in the Northwest Territories that morning. "And I didn't get to say goodbye to my dad or my brother Allan, didn't get to pet my dogs or nothing."[1]

The day she left for the Lestock, Saskatchewan, school, Marlene Kayseas's parents drove her into the town of Wadena. "There was a big truck there. It had a back door and that truck was full of kids and there was no windows on that truck."[2] Larry Beardy travelled by train from Churchill, Manitoba, to the Anglican residential school in Dauphin, Manitoba—a journey of 1,200 kilometres. As soon as they realized that they were leaving their parents behind, the younger children started crying. At every stop, the train took on more children and they would start to cry as well. "That train I want to call that train of tears."[3] Florence Horassi was taken to the Fort Providence, Northwest Territories, school in a small airplane. On its way to the school, the plane stopped at a number of small communities to pick up students. "When the plane took off, there's about six or five older ones, didn't cry, but I saw tears come right out of their eyes. Everybody else was crying. There's a whole plane crying. I wanted to cry, too, 'cause my brother was crying, but I held my tears back and held him."[4]

The arrival at school was often even more traumatizing than the departure from home or the journey. Lily Bruce's parents were in tears when they left her and her brother at the Alert Bay, British Columbia, school.[5] At Fort Chipewyan in northern Alberta, Vitaline Elsie Jenner fought to stay with her mother. "I was screaming and hollering. And in my language I said, 'Mama, Mama, *kâya nakasin*' and in English it was, 'Mom, Mom, don't leave me.' 'Cause that's all I knew was to speak Cree. And so the nun took us."[6]

Nellie Ningewance was raised in Hudson, Ontario, and went to the Sioux Lookout, Ontario, school in the 1950s and 1960s. "When we arrived we had to register that we had arrived, then they took us to cut our hair."[7] Bernice Jacks became very frightened when her hair was cut on her arrival at a school in the Northwest Territories. "I could see my hair falling. And I couldn't do nothing. And I was so afraid my mom ... I wasn't thinking about myself. I was thinking about Mom. I say, 'Mom's gonna be really mad. And June is gonna be angry. And it's gonna be my fault.'"[8]

Marthe Basile-Coocoo recalled feeling a chill on first seeing the Pointe Bleue, Québec, school.

> It was something like a grey day, it was a day without sunshine. It was, it was the impression that I had, that I was only six years old, then, well, the nuns separated us, my brothers, and then my uncles, then I no longer understood. Then that, that was a period there, of suffering, nights of crying, we all gathered in a corner, meaning that we came together, and there we cried. Our nights were like that.[9]

Pauline St-Onge was traumatized by just the sight of the Sept-Îles school in Québec. She fought back when her father tried to take her into the school. "I thought in my child's head I said: 'you would ... you would make me go there, but I will learn nothing, nothing, nothing.'"[10]

Campbell Papequash was taken, against his will, to residential school in 1946. "And after I was taken there they took off my clothes and then they deloused me. I didn't know what was happening but I learned about it later, that they were delousing me; 'the dirty, no-good-for-nothing savages, lousy.'"[11]

Roy Denny was perplexed and frightened by the clothing that the priests and sisters wore at the Shubenacadie, Nova Scotia, school. "We were greeted by this man dressed in black with a long gown. That was the priest, come to find later. And the

"The only building that I knew up to that time, that moment in my life was the one-storey house that we had. And when I got to the residential school, I seen this big monster of a building, and I've never seen any buildings that, that large, that high." – Calvin Myerion, Brandon, Manitoba, school. United Church of Canada Board of Home Missions, 86.158P/ 22N.

nuns with their black, black outfits with the white collar and a white, white collar and, like a breastplate of white."[12] Calvin Myerion recalled being overwhelmed by the size of the Brandon, Manitoba, school. "The only building that I knew up to that time, that moment in my life was the one-storey house that we had. And when I got to the residential school, I seen this big monster of a building, and I've never seen any buildings that, that large, that high."[13] Archie Hyacinthe compared the experience to that of being captured and taken into captivity. "That's when the trauma started for me, being separated from my sister, from my parents, and from our, our home. We were no longer free. It was like being, you know, taken to a strange land, even though it was our, our, our land, as I understood later on."[14] When she first went to the Amos, Québec, school, Margo Wylde could not speak any French. "I said to myself, 'How am I going to express myself? How will I make people understand what I'm saying?' And I wanted to find my sisters to ask them to come and get me. You know it's sad to say, but I felt I was a captive."[15]

On their arrival at residential school, students often were required to exchange the clothes they were wearing for school-supplied clothing. This could mean the loss of homemade clothing that was of particular value and meaning to them. Murray Crowe said his clothes from home were taken and burned at the school that he attended in

Boys at the Sioux Lookout, Ontario, school in the 1930s in their school uniforms. General Synod Archives; Anglican Church of Canada; P75-103-S7-127.

northwestern Ontario.[16] When Wilbur Abrahams's mother sent him to the Alert Bay school in British Columbia, she outfitted him in brand-new clothes. When he arrived at the school, he was told to hand in this outfit in exchange for school clothing. "That was the last time I saw my new clothes. Dare not ask questions."[17] Martin Nicholas of Nelson House, Manitoba, went to the Pine Creek, Manitoba, school in the 1950s. "My mom had prepared me in Native clothing. She had made me a buckskin jacket, beaded with fringes.... And my mom did beautiful work, and I was really proud of my clothes. And when I got to residential school, that first day I remember, they stripped us of our clothes."[18] On her arrival at the Presbyterian school in Kenora, Ontario, Lorna Morgan was wearing "these nice little beaded moccasins that my grandma had made me to wear for school, and I was very proud of them." She said they were taken from her and thrown in the garbage.[19]

Gilles Petiquay, who attended the Pointe Bleue school, was shocked by the fact that each student was assigned a number. "I remember that the first number that I had at the residential school was 95. I had that number—95—for a year. The second number was number 4. I had it for a longer period of time. The third number was 56. I also kept it for a long time. We walked with the numbers on us."[20]

Older brothers were separated from younger brothers, older sisters were separated from younger sisters, and brothers and sisters were separated from each other. Wilbur Abrahams climbed up the steps to the Alert Bay school behind his sisters and started following them to the girls' side of the school. Then, he felt a staff member pulling him by the ear, telling him to turn the other way. "I have always believed that, I think at that particular moment, my spirit left."[21]

When Peter Ross was enrolled at the Immaculate Conception school in Aklavik, Northwest Territories, it was the first time he had ever been parted from his sisters. He said that in all the time he was at the school, he was able to speak with them only at Christmas and on Catholic feast days.[22] Daniel Nanooch recalled that he talked with his sister only four times a year at the Wabasca, Alberta, school. "They had a fence in the playground. Nobody was allowed near the fence. The boys played on this side, the girls played on the other side. Nobody was allowed to go to that fence there and talk to the girls through the fence or whatever, you can't."[23]

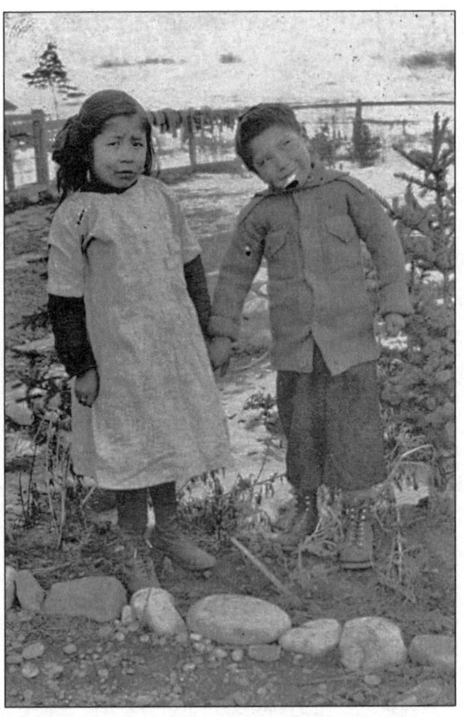

The strict segregation of the sexes at the schools meant that brothers and sisters were quickly separated from one another. General Synod Archives, Anglican Church of Canada, P7538-635.

The only reason Bernice Jacks had wanted to go to residential school was to be with her older sister. But once she was there, she discovered they were to sleep in separate dormitories. On the occasions when she slipped into the older girls' dormitory and crawled into her sister's bed, her sister scolded her and sent her away: "My sister never talked to me like that before."[24] Helen Kakekayash's older sister tried to comfort her when she first arrived at the McIntosh, Ontario, school. She recalled that "she would try to talk to me, and she would get spanked."[25] Bernard Catcheway said that even though he and his sister were both attending the Pine Creek school, they could not communicate with each other. "I couldn't talk to her, I couldn't wave at her. If you did you'd get, you know a push in the head by a nun."[26] On her second day at the Kamloops school in British Columbia, Julianna Alexander went to speak to her brother. "Did I ever get a good pounding and licking, get over there, you can't go over there, you can't talk to him, you know. I said, 'Yeah, but he's my brother.'"[27]

Taken from their homes, stripped of their belongings, and separated from their siblings, residential school children lived in a world dominated by fear, loneliness, and lack of affection.

William Herney, who attended the Shubenacadie school in Nova Scotia, recalled the first few days in the school as being frightening and bewildering. "Within those few days, you had to learn, because otherwise you're gonna get your head knocked off. Anyway, you learned everything. You learned to obey. And one of the rules that you didn't break, you obey, and you were scared, you were very scared."[28] Raymond Cutknife recalled that when he attended the Hobbema school in Alberta, he "lived with fear."[29] Of his years in two different Manitoba schools, Timothy Henderson said, "Every day was, you were in constant fear that, your hope was that it wasn't you today that we're going to, that was going to be the target, the victim. You know, you weren't going to have to suffer any form of humiliation."[30] Shirley Waskewitch said that in Kindergarten at the Catholic school in Onion Lake, Saskatchewan, "I learned the fear, how to be so fearful at six years old. It was instilled in me."[31]

At the Fort Alexander, Manitoba, school, Patrick Bruyere used to cry himself to sleep. "There was, you know, a few nights I remember that I just, you know, cried myself to sleep, I guess, because of, you know, wanting to see my mom and dad."[32] Ernest Barkman, who attended the Pine Creek school, recalled, "I was really lonely and I cried a lot, my brother who was with me said I cried a lot."[33] Paul Dixon, who attended schools in Québec and Ontario, said that at night, children tried to weep silently. "If one child was caught crying, eh, oh, everybody was in trouble."[34] Betsy Annahatak grew up in Kangirsuk, in northern Québec, which was then known as Payne Bay. When her parents were on the land, she lived in a small hostel in the community. "When one person would start crying, all the, all the little girls would start crying; all of us. We were different ages. And we would cry like little puppies or dogs, right into the night, until we go to sleep; longing for our families."[35]

Students' hearts were hardened. Rick Gilbert remembered the Williams Lake, British Columbia, school as a loveless place. "That was one thing about this school was that when you got hurt or got beat up or something, and you started crying, nobody comforted you. You just sat in the corner and cried and cried till you got tired of crying then you got up and carried on with life."[36] Nick Sibbeston, who was placed in the Fort Providence school in the Northwest Territories at the age of five, recalled it as a place where children hid their emotions. "In residential school you quickly learn that you should not cry. If you cry you're teased, you're shamed out, you're even punished."[37] One former student said that during her time at the Sturgeon Landing school in Saskatchewan, she could not recall a staff member ever smiling at a child.[38] Jack Anawak recalled of his time at Chesterfield Inlet, in what is now Nunavut, in the 1950s that "there was no love, there was no feelings, it was just supervisory."[39] Lydia Ross, who attended the Cross Lake school in Manitoba, said, "If you cried, if you got hurt and cried, there was no, nobody to, nobody to comfort, comfort you, nobody to put their arms."[40] Stephen Kakfwi, who attended Grollier Hall in Inuvik and Grandin College in Fort Smith, Northwest Territories, said this lack of compassion affected the way students treated one another. "No hugs, nothing, no comfort. Everything that, I think, happened in the residential schools, we picked it up: we didn't get any hugs; you ain't going to get one out of me I'll tell you that."[41] Victoria McIntosh said that life at the Fort Alexander, Manitoba, school taught her not to trust anyone. "You learn not to cry anymore. You just get harder. And yeah, you learn to shut down."[42]

These accounts all come from statements made by former residential school students to the Truth and Reconciliation Commission of Canada. These events all took place in Canada within the realm of living memory. Like previous generations of residential school children, these children were sent to what were, in most cases, badly constructed, poorly maintained, overcrowded, unsanitary fire traps. Many children were fed a substandard diet and given a substandard education, and worked too hard. For far too long, they died in tragically high numbers. Discipline was harsh and unregulated; abuse was rife and unreported. It was, at best, institutionalized child neglect.

The people who built, funded, and operated the schools offered varying justifications for this destructive intrusion into the lives of Aboriginal families. Through it, they wished to turn the children into farmers and farmers' wives. They wanted the children to abandon their Aboriginal identity and come to know the Christian god. They feared that if the children were not educated, they would be a menace to the social order of the country. Canadian politicians wished to find a cheap way out of their long-term commitments to Aboriginal people. Christian churches sought government support for their missionary efforts. The schools were part of the colonization and conversion of Aboriginal people, and were intended to bring civilization and salvation to their children. These were the rationales that were used to justify making the lives of so many children so unhappy.

The imperial context

> The whole part of the residential school was a part of a bigger scheme of colonization. There was intent; the schools were there with the intent to change people, to make them like others and to make them not fit.
>
> And today, you know, we have to learn to decolonize.
>
> — Shirley Flowers, Statement to the Truth and Reconciliation Commission of Canada[43]

The mandate of the Truth and Reconciliation Commission of Canada requires it to report on "the history, purpose, operation and supervision" of Canada's residential schools. These schools were part of a process that brought European states and Christian churches together in a complex and powerful manner. The history of

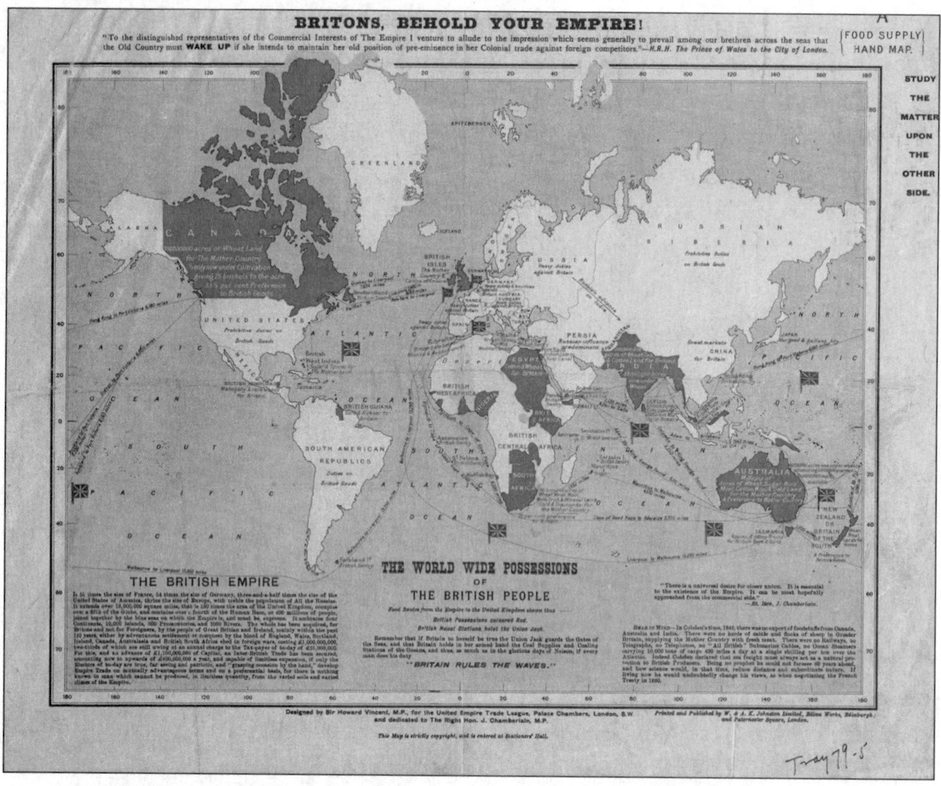

By the end of the nineteenth century, the British Empire spanned the globe. This map was intended to convince Britons of the benefits of empire. In it, Canada was primarily valued for its farmland and as a captive market for British goods. Library and Archives Canada, NMC8207, e011076405-v8.

the schools can be best understood in the context of this relationship between the growth of global, European-based empires and the Christian churches. Starting in the sixteenth century, European states gained control of Indigenous peoples' lands throughout the world. It was an era of mass migration. Millions of Europeans arrived as colonial settlers in nearly every part of the world. Millions of Africans were transported in the European-led slave trade, in which coastal Africans collaborated. Traders from India and China spread throughout the Red Sea and Indian Ocean, bringing with them indentured servants whose lives were little different from those of slaves.[44] The activities of explorers, farmers, prospectors, trading companies, or missionaries often set the stage for expansionary wars, the negotiation and the breaking of Treaties, attempts at cultural assimilation, and the exploitation and marginalization of the original inhabitants of the colonized lands.[45] Over time, Indigenous children in places as distant from one another as East Africa, Australia, and Siberia would be separated from their parents and sent to residential schools.[46]

The spread of European-based empires was set in motion in the fifteenth century when the voyages of maritime explorers revealed potential sources of new wealth to the monarchs of Europe. The Spanish conquest of the Aztecs and the Incas gave Spain, and ultimately all of Europe, access to the resources of North and South America. This not only enriched the Old World, but it also unleashed an unceasing wave of migration, trade, conquest, and colonization.[47] It marked the beginning of the creation of a European-dominated global economy. Although it was led initially by Spain and Portugal, this era of imperial expansion came to be directed by Holland, France, and, in the end, most stunningly by Britain.[48]

Empires were established militarily. They engaged in extensive and violent wars with one another, maintained a military presence on their frontiers, and conducted innumerable military campaigns to put down nationalist uprisings.[49] Colonies were established to be exploited economically. The benefits of empire could come directly as taxes, as precious metals, or as raw materials for industries in the homeland. Colonies often were required to purchase their imports solely from the homeland, making them a captive market.[50]

The mere presence of Indigenous people in these newly colonized lands blocked settler access to the land.[51] To gain control of the land of Indigenous people, colonists negotiated Treaties, waged wars of extinction, eliminated traditional landholding practices, disrupted families, and imposed a political and spiritual order that came complete with new values and cultural practices.[52] Treaty promises often went unfulfilled. United States General William Tecumseh Sherman is quoted as having said, "We have made more than one thousand treaties with the various Indian tribes, and have not kept one of them." In commenting on Sherman's statement in 1886, C. C. Painter, a critic of American Indian policy, observed that the United States had

> never intended to keep them. They were not made to be kept, but to serve a present purpose, to settle a present difficulty in the easiest manner possible, to acquire a desired good with the least possible compensation, and then to be disregarded as soon as this purpose was tainted and we were strong enough to enforce a new and more profitable arrangement.[53]

The outcome was usually disastrous for Indigenous people, while the chief beneficiaries of empire were the colonists and their descendants. Many of the colonies they settled grew to be among the most prosperous societies in the late nineteenth- and early twentieth-century world.[54] Settler colonies often went on to gain political independence. In the case of Canada and the United States of America, these newly created nations spread across North America. As they expanded, they continued to incorporate Indigenous peoples and their lands into empires. Colonialism remains an ongoing process, shaping both the structure and the quality of the relationship between the settlers and Indigenous peoples.

At their height, the European empires laid claim to most of the earth's surface and controlled the seas.[55] Numerous arguments were advanced to justify such extravagant interventions into the lands and lives of other peoples. These were largely elaborations on two basic concepts: 1) the Christian god had given the Christian nations the right to colonize the lands they 'discovered' as long as they converted the Indigenous populations; and 2) the Europeans were bringing the benefits of civilization (a concept that was intertwined with Christianity) to the 'heathen.' In short, it was contended that people were being colonized for their own benefit, either in this world or the next.

In the fifteenth century, the Roman Catholic Church, building on the traditions of the Roman Empire, conceived of itself as the guardian of a universal world order.[56] The adoption of Christianity within the Roman Empire (which defined itself as 'civilized') reinforced the view that to be civilized was to be Christian. The Catholic papacy was already playing a role in directing and legitimizing colonialism prior to Christopher Columbus's voyages to the Americas in the 1490s, largely by granting Catholic kingdoms the right to colonize lands they 'discovered.'[57] In 1493, Pope Alexander VI issued the first of four orders, referred to as "papal bulls" (a term that takes its name from the Latin word for the mould used to seal the document), that granted most of North and South America to Spain, the kingdom that had sponsored Columbus's voyage of the preceding year. These orders helped shape the political and legal arguments that have come to be referred to as the "Doctrine of Discovery," which was used to justify the colonization of the Americas in the sixteenth century. In return, the Spanish were expected to convert the Indigenous peoples of the Americas to Christianity.[58]

Other European rulers rejected the Pope's ability to give away sovereignty over half the world.[59] But they did not necessarily reject the Doctrine of Discovery—they simply modified it. The English argued that a claim to 'discovered lands' was valid if the 'discoverer' was able to take possession of them.[60] Harman Verelst, who promoted the colonization in the eighteenth century of what is now the southern coast of the United States, wrote that "this Right arising from the first discovery is the first and fundamental Right of all European Nations, as to their Claim of Lands in America."[61] This Doctrine of Discovery was linked to a second idea: the lands being claimed were *terra nullius*—no man's land—and therefore open to claim. On the basis of this concept, the British government claimed ownership of the entire Australian continent. (There, the doctrine of *terra nullius* remained the law until it was successfully challenged in court in 1992.)[62] Under this doctrine, imperialists could argue that the presence of Indigenous people did not void a claim of *terra nullius*, since the Indigenous people simply occupied, rather than owned, the land. True ownership, they claimed, could come only with European-style agriculture.[63]

Underlying these arguments was the belief that the colonizers were bringing civilization to savage people who could never civilize themselves. The 'civilizing mission' rested on a belief of racial and cultural superiority. European writers and politicians

A Church Missionary Society school, in Freetown, Sierra Leone. In the nineteenth century, European-based missionary societies established residential schools around the world in an effort to spread the Christian gospel and civilize the 'heathen.' Mary Evans Picture Library, 10825826.

often arranged racial groups in a hierarchy, each with their own set of mental and physical capabilities. The 'special gifts' of the Europeans meant it was inevitable that they would conquer the lesser peoples. Beneath the Europeans, in descending order, were Asians, Africans, and the Indigenous peoples of the Americas and Australia. Some people held that Europeans had reached the pinnacle of civilization through a long and arduous process. In this view, the other peoples of the world had been held back by such factors as climate, geography, and migration. Through a civilizing process, Europeans could, however, raise the people of the world up to their level. This view was replaced in the nineteenth century by a racism that chose to cloak itself in the language of science, and held that the peoples of the world had differing abilities. Some argued that, for genetic reasons, there were limits on the ability of the less-developed peoples to improve. In some cases, it was thought, contact with superior races could lead to only one outcome: the extinction of the inferior peoples.[64]

These ideas shaped global policies towards Indigenous peoples. In 1883, Britain's Lord Rosebery, a future British prime minister, told an Australian audience, "It is on the British race, whether in Great Britain, or the United States, or the Colonies, or wherever it may be, that rest the highest hopes of those who try to penetrate the dark future, or who seek to raise and better the patient masses of mankind."[65] Residential schools were established in the shadow of these ideas. In the year that Rosebery gave this speech, the Canadian government opened its first industrial residential school for Aboriginal people at Battleford on the Canadian Prairies.[66]

The Christian churches not only provided the moral justification for the colonization of other peoples' lands, but they also dispatched missionaries to the colonized nations in order to convert 'the heathen.' From the fifteenth century on, the Indigenous peoples of the world were the objects of a strategy of spiritual and cultural conquest that had its origins in Europe. While they often worked in isolation and under difficult conditions, missionaries were representatives of worldwide organizations that enjoyed the backing of influential individuals in some of the most powerful nations of the world, and which came to amass considerable experience in transforming different cultures.[67] Residential schools figured prominently in missionary work, not only in Canada, but also around the world.

Christian missionaries played a complex but central role in the European colonial project. Their presence helped justify the extension of empires, since they were visibly spreading the word of God to the heathen. If their efforts were unsuccessful, the missionaries might conclude that those who refused to accept the Christian message could not expect the protection of the church or the law, thus clearing the way for their destruction.[68] Although missionaries often attempted to soften the impact of imperialism, they were also committed to making the greatest changes in the culture and psychology of the colonized. They might, for example, seek to have traders give fair prices and to have government officials provide relief in times of need, but they also worked to undermine relationships to the land, language, religion, family relations, educational practices, morality, and social custom.[69]

Missionary zeal was also fuelled by the often violent division that had separated the Christian world into Catholic and Protestant churches. Both Catholics and Protestants invested heavily in the creation of missionary organizations that were intended to engage overseas missionary work. The most well-known Catholic orders were the Franciscans, the Jesuits, and the Oblates. The Oblates originally focused their attention on the poor and working classes of France, but from the 1830s onwards, they engaged in overseas missionary work. They established themselves in eastern Canada, the Pacific Northwest, Ceylon, Texas, and Africa.[70] The Oblates administered a majority of the Roman Catholic residential schools in Canada. They could not have done this work without the support of a number of female religious orders, most particularly the Sisters of Charity (the Grey Nuns), the Sisters of Providence, the Sisters of St. Anne, and the Missionary Oblate Sisters of the Sacred Heart and of Mary Immaculate.

The British-based Church Missionary Society was also a global enterprise. By the middle of the nineteenth century, this Anglican society had missions across the globe in such places as India, New Zealand, West and East Africa, China, and the Middle East. The society's Highbury College in London provided missionaries with several years of training in arithmetic, grammar, history, geography, religion, education, and the administration of schools.[71] By 1901, the Church Missionary Society had an annual income of over 300,000 pounds. It used this money to support 510 male missionaries, 326 unmarried females, and 365 ordained pastors around the world.[72]

The Catholics and Anglicans were not the only European-based missionary societies to take up work in Canada. Presbyterians and Methodists, originally drawing support from the United Kingdom, undertook missionary work among Aboriginal people in the early nineteenth century. On the coast of Labrador, members of the Moravian Brotherhood, an order that had its origins in what is now the Czech Republic, carried out missionary work from the early eighteenth century onwards.[73] Protestant missionary work also depended on the often underpaid and voluntary labour of missionary wives and single women who had been recruited by missionary societies.

Missionaries viewed Aboriginal culture as a barrier to both spiritual salvation and the ongoing existence of Aboriginal people. They were determined to replace traditional economic pursuits with European-style peasant agriculture. They believed that cultural transformation required the imposition of social control and separation from both traditional communities and European settlements. In the light of these beliefs, it is not surprising that they were proponents of an educational world that separated children from the influences of their families and cultures, imposed a new set of values and beliefs, provided a basic elementary education, and created institutions whose daily life reflected Europe's emerging work discipline. In short, they sought to impose the foreign and transforming world of the residential school.

Colonization was undertaken to meet the perceived needs of the imperial powers. The justification offered for colonialism—the need to bring Christianity and civilization to the Indigenous peoples of the world—may have been a sincerely and firmly held belief, but as a justification for intervening in the lives of other peoples, it does not stand up to legal, moral, or even logical scrutiny. The papacy had no authority to give away lands that belonged to Indigenous people. The Doctrine of Discovery cannot serve as the basis for a legitimate claim to the lands that were colonized, if for no other reason than that the so-called discovered lands were already well known to the Indigenous peoples who had inhabited them for thousands of years. The wars of conquest that took place to strip Indigenous peoples of their lands around the globe were not morally just wars; Indigenous peoples were not, as colonists often claimed, subhuman, and neither were they living in violation of any universally agreed-upon set of values. There was no moral imperative to impose Christianity on the Indigenous peoples of the world. They did not need to be 'civilized'; indeed, there is no hierarchy of societies. Indigenous peoples had systems that were complete unto themselves and met their needs. Those systems were dynamic; they changed over time and were capable of continued change.[74] Taken as a whole, the colonial process relied for its justification on the sheer presumption of taking a specific set of European beliefs and values and proclaiming them to be universal values that could be imposed upon the peoples of the world. This universalizing of European values—so central to the colonial

Kahkewaquonaby (Sacred Feathers), also known as Peter Jones, in 1832. He was an Ojibway chief who worked with Methodist officials to establish the Mount Elgin residential school in Muncey, Ontario. Toronto Public Library, X2-25.

project—that was extended to North America served as the prime justification and rationale for the imposition of a residential school system on the Indigenous peoples of Canada.

Residential schools in pre-Confederation Canada

In Canada, residential schooling was closely linked to colonization and missionary crusades. The first boarding school for Aboriginal people in what is now Canada was established in the early seventeenth century near the French trading post at the future site of Québec City. At this Roman Catholic school, missionaries hoped to both 'civilize' and 'Christianize' young Aboriginal boys.[75] The school was a failure: parents were reluctant to send their children, and the students were quick to run away and return home.[76] Later efforts in New France met with no greater success.[77] After the British conquest of New France in 1763, the idea of residential schooling lay dormant until the early nineteenth century. In the first decade of that century, the New England Company, a British-based missionary society, funded a boarding school operation in Sussex Vale, New Brunswick. The goals were to teach young Mi'kmaq and Maliseet children trades and to convert them to Protestantism.[78] In the 1820s, John West, an Anglican missionary from England, opened a boarding school for Aboriginal students at Red River.[79] Although these efforts also failed to take root, in 1834, the Mohawk Institute, a mission school on the Grand River in what is now Ontario, began taking in boarders.[80] This school would remain in operation until 1970.[81]

In 1847, Egerton Ryerson, the superintendent of schools for Upper Canada, recommended the establishment of residential schools in which Aboriginal students would be given instruction in "English language, arithmetic, elementary geometry, or knowledge of forms, geography and the elements of general history, natural history and agricultural chemistry, writing, drawing and vocal music, book-keeping (especially in reference to farmers' accounts) religion and morals."[82] This he thought of as "a plain English education adapted to the working farmer and mechanic. In this their object is identical with that of every good common school." Pupils should be "taught agriculture, kitchen gardening, and mechanics, so far as mechanics is connected with making and repairing the most useful agricultural implements."[83]

After the release of Ryerson's report, Methodist missionaries operated a number of boarding schools in southern Ontario in the 1850s.[84] One of them, the Mount Elgin school at Munceytown (later, Muncey), did not close until 1946.[85] The first of what would be a string of Roman Catholic residential schools in what is now British Columbia opened in the early 1860s.[86] A school in Fort Providence in what is now the Northwest Territories began taking in students in 1867.[87]

The colonization of the Northwest

After the Canadian state was established in 1867, the federal government began making small per-student grants to many of the church-run boarding schools. Federal government involvement in residential schooling did not begin in earnest until the 1880s. The catalyst for this expansion was the 1870 transfer of much of contemporary Alberta, Saskatchewan, Manitoba, northern Québec, northern Ontario, the Northwest Territories, and Nunavut from the Hudson's Bay Company to the Canadian government. The following year, British Columbia was brought into Confederation by the promise of a continental rail link.

Canadian politicians intended to populate the newly acquired lands with settlers from Europe and Ontario. These settlers were expected to buy goods produced in central Canada and ship their harvests by rail to western and eastern ports and then on to international markets. Settling the "Northwest"—as this territory came to be known—in this manner meant colonizing the over 40,000 Indigenous people who lived there.[88]

The Rupert's Land Order of 1870, which transferred much of the Northwest to Canadian control, required that "the claims of the Indian tribes to compensation for lands required for purposes of settlement will be considered and settled in conformity with the equitable principles which have uniformly governed the British Crown in its dealings with the aborigines."[89] These principles had been set down in the Royal Proclamation of 1763, which placed limits on the conditions under which Aboriginal land could be transferred. "If at any Time any of the Said Indians should be inclined to dispose of the said Lands," they could do so, but land could be sold only to the Crown, and the sale had to be at a meeting of Indians that had been held specifically for that purpose.[90] The Royal Proclamation, in effect, ruled that any future transfer of 'Indian' land would take the form of a Treaty between sovereigns.[91] In this, it stands as one of the clearest and earliest expressions of what has been identified as a long-standing element of Canadian Aboriginal policy.[92]

The signing of Treaty 1 at Lower Fort Garry, 1871. To gain control of the land of Indigenous people, colonists negotiated Treaties, waged wars of extinction, eliminated traditional landholding practices, disrupted families, and imposed new political and spiritual order that came complete with new values and cultural practices. Provincial Archives of Manitoba, N11975.

To enable the colonization of the Northwest, in 1871, the federal government began negotiating the first in a series of what came to be termed as "Numbered Treaties" with the First Nations of western and northern Canada. The only alternative to negotiating Treaties would have been to ignore the legal obligations of the Rupert's Land Order and attempt to subdue the First Nations militarily, but that would have been a very costly proposition. In 1870, when the entire Canadian government budget was $19 million, the United States was spending more than that—$20 million a year—on its Indian Wars alone. Despite all these pressures, the government took a slow and piecemeal approach to Treaty making.[93]

Through the Treaties, Aboriginal peoples were seeking agricultural supplies and training as well as relief during periods of epidemic or famine in a time of social and economic transition.[94] They saw the Treaty process as establishing a reciprocal relationship that would be lasting.[95] The goal was to gain the skills that would allow them to continue to control their own destinies and retain their culture and identity as Aboriginal people. As Ahtahkakoop (Star Blanket) said, "We Indians can learn the ways of living that made the white man strong."[96] The provisions varied from Treaty to Treaty, but they generally included funds for hunting and fishing supplies, agricultural assistance, yearly payments for band members (annuities), and an amount of reserve lands based on the population of the band.[97] First Nations never asked for residential schools as part of the Treaty process, and neither did the government suggest that such schools would be established. The education provisions also varied in different Treaties, but promised to pay for schools on reserves or teachers. The federal government was slow to live up to its Treaty obligations. For example, many First Nations were settled on reserves that were much smaller than they were entitled to, while others were not provided with any reserve.[98] Some obligations remain unfulfilled to this day. The commitment to establish on-reserve schools was also ignored in many cases. As a result, parents who wished to see their children educated were forced to send them to residential schools.[99]

The assimilation policy

From the Canadian government's perspective, the most significant elements in the Treaties were the written provisions by which the First Nations agreed to "cede, release, surrender, and yield" their land to the Crown.[100] In the Treaty negotiations, however, federal officials left the impression that the government intended the Treaties to establish a permanent relationship with First Nations. Treaty Commissioner Alexander Morris told the Cree in 1876, "What I trust and hope we will do is not for to-day and tomorrow only; what I will promise, and what I believe and hope you will take, is to last as long as the sun shines and yonder river flows."[101] In reality, the federal government policy was very different from what Morris said. The intent of the government's policy, which was firmly established in legislation at the time that the Treaties had been negotiated, was to assimilate Aboriginal people into broader Canadian society. At the end of this process, Aboriginal people were expected to have ceased to exist as a distinct people with their own governments, cultures, and identities.

The federal *Indian Act*, first adopted in 1876, like earlier pre-Confederation legislation, defined who was and who was not an 'Indian' under Canadian law.[102] The Act also defined a process through which a person could lose status as an Indian. Women, for example, could lose status simply by marrying a man who did not have status. Men

This "Sun Dance" ceremony was one of the Aboriginal spiritual practices outlawed by the federal government in the nineteenth century. Library and Archives Canada, Trueman, C-0104106.

could lose status in a number of ways, including graduating from a university. Upon giving up their status, individuals also were granted a portion of the band's reserve land.[103]

First Nations people were unwilling to surrender their Aboriginal identity in this manner. Until 1920, other than women who involuntarily lost their Indian status upon marriage to a non-status individual, only 250 'Indians' voluntarily gave up their status.[104] In 1920, the federal government amended the *Indian Act* to give it the power to strip individuals of their status against their will. In explaining the purpose of the amendment to a parliamentary committee, Indian Affairs Deputy Minister Duncan Campbell Scott said that "our object is to continue until there is not a single Indian in Canada that has not been absorbed into the body politic, and there is no Indian question, and no Indian Department that is the whole object of this Bill."[105] The other major element in the bill that Scott was referring to empowered the government to compel parents to send their children to residential schools. Residential schooling was always more than simply an educational program: it was an integral part of a conscious policy of cultural genocide.

Further evidence of this assault on Aboriginal identity can be found in amendments to the *Indian Act* banning a variety of Aboriginal cultural and spiritual practices. The two most prominent of these were the west-coast Potlatch and the Prairie Thirst Dance (often referred to as the "Sun Dance").[106] Residential school principals had been in the forefront of the campaign to ban these ceremonies, and also urged the government to enforce the bans once they were put in place.[107]

The Aboriginal right to self-government was also undermined. The *Indian Act* gave the federal government the authority to veto decisions made by band councils and to depose chiefs and councillors. The Act placed restrictions on First Nations farmers' ability to sell their crops and take out loans. Over the years, the government also assumed greater authority as to how reserve land could be disposed of: in some cases, entire reserves were relocated against the will of the residents. The *Indian Act* was a piece of colonial legislation by which, in the name of 'protection,' one group of people ruled and controlled another.

The industrial school initiative

It was in keeping with this intent to assimilate Aboriginal peoples and, in the process, to eliminate its government-to-government relationship with First Nations that the federal government dramatically increased its involvement in residential schooling in the 1880s. In December 1878, J. S. Dennis, the deputy minister of the Department of the Interior, prepared a memorandum for Prime Minister Sir John A. Macdonald on the country's Aboriginal policy. Dennis advised Macdonald that the long-term goal should be to instruct "our Indian and half-breed populations" in farming, raising cattle, and the mechanical trades, rendering them self-sufficient. This would pave the way "for their emancipation from tribal government, and for their final absorption into the general community." Dennis argued that residential schools were key to fulfilling these goals. It was his opinion that in a short time, schools might become "self-sustaining institutions."[108]

In the following year, Nicholas Davin, a failed Conservative candidate, carried out a brief study of the boarding schools that the United States government had established for Native Americans. He recommended that Canada establish a series of such schools on the Prairies. Davin acknowledged that a central element of the education provided at these schools would be directed towards the destruction of Aboriginal spirituality. Since all civilizations were based on religion, it would be inexcusable, he thought, to do away with Aboriginal faith "without supplying a better [one]." For this

The Qu'Appelle school at Lebret in what is now Saskatchewan opened in 1884. O.B. Buell, Library and Archives Canada, PA-182246.

reason, he recommended that while the government should fund the schools, the churches should operate them.[109]

The decision to continue to rely on the churches to administer the schools on a day-to-day basis had serious consequences. The government constantly struggled, and failed, to assert control over the churches' drive to increase the number of schools they operated. At various times, each denomination involved in school operation established boarding schools without government support or approval, and then lobbied later for per capita funding. When the churches concluded, quite legitimately, that the per capita grant they received was too low, they sought other types of increases in school funding. Building on their network of missions in the Northwest, the Catholics quickly came to dominate the field, usually operating twice as many schools as did the Protestant denominations. Among the Protestant churches, the Anglicans were predominant, establishing and maintaining more residential schools than the Methodists or the Presbyterians. The United Church, created by a union of Methodist and Presbyterian congregations, took over most of the Methodist and Presbyterian schools in the mid-1920s. Presbyterian congregations that did not participate in the union established the Presbyterian Church in Canada and retained responsibility for two residential schools. In addition to these national denominations, a local Baptist mission ran a residence for Aboriginal students in Whitehorse in the 1940s and 1950s, and a Mennonite ministry operated three schools in northwestern Ontario in the 1970s and 1980s. Each faith, in its turn, claimed government discrimination against it. Competition for converts meant that churches sought to establish schools in the same locations as their rivals, leading to internal divisions within communities and expensive duplication of services.

The model for these residential schools for Aboriginal children, both in Canada and the United States, did not come from the private boarding schools to which members of the economic elites in Britain and Canada sent their children. Instead, the model came from the reformatories and industrial schools that were being constructed in Europe and North America for the children of the urban poor. The British parliament adopted the *Reformatory Schools Act* in 1854 and the *Industrial Schools Act* in 1857.[110] By 1882, over 17,000 children were in Britain's industrial schools.[111] Under Ontario's 1880 *Act for the Protection and Reformation of Neglected Children*, a judge could send children under the age of fourteen to an industrial school, where they might be required to stay until they turned eighteen.[112] Such schools could be dangerous and violent places. At the Halifax Boys Industrial School, first offenders were strapped, and repeat offenders were placed in cells on a bread-and-water ration. From there, they might be sent to the penitentiary.[113] The Canadian government also drew inspiration from the United States. There, the first in a series of large-scale, government-operated, boarding schools for Native Americans opened in 1879 in a former army barracks in Carlisle, Pennsylvania.[114]

On the basis of Davin's report and developments in the United States, the federal government decided to open three industrial schools. The first one opened in Battleford in what is now Saskatchewan in 1883. It was placed under the administration of an Anglican minister. The following year, two more industrial schools opened: one at Qu'Appelle in what is now Saskatchewan, and one at High River in what is now Alberta. Both these schools were administered by principals nominated by the Roman Catholic Oblate order. The federal government not only built these schools, but it also assumed all the costs of operating them. Recruiting students for these schools was difficult. According to the Indian Affairs annual report, in 1884, there were only twenty-seven students at the three schools.[115]

Unlike the church-run boarding schools, which provided a limited education with a heavy emphasis on religious instruction, the industrial schools were intended to prepare First Nations people for integration into Canadian society by teaching them basic trades, particularly farming. Generally, industrial schools were larger than boarding schools, were located in urban areas, and, although church-managed, usually required federal approval prior to construction. The boarding schools were smaller institutions, were located on or near reserves, and provided a more limited education. The differences between the industrial schools and the boarding schools eroded over time. By the 1920s, the federal government ceased to make any distinction between them, referring to them simply as "residential schools."

In justifying the investment in industrial schools to Parliament in 1883, Public Works Minister Hector Langevin argued that

> if you wish to educate these children you must separate them from their parents during the time that they are being educated. If you leave them in the family they may know how to read and write, but they still remain savages, whereas by separating them in the way proposed, they acquire the habits and tastes—it is to be hoped only the good tastes—of civilized people.[116]

The federal government entered into residential schooling at a time when it was colonizing Aboriginal lands in western Canada. It recognized that, through the Treaties, it had made commitments to provide Aboriginal people with relief in periods of economic distress. It also feared that as traditional Aboriginal economic pursuits were marginalized or eliminated by settlers, the government might be called upon to provide increased relief. In this context, the federal government chose to invest in residential schooling for a number of reasons. First, it would provide Aboriginal people with skills that would allow them to participate in the coming market-based economy. Second, it would further their political assimilation. It was hoped that students who were educated in residential schools would give up their status and not return to their reserve communities and families. Third, the schools were seen as engines of cultural and spiritual change: 'savages' were to emerge as Christian 'white men.' There was also a national security element to the schools. Indian Affairs official Andsell Macrae observed that "it is unlikely that any Tribe or Tribes would give trouble of a serious nature to the Government whose members had children completely under Government control."[117] Duncan Campbell Scott succinctly summarized Indian Affairs' goals for the schools in 1909: "It includes not only a scholastic education, but instruction in the means of gaining a livelihood from the soil or as a member of an industrial or mercantile community, and the substitution of Christian ideals of conduct and morals for aboriginal concepts of both."[118] The achievement of such invasive and ambitious goals would require a substantial level of funding. This was never forthcoming.

Funding: The dream of self-supporting schools

In announcing the construction of the three initial industrial schools, Indian Commissioner Edgar Dewdney said that although the starting costs would be high, he could see no reason why the schools would not be largely self-supporting in a few years, due to the skills in farming, raising stock, and trades that were being taught to the students.[119] In supporting an Anglican proposal for two industrial schools in Manitoba, Indian Affairs Deputy Minister Lawrence Vankoughnet wrote to Prime Minister Macdonald that it would be "well to give a Grant of money annually to each school established by any Denomination for the industrial training of Indian children." He said that system worked well in Ontario, and it "costs the Government less than the whole maintenance of the School would cost and it enlists the sympathies and assistance of the religious denominations in the education and industrial training of the Indian children."[120]

The government believed that between the forced labour of students and the poorly paid labour of missionaries, it could operate a residential school system on a nearly cost-free basis. The missionaries and the students were indeed a source of cheap labour—but the government was never happy with the quality of the teaching and, no matter how hard students worked, their labour never made the schools self-supporting. Soon after the government established the industrial schools, it began to cut salaries.[121] Initially, the federal government covered all the costs of operating the industrial schools. In 1891, this policy was abandoned in favour of one by which schools received a fixed amount per student (referred to as a "per capita grant").[122] The system both intensified the level of competition among churches for students and encouraged principals to accept students who should have been barred from admission because they were too young or too sick.[123]

The government never adequately responded to the belated discovery that the type of residential school system that officials had envisioned would cost far more than politicians were prepared to fund. In the early twentieth century, chronic underfunding led to a health crisis in the schools and a financial crisis for the missionary societies. Indian Affairs, with the support of leading figures in the Protestant churches, sought to dramatically reduce the number of residential schools, replacing them with day schools. The government abandoned the plan when it failed to receive the full support of all the churches involved in the operation of the schools.[124] Instead, in 1911, the federal government finally implemented a significant increase to the per capita grant received by boarding schools and attempted to impose basic health standards for the schools. This resulted in a short-term improvement. However, inflation eroded the value of the grant increase, and the grant was actually reduced repeatedly during the Great Depression and at the start of the Second World War.[125]

Funding for residential schools was always lower than funding for comparable institutions in Canada and the United States that served the general population. In 1937, Indian Affairs was paying, on average, $180 a year per student. This was less than a third of the per capita costs at that time for the Manitoba School for the Deaf ($642.40) and the Manitoba School for Boys ($550). In the United States, the annual per capita cost at the Chilocco Indian Residential School in Oklahoma in 1937 was $350. According to the American Child Welfare League, the per capita costs for well-run institutions in that country ranged between $313 and $541.[126] It would not be until the 1950s that changes were made in the funding system in Canada that were intended to ensure that the schools could recruit qualified teachers and improve the student

Aboriginal family at the Elkhorn, Manitoba, school. Indian Affairs took the position that once parents enrolled their children in a residential school, only the government could determine when they would be discharged. General Synod Archives, Anglican Church of Canada, P75-103-S8-56.

diets.[127] Even these improvements did not end the inequity in residential school funding. In 1966, residential schools in Saskatchewan were spending between $694 and $1,193 a year per student.[128] Comparable child-welfare institutions in Canada were spending between $3,300 and $9,855 a year. In the United States, the annual cost of residential care per child was between $4,500 and $14,059.[129]

Compelling attendance

It was not until 1894 that the federal government put in place regulations relating to residential school attendance. Under the regulations adopted in that year, residential school attendance was voluntary. However, if an Indian agent or justice of the peace thought that any "Indian child between six and sixteen years of age is not being properly cared for or educated, and that the parent, guardian or other person having charge or control of such child, is unfit or unwilling to provide for the child's education," he could issue an order to place the child "in an industrial or boarding school, in which there may be a vacancy for such child."

The Roman Catholic school in Fort George, Quebec, opened in 1931. Deschâtelets Archives.

If a child placed in the school under these regulations left a residential school without permission, or did not return at a promised time, school officials could get a warrant from an Indian agent or a justice of the peace authorizing them (or a police officer, truant officer, or employee of the school or Indian Affairs) to "search for and take such child back to the school in which it had been previously placed." With a warrant, one could enter—by force if need be—any house, building, or place named in the warrant and remove the child. Even without a warrant, Indian Affairs employees and constables had the authority to arrest a student in the act of escaping from a residential school and return the child to the school.[130]

It was departmental policy that no child could be discharged without departmental approval—even if the parents had enrolled the child voluntarily. The government had no legislative basis for this policy. Instead, it relied on the admission form that parents were supposed to sign. (In some cases, school staff members signed these forms.)[131] By 1892, the department required that all parents sign an admission form when they enrolled their children in a residential school. In signing the form, parents gave their consent that "the Principal or head teacher of the Institution for the time being shall be the guardian" of the child. In that year, the Department of Justice provided Indian Affairs with a legal opinion to the effect that "the fact of a parent having signed such an application is not sufficient to warrant the forcible arrest against the parents' will of a truant child who has been admitted to an Industrial School pursuant to the application." It was held that, without legislative authority, no form could provide school administrators with the power of arrest.[132] Despite this warning, well into the twentieth century, Indian Affairs would continue to enforce policies regarding attendance for which it had no legal authority.[133] This is not the only example of the government's use of unauthorized measures. In the 1920s, students were to be discharged from residential school when they turned sixteen. Despite this, William Graham, the Indian commissioner, refused to authorize discharge until the students turned eighteen. He estimated that, on this basis, he rejected approximately 100 applications for discharge a year.[134]

In 1920, the *Indian Act* was amended to allow the government to compel any First Nations child to attend residential school. However, residential school was never compulsory for all First Nations children. In most years, there were more First Nations children attending Indian Affairs day schools than residential schools. During the early 1940s, this pattern was reversed. In the 1944–45 school year, there were 8,865 students in residential schools, and 7,573 students in Indian Affairs day schools. In that year, there were reportedly 28,429 school-aged Aboriginal children. This meant that 31.1% of the school-aged Aboriginal children were in residential school.[135]

Regulation

The residential school system operated with few regulations; those that did exist were in large measure weakly enforced. The Canadian government never developed anything approaching the education acts and regulations by which provincial governments administered public schools. The key piece of legislation used in regulating the residential school system was the *Indian Act*. This was a multi-purpose piece of legislation that defined and limited First Nations life in Canada. The Act contained no education-related provisions until 1884. There were no residential school–specific regulations until 1894. These dealt almost solely with attendance and truancy.

It was recognized by those who worked within the system that the level of regulation was inadequate. In 1897, Indian Affairs education official Martin Benson wrote, "No regulations have been adopted or issued by the Department applicable to all its schools, as had been done by the Provincial Governments."[136] The situation did not improve over time. The education section of the 1951 *Indian Act* and the residential school regulations adopted in 1953 were each only four pages in length.[137] By comparison, the Manitoba *Public Schools Act* of 1954 was ninety-one pages in length.[138] In addition to the Act, the Manitoba government had adopted nineteen education-related regulations.[139]

It is also apparent that many key people within the system had little knowledge of the existing rules and regulations. In 1922, an Indian agent in Hagersville, Ontario, inquired of departmental headquarters if there had been any changes in the regulations regarding education since the adoption of a set of education regulations in 1908.

His question suggests he was completely unaware of major changes to the *Indian Act* regarding education that had supplanted previous regulations in 1920.[140] In 1926, J. K. Irwin, the newly appointed principal of the Gordon's school in Saskatchewan, discovered upon taking office that he could not find any "laid down regulations as to the duties and powers of a Principal of an Indian Boarding School." He wrote to Indian Affairs, asking for a copy of such regulations, since he wanted to know "exactly what I am to do and what powers I have."[141] Departmental secretary J. D. McLean informed him that "there are no printed regulations concerning the duties and powers of the principal of an Indian residential school."[142]

The system was so unregulated that in 1968, after Canada had been funding residential schools for 101 years, Indian Affairs Deputy Minister J. A. MacDonald announced, "For the first time we have set down in a precise and detailed manner the criteria which is to be used in future in determining whether or not an Indian child is eligible for these institutions."[143]

Expansion and decline

From the 1880s onwards, residential school enrolment climbed annually. According to federal government annual reports, the peak enrolment of 11,539 was reached in the 1956–57 school year.[144] (For trends, see Graph 1.) Most of the residential schools were located in the northern and western regions of the country. With the exception of Mount Elgin and the Mohawk Institute, the Ontario schools were all in northern or northwestern Ontario. The only school in the Maritimes did not open until 1930.[145] Roman Catholic and Anglican missionaries opened the first two schools in Québec in the early 1930s.[146] It was not until later in that decade that the federal government began funding these schools.[147]

The number of schools began to decline in the 1940s. Between 1940 and 1950, for example, ten school buildings were destroyed by fire.[148] As Graph 2 illustrates, this decrease was reversed in the mid-1950s, when the federal department of Northern Affairs and National Resources dramatically expanded the school system in the Northwest Territories and northern Québec. Prior to that time, residential schooling in the North was largely restricted to the Yukon and the Mackenzie Valley in the Northwest Territories. Large residences were built in communities such as Inuvik, Yellowknife, Whitehorse, Churchill, and eventually Iqaluit (formerly Frobisher Bay). This expansion was undertaken despite reports that recommended against the establishment of residential schools, since they would not provide children with the skills necessary to live in the North, skills they otherwise would have acquired in their home communities.[149] The creation of the large hostels was accompanied by the opening of

Graph 1
Residential school enrolment, 1869–70 to 1965–66

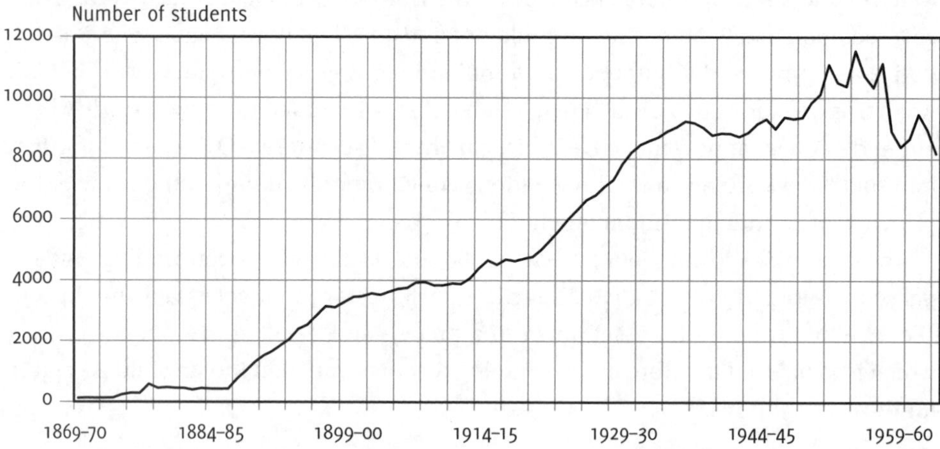

Source: Indian Affairs and Northern Affairs annual reports. After the 1965–66 school year, Indian Affairs stopped reporting on annual residential school enrolment.

Graph 2
Number of residential schools and residences, 1867–1998

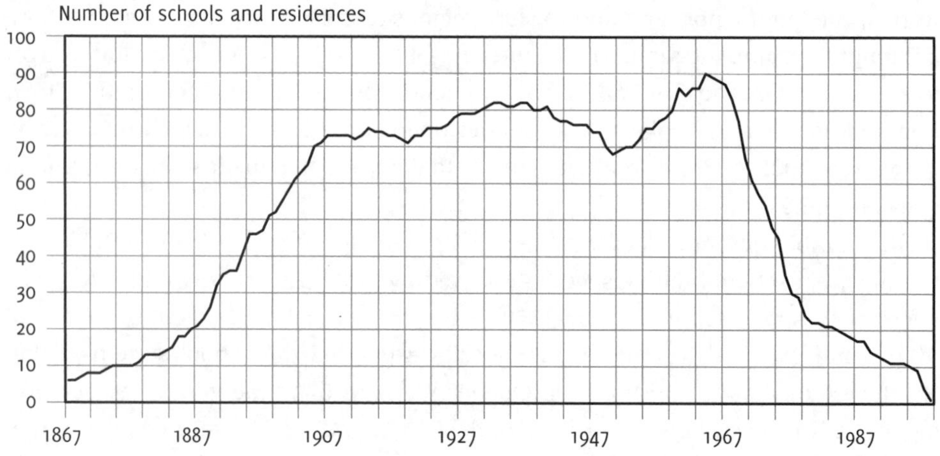

Source: Indian and Northern Affairs Canada, Indian Residential Schools of the Indian Residential Schools Settlement Agreement 2011.

Fleming Hall, the Anglican-run hostel opened by the federal government in Fort McPherson, Northwest Territories, as part of its expansion of residential schools in northern Canada in the late 1950s and early 1960s. General Synod Archives, Anglican Church of Canada, P8454-66.

what were termed "small hostels" in the smaller and more remote communities of the eastern Arctic and the western Northwest Territories.

Policy towards Métis and Inuit students

Many of the early advocates of residential schooling in Canada expected that the schools would take in both Aboriginal children who had status under the *Indian Act* (in other words, they were Indians as defined by the Act) as well as Aboriginal children who, for a variety of reasons, did not have status. The federal government classed these individuals alternately as "non-status Indians," "half-breeds," or "Métis."[150]

The early church-run boarding schools made no distinction between status and non-status or Métis children.[151] The federal government position on the matter was constantly shifting. It viewed the Métis as members of the 'dangerous classes' whom the residential schools were intended to civilize and assimilate.[152] This view led to the

Métis children at the Dawson City, Yukon, residence. General Synod Archives, Anglican Church of Canada, P75-103-S8-264.

adoption of policies that allowed for the admission of Métis children to the schools at various times.[153] However, from a jurisdictional perspective, the federal government believed that the responsibility for educating and assimilating Métis people lay with provincial and territorial governments. There was a strong concern that if the federal government began providing funding for the education of some of the children the provinces and territories were responsible for, it would find itself subject to having to take responsibility for the rest.[154] When this view dominated, Indian agents would be instructed to remove Métis students from residential schools.[155]

Despite their perceived constitutional responsibility, provincial and territorial governments were reluctant to provide services to Métis people. They did not ensure that there were schools in Métis communities, or work to see that Métis children were admitted and welcomed into the general public school system.[156] Many Métis parents who wished to see their children educated in schools had no option but to try to have them accepted into a residential school. In some cases, these would be federally funded schools, but, in other cases, Métis students attended church-run schools or residences that did not receive federal funding.[157]

Provincial governments slowly began to provide increased educational services to Métis students after the Second World War. As a result, Métis children lived in residences and residential schools that were either run or funded by provincial governments. The Métis experience is an important reminder that the impacts of residential schooling extend beyond the formal residential school program that Indian Affairs operated.[158]

Inuit children were recruited to a school in Shingle Point in the Yukon in the 1920s. General Synod Archives, Anglican Church of Canada, P9901-589.

Prior to the 1950s, most of the students who attended schools in the Northwest Territories were either First Nations or Métis. As late as 1949, only 111 Inuit students were receiving full-time schooling in the North.[159] The hostel system that Northern Affairs established in the Northwest Territories in the mid-1950s did not restrict admission to First Nations students. It was only at this point that large numbers of Inuit children began attending residential schools. The impact of the schools on the Inuit was complex. Some children were sent to schools thousands of kilometres from their homes, and went years without seeing their parents. In other cases, parents who had previously been supporting themselves by following a seasonal cycle of land- and marine-based resource harvesting began settling in communities with hostels so as not to be separated from their children.

Because of the majority of the Aboriginal population in two of the three northern territories, the per capita impact of the schools in the North is higher than anywhere else in the country. And, because the history of these schools is so recent, not only are there many living Survivors today, but there are also many living parents of Survivors. For these reasons, both the intergenerational impacts and the legacy of the schools, the good and the bad, are particularly strongly felt in the North.

The integration policy

By 1945, the Indian Affairs residential school system, starved for funding for fifteen years, was on the verge of collapse.[160] Not only was the existing Indian Affairs education system lacking money and resources, but also there were no school facilities of any sort for 42% of the school-aged First Nations children.[161] Having concluded that it was far too expensive to provide residential schooling to these students, Indian Affairs began to look for alternatives. One was to expand the number of Indian Affairs day schools. From 1945–46 to 1954–55, the number of First Nations students in Indian Affairs day schools increased from 9,532 to 17,947.[162] In 1949, the Special Joint Committee of the Senate and House of Commons Appointed to Examine and Consider *The Indian Act* recommended "that wherever and whenever possible Indian children should be educated in association with other children."[163] In 1951, the *Indian Act* was amended to allow the federal government to enter into agreements with provincial governments and school boards to have First Nations students educated in public schools.[164] By 1960, the number of students attending "non-Indian" schools (9,479) had surpassed the number living in residential schools (9,471).[165] The transfer of First Nations students into the public school system was described as "integration." By then, the overall policy goal was to restrict the education being given in Indian Affairs schools to the lower grades. Therefore, it was expected that during the course of their schooling, at least half of the students then in Indian Affairs schools would transfer to a 'non-Indian' school.[166]

The integration policy was opposed by some of the church organizations. Roman Catholic church officials argued that residential schooling was preferable for three reasons: 1) teachers in public schools were not prepared to deal with Aboriginal students; 2) students in public schools often expressed racist attitudes towards Aboriginal students; and 3) Aboriginal students felt acute embarrassment over their impoverished conditions, particularly in terms of the quality of the clothing they wore and the food they ate.[167] These were all issues that students and parents raised, as well.[168]

Child-welfare facilities

From the 1940s onwards, residential schools increasingly served as orphanages and child-welfare facilities. By 1960, the federal government estimated that 50% of the children in residential schools were there for child-welfare reasons. What has come to be referred to as the "Sixties Scoop"—the dramatic increase in the apprehension of Aboriginal children from the 1960s onwards—was in some measure simply a transferring of children from one form of institution, the residential school, to another, the child-welfare agency.[169] The schools were not funded or staffed to function as child-welfare institutions. They failed to provide their students with the appropriate level of personal and emotional care children need during their childhood and adolescence. This failure applied to all students, but was of particular significance in the case of the growing number of social-welfare placements in the schools.[170] Some children had to stay in the schools year-round because it was thought there was no safe home to which they could return. The residential school environment was not a safer or more loving haven. These children spent their entire childhoods in an institution.

The closure of residential schools, which commenced in earnest in 1970, was accompanied by a significant increase in the number of children being taken into care by child-welfare agencies.[171] By the end of the 1970s, the transfer of children from residential schools was nearly complete in southern Canada, and the impact of the Sixties Scoop was in evidence across the country. In 1977, Aboriginal children accounted for 44% of the children in care in Alberta, 51% of the children in care in Saskatchewan, and 60% of the children in care in Manitoba.[172] In those residences that remained in operation, the percentage of social-welfare cases remained high.[173]

The road to closure, 1969

In 1968, the federal government drastically restructured the residential school system by dividing the schools into residences and day schools, each with a principal or administrator.[174] In June of the following year, the federal government took direct control over all the schools in southern Canada.[175] Because churches were allowed to continue to appoint the residence administrators, their presence continued in many schools in the coming years. They were, however, no longer directly responsible for the facilities.[176] In 1969, the federal government also began to transfer the hostels and day schools in the Yukon and Northwest Territories to their respective territorial governments. Most of the small hostels in the eastern Arctic and Nunavik (Arctic Québec) were closed by the end of 1971. (Four small hostels were also operated in the western and central Arctic. The last of these, located at Cambridge Bay, did not close until the late 1990s.)[177]

Having assumed control over the southern Canadian schools in 1969, the federal government commenced what would prove to be a protracted process of closing the system down. According to the Indian Affairs annual report for 1968–69, the department was responsible for sixty residences. Two years later, the number was down to forty-five.[178] The government takeover of the residential schools also coincided with the release of the federal government's White Paper on "Indian Policy." This document proposed a massive transfer of responsibility for First Nations people from the federal to provincial governments.[179] It called for the repeal of the *Indian Act*, the winding up of the Department of Indian Affairs, and the eventual extinguishment of the Treaties.[180] The recently formed National Indian Brotherhood (NIB) described the White Paper as a document intended to bring about "the destruction of a Nation of People by legislation and cultural genocide."[181] In its response, the NIB proposed "Indian Control of Indian Education."[182] In 1971, Indian Affairs Minister Jean Chrétien announced that, in the face of First Nations resistance, the federal government was abandoning the policy directions outlined in the White Paper.[183]

By then, First Nations communities had already taken over one residential school. In the summer of 1970, parents of children at the Blue Quills, Alberta, school occupied the school, demanding that its operation be turned over to a First Nations education authority. They took this measure in response to reports that the school was to be turned into a residence and their children were to be educated at a nearby public school. The Blue Quills conflict was the result of both long-standing local dissatisfaction with the administration of the school and First Nations opposition to the policy of integration.[184] It was estimated that over 1,000 people participated in the sit-in, with rarely fewer than 200 people being at the school on any given day.[185] Seventeen days after the sit-in commenced, Minister Jean Chrétien announced that the school would be transferred to the Blue Quills Native Education Council.[186] In coming years, the Qu'Appelle, Prince Albert, Duck Lake, Lestock, and Grayson facilities in Saskatchewan were also taken over by First Nations authorities. The Christie residence in Tofino, British Columbia, was also operated briefly by an Aboriginal authority.[187]

The federal government, however, remained committed to the closing of the facilities. Because of the government's lengthy history of underfunding residential schools, many of the schools were in poor repair. Between 1995 and 1998, the last seven residences in southern Canada were closed.[188]

Starting in the 1970s, territorial governments, in which former residential school students were serving as cabinet ministers, also began expanding the number of day schools as part of a campaign to close residential schools in the North. The last large hostel in the Yukon closed in 1985.[189] By 1986, there were only three large hostels operating in the Northwest Territories.[190] Grollier Hall, the last large hostel in the North, closed in 1997.[191] If one dates the residential school system back to the early 1830s, when the Mohawk Institute first took in boarders, the system had been in operation for over 160 years. The closing of the schools did not mark the end of the history of residential schooling in Canada. By the 1990s, former students had begun to make Canadians aware of the tremendous harm that the residential school experience had caused to Aboriginal people and Aboriginal communities.

The classroom in the Moose Factory, Ontario, school. General Synod Archives, Anglican Church of Canada, P7538-970.

The school experience

Education: "The children's work was merely memory work."

As educational institutions, the residential schools were failures, and regularly judged as such. In 1923, former Regina industrial school principal R. B. Heron delivered a paper to a meeting of the Regina Presbytery of the Presbyterian Church that was highly critical of the residential school system. He said that parents generally were anxious to have their children educated, but they complained that their children "are not kept regularly in the class-room; that they are kept out at work that produces revenue for the School; that when they return to the Reserves they have not enough education to enable them to transact ordinary business—scarcely enough to enable them to write a legible letter."[192] The schools' success rate did not improve. From 1940–41 to 1959–60, 41.3% of each year's residential school Grade One enrolment was not promoted to Grade Two.[193] Just over half of those who were in Grade Two would get to Grade Six.[194]

Members of the Croissés, a religious society for youth at the Fort Frances, Ontario, school. St. Boniface Historical Society Archives, Fond of the Grey Nuns of Manitoba, 03/31/1.

Many principals and teachers had low expectations of their students. Wikwemikong, Ontario, principal R. Baudin wrote in 1883, "What we may reasonably expect from the generality of children, is certainly not to make great scholars of them. Good and moral as they may be, they lack great mental capacity." He did not think it wise to expect them to "be equal in every respect to their white brethren."[195] In preparing a 1928 report on the Anglican school at Onion Lake, a Saskatchewan government school inspector expressed his belief that "in arithmetic abstract ideas develop slowly in the Indian child."[196] Some thought it was a risky matter to give the students too much education. Mount Elgin principal S. R. McVitty wrote in 1928 that "classroom work is an important part of our training, but not by any means the most important." He added, "In the case of the Indian 'a little learning is a dangerous thing.'"[197]

Much of what went on in the classroom was simply repetitious drill. A 1915 report on the Roman Catholic school on the Blood Reserve in Alberta noted, "The children's work was merely memory work and did not appear to be developing any deductive power, altogether too parrot like and lacking expression."[198] A 1932 inspector's report from the Grayson, Saskatchewan, school suggests there had been little change. "The teaching as I saw it today was merely a question of memorizing and repeating a mass of, to the children, 'meaningless' facts."[199]

The classrooms were often severely overcrowded. At the Qu'Appelle school in 1911, Sister McGurk had seventy-five girls in her junior classroom. The inspector of Roman Catholic schools reported to Ottawa that this was an "almost impossible" situation.[200]

In 1915, two teachers were responsible for 120 students at the Coqualeetza Institute in Chilliwack, British Columbia.[201] In 1928, there were sixty students in the junior classroom at the Alberni, British Columbia, school.[202]

The Indian Affairs schools branch maintained that the principals and the staff were "appointed by the church authorities, subject to the approval of the Department as to qualifications."[203] In reality, the churches hired staff and the government then automatically approved their selections.[204] The churches placed a greater priority on religious commitment than on teaching ability.[205] Because the pay was so low, many of the teachers lacked any qualification to teach.[206] In 1908, Indian Affairs inspector F. H. Paget reported that at the Battleford school, "frequent changes in the staff at this school has not been to its advantage." The problem lay not with the principal, but with the fact that "more profitable employment is available in the District and, furthermore, the salaries paid are not as high as are paid in other public institutions."[207] When a British Columbia Indian agent recommended that schools be required to hire only qualified staff, he was told by his superior, British Columbia Indian Superintendent A. W. Vowell, that such a requirement would result in the churches' applying for "larger grants." And, as Vowell understood it, Indian Affairs "is not at present disposed to entertain requests for increased grants to Indian boarding and industrial schools."[208] In 1955, 55 (23%) of the 241 teachers in residential schools directly employed by Indian Affairs had no teacher's certificate.[209] In 1969, Indian Affairs reported it was still paying its teachers less than they could make in provincial schools. "As a result, there are about the same number of unqualified teachers, some 140, in federal schools [residential and non-residential] now, as ten years ago."[210]

In the minds of some principals, religious training was the most valuable training the schools provided. In 1903, Brandon, Manitoba, principal T. Ferrier wrote that "while it is very important that the Indian child should be educated, it is of more importance that he should build up a good clean character." Such a heavy emphasis was required, in Ferrier's opinion, to "counteract the evil tendencies of the Indian nature."[211] Louise Moine recalled that religious instruction and observation were a constant part of life at the Qu'Appelle school in the early twentieth century: "From the time we got out of bed at the sound of the bell, we went down on our knees to pray. After we had washed and dressed, we headed for the chapel to attend Low mass which was always held at 7 a.m."[212] The staff handbook for the Presbyterian school in Kenora in the 1940s stated it was expected that, upon leaving the school, most students would "return to the Indian Reserves from which they had come." Given this future, staff members were told that "the best preparation we can give them is to teach them the Christian way of life."[213]

Not surprisingly, many of those who succeeded academically followed careers in the church. Coqualeetza graduate Peter Kelly became a Methodist Church minister. Emmanuel College graduate Edward Ahenakew became an Anglican minister. Others worked for government or taught school. Qu'Appelle graduate Daniel Kennedy became an interpreter and general assistant for the Assiniboine Indian Agency. Joseph Dion, a graduate of the Onion Lake school, taught school for many years in Saskatchewan. Still others pursued business and professional careers. After attending the Mohawk Institute, Beverly Johnson went to Hellmuth College in London, Ontario, where he excelled at sports and drama. He then went to work for the New York Life Insurance Company in Pennsylvania. A graduate of the Mohawk Institute, N. E. Lickers, was called to the bar in 1938 and was described by the *Branford Expositor* as the "First Ontario Indian Lawyer." [214]

Despite these successes, little encouragement generally was offered to students who wished to pursue further education. Oliver Martin, who was raised on the Six Nations Reserve in Ontario and went on to become an Ontario magistrate, recalled being told by Indian Affairs Deputy Minister Duncan Campbell Scott: "It's no use sending you Indians to school you just go back to the reserve anyway."[215]

For many students, classroom life was foreign and traumatic. David Charleson said he found the regimentation at the Christie, British Columbia, school so disturbing that he "never wanted to learn, so I jumped into my shell. I took Kindergarten twice because of what happened to me. I didn't want to learn."[216] At the Birtle school in Manitoba, Isabelle Whitford said, she had a hard time adjusting to the new language and the classroom discipline. "Every time I couldn't get an answer, like, you know, she would pull my ears and shake my head."[217] Betsy Olson described class work at the Prince Albert, Saskatchewan, school as a torment, in which her "spelling was always 30, 40, it was way down. And when we did spelling, sometimes I freeze, I couldn't move, I just scribbled because I couldn't move my hand."[218] Leona Agawa never felt comfortable in the classroom at the Spanish, Ontario, school. For much of her time in school, she was frightened or intimidated. "I'd hear my name, but I never got to answer. I stood up, never got to answer what they were saying when they sat me down. And I'd get a good slap after, after you, you leave there for not being nice in school."[219]

Since the 1920s, Indian Affairs had required residential schools to adopt provincial curricula.[220] The department had also asked provincial governments to have their school inspectors inspect Indian Affairs schools.[221] The wisdom of this practice had been questioned during the hearings of the Special Joint Committee of the Senate and House of Commons inquiry into the *Indian Act* in the 1940s. Andrew Moore, a secondary school inspector for the Province of Manitoba, told the committee members that Indian Affairs took full responsibility for all aspects of First Nations education, including curriculum.[222] Provincial education departments, including the one he worked for, were "not organized or not interested in Indian schools."[223]

In 1963, D. W. Hepburn, the former principal of the federal school in Inuvik, published an article with the ominous headline "Northern Education: Façade for Failure." He argued that the education being provided in the new federal schools was "hopelessly inadequate. The reasons for this failure are clear: the aims of education set forth

Grandin College in Fort Smith, Northwest Territories, developed a positive reputation as a "leadership factory" for the North. Deschâtelets Archives.

by the Department are thoroughly confused, the curriculum is inappropriate, and many current practices of the system are not only ill-conceived but actually harmful."[224] Although 60% of the students at the Inuvik school were in the first three grades, few teachers had any background in primary education, and "almost none has any special training in native education, and will receive none from the Department."[225] The schools were producing individuals who "lack not only the skills required for most permanent wage employment but also those necessary for the traditional economy."[226]

The decision to leave curriculum to provincial education departments meant that Aboriginal students were subjected to an education that demeaned their history, ignored their current situation, and did not even recognize them or their families as citizens. This was one of the reasons for the growing Aboriginal hostility to the Indian Affairs integration policy. An examination of the treatment of Aboriginal people in provincially approved textbooks reveals a serious and deep-rooted problem. In response to a 1956 recommendation that textbooks be developed that were relevant to Aboriginal students, Indian Affairs official R. F. Davey commented, "The preparation of school texts is an extremely difficult matter." It was his opinion that "there are other needs which can be met more easily and should be undertaken first."[227] In the following years, assessments of public-school textbooks showed that they continued to perpetuate racist stereotypes of Aboriginal people.[228] A 1968 survey pointed out that in some books, the word *squaw* was being used to describe Aboriginal women, and the word *redskins* used to describe Aboriginal people.[229]

Students also noted that the curriculum belittled their ancestry. Mary Courchene said, "Their only mandate was to Christianize and civilize; and it's written in black and white. And every single day we were reminded."[230] Lorna Cochrane could never forget an illustration in a social studies text. "There was a picture of two Jesuits laying in the snow, they were murdered by these two 'savages.' And they had this what we call 'a blood-curdling look' on their faces is how I remember that picture."[231] When the curriculum was not racist, it was bewildering and alienating. Many students could not identify with the content of the classroom materials. For instance, Lillian Elias remembers that "when I looked at Dick and Jane I thought Dick and Jane were in heaven when I saw all the green grass. That's how much I knew about Dick and Jane."[232]

Some students said that the limits of the education they had received in residential school became apparent when they were integrated into the public school system.[233] Many said there was no expectation that they would succeed. Walter Jones never forgot the answer that a fellow student at the Alberni, British Columbia, school was given when he asked if he would be able to go to Grade Twelve. "That supervisor said, 'You don't need to go that far,' he says. He says, 'Your people are never going to get education to be a professional worker, and it doesn't matter what lawyer, or doctor, or electrician, or anything, that a person has to go to school for.'"[234]

Some northern schools developed reputations for academic success. Grandin College in Fort Smith was established originally to recruit young people for the Catholic ministry. A new principal, Jean Pochat, decided to focus on providing young men and women with leadership training.[235] The school became known as a "leadership factory," producing numerous future government leaders for the North.[236] Students who attended the Churchill Vocational Centre spoke about how they were taught by open-minded teachers who were willing to expose them to the social and political changes taking place across the world in the 1960s.[237] John Amagoalik wrote that at the Churchill Vocational Centre, "we had excellent teachers. To this day we still talk about them.... They treated us as ordinary people. We had never experienced this sort of attitude before and it was, in a way, liberating to be with new teachers that treated you as their equal."[238] David Simailak spoke of how his time at residential school gave him a series of new opportunities. He fondly remembers excelling at math and spelling competitions, and travelling to Montreal for Expo '67.[239]

Specific teachers were remembered with gratitude. When Roddy Soosay lived in residence, he attended a local public school. He credited his high school principal at the Ponoka, Alberta, public school for pushing him to succeed.[240] Martha Loon said that at the Poplar Hill, Ontario, school in the 1980s, there were staff members who befriended and helped her and her siblings. There was one staff member to whom she could tell all her problems. "I could say anything to her, and we'd go for walks sometimes. So, I could tell her anything and she wouldn't, she wouldn't say anything

Carpenter's shop in the Battleford school, 1894. Saskatchewan Archives Board, R-B7.

to other staff members about it. So, in a way, that's, you know, gave me a chance to express my frustrations, and the things that I didn't like."[241]

Other students were able to concentrate on their studies. Frederick Ernest Koe said that at Stringer Hall in Inuvik, he devoted all his energies to his school work. "You kind of develop a protective mechanism on the shell that you didn't rat on anybody, you kind of behave, you followed orders and things would go smooth."[242] Madeleine Dion Stout succeeded academically at the Blue Quills school, but she did not credit the school for her success. "It's not residential school that made me a good student. My, the fundamental values and good example I had before I went to residential school by my grandfather and my parents, and all the old people on the reserve where I grew up are the ones who made me a good student."[243]

Work: "No idleness here."

Student education was further undermined by the amount of work the students had to do to support the schools. Because Indian Affairs officials had anticipated that the residential schools would be self-sufficient, students were expected to raise or grow and prepare most of the food they ate, to make and repair much of their clothing, and to maintain the schools. As a result, most of the residential schools operated on what was referred to as the "half-day system." Under this system—which amounted to

Mount Elgin, Ontario, laundry room. Clothes wringers, such as the one shown here, were a source of injury at a number of residential schools. The United Church of Canada Archives, 90.162P1173.

institutionalized child labour—students were in class for half the day and in what was supposed to be vocational training for the other half. Often, as many students, teachers, and inspectors observed, the time allocated for vocational training was actually spent in highly repetitive labour that provided little in the way of training. Rather, it served to maintain the school operations.

The half-day system was not a formally mandated system. Some schools did not use it, and those that did use it implemented it on their own terms. When, in 1922, Indian Affairs education official Russell Ferrier recommended that the Chapleau, Ontario, school implement the half-day system, he had to rely on his memory of visits to other schools in order to describe how the system operated. Indian Affairs had no official written description of the system.[244] This is telling evidence of the haphazard way in which residential schools were managed.

While the half-day system was supposed to apply only to the older students, the reality was that every student worked. Above and beyond the half-day that students spent in vocational training, it was not uncommon for them to perform daily chores both before and after school. As a result, students often spent more than half a day working for the school. At High River, Alberta, in the 1880s, students who were not learning a trade were expected to put in two hours a day of chores in the winter and four hours in the summer. According to Principal E. Claude, "To these youngest ones pertained the weeding of the garden and the house work on their side of the school, and I must say, that this summer none denied our watchword, 'No idleness here,' as all work was exclusively done by the pupils."[245]

From the time the schools were opened, parents and inspectors raised concerns about just how much work students were being required to do. Inspector T. P. Wadsworth claimed in 1884 that the boys at the Battleford school generally enjoyed their chores, but added that he would protest "against forcing these little fellows to haul water every day and all day from the river in winter, as was the case last year."[246] In 1886, Qu'Appelle school principal Joseph Hugonnard wrote, "During the summer they have more manual labor and recreation. The parents cannot understand that the pupils are here to learn how to work as well as to read and write, we therefore cannot at present devote too much time to the former."[247] Inspector Wadsworth returned to the issue of overwork in 1893, when he said that much of the farm work at the Middlechurch, Manitoba, school was too much for the boys. The girls were also set to work in the laundry at a "tender age."[248] Gilbert Wuttunee, who attended the Battleford school in the first decade of the twentieth century, recalled, "They didn't do any farm work or any kind of work until you got to, at that time, standard three, whether you were nine years old or fifteen years old." After he turned nine, he "never saw another full day of school until I left." By then, the school had drastically reduced the number of trades it taught: "There was just blacksmithing, carpentering and farming."[249] According to Lillian Elias, each fall, a barge would arrive in Aklavik, loaded with logs for the school furnace. The students would form a long chain leading from the barge to the furnace room and, with the assistance of the school staff, unload the barge.[250]

The work was inadequately supervised and often dangerous. There are accounts of students' getting hands caught in power equipment in the school laundries, the kitchens, workshops, and fields.[251] Principals tended to place the blame on student carelessness and neglected to report such injuries to the government. Several injuries were recorded only after the student's parents complained or the government received a bill for the hospital treatment of a student.[252] In December 1935, a mangle (a type of clothes wringer) at the Qu'Appelle school crushed several fingers on Florence McLeod's right hand, which were amputated. The school principal, G. Leonard, stressed that "this mangle has been in use at this school for several years and all the girls are familiar with its operation." Indian Affairs secretary A. F. MacKenzie concluded that "all the necessary precautions were taken, and, while the accident to Florence McLeod is regretted, it was through no fault of the school management."[253] The school's failure to protect its students can be seen in the fact that McLeod's father, Henry, had been injured in a similar fashion when he was a student at the same school.[254] In 1941, a twelve-year-old boy lost all the fingers on one hand in an accident in the Brandon, Manitoba, school barn.[255] Eight years later, fifteen-year-old Rodney Beardy died in a tractor accident at the same school.[256] A student at the Edmonton school lost a foot in 1944 after an accident during the operation of a machine used in the preparation of fodder.[257] Two boys from the Birtle, Manitoba, school were injured in a truck accident in 1942. From Indian Affairs correspondence, it appears that the accident involved a truck carrying seventy boys who were being taken from the school to the fields to do farm work. Indian Affairs official R. A. Hoey criticized the principal for allowing the practice to take place, noting that "it is almost unbelievable that the principal should permit 70 pupils to be conveyed in a truck."[258]

Even though the half-day system was supposedly eliminated in the early 1950s, students continued to be overworked.[259] After Sam Ross ran away from the Birtle school in 1959, he told Indian Affairs official J. R. Bell that he wanted to continue his education, but had been forced to work "too hard" at the school. He said that from September to Christmas of the previous year, he had worked in the school barn every day between "6:00 A.M. and 7:00 A.M. and from 8:00 A.M. to 9:00 A.M. again at recess, from 4:00 P.M. to 6:00 P.M. and had had to stoke up the furnace with coal at 10:00 o'clock before retiring." Ross said that "he liked school but not working like a hired hand." Bell recommended that the amount of student labour being done at the Birtle school be investigated.[260]

Language and culture: "The Indian language is indeed seldom heard in the institution."

The government's hostile approach to Aboriginal languages was reiterated in numerous policy directives. In 1883, Indian Commissioner Edgar Dewdney instructed Battleford school principal Thomas Clarke that great attention was to be given "towards imparting a knowledge of the art of reading, writing and speaking the English language rather than that of Cree."[261] In 1889, Deputy Minister of Indian Affairs Lawrence Vankoughnet informed Bishop Paul Durieu that in the new Cranbrook, British Columbia, school, mealtime conversations were to be "conducted exclusively in the English language." The principal was also to set a fixed time during which Aboriginal languages could be spoken.[262] In 1890, Indian Commissioner Hayter Reed proposed, "At the most the native language is only to be used as a vehicle of teaching and should be discontinued as such as soon as practicable." English was to be the primary language of instruction, "even where French is taught."[263] The Indian Affairs "Programme of Studies for Indian Schools" of 1893 advised, "Every effort must be made to induce pupils to speak English, and to teach them to understand it; unless they do the whole work of the teacher is likely to be wasted."[264]

Principals regularly reported on their success in suppressing Aboriginal languages. In 1887, Principal E. Claude boasted that his thirty students at the High River school "all understand English passably well and few are unable to express themselves in English. They talk English in recreation. I scarcely need any coercive means to oblige

Inuit students at the Joseph Bernier School, Chesterfield Inlet, 1956. Diocese of Churchill-Hudson Bay.

them to do so."[265] In 1898, the Kamloops principal reported that "English is the only language used at all times by the pupils."[266] That same year, the Mission, British Columbia, principal wrote, "English is the common language of the school, the Indian language is indeed seldom heard in the institution, except with the newly arrived pupils."[267] The 1898 report from the principal of the Anglican school at Onion Lake indicated that the school was one of the few exceptions. There, the children were taught to "read and write both Cree and English."[268] Inspectors viewed the continued use of Aboriginal languages by the students as a sign of failure. The principal of the Red Deer school was taken to task in 1903 by an inspector who felt that a "serious drawback to school work, as well as an evidence of bad discipline, was the use of the Cree language, which was quite prevalent."[269]

This policy of language suppression continued well into the twentieth century. After a 1935 tour of Canada, Oblate Superior General Théodore Labouré expressed concern over the strict enforcement of prohibitions against speaking Aboriginal languages. In his opinion, "The forbidding of children to speak Indian, even during recreation, was so strict in some of our schools that any lapse would be severely punished—to the point that children were led to consider it a serious offense."[270]

Students had strong memories of being punished for 'speaking Indian.' Mary Angus, who attended the Battleford school in the late nineteenth century, said that students caught speaking their own language were given a close haircut: "All the hair cut to be as a man, that what they do, for us not to talk. We were afraid of that, to have our hair cut."[271] At the Fraser Lake school in British Columbia, Mary John said she could speak her own language only in whispers.[272] Melvina McNabb was seven years old when she was enrolled in the File Hills school, and "I couldn't talk a word of English. I talked Cree and I was abused for that, hit, and made to try to talk English."[273] Raymond Hill, who was a student at the Mohawk Institute in Brantford in the early years of the twentieth century, said, "I lost my language. They threatened us with a strapping if we spoke it, and within a year I lost all of it. They said they thought we were talking about them."[274]

Language use often continued in secret. Mary Englund recalled that while Aboriginal languages were banned at the Mission school in the early twentieth century, children would still speak it to one another.[275] Clyde Peters said he stopped speaking his Aboriginal language at the Mount Elgin school after he found out the school punished students for doing so. "I never got the strap for it but I was warned enough that I didn't do it." Even after that, he and his friends would speak to each other when they thought no one else could hear them. "When we'd go up in the dormitories in the evening I had a friend from Sarnia who I could talk with."[276]

Many of the students came to the school fluent in an Aboriginal language, with little or no understanding of French or English. This trend continued well into the post-war period. For these children, the first few months in the school were disorienting and frightening. Arthur McKay arrived at the Sandy Bay, Manitoba, school in the early 1940s with no knowledge of English. "They told me not to speak my language and everything, so I always pretended to be asleep at my desk so they wouldn't ask me anything."[277] Peter Nakogee recalled being punished for writing in his notebook in Cree syllabics at the Fort Albany, Ontario, school.[278]

Meeka Alivaktuk came to the Pangnirtung school in what is now Nunavut with no knowledge of English. When she failed to obey an instruction because she did not understand it, she was slapped on the hands. "That's how my education began."[279] On his first day of school in Pangnirtung, the teacher overheard Sam Kautainuk speaking to a friend in Inuktitut. "He took a ruler and grabbed my head like this and then smacked me in the mouth with the ruler four times."[280]

At the Qu'Appelle school in the mid-1960s, Greg Rainville said, he was punished for failing to carry out instructions given to him in a language he did not understand. "The nuns would get frustrated with you when they talked to you in French or English, and you're not knowing what they're talking about, and you're pulled around by the ear."[281] At the Shubenacadie school, a staff member once caught William Herney speaking Mi'kmaq with his brother. She strapped him and then washed his mouth out with soap.[282] Alphonsine McNeely underwent the same punishment at the Roman Catholic school at Aklavik in the 1940s.[283] Pierrette Benjamin said she was forced to eat soap at the La Tuque school. "The principal, she put it in my mouth, and she said, 'Eat it, eat it.'"[284]

The language policy disrupted families. When John Kistabish left the Amos, Québec, school, he could no longer speak Algonquin, and his parents could not speak French, the language that he had been taught in the school. As a result, he found it almost impossible to communicate with them about the abuse he experienced at the school. "I had tried to talk with my parents, and, no, it didn't work.... We were well anyway because I knew that they were my parents, when I left the residential school, but the communication wasn't there."[285]

Culture was attacked as well as language. In his memoirs, Stoney Chief John Snow tells of how at the Morley, Alberta, school, the "education consisted of nothing that had any relationship to our homes and culture. Indeed Stoney culture was condemned explicitly and implicitly." He recalled being taught that the only good people on earth were non-Indians and, specifically, white Christians.[286] Andrew Bull Calf recalled that at the residential school in Cardston, Alberta, students were not only punished for speaking their own languages, but they also were discouraged from participating in traditional cultural activities.[287] Evelyn Kelman recalled that the principal at the Brocket, Alberta, school warned students that if they attended a Sun Dance that was to be held during the summer, they would be strapped on their return to school.[288] Marilyn Buffalo recalled being told by Hobbema, Alberta, school staff that the Sun Dance was 'devil worship.'[289] One year, Sarah McLeod returned to the Kamloops school with a miniature totem pole that a family member had given her for her birthday. When she proudly showed it to one of the nuns, it was taken from her and thrown out. She was told that it was nothing but devilry.[290]

School officials did not limit their opposition to Aboriginal culture to the classroom. In 1942, Gleichen, Alberta, principal John House became involved in a campaign to have two Blackfoot chiefs deposed, in part because of their support for traditional dance ceremonies.[291] In 1943, F. E. Anfield, the principal of the Alert Bay, British Columbia, school, wrote a letter encouraging former students not to participate in local Potlatches, implying that such ceremonies were based on outdated superstition, and led to impoverishment and family neglect.[292]

Even when it did not directly disparage Aboriginal culture, the curriculum undermined Aboriginal identity. Thaddee Andre, who attended the Sept-Îles, Québec, school in the 1950s, recalled how as a student he wanted "to resemble the white man, then in the meantime, they are trying by all means to strip you of who you are as an Innu. When you are young, you are not aware of what you are losing as a human being."[293]

It was not until the 1960s that attitudes began to change about the place of Aboriginal language and culture in residential schools.[294] Alex Alikashuak said that at the Churchill school, which operated in the 1960s, there were no restrictions on the use of Aboriginal languages. He recalled, "The only time, real time we spoke English was when we were in the classroom, or we're talking to one of the administration staff, and or somebody from town that's not Inuit, but otherwise we, everybody spoke our language."[295] The Canadian Welfare Council's 1967 report on nine Saskatchewan residential schools described "an emphasis on relating course content to the Indian culture" as "imaginative" and a sign of progress in "making the educational experience meaningful for the Indian child."[296] By 1968, the Roman Catholic school in Cardston was incorporating Blackfoot into its educational program.[297] In some schools, Aboriginal teachers were brought in to teach dancing and singing.[298] However, as late as the 1969–70 school year, there were only seven Indian Affairs schools that offered courses in Aboriginal languages or used Aboriginal languages as the language of instruction.[299]

Despite the encouragement that was offered in some schools, and the students' efforts to keep their language alive, the overall impact was language loss. Of her experiences at the Baptist school in Whitehorse and the Anglican school in Carcross, Rose Dorothy Charlie said, "They took my language. They took it right out of my mouth. I never spoke it again."[300] In some cases, the residential school experience led parents to decide not to teach their children an Aboriginal language. Both of Joline Huskey's parents attended residential school in the Northwest Territories. As a result of their experience in the schools, they raised their daughter to speak English.[301] When Bruce Dumont was sent to residential school in Onion Lake, Saskatchewan, his mother warned him not to speak Cree.[302]

Arranging and blocking marriages

Through the residential schools, Indian Affairs and church officials sought to extend their control into the most intimate aspects of the lives of Aboriginal children. Indian Affairs officials believed that because the department had spent money educating students, it had gained the right to determine whom they married. Government officials feared that if students married someone who had not also been educated at a residential school, they would revert to traditional 'uncivilized' ways.[303] The control of marriage was part of the ongoing policy of forced assimilation. In 1890, Indian Commissioner Hayter Reed criticized Qu'Appelle principal Joseph Hugonnard for allowing female students from the Qu'Appelle school to marry boys who had not gone to school, without first getting Indian Affairs' approval. Reed argued, "The contention that the parents have the sole right to decide such matters cannot for one moment be admitted."[304]

The government not only encouraged marriage between students, but it also began to make marriage part of the process of getting out of residential school. In his annual report for 1896, Deputy Minister Hayter Reed wrote, "It is considered advisable, where pupils are advanced in years and considered capable of providing for themselves, to bring about a matrimonial alliance, either at the time of being discharged from the school or as soon after as possible."[305] In other words, the principals were expected to arrange marriages for the older students.

Principals regularly reported and celebrated student marriages, and, indeed, did often arrange them.[306] Reverend P. Claessen, principal of the Kuper Island school, reported in 1909 that he had succeeded in "engaging one of our leaving girls with one of our best old boys."[307] Kamloops school principal A. M. Carion reported, "It is gratifying to note again that since my last report, two more couples of ex-pupils have been united in the bonds of holy wedlock. The ex-pupils who marry other ex-pupils are better able to retain the habits of civilized life, which they acquired at the school."[308]

Efforts were also made to block marriages deemed to be unsuitable. In 1895, Indian agent Magnus Begg told members of the Blackfoot Reserve that "no young man could marry a girl from an Industrial or board [sic] School without having prepared a house with two rooms, and owning cows, with the necessary stabling, &c."[309] In that same year, principals and Indian agents were instructed to seek departmental permission prior to allowing students to marry.[310]

Principals continued to arrange marriages into the 1930s. In 1936, the principal of the Roman Catholic school at Onion Lake prepared a list of students who had turned sixteen and who, he believed, should not be discharged. He noted that he insisted on keeping the students, since he would "always try to marry them as soon as they leave the school." He wanted to keep one eighteen-year-old student in the school until the fall threshing was complete. Then, she would be married to a former pupil. He wanted to keep another eighteen-year-old until "she gets married during the year."[311] In 1922, the head of the Presbyterian Church's Winnipeg Committee on Indian Work urged the government to make it "unlawfull [sic] for a pupil or ex-pupil of the School to marry or be married without the permission of the Indian Agent." The Presbyterians proposed that the children of such unauthorized marriages be denied Treaty annuities until they reached the age of twenty-one and be prohibited from attending school.[312] Although the measure was not adopted, it is reflective of the church's lack of respect for the autonomy of Aboriginal people.

Food: "Always hungry"

In his memoir of his years as a student at the Mount Elgin school in southern Ontario in the early twentieth century, Enos Montour wrote that the boys "were always hungry. Grub was the beginning and end of all conversations."[313] According to Eleanor Brass, the dinners at the File Hills, Saskatchewan, school consisted "of watery soup with no flavour, and never any meat." One winter, it seemed to her that they ate fish every day.[314] In fair weather, the boys would trap gophers and squirrels, and roast them over open fires to supplement their meagre diets. Sometimes, they would share these

Ahousaht, British Columbia, students in the school cafeteria. British Columbia Archives, PN-15589.

treats with the girls at the school.[315] Mary John, who attended the Fraser Lake, British Columbia, school, recalled that the meals were dull and monotonous: a regular diet of porridge interspersed with boiled barley and beans, and bread covered with lard. Weeks might go by without any fish or meat; sugar and jam were reserved for special occasions.[316] A former student of the Hay River school in the Northwest Territories recalled that in the years following the First World War, he "didn't see jam from the time I got off the boat to the time I got back on to come back down."[317] Another student from that school recalled a constant diet of fish: "They would boil it up real good until the meat falls away, the bones and scales all floating around, then mix in flour and serve it up. I won't use flour for my dogs because there's not much good in it."[318]

The reports of government inspectors confirm these student memories. An 1895 report on an inspection of the Middlechurch school concluded, "The 'bill of fare' is plain. I believed it to be barely sufficient for the older pupils, who have now, at fifteen to eighteen years of age, larger apetites [sic] than they will have when older."[319] In 1918, Indian agent John Smith inspected the Kamloops school and reported his "suspicion that the vitality of the children is not sufficiently sustained from a lack of nutritious food, or enough of the same for vigorous growing children."[320] A local doctor concurred, writing that "for some months past the food supplied has been inadequate for the needs of the children."[321] There were some positive assessments, but Indian

Students working in the kitchen at the Cross Lake, Manitoba, school in the early 1920s. St. Boniface Historical Society Archives; Roman Catholic Archbishop of Keewatin-The Pas Fonds; N1826.

Affairs official Martin Benson questioned their accuracy. "In almost every instance when meals are mentioned by Inspectors they are said to be well cooked. I doubt very much whether they ever took a full regulation school meal of bread and dripping, or boiled beef and potatoes." In Benson's opinion, "The bill of fare is decidedly monotonous and makes no allowance for peculiarities of taste or constitution."[322]

When funding was cut during the Depression of the 1930s, it was the students who paid the price—in more ways than one. At the end of the 1930s, it was discovered that the cook at the Presbyterian school at Kenora was actually selling bread to the students, at the rate of ten cents a loaf. When asked if the children got enough to eat at meals, she responded, "Yes, but they were always hungry." The Indian agent ordered an end to the practice.[323] The fact that hungry students would be reduced to buying bread to supplement their meals in 1939 highlights the government's failure to provide schools with the resources needed to feed students adequately.

Milk was in constant shortage at many schools, in part due to the poor health and small size of the school dairy herds.[324] As late as 1937, disease among the cows at the Kamloops school had cut milk production by 50%. To the principal's frustration,

Ottawa refused to fund the construction of an additional barn, which would have allowed for an increase in milk production and the isolation of sick animals.[325] Even when the dairy herds were producing satisfactorily, the students did not always get the full benefit. Often, the milk was separated, with the skimmed milk served to the children.[326] The milk fat was turned to butter and cream, which was frequently sold to raise funds for the schools. Inspector W. Murison noted in 1925 that the cows at the Elkhorn, Manitoba, school were producing enough milk for the school, but the students were not getting "the full benefit of this milk as I found that they were making about 30 lbs. of butter a week, and a great deal of the milk given the children is separated milk, which has not much food value."[327]

In 1942, the federal government issued Canada's Official Food Rules, an early version of the Canada Food Guide.[328] Inspectors quickly discovered that residential school diets did not measure up to the Food Rules. Dr. L. B. Pett, the head of the federal government's Nutrition Division, concluded in 1947, on the basis of inspections his staff had done, that "no school was doing a good feeding job."[329] It was not until the late 1950s that the federal government adopted a residential school food allowance calculated to provide a diet deemed "fully adequate nutritionally."[330] Even with the increase in funding, schools still had difficulty providing students with adequate meals. A 1966 dietician's report on Yukon Hall in Whitehorse observed that although the Canada Food Guide requirements were being met, "because of the appetite of this age group, the staff are finding 66¢ per day per student is limiting."[331] In 1969, an official at Coudert Hall in Whitehorse wrote, "The $0.80 alloted [sic] per student for food is not sufficient. In the north we find prices sky high." To cope with the problem, the residence sometimes had to buy "less meat and served maccaroni [sic] products."[332] A November 1970 inspection of the Dauphin, Manitoba, school noted that the "menu appears to be short of the recommended two servings of fruit per day."[333]

In their home communities, many students had been raised on food that their parents had hunted, fished, or harvested. These meals were very different from the European diets served at the schools. This change in diet added to the students' sense of disorientation. Daisy Diamond found the food at residential school to be unfamiliar and unpalatable. "When I was going to Shingwauk, the food didn't taste very good, because we didn't have our traditional food there, our moose meat, our bannock, and our berries."[334] Dora Fraser, from the eastern Arctic, found it difficult to adjust to the food served in the hostels. "We were eating canned food, beans, peas, red beans. The food was terrible."[335] Even when traditional foods were prepared, the school cooks made them in ways that were unfamiliar and unappetizing to the students. Ellen Okimaw, who attended the Fort Albany, Ontario, school, had vivid memories of poorly cooked fish served at the schools. The school cook had simply "dumped the whole thing, and boiled them like that, just like that without cleaning them."[336]

Bernard Catcheway recalled that in the 1960s at the Pine Creek, Manitoba, school, "we had to eat all our food even though we didn't like it. There was a lot of times there I seen other students that threw up and they were forced to eat their own, their own vomit."[337] Bernard Sutherland recalled students at the Fort Albany school being forced to eat food that they had vomited. "I saw in person how the children eat their vomit. When they happened to be sick. And they threw up while eating."[338] These abuses led in 1999 to the conviction of Anna Wesley, a former staff member of the Fort Albany school, on three charges of administering a noxious substance.[339]

Some schools did make allowances for traditional foods. Simon Awashish recalled being allowed to trap for food while attending the Amos, Québec, school.

> When we brought in hares, we were asked if ... there was some members of our nation that came to work in the kitchen, and we asked them to cook the hare for us in the traditional Atikameg way, in order to keep some sort of contact with our traditional food that we had before, before we were separated from our community.[340]

Students who spoke of hunger also spoke of their efforts to improve their diet secretly. Woodie Elias recalled being hungry all the time at the Anglican school in Aklavik. "Once in a while we go raid the cellar and you can't call that stealing; that was our food."[341] When Dorothy Nolie helped out in the Alert Bay school kitchen, she and her co-workers would eat bread as they sliced it. "Kids would come to me and ask me for bread, and I'd sneak it to them."[342] At the Moose Factory school in Ontario, Nellie Trapper said, students "used to steal food, peanut butter, whatever's cooking in a pot. There were big pots in there. I remember taking figs from that pot."[343]

Complaints about the limited, poorly prepared, monotonous diet were intensified by the fact that at many schools, the students knew the staff members were being served much better fare than they had. At the school she attended in Saskatchewan, Inez Dieter said, "the staff used to eat like kings, kings and queens." Like many students, she said, she used the opportunity of working in the staff dining room to help herself to leftovers. "I'd steal that and I'd eat, and I'd feel real good."[344] Gladys Prince recalled how, at the Sandy Bay school in Manitoba, the "priests ate the apples, we ate the peelings. That is what they fed us. We never ate bread. They were stingy them, their own, their own baking."[345] When Frances Tait was given a position in the staff dining room, she said, she thought she had "died and gone to heaven 'cause even eating their leftovers were better than what we got."[346] Hazel Bitternose, who attended schools in Lestock and Qu'Appelle, said she enjoyed working in the priests' dining room. "They had some good food there and I used to sneak some food and able to feed myself good there. So that's why I liked to work there."[347]

The federal government knowingly chose not to provide schools with enough money to ensure that kitchens and dining rooms were properly equipped, that cooks were properly trained, and, most significantly, that food was purchased in sufficient quantity and quality for growing children. It was a decision that left thousands of Aboriginal children vulnerable to disease.

Health: "For sickness, conditions at this school are nothing less than criminal."

The number of students who died at Canada's residential schools is not likely ever to be known in full. The most serious gap in information arises from the incompleteness of the documentary record. Many records have simply been destroyed. According to a 1935 federal government policy, school returns could be destroyed after five years, and reports of accidents after ten years. This led to the destruction of fifteen tonnes of waste paper. Between 1936 and 1944, 200,000 Indian Affairs files were destroyed.[348] Health records were regularly destroyed. For example, in 1957, Indian and Northern Health Services was instructed to destroy "correspondence re routine arrangements re medical and dental treatments of Indians and Eskimos, such as transportation, escort services, admission to hospital, advice on treatment, requests for treatment, etc." after a period of two years. Reports by doctors, dentists, and nurses were similarly assigned a two-year retention period.[349]

Often, the existing record lacks needed detail. For example, it was not uncommon for principals, in their annual reports, to state that a specific number of students had died in the previous year, but not to name them.[350] It was not until 1935 that Indian Affairs adopted a formal policy on how deaths at the schools were to be reported and investigated.[351]

There can be no certainty that all deaths were, in fact, reported to Indian Affairs—the Truth and Reconciliation Commission of Canada has located reports of student deaths in church records that are not reported in government documents.[352] In some cases, school officials appear not to have recognized a responsibility to report student deaths to provincial vital statistics officials, meaning that these records may also be deficient.[353]

As part of its work, the Truth and Reconciliation Commission of Canada has established a National Residential School Student Death Register. The creation of this register marks the first effort in Canadian history to properly record the number of students who died in residential schools. The register is made of up three sub-registers:

1) the Register of Confirmed Deaths of Named Residential School Students (the "Named Register");

2) the Register of Confirmed Deaths of Unnamed Residential School Students (the "Unnamed Register"); and

Graph 3

Residential school death rates for 1,000 students, Named and Unnamed registers combined, 1869 to 1965

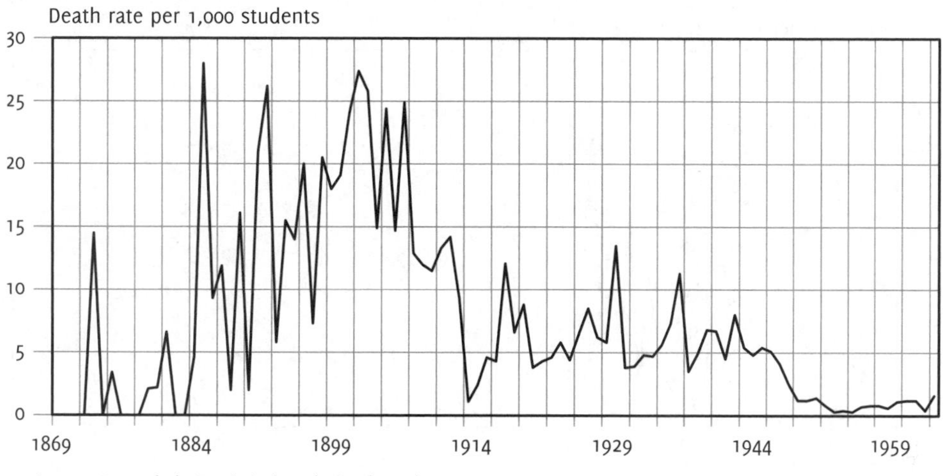

Source: Rosenthal, "Statistical Analysis of Deaths," 11.

Graph 4

Comparative death rates per 1,000 population, residential schools (Named and Unnamed registers combined) and the general Canadian population of school-aged children, using five-year averages from 1921 to 1965.

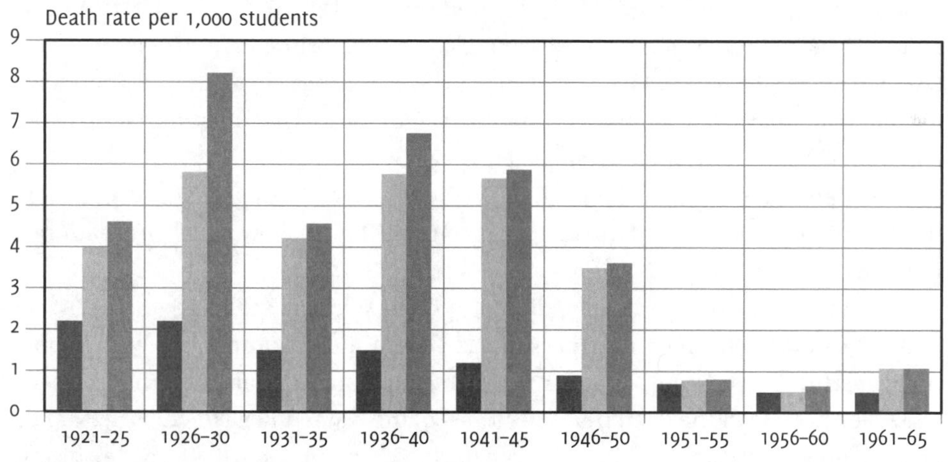

Source: Fraser, Vital Statistics and Health, Table B35-50, http://www.statcan.gc.ca/pub/11-516-x/section-b/4147437-eng.htm; Rosenthal, "Statistical Analysis of Deaths," 13.

Graph 5

Residential school tuberculosis death rates per 1,000 population, Named and Unnamed registers combined, 1869–1965

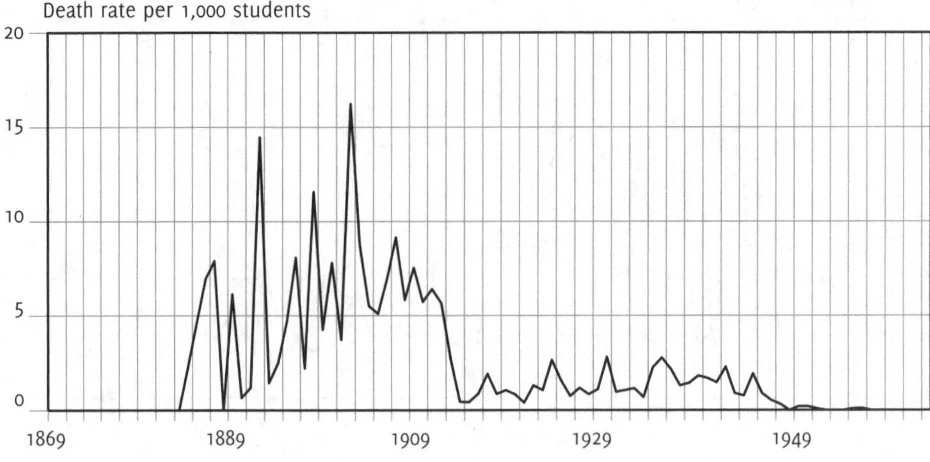

Source: Rosenthal, "Statistical Analysis of Deaths," 97–99.

3) the Register of Deaths that Require Further Investigation (to determine if they should be placed on either the Named or Unnamed register).

A January 2015 statistical analysis of the Named Register for the period from 1867 to 2000 identified 2,040 deaths. The same analysis of a combination of the Named and Unnamed registers identified 3,201 reported deaths. The greatest number of these deaths (1,328 on the Named Register and 2,434 on the Named and Unnamed registers) took place prior to 1940. Graph 3 shows the overall death rate per 1,000 students for the residential schools during this period (figures are based on information in the combined Named and Unnamed registers).

This graph suggests that the peak of the health crisis in the schools occurred in the late nineteenth and early twentieth centuries. It also shows that the death rate remained high until the 1950s.

The death rates for Aboriginal children in the residential schools were far higher than those experienced by members of the general Canadian population. Graph 4 compares the death rate per 1,000 of the general population of Canadian children aged five to fourteen with the death rates per 1,000 of the Named Register and the Named and Unnamed registers combined. (Given the limitations in Statistics Canada's historical data, the death rates are provided as five-year averages.) As can be seen, until the 1950s Aboriginal children in residential schools died at a far higher rate than school-aged children in the general population. It is only in the 1950s that the residential school death rates declined to a level comparable to that of the general school-aged population. As late as the 1941–45 period, the Named and Unnamed Combined

The Roman Catholic school at Sturgeon Landing, Saskatchewan, was destroyed by fire in September 1952. There was no loss of life. St. Boniface Historical Society Archives, Roman Catholic Archbishop of Keewatin-The Pas Fonds, N3637.

residential school death rate was 4.90 times higher than the general death rate. In the 1960s, even though the residential school death rates were much lower than their historic highs, they were still double those of the general school-aged population.

In nearly 50% of the cases (both in the Named and Unnamed registers), there is no recorded cause of death. From those cases where the cause of death was reported, it is clear that until the 1950s, the schools were the sites of an ongoing tuberculosis crisis. Tuberculosis accounted for just less than 50% of the recorded deaths (46.2% for the Named Register, and 47% for the Named and Unnamed registers combined). The tuberculosis death rate remained high until the 1950s: its decline coincides with the introduction of effective drug treatment. The next most frequently recorded causes of death were influenza (9.2% on the Named Register, and 9.1% of the deaths on the combined Named and Unnamed registers), pneumonia (6.9% on the Named Register, and 9.1% of the deaths on the combined Named and Unnamed registers), and general lung disease (3.4% on the Named Register, and 5.5% of the deaths on the combined Named and Unnamed registers). Graph 5 shows the residential school tuberculosis death rate (figures are based on information in the combined Named and Unnamed registers).

The tuberculosis health crisis in the schools was part of a broader Aboriginal health crisis that was set in motion by colonial policies that separated Aboriginal people from their land, thereby disrupting their economies and their food supplies. This crisis was particularly intense on the Canadian Prairies. Numerous federal government policies contributed to the undermining of Aboriginal health. During a period of starvation,

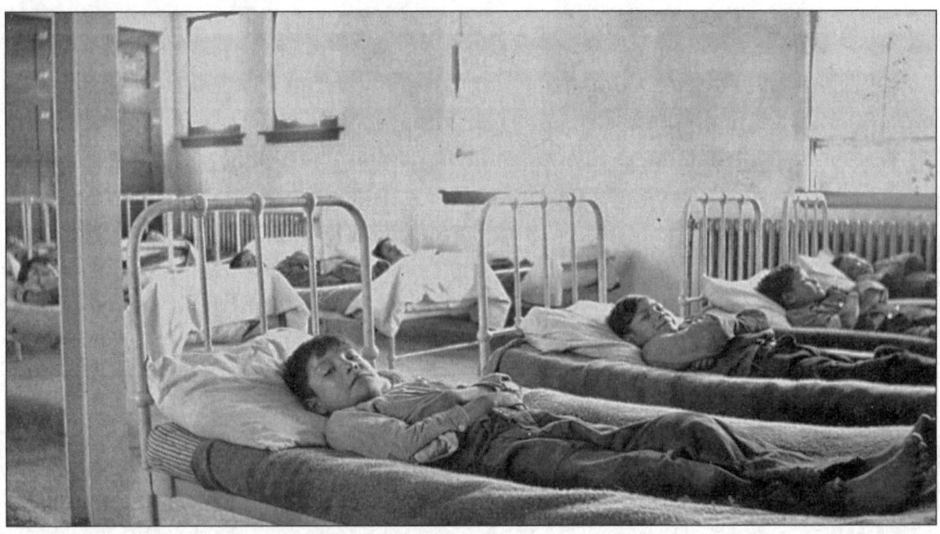

Old Sun's, Alberta, dormitory. Diseases such as tuberculosis could spread quickly in crowded dormitories. General Synod Archives, Anglican Church of Canada, P75-103-S7-167.

rations were withheld from bands in an effort to force them to abandon the lands that they had initially selected for their reserves. In making the Treaties, the government had promised to provide assistance to First Nations to allow them to make a transition from hunting to farming. This aid was slow in coming and inadequate on arrival. Restrictions in the *Indian Act* made it difficult for First Nations farmers to sell their produce or borrow money to invest in technology. Reserve land was often agriculturally unproductive. Reserve housing was poor and crowded, sanitation was inadequate, and access to clean water was limited. Under these conditions, tuberculosis flourished. Those people it did not kill were often severely weakened and likely to succumb to measles, smallpox, and other infectious diseases.[354]

For Aboriginal children, the relocation to residential schools was generally no healthier than their homes had been on the reserves. In 1897, Indian Affairs official Martin Benson reported that the industrial schools in Manitoba and the Northwest Territories had been "hurriedly constructed of poor materials, badly laid out, without due provision for lighting, heating or ventilation." In addition, drainage was poor, and water and fuel supplies were inadequate.[355] Conditions were not any better in the church-built boarding schools. In 1904, Indian Commissioner David Laird echoed Benson's comments when he wrote that the sites for the boarding schools on the Prairies seemed "to have been selected without proper regard for either water-supply or drainage. I need not mention any school in particular, but I have urged improvement in several cases in regard to fire-protection."[356]

Students' health depended on clean water, good sanitation, and adequate ventilation. But little was done to improve the poor living conditions that were identified at the beginning of the twentieth century. In 1940, R. A. Hoey, who had served as the Indian Affairs superintendent of Welfare and Training since 1936, wrote a lengthy assessment of the condition of the existing residential schools. He concluded that many schools were "in a somewhat dilapidated condition" and had "become acute fire hazards." He laid responsibility for the "condition of our schools, generally," upon their "faulty construction." This construction, he said, had failed to meet "the minimum standards in the construction of public buildings, particularly institutions for the education of children."[357] By 1940, the government had concluded that future policy should concentrate on the expansion of day schools for First Nations children. As a result, many of the existing residential school buildings were allowed to continue to deteriorate. A 1967 brief from the National Association of Principals and Administrators of Indian Residences—which included principals of both Catholic and Protestant schools—concluded, "In the years that the Churches have been involved in the administration of the schools, there has been a steady deterioration in essential services. Year after year, complaints, demands and requests for improvements have, in the main, fallen upon deaf ears."[358]

When E. A. Côté, the deputy minister responsible for Indian Affairs, met with church and school representatives to discuss the brief, he told them that only emergency repairs would be undertaken at schools that Indian Affairs intended to close.[359]

The badly built and poorly maintained schools constituted serious fire hazards. Defective firefighting equipment exacerbated the risk, and schools were fitted with inadequate and dangerous fire escapes. Lack of access to safe fire escapes led to high death tolls in fires at the Beauval and Cross Lake schools.[360] The Truth and Reconciliation Commission of Canada has determined that at least fifty-three schools were destroyed by fire. There were at least 170 additional recorded fires. At least forty students died in residential school fires.[361] The harsh discipline and jail-like nature of life in the schools meant that many students sought to run away. To prevent this, many schools deliberately ignored government instructions in relation to fire drills and fire escapes. These were not problems only of the late nineteenth or early twentieth centuries. Well into the twentieth century, recommendations for improvements went unheeded, and dangerous and forbidden practices were widespread and entrenched. In the interests of cost containment, the Canadian government placed the lives of students and staff at risk for 130 years.

The buildings were not only fire traps. They were also incubators of disease. Rather than helping combat the tuberculosis crisis in the broader Aboriginal community, the poor condition of the schools served to intensify it. The 1906 annual report of Dr. Peter Bryce, the chief medical officer for Indian Affairs, observed that "the Indian population of Canada has a mortality rate of more than double that of the whole population, and in some provinces more than three times." Tuberculosis was the prevalent cause of death. He described a cycle of disease in which infants and children were infected

Dr. Peter Bryce, Indian Affairs chief medical officer, recommended in 1909 that Canada's residential schools be turned into sanatoria and placed under his administration. Library and Archives Canada, Topley Studio, a042966.

at home and sent to residential schools, where they infected other children. The children infected in the schools were "sent home when too ill to remain at school, or because of being a danger to the other scholars, and have conveyed the disease to houses previously free."[362] The following year, Bryce published a damning report on the conditions at prairie boarding schools. In an age when fresh air was seen as being central to the successful treatment of tuberculosis, he concluded that, with only a few exceptions, the ventilation at the schools was "extremely inadequate."[363]

He found the school staff and even physicians

> inclined to question or minimize the dangers of infection from scrofulous or consumptive pupils [*scrofula* and *consumption* were alternate names for types of tuberculosis] and nothing less than peremptory instructions as to how to deal with cases of disease existing in the schools will eliminate this ever-present danger of infection.[364]

He gave the principals a questionnaire to complete regarding the health condition of their former students. The responses from fifteen schools revealed that "of a total of 1,537 pupils reported upon nearly 25 per cent are dead, of one school with an absolutely accurate statement, 69 per cent of ex-pupils are dead, and that everywhere the almost invariable cause of death given is tuberculosis." He drew particular attention to the fate of the thirty-one students who had been discharged from the File Hills school: nine were in good health, and twenty-two were dead.[365]

The extent of the health crisis was so severe that some people within the federal government and the Protestant churches became convinced that the only solution was to close the schools and replace them with day schools. However, the Indian Affairs minister of the day, Frank Oliver, refused to enact the plan without the support of the churches involved. The plan foundered for lack of Roman Catholic support. During the same period, Bryce recommended that the federal government take over all the schools and turn them into sanatoria under his control. This plan was rejected because it was viewed as being too costly, and it was thought that it would have met with church opposition.[366]

Instead of closing schools or turning them into sanatoria, the government's major response to the health crisis was the negotiation in 1910 of a contract between Indian Affairs and the churches. This contract increased the grants to the schools and imposed a set of standards for diet and ventilation. The contract also required that students not be admitted "until, where practicable, a physician has reported that the child is in good health."[367]

As noted earlier, although the contract led to improvements in the short term, inflation quickly eroded the benefit of the increase in grants. The situation was worsened by the cuts to the grants that were repeatedly imposed during the Great Depression of the 1930s. The underfunding created by the cuts guaranteed that students would be poorly fed, clothed, and housed. As a result, children were highly susceptible to tuberculosis. And, because the government was slow to put in place policies that would have prohibited the admission of children with tuberculosis, and ineffective in enforcing such policies once they were developed, healthy children became infected. As late as the 1950s, at some schools, pre-admission medical examinations appear to have been perfunctory, ineffective, or non-existent.[368] In the long run, the 1910 contract proved to be no solution for the tuberculosis crisis.

The schools often lacked adequate facilities for the treatment of sick children. In 1893, Indian Affairs inspector T. P. Wadsworth reported that at the Qu'Appelle school, the "want of an infirmary is still very much felt."[369] Those infirmaries that existed were often primitive. On an 1891 visit to the Battleford school, Indian Commissioner Hayter Reed concluded that the hospital ward was in such poor shape that they had been obliged to move the children in it to the staff sitting room. According to Reed, "The noise, as well as the bad smells, come from the lavatory underneath."[370] Proposals to construct a small hospital at the Red Deer school in 1901 were not implemented.[371] There were also reports of inadequate isolation facilities at the Regina school (1901), the Anglican school in Onion Lake, Saskatchewan (1921), the Mission, British Columbia, school (1924), and the Muncey, Ontario, school (1935).[372] When diphtheria broke out at Duck Lake, Saskatchewan, in 1909, the nine students who fell ill were placed in a "large isolated house."[373]

Even though the 1910 contract required all schools to have hospital accommodation to prevent the spread of infectious disease, many schools continued to be without a proper infirmary. The 1918 global influenza epidemic left four children dead at the Red Deer, Alberta, school. When the influenza epidemic subsided, Principal J. F. Woodsworth complained to Indian Affairs, "For sickness, conditions at this school are nothing less than criminal. We have no isolation ward and no hospital equipment of any kind."[374] The Roman Catholic principals petitioned the federal government for the establishment of sick rooms, under the supervision of a competent nurse, at each school in 1924. At the same time, they objected to the sanitary inspection of the schools by government-appointed nurses, since they recommended changes "leading to the transformation of our schools into hospitals or sanatoriums."[375] There were also regular reports that schools could not afford to hire needed nursing staff.[376] Indian Affairs officials continued to be critical of the quality of care provided by school infirmaries at the end of the 1950s.[377] Complaints from principals make it clear that into the late 1960s, there were still severe limitations on the range of health services being provided to residential school students.[378]

General Aboriginal health care was never a priority for the Canadian government. Tuberculosis among Aboriginal people largely was ignored unless it threatened the general Canadian population.[379] In 1937, Dr. H. W. McGill, the director of Indian Affairs, sent out an instruction that Indian health-care services "must be restricted to those required for the safety of limb, life or essential function." Hospital care was to be limited, spending on drugs was cut in half, and sanatoria and hospital treatment for chronic tuberculosis were eliminated.[380]

The high death rates led many parents to refuse to send their children to residential school. In 1897, Kah-pah-pah-mah-am-wa-ko-we-ko-chin (also known as Tom) was deposed from his position as a headman of the White Bear Reserve in what is now Saskatchewan for his vocal opposition to residential schools. In making his case for a school on the reserve, he pointed to the death rate at the Qu'Appelle industrial school, adding, "Our children are not strong. Many of them are sick most of the time, many of the children sent from this Reserve to the Schools have died.[381]

Death casts a long shadow over many residential school memories. Louise Moine attended the Qu'Appelle school in the early twentieth century. She recalled one year when tuberculosis was "on the rampage in that school. There was a death every month on the girls' side and some of the boys went also."[382] Of his years at the Roman Catholic school in Onion Lake, Joseph Dion recalled, "My schoolmates and I were not long in concluding that the lung sickness was fatal, hence as soon as we saw or heard of someone spitting blood, we immediately branded him for the grave. He had consumption: he had to die."[383] Simon Baker's brother Jim died from spinal meningitis at the Lytton, British Columbia, school. "I used to hear him crying at night. I asked the principal to take him to the hospital. He didn't. After about two weeks, my brother was in so much pain, he was going out of his mind. I pleaded with the principal for days to take him to a doctor."[384]

Ray Silver said that he always blamed the Alberni school for the death of his brother Dalton. "He was a little guy, laying in the bed in the infirmary, dying, and I didn't know 'til he died. You know that's, that was the end of my education."[385] The death of a child often prompted parents to withdraw the rest of their children from a school. One former student said her father came to the school when her sister became ill at the Anglican school at Aklavik, Northwest Territories. "He came upstairs and there we were. He cried over us. He took me home. He put her in a hospital, and she died."[386]

The high deaths rates in the schools were, in part, a reflection of the high death rates among the Aboriginal community in general. Indian Affairs officials often tried to portray these rates as simply the price that Aboriginal people had to pay as part of the process of becoming civilized. In reality, these rates were the price they paid for being colonized.[387] Aboriginal livelihoods were based on access to the land; colonization disrupted that access and introduced new illnesses to North America. Colonial policies helped wiped out food sources and confined Aboriginal people to poorly located reserves, with inadequate sanitation and shelter. The schools could have served as institutions to help counter these problems. To do that, however, they would have had to have been properly constructed, maintained, staffed, and supplied. Government officials were aware of this. They were also aware that death rates among students at residential schools were disproportionately high. It would be wrong to say the government did nothing about this crisis: the 1910 contract did provide a substantial funding increase to the schools. But the federal government never made the type of sustained investment in Aboriginal health, in either the communities or the schools, that could have addressed this crisis—which continues to the present. The non-Aboriginal tuberculosis death rate declined before the introduction of life-saving drugs. It was brought down by improvements in diet, housing, sanitation, and medical attention. Had such measures been taken by the federal government earlier, they would have reduced both the Aboriginal death rates and the residential school students' death rates. By failing to take adequate measures that had been recommended to it, the federal government blighted the health of generations of Aboriginal people.

Burial policy

Many of the early schools were part of larger church mission centres that might include a church, a dwelling for the missionaries, a farm, a sawmill, and a cemetery. The mission cemetery might serve as a place of burial for students who died at school, members of the local community, and the missionaries themselves. For example, the cemetery at the Roman Catholic St. Mary's mission, near Mission, British Columbia, was intended originally for priests and nuns from the mission as well as for students from the residential school.[388]

During the influenza pandemic of 1918–19, many of the schools and missions were overwhelmed. At the Fort St. James school and mission in British Columbia, the dead were buried in a common grave.[389] At the Red Deer school, four students who died there were buried two to a grave to save costs.[390] In some cases, student and staff graves were treated differently. At the Spanish, Ontario, school, the graves of staff members were marked with headstones that, in the case of former priests and nuns, provided

Residential school students at the Roman Catholic cemetery in Fort George, Québec. Deschâtelets Archives.

name and date of birth and death. The burial spots of students were identified only by plain white crosses.[391]

The general Indian Affairs policy was to hold the schools responsible for burial expenses when a student died at school. The school generally determined the location and nature of that burial.[392] Parental requests to have children's bodies returned home for burial were generally refused as being too costly.[393] In her memoirs, Eleanor Brass recalled how the body of one boy, who hung himself at the File Hills school in the early twentieth century, was buried on the Peepeekisis Reserve, even though his parents lived on the Carlyle Reserve.[394] As late as 1958, Indian Affairs refused to return the body of a boy who had died at a hospital in Edmonton to his northern home community in the Yukon.[395]

The reluctance to pay the cost of sending the bodies of children from residential schools home for burial ceremonies continued into the 1960s. Initially, for example, Indian Affairs was initially unwilling to pay to send the body of twelve-year-old Charlie Wenjack back to his parents' home community in Ogoki, Ontario, in 1966.[396] When Charles Hunter drowned in 1974 while attending the Fort Albany school, it was decided, without consultation with his parents, to bury him in Moosonee rather than send him home to Peawanuck near Hudson Bay. It was not until 2011, after significant public efforts made on his behalf by his sister Joyce, who had never got to meet her older brother, that Charles Hunter's body was exhumed and returned to Peawanuck for a community burial. The costs were covered by funds that the *Toronto Star* raised from its readership.[397]

A school closing might mean the cemetery would be left unattended. When the Battleford school closed in 1914, Principal E. Matheson reminded Indian Affairs that there was a school cemetery that contained the bodies of seventy to eighty individuals, most of whom were former students. He worried that unless the government took steps to care for the cemetery, it would be overrun by stray cattle.[398] In short, throughout the system's history, children who died at school were buried in school or mission cemeteries, often in poorly marked graves. The closing of the schools has led, in many cases, to the abandonment of these cemeteries.

Discipline: "Too suggestive of the old system of flogging criminals"

When Indian agent D. L. Clink returned a runaway student to the Red Deer industrial school in 1895, he noted that the boy's head was bruised from where a teacher had hit him with a stick. The school principal, John Nelson, told Clink that he "had been severe with him before but he would be more severe now." Worried that if he "left the boy he would be abused," Clink took the boy away from the school. He also recommended to Indian Affairs that the teacher who had struck the student be dismissed and brought up on charges, since "his actions in this and other cases would not be tolerated in a white school for a single day in any part of Canada."[399] Clink's report led Indian Affairs Deputy Minister Hayter Reed to direct his staff:

> Instructions should be given, if not already sent, to the Principals of the various schools, that children are not to be whipped by anyone save the Principal, and even when such a course is necessary, great discretion should be used and they should not be struck on the head, or punished so severely that bodily harm might ensue. The practice of corporal punishment is considered unnecessary as a general measure of discipline and should only be resorted to for very grave offences and as a deterrent example.[400]

Reed's instruction underlines a number of the recurrent problems with the Indian Affairs approach to discipline in residential schools. First, Reed, who had previously been the Indian commissioner in western Canada, did not know whether there were regulations dealing with school discipline. Second, his directive is vague: while it indicates where students should *not* be struck, it does not specify where they could be struck, or place limits on what students could be struck with; and neither are there limits on the number of blows. Third, it is not clear that these instructions were ever issued to the principals. If they were, they were soon lost and forgotten. In later years, when conflicts arose over discipline at the schools, Indian Affairs officials made no reference to the policy. In 1920, Canon S. Gould, the general secretary of the Missionary

The Mohawk Institute in Brantford, Ontario, was just one of the schools that had specific "punishment rooms." General Synod Archives, Anglican Church of Canada, P75-103-S4-507.

Society of the Church of England in Canada, asked Deputy Minister Campbell Scott, "Is corporal punishment for disciplinary purposes recognized, or permitted in the Indian Boarding schools?" He noted that whether or not it was permitted, he imagined that it was applied in every residential school in the country.[401] The first—and only—evidence of a nation-wide discipline policy for residential schools that the Truth and Reconciliation Commission of Canada has been able to locate in the documents reviewed to date was issued in 1953.[402]

The failure to establish and enforce a national policy on discipline meant that students were subject to disciplinary measures that would not, as Clink noted in 1895, be tolerated in schools for non-Aboriginal children. Four years after Reed asked his staff to issue instructions on corporal punishment, Indian Commissioner David Laird reported that several children had been "too severely punished" at the Middlechurch school. "Strappings on the bare back," he wrote, was "too suggestive of the old system of flogging criminals."[403]

Corporal punishment was often coupled with public humiliation. In December 1896 in British Columbia, the Kuper Island school's acting principal gave two boys "several lashes in the Presence of the Pupils" for sneaking into the girls' dormitory at night.[404] When, in 1934, the principal of the Shubenacadie school could not determine who had stolen money and chocolates from a staff member, he had the suspects thrashed with a seven-thonged strap and then placed on bread-and-water diets.[405]

Some schools had a specific room set aside to serve as a "punishment room."[406] After a 1907 inspection of the Mohawk Institute in Brantford, the Ontario inspector for

Indian agencies, J. G. Ramsden, reported, "I cannot say that I was favourably impressed with the sight of two prison cells in the boys [sic] play house. I was informed, however, that these were for pupils who ran away from the institution, confinement being for a week at a time when pupils returned."[407] In 1914, a father successfully sued the Mohawk Institute principal for locking his daughter in a cell for three days on what was described as a "water diet."[408]

Boys at the Anglican school in Brocket, Alberta, were chained together as punishment for running away in 1920.[409] At the Gleichen, Alberta, school, a principal was accused of shackling a boy to his bed and beating him with a quirt (a riding whip) until his back bled. The principal admitted to having beaten the boy with the whip, but denied breaking the boy's skin.[410]

Abusive punishment often prompted children to run away. The father of Duncan Sticks, a boy who died from exposure after running away from the Williams Lake school in British Columbia, told a coroner's inquest in 1902 that, in the past, his son had run away because he had been "beaten with a quirt."[411] A boy who ran away from the Anglican school in The Pas, after being severely beaten by the principal, nearly died of exposure.[412]

The violent nature of the discipline at the schools came as a shock to students. Isabelle Whitford said that prior to coming to the Sandy Bay school, she had never been physically disciplined. "All my dad have to do was raise his voice, and we knew what he meant. So, when I first got hit by the nuns, it was really devastating 'cause how can they hit me when my parents didn't hit me, you know?"[413] Rachel Chakasim said that at the Fort Albany school, "I saw violence for the first time. I would see kids getting hit. Sometimes in the classrooms, a yardstick was being used to hit."[414]

Fred Brass said that his years at the Roman Catholic school at Kamsack, Saskatchewan, were "the hellish years of my life. You know to be degraded by our so-called educators, to be beat by these people that were supposed to have been there to look after us, to teach us right from wrong. It makes me wonder now today a lot of times I ask that question, who was right and who was wrong?"[415] According to Geraldine Bob, the staff members at the Kamloops school she attended were not able to control their tempers once they began to punish a student. "They would just start beating you and lose control and hurl you against the wall, throw you on the floor, kick you, punch you."[416]

It was a common practice to shave the heads of students who ran away. William Antoine recalled that at the Spanish, Ontario, school, this was done in front of the other students. "They got all the boys to look at what is happening to this boy, what they were doing to him because he ran away. They cut all his hair off and they pulled, pulled his pants down and he was kneeling on the floor, and holding onto the chair."[417] Eva Simpson said that at the Catholic school in The Pas, her cousin's head was shaved for running away.[418]

Many students spoke of teachers punishing them by pulling their ears. At Sioux Lookout, Dorothy Ross said, "one time me and this other girl were, we were, were fooling around, we were teasing each other in our own language, we got, I got caught. She pulled my ear so hard."[419] Archie Hyacinthe could recall that in the classrooms of the Roman Catholic school in Kenora, "every time we didn't listen, they would tug us behind the ear, or behind the neck, or on the elbows."[420] Jonas Grandjambe recalled how the nun in charge of the boys' dormitory at the Roman Catholic school in Aklavik, in the Northwest Territories, would "grab our ear and twist it."[421] Delores Adolph said that the discipline she received at the Mission school impaired her hearing.[422] Joseph Wabano said that at the Fort Albany, Ontario, school, the staff would hit students with a one-inch-thick board.[423] Noel Starblanket recalled being constantly "slapped on the side of the head" at the Qu'Appelle school. One teacher struck him in the face and broke his nose.[424]

Mervin Mirasty said that at the Beauval, Saskatchewan, school, boys who were caught throwing snowballs were punished with blows to their hands from the blade of a hockey stick.[425] As a punishment, Nellie Trapper, who attended the Moose Factory, Ontario, school in the 1950s, was assigned to "scrubbing the stair, the stairwell with a toothbrush, me and this other girl. Like, I don't remember what I did wrong, but that was something that I won't forget. I remember sitting on the steps, and she, our supervisor was standing there, watching us."[426] Former students also spoke of how, in winter, they might be forced to stand or sit, inadequately clothed, in the snow as a form of punishment.

It was not uncommon for residential school students, traumatized by being placed in such a harsh and alien environment, to wet their beds. These students were subjected to humiliating punishments. Wendy Lafond said that at the Prince Albert, Saskatchewan, school, "if we wet our beds, we were made to stand in the corner in our pissy clothes, not allowed to change."[427] Don Willie recalled that students who wet their beds were publicly humiliated at the Alert Bay school. "And they used to, they used to line up the wet bed, bedwetters, and line them up in the morning, and parade them through, parade them through breakfast, the breakfast area, pretty much to shame them."[428]

Policies that were seen as being unacceptable in the early twentieth century were still in place in the 1960s. Many students compared residential schools to jails: some spoke of being locked up in dormitories, broom closets, basements, and even crawl spaces. In 1965, students who ran away from the Presbyterian school in Kenora were locked up with just a mattress on the floor and put on a bread-and-milk diet.[429] Students were still being locked up in what was referred to as the "counselling" room at the Poplar Hill, Ontario, school in the 1980s.[430] Despite the fact that Indian Affairs had given orders to abandon the practice, students were still having their hair cropped into the 1970s.[431] In the 1990s, students at the Gordon's, Saskatchewan, school were still being struck, and pushed into lockers and walls by one staff member.[432]

The failure to develop, implement, and monitor effective discipline sent an unspoken message that there were no real limits on what could be done to Aboriginal children within the walls of a residential school. The door had been opened early to an appalling level of physical and sexual abuse of students, and it remained open throughout the existence of the system.

Abuse: "And he did awful things to me."

From the nineteenth century onwards, the government and churches were well aware of the risk that staff might sexually abuse residential school students. As early as 1886, Jean L'Heureux, who worked as a translator for Indian Affairs and a recruiter for Roman Catholic schools in Alberta, was accused of sexually abusing boys in his care. The officials responsible for the schools recognized that his actions were not appropriate. Despite this, there is no record of a criminal investigation being carried out at the time.[433] When new allegations against L'Heureux emerged in 1891, he was allowed to resign. In dealing with the matter, Indian Affairs Deputy Minister Lawrence Vankoughnet hoped "it would not be necessary to state the cause which led to the same [the resignation]."[434]

When it came to taking action on the abuse of Aboriginal children, early on, Indian Affairs and the churches placed their own interests ahead of the children in their care and then covered up that victimization. It was cowardly behaviour.

This set the tone for the way the churches and government would treat the sexual abuse of children for the entire history of the residential school system. Complaints often were ignored. In some cases where allegations were made against a school principal, the only measure that Indian Affairs took was to contact the principal.[435] In at least one case, Indian Affairs officials worked with school officials to frustrate a police investigation into abuse at a school. When attempting to return some runaway boys to the Kuper Island school in 1939, British Columbia Provincial Police officers concluded that there was good reason to believe the boys had run away because they were being sexually abused at the school. The police launched an investigation and refused to return the boys to the school.[436] When Indian Affairs officials finally investigated, they concluded that the allegations had merit. However, to protect the school's reputation, the local Indian Affairs official advised the suspected abusers to leave the province, allowing them to avoid prosecution.[437] Nothing was done for the students who had been victimized or for their parents.

These patterns persisted into the late twentieth century. Officials continued to dismiss Aboriginal reports of abuse.[438] In some cases, staff members were not fired, even

In 1939, Indian Affairs officials recommended that Kuper Island school staff suspected of sexually abusing students leave the province, allowing them to avoid prosecution. British Columbia Archives, pdp05505.

after being convicted of assaulting a student.[439] Complaints were improperly investigated. For example, charges of sexual impropriety made against the principal of the Gordon's school were investigated by a school staff member in 1956.[440] Church officials failed to report cases of abuse to Indian Affairs, and Indian Affairs failed to report cases of abuse to families.[441] It was not until 1968 that Indian Affairs began to compile and circulate a list of former staff members who were not to be hired at other schools without the approval of officials in Ottawa.[442] The churches and the government remained reluctant to take matters to the police. As a result, prosecutions were rare.

In the documents it has reviewed, the Truth and Reconciliation Commission of Canada has identified over forty successful convictions of former residential school staff members who sexually or physically abused students.[443] Most of these prosecutions were the result of the determination of former students to see justice done.

The full extent of the abuse that occurred in the schools is only now coming to light. As of January 31, 2015, the Independent Assessment Process (IAP), established under the Indian Residential Schools Settlement Agreement (IRSSA) had received 37,951 claims for injuries resulting from physical and sexual abuse at residential schools. The IAP is a mechanism to compensate former students for sexual and physical abuse experienced at the schools and the harms that arose from the assaults. By the end of 2014, the IAP had resolved 30,939 of those claims, awarding $2,690,000,000 in compensation.[444] The Common Experience Payment (CEP) established under IRSSA provided compensation to individuals who attended a school on the IRSSA's approved list of schools. The CEP recognized the claims of 78,748 former residential school students. Although claims for compensation under the IAP could be made by non-residential school students who were abused at the schools, the vast majority of IAP claims were made by former residential school students. The number of claims for compensation for abuse is equivalent to approximately 48% of the number of former students who were eligible to make such claims. This number does not include those former students who died prior to May 2005.

As the numbers demonstrate, the abuse of children was rampant. From 1958, when it first opened, until 1979, there was never a year in which Grollier Hall in Inuvik did not employ at least one dormitory supervisor who would later be convicted for sexually abusing students at the school. Joseph Jean Louis Comeau, Martin Houston, George Maczynski, and Paul Leroux all worked at Grollier Hall during this period. All were convicted of abusing Grollier Hall students.[445] William Peniston Starr served as director of the Gordon's, Saskatchewan, residence from 1968 until 1984.[446] Prior to that, he worked at a series of schools in Alberta and Québec.[447] In 1993, he was convicted of ten counts of sexually assaulting Gordon's school students.[448] Arthur Plint worked as a boys' supervisor at the Alberni residential school for two five-year periods between 1948 and 1968. In 1995, he pleaded guilty to eighteen counts of indecent assault. In sentencing him to eleven years in jail, Justice D. A. Hogarth described Plint as "a sexual terrorist."[449]

Physical abuse and sexual abuse often were intertwined. Jean Pierre Bellemare, who attended the Amos, Québec, school, spoke for many students when he told the Commission that he had been subjected to "physical violence, verbal violence, touchings, everything that comes with it."[450] Andrew Yellowback was "sexually, physically, emotionally, and mentally abused" at the Cross Lake, Manitoba, school for eight years.[451] There was no single pattern of abuse: students of both sexes reported assaults from staff members of both the opposite sex and the same sex as themselves.[452]

First-year students, traumatized by separation from their parents and the harsh and alien regime of the school, were particularly vulnerable to abusive staff members who sought to win their trust through what initially appeared to be simple kindness. In some cases, this might involve little more than extra treats from the school canteen. This favouritism, however, was often the prelude to a sexual assault that left the student scared and confused.[453]

Many students spoke of having been raped at school.[454] These were moments of terror. Josephine Sutherland was cornered by one of the lay brothers in the Fort Albany school garage: "I couldn't call for help, I couldn't. And he did awful things to me."[455] Other students recalled being assaulted in the church confessional.[456] A student in the change room would suddenly have a bag pulled over his head.[457] The abuse could begin with an instruction to report to the shower room in the middle of the night or to take lunch to a staff member's room.[458] An abusive staff person might stalk a student, blocking her or his way, or grope a passing student.[459] Female students spoke of how some staff members took advantage of their innocence, rubbing against them sexually while they were sitting on their laps.[460] Abuse also took the form of voyeuristic humiliation: some staff insisted on watching the students shower.[461]

Some dormitory supervisors used their authority to institute dormitory-wide systems of abuse. Many students spoke of the fear and anxiety that spread across their dormitories in the evenings.[462] They went to bed fearful that they might be called into the supervisor's room.[463] To protect themselves, some students attempted to never be alone.[464] Older children sometimes sought to protect younger ones.[465]

Most students came to school with little knowledge or understanding of sexual activity, let alone the types of sexual abuse to which they might be subjected. Abuse left them injured, bewildered, and often friendless or subject to ridicule by other students.[466] Many students thought they were the only children being abused. This confusion made it difficult for them to describe or report their abuse.[467] Some were told they would face eternal damnation for speaking of what had been done to them.[468]

Many students fought back against their far larger and more powerful assailants, especially as they got older and stronger.[469] Some succeeded in forcing their tormentors to leave them alone.[470] Many others, such as Lawrence Waquan, concluded that there was "nothing you can do."[471] Some students ran away from school in an attempt to escape abuse.[472] Others begged their parents not to return them to school after a break.[473]

Some students never reported abuse for fear they would not be believed.[474] Other students who did report abuse were told that they were to blame.[475] In some cases, school officials took immediate action when abuse was reported to them, but the rarity of such actions is itself noteworthy.[476] Former students spoke of how betrayed they felt when nothing was done about their complaints.[477] Many simply felt too ashamed to ever speak of the abuse.[478] Family members often refused to believe their children's reports of abuse, intensifying their sense of isolation and pain.[479] This was especially so within families that had adopted Christianity, and could not believe that the people of God looking after their children would ever do such things.[480]

The impact of abuse was immediate and long-lasting. It destroyed the students' ability to function in the school, and led many to turn to self-destructive behaviours.[481]

Staff abuse of children created conditions for the student abuse of other students. Every school system has to deal with school bullies, student cliques, and inter-student conflict. It is part of the socialization process. Ideally, corrective lessons in how to treat others well are taught, as well as shown by example. Residential school staff had a responsibility not only to model such behaviour, but also to protect students from being victimized. In many cases, they failed to provide that protection. Conflicts between students are not unique to residential schools, but they take on greater significance in a residential school setting where children cannot turn to adult family members for comfort, support, and redress. The moral influences that a child's home community can exert are also absent. Instead, the children were left vulnerable and unprotected. Residential schools failed to live up to their responsibility to protect students from being victimized by other students.

Older or bigger students used force—or the threat of force—to establish their dominance over younger students. In some cases, this dominance was used to coerce younger or smaller students to participate in sexual acts. In other cases, bullies forced vulnerable students to turn over their treats, their food, or their money, or to steal on their behalf. In addition, bullies might simply seek a measure of sadistic satisfaction from beating those who were weaker. Bullies operated individually or in groups. Such groups were often formed initially as a defensive response to the level of violence within the school, but, over time, would take on their own offensive characteristics. Sometimes, such groups not only focused their anger and/or frustration on other students, but also sought to disrupt the general operation of the school. The fact that Catholic and Protestant church leaders continued to disparage one another's religions throughout this period meant that conflicts between students could also take on religious overtones, particularly in communities with more than one residential school, such as Inuvik in the Northwest Territories.

Student victimization of students was an element of the broader abusive and coercive nature of the residential school system. Underfed, poorly housed, and starved for affection, students often formed groups based on age, community of origin, or First Nation. Such groups gave students a measure of identity and status, but also provided protection to their members and dominated more vulnerable students.

William Garson recalled that at the Elkhorn, Manitoba, school, "we were always like hiding in the corners; you know away from any abusement. From other, older, from older, elder boys, students."[482] Percy Thompson said that at the Hobbema school, "one bully used to come at me and he'd pretend he was going to talk to me and all of sudden hit me in the belly. And of course I gag, gag, and he'd laugh his head off and, you know, to see me in such a predicament."[483] Alice Ruperthouse spoke of "the cruelty of the other children" at the Amos, Québec, school. "It was, you know, like in a jungle. Like in a jungle, you don't know what's going to come out but you know you had to watch out."[484] Albert Elias felt that the classroom at the Anglican school in Aklavik "was the safest place to be in 'cause that's where nobody could beat me up. I dreaded recesses and lunches and after school, I dreaded those times."[485]

Bullying might start shortly after arrival. In some schools, all new male students were put through a hazing. Denis Morrison said that each new arrival at the Fort Frances school underwent a beating. "They used to initiate you, like, they would beat the hell out of you, the other kids would. It wasn't anybody else, it was the other kids, the older ones, eh."[486] Bob Baxter recalled that there were student gangs at the Sioux Lookout school. He was beaten up and knifed on one occasion. He had a vivid memory of people tying him to his bed and throwing hot water over him.[487] Clara Quisess said that at the Fort Albany school in Ontario, older girls would threaten the younger ones with knives.[488] Louisa Birote recalled that the girls at the La Tuque, Québec, school all formed themselves into hostile groups. "We hated each other. So, this little gang didn't like the other gang. That's the way at the school, that's what we were taught, fears, and we were scared, and I went to hide in what we called the junk room, the junk closet."[489]

A lack of adequate supervision in the schools and residences meant that such domination could give rise to physical and sexual abuse. The assaults ranged from being forced to kiss someone, to being forced to simulate a sex act, to being raped. In some cases, victims were given small treats to encourage them to be silent; in other cases, they were told they would be killed if they reported the assault.[490] Agnes Moses recalled being molested by older girls at a hostel in northern Canada. "I never quite understood it, and it really wrecked my life, it wrecked my life as a mother, a wife, a woman, and sexuality was a real, it was a dirty word for us."[491] The experience of being abused at a British Columbia school by a group of boys left Don Willie distrustful of most people. "The only, only friends I kept after that were my relatives."[492]

Complaints were infrequent, as students had good reason not to report their abuse. Some feared that bullies would retaliate if they were reported. Others were ashamed of what had been done to them, and some did not fully understand what had been done to them. Many students feared they would not be believed—or would be blamed for somehow bringing the abuse upon themselves. Still others were further punished when they did tell. So, rather than report the abuse, many students chose to fight back; to seek admission into a receptive group, where violence could be fought with violence; or to endure the pain in silence. This victimization left many students feeling intensely betrayed, fearful, isolated, and bereft of home teachings and protection. The betrayal by fellow students has contributed significantly to the schools' long-term legacy of continuing division and distrust within Aboriginal communities. The residential school system's shameful inability to protect students from such victimization, even from among themselves, represents one of its most significant and least-understood failures.

Sports and culture: "It was a relief."

Many students stated that sports helped them make it through residential school. Christina Kimball attended the Roman Catholic school near The Pas, where she experienced physical, sexual, and emotional abuse. She believes that it was only through her involvement with sports that she survived. "I was very sports-oriented. I played baseball. Well, we play baseball, and even hockey. We had a hockey team. That has benefited, benefited me in a way 'cause I loved playing sports. Well, that's one way, too. I don't know how I did it but I was pretty good in sports."[493] Noel Starblanket said that at the Qu'Appelle school, "I had some good moments, in particular in the sports side, 'cause I really enjoyed sports. I was quite athletic, and basically that's what kept

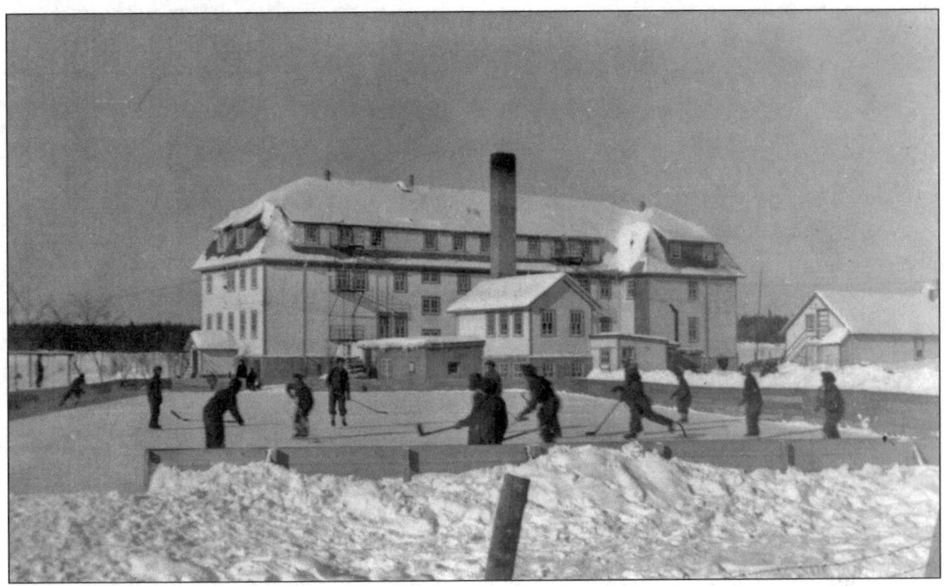

Boys playing hockey at the McIntosh, Ontario, school. Many students said that they would not have survived their residential school years, were it not for sports. St. Boniface Historical Society, Oblates of Mary Immaculate, Manitoba Province Fonds, SHSB 29362.

me alive, that's what kept me going was the sports."[494] At the Lestock school, Geraldine Shingoose took refuge in extracurricular activities.

> One of the good things that I would do to try and get out of just the abuse was try to, I would join track-meet, try and be, and I was quite athletic in boarding school. And I also joined the band, and I played a trombone. And, and that was something that took me away from the school, and just to, it was a relief.[495]

Paul Andrew spent seven years at Grollier Hall in Inuvik. One of his strongest and most positive memories related to school sports. "There were times when I felt dumb and stupid. But put me in a gym, there was not too many people better than I am."[496]

Recreational activities were always underfunded and undersupplied at the schools. A national survey of Indian Affairs schools (both day and residential) in 1956 concluded:

> In most of the schools there appeared to be little or no physical education program. A number of schools had no facilities for such activities. Basement areas were obviously designed for playing areas, but they were very inadequate and were utilized for storage or for assembly purposes. A large number of school sites were not properly cleared, graded, and prepared for playing purposes. Many were still in the wild state; others were overgrown with shrubs, thistles, grasses and other weeds presenting a very unkempt and neglected appearance.[497]

Grandin College girls' basketball team, Northwest Territories. One Grandin student wrote in the school newsletter, "At Grandin, Education comes first." Although students could participate in school sports teams, "if you are behind in your school work, you are forced to quit your sports." Deschâtelets Archives.

Oblate Provincial L. Poupore wrote to Indian Affairs about conditions at the Williams Lake, British Columbia, school in 1957. He pointed out that a year and half earlier, he had informed Indian Affairs about the need for a school gymnasium. At that time, he said, "The boys' play room, a room about 35 by 60, was a scene of bedlam during recreation periods. There were about 150 boys trying to play; the mud they had brought in on their feet had dried and there was so much dust in the room that you could not recognize a boy at the opposite end." Although the department had assured him the construction of a gymnasium would be a priority, nothing had been done, and "the problem of playroom space is worse than ever."[498]

Despite the lack of financial support, hockey teams from a number of schools achieved considerable success in the 1940s and 1950s. Teams from Duck Lake and Qu'Appelle in Saskatchewan, in particular, established enviable records. The Duck Lake school team, the St. Michael's Indians, won the championship of an eight-team league in the Rosthern area in 1946.[499] In 1948, the same team, coached by Father G.-M. Latour, won the northern Saskatchewan midget hockey championship. The following year, it won the provincial championship.[500] According to the *Prince Albert Daily Herald*, "While the Duck Lake boys were outweighed in their midget series they made it up in hockey know-how, skating ability and shooting accuracy. Their drives, from any angle, had the Regina players scared and baffled at the same time."[501] Among the players on the 1949 Duck Lake provincial championship team was Fred Sasakamoose, who went on to become the first status Indian to play in the National Hockey League.[502]

While hockey dominated boys' sports in most residential schools, British Columbia residential schools gained renown for their boxers. In 1947, the Roman Catholic school at Sechelt in North Vancouver advertised for a volunteer to run a school athletics program. Navy veteran Alex Strain took on the job. At the time, the school had no recreation program and no facilities. Under Strain's direction, the students cleared out a storage building and turned it into a gymnasium. Putting in four days of volunteer work a week, Strain created what *Vancouver Sun* reporter Gerry Pratt described as "the smoothest tumbling team in the province." He then established a boxing program at the school. The limits of the first ring were marked out by four rows of chairs. The first punching bag was a navy duffle bag filled with tumbling mats. After two years, Strain purchased a used truck and took the students on a boxing tour of Vancouver Island. After four years in existence, the team had won over 100 trophies. Sister John Lawrence made robes and shorts for each member of the team and also served as trainer.[503] Frederick Baker, the winner of the first national Tom Longboat award, was a member of the Sechelt boxing team. Baker had won three championships in 1948, two in 1949, one in 1950, and one in 1951.[504]

Painter Judith Morgan attended the Alberni, British Columbia, school in the 1940s. Royal British Columbia Museum, Image G-02437.

Other students sought solace in the arts. A number of former residential school students went on to prominent careers in the visual arts, including Alex Janvier, Jackson Beardy, Judith Morgan, and Norval Morrisseau. Some, such as Beardy, were encouraged in their artistic endeavours by sympathetic staff.[505] Like sports, cultural activities were underfunded. They were also often intended to encourage assimilation. In 1967, the students attending the Shingwauk, Ontario, school put on a four-act play called *Arrow to the Moon*. One act used a dialogue between an Elder and a young man to contrast what were seen as the old and new ways open to Aboriginal people. Billy Diamond played the role of the young man, who concludes at the scene's end, "The new ways show a way to work and live but the old ways have shown us how to die." The performance was filmed and shown to the James Bay Cree, who refrained from making any public comment, but were shocked to discover the degree to which their children were being manipulated.[506]

Albert Canadien recalled in his memoirs from Akaitcho Hall:

> A few of the boys had guitars and there were other instruments in the common room. Sometimes, a few of the boys would get together and play to pass the time. John, the boys' supervisor, noticed this was going on and took an interest, encouraging us to play and sing.
>
> At first we got together just for fun. But eventually ... we formed a band. There were five or six of us, and we call ourselves the Arctic Ramblers. We had guitars, fiddle, bass guitar, drums, and there was even a piano for a while.

They played at dances at the residence and in Hay River.[507] Canadien went on to play in the Chieftones, a rock-and-roll band that toured extensively across North America.[508]

On the rinks, the athletic fields, and parade grounds, or in the arts and handicraft rooms and on performance stages, many students found a way to express themselves, and, through that, gained the opportunity to explore their own talents and sometimes other parts of the country or the world. Most importantly, they gained some confidence in their ability to achieve.

Resistance: "I am the father of this child."

Parents and children developed a variety of strategies to resist residential schooling. Parents might refuse to enrol students, refuse to return runaways, or they might refuse to return students to school at the end of the summer holidays. They also called on the government to increase school funding; to establish day schools in their home communities; and to improve the quality of education, food, and clothing. In taking such measures, they often put themselves at risk of legal reprisals. Almost invariably, the system declined to accept the validity of parental and student criticisms. Parental influences were judged by school and government officials to be negative and backward. The schools also suspected parents of encouraging their children in acts of disobedience.[509] Once parents came to be viewed as the 'enemy,' their criticisms, no matter how valid, could be discounted.

Prior to 1920, when the *Indian Act* was amended to allow Indian Affairs to compel children to attend residential school, the most effective form of resistance that parents could make was to simply refuse to enrol their children. This measure was so effective that it contributed to the closure of a number of residential schools. The Battleford, Saskatchewan, school, which had a capacity of 150 students, had an enrolment of thirty-five in 1915.[510] The school was closed two years later.[511] The High River, Alberta,

Students at the Kitamaat, British Columbia, school. In 1922, parents refused to return their children to school after the death of one student. The United Church of Canada Archives, 93.049P1835.

school could also hold over 100 students, but by 1922, the year it closed, the school had an enrolment of only forty.[512] The Middlechurch, Manitoba, school was not rebuilt after it burned down in 1906, in large measure because it could not recruit enough students.[513] For similar reasons, the St. Boniface, Manitoba, school closed in 1905; the Calgary, Alberta, school closed in 1907; the Regina, Saskatchewan, school closed in 1910; the Elkhorn, Manitoba, school closed in 1919; and the Red Deer, Alberta, school closed in 1919.[514]

By refusing to enrol their children in the industrial schools on the Prairies, parents not only undermined the federal government's assimilation policies, but also deprived the schools of per capita grant revenue and student labour. As a result, the industrial schools ran significant deficits, and overworked and underfed the children they did recruit. This led other parents to withdraw their children from the schools. This was never a risk-free choice for parents. Often, residential schools were the only available schools. Parents who wished to see their children schooled had few, if any, options.[515]

Sometimes, government officials also took reprisals against parents who kept their children out of school, in some cases denying them food rations and Treaty payments.[516] Parents continued to keep their children out of school well into the twentieth century: in 1941, only forty-five students were enrolled in the Fort Providence school, which had an authorized attendance of 100.[517]

In at least one instance, parents home-schooled their children. In 1941, Muriel, Doreen, and Kathleen Steinhauer were kept home from the Edmonton residential school because their parents were not satisfied with the progress they were making at the school. Their mother, Isabel, had been a schoolteacher prior to her marriage, and home-schooled the children.[518]

Sometimes, parents took their children out of school against the wishes of the principal. In 1904, a husband and wife attempted to remove their daughter from the Kuper Island school. When Principal G. Donckele informed them that when they signed the admission form, they had given the government the right to determine when their daughter would be discharged, the father said, "I am the father of this child and I do not care for what you and the government have to say about it." After being told that he could be prosecuted, the father left with his daughter anyway.[519]

In 1913, when a mother removed her daughter from the Fort Resolution school, the Mounted Police were called in and the mother surrendered the girl to the school.[520] In response to the death of a student in 1922, local parents withdrew their children from the Kitamaat, British Columbia, residential school. They agreed to return them only on the condition that the principal "sign her name to a paper before us that she would see that the children got all the food they wanted, that they would be well cared for, and be supplied with sufficient clothing."[521]

In March 1948, the principal of the Roman Catholic school at Cardston, Alberta, struck a father who was attempting to take his son out of the school. In discussing the issue with Indian Affairs, the Blood Indian Council insisted on having the record note that this was "not the first time that Father Charron had hit an Indian."[522]

It was not uncommon for the parents of an entire community or region to refuse to return their children to school. In the fall of 1926, for example, parents from communities in Manitoba's Interlake region announced they were not sending their children back to the Elkhorn school. According to the parents, the children were not well fed, the older boys compelled the younger boys to steal, and all children were poorly clothed.[523] In October 1927, seventy-five school-aged children from the Blood Reserve in Alberta either had not returned to school or had not been enrolled in school. It took a letter from the police, plus a follow-up visit from the Indian agent, to fill the Anglican and Catholic schools on the reserve.[524] Two weeks after the start of the 1940 school year, fifty-four students had yet to return to the Fraser Lake, British Columbia, school. The police were called in, and by October 2, twenty-five of the students had been returned.[525] This form of parental action was common throughout the 1940s.[526]

Parents were eager to have their children properly educated, and often proposed realistic and effective solutions. In 1905, parents of children attending the Roman Catholic boarding school in Squamish, British Columbia, petitioned to have the school converted into an industrial school. The request was not granted, despite the fact that Indian Affairs officials recognized that the boarding school grant allowed for only "the bare necessities in the line of food and clothing."[527]

Some First Nations leaders who had originally supported residential schools later publicly regretted their decision. Chief Napahkesit of the Pine Creek Band in Manitoba said in 1917 that he was sorry he had ever supported the construction of the Pine Creek school. According to the local Indian agent, the chief felt "the children know less when they come out than they did when they went in." What was needed, the chief said, was a day school.[528] Calls for day schools were, in fact, a common parental request.[529] A 1949 call from parents for a day school at the Cowessess Reserve eventually proved to be successful.[530]

Parents might also demand the dismissal of a principal.[531] In 1917, to back up their call for the resignation of the Shoal Lake school principal, parents refused to return their children to the school.[532] In this case, the principal did resign.[533] The parents of the Kahkewistahaw Band unsuccessfully petitioned the federal government to remove a teacher from the Round Lake, Saskatchewan, school in July 1949. They said that "the children's report cards are very unsatisfactory, worst ever received, and she abuses the children too much.[534] Parents also complained that their children were not learning the skills they needed to survive. Chief Kejick of the Shoal Lake Band told Indian Affairs officials in 1928 that the students from his reserve "did not know how to make a living when they left school and would like trades taught."[535] Eight years later, Charlie Shingoose of the Waywayseecappo Band sought to have his fifteen-year-old son discharged from the Birtle school so he could teach him to "work, trap, etc."[536]

Parents also hired lawyers to press their cases for investigations into the deaths of children who had run away, to complain about the harshness of discipline, to advocate on behalf of children who had been injured working at the schools, and to attempt to have their children discharged from school.[537]

One of the more unusual protests was mounted by First Nations people (Dene) in the Northwest Territories, who, in 1937, refused to accept their Treaty payments in protest of conditions at the Fort Resolution school. Their children, they said, were "living in hell."[538]

Residential schools also came under criticism from early First Nations organizations. At its meeting in Saddle Lake, Alberta, in 1931, the League of Indians of Canada called for the construction of more day schools to augment residential schools.[539] The following year, the league, by then known as the League of Indians of Western Canada, called for the closure of boarding schools.[540] The league also recommended that only qualified teachers be hired to work at residential schools, that medical examinations be given to students before they were sent to the schools, and that the half-day system be changed to allow for greater class time.[541]

In an effort to bring their own residential schooling to an end, some students attempted to burn their schools down. There were at least thirty-seven such attempts,

Boys cutting wood at the Williams Lake, British Columbia, school in either the late nineteenth or early twentieth century. In February 1902 Duncan Sticks froze to death after running away from the school. Museum of the Cariboo Chilcotin.

two of which ended in student and staff deaths.[542] For students, the most effective form of resistance was to run away. The principal of the Shingwauk Home in Sault Ste. Marie, Ontario, school in the 1870s, E. F. Wilson, devoted a chapter of his memoirs to the topic of "Runaway Boys." It included the story of three boys who tried to make their way home by boat. They were found alive more than ten days later, stranded on an island in the North Channel of Lake Huron.[543]

After 1894, children enrolled in a residential school (or who had been placed there by government order because it was felt that they were not being properly cared for by their parents) but who were refusing to show up at school were considered to be "truant." Under the *Indian Act* and its regulations, they could be returned to the school against their will. Children who ran away from residential schools were also considered to be truants. Parents who supported their children in their truancy were often threatened with prosecution.[544]

Most runaway students headed for their home communities. Students knew they might be caught, returned, and punished. Still, they believed the effort to make it home and have a measure of freedom was worth it. In some cases, in fact, the schools failed to force runaways to return.[545] Some students eluded capture. Instead of heading home, some went to work for local farmers and, as a result, were able to avoid their pursuers for considerable periods of time.[546]

Running away could be risky. At least thirty-three students died, usually due to exposure, after running away from school.[547] In a significant number of cases, parents and Indian Affairs officials concluded that the deaths could have been prevented if school officials had mounted earlier and more effective searches and notified police officials and family members.[548] In the case of Charles and Tom Ombash, two brothers who ran away from the Sioux Lookout school on October 5, 1956, school officials waited until November before informing police or Indian Affairs.[549] The boys were never found—community members continued to search for their remains decades after their disappearance.[550]

These deaths date back to the beginning of the twentieth century. However, the first system-wide policy outlining the procedures to be taken when a child ran away from school that the Truth and Reconciliation Commission of Canada has located in the documents it has reviewed dates from 1953. This was seventy-five years after the government began its residential school system. That policy simply stated, "The principal shall take prompt action to effect the return to school of any truant pupil, and shall report promptly to the Superintendent, Indian Agency, every case of truancy."[551] The nature of the prompt action was undefined. In particular, there was no requirement to contact either the child's parents or the police. It was not until 1971 that a more encompassing, nation-wide, policy was announced.[552]

In pursuing children to their parents' homes, the actions of school employees could be both invasive and disrespectful.[553] In the town of Lebret, Saskatchewan, "all the houses were checked" by the police as part of a search for two runaways from the File Hills school in 1935.[554]

Running away was not in itself a crime. However, most students were wearing school-issued clothing when they ran away, and, in some cases, principals tried, and even succeeded, in having them prosecuted for stealing the clothing they were wearing.[555] Students who ran away numerous times also could be charged under the *Juvenile Delinquents Act*. In such cases, they could be sentenced to a reformatory until they turned twenty-one.[556]

The 1894 *Indian Act* amendments made parents who did not return truants to school subject to prosecution. The Mounted Police were often called in to force parents to send their children to school.[557] The Blue Quills, Alberta, school journal entry for May 1, 1932, reads: "The savages having received the order to bring their children to school unless they want the police to get involved, some parents did obey the order today. But there are still those who turn a deaf ear."[558] In 1937, a father who refused to return his son to the Sandy Bay, Manitoba, school was sentenced to ten days in jail. To prevent him from running away again, the boy was sent to a school in Saskatchewan.[559]

Parents were often outraged at having to return runaways. Wallace Hahawahi's father was reported as being "very indignant" at the prospect of sending his son back to the Brandon school in 1936. The boy was over sixteen and needed to help out at home. In this case, the father's argument prevailed and the boy was discharged.[560] Another runaway from the same school, Kenneth Thompson, told the police, "I am a Treaty Indian of Assiniboine Indian Reserve, I am 17 year of Age. I wish to state the reason I ran away from school was because I have to work too hard in fact I do not study at all. I am working around the school all the time. I consider if I have to work I may as well work at home for my father."[561] Despite his argument, he was returned to the school.[562]

Indian agents often referred to ongoing truancy issues at specific schools as "epidemics." The agents viewed such epidemics as a sign of underlying problems at a school. In 1928, Indian agent J. Waddy wrote that at the Anglican school in The Pas, "hardly a day goes bye [sic] that one or more do not take leave on their own account."[563] In 1935, ten pupils ran away from the Birtle, Manitoba, school.[564] In the closing years of the 1930s, the Shubenacadie school in Nova Scotia experienced continual truancy problems. It was not uncommon for some students to make numerous attempts to leave the school. On the morning of July 7, 1937, Andrew Julian decided not to join the other boys assigned to milk the school's dairy herd. Instead, he headed for Truro, where he was reported as being sighted in the rail yard. He was not located until the end of the month. By then, he had made it to Nyanza in Cape Breton, a distance of 260 miles (418.4 kilometres) from the school.[565] The following year, Steven Labobe (also given as LaBobe) managed to make it back to his home on Prince Edward Island. The principal decided not to demand the boy's return.[566] Other boys were not so lucky. One boy, who ran away five times, was eventually placed in a private reformatory.[567]

Many students said they ran away to escape the discipline of the school. Ken Lacquette attended residential schools in Brandon and Portage la Prairie, Manitoba. "They used to give us straps all the time with our pants down they'd give us straps right in the public. Then ... this started happening, after awhile when I was getting old enough I started taking off from there, running away."[568] Others were seeking to escape something far more sinister than corporal punishment. After being subjected to ongoing sexual abuse, Anthony Wilson ran away from the Alberni school.[569]

In the 1940s, Arthur McKay regularly ran away from the Sandy Bay school. "I didn't even know where my home was, the first time right away. But these guys are the ones; my friends were living in nearby reserve, what they call Ebb and Flow, that's where they were going so I followed."[570] Ivan George and a group of his friends ran away from the Mission, British Columbia, school when he was eleven years old. They were strapped on their return. Despite this, he ran away two more times that school year.[571]

Muriel Morrisseau ran away from the Fort Alexander school almost every year she was at the school. The experience was often frightening. "I remember running away again trying to cross the river and it started freezing up, we all got scared, we had to come back again with a tail under our legs."[572] Isaac Daniels ran away from the Prince Albert, Saskatchewan, school with two older boys. Their escape route involved crossing a railway bridge. Partway across, Daniels became too frightened to continue and turned back.[573] Dora Necan ran away from the Fort Frances school with a friend. They made it to the United States and stayed there for three days before returning to the school.[574] Nellie Cournoyea was sheltered by Aboriginal families along her route when she ran away from an Anglican hostel in the Northwest Territories after a confrontation with a teacher.[575] When Lawrence Waquan ran away from the Fort Chipewyan school in 1965, there were no roads and no one along the way to support him. "I walked from Fort Chipewyan in northern Alberta to Fort Smith, 130 miles. It took me about five days. I was only about sixteen. And I just ate berries and drank water to survive."[576]

When Beverley Anne Machelle and her friends ran away from the Lytton, British Columbia, school, they had to contend with the school's isolated and mountainous location.

> It was halfway down this big hill, and then from there you could see town. And we got halfway down there, and we were all feeling, like, woo-hoo, you know, and we got out of there, and, and we're gonna go do something fun, and, and then we got halfway down, and then we realized, well, we have no money, and we have no place to go. There was no place to go. There was no safe place to go.[577]

The girls at the Sioux Lookout school rebelled in 1955 when they were all sent to bed early after a number of girls had been caught stealing. They barricaded themselves in their dormitory and refused to allow any staff to enter.[578] There was a similar revolt in Edmonton in the 1960s, when students blocked staff entry to the dormitory at night, to protest the abuse of students.[579]

Collectively and individually, parents and students did resist the residential school attack on Aboriginal families and communities. On occasion, they won small victories: a child might be discharged; a day school might be built. However, as long as Aboriginal people were excluded from positions of control over their children's education, the root causes of the conflict remained unresolved.

The staff: "My aim was to do something good."

For most of their history, residential schools were staffed by individuals who were recruited by Christian missionary organizations. Generally, the churches appointed a priest or minister, as opposed to an educator, as the principal. The Roman Catholic schools could draw staff from a number of Catholic religious orders, whose members had made explicit vows of obedience, poverty, and chastity. In the spirit of those vows, they would be obliged to go where they were sent, would not expect payment, and would have no families to support. Indian Commissioner David Laird believed that since members of Roman Catholic religious orders received very little in exchange for

Staff outside the entrance of the Brandon, Manitoba, school in 1946. National Film Board of Canada. Photothèque, Library and Archives Canada, PA-048575.

their services, the Roman Catholic schools could "afford to have a much larger staff than where ordinary salaries are paid, and there is consequently less work for each to do, without interfering with the quality of the work done."[580] The Protestant schools recruited many of their staff members through missionary organizations.

Many of the early school staff members believed they were participating in a moral crusade. In her history of the McDougall Orphanage, the predecessor of the Morley school in Alberta, Mrs. J. McDougall described the work of the mission and orphanage as "going out after the wild and ignorant and bringing them into a Christian home and blessing the body, culturing the mind and trying to raise spiritual vision."[581]

Staff members were often motivated by a spirit of adventure as well as a religious commitment. As a young seminary student in Corsica, a French island in the Mediterranean, Nicolas Coccola wanted more than a life as a priest. In his memoir, he wrote, "The desire of foreign missions with the hope of martyrdom appeared to me as a higher calling." He ended up living out his life as a residential school principal in British Columbia.[582] As a small boy in England in the middle of the nineteenth century, Gibbon Stocken read with enthusiasm the missionary literature sent to him by an aunt. When he turned seventeen, he volunteered his services to the Anglican Church Missionary Society. He hoped to be sent to India. Instead, he was offered a position on the Blackfoot Reserve in what is now southern Alberta.[583] British-born nurse and midwife Margaret Butcher managed to get to India, where she worked for a British family. From there, she made her way to British Columbia, where she worked with a Methodist mission to Japanese immigrants.[584] In 1916, she was on her way to a job at the Methodist residential school in Kitamaat, British Columbia.[585]

This mix of motivations continued throughout the system's history. Lorraine Arbez, who worked at the Qu'Appelle school in the 1950s, said, "I chose this career to work with the children and my aim was to do something good with them and I hope I was of some use."[586] For Noreen Fischbuch, who worked at schools in Ontario and Alberta in the 1950s and 1960s, the residential schools offered much-needed experience: "As far as I was concerned, it was a teaching job, it was with the kids and I liked the kids.... The kids were getting an education; I had a job."[587] George Takashima, who taught at Sioux Lookout, explained, "I was just sort of adventuresome, you might say."[588]

Almost all the staff members were poorly paid. Government officials took the position that because many of the staff members belonged to missionary organizations, pay was a "minor consideration."[589] As a result, the schools had problems recruiting and keeping staff. Alexander Sutherland of the Methodist Church was particularly outspoken about the link between low wages and the difficulties the schools had in recruiting staff. In 1887, he wrote to the minister of Indian Affairs about the "difficulty of obtaining efficient and properly qualified teachers, on account of the meagre salaries paid."[590] The issue of low pay never went away. More than half a century later, in 1948, C. H. Birdsall, the chair of the United Church committee responsible for the Edmonton school, complained that it "is impossible for the Residential School to offer salaries in competition with" rates that Indian Affairs was paying teachers at day schools. Given the inadequate quality of accommodation, equipment, and staff at the school, he felt that it was "doubtful the present work with Indian Children could properly be called education."[591] Many of the Catholic schools survived on what amounted to volunteer labour. In 1948, Sechelt principal H. F. Dunlop informed Ottawa, "If this school kept out of the red during the past year it was largely due to the fact that four Oblates, working here full time, received in salaries from Jan 1947 to Jan 1948 the grand total of $1800."[592] As late as 1960, the nuns at the Christie Island school were being paid $50 a month—a fact that made Principal A. Noonan "feel like a heel."[593]

Many qualified and experienced people worked in the schools. Miss Asson, the matron at the Kitamaat school in 1930, was a graduate of the Ensworth Deaconess Hospital in St. Joseph, Missouri. She had also trained as a deaconess in Toronto, and worked in China from 1909 to 1927.[594] The matron at the Anglican Wabasca, Alberta, school in 1933 was a nurse.[595] Among the staff at the Norway House school in the early twentieth century were the sisters Charlotte Amelia and Lilian Yeomans. Charlotte had trained as a nurse, and Lilian was one of the first women in Canada to qualify as a doctor.[596] Theresa Reid had four years of teaching experience and a teaching certificate before she applied to work at Norway House,[597] George Takashima had a teaching

The chief cook at Lapointe Hall in Fort Simpson, Northwest Territories. The schools were highly dependent on female labour. Northwest Territories Archives, N-1992-255-0144.

certificate,[598] and Olive Saunders had a university degree and several years of teaching experience.[599] In 1966, E. O. Drouin, the principal of the Roman Catholic school in Cardston, boasted that out of the twenty-one people on his staff, ten had university degrees. Drouin, himself, had left his position as a university professor to go to work at the school.[600]

A number of people devoted their adult lives to working in residential schools. At least twelve principals died in office.[601] Kuper Island principal George Donckele resigned in January 1907; by June of that year, he was dead.[602] Sherman Shepherd served at the Anglican schools in Shingle Point on the Arctic Ocean in the Yukon, Aklavik (Northwest Territories), Fort George (Québec), and Moose Factory (Ontario), resigning in 1954 after twenty-five years of service in northern Canada.[603] Others worked into their old age, since, due to low pay, their savings were also low and pensions were minimal. When the seventy-three-year-old matron of the Ahousaht school in British Columbia retired in 1929, Principal W. M. Wood recommended that she be given an honorarium of a month's salary as appreciation for her years of service. Woods noted that she was "retiring with very limited means."[604]

Such long service was not the norm. Because the pay was often low and the working and living conditions were difficult, turnover was high throughout the system's history. From 1882 to 1894, there was what amounted to an annual full turnover of teachers at the Fort Simpson (now Port Simpson), British Columbia, school. At one point, all the teaching was being done by the local Methodist missionary Thomas Crosby, his wife, Emma, and the school matron.[605] Between January 1958 and March 1960, a period of just over two years, the Alert Bay school lost fifty-eight staff members. Of these, nineteen had been fired because they were deemed to be incompetent. Eight others left because they were angry with the principal.[606] In 1958, the Benedictine Sisters announced that their order would no longer be providing the Christie, British Columbia, school with staff from its monastery in Mount Angel, Oregon. According to the prioress of the Benedictine monastery, Mother Mary Gemma, meeting residential school needs had left the members of the order physically and mentally exhausted.

"One of my youngest teachers had to have shock treatments this year and two others may have to." In the previous two and a half years, the order had lost fourteen teachers.[607] These examples are confirmed by the overall statistics. The average annual turnover rate for all Indian Affairs schools from 1956–57 to 1963–64 was 25%.[608]

The schools were heavily dependent on female labour. The Roman Catholics relied on female religious orders to staff and operate the residential schools.[609] The Protestants were equally reliant upon the underpaid work of female staff. Austin McKitrick, the principal of the Presbyterian school at Shoal Lake in northwestern Ontario, acknowledged this when he wrote in 1901, "I think if we men were to put ourselves in the places of some overworked, tired-out women, we would perhaps not stand it so patiently as they often do."[610] One missionary wrote that, knowing what he did about what was expected of female missionaries, he would discourage any daughter of his from working for the Methodist Women's Missionary Society.[611]

Although women usually worked in subordinate roles, the 1906 Indian Affairs annual report listed eleven female principals. All worked at boarding schools, as opposed to industrial schools. Seven of them were Roman Catholic, two were Anglican, one was Methodist, and one was Presbyterian.[612] One of these principals was Kate Gillespie. After teaching at day schools on reserves near Kamsack and Prince Albert, she was appointed principal of the File Hills school in 1901, a position she held until her marriage in 1908.[613]

The schools employed many more people than principals and teachers. Most schools were mini-communities. There were cooks, seamstresses, housekeepers, matrons, disciplinarians, farmers, carpenters, blacksmiths, engineers (to operate the heating and electrical generators), shoemakers, and even bandmasters.[614] Smaller schools such as the United Church Crosby Girls' Home in Port Simpson, British Columbia, made do with a staff of only three people in 1935.[615] The Roman Catholic school at Kamloops, British Columbia, had at least nineteen staff in that same year.[616] The Prince Albert, Saskatchewan, residence had over fifty employees during the 1966–67 school year.[617]

Workloads were heavy, and time off was rare. The seven-day week was the norm for many employees. An 1896 report on the Mount Elgin school noted, "No holidays are given or allowed to the staff; all days or parts of days lost time are deducted from their wages."[618] The policy at the Anglican schools into the 1920s was to allow "one full day off duty each month."[619] Indian agent F. J. C. Ball predicted that a sixty-three-year-old employee of the Lytton school was headed for a nervous breakdown in 1922. According to Ball, the man was "acting as teacher, minister, janitor and general handy man around the School. He also has charge of the boys [sic] dormitory at night."[620]

Staff meals were generally superior to those provided to the students. Staff members, particularly in the early years of the system, had greater immunity than their students to many of the diseases that plagued residential schools. Despite this, the living conditions that prevailed in many schools took a toll on staff. In 1896, E. B. Glass, the principal of the Whitefish Lake school in what is now Alberta, said the deterioration in the health of one staff member was the result of having to work in an inadequately heated and poorly insulated schoolhouse in which the "cold wind whistled up through the floor." Glass said that "the Department which charges itself with building, repairing and furnishing school houses, should also charge itself with neglect and the suffering endured by the teacher from that neglect."[621]

Disease and illness also claimed the children of married staff members. Emma Crosby, who helped found the Crosby Girls' Home in Port Simpson in the late 1870s, buried four of her children at Port Simpson. Two of them had succumbed to diphtheria.[622] Elizabeth Matheson, the wife of the Onion Lake principal, lost a daughter to whooping cough and a son to meningeal croup in the early years of the twentieth century.[623] During her fourth pregnancy, Elizabeth Matheson was so depressed that she considered suicide.[624]

Missionary staff, particularly in the early years of the system, were extremely hostile to Aboriginal culture.[625] They commonly described Aboriginal people as "lazy."[626] The long-time principal of the Shubenacadie school in Nova Scotia, J. P. Mackey, was expressing these views in the 1930s. In one letter, he described Aboriginal people as natural liars. "For myself, I never hope to catch up with the Indian and his lies, and in fact I am not going to try."[627] Others, however, spoke out on behalf of Aboriginal people. Hugh McKay, the superintendent of Presbyterian missionary work among Aboriginal people, criticized the federal government for failing to implement its Treaty promises and for failing to alleviate the hunger crisis on the Prairies.[628] Similarly, William Duncan, the Anglican missionary at Metlakatla, British Columbia, advised the Tsimshian on how to advance arguments in favour of Aboriginal title.[629]

Sometimes, staff protested the way students were treated. When two staff members of the Prince Albert, Saskatchewan, school resigned in 1952, they complained of the harsh disciplinary regime at the school.[630] In 1957, Helen Clafton, an ex-dormitory supervisor, wrote of how, at the Lytton, British Columbia, school, "the 'strap' is altogether too much in evidence."[631]

Aboriginal people also worked for the schools. The Mohawk Institute hired former student Isaac Barefoot to work as a teacher in 1869. Barefoot went on to serve as acting principal and was later ordained as an Anglican minister.[632] Another former student, Susan Hardie, obtained her teaching certificate in 1886.[633] She was the school governess as early as 1894, and was paid $200 a year.[634] She retired at the beginning of the 1936–37 school year.[635] A young Oneida woman, Miss Cornelius, taught at the Regina school in the early twentieth century.[636] She left the following year, lured away to a better paying school in the United States.[637] In the early 1930s, the Brandon school hired former student Lulu Ironstar as a teacher.[638] But these were exceptions, not the rule. As late as 1960, there were only twenty-three First Nations teachers working in residential schools across the country. Nineteen taught academic subjects and the other four taught home economics and industrial arts.[639] Stan McKay, who was educated at the Birtle and Brandon residential schools, taught in the Norway House, Manitoba, school in the 1960s. Although there was much that he enjoyed about the work, he left after two years. In his opinion, the education he was being forced to provide was not relevant to the lives of the children. There was, for example, a heavy emphasis on English, and no recognition of the role of Cree in the communities from which the children came. "They were doomed to fail under the system that existed. The majority of them would certainly and did."[640]

Miss Cornelius, an Oneida woman, taught at the Regina, Saskatchewan, school in the early twentieth century. Saskatchewan Archives Board, R-B992.

Verna Kirkness, who was raised on the Fisher River First Nation in Manitoba, taught at both the Birtle and Norway House schools.[641] She did not like the atmosphere at the Birtle school, where, she felt, administrators discouraged students from spending additional time with her. In her memoir, she wrote that she "wondered if they were afraid the children would tell me things about their lives away from the classroom."[642]

It was in the 1960s that a number of Aboriginal people were promoted to the position of school principal. Ahab Spence, a former residential school student, was appointed principal of the Sioux Lookout school in 1963.[643] Under Spence's administration, the school had a staff of twenty-three, half of whom were Aboriginal.[644] Colin Wasacase became the principal of the Presbyterian school in Kenora in 1966.[645] In keeping with past practice, his wife was made school matron.[646] This trend continued into the 1970s, when Aboriginal people were appointed to administrative positions at numerous residential schools, including those in Mission and Kamloops, British Columbia; Blue Quills, Alberta; Prince Albert, Duck Lake, and Qu'Appelle, Saskatchewan; and Fort George, Québec.[647] Although the total number of schools declined rapidly from 1969 onwards, they became a significant source of Aboriginal employment, particularly in Saskatchewan, where six schools were operated by First Nations educational authorities. Of the 360 people working in the Saskatchewan schools in 1994, 220 were of Aboriginal ancestry—almost two-thirds of the total.[648]

Most of the Aboriginal people who were hired by the schools worked as cooks, cleaners, and handymen. In 1954, Mrs. Clair, a Cree woman who had attended the school at Lac La Ronge, Saskatchewan, was working at the Carcross school in the Yukon. She was described by a superintendent as a "very fine person, willing worker and everyone likes her. Can certainly get the most out of the children."[649] At the Wabasca, Alberta, school, Alphonse Alook was seen as being "a tower of strength to the Principal especially of late. Can do fair carpentering and is loyal to the school. Principal recommends an increase in his salary."[650] Four young Aboriginal women, three of whom were sisters, had been hired to work at the Fort George, Québec, school in 1953.[651] A 1956 report on three of them said, "The Herodier girls are all doing a fine job." They were not, however, being housed in the same way as non-Aboriginal staff. The report observed that it was fortunate that "the native girls do not mind doubling up in cramped quarters otherwise staff accommodation would be insufficient."[652]

A number of former Aboriginal staff members felt they helped make an important difference in the lives of the students. Jeanne Rioux went to the Edmonton school and later worked as a supervisor at the Hobbema school in Alberta. There, she challenged staff about the way they disciplined children.[653] Mary Chapman was a former residential school student who later worked in the kitchen of the Kuper Island school. At her prompting, the school began serving students and staff the same meals. It was her rule that "if we run out of roast, the kids run out of roast, I don't give them bologna, I take the roast from the staff and I give it to them."[654] Vitaline Elsie Jenner, who had unhappily attended the Fort Chipewyan, Alberta, residential school, worked as a girls' supervisor at Breynat Hall, the Roman Catholic residence at Fort Smith, Northwest Territories. To her surprise, she enjoyed most of the experience. She recalled being asked by one staff person what sort of games she thought the children would like to play to make them feel at home. "I said, 'You know I bet you they all want to be hugged, like I was in that residential school. 'Cause you know what? They're away from their parents.'"[655]

Former staff and the children of former staff members have expressed the view that much of the discussion of the history of residential schools has overlooked both the positive intent with which many staff members approached their work, and the positive accomplishments of the school system. Although they certainly believed the system was underfunded, they also believed that they and their parents devoted much of their lives to educating and caring for Aboriginal children.

Most of the staff members did not make a career in residential schools, spending only a year or two at a school before moving on. Others stayed for many years in conditions that were often very different from what they grew up with, working for low pay, and living in cramped and confined quarters with, at times, less than congenial colleagues. They spent their time teaching, cooking, cleaning, farming, and supervising children. On their own, these can be seen as positive, not negative, activities. For the most part, the school staff members were not responsible for the policies that separated children from their parents and lodged them in inadequate and underfunded facilities. In fact, many staff members spent much of their time and energy attempting to humanize a harsh and often destructive system. Along with the children's own resilience, such staff members share credit for any positive results of the schools.

Agreement and apologies

During the years in which the federal government was slowly closing the residential school system, Aboriginal people across the country were establishing effective regional and national organizations. In the courts and the legislatures, they argued for the recognition of Aboriginal rights, particularly the right to self-government. They forced the government to withdraw its 1969 White Paper that aimed at terminating Aboriginal rights, they placed the settling of land claims on the national agenda, ensured that Aboriginal rights were entrenched in the Constitution, and saw the creation of a new jurisdiction within Canada—the territory of Nunavut—with an Inuit majority population. These developments were part of a global movement asserting the rights of Indigenous peoples. Canadian Aboriginal leaders played a key role in this movement. For example, they were central in the creation of the World Council of Indigenous Peoples in 1975.[656] The work of the council laid the groundwork for the 2007 *United Nations Declaration on the Rights of Indigenous Peoples*.[657]

From the 1960s onwards, many people within the churches began to re-evaluate both the broader history of the relations between the churches and Aboriginal peoples, and the specific history of the residential schools. Many church organizations provided support to Aboriginal campaigns on such issues as land and Treaty rights. In the 1980s, the churches began to issue apologies to Aboriginal people. One of the first of these, issued in 1986 by the United Church of Canada, focused on the destructive impact that church missionary work had on Aboriginal culture.[658] The Oblate order offered an apology in 1991 that referred to the residential schools.[659] Apologies relating specifically to their roles in operating residential schools were issued by the Anglicans in 1993, the Presbyterians in 1994, and the United Church in 1998.[660]

Aboriginal people also began both individually and collectively to push for the prosecution of individuals who had abused students at residential schools and for compensation for former students. In 1987, Nora Bernard, a former student of the Shubenacadie residential school, began interviewing fellow Survivors in the kitchen of her home in Truro, Nova Scotia.[661] In 1995, she formed the Shubenacadie Indian Residential School Survivors Association and started registering Survivors. The work of former students from the schools in places as distant as Fort Albany, Ontario; Chesterfield Inlet, then in the Northwest Territories; and Williams Lake, British Columbia, led to several police investigations, and a limited number of prosecutions and convictions. They also led to the creation of local and national organizations of former residential school students. Phil Fontaine, then Grand Chief of the Assembly of Manitoba Chiefs, placed the issue on the national agenda in October 1990 when he spoke publicly about the abuse that he and his fellow students had experienced at the Fort Alexander school.[662]

Former students also filed lawsuits against the federal government and the churches over the treatment that they received in the schools. Although they were successful in a number of these cases, courts were not willing to provide compensation for some issues of importance to Aboriginal peoples, such as the loss of language and culture. By October 2001, more than 8,500 residential school Survivors had filed lawsuits against the federal government, the churches, related organizations, and, where possible, the individual who committed the abuse.[663] By 2005, it was estimated that the volume surpassed 18,000 lawsuits.[664] Former students also commenced class-action lawsuits for compensation. Although lower courts rejected their right to pursue such claims, in 2004, the Ontario Court of Appeal ruled that one of these cases (known as the "Cloud case") should be allowed to proceed.[665] Within months, the federal government agreed to enter into a process intended to negotiate a settlement to the growing number of class-action suits. The Indian Residential Schools Settlement Agreement (IRSSA) was reached in 2006 and approved by the courts in the following year. The IRSSA has five main components: 1) a Common Experience Payment; 2) an Independent Assessment Process; 3) support for the Aboriginal Health Foundation; 4) support for residential school commemoration; and 5) the establishment of a Truth and Reconciliation Commission of Canada. Through the Common Experience Payment, former students would receive a payment of $10,000 for the first year that they attended a residential school, and an additional $3,000 for each additional year or partial year of attendance. The Independent Assessment Process adjudicated and compensated the claims of those students who were physically or sexually abused at the schools. Funding was also provided to the Aboriginal Healing Foundation to support initiatives addressing the residential school legacy. The Settlement Agreement committed the federal government to funding initiatives to commemorate the residential school experience. The Truth and Reconciliation Commission of Canada was mandated to tell Canadians about the history of residential schools and the impact those schools had on Aboriginal peoples, and to guide a process of reconciliation.

The court approval of the IRSSA in 2007 was followed in June 2008 with Prime Minister Stephen Harper's apology on behalf of Canada. In his statement, the prime minister recognized that the primary purpose of the schools had been to remove children from their homes and families in order to assimilate them better into the dominant culture. Harper said, "These objectives were based on the assumption Aboriginal cultures and spiritual beliefs were inferior and unequal. Indeed, some sought, as it was infamously said, 'to kill the Indian in the child.' Today, we recognize that this policy of assimilation was wrong, has caused great harm, and has no place in our country."[666]

Canada's Aboriginal leaders along with a number of former residential schools students were present on the floor of the House of Commons when Prime Minister Stephen Harper delivered his 2008 apology. Clockwise from the left: former student Don Favel; former student Mary Moonias; former student Mike Cachagee, President of the National Residential School Survivors Society; former student Crystal Merasty; former student Piita Irniq; Patrick Brazeau, National Chief of the Congress of Aboriginal Peoples; Mary Simon, President of the Inuit Tapiriit Kanatami; Phil Fontaine, National Chief of the Assembly of First Nations; Beverley Jacobs, President of the Native Women's Association of Canada; Clem Chartier, President of the Métis National Council. Former student Marguerite Wabano is obscured by Phil Fontaine's headdress. Canadian Press: Fred Chartrand.

The prime minister was joined by the leaders of the other parties represented in the Canadian House of Commons. The Liberal leader of the opposition, the Honourable Stéphane Dion, recognized that the government's policy had "destroyed the fabric of family in First Nations, Métis and Inuit communities. Parents and children were made to feel worthless. Parents and grandparents were given no choice. Their children were stolen from them."[667] The Bloc Québecois leader, the Honourable Gilles Duceppe, asked Canadians to "picture a small village, a small community. Now picture all of its children, gone. No more children between seven and sixteen playing in the lanes or the woods, filling the hearts of their elders with their laughter and joy."[668] The New Democratic Party leader, the Honourable Jack Layton, called on Canadians to help

> reverse the horrific and shameful statistics afflicting Aboriginal populations, now: the high rates of poverty, suicide, the poor or having no education, over-

> crowding, crumbling housing, and unsafe drinking water. Let us make sure that all survivors of the residential schools receive the recognition and compensation that is due to them.[669]

In his response, Phil Fontaine, then National Chief of the Assembly of First Nations, said the apology marked a new dawn in the relationship between Aboriginal people and the rest of Canada. He also called attention to the "brave survivors," who, by "the telling of their painful stories, have stripped white supremacy of its authority and legitimacy. The irresistibility of speaking truth to power is real."[670] National Chief of the Congress of Aboriginal Peoples Patrick Brazeau spoke of how the resiliency, courage, and strength of residential school Survivors had inspired all Aboriginal people.[671] Mary Simon, President of the Inuit Tapiriit Kanatami, said, in tackling the hard work that remained to be done, "Let us now join forces with the common goal of working together to ensure that this apology opens the door to a new chapter in our lives as aboriginal peoples and in our place in Canada."[672] Clem Chartier, President of the Métis National Council, noted that he had attended a residential school, and pointed out that many issues regarding the relationship between Métis people and residential schools still were not resolved. He said, "I also feel deeply conflicted, because there is still misunderstanding about the situation of the Métis Nation, our history and our contemporary situation."[673] Beverley Jacobs, President of the Native Women's Association of Canada, spoke of how Aboriginal communities were recovering their traditions. "Now we have our language still, we have our ceremonies, we have our elders, and we have to revitalize those ceremonies and the respect for our people not only within Canadian society but even within our own peoples."[674]

The Settlement Agreement and the formal apology by Prime Minister Stephen Harper represent the culmination of years of political struggle, changes in societal attitudes, court decisions, and negotiation. Through it all, the Survivors kept the issue alive.

These events do not bring the residential school story to an end. The legacy of the schools remains. One can see the impact of a system that disrupted families in the high number of Aboriginal children who have been removed from their families by child-welfare agencies. An educational system that degraded Aboriginal culture and subjected students to humiliating discipline must bear a portion of responsibility for the current gap between the educational success of Aboriginal and non-Aboriginal Canadians. The health of generations of Aboriginal children was undermined by inadequate diets, poor sanitation, overcrowded conditions, and a failure to address the tuberculosis crisis that was ravaging the country's Aboriginal community. There should be little wonder that Aboriginal health status remains far below that of the general population. The over-incarceration and over-victimization of Aboriginal people also have links to a system that subjected Aboriginal children to punitive discipline and exposed them to physical and sexual abuse.

The history of residential schools presented in this report commenced by placing the schools in the broader history of the global European colonization of Indigenous peoples and their lands. Residential schooling was only a part of the colonization of Aboriginal people. The policy of colonization suppressed Aboriginal culture and languages, disrupted Aboriginal government, destroyed Aboriginal economies, and confined Aboriginal people to marginal and often unproductive land. When that policy resulted in hunger, disease, and poverty, the federal government failed to meet its obligations to Aboriginal people. That policy was dedicated to eliminating Aboriginal peoples as distinct political and cultural entities and must be described for what it was: a policy of cultural genocide.

Despite being subjected to aggressive assimilation policies for nearly 200 years, Aboriginal people have maintained their identity and their communities. They continue to assert their rights to self-governance. In this, they are not alone. Like the Settlement Agreement in Canada, the *United Nations Declaration on the Rights of Indigenous Peoples* is a milestone in a global campaign to recognize and respect the rights of Indigenous peoples. It is time to abandon the colonial policies of the past, to address the legacy of the schools, and to engage in a process of reconciliation with the Aboriginal people of Canada.

The legacy

I want Canadians to understand that [the legacy of the residential schools] does not just affect the lives of the person who actually attended the school, but family members, such as spouses and children, are also very deeply affected about this sad legacy in history.

— Johanne Coutu-Autut, spouse of former Turquetil Hall resident[1]

Residential schools are a tragic part of Canada's history. But they cannot simply be consigned to history. The legacy from the schools and the political and legal policies and mechanisms surrounding their history continue to this day. This is reflected in the significant educational, income, health, and social disparities between Aboriginal people and other Canadians. It is reflected in the intense racism some people harbour against Aboriginal people and in the systemic and other forms of discrimination Aboriginal people regularly experience in this country. It is reflected too in the critically endangered status of most Aboriginal languages.

Current conditions such as the disproportionate apprehension of Aboriginal children by child-welfare agencies and the disproportionate imprisonment and victimization of Aboriginal people can be explained in part as a result or legacy of the way that Aboriginal children were treated in residential schools and were denied an environment of positive parenting, worthy community leaders, and a positive sense of identity and self-worth. The schools could be brutal places, as Joseph Martin Larocque, a former student at the Beauval residential school in Saskatchewan, told the Truth and Reconciliation Commission of Canada.

[Residential school] was a very harsh environment. They, they treated us like criminals.... You, you had to, it's like a prison. But we were small kids, and we didn't understand. We didn't understand harsh discipline. We, we understood love from our, our parents. But the harsh discipline was hard to take, and that happened to everybody, not only me.[2]

The impacts of the legacy of residential schools have not ended with those who attended the schools. They affected the Survivors' partners, their children, their grandchildren, their extended families, and their communities. Children who were abused in the schools sometimes went on to abuse others. Many students who spoke to the Commission said they developed addictions as a means of coping. Students who were treated and punished like prisoners in the schools often graduated to real prisons. For many, the path from residential school to prison was a short one. Mervin Mirasty was a student at the Beauval residential school.

> I ran away from school. I'd go out, I'd walk around town, and steal whatever I could steal.... I started stealing cars. I got caught at fifteen. I ended up in jail. From that point of fifteen years old 'til ... to the year 2000, I got sentenced to twenty-five years all together, twenty-five years all together. And I don't know what I was fighting, what I was trying to do. I didn't care who I stole from. I drank. I started drinking when I was about seventeen, eighteen. I drank, I stole, I hardly worked. I used the system, the welfare system, and plus I stole, and I drank.[3]

Children exposed to strict and regimented discipline in the schools sometimes found it difficult to become loving parents. Genine Paul-Dimitracopoulos's mother was placed in the Shubenacadie residential school in Nova Scotia at a very early age. Paul-Dimitracopoulos told the Commission that knowing this, and what the school was like, helped her understand "how we grew up because my mom never really showed us love when we were kids coming up. She, when I was hurt or cried, she was never there to console you or to hug you. If I hurt myself she would never give me a hug and tell me it would be okay. I didn't understand why."[4] Alma Scott of Winnipeg told the Commission that as "a direct result of those residential schools because I was a dysfunctional mother.... I spent over twenty years of my life stuck in a bottle in an addiction where I didn't want to feel any emotions so I numbed out with drugs and with alcohol.... That's how I raised my children, that's what my children saw, and that's what I saw."[5]

The Commission is convinced that genuine reconciliation will not be possible until the complex legacy of the schools is understood, acknowledged, and addressed. Parliament and the Supreme Court have recognized that the legacy of residential schools should be considered when sentencing Aboriginal offenders. Although these have been important measures, they have not been sufficient to address the grossly disproportionate imprisonment of Aboriginal people, which continues to grow, in part because of a lack of adequate funding and support for culturally appropriate alternatives to imprisonment.

More First Nations child-welfare agencies have been established, but the disproportionate apprehension of Aboriginal children also continues to grow. In part, this has happened because of a lack of adequate funding for culturally appropriate supports that would allow children to remain safely with their families, or to allow children to be placed in foster or adoptive environments that are culturally appropriate and capable of giving children a sense of identity, self-respect, and self-worth.

Many of the individual and collective harms have not yet been redressed, even after the negotiated out-of-court settlement of the residential school litigation in 2006, and Canada's apology in 2008. In fact, some of the damages done by residential schools to Aboriginal families, languages, education, and health may be perpetuated and even worsened as a result of current governmental policies. New policies can easily be based on a lack of understanding of Aboriginal people, similar to that which motivated the schools. For example, current child-welfare and health policies that fail to take into account the importance of community in raising children can result in inappropriate decision making. We must learn from the failure of the schools in order to ensure that the mistakes of the past are not repeated in the future.

Despite the challenges and failings in responding to the legacy of residential schools, and a concern that the federal government may have lost a sense of urgency on these issues since the 2006 Indian Residential Schools Settlement Agreement and Canada's apology in 2008, the Commission is nonetheless cautiously optimistic that promising pathways to constructive reforms do exist. These could include new strategies based on respect for Aboriginal self-determination and for Canada's obligations under Treaties, and Canada's endorsement of the new *United Nations Declaration on the Rights of Indigenous Peoples.*

In its February 2012 *Interim Report,* the Commission observed that the *United Nations Declaration* provides a valuable framework for working towards ongoing reconciliation between Aboriginal and non-Aboriginal Canadians. We continue to encourage all governments, and all the legal parties to the Settlement Agreement, to use it as such a framework.[6]

The Government of Canada initially refused to adopt the *Declaration.* When it finally did endorse the *Declaration,* it did not fully embrace its principles, saying that "it is a non-legally binding document that does not reflect customary international law nor change Canadian laws."[7] The Commission is convinced that a refusal to respect the rights and remedies in the *Declaration* will serve to further aggravate the legacy of residential schools, and will constitute a barrier to progress towards reconciliation.

Child welfare

Residential schools, as acknowledged by the prime minister's own admission in his 2008 official apology from Canada, were an attack on Aboriginal children and families. They were based on racist attitudes that considered Aboriginal families as being frequently unfit to care for their children. By removing children from their communities and by subjecting them to strict discipline, religious indoctrination, and a regimented life more akin to life in a prison than a family, residential schools often harmed the subsequent ability of the students to be caring parents. In many ways, the schools were more a child-welfare system than an educational one. A survey in 1953 suggested that of 10,112 students then in residential schools, 4,313 were either orphans or from what were described as "broken homes."[8] From the 1940s onwards, residential schools increasingly served as orphanages and child-welfare facilities. By 1960, the federal government estimated that 50% of the children in residential schools were there for child-welfare reasons.[9]

The residential school experience was followed by the "Sixties Scoop"—the wide-scale national apprehension of Aboriginal children by child-welfare agencies. Child-welfare authorities removed thousands of Aboriginal children from their families and communities and placed them in non-Aboriginal homes without taking steps to preserve their culture and identity. Children were placed in homes across Canada, in the United States, and even overseas. This practice actually extended well beyond the 1960s, until at least the mid- to late 1980s.[10]

Today, the effects of the residential school experience and the Sixties Scoop have adversely affected parenting skills and the success of many Aboriginal families. These factors, combined with prejudicial attitudes toward Aboriginal parenting skills and a tendency to see Aboriginal poverty as a symptom of neglect, rather than as a consequence of failed government policies, have resulted in grossly disproportionate rates of child apprehension among Aboriginal people. A 2011 Statistics Canada study found that 14,225 or 3.6% of all First Nations children aged fourteen and under were in foster care, compared with 15,345 or 0.3% of non-Aboriginal children.[11] As Old Crow Chief Norma Kassi said at the Northern National Event in Inuvik, "The doors are closed at the residential schools but the foster homes are still existing and our children are still being taken away."[12] The Commission agrees: Canada's child-welfare system has simply continued the assimilation that the residential school system started.

Canada's child-welfare crisis has not gone unnoticed in the international community. In 2012, the United Nations Committee on the Rights of the Child expressed to Canada its concern about the frequent removal of children in Canada from families as a "first resort" in cases of neglect, financial hardship, or disability. In its report, the committee singled out the frequency with which Aboriginal children are placed outside their communities.[13] Noting that Canada had failed to act on its own auditor general's findings of inequitable child-welfare funding, the committee concluded that "urgent measures" were needed to address the discriminatory overrepresentation of Aboriginal children in out-of-home care.[14]

Disturbing data

The First Nations Component of the Canadian Incidence Study of Reported Child Abuse and Neglect, designed by the Public Health Agency of Canada and its provincial, academic, and agency partners, confirmed that Aboriginal children in the geographic areas studied are also significantly overrepresented as subjects of child maltreatment investigations. For every 1,000 First Nations children, there were 140.6 child maltreatment-related investigations, as compared with 33.5 investigations for non-Aboriginal children.[15] The rate of investigations involving First Nations children was 4.2 times the rate of non-Aboriginal investigations.[16] The study also found that in the population under review, those allegations were more likely to be substantiated in the cases of First Nations children. This was true for all categories of maltreatment, but the difference was most extreme for investigations of neglect.[17] Investigations of First Nations families for neglect were substantiated at a rate eight times greater than for the non-Aboriginal population.[18]

An analysis of the Canadian Incidence Study confirmed that poverty and social stressors are major factors in child-welfare investigations involving Aboriginal families. Aboriginal parents were more likely to experience a host of serious risk factors, including domestic violence, alcohol abuse, lack of social supports, drug or solvent abuse, and a history of living in foster care or group homes.[19] The direct connection between Aboriginal poverty and high child-welfare apprehensions has been known for half a century. Yet, Aboriginal children are still taken away from their parents because their parents are poor.

Researchers suggest that clear standards are needed to guide apprehensions, and that the provision of family supports and prevention services might be a better response to concerns than removal of the child.[20] There must be a commitment to reducing the number of Aboriginal children in care and developing supports to keep families together. Child-welfare workers must bring to their work an understanding of Aboriginal culture as well as an understanding of the lasting harms caused by residential schools.

Call to Action

1) We call upon the federal, provincial, territorial, and Aboriginal governments to commit to reducing the number of Aboriginal children in care by:

   i. Monitoring and assessing neglect investigations.

   ii. Providing adequate resources to enable Aboriginal communities and child-welfare organizations to keep Aboriginal families together where it is safe to do so, and to keep children in culturally appropriate environments, regardless of where they reside.

iii. Ensuring that social workers and others who conduct child-welfare investigations are properly educated and trained about the history and impacts of residential schools.

iv. Ensuring that social workers and others who conduct child-welfare investigations are properly educated and trained about the potential for Aboriginal communities and families to provide more appropriate solutions to family healing.

v. Requiring that all child-welfare decision makers consider the impact of the residential school experience on children and their caregivers.

Better research and data are also required in order to monitor and develop strategies to reduce the overrepresentation of Aboriginal children in care.

Call to Action

2) We call upon the federal government, in collaboration with the provinces and territories, to prepare and publish annual reports on the number of Aboriginal children (First Nations, Inuit, and Métis) who are in care, compared with non-Aboriginal children, as well as the reasons for apprehension, the total spending on preventive and care services by child-welfare agencies, and the effectiveness of various interventions.

Death and abuse of children in care

The child-welfare system apprehends too many Aboriginal children while, at the same time, failing to protect them. The Commission heard many stories of mistreatment in foster homes. One woman told us that her foster parents physically and sexually abused her. Her Aboriginal identity was constantly disparaged. She said, "[My foster parents were] adamant about Aboriginal culture being less than human, living as dirty bush people, eating rats. It made me not want to be one of those people. And for years, I didn't know how to be proud of who I was because I didn't know who I was."[21]

Linda Clarke was placed in a foster home with three other children.

> In that foster home there was a pedophile, and I don't [know] what was happening to anybody else, but I became his target. The mother used to always send me to do errands with him. And so every time, he would make me do things to him and then he would give me candy. Also, in that home there was no hugging of us foster kids or anything like that. And I carried a great guilt for

many, many years, because sometimes I didn't want to resist it, I just.... But I knew it was very bad.[22]

Sometimes, child-welfare placements end in tragedy. Where there are province-specific statistics available, the findings suggest that in some parts of the country, Aboriginal children who come into contact with child-welfare authorities are significantly more likely to die.

Research in Alberta indicated that 78% of children who have died in foster care between 1999 and mid-2013 were Aboriginal.[23] Since Aboriginal children, a minority of the overall population, represent 59% of children in care in Alberta, the rate of Aboriginal child deaths in care is even more disproportionate than the apprehension rate. Of the seventy-four recorded deaths of Aboriginal children in care, thirteen were due to accidents, twelve children committed suicide, and ten children were the victims of homicide.[24] Forty-five of these Aboriginal children died while in the care of a provincial child-welfare agency, and twenty-nine died in the care of an on-reserve First Nations child and family service agency.

Delivery of child-welfare services

There are over 300 child-welfare agencies in Canada operating under provincial and territorial jurisdiction. In addition, Canada provides funding to over 100 agencies delivering child and family services to First Nations families under the framework of provincial legislation.[25] In 2010–11, there were 9,241 First Nations children outside the parental home and in the care of these First Nations child and family service agencies, representing 5.5% of on-reserve children.[26] A few larger Canadian cities (such as Toronto and Vancouver) also have Aboriginal child and family service agencies.[27] In Manitoba, there is also an agency serving Métis families. There are, however, no Aboriginally controlled agencies in the three northern territories; child-welfare services to Aboriginal families there are provided through the same government agencies that serve all children. In two out of the three territories, Aboriginal people make up a majority of the members in their legislatures and cabinets.

Although the federal government acknowledges its responsibility for child-welfare services to First Nations families, Métis communities are not well served. The Commission believes that adequately funded, Métis-specific, child and family services must be made available to Métis children and families. The Government of Canada should not let unresolved jurisdictional disputes stand in the way of the acceptance of such responsibilities. Similarly, the Commission believes the Government of Canada should ensure the development of adequately resourced Inuit child-welfare services in the North and in urban centres such as Ottawa and Montreal that have a significant Inuit population.

Lack of adequate funding

Proof of the effectiveness of First Nations child and family service agencies is still preliminary, but anecdotal evidence and case studies suggest that First Nation agencies are more effective than non-Aboriginal agencies in providing service to First Nation clients.[28] But, it is troubling that the ability of First Nations child and family services agencies to develop culturally appropriate services has been constrained by limited funding. Of twelve First Nations agencies surveyed in 2005, 83.4% reported that they did not receive adequate funds to ensure culturally appropriate services.[29] It is clear that the way in which Canada has funded Aboriginal child welfare has hampered First Nations agencies in providing effective services. This shortfall continues to inflict pain on Aboriginal families and communities, and contributes to the continuing overrepresentation of Aboriginal children in foster care.

Jurisdictional disputes

Jurisdictional responsibility for child welfare is intensely contested. Historically, the federal government and provincial and territorial governments have tried to shift responsibility for Aboriginal child services from one level of government to another. The federal position is that responsibility for child and family services lies solely within the jurisdiction of the provinces and territories. Canada contends that the federal government is responsible for funding only on-reserve services. In contrast, the provinces maintain that the federal government has constitutional responsibility for 'Indians,' and argue that Ottawa has off-loaded that responsibility to the provinces to provide services to an increasingly urban, non-reserve population.[30]

The result is that there are often disputes over which level of government or department is responsible for paying costs. The repercussions of these disputes can be serious, with Aboriginal children paying the highest price—in particular, children with complex developmental, mental health, and physical health issues.[31]

In 2007, the House of Commons unanimously supported the adoption of "Jordan's Principle," named in honour of a Manitoba infant born with complex medical needs who spent all of his short life in hospital, caught up in a federal–provincial jurisdictional dispute over responsibility for funding his care.[32] According to Jordan's Principle, the government department that is first contacted for a service available only off-reserve must pay for it and later pursue reimbursement for the expenses.[33] But Jordan's Principle was not passed into law; rather, it is a statement of principle by the Canadian parliament.[34] Many inter-governmental cases of disputed responsibility continue.

Call to Action:

3) We call upon all levels of government to fully implement Jordan's Principle.

Improving outcomes for children

Although there is now considerable Aboriginal control of child-welfare services, Aboriginal agencies still struggle for adequate funding. There is a need for more funding and research into preventive services that can support Aboriginal families. At the same time, many of the conditions that result in disproportionate Aboriginal involvement in the child-welfare system are related to more intractable legacies of residential schools, including poverty, addictions, and domestic and sexual violence. We believe that in order to redress the legacy of residential schools and to move towards more respectful and healthy relationships, the Government of Canada, in meaningful consultation with First Nations, Inuit, and Métis communities, must recognize and address the broader context of the child-welfare crisis. This includes matters of child poverty, housing, water, sanitation, food security, family violence, addictions, and educational inequities. Effective child-welfare reform will require both measureable targets and timelines for reducing the numbers and proportion of Aboriginal children in care, greater consistency in the system's regulatory framework, and the acknowledgement of the central role of Aboriginal agencies.

Canada has rejected First Nations' demands to operate services in accordance with traditional laws and traditional justice systems. By contrast, in the United States, tribal courts have played an important role in the child-welfare system since 1978. These courts have exclusive jurisdiction over custody proceedings involving Native American children living on a reservation. They may also play a role in Native American child-custody cases where the child lives outside a reservation.[35] While not perfect, the American system has led to greater tribal authority over the placement of Indigenous children, as well as the expansion of family preservation programs. Indigenous children are still removed from their homes in disproportionately high numbers, but the rate of overrepresentation has decreased. The rate of placement with non-Indigenous caregivers has also decreased.[36]

Call to Action

4) We call upon the federal government to enact Aboriginal child-welfare legislation that establishes national standards for Aboriginal child apprehension and custody cases and includes principles that:

i. Affirm the right of Aboriginal governments to establish and maintain their own child-welfare agencies.

ii. Require all child-welfare agencies and courts to take the residential school legacy into account in their decision making.

iii. Establish, as an important priority, a requirement that placements of Aboriginal children into temporary and permanent care be culturally appropriate.

There is also a human dimension to improving outcomes for Aboriginal children. The intergenerational impact of the residential school experience has left some families without strong role models for parenting. An investment in culturally appropriate programs in Aboriginal communities has the potential to improve parenting skills and enable more children to grow up safely in their own families and communities.

Call to Action

5) We call upon the federal, provincial, territorial, and Aboriginal governments to develop culturally appropriate parenting programs for Aboriginal families.

Education

The residential school system failed as an education system. It was based on racist assumptions about the intellectual and cultural inferiority of Aboriginal people—the belief that Aboriginal children were incapable of attaining anything more than a rudimentary elementary-level or vocational education. Consequently, for most of the system's history, the majority of students never progressed beyond elementary school. The government and church officials who operated the residential schools ignored the positive emphasis that the Treaties and many Aboriginal families placed on education. Instead, they created dangerous and frightening institutions that provided little learning.

In their mission to 'civilize' and Christianize, the school staff relied on corporal punishment to discipline their students. That punishment often crossed the line into physical abuse. Although it is employed much less frequently now, corporal punishment is still legally permissible in schools and elsewhere under Canadian law. Section 43 of the *Criminal Code* says: "Every schoolteacher, parent or person standing in the place of a parent is justified in using force by way of correction toward a pupil or child, as the case may be, who is under his care, if the force does not exceed what is reasonable under the circumstances." The Commission believes that corporal punishment is a relic of a discredited past and has no place in Canadian schools or homes.

Call to Action

6) We call upon the Government of Canada to repeal Section 43 of the *Criminal Code* of Canada.

The objectives of the schools were to strip away Aboriginal children's identities and assimilate them into Western Christian society. Doris Young, who attended the Elkhorn residential school in Manitoba, described the experience as a systematic attack on her identity as a Cree person.

> Those schools were a war on Aboriginal children, and they took away our identity. First of all, they gave us numbers, we had no names, we were numbers, and they cut our hair. They took away our clothes, and gave us clothes ... we all looked alike. Our hair was all the same, cut us into bangs, and straight short, straight hair up to our ears.... They took away our moccasins, and gave us shoes. I was just a baby. I didn't actually wear shoes, we wore moccasins. And so our identity was immediately taken away when we entered those schools.[37]

In addition to the emotional and psychological damage they inflicted, one of the most far-reaching and devastating legacies of residential schools has been their impact on the educational and economic success of Aboriginal people. The lack of role models and mentors, insufficient funds for the schools, inadequate teachers, and unsuitable curricula generally taught in a foreign language—and sometimes by teachers who were also not proficient in the language of instruction—have all contributed to dismal success rates for Aboriginal education. These conditions were compounded for many students by the challenges of trying to learn in environments rendered traumatic by homesickness, hunger, fear, abuse, and institutionalized helplessness. The Commission has heard many examples of students who attended residential school for eight or more years, but left with nothing more than Grade Three achievement, and sometimes without even the ability to read. According to Indian Affairs annual reports, in the 1950s, only half of each year's enrolment got to Grade Six.[38]

Poor educational achievement has led to the chronic unemployment or under-employment, poverty, poor housing, substance abuse, family violence, and ill health that many former students of the schools have suffered as adults. Although educational success rates are slowly improving, Aboriginal Canadians still have dramatically lower educational and economic achievements than other Canadians.

Education is a fundamental human and Aboriginal right, guaranteed in Treaties, in international law, and in the Canadian Charter of Rights and Freedoms. In particular, the *United Nations Declaration on the Rights of Indigenous Peoples* contains a powerful statement on the right to education under community control. The *Declaration* states, "Indigenous peoples have the right to establish and control their educational systems and institutions providing education in their own languages, in a manner appropriate to their cultural methods of teaching and learning."[39] The Commission believes that fulfilling the promise of the *Declaration* will be key to overcoming the legacy of the residential schools.

Education and the income gap

It is not surprising that, faced with terrible conditions and mostly ineffective teaching, many students left school as soon as they could. A 2010 study of Aboriginal parents and children living off reserves found that the high school completion rate is lower for former residential school students (28%) than for those who did not attend (36%).[40] Only 7% of the parents who attended residential school have obtained a university degree, compared with 10% for those Aboriginal parents who had never attended these institutions.[41]

Although secondary school graduation rates for all Aboriginal people have improved since the closure of the schools, considerable gaps remain when compared with the rates for the non-Aboriginal population. For example, according to the 2006 census, 34% of Aboriginal adults had not graduated from high school, compared with only 15% of their non-Aboriginal counterparts.[42] In the 2011 census, these numbers improved slightly, with 29% of Aboriginal people not graduating from high school, compared with 12% in the non-Aboriginal population.[43]

It is significant that the lowest levels of educational success are in those communities with the highest percentages of descendants of residential school Survivors: First Nations people living on reserves, and Inuit. Both groups have a high school completion rate of 41% or less.[44]

The statistics for First Nations people living off reserves and for Métis are somewhat better. More than 60% of First Nations people living off reserves and 65% to 75% of Métis people have graduated from high school (although these results are still below the national average).[45]

Lower educational attainment for the children of Survivors has severely limited their employment and earning potential, just as it did for their parents. Aboriginal people have lower median after-tax income, are more likely to experience unemployment, and are more likely to collect employment insurance and social assistance benefits.[46] This situation is true for all Aboriginal groups, with some variations. In 2009, the Métis unemployment rate for persons aged twenty-five to fifty-four was 9.4%, while the non-Aboriginal rate was 7.0%.[47] In 2006, the Inuit unemployment rate was 19%.[48] The true rates of unemployment for people living on reserves are difficult to ascertain because of limited data collection.[49]

Aboriginal people also have incomes well below their non-Aboriginal counterparts. The median income for Aboriginal people in 2006 was 30% lower than the median income for non-Aboriginal workers ($18,962 versus $27,097, respectively).[50] The gap narrows when Aboriginal people obtain a university degree, which they do at a far lower rate.[51] Not surprisingly, the child poverty rate for Aboriginal children is also very high—40%, compared with 17% for all children in Canada.[52] The income gap is pervasive: non-Aboriginal Canadians earn more than Aboriginal workers no matter whether they work on reserves, off reserves, or in urban, rural, or remote locations.[53]

The proportion of Aboriginal adults below the poverty line, regardless of age and gender, is much higher than that of non-Aboriginal adults, with differences ranging from 7.8% for adult men aged sixty-five or older, to 22.5% for adult women aged sixty-five or older.[54] The depth of poverty is also much greater, with Aboriginal people having an average income that falls further below the poverty line on average than that of non-Aboriginal adults, and their poverty is more likely to have persisted for a significant period of time.[55]

Call to Action

7) We call upon the federal government to develop with Aboriginal groups a joint strategy to eliminate educational and employment gaps between Aboriginal and non-Aboriginal Canadians.

Funding inequities

Present-day Aboriginal education in Canada is made up of a mix of models. The federal government funds schools on reserves, with the actual operation of those schools often delegated to the local First Nation. Aboriginal children who do not live on reserves are educated through the provincial or territorial school systems. In addition, there are a few education systems completely run and managed by First Nations through self-government and other types of intergovernmental agreements.

There are approximately 72,000 students attending 518 First Nation schools.[56] Despite those numbers, many children must still leave their homes and families behind if they wish to obtain a higher education, even at the high school level.

Since 1973, the Government of Canada has claimed that it is committed to devolving control of education to First Nations people.[57] However, the interpretation of "Indian control" offered by the Government of Canada bears little resemblance to the vision of First Nations. The government's version of the term has entailed the devolution of federal education programs to First Nations, without the benefit of adequate funding or statutory authority.[58] Indeed, when devolution began, it was designed to occur without any additional expense. This meant that former Indian Affairs-operated schools, which were already substandard compared with provincial norms, were handed over to the First Nation bands to run, but without giving the bands the means to operate them effectively. As a result, the curriculum for the majority of First Nation schools is virtually identical to that found in the provincial and territorial schools.[59] This approach is not significantly different from the approach during the residential school era, when Indigenous communities had no say in the content and language of their children's schooling.

The funding formula for First Nations schools was last updated in 1996, and does not take into account the range of basic and contemporary education components needed to deliver a good-quality education in the twenty-first century, such as information and communication technologies, sports and recreation, language proficiency, and library services.[60] Worse still, since 1996, funding growth for First Nations education has been capped at 2%, an amount that has been insufficient to keep pace with either inflation or the rapid increases in the Aboriginal student population.[61] Meanwhile, between 1996 and 2006, funding to provincial and territorial school systems increased annually by 3.8%, almost double the increase for reserve schools.[62] The underfunding of reserve schools likely violates Treaty promises about education, and makes it very difficult to overcome the educational and consequent income gaps.

In many cases, the fees that First Nations are charged when they send their children to provincial schools are higher than the amount of funding they receive from Canada per student.[63]

Calls to Action

8) We call upon the federal government to eliminate the discrepancy in federal education funding for First Nations children being educated on reserves and those First Nations children being educated off reserves.
9) We call upon the federal government to prepare and publish annual reports comparing funding for the education of First Nations children on and off reserves, as well as educational and income attainments of Aboriginal peoples in Canada compared with non-Aboriginal people.

Education reform

Since 2011, three major reports on First Nations education have concluded that the status quo is unacceptable and that there is a need for a complete restructuring based on principles of self-government, a culturally relevant curriculum, and stable funding. All three reports agree that Aboriginal peoples themselves must lead and control the process of change.[64]

In October 2013, the government released the text of the proposed First Nations Education Act. The bill itself provided no guarantee of increased or stable funding of First Nations schools, leaving such matters to be resolved through regulations, with no assurance of equity in the distribution of resources to educate First Nations children in First Nations schools or in provincial schools. In February 2014, the Government of Canada and the Assembly of First Nations announced an agreement on a new basis for First Nations education reform and legislation. The agreement called for over $2 billion in new funding to reserve schools, and replaced the 2% cap on annual increases with a 4.5% annual increase and $1.25 billion from 2016–17 to 2018–19. However, after opposition from Aboriginal leaders, the proposed legislation was put on hold, pending agreement on the principles for a new Act.

Based on all that it has heard from thousands of former students and family members throughout the country, the Commission is convinced that such an Act must recognize the importance of education in strengthening the cultural identity of Aboriginal people and providing a better basis for success. Albert Marshall, a former student of the Shubenacadie residential school in Nova Scotia, made this point forcefully to the Commission.

> The current education system has been designed to completely eradicate who I am and to kill that Indian Mi'kmaq spirit that's in me. But I do know I need knowledge and I need education. But the kind of education I need has to be reflective of who I am as a Mi'kmaq. And that knowledge that I get, that I will receive, I have a responsibility with that knowledge to pass it down so others will benefit from it.... The kind of legacy that I want to leave my children in the future generations is one of which they will be able to excel, they will be able to compete without having to worry about is the education system going to further eradicate their selves.[65]

Call to Action

10) We call upon the federal government to draft new Aboriginal education legislation with the full participation and informed consent of Aboriginal peoples. The new legislation would include a commitment to sufficient funding and would incorporate the following principles:

    i. Providing sufficient funding to close identified educational achievement gaps within one generation.

    ii. Improving education attainment levels and success rates.

    iii. Developing culturally appropriate curricula.

    iv. Protecting the right to Aboriginal languages, including the teaching of Aboriginal languages as credit courses.

v. Enabling parental and community responsibility, control, and accountability, similar to what parents enjoy in public school systems.

vi. Enabling parents to fully participate in the education of their children.

vii. Respecting and honouring Treaty relationships.

Métis and Inuit education

Provincial and territorial schools are the only option for Métis students, other Aboriginal children without recognized status, and those First Nation and Inuit children who do not live on reserves or who do live on reserves but attend provincial schools. Their educational outcomes are not significantly better than those who attend First Nation schools on reserves or in their home communities.[66] Jurisdictional disputes between the federal and provincial governments over responsibility for Métis education continue to be a major obstacle to ensuring that Métis people have control over the education of their young people. The Métis remain without recognized jurisdiction and authority even though they have equal protection under Section 35 of the Constitution.[67] The result is that Métis children generally are educated in public or Catholic school systems in which school boards are not specifically held accountable for the education needs of Métis children.[68] The Commission believes all levels of government should consult with Métis parents, communities, and national organizations to provide Métis-specific educational programming.

Inuit students face one of the largest gaps in terms of educational attainment. A disproportionately high number of northern parents are residential school Survivors or intergenerational Survivors. Inuit are among Canada's youngest citizens, with a median age of twenty-two. In response to the intense needs of its young population, Inuit peoples have been leading the way to dramatic change. Inuit education is on the cusp of significant transformation, with some of the most promising models for self-governing education coming out of northern communities. But these changes have not been without obstacles. Some regions have a greater capacity to develop the necessary resources than others. A shortage of bilingual educators is one of the greatest barriers to expanding bilingual education in Inuit schools. There is also a lack of teaching and reading materials in Inuit languages.[69]

Another major problem is the lack of supports both within and outside the education system that are necessary to ensure student success. Inuit educators have long recognized that it is important to begin working with children as early as possible, but the North lacks good-quality daycare and preschool spaces.[70]

Post-secondary education

To help close the income and employment gap, Aboriginal people need increased access to post-secondary education. Only 8.7% of First Nations people, 5.1% of Inuit, and 11.7% of Métis have a university degree, according to the 2011 census.[71] The federal auditor general has commented: "In 2004, we noted that at existing rates, it would take 28 years for First Nations communities to reach the national average. More recent trends suggest that the time needed may be still longer."[72] The barriers to post-secondary education have had profound effects. Geraldine Bob attended residential school at Kamloops, British Columbia. She told the Commission at a Community Hearing in Fort Simpson, Northwest Territories, that poor education and negative experiences at residential school delayed her attendance at university and her entry into the workforce as a teacher. She suggested that

> the residential school system owes me those lost years. You know, I lost my retirement; I have to keep working, I don't have a good retirement fund because it was so late when I went to school. And I've proven that I can go to university and be successful as a teacher. So ... that little tiny bit of Common Experience Payment doesn't compensate for all that loss.[73]

Almost no one with some university or college education who spoke to the Commission had been able to obtain that education directly after high school. Most, like Geraldine Bob, had lost years to the time it took them to heal enough to even consider the possibility of upgrading their schooling.

If access to post-secondary education is to be improved, increasing the rates of secondary school completion is an important step. But even for those who qualify for a university program, there are significant obstacles. Federal funding for post-secondary education suffers from the same 2% funding cap that has been imposed on elementary and secondary schools since 1996. The First Nations Education Council estimates that there is a backlog of over 10,000 First Nations students waiting for post-secondary funding, with an additional $234 million required to erase that backlog and meet current demands.[74] The financial barriers and other difficulties that Aboriginal people face in attending post-secondary institutions deprive the Canadian workforce of the social workers, teachers, health-care workers, tradespeople, legal professionals, and others who can help address the legacy of residential schools.

Call to Action

11) We call upon the federal government to provide adequate funding to end the backlog of First Nations students seeking a post-secondary education.

Early childhood education programs

Aboriginal families continue to suffer from a general lack of early childhood education programs. The Assembly of First Nations reported that, according to 2011 data, 78% of children up to the age of five have no access to licensed daycare, let alone to intensive early childhood programs.[75] Such programs are vital to support the development of young children and, by extension, address some of the deficit in parenting skills that is the legacy of residential schools.

Call to Action

12) We call upon the federal, provincial, territorial, and Aboriginal governments to develop culturally appropriate early childhood education programs for Aboriginal families.

To close the education and income gaps, there needs to be stable and adequate funding of Aboriginal education that takes into account the challenges of the legacy of residential schools as well as other challenges faced by Aboriginal people. In addition to fair and adequate funding, there is also a need to maximize Aboriginal control over Aboriginal education, and to facilitate instruction in Aboriginal cultures and languages. These educational measures will offer a realistic prospect of reconciliation on the basis of equality and respect.

Language and culture

In a study of the impact of residential schools, the Assembly of First Nations noted in 1994 that

> language is necessary to define and maintain a world view. For this reason, some First Nation elders to this day will say that knowing or learning the native language is basic to any deep understanding of a First Nation way of life, to being a First Nation person. For them, a First Nation world is quite simply not possible without its own language. For them, the impact of residential school silencing their language is equivalent to a residential school silencing their world.[76]

The Royal Commission on Aboriginal Peoples similarly noted the connection between Aboriginal languages and what it called a "distinctive world view, rooted in the stories of ancestors and the environment." The Royal Commission added that Aboriginal languages are a "tangible emblem of group identity" that can provide "the individual a sense of security and continuity with the past ... maintenance of the language and group identity has both a social-emotional and a spiritual purpose."[77]

Residential schools were a systematic, government-sponsored attempt to destroy Aboriginal cultures and languages and to assimilate Aboriginal peoples so that they no longer existed as distinct peoples. English and, to a far lesser degree, French were the only languages permitted to be used in most schools. Students were punished—often severely—for speaking their own languages. Michael Sillett, a former student at the North West River residential school in Newfoundland and Labrador, told the Commission, "Children at the dorm were not allowed to speak their mother tongue. I remember several times when other children were slapped or had their mouths washed out for speaking their mother tongue; whether it was Inuktitut or Innu-aimun. Residents were admonished for just being Native."[78] As late as the 1970s, students at schools in northwestern Ontario were not allowed to speak their language if they were in the presence of a staff member who could not understand that language.[79] Conrad Burns, whose father attended the Prince Albert school, named this policy for what it was: "It was a cultural genocide. People were beaten for their language, people were beaten because ... they followed their own ways."[80]

Rights to culture and language, and the need for remedies for their loss, have long been recognized in international law.[81] They are specifically acknowledged in the *United Nations Declaration of the Rights of Indigenous Peoples,* which has recognized the critical state of Aboriginal languages. Article 8:1 of the *Declaration* recognizes that "Indigenous peoples and individuals have the right not to be subjected to forced assimilation or destruction of their culture." Article 8:2 provides that "states shall provide effective mechanisms for prevention of and redress for any form of forced assimilation or integration."

The *Declaration* also includes specific recognition of the right to revitalize and transmit Aboriginal languages in Article 13:1, which recognizes that "Indigenous peoples have the right to revitalize, use, develop and transmit to future generations their histories, languages, oral traditions, philosophies, writing systems and literatures, and to designate and retain their own names for communities, places and persons." Article 14 provides for educational language rights of the type that Canadians already know and experience, with respect to anglophone and francophone minorities. Article 14:1 provides similarly that "Indigenous peoples have the right to establish and control their educational systems and institutions providing education in their own languages, in a manner appropriate to their cultural methods of teaching and learning," and Article 14:3 provides: "States shall, in conjunction with indigenous peoples, take effective measures, in order for indigenous individuals, particularly children, including those living outside their communities, to have access, when possible, to an education in their own culture and provided in their own language." Article 16 provides that Indigenous peoples "have the right to establish their own media in their own languages and to have access to all forms of non-indigenous media without discrimination," and that states "shall take effective measures to ensure that State-owned media duly reflect indigenous cultural diversity."[82]

The attempt to assimilate students by denying them access to, and respect for, their Aboriginal language and culture often meant that the students became estranged from their families and communities. Agnes Mills, a former student at All Saints residential school in Saskatchewan, told the Commission her story.

> And one of the things that residential school did for me, I really regret, is that it made me ashamed of who I was.... And I wanted to be white so bad, and the worst thing I ever did was I was ashamed of my mother, that honourable woman, because she couldn't speak English. She never went to school, and they told us that, we used to go home to her on Saturdays, and they told us that we couldn't talk Gwich'in to her and, and she couldn't, like couldn't communicate. And my sister was the one that had the nerve to tell her, "We can't talk Loucheux to you, they told us not to."[83]

Mary Courchene, formerly a student at the residential schools at Fort Alexander in Manitoba and Lebret in Saskatchewan, had a similar interaction with her family.

> And I looked at my dad, I looked at my mom, I looked at my dad again. You know what? I hated them. I just absolutely hated my own parents. Not because I thought they abandoned me; I hated their brown faces. I hated them because they were Indians.... So I, I looked at my dad and I challenged him and I said, "From now on we speak only English in this house," I said to my dad. And you know when we, when, in a traditional home where I was raised, the first thing that we all were always taught was to respect your Elders and never to, you know, to challenge them. And here I was, eleven years old, and I challenged ... my dad looked at me and I, and I thought he was going to cry. In fact his eyes filled up with tears. He turned to my mom and he says, ... "Then I guess we'll never speak to this little girl again. I don't know her."[84]

Some Survivors refused to teach their own children their Aboriginal languages and cultures because of the negative stigma that had come to be associated with them during their school years. This has contributed significantly to the fragile state of Aboriginal languages in Canada today.

Many of the almost ninety surviving Aboriginal languages in Canada are under serious threat of extinction. In the 2011 census, 14.5% of the Aboriginal population reported that their first language learned was an Aboriginal language.[85] In the previous 2006 census, 18% of those who identified as Aboriginal had reported an Aboriginal language as their first language learned, and a decade earlier, in the 1996 census, the figure was 26%. This indicates nearly a 50% drop in the fifteen years since the last residential schools closed. There are, however, variations among Aboriginal peoples: 63.7% of Inuit speak their Indigenous language, compared with 22.4% of First Nations people and only 2.5% of Métis people.[86]

Some languages are close to extinction because they have only a few remaining speakers of the great-grandparent generation. The United Nations Educational, Scientific and Cultural Organization (UNESCO) lists 36% of Canada's Aboriginal languages as being critically endangered, in the sense that they are used only by great-grandparent generations; 18% are severely endangered, in the sense that they are used by the great-grandparent and grandparent generations; and 16% are definitely endangered, in the sense that they are used by the parental and the two previous generations. The remaining languages are all vulnerable.[87] If the preservation of Aboriginal languages does not become a priority both for governments and for Aboriginal communities, then what the residential schools failed to accomplish will come about through a process of systematic neglect.

Language rights

In interpreting Aboriginal and Treaty rights under Section 35(1) of the *Constitution Act, 1982*, the Supreme Court of Canada has stressed the relation of those rights to the preservation of distinct Aboriginal cultures.[88] The Commission concurs. The preservation of Aboriginal languages is essential and must be recognized as a right.

Call to Action

13) We call upon the federal government to acknowledge that Aboriginal rights include Aboriginal language rights.

Government programs

At a time when government funding is most needed to protect Aboriginal languages and culture, Canada has not upheld commitments it previously made to fund such programs. In 2002, the federal government promised $160 million for the creation of a centre for Aboriginal languages and culture and a national language strategy.[89] But, in 2006, the government retreated from that commitment, pledging instead to spend $5 million per year in "permanent funding" for the Aboriginal Languages Initiative (ALI), which had been started in 1998.[90] The ALI is a program of government-administered heritage subsidies. It is not based on the notion of respectful nation-to-nation relations between Canada and Aboriginal peoples. Neither does it provide Aboriginal people with the opportunity to make decisions for themselves about how to allocate scarce resources and how to administer programs. Many who appeared before the Truth and Reconciliation Commission of Canada were skeptical about the government's commitment to preserve Aboriginal languages. As Michael Sillett told us, "I cannot see the federal government putting out the money that's necessary for full restitution, you know.... I can't bring back my language; I lost that. I lost my culture, you know."[91]

Other than ALI, the only significant programs for language preservation are the Canada-Territorial Language Accords ($4.1 million annual budget), which support territorial government-directed Aboriginal language services, supports, and community projects in Nunavut and the Northwest Territories. In Yukon, language revitalization and preservation projects are supported through transfer agreements with ten of the eleven self-governing Yukon First Nations.[92]

The combined total annual federal budget for these Aboriginal languages programs is $9.1 million. By way of comparison, the Official Languages Program for English and French is projected to receive funding as follows:

- 2012–13: $353.3 million
- 2013–14: $348.2 million
- 2014–15: $348.2 million[93]

The resources committed to Aboriginal language programs are far fewer than what is committed to French in areas where French speakers are in the minority. For example, the federal government provides support to the small minority of francophones in Nunavut in the amount of approximately $4,000 per individual annually. In contrast, funding to support Inuit-language initiatives is estimated at $44 per Inuk per year.[94]

The Commission believes that a multi-pronged approach to Aboriginal language preservation—if implemented, honourably resourced, and sustained— might prevent further increase in the litigation of Aboriginal language rights, and the increased international criticism of Canada's policy towards Aboriginal-language rights. This approach will require full, good-faith consultation, which recognizes that although Aboriginal communities have the necessary knowledge, particularly among their Elders, to preserve their own languages, additional support is needed. The outcome of the consultation should be legislation and policies that affirm the importance of Canada's Indigenous languages, and allocate adequate funding to ensure their preservation.

Calls to Action

14) We call upon the federal government to enact an Aboriginal Languages Act that incorporates the following principles:

    i. Aboriginal languages are a fundamental and valued element of Canadian culture and society, and there is an urgency to preserve them.

    ii. Aboriginal language rights are reinforced by the Treaties.

iii. The federal government has a responsibility to provide sufficient funds for Aboriginal-language revitalization and preservation.

iv. The preservation, revitalization, and strengthening of Aboriginal languages and cultures are best managed by Aboriginal people and communities.

v. Funding for Aboriginal language initiatives must reflect the diversity of Aboriginal languages.

15) We call upon the federal government to appoint, in consultation with Aboriginal groups, an Aboriginal Languages Commissioner. The commissioner should help promote Aboriginal languages and report on the adequacy of federal funding of Aboriginal-languages initiatives.

In addition to promoting the use of Aboriginal languages, an Aboriginal Languages Commissioner would also educate non-Aboriginal Canadians about the richness and value of Aboriginal languages and how strengthening those languages can enhance Canada's international reputation.

Aboriginal people recognize how important it is for their children to speak and understand an Aboriginal language. Sabrina Williams, an intergenerational Survivor from British Columbia, expressed that need.

> I didn't realize until taking this language class how much we have lost—all the things that are attached to language: it's family connections, it's oral history, it's traditions, it's ways of being, it's ways of knowing, it's medicine, it's song, it's dance, it's memory. It's everything, including the land.... And unless we inspire our kids to love our culture, to love our language ... our languages are continually going to be eroded over time. So, that is daunting. Yeah. So, to me that's part of what reconciliation looks like.[95]

Language instruction may require innovative approaches, including the use of Elders and others as teachers and the use of immersion programs. Education institutions must be flexible and responsive in their attempts to encourage the teaching of Aboriginal languages. They should be prepared to draw on the available resources within Aboriginal communities to facilitate the teaching and transmission of Aboriginal languages. More formal training opportunities are also required.

Call to Action

16) We call upon post-secondary institutions to create university and college degree and diploma programs in Aboriginal languages.

Reclaiming names

As a result of the residential school experience, many Aboriginal people lost their language and lost touch with their culture. Many also suffered a loss of a different sort. It was common for residential school officials to give students new names. At the Aklavik Anglican school in the Northwest Territories, a young Inuit girl named Masak became "Alice"—she would not hear her old name until she returned home.[96] At the Qu'Appelle school in Saskatchewan, Ochankugahe (Path Maker) became Daniel Kennedy, named for the biblical Daniel, and Adélard Standing Buffalo was named for Adélard Langevin, the Archbishop of St. Boniface.[97] Survivors and their families who have sought to reclaim the names that were taken from them in residential schools have found the process to be both expensive and time consuming. We believe that measures should be put in place to reduce the burden placed on those who seek to reclaim this significant portion of their heritage.

Call to Action

17) We call upon all levels of government to enable residential school Survivors and their families to reclaim names changed by the residential school system by waiving administrative costs for a period of five years for the name-change process and the revision of official identity documents, such as birth certificates, passports, driver's licenses, health cards, status cards, and social insurance numbers.

Health

Residential schools endangered the health and well-being of the children who attended them. Many students succumbed to infectious disease, particularly tuberculosis. Sexual and physical abuse, as well as separation from families and communities, caused lasting trauma for many others. The effects of this trauma were often passed on to the children of the residential school Survivors and sometimes to their grandchildren. Residential schools also posed a threat to the mental health of students through the pervasive assumptions and assertions they made about the inferiority of Aboriginal peoples, cultures, and languages. This disregard for Aboriginal health and well-being was consistent with the long-established patterns of colonialism: the introduction of new diseases, the disruption of traditional food sources, and the concentration of people on unproductive land and the housing of them in cramped, unsanitary dwellings.

The schools undermined Aboriginal health by failing to feed and clothe the children properly and housing them in poorly constructed and dangerous buildings. The schools did not properly screen out sick and infectious children, and often lacked adequate treatment facilities. As Ruby Firth, a former student at Stringer Hall in the Northwest Territories, told the Commission, those conditions had a lasting effect.

> I've got chronic bronchitis today. Every winter I get pneumonia like two or three times and I'm on two puffers 'cause when I was in Stringer Hall residential school they used to put us in these little skinny red coats that weren't even warm enough for winter. And we used to have to walk across the street to go to school.... Both my lungs are 50% scarred from having pneumonia seven times in [residential school]. That's always going to be there, it's never going to go away.[98]

There were also lasting psychological and emotional impacts. Sonia Wuttunee-Byrd described the damage that residential school caused her.

> I lost my braids, my beautiful hair was cut, and I felt like my identity was so confused, I didn't know who I was. What is even worse is that they started to sexually take advantage of me and abuse me, not one, not two, but many, many people for a very long time, until I was sixteen. I started to really deteriorate. I became very sick and anorexic, and really started to go downhill. At one point I only weighed sixty-six pounds, and that was it, I had no desire to live. The doctor said, "You have a month to live, go home." He said to my family, "Take her home, she is going to die."... I would say to Mom and Dad, and they never understood why I was crying. The school always said, "Sonia is a fantastic student, she is doing so well," but inside it was torment. I held everything in and didn't tell anybody for twenty years.[99]

Katherine Copenace, a former student at the St. Mary's residential school in Ontario, told the Commission about her struggles.

> The residential school students suffered physical, sexual, spiritual, and most of all emotional abuse and my dad used to say to me, "Emotional abuse is more damaging than physical abuse. Your physical hurts heal." That's what he used to say. When I got older, I had thoughts of suicide, inflicting pain on myself which I did. I used to slash my arms, pierce my arms, my body and I destroyed myself with alcohol which the government introduced of course.[100]

The children in residential schools were powerless to take healing measures. They were denied access to traditional foods and to families, traditional healers, and communities who could have helped them, according to Aboriginal ways, to deal with the physical, mental, emotional, and spiritual elements of ill health. Because of the isolated location of many of the schools, students were also often denied access to 'Western' doctors and nurses. This double denial of health care, based in government policy, continues to this day, due to the relative isolation of many Aboriginal communities, many of which have no road access, and limited access to local health resources.

Health care is a right enshrined in international and constitutional law as well as in Treaties. The *United Nations Declaration on the Rights of Indigenous Peoples* recognizes that Indigenous peoples have the right to physical and mental integrity, as well as the right to equal enjoyment of the highest attainable standard of physical and mental health. In taking measures to achieve these goals, states are obligated to pay particular attention to the rights and special needs of Elders, women, youth, children, and persons with disabilities.[101] Indigenous peoples have the right to be actively involved in developing, determining, and administering health programs that affect them.[102] Indigenous peoples also have the right to traditional medicines and to maintain their traditional health practices.[103]

The Numbered Treaties also established additional legal obligations concerning Aboriginal health and wellness.[104] The right to medical care was recognized in Treaties 6, 7, 8, 10, and 11.[105] Treaty 6 explicitly included provision of a "medicine chest" and relief from "pestilence."[106] However, the right to health is not limited to these Treaties. The Treaty negotiations included many references to the protection of, and non-interference with, traditional ways of life.[107]

Call to Action

18) We call upon the federal, provincial, territorial, and Aboriginal governments to acknowledge that the current state of Aboriginal health in Canada is a direct result of previous Canadian government policies, including residential schools, and to recognize and implement the health-care rights of Aboriginal people as identified in international law and constitutional law, and under the Treaties.

The health gap

There are troubling gaps in health outcomes between Aboriginal and non-Aboriginal Canadians. For example:

- The infant mortality rates for First Nations and Inuit children range from 1.7 to over 4 times the non-Aboriginal rate.[108]
- From 2004 to 2008, the "age-specific mortality rate" at ages one to nineteen in the Inuit homelands was 188.0 deaths per 100,000 person-years at risk, compared with only 35.3 deaths per 100,000 in the rest of Canada.[109]
- First Nations people aged forty-five and older have nearly twice the rate of diabetes as the non-Aboriginal population.[110]

- First Nations people were six times more likely than the general population to suffer alcohol-related deaths, and more than three times more likely to suffer drug-induced deaths.[111]

The overall suicide rate among First Nation communities is about twice that of the total Canadian population. For Inuit, the rate is still higher: six to eleven times the rate for the general population. Aboriginal youth between the ages of ten and twenty-nine who are living on reserves are five to six times more likely to die by suicide than non-Aboriginal youth.[112]

Measuring progress

Obtaining precise information on the state of health of Aboriginal people in Canada is difficult. The most complete information about comparative health outcomes is out of date, much of it coming from the 1990s. Unlike in other countries, the Canadian government has not provided a comprehensive list of well-being indicators comparing Aboriginal and non-Aboriginal populations. The lack of accessible data on comparable health indicators means that these issues receive less public, media, and political attention. In Australia, the government has set a timeline for closing the gap in health outcomes between Aboriginal and non-Aboriginal citizens. The Australian prime minister reports annually on the progress being made to close the gaps in targets related to life expectancy and mortality rates for Indigenous children.[113] Canada must do likewise.

Call to Action

19) We call upon the federal government, in consultation with Aboriginal peoples, to establish measurable goals to identify and close the gaps in health outcomes between Aboriginal and non-Aboriginal communities, and to publish annual progress reports and assess long-term trends. Such efforts would focus on indicators such as: infant mortality, maternal health, suicide, mental health, addictions, life expectancy, birth rates, infant and child health issues, chronic diseases, illness and injury incidence, and the availability of appropriate health services.

In 2003, the First Ministers' Accord on Health Care Renewal recognized the obvious: that Aboriginal peoples face serious health challenges. The accord committed to making the reduction of the gap in health status between Aboriginal and non-Aboriginal peoples a national priority. More than a decade later, that gap remains. In fact, the federal government has moved backwards on issues of Aboriginal health since the signing of the Indian Residential Schools Settlement Agreement and Canada's apology to Survivors. It has terminated funding to a number of Aboriginal health organizations, including the Aboriginal Healing Foundation and the National Aboriginal Health Organization. These organizations were committed to models of research and treatment in which Aboriginal communities have ownership, control, access, and possession. Their loss significantly limits the development of accurate information about health issues and solutions under Aboriginal control. Health Canada has also cut funding for a number of Aboriginal primary health programs, including programs that address diabetes, fetal alcohol spectrum disorder, youth suicide, infectious diseases, and maternal and child health.[114] These cuts have had a serious impact on Aboriginal communities.

Trudy King, a former student at Grandin College residential school, is from Fort Resolution in the Northwest Territories.

> When I lost my son here in 2003, I needed counselling for me and my children. I couldn't get help here anywhere. There was the health and social services coordinator here that I begged and begged to help us, and she said, "There's no monies. We don't have monies to get counselling for you and your kids." I couldn't go anywhere. Nobody would help us, and, and I didn't, and it was in 2003. There has to be help out there for people that want, are crying for help. I couldn't get it. My kids couldn't get it.[115]

A former student at Guy Hill residential school in Manitoba, M. R. E. Linklater, also emphasized the need for more community-based services when she spoke with the Commission.

> More programs should be put on for our children and our grandchildren and our great-grandchildren 'cause they need to understand why their parents are the way they are. Why so many of our people are so into alcohol and drug addiction, and for myself, I know why, it's to survive or not to go back there. Our children need more education, support, more programs, not to cut the programs that they have in place.[116]

Health reforms often involve Aboriginal people in complex jurisdictional disputes and tripartite negotiations with both the federal and provincial or territorial governments. Such jurisdictional disputes have particularly affected Métis, non-status, and urban Aboriginal people, as the federal government insists that providing services to these groups is a provincial and territorial responsibility.

Call to Action

20) In order to address the jurisdictional disputes concerning Aboriginal people who do not reside on reserves, we call upon the federal government to recognize, respect, and address the distinct health needs of the Métis, Inuit, and off-reserve Aboriginal peoples.

Aboriginal healing practices

Aboriginal health practices and beliefs, like Aboriginal peoples themselves, are diverse. However, an holistic approach to health is common to many Aboriginal cultures and has also been increasingly validated by 'Western' medicine. A belief shared among many Inuit, Métis, and First Nation people is that a sacred connection exists among people, the Earth, and everything above it, upon it, and within it. For purposes of healing, this means activities such as "on-the-land" or "bush" healing camps where participants can experience the healing power of the natural world. Traditional practices can also include sweat lodges, cedar baths, smudging, the lighting of the Qulliq (a stone lamp used by the Inuit for ceremonial purposes), and other spiritual ceremonies.[117] Best practices for Aboriginal wellness involve a range of services from mainstream health care to traditional practices and medicines, all under community leadership and control. Such an integrated approach has the power to improve the lives of all community members.

Calls to Action

21) We call upon the federal government to provide sustainable funding for existing and new Aboriginal healing centres to address the physical, mental, emotional, and spiritual harms caused by residential schools, and to ensure that the funding of healing centres in Nunavut and the Northwest Territories is a priority.

22) We call upon those who can effect change within the Canadian health-care system to recognize the value of Aboriginal healing practices and use them in the treatment of Aboriginal patients in collaboration with Aboriginal healers and Elders where requested by Aboriginal patients.

Overcoming the health legacy of the residential schools will require a long-term investment in Aboriginal communities, so that communities can revive their capacity to heal themselves. One key investment will be the training of more Aboriginal health and social service professionals. The work that Health Canada's community cultural and traditional knowledge healing team members did in support of this Commission and other Settlement Agreement processes is but one example of the invaluable service these professionals can provide.

Call to Action

23) We call upon all levels of government to:

i. Increase the number of Aboriginal professionals working in the health-care field.

ii. Ensure the retention of Aboriginal health-care providers in Aboriginal communities.

iii. Provide cultural competency training for all health-care professionals.

Closing the gap in health outcomes will come about only as part of a comprehensive strategy of change. To be more effective in improving health outcomes, non-Aboriginal medical practitioners must develop a better understanding of the health issues facing Canada's Aboriginal peoples and of the legacy of residential schools.

Call to Action

24) We call upon medical and nursing schools in Canada to require all students to take a course dealing with Aboriginal health issues, including the history and legacy of residential schools, the *United Nations Declaration on the Rights of Indigenous Peoples,* Treaties and Aboriginal rights, and Indigenous teachings and practices. This will require skills-based training in intercultural competency, conflict resolution, human rights, and anti-racism.

Justice

Residential schools inflicted profound injustices on Aboriginal people. Aboriginal parents were forced, often under pressure from the police, to give up their children to the schools. Children were taken far from their communities to live in frightening custodial institutions, which felt like prisons. The children who attended residential schools were often treated as if they were offenders and were often victimized.

This pattern of disproportionate imprisonment and victimization of Aboriginal people continues to this day. The continued failure of the justice system denies Aboriginal people the safety and opportunities that most Canadians take for granted. Redress to the racist and colonial views that inspired the schools, and effective and long-term solutions to the crime problems that plague too many Aboriginal communities, call for increased use of Aboriginal justice, based on Aboriginal laws and healing practices.

To understand the full legacy of the harms of the schools, it is important to examine how the Canadian legal system responded to residential school abuse. Relatively few prosecutions for abuse resulted from police investigations. In some cases, the federal government actually compromised these investigations—and the independence of the Royal Canadian Mounted Police (RCMP)—to defend its own position in civil cases brought against it by residential school Survivors.

RCMP independence compromised

In late 1994, the RCMP established the E Division Task Force to investigate allegations of abuse in British Columbia residential schools. There is evidence, however, that RCMP investigations into abuse were adversely influenced by the federal government's strategic interests in defending itself in the many civil lawsuits commenced by former students. For example, the government demanded that the RCMP hand over its investigation files related to abuse at the Kuper Island school. Despite some initial objections, the RCMP eventually did turn over the files.[118] This was done without due regard for the privacy rights of the complainants in the case, and, in effect, gave the government an advantage in defending itself. When the police force requested the return of these files, the government declined, and then further refused to disclose the information it had received to the Survivors who had brought the civil lawsuits.[119]

Affidavits filed by RCMP officers suggest that the federal government's interest in defending itself in civil litigation interfered with police investigations into crimes committed at the residential schools. Although a judge eventually ordered that Survivors should have the same access to RCMP criminal investigation material regarding offences at the Kuper Island school as the government, the whole affair meant Survivors could reasonably conclude that the RCMP was acting as an agent of the federal government, rather than as an impartial enforcer of the law.[120]

Call to Action

25) We call upon the federal government to establish a written policy that reaffirms the independence of the Royal Canadian Mounted Police to investigate crimes in which the government has its own interest as a potential or real party in civil litigation.

Unnecessary insistence on corroboration

The RCMP E Division Task Force final report notes that "a very common situation that kept occurring over and over again" was that Crown counsel refused to prosecute without corroboration in the form of physical evidence.[121] This approach was based on an unwillingness to take the complainant's own evidence as sufficient to justify a prosecution. It betrays an unwillingness to take the evidence of Aboriginal people as being worthy of belief. At best, the refusal to prosecute without corroboration was based on a belief that the denial of any accused person who occupied a position of authority at the schools would be sufficient to create a reasonable doubt about guilt.

Since 1982, the requirement for corroboration was specifically dropped for sexual offences, and it was never required for non-sexual offences.[122] The Commission is concerned that a continued insistence on corroboration has resulted in discriminatory treatment of Aboriginal victims.

Few criminal prosecutions

The Commission has been able to identify fewer than fifty convictions stemming from allegations of abuse at residential schools. This figure is insignificant compared with the nearly 38,000 claims of sexual and serious physical abuse that were submitted as part of the Independent Assessment Process (IAP), set up under the Settlement Agreement.[123]

Although there were not many prosecutions for sexual abuse, there were even fewer charges of physical abuse brought against former school staff. The RCMP's own report suggests that the E Division Task Force viewed physical assaults against Aboriginal children as being less serious than sexual abuse. The RCMP attributed complaints by former students about assaults as evidence of a "culture clash between the rigid, 'spare the rod, spoil the child' Christian attitude, and the more permissive Native tradition of child-rearing."[124] This preconception undoubtedly affected the number of prosecutions that occurred for physical abuse at the schools.

Civil litigation

Having generally failed to find justice through police investigations and criminal prosecutions, residential school Survivors increasingly turned to the civil justice system in the 1990s, bringing lawsuits against abusers as well as the federal government and the churches that operated the schools. The Canadian legal system, however, was prepared to consider only some of the harms that the Survivors suffered—generally, those harms caused by sexual and sometimes physical abuse. It refused to consider on the merits the Survivors' claims relating to loss of language, culture, family attachment, and violation of Treaty rights to education. The Canadian legal system refused to consider the claims that Survivors brought on behalf of their parents and their children. It also refused to provide remedies for the collective harms that residential schools caused to Aboriginal nations and communities.

Residential school litigation has been extremely complex, expensive, and lengthy. It has been especially difficult for the Survivors, many of whom were revictimized through explicit questioning and adversarial treatment by the Government of Canada, the churches, and even their own lawyers.

Limitation periods

Within the Canadian justice system, complainants in civil proceedings have a limited period of time in which to file suit. If they wait too long after the harm they have suffered, they may not be allowed to pursue their claim because of a provincial statute of limitation. Although statutes of limitation can protect defendants in civil lawsuits, they can also have the effect of denying plaintiffs the opportunity to have the truth of their allegation determined in court. This is most dramatically true for child victims, who have neither the means nor the knowledge to pursue claims of harm until much later, when the time period for a claim may very well have run out.

A statute of limitation defence has to be raised by the defendant. In its 2000 report on responding to child abuse in institutions, the Law Commission of Canada recommended that the federal government should not rely solely on statute of limitation defences.[125] Nevertheless, the Government of Canada and the churches have frequently and successfully raised these defences in residential school litigation. The Commission believes that the federal government's successful use of statute of limitation defences has meant that Canadian courts and Canadians in general have considered only a small part of the harms of residential schools, mostly those caused by sexual abuse. Some provinces have amended their limitation statutes to enable civil prosecutions for a wider range of offences. We urge others to follow suit.

Call to Action

26) We call upon the federal, provincial, and territorial governments to review and amend their respective statutes of limitations to ensure that they conform with the principle that governments and other entities cannot rely on limitation defences to defend legal actions of historical abuse brought by Aboriginal people.

Educating lawyers

The criminal prosecution of abusers in residential schools and the subsequent civil lawsuits were a difficult experience for Survivors. The courtroom experience was made worse by the fact that many lawyers did not have adequate cultural, historical, or psychological knowledge to deal with the painful memories that the Survivors were forced to reveal. The lack of sensitivity that lawyers often demonstrated in dealing with residential school Survivors resulted, in some cases, in the Survivors' not receiving appropriate legal service. These experiences prove the need for lawyers to develop a greater understanding of Aboriginal history and culture as well as the multi-faceted legacy of residential schools.

Calls to Action

27) We call upon the Federation of Law Societies of Canada to ensure that lawyers receive appropriate cultural competency training, which includes the history and legacy of residential schools, the *United Nations Declaration on the Rights of Indigenous Peoples*, Treaties and Aboriginal rights, Indigenous law, and Aboriginal–Crown relations. This will require skills-based training in intercultural competency, conflict resolution, human rights, and anti-racism.

28) We call upon law schools in Canada to require all law students to take a course in Aboriginal people and the law, which includes the history and legacy of residential schools, the *United Nations Declaration on the Rights of Indigenous Peoples*, Treaties and Aboriginal rights, Indigenous law, and Aboriginal–Crown relations. This will require skills-based training in intercultural competency, conflict resolution, human rights, and anti-racism.

Aftermath of the Settlement Agreement

During the 1990s, the number of civil lawsuits against Canada and the churches that ran the schools steadily increased. Many of these claims were combined into class actions that were certified by provincial courts. In May 2005, the Government of Canada appointed former Supreme Court Justice Frank Iacobucci as its chief negotiator to help reach a settlement agreement among the many parties involved in litigation: representatives from Aboriginal communities, church groups, the federal government, and Survivors represented by various law firms. The parties reached an agreement in principle in November 2005. The details of the Indian Residential Schools Settlement Agreement were finalized and approved by the federal cabinet on May 10, 2006. The thousands of legal claims made against the federal government and the churches were concluded and settled under the terms of the Settlement Agreement.[126]

Because the Settlement Agreement would involve the termination of a number of class-action proceedings that the courts had already authorized, it was necessary for courts in most provinces and territories to consider whether the Settlement Agreement was a fair resolution of the claims and, in particular, whether it adequately protected the interests of all the class members.

The Settlement Agreement included a Common Experience Payment (CEP) for everyone who attended one of the residential schools listed in the Agreement. In addition to the CEP, an Independent Assessment Process (IAP) was established to pay compensation to those who suffered sexual or serious physical assaults, such as severe beating, whipping, and second-degree burning, at the schools. The process also included compensation for assaults by other students if they were the result of a lack of reasonable supervision.

The IAP was designed to be an easier process for complainants than litigation. Hearings are held in private with cultural supports for the claimants and health supports provided by Health Canada. In contrast to the protracted nature of much civil litigation, hearings are supposed to be held within nine months, with decisions due shortly after the hearings.

In their statements to the Commission, some Survivors have expressed concerns about the IAP abuse hearing process because it did not allow them to face their abusers directly. Bernard Catcheway, a former student at Pine Creek residential school in Manitoba, told the Commission,

> You know and [my abuser's] still alive. I think she's eighty-nine years old according to when I went to my hearing three years ago. I wanted her so badly to come to that hearing, you know, but because of her age and because of her, I guess, incompetency, you know, she chose not to be there. I would have loved for her to, to meet her at that time, to basically say I, you know, to say whatever it was that made her do things to us, I was going to say, "I forgive you." But I never got a chance to say that.[127]

Other claimants, such as Amelia Galligos-Thomas, a former student at Sechelt residential school in British Columbia, criticized the IAP's delay in hearing and settling claims.

> I've been waiting five years now for my appeal, and it hasn't happened yet. And it's almost time for them to stop giving the money out to us. And they opened up all our wounds, for what? To turn us all down? And some people are dying.... My sister's doing drugs, like, 'cause she's tired of waiting. She's living on the streets. So, so, why did they do this to us, again? They hurt us again. They shouldn't go back on their word to us. They already hurt us. Stop hurting us.[128]

Exclusions from the Settlement

Not all Survivors of residential school abuse were included in the Settlement Agreement. For example, day school students, many Métis students, and pupils from schools in Newfoundland and Labrador have been excluded, as have students who attended government-funded schools that were not identified as residential schools. These exclusions have led to new civil lawsuits against the government. The Commission urges all parties to seek expedited means of resolving this litigation.

Call to Action

29) We call upon the parties and, in particular, the federal government, to work collaboratively with plaintiffs not included in the Indian Residential Schools Settlement Agreement to have disputed legal issues determined expeditiously on an agreed set of facts.

Overrepresentation of Aboriginal people in prison

The dramatic overrepresentation of Aboriginal people in Canada's prison system continues to expand. In 1995–96, Aboriginal people made up 16% of all those sentenced to custody. By 2011–12, that number had grown to 28% of all admissions to sentenced custody, even though Aboriginal people make up only 4% of the Canadian adult population.[129] The situation of women is even more disproportionate: in 2011–12, 43% of admissions of women to sentenced custody were Aboriginal.[130]

The causes of the over-incarceration of Aboriginal people are complex. The convictions of Aboriginal offenders frequently result from an interplay of factors, including the intergenerational legacy of residential schools. Aboriginal overrepresentation in prison reflects a systemic bias in the Canadian justice system. Once Aboriginal persons are arrested, prosecuted, and convicted, they are more likely to be sentenced to prison than non-Aboriginal people. In 2011–12, Aboriginal people made up 21% of those who received probation or conditional sentences (under which a defendant is found guilty but allowed to remain in the community).[131]

Parliament has recently passed legislation to prescribe mandatory minimum sentences of imprisonment for certain offences. Judges are required to impose these mandatory minimums. Additional restrictions have also been placed on community sanctions. These decisions have further contributed to the over-incarceration of Aboriginal people in prison. It is assumed that locking up offenders makes communities safer, but there is no evidence to demonstrate that this is indeed the case. There are concerns that Aboriginal people are not receiving culturally appropriate rehabilitative programs in federal prisons, and they are even less likely to have access to such programs in provincial correctional institutions for those people serving sentences of less than two years.

Violence and criminal offending are not inherent in Aboriginal people. They result from very specific experiences that Aboriginal people have endured, including the intergenerational legacy of residential schools. It should not be surprising that those who experienced and witnessed very serious violence against Aboriginal children in the schools frequently became accustomed to violence in later life. One intergenerational Survivor recalled that her mother

> never talked about it very much or never expressed it. And she was very quiet, and she had issues with alcohol, and I saw that, and that was basically the only time that she was really aggressive I guess is during those times when she drank.... And my father was also very aggressive. It was a very violent home actually. My brothers used to fight each other, and my brothers would fight my dad, and my mom and my dad would fight, and a lot of violence in the home, actually to the point where my brother, my oldest brother, killed my, one of our other brothers in the home ... when I was nine, and I saw the whole thing.[132]

The Commission heard numerous accounts of the hardships experienced by former residential school students who became involved with the justice system. For many, there were painful parallels between their time in school and their time in jail. For Daniel Andre, the road from Grollier Hall in Inuvik in the Northwest Territories led, inevitably, to jail.

> I knew that I needed help to get rid of what happened to me in residential school. Like, everywhere I went, everything I did, all the jobs I had, all the towns I lived in, all the people I met, always brought me back to, to being in residential school, and being humiliated, and beaten, and ridiculed, and told I was a piece of garbage, I was not good enough, I was, like, a dog.... So, one of the scariest things for me being in jail is being humiliated in front of everybody, being made, laughed at, and which they do often 'cause they're just, like, that's just the way they are. And a lot of them are, like, survival of the fittest. And, like, if you show weakness, they'll, they'll just pick on you even more and ... I had to, to survive. I had to be strong enough to survive. I had to, I had to build up a system where I became a jerk. I became a bad person. I became an asshole. But I survived, and learnt all those things to survive.[133]

It should not be surprising that those who were sexually abused in the schools as children sometimes perpetuated sexual violence later in their lives. It should not be surprising that those who were taken from their parents and exposed to harsh and regimented discipline in the schools and disparagement of their culture and families often became poor and sometimes violent parents later in their lives. It should not be surprising that those who were exposed to poor education and to spiritual and cultural abuse in the schools later turned to alcohol and drugs as a means to cope and try to forget. The consequences for many students and their families were tragic.

Grace Campbell is an intergenerational Survivor.

> When I was drinking a lot of things happened to me ... I had to do things and a lot of times I just about got killed and then, I thought it was easy. Easy drinking, easy to get the way I was living and I didn't like it. I was selling my body and I didn't like it. At the time I didn't know it but when I look back, some of those creeps I hung with, men and guns and everything, like you know. I was losing my drinking buddies though; they were being murdered and dying.[134]

Action is required now to overcome the legacy of residential schools that has played a major role in the over-incarceration of Aboriginal people.

Call to Action

30) We call upon federal, provincial, and territorial governments to commit to eliminating the overrepresentation of Aboriginal people in custody over the next decade, and to issue detailed annual reports that monitor and evaluate progress in doing so.

Community programs

In 1996, Parliament legislated principles that would allow offenders who might otherwise be imprisoned to serve their sentences in the community. A centrepiece of these reforms was Section 718.2(e) of the *Criminal Code,* which instructs judges that "all available sanctions other than imprisonment that are reasonable in the circumstances should be considered for all offenders, with particular attention to the circumstances of aboriginal offenders."[135]

In 1999, in *R. v. Gladue,* the Supreme Court stated that Section 718.2(e) of the *Criminal Code* was enacted in response to alarming evidence that Aboriginal peoples were incarcerated disproportionately to non-Aboriginal people in Canada.[136] The court stressed that this section is a remedial provision, enacted specifically to oblige the judiciary to make special efforts to find reasonable alternatives to imprisonment for Aboriginal offenders and to take into account the background and systemic factors that bring Aboriginal people into contact with the justice system.[137]

In some jurisdictions, the *Gladue* decision has resulted in the production of more extensive pre-sentence, or "Gladue," reports that detail the background and contextual circumstances of Aboriginal offenders. These reports help inform judges' sentencing decisions and are meant to encourage alternative options to incarceration. However, bringing these reports to court has not been without difficulty and controversy. Some jurisdictions provide few resources for the intensive, specialized, and culturally sensitive work that is necessary to produce an adequate Gladue report, despite the clear mandate given by the Supreme Court.[138]

In 2012, the Supreme Court revisited and reaffirmed *Gladue*. In *R. v. Ipeelee*, the Supreme Court pointed out that some judges had erred in their application of *Gladue* by concluding that it did not apply to serious offences or that it required an offender to demonstrate a causal connection between the commission of the crime and the legacy of residential schools or other background or contextual factors that help explain why an Aboriginal offender is before the courts.[139]

Even if excellent Gladue reports were prepared from coast to coast, they would still fail to make a difference in the amount of Aboriginal overrepresentation in the prison system without the addition of realistic alternatives to imprisonment, including adequate resources for intensive community programs that can respond to the conditions that caused Aboriginal offending.

Call to Action:

31) We call upon the federal, provincial, and territorial governments to provide sufficient and stable funding to implement and evaluate community sanctions that will provide realistic alternatives to imprisonment for Aboriginal offenders and respond to the underlying causes of offending.

A failure to provide sufficient and stable resources for the community and treatment programs that are necessary to implement *Gladue* and *Ipeelee* helps explain why those decisions have not slowed increasing Aboriginal overrepresentation in prison. In addition to these significant challenges, there are now new barriers to implementing effective and just alternative sentences for Aboriginal offenders.

Mandatory minimum sentences

One of the most dramatic examples of the trend towards mandatory minimum sentence is the *Safe Streets and Communities Act* (Bill C-10), which came into force in 2012. The Act specifies minimum sentences that judges must impose for certain crimes. As a result of the new legislation, certain offences are no longer eligible for a conditional sentence.[140]

Bill C-10 and other similar *Criminal Code* amendments have undermined the 1996 reforms that required judges to consider all reasonable alternatives to imprisonment, with particular attention to the circumstances of Aboriginal offenders. The

Commission believes that the recent introduction of mandatory minimum sentences and restrictions on conditional sentences will increase Aboriginal overrepresentation in prison. Such developments are preventing judges from implementing community sanctions even when they are consistent with the safety of the community and even when they have a much greater potential than imprisonment to respond to the intergenerational legacy of residential schools that often results in offences by Aboriginal persons.[141]

Call to Action

32) We call upon the federal government to amend the *Criminal Code* to allow trial judges, upon giving reasons, to depart from mandatory minimum sentences and restrictions on the use of conditional sentences.

Offenders with FASD

There is another link between the substance abuse that has plagued many residential school Survivors and the over-incarceration of Aboriginal people. Fetal alcohol spectrum disorder (FASD) is a permanent brain injury caused when a woman's consumption of alcohol during pregnancy affects her fetus. The disabilities associated with FASD include memory impairments, problems with judgment and abstract reasoning, and poor adaptive functioning.[142] It is a debilitating cognitive impairment, which children must live with for the rest of their lives, through no fault of their own. A study done for the Aboriginal Healing Foundation drew links among the intergenerational trauma of residential schools, alcohol addictions, and FASD.[143] The study concluded that the "residential school system contributed to the central risk factor involved, substance abuse, but also to factors shown to be linked to alcohol abuse, such as child and adult physical, emotional and sexual abuse, mental health problems and family dysfunction."[144]

About 1% of Canadian children are born with some form of disability related to prenatal alcohol consumption, but estimates from Canada and the United States suggest that 15% to 20% of prisoners have FASD.[145] A recent Canadian study found that offenders with FASD had much higher rates of criminal involvement than those without FASD, including more juvenile and adult convictions.[146] The Commission believes there is a need to take urgent measures both to prevent FASD and to better manage its harmful consequences. There is a clear need in Aboriginal communities for more programming that addresses the problems of addiction and FASD.

Call to Action

33) We call upon the federal, provincial, and territorial governments to recognize as a high priority the need to address and prevent Fetal Alcohol Spectrum Disorder (FASD), and to develop, in collaboration with Aboriginal people, FASD preventive programs that can be delivered in a culturally appropriate manner.

It is challenging for courts to deal with offenders with FASD, because obtaining an official diagnosis entails a long and costly process of multidisciplinary referrals. Even if trial judges have been educated about the symptoms of FASD, they are generally unable to take notice of FASD without evidence of a diagnosis.[147] Clearly, better diagnostic tools are needed, accompanied by sufficient resources for intensive community programs as realistic alternatives to jail and as support for people living with FASD to avoid repeated conflicts with the law.

The recent enactment of mandatory minimum sentences for some offences further complicates the situation of offenders with FASD because it denies judges the flexibility to consider individual circumstances in their sentencing. There is a danger that prison will be used unnecessarily as another expensive crisis intervention for Aboriginal offenders with FASD, even though culturally appropriate supports in the community could often be a more appropriate approach.[148] As well as amending mandatory minimum sentencing laws, the federal government can do much more to tailor correctional and parole resources to facilitate the reintegration of offenders with FASD into their communities.

Call to Action

34) We call upon the governments of Canada, the provinces, and territories to undertake reforms to the criminal justice system to better address the needs of offenders with Fetal Alcohol Spectrum Disorder (FASD), including:

   i. Providing increased community resources and powers for courts to ensure that FASD is properly diagnosed, and that appropriate community supports are in place for those with FASD.

   ii. Enacting statutory exemptions from mandatory minimum sentences of imprisonment for offenders affected by FASD.

   iii. Providing community, correctional, and parole resources to maximize the ability of people with FASD to live in the community.

   iv. Adopting appropriate evaluation mechanisms to measure the effectiveness of such programs and ensure community safety.

Cultural services in prisons and jails

Studies based on interviews with Aboriginal inmates have confirmed that Aboriginal culture and spirituality can contribute to the healing of the inmates, to increased self-esteem, and to positive changes in lifestyle that make release and reintegration a real possibility.[149] Research suggests that recidivism rates for Aboriginal offenders who had participated in spiritual activities (such as sweat lodge ceremonies) were lower than for those who had not.[150]

However, Aboriginal people receive few services in provincial correctional facilities that are designed for those serving sentences of two years less a day or are awaiting trial. Only a few provinces, such as British Columbia, have Aboriginal justice strategies that include cultural awareness training for officials and contracting with Aboriginal communities to provide spiritual leadership, counselling, and cultural programming for prisoners. [151]

The need for cultural programs in jail was expressed by a former residential school student who was an inmate at a correctional facility in Yellowknife. The Survivor told the Commission, "It would be nice if our own people would come in here and teach us about life ... you know, how to live. This is not the way of life for us. It's not the way for us people. But if they would teach a program like that, that will catch somebody for sure."[152]

There are some federal programs that appear to be working, but Aboriginal inmates do not have access to these programs in all parts of the country. For example, although Aboriginal healing lodges within correctional facilities have great potential to assist Aboriginal inmates, there are only four such lodges run by Correctional Services Canada and four run by Aboriginal communities under Section 81 of the *Corrections and Conditional Release Act*.[153] Lack of funding and difficulties in recruiting and training staff are obstacles to successful expansion of the healing lodge resources. In addition, prisoners must be classified as "minimum security" to be eligible, and 90% of Aboriginal inmates are assigned "medium" or "maximum" security classifications.

Calls to Action

35) We call upon the federal government to eliminate barriers to the creation of additional Aboriginal healing lodges within the federal correctional system.

36) We call upon the federal, provincial, and territorial governments to work with Aboriginal communities to provide culturally relevant services to inmates on issues such as substance abuse, family and domestic violence, and overcoming the experience of having been sexually abused.

Parole and community supports

Aboriginal offenders face many challenges in obtaining parole from prison and beginning their transition back into the community. For many Aboriginal inmates seeking parole, their criminal history is a major factor held against them. Although some research has concluded that criminal history is a reliable risk predictor for both Aboriginal and non-Aboriginal inmates, systemic discrimination related to poverty and the legacy of residential schools undoubtedly disadvantages Aboriginal offenders.[154] Just as some courts have the benefit of background and contextual information contained in pre-sentencing reports, parole hearings need a full understanding of an offender's circumstances when making their decisions.

When the National Parole Board grants parole, correctional programming continues. The early stages of parole are often spent in a residential correctional facility: a halfway house. Although it is not a prison, a halfway house requires the offender to reside there and not be absent except under specific exceptions (for example, supervised absences or employment). It is intended as a transitional phase in an offender's parole, neither full incarceration nor full freedom in the community, with the goal of gradual reintegration into the community. Unfortunately, there are too few halfway houses that provide programming specifically for Aboriginal offenders.

Call to Action

37) We call upon the federal government to provide more supports for Aboriginal programming in halfway houses and parole services.

Overrepresentation of youth

The youth justice system, perhaps even more than the adult criminal justice system, is failing Aboriginal families. Aboriginal girls make up 49% of the youth admitted to custody, and Aboriginal boys are 36% of those admitted to custody.[155] The current law regarding young people accused of crimes is the *Youth Criminal Justice Act*, which was introduced in 2002. One of the key objectives of the Act is to reserve jail for the most violent or habitual offenders. Even in such cases, one of the express goals of the youth criminal justice system is to address the circumstances underlying a young person's offending behaviour in order to rehabilitate and reintegrate them.[156] The Act has the flexibility to allow Aboriginal communities to have some measure of control over the youth process and to ensure Aboriginal perspectives are considered in individual cases.

By many objective measures, the *Youth Criminal Justice Act* has been a success. Since it came into effect, there has been a steady decline in youth crime, youth court caseloads, and youth supervised on community sentences and in custody.[157] But one thing the Act has not succeeded in doing is reducing the overrepresentation of Aboriginal youth in the criminal justice system.[158] The great vulnerability and disadvantage experienced by so many Aboriginal youth undoubtedly contribute to their overrepresentation, a factor that is intimately tied to the legacy of the residential schools. Many of today's Aboriginal children and youth live with the legacy of residential schools every day, as they struggle to deal with high rates of addictions, fetal alcohol disorder, mental health issues, family violence, incarceration of parents, and the intrusion of child-welfare authorities. All these factors place them at greater risk of involvement with crime.

The growing overrepresentation of Aboriginal youth in custody mirrors and is likely related to the even more dramatic overrepresentation of Aboriginal children in the care of child-welfare agencies. Research in British Columbia found that 35.5% of youth in care are also involved in the youth justice system, as compared with only 4.4% of youth who are not in care.[159] The Commission believes that there are ways to reduce the growing overrepresentation of Aboriginal youth, but that they will be found primarily outside the justice system. There is an urgent need to support Aboriginal families and alleviate the poverty experienced by many Aboriginal communities. The federal government should take the lead by committing the resources necessary to eliminating the overrepresentation of Aboriginal children and youth in care and custody. Part of that commitment should include collecting and publishing better data to measure progress.

Call to Action

38) We call upon the federal, provincial, territorial, and Aboriginal governments to commit to eliminating the overrepresentation of Aboriginal youth in custody over the next decade.

Victimization of Aboriginal people

An astonishing number of Aboriginal children were victims of crime in residential schools. By the end of 2014, the Independent Assessment Process had resolved 30,939 sexual or serious physical abuse claims, awarding $2.69 billion in compensation.[160] Although not every case would have involved a criminal act, the vast majority did, easily allowing anyone to conclude that the Indian Residential Schools Settlement Agreement involved the largest single recognition of criminal victimization in

Canadian history. This victimization of children has carried profound and long-lasting effects. Ruby Firth, a former student at Stringer Hall, told the Commission,

> All through my, residential school ... I was a victim. They put me in that frame of mind where I was a victim. I was four years old being a victim. Five years old, couldn't stop it. Six years old, couldn't stop it. Seven years old, couldn't stop it. So at some point my brain is going to say, "This is never going to stop!" So that's what I was doing in my adult life too because it didn't stop in my childhood, I was doing that in my adult, "This is never going to stop."[161]

The justice system continues to fail Aboriginal victims of crime. There are few services available for Aboriginal victims of crime. Victim compensation schemes are often lacking and often fail to recognize the distinct needs of Aboriginal victims of crime.

The statistics are startling. Aboriginal people are 58% more likely to be victimized by crime.[162] Aboriginal women report being victimized by violent crime at a rate almost three times higher than non-Aboriginal women—13% of Aboriginal women reported being victimized by violent crime in 2009.[163] In the same year, one in ten Aboriginal people reported being a victim of a non-spousal violent crime, more than double the rate reported by non-Aboriginal people.

It is difficult to obtain accurate information about the rate of victimization in Aboriginal communities. According to some studies, less than one-third of victims of crime report their victimization to police, and police forces across the country do not have a consistent method for recording the Aboriginal identity of victims.[164] Statistics Canada does not provide the kinds of supports necessary to permit some Aboriginal victims to comfortably disclose their experience to researchers. The most recent Statistics Canada data on homicide and family violence fail to report how many victims were Aboriginal, although older data suggest the homicide victimization rate of Aboriginal people between 1997 and 2000 was seven times that of non-Aboriginal people.[165]

Call to Action

39) We call upon the federal government to develop a national plan to collect and publish data on the criminal victimization of Aboriginal people, including data related to homicide and family violence victimization.

This data should be used to guide the development and funding of culturally appropriate services for Aboriginal victims of crime and to help make measureable reductions in the overrepresentation of Aboriginal people among crime victims.

Call to Action

40) We call upon all levels of government, in collaboration with Aboriginal people, to create adequately funded and accessible Aboriginal-specific victim programs and services with appropriate evaluation mechanisms.

Violence against Aboriginal women and girls

The overrepresentation of Aboriginal women and girls among crime victims is particularly disturbing. Aboriginal women and girls are more likely than other women to experience risk factors for violence. They are disproportionately young, poor, unemployed, and likely to have been involved with the child-welfare system and to live in a community marked by social disorder.[166]

Velma Jackson, who attended the Blue Quills residential school in Alberta, told the Commission her story.

> A lot of other girls my age were [in Blue Quills], but I only know of one that survived, all the rest are dead today. Some died on the street. Some died prostituting. Others into alcoholism got run over by vehicles. But their children are still alive today.... I can't to this day wear a dress because of all the things that happened in the school. It was like a sanctuary for pedophiles I would call it, that's probably why I blocked out so much of my life is because of that.[167]

The most disturbing aspect of this victimization is the extraordinary number of Aboriginal women who have been murdered or are reported as missing. A report by the RCMP, released in 2014, found that between 1980 and 2012, 1,017 Aboriginal women and girls were killed and 164 were missing. Two hundred and twenty-five of these cases remain unsolved.[168]

More research is needed, but the available information suggests a devastating link between the large numbers of missing and murdered Aboriginal women and the many harmful background factors in their lives. These include: overrepresentation of Aboriginal children in child-welfare care; domestic and sexual violence; racism, poverty, and poor educational and health opportunities in Aboriginal communities; discriminatory practices against women related to band membership and Indian status; and inadequate supports for Aboriginal people in cities. This complex interplay of factors—many of which are part of the legacy of residential schools—needs to be examined, as does the lack of success of police forces in solving these crimes against Aboriginal women.

Call to Action

41) We call upon the federal government, in consultation with Aboriginal organizations, to appoint a public inquiry into the causes of, and remedies for, the disproportionate victimization of Aboriginal women and girls. The inquiry's mandate would include:

    i. Investigation into missing and murdered Aboriginal women and girls.

    ii. Links to the intergenerational legacy of residential schools.

Strategies for change

Multi-pronged strategies are necessary to respond to the harmful legacy of residential schools, as demonstrated in part by the overrepresentation of Aboriginal people among prisoners and crime victims. Compiling better data on Aboriginal overrepresentation in the justice system is a starting point. Collection of this data must be coupled with developing measurable goals for reducing this overrepresentation and providing the resources necessary to reach those goals. The approach must be an holistic and culturally appropriate one that addresses the need for improvements in health, education, and economic development in Aboriginal communities.

Any strategy aimed at reducing Aboriginal offending and victimization must also include recognition of the rights of Aboriginal communities to develop their own justice systems as part of a larger commitment to Aboriginal self-determination and self-government. These rights are grounded in international and constitutional law as well as in the Treaties. Aboriginal forms of justice may be as diverse as Canada's Aboriginal peoples themselves. It is a central conclusion of the Truth and Reconciliation Commission of Canada that recognition of the Aboriginal right to self-determination, more appropriate funding allocations for services from governments, and methodical tracking of progress are the preconditions for redressing the disastrous legacy of residential schools and aiding the long process of reconciliation within Canada.

Call to Action

42) We call upon the federal, provincial, and territorial governments to commit to the recognition and implementation of Aboriginal justice systems in a manner consistent with the Treaty and Aboriginal rights of Aboriginal peoples, the *Constitution Act, 1982*, and the *United Nations Declaration on the Rights of Indigenous Peoples*, endorsed by Canada in November 2012.

The Commission is convinced that genuine reconciliation will not be possible until the broad legacy of the schools is both understood and addressed. Governments in Canada spend billions of dollars each year in responding to the symptoms of the intergenerational trauma of residential schools. Much of this money is spent on crisis interventions related to child welfare, family violence, ill health, and crime. Despite genuine reform efforts, the dramatic overrepresentation of Aboriginal children in foster care, and among the sick, the injured, and the imprisoned, continues to grow. Only a real commitment to reconciliation will reverse the trend and lay the foundation for a truly just and equitable nation.

The challenge of reconciliation

Setting the context

Canada has a long history of colonialism in relation to Aboriginal peoples. That history and its policies of cultural genocide and assimilation have left deep scars on the lives of many Aboriginal people, on Aboriginal communities, as well as on Canadian society, and have deeply damaged the relationship between Aboriginal and non-Aboriginal peoples. It took a long time for that damage to have been done and for the relationship we see to have been created, and it will take us a long time to fix it. But the process has already begun.

An important process of healing and reconciling that relationship began in the 1980s with church apologies for their treatment of Aboriginal peoples and disrespect of their cultures. It continued with the findings of the Royal Commission on Aboriginal Peoples, along with court recognition of the validity of the Survivors' stories. It culminated in the Indian Residential Schools Settlement Agreement and the prime minister of Canada's apology in Parliament in June 2008, along with the apologies of all other parliamentary leaders. That process of healing and reconciliation must continue. The ultimate objective must be to transform our country and restore mutual respect between peoples and nations.

Reconciliation is in the best interests of all of Canada. It is necessary not only to resolve the ongoing conflicts between Aboriginal peoples and institutions of the country, but also in order for Canada to remove a stain from its past and be able to maintain its claim to be a leader in the protection of human rights among the nations of the world. Canada's historical development, as well as the view held strongly by some that the history of that development is accurate and beneficent, raises significant barriers to reconciliation in the twenty-first century.

No Canadian can take pride in this country's treatment of Aboriginal peoples, and, for that reason, all Canadians have a critical role to play in advancing reconciliation in ways that honour and revitalize the nation-to-nation Treaty relationship.

At the Truth and Reconciliation Commission of Canada's (TRC) Traditional Knowledge Keepers Forum held in June 2014, Chief Ian Campbell said, "Our history is your history, as Canada ... until Canada accepts that ... this society will never flourish to its full potential."[1]

The history and destructive legacy of the residential school system is a powerful reminder that Canada disregarded its own historical roots. Canada's determination to assimilate Aboriginal peoples, in spite of the early relationship established at first contact and formalized and maintained in Treaties, attests to that fact. As Gerry St. Germain (Métis), then a Canadian senator, said,

> There can be no doubt that the founders of Canada somehow lost their moral compass in their relations with the people who occupied and possessed the land.... While we cannot change history, we can learn from it and we can use it to shape our common future.... This effort is crucial in realizing the vision of creating a compassionate and humanitarian society, the society that our ancestors, the Aboriginal, the French and the English peoples, envisioned so many years ago—our home, Canada.[2]

Aboriginal peoples have always remembered the original relationship they had with early Canadians. That relationship of mutual support, respect, and assistance was confirmed by the Royal Proclamation of 1763 and the Treaties with the Crown that were negotiated in good faith by their leaders. That memory, confirmed by historical analysis and passed down through Indigenous oral histories, has sustained Aboriginal peoples in their long political struggle to live with dignity as self-determining peoples with their own cultures, laws, and connections to the land.

The destructive impacts of residential schools, the *Indian Act*, and the Crown's failure to keep its Treaty promises have damaged the relationship between Aboriginal and non-Aboriginal peoples. The most significant damage is to the trust that has been broken between the Crown and Aboriginal peoples. That broken trust must be repaired. The vision that led to that breach in trust must be replaced with a new vision for Canada; one that fully embraces Aboriginal peoples' right to self-determination within, and in partnership with, a viable Canadian sovereignty. If Canadians fail to find that vision, then Canada will not resolve long-standing conflicts between the Crown and Aboriginal peoples over Treaty and Aboriginal rights, lands, and resources, or the education, health, and well-being of Aboriginal peoples. Reconciliation will not be achieved, and neither will the hope for reconciliation be sustainable over time. It would not be inconceivable that the unrest we see today among young Aboriginal people could grow to become a challenge to the country's own sense of well-being and its very security.

Reconciliation must become a way of life. It will take many years to repair damaged trust and relationships in Aboriginal communities and between Aboriginal and non-Aboriginal peoples. Reconciliation not only requires apologies, reparations, the relearning of Canada's national history, and public commemoration, but also needs real social, political, and economic change. Ongoing public education and dialogue are essential to reconciliation. Governments, churches, educational institutions, and Canadians from all walks of life are responsible for taking action on reconciliation in concrete ways, working collaboratively with Aboriginal peoples. Reconciliation begins with each and every one of us.

The Aboriginal and non-Aboriginal youth of our country have told the Commission that they want to know the truth about the history and legacy of residential schools. They want to understand their responsibilities as parties to the same Treaties—in other words, as Treaty people. They want to learn about the rich contributions that Aboriginal peoples have made to this country. They understand that reconciliation involves a conversation not only about residential schools, but also about all other aspects of the relationship between Aboriginal and non-Aboriginal peoples.

As Commissioners, we believe that reconciliation is about respect. That includes both self-respect for Aboriginal people and mutual respect among all Canadians. All young people need to know who they are and from where they come. Aboriginal children and youth, searching for their own identities and places of belonging, need to know and take pride in their Indigenous roots. They need to know the answers to some very basic questions. Who are my people? What is our history? How are we unique? Where do I belong? Where is my homeland? What is my language and how does it connect me to my nation's spiritual beliefs, cultural practices, and ways of being in the world? They also need to know why things are the way they are today. That requires an understanding of the history of colonization, including the residential school system and how it has affected their families, communities, their people, and themselves.

Of equal importance, non-Aboriginal children and youth need to comprehend how their own identities and family histories have been shaped by a version of Canadian history that has marginalized Aboriginal peoples' history and experience. They need to know how notions of European superiority and Aboriginal inferiority have tainted mainstream society's ideas about, and attitudes towards, Aboriginal peoples in ways that have been profoundly disrespectful and damaging. They too need to understand Canada's history as a settler society and how assimilation policies have affected Aboriginal peoples. This knowledge and understanding will lay the groundwork for establishing mutually respectful relationships.

The Royal Commission on Aboriginal Peoples

In the summer of 1990, at Oka, Québec, the Mohawks of Kanesatake, the government of Québec, the Québec provincial police, and the Canadian military became embroiled in a violent confrontation over the town's plan to develop a golf course on Mohawk burial grounds located in a forested area known as "The Pines." The Mohawks' claim to that land and demands for the recognition of their traditional territory had gone unheeded for years by the federal government. The resulting confrontation, according to historian J. R. Miller, was "proof of Canada's failed Indian [land] claims policy."[3] What had begun as a peaceful act of resistance by Mohawk people defending their lands took a violent turn.[4] The "Oka crisis," as it became widely known in the media, led to a seventy-eight-day standoff and involved armed resistance led by militarily trained Mohawk warriors.[5] It was an event that shook Canada's complacency about Aboriginal demands to the core. Shortly after an end to the siege had been negotiated, Prime Minister Brian Mulroney wrote:

> The summer's events must not be allowed to over-shadow the commitment that my government has made to addressing the concerns of aboriginal people.... These grievances raise issues that deeply affect all Canadians and therefore must be resolved by all Canadians working together.... The government's agenda responds to the demands of aboriginal peoples and has four parts: resolving land claims; improving the economic and social conditions on reserves; defining a new relationship between aboriginal peoples and governments; and addressing the concerns of Canada's aboriginal peoples in contemporary Canadian life. Consultation with aboriginal peoples and respect for the fiduciary responsibilities of the Crown are integral parts of the process. The federal government is determined to create a new relationship among aboriginal and non-aboriginal Canadians based on dignity, trust and respect.[6]

The Government of Canada subsequently created a Royal Commission to look into the state of affairs of Aboriginal peoples in Canada. The Royal Commission provided a glimpse into just how bad things had become.

In 1996, the Royal Commission on Aboriginal Peoples (RCAP) put forward a bold and comprehensive vision of reconciliation. The RCAP report observed that if Canada was to thrive in the future, the relationship between Aboriginal peoples and the Crown must be transformed. The report concluded that the policy of assimilation was a complete failure and that Canada must look to the historical Treaty relationship to establish a new relationship between Aboriginal and non-Aboriginal peoples, based on the principles of mutual recognition, mutual respect, sharing, and mutual responsibility.[7]

The Royal Commission emphasized that Aboriginal peoples' right to self-determination is essential to a robust upholding of Canada's constitutional obligations to Aboriginal peoples and compliance with international human rights law. In other words, the RCAP report saw reconciliation as placing a heavy onus on the Government of Canada to change its conduct and to see the validity of the Aboriginal perspective of how the relationship should be in the future.

In the years following the release of the RCAP report, developing a national vision of reconciliation has proved to be challenging. In principle, Aboriginal peoples, governments, and the courts agree that reconciliation is needed. In practice, it has been difficult to create the conditions for reconciliation to flourish.

The Indian Residential Schools Settlement Agreement, including the creation of the Truth and Reconciliation Commission of Canada, was an attempt to resolve the thousands of lawsuits brought against the government for cases of historical abuse. Its implementation has also been challenging. Canada and the churches have made apologies to Survivors, their families, and communities. Yet, Canadian government actions continue to be unilateral and divisive, and Aboriginal peoples continue to resist such actions. Negotiations on Treaties and land-claims agreements continue with a view to reconciling Aboriginal title and rights with Crown sovereignty. However, many cases remain unresolved. The courts have produced a body of law on reconciliation in relation to Aboriginal rights, which has established some parameters for discussion and negotiations, but there remains no ongoing national process or entity to guide that discussion. What is clear to this Commission is that Aboriginal peoples and the Crown have very different and conflicting views on what reconciliation is and how it is best achieved. The Government of Canada appears to believe that reconciliation entails Aboriginal peoples' acceptance of the reality and validity of Crown sovereignty and parliamentary supremacy, in order to allow the government to get on with business. Aboriginal people, on the other hand, see reconciliation as an opportunity to affirm their own sovereignty and return to the 'partnership' ambitions they held after Confederation.

The *United Nations Declaration on the Rights of Indigenous Peoples* as a framework for reconciliation

Aboriginal peoples in Canada were not alone in the world when it came to being treated harshly by colonial authorities and settler governments. Historical abuses of Aboriginal peoples and the taking of Indigenous lands and resources throughout the world have been the subject of United Nations' attention for many years. On September 13, 2007, after almost twenty-five years of debate and study, the United Nations (UN) adopted the *Declaration on the Rights of Indigenous Peoples.* As a declaration, it calls upon member states to adopt and maintain its provisions as a set of "minimum standards for the survival, dignity and well-being of the indigenous peoples of the world."[8]

The Commission concurs with the view of S. James Anaya, UN Special Rapporteur on the Rights of Indigenous Peoples, who observed,

> It is perhaps best to understand the Declaration and the right of self-determination it affirms as instruments of reconciliation. Properly understood, self-determination is an animating force for efforts toward reconciliation—or, perhaps, more accurately, conciliation—with peoples that have suffered oppression at the hands of others. Self-determination requires confronting

> and reversing the legacies of empire, discrimination, and cultural suffocation. It does not do so to condone vengefulness or spite for past evils, or to foster divisiveness but rather to build a social and political order based on relations of mutual understanding and respect. That is what the right of self-determination of indigenous peoples, and all other peoples, is about.[9]

Canada, as a member of the United Nations, initially refused to adopt the *Declaration*. It joined the United States, Australia, and New Zealand in doing so. It is not coincidence that all these nations have a common history as part of the British Empire. The historical treatment of Aboriginal peoples in these other countries has strong parallels to what happened to Aboriginal peoples in Canada. Specifically, Canada objected to the *Declaration*'s

> provisions dealing with lands, territories and resources; free, prior and informed consent when used as a veto; self-government without recognition of the importance of negotiations; intellectual property; military issues; and the need to achieve an appropriate balance between the rights and obligations of Indigenous peoples, member States and third parties.[10]

Although these four countries eventually endorsed the *Declaration*, they have all done so conditionally. In 2010, Canada endorsed the *Declaration* as a "non-legally binding aspirational document."[11] Despite this endorsement, we believe that the provisions and the vision of the *Declaration* do not currently enjoy government acceptance. However, because Canada has accepted the *Declaration*, we hold the federal government to its word that it will genuinely aspire to achieve its provisions.

In 2011, Canadian churches and social justice advocacy groups who had campaigned for Canada's adoption of the *Declaration* urged the federal government to implement it. However, Canada's interpretation of the *Declaration* remained unchanged. On September 22, 2014, at the World Conference on Indigenous Peoples (WCIP) in New York, the United Nations General Assembly adopted an action-oriented "Outcome Document" to guide the implementation of the *Declaration*. Member states from around the world committed, among other things, to the following:

> Taking, in consultation and cooperation with indigenous peoples, appropriate measures at the national level, including legislative, policy, and administrative measures, to achieve the ends of the *Declaration*, and to promote awareness of it among all sectors of society, including members of legislatures, the judiciary and the civil service.... [para. 7] We commit ourselves to cooperating with indigenous peoples, through their own representative institutions, to develop and implement national action plans, strategies or other measures, where relevant, to achieve the ends of the Declaration [para. 8] ... [and also] encourage the private sector, civil society and academic institutions to take an active role in promoting and protecting the rights of indigenous peoples. [para. 30][12]

The "Outcome Document" represented an important step forward with regard to implementing the *Declaration* in practical terms. The development of national action plans, strategies, and other concrete measures will provide the necessary structural and institutional frameworks for ensuring that Indigenous peoples' right to self-determination is realized across the globe.

Canada issued a formal statement at the WCIP, objecting to certain paragraphs of the document related to the principle of obtaining the "free, prior and informed consent" (FPIC) of Indigenous peoples when states are making decisions that will affect their rights or interests, including economic development on their lands. Canada said,

> Free, prior and informed consent, as it is considered in paragraphs 3 and 20 of the WCIP Outcome Document, could be interpreted as providing a veto to Aboriginal groups and in that regard, cannot be reconciled with Canadian law, as it exists.... Canada cannot support paragraph 4, in particular, given that Canadian law, recently reaffirmed in a Supreme Court of Canada decision, states the Crown may justify the infringement of an Aboriginal or Treaty right if it meets a stringent test to reconcile Aboriginal rights with a broader public interest.[13]

In a public statement, Indigenous leaders and their supporters said that Canada's concerns were unfounded, noting that

> the notion that the *Declaration* could be interpreted as conferring an absolute and unilateral veto power has been repeatedly raised by Canada as a justification for its continued opposition to the *Declaration*. This claim, however, has no basis either in the *UN Declaration* or in the wider body of international law. Like standards of accommodation and consent set out by the Supreme Court of Canada, FPIC in international law is applied in proportion to the potential for harm to the rights of Indigenous peoples and to the strength of these rights. The word "veto" does not appear in the *UN Declaration*.... Canada keeps insisting that Indigenous peoples don't have a say in development on their lands. This position is not consistent with the *UN Declaration on the Rights of Indigenous Peoples*, decisions by its own courts, or the goal of reconciliation.[14]

Reflecting on the importance of the *Declaration* to First Nations, Inuit, and Métis peoples in Canada, Grand Chief Edward John, Hereditary Chief of the Tl'azt'en Nation in northern British Columbia, explained,

> We have struggled for generations for recognition of our rights. We have fought for our survival, dignity and well-being, and the struggle continues. Canada's denial of First Nations' land rights falls well short of the minimum standards affirmed by the *Declaration* and demonstrates a clear failure by Canada to implement its human rights obligations. Prime Minister Harper's apology for Canada's role in the Indian Residential Schools acknowledged that the policy of assimilation was wrong and has no place in our country. Yet Canada's policy of denying Aboriginal title and rights is premised on the same attitude of

> assimilation. It is time for this attitude and the policies that flow from it to be cast aside. The *Declaration* calls for the development of new relationships based on recognition and respect for the inherent human rights of Indigenous peoples.[15]

The TRC considers "reconciliation" to be an ongoing process of establishing and maintaining respectful relationships at all levels of Canadian society. The Commission therefore believes that the *United Nations Declaration on the Rights of Indigenous Peoples* is the appropriate framework for reconciliation in twenty-first-century Canada. Studying the *Declaration* with a view to identifying its impacts on current government laws, policy, and behaviour would enable Canada to develop a holistic vision of reconciliation that embraces all aspects of the relationship between Aboriginal and non-Aboriginal Canadians, and to set the standard for international achievement in its circle of hesitating nations.

Aboriginal peoples' right to self-determination must be integrated into Canada's constitutional and legal framework and civic institutions, in a manner consistent with the principles, norms, and standards of the *Declaration*. Aboriginal peoples in Canada have Aboriginal and Treaty rights. They have the right to access and revitalize their own laws and governance systems within their own communities and in their dealings with governments. They have a right to protect and revitalize their cultures, languages, and ways of life. They have the right to reparations for historical harms.

In 2014, the Supreme Court of Canada ruled that the Tsilhqot'in peoples have Aboriginal title to their lands in northern British Columbia, and "ownership rights similar to those associated with fee simple, including: the right to decide how the land will be used; the right of enjoyment and occupancy of the land; the right to possess the land; the right to the economic benefits of the land; and the right to pro-actively use and manage the land."[16] The court said, "Governments and individuals proposing to use or exploit land, whether before or after a declaration of Aboriginal title, can avoid a charge of infringement or failure to adequately consult by obtaining the consent of the interested Aboriginal group."[17]

In the face of growing conflicts over lands, resources, and economic development, the scope of reconciliation must extend beyond residential schools to encompass all aspects of Aboriginal and non-Aboriginal relations and connections to the land. Therefore, in our view, it is essential that all levels of government endorse and implement the *Declaration*. The Commission urges the federal government to reverse its position and fully endorse the "Outcome Document." We believe that the federal government must develop a national action plan to implement the *Declaration*. This would be consistent with the direction provided by the Supreme Court of Canada. More importantly, it would be consistent with the achievement of reconciliation.

Calls to Action

43) We call upon federal, provincial, territorial, and municipal governments to fully adopt and implement the United Nations *Declaration on the Rights of Indigenous Peoples* as the framework for reconciliation.

44) We call upon the Government of Canada to develop a national action plan, strategies, and other concrete measures to achieve the goals of the United Nations *Declaration on the Rights of Indigenous Peoples.*

Doctrine of Discovery

Earlier in this report, we recalled how European states relied on the Doctrine of Discovery and the concept of *terra nullius* (lands belonging to no one) to justify empire building and the colonization of Aboriginal peoples and their lands in North America and across the globe. Far from being ancient history with no relevance for reconciliation today, the Doctrine of Discovery underlies the legal basis on which British Crown officials claimed sovereignty over Indigenous peoples and justified the extinguishment of their inherent rights to their territories, lands, and resources.

Speaking at the Manitoba National Event in 2010, former day school student, political leader, and educator Sol Sanderson explained the importance of making the connection between the policies and practices of imperialism and colonization and the need for transformative change in Canadian society.

> What were the objectives of those empire policies? Assimilation, integration, civilization, Christianization and liquidation. Who did those policies target? They targeted the destruction of our Indigenous families worldwide. Why? Because that was the foundation of our governing systems. They were the foundations of our institutions, and of our societies of our nations. Now those policies still form the basis of Canadian law today, not just in the *Indian Act* [that] outlawed our traditions, our customs, our practices, our values, our language, our culture, our forms of government, our jurisdiction.... They say we have constitutionally protected rights in the form of inherent rights, Aboriginal rights and Treaty rights, but we find ourselves in courts daily defending those rights against the colonial laws of the provinces and the federal government. Now, we can't allow that to continue.[18]

From 2010 to 2014, the United Nations Permanent Forum on Indigenous Issues undertook a number of studies and reports on the Doctrine of Discovery. During this same time period, the Settlement Agreement churches also began to examine the Christian thinking that had justified taking Indigenous lands and removing children from their families and communities. Writing about the Roman Catholic foundations of Aboriginal land claims in Canada, historian Jennifer Reid explains why the Doctrine remains relevant today.

> Most non-Aboriginal Canadians are aware of the fact that Indigenous peoples commonly regard land rights as culturally and religiously significant. Fewer non-natives, I suspect, would consider their own connection with property in the same light, and fewer still would regard the legal foundation of all land rights in Canada as conspicuously theological. In fact, however, it is. The relationship between law and land in Canada can be traced to a set of fifteenth-century theological assumptions that have found their way into Canadian law.... The Doctrine of Discovery was the legal means by which Europeans claimed rights of sovereignty, property, and trade in regions they allegedly discovered during the age of expansion. These claims were made without consultation or engagement of any sort with the resident populations in these territories—the people to whom, by any sensible account, the land actually belonged. The Doctrine of Discovery has been a critical component of historical relationships between Europeans, their descendants, and Indigenous peoples, and it underlies their legal relationships to this day, having smoothly and relatively uncritically transitioned from Roman Catholic to international law.[19]

In April 2010, the Permanent Observer Mission of the Holy See (the UN representative from the Roman Catholic Vatican) issued a statement regarding the Doctrine of Discovery at the ninth session of the UN Permanent Forum on Indigenous Issues.[20] The statement noted that earlier papal bulls regarding territorial expansion and the forced conversion of Indigenous peoples had subsequently been abrogated or annulled by the Roman Catholic Church.

> Regarding the question of the doctrine of discovery and the role of the Papal Bull *Inter Coetera*, the Holy See notes that *Inter Coetera,* as a source of international law ... was first of all abrogated by the Treaty of Tordesilles in 1494, and that Circumstances have changed so much that to attribute any juridical value to such a document seems completely out of place.... In addition, it was also abrogated by other Papal Bulls, for example, *Sublimis Deus* in 1537, which states, *"Indians and all other people who may later be discovered by Christians, are by no means to be deprived of their liberty or the possession of their property ... should the contrary happen, it shall be null and have no effect."* This view was expanded upon and reinforced in *Immensa Pastorum* of [Pope] Benedict XIV of 20 December 1741 and a number of other Papal Encyclicals, statements and decrees. If any doubt remains, it is abrogated by Canon 6 of the Code of Canon Law of 1983 which abrogates in general all preceding penal and disciplinary laws.... Therefore, for International Law and for the Catholic Church Law, the Bull *Inter Coetera* is a historic remnant with no juridical, moral or doctrinal value.... The fact that juridical systems may employ the "Doctrine of Discovery" as a juridical precedent is now therefore a characteristic of the laws of those

> states and is independent of the fact that for the Church the document has had no value for centuries. The refutation of this doctrine is therefore now under the competence of national authorities, legislators, lawyers and legal historians.[21]

For many, that Catholic statement was inadequate. The doctrine's influence in Western law and its destructive consequences for Indigenous peoples have been well documented by scholars and other experts.[22]

In 2014, the North American representative to the UN Permanent Forum on Indigenous Issues, Grand Chief Edward John, tabled the "Study on the Impacts of the Doctrine of Discovery on Indigenous Peoples, Including Mechanisms, Processes, and Instruments of Redress." The study concluded:

> With regard to land dispossessions, forced conversions of non-Christians, the deprivation of liberty and the enslavement of indigenous peoples, the Holy See reported that an "abrogation process took place over the centuries" to invalidate such nefarious actions. Such papal renunciations do not go far enough. There is a pressing need to decolonize from the debilitating impacts and ongoing legacy of denial by states of indigenous peoples' inherent sovereignty, laws, and title to the lands, territories, and resources. At the same time, there is a growing movement among faith-based bodies to repudiate the doctrine of discovery.[23]

In 2010, the Anglican Church of Canada was the first of the Settlement Agreement churches in Canada to reject the Doctrine of Discovery and to "review the Church's policies and programs with a view to exposing the historical reality and impact of the Doctrine of Discovery and eliminating its presence in its contemporary policies, program, and structures."[24] In 2013, the Anglican Church established a Commission on Discovery, Reconciliation, and Justice, which had three goals:

1) to examine the Anglican Church of Canada's policies and practices and revise them as necessary to be consistent with its repudiation of the Doctrine of Discovery;
2) to look into the question of "what is reconciliation"; and
3) to review the church's commitment to addressing long-standing injustices borne by Indigenous peoples in Canada.

The Commission on Discovery will table a final report to the Anglican General Synod in 2016.[25]

In February 2012, the Executive Committee of the World Council of Churches (WCC) also repudiated the Doctrine of Discovery. The WCC represents over 500 million Christians, in more than 110 countries, in 345 member churches, including three of the Settlement Agreement churches.[26] The WCC statement denounced the Doctrine of Discovery and urged governments to "dismantle the legal structures and policies based on the Doctrine of Discovery ... [and to] ensure that they conform to the *United Nations Declaration on the Rights of Indigenous Peoples.*" The statement expressed solidarity with Indigenous peoples and affirmed their rights of self-determination and self-governance. The WCC also asked its member churches to support Indigenous self-determination in spiritual matters and education of all members of their churches.[27]

The United Church of Canada responded to this call. At its meeting in March 2012, the Executive of the General Council of the United Church "agreed unanimously to disown the Doctrine of Discovery, a historical concept which has been used to rationalize the enslavement and colonization of Indigenous peoples around the world."[28]

At the eleventh session of the UN Permanent Forum in May 2012, KAIROS, an interchurch social justice advocacy organization, made a joint statement with the Assembly of First Nations, Chiefs of Ontario, Grand Council of the Crees (Eeyou Istchee), Amnesty International, and the Canadian Friends Service Committee (Quakers) on the Doctrine of Discovery. The statement said that "while churches have begun to repudiate this racist doctrine, States around the world have not." It recommended that states, in conjunction with Indigenous peoples, undertake legal and policy reform to remove "any remnants of doctrines of superiority, including 'discovery,' as a basis for the assumed sovereignty over Indigenous peoples and their lands and resources."[29]

In his report to the UN Permanent Forum, Grand Chief Edward John focused on how Canadian courts have dealt with sovereignty issues.

> The highest court of Canada has recognized the need for reconciliation of "pre-existing aboriginal sovereignty with assumed Crown sovereignty." The Supreme Court has taken judicial notice of "such matters as colonialism, displacement and residential schools," which demonstrate how "assumed" sovereign powers were abused throughout history. The root cause of such abuse leads back to the Doctrine of Discovery and other related fictitious constructs which must therefore be addressed.[30]

At the thirteenth session of the UN Permanent Forum in May 2014, Haudenosaunee Faithkeeper Oren Lyons spoke about the principles of good governance as they relate to the *United Nations Declaration.* He said,

> We recognize the Doctrine of Discovery and its long-term effects on our peoples led to the atrocities we faced in residential and boarding schools, both in Canada and the U.S.... the Doctrine of Discovery has been invoked as a justification for the ongoing exploitation of our lands, territories, and resources and directly violates Article 7 paragraph 2 of the UNDRIP [the *Declaration*].[31]

The Doctrine of Discovery and the related concept of *terra nullius* underpin the requirement for Aboriginal peoples to prove their pre-existing occupation of the land in court cases or to have their land and resource rights extinguished in contemporary Treaty and land-claims processes. Such a requirement does not conform to international law or contribute to reconciliation. Such concepts are a current manifestation of historical wrongs and should be formally repudiated by all levels of Canadian government.

Our intention in so concluding is to highlight that there is an important distinction to be drawn between the Doctrine of Discovery and its related concepts and the several inherently unjust policies, laws, and principles to which they have given rise over the years. It would not be enough to simply repudiate the Doctrine of Discovery, for example, while still maintaining the requirement for Aboriginal people to prove the validity of their existence and territoriality. We would not suggest that the repudiation of the Doctrine of Discovery necessarily gives rise to the invalidation of Crown sovereignty. The Commission accepts that there are other means to establish the validity of Crown sovereignty without undermining the important principle established in the Royal Proclamation of 1763, which is that the sovereignty of the Crown requires that it recognize and deal with Aboriginal title in order to become perfected. It must not be forgotten that the terms of the Royal Proclamation were explained to, and accepted by, Indigenous leaders during the negotiation of the Treaty of Niagara of 1764.

Treaties: Honouring the past and negotiating the future

It is important for all Canadians to understand that without Treaties, Canada would have no legitimacy as a nation. Treaties between Indigenous nations and the Crown established the legal and constitutional foundation of this country.

Elder Fred Kelly emphasized that Treaty making and Aboriginal peoples' ways of resolving conflict must be central to reconciliation. He said,

> There are those who believe that a generic reconciliation process is a Western-based concept to be imposed on the Aboriginal peoples without regard to their own traditional practices of restoring personal and collective peace and harmony. We must therefore insist that the Aboriginal peoples have meaningful participation in the design, administration, and evaluation of the reconciliation process so that it is based on their local culture and language. If reconciliation is to be real and meaningful in Canada, it must embrace the inherent right of self-determination through self-government envisioned in the treaties....
>
> Where government refuses to implement Aboriginal rights and the original spirit and intent of the treaties, the citizens of Canada must take direct action to forcefully persuade its leadership. Treaties and memoranda of agreement are simply the stage-setting mechanisms for reconciliation. There must be action ... all Canadians have treaty rights.... It is upon these rights and obligations that our relationship is founded.[32]

If Canada's past is a cautionary tale about what not to do, it also holds a more constructive history lesson for the future. The Treaties are a model for how Canadians, as diverse peoples, can live respectfully and peacefully together on these lands we now share.

The Royal Proclamation of 1763 and Treaty of Niagara, 1764

The history of Treaty making in Canada is contentious. Aboriginal peoples and the Crown have interpreted the spirit and intent of the Treaties quite differently. Generally, government officials have viewed the Treaties as legal mechanisms by which Aboriginal peoples ceded and surrendered their lands to the Crown. In contrast, First Nations, Inuit, and Métis peoples understand Treaties as a sacred obligation that commits both parties to maintain respectful relationships and share lands and resources equitably.

Indigenous peoples have kept the history and ongoing relevance of the Treaties alive in their own oral histories and legal traditions. Without their perspectives on the history of Treaty making, Canadians know only one side of this country's history. This story cannot simply be told as the story of how Crown officials unilaterally imposed Treaties on Aboriginal peoples; they were also active participants in Treaty negotiations.[33] The history and interpretation of Treaties and the Aboriginal–Crown relationship as told by Indigenous peoples enriches and informs our understanding of why we are all Treaty people.[34] This is evident, for example, in the story of the Royal Proclamation of 1763 and its relationship to the Treaty of Niagara of 1764. The Royal Proclamation, which was issued by colonial officials, tells only half this story.

On October 7, 1763, King George III issued a Royal Proclamation by which the British Crown first recognized the legal and constitutional rights of Aboriginal peoples in Canada. In the Royal Proclamation of 1763, the British declared that all lands west of the established colonies belonged to Aboriginal peoples and that only the Crown could legally acquire these lands by negotiating Treaties.

At a time when Aboriginal peoples still held considerable power and conflicts with settlers were increasing, British officials sought to establish a distinct geographical area that would remain under the jurisdiction of Indigenous nations until Treaties were negotiated.

Anishinaabe legal scholar John Borrows notes that the Royal Proclamation can be fully understood only in relation to the Treaty of Niagara, in which the terms of the proclamation were ratified by Indigenous nations in 1764. As Borrows explains, the Indigenous leaders who negotiated the Treaty of Niagara with the Crown did so with the understanding that they would remain free and self-determining peoples. Borrows observes:

> The Proclamation uncomfortably straddled the contradictory aspirations of the Crown and First Nations when its wording recognized Aboriginal rights to land by outlining a policy that was designed to extinguish these rights.... The different objectives that First Nations and the Crown had in the formulation of the principles surrounding the Proclamation is the reason for the different visions embedded within its text. Britain was attempting to secure territory and jurisdiction through the Proclamation, while the First Nations were concerned with preserving their lands and sovereignty.[35]

The Royal Proclamation was ratified by over 2,000 Indigenous leaders who had gathered at Niagara in the summer of 1764 to make a Treaty with the Crown.[36] The Treaty negotiations, like earlier trade and peace and friendship Treaties, were conducted in accordance with Indigenous law and diplomatic protocol. John Borrows presents evidence that Aboriginal peoples, some fifty-four years after the Treaty of Niagara was negotiated and ratified, still remembered the promises that were made by the Crown. In 1818, a Crown representative, Captain Thomas G. Anderson, gave the following account of a meeting between Anishinaabe peoples and the Crown at Drummond Island in Lake Huron.

> The Chiefs did decamp, laying down a broad Wampum Belt, made in 1764.... Orcata [an Anishinaabe] speaker ... holding the Belt of 1764 in his hand ... said: Father, this my ancestors received from our Father, Sir. W. Johnson. You sent word to all your red children to assemble at the crooked place (Niagara). They heard your voice—obeyed the message—and the next summer met you at the place. You then laid this belt on a mat, and said—'Children, you must all touch this Belt of Peace. I touch it myself, that we may all be brethren united, and hope our friendship will never cease. I will call you my children; will send warmth (presents) to your country; and your families shall never be in want. Look towards the rising sun. My Nation is as brilliant as it is, and its word cannot be violated.' Father, your words were true—all you promised came to pass. On giving us a Belt of Peace, you said—'If you should ever require my assistance, send this Belt, and my hand will be immediately stretched forth to assist you.' Here the speaker laid down the Belt.[37]

Over the years, Indigenous leaders involved in Treaty negotiations not only used wampum belts to recount the Treaty of Niagara, but also presented original copies of the Royal Proclamation to government officials. In 1847, a colonial official reported,

> The subsequent proclamation of His Majesty George Third, issued in 1763, furnished them with a fresh guarantee for the possession of their hunting grounds and the protection of the crown. This document the Indians look upon as their charter. They have preserved a copy of it to the present time, and have referred to it on several occasions in the representations to government.[38]

On October 7, 2013, Canada marked the 250th anniversary of the Royal Proclamation of 1763. The governor general of Canada, His Excellency the Right Honourable David Johnston, spoke about the proclamation's importance.

> This extraordinary document is part of the legal foundation of Canada. It is enshrined in the Constitution Act of 1982, and it sets out a framework of values or principles that have given us a navigational map over the course of the past two-and-a-half centuries.... Its guiding principles—of peace, fairness and respect—established the tradition of treaty-making, laid the basis for the recognition of First Nations rights, and defined the relationship between First Nations peoples and the Crown.... All history reverberates through the ages, but the Royal Proclamation is uniquely alive in the present-day. Not only is it a living constitutional document, its principles are of great relevance to our situation today, in 2013, and to our shared future.... Without a doubt, we have faced, and are facing challenges, and we have much hard work to do on the road to reconciliation, but it is a road we must travel together. In modern time, the successful conclusion of comprehensive land claims agreements are an example of the principles of the Royal Proclamation in action.[39]

Across the country, Indigenous peoples also commemorated the anniversary, calling on Canadians to honour the spirit and intent of the Royal Proclamation. In British Columbia, where very few Treaties were signed, the First Nations Summit leaders issued a statement reminding Canadians that the principles set out in the proclamation were still relevant in present-day Canada. They said,

> With Confederation, the First Nations–Crown relationship has regrettably been guided by federal control under the constraints of the *Indian Act*, not by the principles articulated in the Proclamation.... The time has arrived for all Canadians to move into an era of recognition and reconciliation between First Nations and the Crown. Although there is general recognition of Aboriginal title and rights, far too often these rights exist without an effective remedy. There are many solutions that have the potential of moving us to where we need to be. Such solutions include the negotiation of modern-day treaties, agreements and other constructive arrangements, consistent with the principles of the Proclamation.[40]

Across the river from the parliament buildings in Ottawa that October, Idle No More supporters gathered in Gatineau, Québec, at the Canadian Museum of Civilization, to commemorate the Royal Proclamation as part of a national and international day of action. One of the organizers, Clayton Thomas-Muller, said, "We are using this founding document of this country and its anniversary to usher in a new era of reconciliation of Canada's shameful colonial history, to turn around centuries of neglect and abuse of our sacred and diverse nations."[41]

In Toronto, the focus was on the Gus-Wen-Tah, or Two-Row Wampum Treaty belt, used by the Mohawk in Treaty negotiations with colonial European officials.[42] As Aboriginal and non-Aboriginal people gathered to mark the historic day, speaker Davyn Calfchild said, "Everyone needs to learn about the Two-Row and the nation-to-nation relationships it represents. It's not just for Native people; it's for non-Native people too." The gathering ended with a march as people carried a replica of the Two-Row Wampum through the streets of the city.[43] Those who commemorated the Royal Proclamation and the Two-Row Wampum emphasized that the principles and practices that cemented the Treaty relationship remain applicable today.

The Royal Proclamation of 1763, in conjunction with the Treaty of Niagara of 1764, established the legal and political foundation of Canada and the principles of Treaty making based on mutual recognition and respect. A Royal Proclamation is also an important symbol. Issued at the highest level, it sends a message to all citizens about the values and principles that define the country. There is a need for a new proclamation that reaffirms the long-standing, but often disregarded, commitments between Canada and Aboriginal peoples. The proclamation would include an official disavowal of the Doctrine of Discovery and commitment to the full implementation of the *United Nations Declaration.*

Call to Action

45) We call upon the Government of Canada, on behalf of all Canadians, to jointly develop with Aboriginal peoples a Royal Proclamation of Reconciliation to be issued by the Crown. The proclamation would build on the Royal Proclamation of 1763 and the Treaty of Niagara of 1764, and reaffirm the nation-to-nation relationship between Aboriginal peoples and the Crown. The proclamation would include, but not be limited to, the following commitments:

   i. Repudiate concepts used to justify European sovereignty over Indigenous lands and peoples such as the Doctrine of Discovery and *terra nullius.*

   ii. Adopt and implement the *United Nations Declaration on the Rights of Indigenous Peoples* as the framework for reconciliation.

   iii. Renew or establish Treaty relationships based on principles of mutual recognition, mutual respect, and shared responsibility for maintaining those relationships into the future.

   iv. Reconcile Aboriginal and Crown constitutional and legal orders to ensure that Aboriginal peoples are full partners in Confederation, including the recognition and integration of Indigenous laws and legal traditions in negotiation and implementation processes involving Treaties, land claims, and other constructive agreements.

The principles enunciated in the new Royal Proclamation will serve as the foundation for an action-oriented Covenant of Reconciliation, which points the way forward toward an era of mutual respect and equal opportunity.

Calls to Action

46) We call upon the parties to the Indian Residential Schools Settlement Agreement to develop and sign a Covenant of Reconciliation that would identify principles for working collaboratively to advance reconciliation in Canadian society, and that would include, but not be limited to:

   i. Reaffirmation of the parties' commitment to reconciliation.

   ii. Repudiation of concepts used to justify European sovereignty over Indigenous lands and peoples, such as the Doctrine of Discovery and *terra nullius*, and the reformation of laws, governance structures, and policies within their respective institutions that continue to rely on such concepts.

   iii. Full adoption and implementation of the *United Nations Declaration on the Rights of Indigenous Peoples* as the framework for reconciliation.

   iv. Support for the renewal or establishment of Treaty relationships based on principles of mutual recognition, mutual respect, and shared responsibility for maintaining those relationships into the future.

   v. Enabling those excluded from the Settlement Agreement to sign onto the Covenant of Reconciliation.

   vi. Enabling additional parties to sign onto the Covenant of Reconciliation.

Governments at all levels of Canadian society must also commit to a new framework for reconciliation to guide their relations with Aboriginal peoples.

Call to Action

47) We call upon federal, provincial, territorial, and municipal governments to repudiate concepts used to justify European sovereignty over Indigenous peoples and lands, such as the Doctrine of Discovery and *terra nullius*, and to reform those laws, government policies, and litigation strategies that continue to rely on such concepts.

Churches and faith groups also have an important role to play in fostering reconciliation through support for the *United Nations Declaration* and repudiation of the Doctrine of Discovery.

Calls to Action:

48) We call upon the church parties to the Settlement Agreement, and all other faith groups and interfaith social justice groups in Canada who have not already done so, to formally adopt and comply with the principles, norms, and standards of the *United Nations Declaration on the Rights of Indigenous Peoples* as a framework for reconciliation. This would include, but not be limited to, the following commitments:

   i. Ensuring that their institutions, policies, programs, and practices comply with the *United Nations Declaration on the Rights of Indigenous Peoples.*

   ii. Respecting Indigenous peoples' right to self-determination in spiritual matters, including the right to practise, develop, and teach their own spiritual and religious traditions, customs, and ceremonies, consistent with Article 12:1 of the *United Nations Declaration on the Rights of Indigenous Peoples.*

   iii. Engaging in ongoing public dialogue and actions to support the *United Nations Declaration on the Rights of Indigenous Peoples.*

   iv. Issuing a statement no later than March 31, 2016, from all religious denominations and faith groups, as to how they will implement the *United Nations Declaration on the Rights of Indigenous Peoples.*

49) We call upon all religious denominations and faith groups who have not already done so to repudiate concepts used to justify European sovereignty over Indigenous lands and peoples, such as the Doctrine of Discovery and *terra nullius.*

Revitalizing Indigenous law: Truth, reconciliation, and access to justice

Until recently, Canadian law was used by Canada to suppress truth and deter reconciliation. Parliament's creation of assimilative laws and regulations facilitated the oppression of Aboriginal cultures and enabled the residential school system. In addition, Canada's laws and associated legal principles fostered an atmosphere of secrecy and concealment. When children were abused in residential schools, the law, and the ways in which it was enforced (or not), became a shield behind which churches, governments, and individuals could hide to avoid the consequences of horrific truths. Decisions not to charge or prosecute abusers allowed people to escape the harmful consequences of their actions. In addition, the right of Aboriginal communities and leaders to function in accordance with their own customs, traditions, laws, and cultures was taken away by law. Those who continued to act in accordance with those cultures could be, and were, prosecuted. Aboriginal people came to see law as a tool of government oppression.

To this point, the country's civil laws continued to overlook the truth that the extinguishment of peoples' languages and cultures is a personal and social injury of the deepest kind. It is difficult to understand why the forced assimilation of children through removal from their families and communities—to be placed with people of another race for the purpose of destroying the race and culture from which the children come—can be deemed an act of genocide under Article 2(e) of the UN's Convention on Genocide, but is not a civil wrong.

Failure to recognize such truths hinders reconciliation. Many Aboriginal people have a deep and abiding distrust of Canada's political and legal systems because of the damage they have caused. They often see Canada's legal system as being an arm of a Canadian governing structure that has been diametrically opposed to their interests. Not only has Canadian law generally not protected Aboriginal land rights, resources, and governmental authority, despite court judgments, but it has also allowed, and continues to allow, the removal of Aboriginal children through a child-welfare system that cuts them off from their culture. As a result, law has been, and continues to be, a significant obstacle to reconciliation. This is the case despite the recognition that courts have begun to show that justice has historically been denied and that such denial should not continue. Given these circumstances, it should come as no surprise that formal Canadian law and Canada's legal institutions are still viewed with suspicion within many Aboriginal communities.

Yet, that is changing. Court decisions since the repatriation of Canada's Constitution in 1982 have given hope to Aboriginal people that the recognition and affirmation of their existing Treaty and Aboriginal rights in Section 35 of the *Constitution Act, 1982* may be an important vehicle for change. However, the view of many Aboriginal people is that the utilization of the Government of Canada's court is fraught with danger. Aboriginal leaders and communities turn to Canada's courts literally because there is no other legal mechanism. When they do so, it is with the knowledge that the courts still are reluctant to recognize their own traditional means of dispute resolution and law.

Reconciliation will be difficult to achieve until Indigenous peoples' own traditions for uncovering truth and enhancing reconciliation are embraced as an essential part of the ongoing process of truth determination, dispute resolution, and reconciliation. No dialogue about reconciliation can be undertaken without mutual respect as shown through protocols and ceremony. Just as the mace, for example, is essential to a session of Parliament, the presence of the pipe for some Tribes would be necessary to a formal process of reconciliation.

The road to reconciliation also includes a large, liberal, and generous application of the concepts underlying Section 35(1) of Canada's Constitution, so that Aboriginal rights are implemented in a way that facilitates Aboriginal peoples' collective and individual aspirations. The reconciliation vision that lies behind Section 35 should not be seen as a means to subjugate Aboriginal peoples to an absolutely sovereign Crown, but as a means to establish the kind of relationship that should have flourished since Confederation, as was envisioned in the Royal Proclamation of 1763 and the post-Confederation Treaties. That relationship did not flourish because of Canada's failure to live up to that vision and its promises. So long as the vision of reconciliation in Section 35(1) is not being implemented with sufficient strength and vigour, Canadian law will continue to be regarded as deeply adverse to realizing truth and reconciliation for many First Nations, Inuit, and Métis people. To improve Aboriginal peoples' access to justice, changes must occur on at least two fronts: nationally, and within each Aboriginal community.

The *United Nations Declaration on the Rights of Indigenous Peoples* and the UN "Outcome Document" provide a framework and a mechanism to support and improve access to justice for Indigenous peoples in Canada. Under Article 40 of the *Declaration*,

> Indigenous peoples have the right to access to and prompt decision through just and fair procedures for the resolution of conflicts and disputes with States or other parties, as well as to effective remedies for all infringements of their individual and collective rights. Such a decision shall give due consideration to the customs, traditions, rules and legal systems of the indigenous peoples concerned and international human rights.[44]

In 2013, the UN Expert Mechanism on the Rights of Indigenous Peoples issued a study, "Access to Justice in the Promotion and Protection of the Rights of Indigenous Peoples." It made several key findings that are relevant to Canada. The international study noted that states and Indigenous peoples themselves have a critical role to play in implementing Indigenous peoples' access to justice. Substantive changes are required within the criminal legal system and in relation to Indigenous peoples' rights to their lands, territories, and natural resources; political self-determination; and community well-being.[45] The study made several key findings and recommendations, including the following:

> The right to self-determination is a central right for indigenous peoples from which all other rights flow. In relation to access to justice, self-determination affirms their right to maintain and strengthen indigenous legal institutions, and to apply their own customs and laws.
>
> The cultural rights of indigenous peoples include recognition and practice of their justice systems ... as well as recognition of their traditional customs, values and languages by courts and legal procedures.
>
> Consistent with indigenous peoples' right to self-determination and self-government, States should recognize and provide support for indigenous peoples' own justice systems and should consult with indigenous peoples on the best means for dialogue and cooperation between indigenous and State systems.
>
> States should recognize indigenous peoples' rights to their lands, territories and resources in laws and should harmonize laws in accordance with indigenous peoples' customs on possession and use of lands. Where indigenous peoples have won land rights and other cases in courts, States must implement these decisions. The private sector and government must not collude to deprive indigenous peoples of access to justice.
>
> Indigenous peoples should strengthen advocacy for the recognition of their justice systems.
>
> Indigenous peoples' justice systems should ensure that indigenous women and children are free from all forms of discrimination and should ensure accessibility to indigenous persons with disabilities.
>
> Indigenous peoples should explore the organization and running of their own truth-seeking processes.[46]

These conclusions are consistent with this Commission's own views. We also concur with the 2014 report issued by S. James Anaya, the United Nations Special Rapporteur on the Rights of Indigenous Peoples, about the state of Canada's relationship with Indigenous peoples. He concluded that the

> Government of Canada has a stated goal of reconciliation, which the Special Rapporteur heard repeated by numerous government representatives with whom he met. Yet even in this context, in recent years, indigenous leaders have expressed concern that progress towards this goal has been undermined by actions of the Government that limit or ignore the input of indigenous governments and representatives in various decisions that concern them.... [D]

> espite positive steps, daunting challenges remain. Canada faces a continuing crisis when it comes to the situation of indigenous peoples of the country. The well-being gap between aboriginal and non-aboriginal people in Canada has not narrowed over the last several years, treaty and aboriginal claims remain persistently unresolved, indigenous women and girls remain vulnerable to abuse, and overall there appear to be high levels of distrust among indigenous peoples towards government at both the federal and provincial levels.[47]

In Canada, law must cease to be a tool for the dispossession and dismantling of Aboriginal societies. It must dramatically change if it is going to have any legitimacy within First Nations, Inuit, and Métis communities. Until Canadian law becomes an instrument supporting Aboriginal peoples' empowerment, many Aboriginal people will continue to regard it as a morally and politically malignant force. A commitment to truth and reconciliation demands that Canada's legal system be transformed. It must ensure that Aboriginal peoples have greater ownership of, participation in, and access to its central driving forces. Canada's Constitution must become truly a constitution for all of Canada.[48] Aboriginal peoples need to become the law's architects and interpreters where it applies to their collective rights and interests. Aboriginal peoples need to have more formal influence on national legal matters to advance and realize their diverse goals.

At the same time, First Nations, Inuit, and Métis peoples need greater control of their own regulatory laws and dispute-resolution mechanisms. Aboriginal peoples must be recognized as possessing the responsibility, authority, and capability to address their disagreements by making laws within their communities. This is necessary to facilitating truth and reconciliation within Aboriginal societies.

Law is necessary to protect communities and individuals from the harmful actions of others. When such harm occurs within Aboriginal communities, Indigenous law is needed to censure and correct citizens when they depart from what the community defines as being acceptable. Any failure to recognize First Nations, Inuit, and Métis law would be a failure to affirm that Aboriginal peoples, like all other peoples, need the power of law to effectively deal with the challenges they face.

The Commission believes that the revitalization and application of Indigenous law will benefit First Nations, Inuit, and Métis communities, Aboriginal–Crown relations, and the nation as a whole. For this to happen, Aboriginal peoples must be able to recover, learn, and practise their own, distinct, legal traditions. That is not to say that the development of self-government institutions and laws must occur at the band or village level. In its report, the Royal Commission on Aboriginal Peoples spoke about the development of self-government by Aboriginal nations:

> We have concluded that the right of self-government cannot reasonably be exercised by small, separate communities, whether First Nations, Inuit or Métis.

> It should be exercised by groups of a certain size—groups with a claim to the term 'nation'.
>
> The problem is that the historical Aboriginal nations were undermined by disease, relocations and the full array of assimilationist government policies. They were fragmented into bands, reserves and small settlements. Only some operate as collectivities now. They will have to reconstruct themselves as nations.[49]

We endorse the approach recommended by the Royal Commission.

Indigenous law, like so many other aspects of Aboriginal peoples' lives, has been impacted by colonization. At the TRC's Knowledge Keepers Forum in 2014, Mi'kmaq Elder Stephen Augustine spoke about the Mi'kmaq concept for "making things right." He shared a metaphor about an overturned canoe in the river. He said, "We'll make the canoe right and ... keep it in water so it does not bump on rocks or hit the shore.... [When we tip a canoe] we may lose some of our possessions.... Eventually we will regain our possessions [but] they will not be the same as the old ones."[50]

When we consider this concept in relation to residential schools, we have repeatedly heard that they caused great and obvious loss. The Mi'kmaq idea for "making things right" implies that sometimes, in certain contexts, things can be made right—but the remedy might not allow us to recapture what was lost. Making things right might involve creating something new as we journey forward. Just as the Canadian legal system has evolved over time, Indigenous law is not frozen in time. Indigenous legal orders adapt with changing circumstances. The development and application of Indigenous law should be regarded as one element of a broader holistic strategy to deal with the residential schools' negative effects.

There are diverse sources of Indigenous law that hold great insight for pursuing reconciliation. In 2012, the TRC partnered with the University of Victoria Faculty of Law's Indigenous Law Clinic, and the Indigenous Bar Association, to develop a national research initiative, the "Accessing Justice and Reconciliation (AJR) Project." Working with seven community partners, the AJR project examined six different legal traditions across the country: Coast Salish (Snuneymuxw First Nation, Tsleil-Waututh Nation); Tsilhqot'in (Tsilhqot'in National Government); Northern Secwepemc (T'exelc Williams Lake Indian Band); Cree (Aseniwuche Winewak Nation); Chippewas of Nawash Unceded First Nation # 27); and Mi'kmaq (Mi'kmaq Legal Services Network, Eskasoni).

The AJR report concluded that many more Aboriginal communities across the country would benefit from recovering and revitalizing their laws. Doing so would enable First Nations, Inuit, and Métis communities to remedy community harms and resolve internal conflicts as well as external conflicts with governments more effectively. Professor Val Napoleon, the project's academic lead, and Hadley Friedland, the project coordinator, said,

> We believe there is much hope that even the process of intentionally and seriously continuing ... [this work] will contribute to a truly robust reconciliation in Canada.... This work is vital for the future health and strength of Indigenous societies and has much to offer Canada as a whole.... Legal traditions are not only prescriptive, they are descriptive. They ascribe meaning to human events, challenges and aspirations. They are intellectual resources that we use to frame and interpret information, to reason through and act upon current problems and projects, to work toward our greatest societal aspirations. Finding ways to support Indigenous communities to access, understand and apply their own legal principles today is not just about repairing the immense damages from colonialism. As Chief Doug S. White III (Kwulasultun) puts it ... "Indigenous law is the great project of Canada and it is the essential work of our time. It is not for the faint of heart, it is hard work. We need to create meaningful opportunities for Indigenous and non-Indigenous people to critically engage in this work because all our futures depend on it."[51]

Call to Action:

50) In keeping with the *United Nations Declaration on the Rights of Indigenous Peoples,* we call upon the federal government, in collaboration with Aboriginal organizations, to fund the establishment of Indigenous law institutes for the development, use, and understanding of Indigenous laws and access to justice in accordance with the unique cultures of Aboriginal peoples in Canada.

Reconciliation and accountability

Victims of violence; holders of rights

Survivors are more than just victims of violence. They are also holders of Treaty, constitutional, and human rights.[52] They are women and men who have resilience, courage, and vision. Many have become Elders, community leaders, educators, lawyers, and political activists who are dedicated to revitalizing their cultures, languages, Treaties, laws, and governance systems. Through lived experience, they have gained deep insights into what victims of violence require to heal. Equally important, they have provided wise counsel to political leaders, legislators, policymakers, and all citizens about how to prevent such violence from happening again.

The Commission agrees with Anishinaabe scholar and activist Leanne Simpson, who has urged Canadians not to think about reconciliation in narrow terms or to view Survivors only as victims. She said:

> If reconciliation is focused only on residential schools rather than the broader set of relationships that generated policies, legislation, and practices aimed at assimilation and political genocide, then there is a risk that reconciliation will "level the playing field" in the eyes of Canadians.... I also worry that institutionalization of a narrowly defined "reconciliation" subjugates treaty and nation-based participation by locking our Elders—the ones that suffered the most directly at the hands of the residential school system—into a position of victimhood. Of course, they are anything but victims. They are our strongest visionaries and they inspire us to vision alternative futures.[53]

Speaking at the British Columbia National Event, Honorary Witness and former lieutenant governor of British Columbia, the Honourable Steven Point, said:

> We got here to this place, to this time, because Aboriginal Survivors brought this [residential schools] to the Supreme Court of Canada. The churches and the governments didn't come one day and say, "Hey, you know, we did something wrong and we're sorry. Can you forgive us?" Elders had to bring this matter to the Supreme Court of Canada. It's very like the situation we have with Aboriginal rights, where nation after nation continues to seek the recognition of their Aboriginal title to their own homelands.[54]

The Commission believes that Survivors, who took action to bring the history and legacy of the residential schools to light, who went to court to confront their abusers, and who ratified the Settlement Agreement, have made a significant contribution to reconciliation. The Truth and Reconciliation Commission of Canada was not established because of any widespread public outcry, demanding justice for residential school Survivors.[55] Neither did the Settlement Agreement, including the TRC, come about only because government and church defendants, faced with huge class-action lawsuits, decided it was preferable to litigation. Focusing only on the motivations of the defendants does not tell the whole story. It is important not to lose sight of the many ways in which Aboriginal peoples have succeeded in pushing the boundaries of reconciliation in Canada.

From the early 1990s onward, Aboriginal people and their supporters had been calling for a public inquiry into the residential school system. The Royal Commission on Aboriginal Peoples made this same recommendation in 1996. A majority of Survivors ratified the Settlement Agreement, in part because they were dissatisfied with the litigation process. Survivors wanted a public forum such as a truth and reconciliation commission so that Canada could hear their unvarnished truths about the residential schools. Survivors also wanted a formal apology from Canada that acknowledged the country's wrongdoing.[56] Due in large part to their efforts, the prime minister delivered a national apology to Survivors on behalf of the government and non-Aboriginal Canadians.

Although societal empathy for Aboriginal victims of abuse in residential schools is important, this alone will not prevent similar acts of violence from recurring in new institutional forms. There is a need for a clear and public recognition that Aboriginal peoples must be seen and treated as much more than just the beneficiaries of public good will. As holders of Treaty, constitutional, and human rights, they are entitled to justice and accountability from Canada to ensure that their rights are not violated.

In his initial report, tabled in August of 2012, Pablo de Greiff, the first UN Special Rapporteur on the Promotion of Truth, Justice, Reparation and Guarantees of Non-Recurrence, pointed out that in countries where prosecuting individual perpetrators of criminal acts involving human rights violations has been difficult, other measures such as truth-seeking forums, reparations, and institutional reforms are especially critical. Such measures enable victims of state violence to develop some confidence in the legitimacy and credibility of the state's justice system. But de Greiff cautions that implementing these measures alone does not guarantee that reconciliation will follow. Apologies, commemoration, public memorials, and educational reform are also required in order to transform social attitudes and foster long-term reconciliation.[57]

The Treaty, constitutional, and human rights violations that occurred in and around the residential school system confirm the dangers that exist for Aboriginal peoples when their right to self-determination is ignored or limited by the state, which purports to act "in their best interests." Historically, whenever Aboriginal peoples have been targeted as a specific group that is deemed by government to be in need of protective legislation and policies, the results have been culturally and ethnically destructive.

For Aboriginal peoples in Canada, the protection and exercise of their right to self-determination is the strongest antidote to further violation of their rights. In the coming years, governments must remain accountable for ensuring that Aboriginal peoples' rights are protected and that government actions do, in fact, repair trust and foster reconciliation. Repairing trust begins with an apology, but it involves far more than that.

Moving from apology to action

From the outset, this Commission has emphasized that reconciliation is not a one-time event; it is a multi-generational journey that involves all Canadians. The public apologies and compensation to residential school Survivors, their families, and communities by Canada and the churches that ran the residential schools marked the beginning, not the end, of this journey. Survivors needed to hear government and church officials admit that the cultural, spiritual, emotional, physical, and sexual abuse that they suffered in the schools was wrong and should never have happened, but they needed more.

The children and grandchildren of Survivors needed to hear the truth about what happened to their parents and grandparents in the residential schools. At the Commission's public events, many Survivors spoke in the presence of their children and grandchildren for the first time about the abuses they had suffered as children, and about the destructive ways of behaving they had learned at residential school. Many offered their own heartfelt apologies to their families for having been abusive, or unable to parent, or simply to say "I love you."

Apologies are important to victims of violence and abuse. Apologies have the potential to restore human dignity and empower victims to decide whether they accept an apology or forgive a perpetrator. Where there has been no apology, or one that victims believe tries to justify the behaviour of perpetrators and evade responsibility, reconciliation is difficult, if not impossible, to achieve. The official apologies from Canada and the churches sent an important message to all Canadians that Aboriginal peoples had suffered grievous harms at the hands of the state and church institutions in the schools, and that, as the parties responsible for those harms, the state and the churches accepted their measure of responsibility. The apologies were a necessary first step in the process of reconciliation.

The history and destructive legacy of residential schools is a sober reminder that taking action does not necessarily lead to positive results. Attempts to assimilate First Nations, Inuit, and Métis peoples into mainstream Canadian society were a dismal failure. Despite the devastating impacts of colonization, Indigenous peoples have always resisted (though in some places not always successfully) attacks on their cultures, languages, and ways of life.

If Canadians are to keep the promise of the apologies made on their behalf—the promise of "never again!"—then we must guard against simply replicating the assimilation policies of the past in new forms today. As TRC Honorary Witness Wab Kinew said, "The truth about reconciliation is this: It is not a second chance at assimilation. It should not be a kinder, gentler evangelism, free from the horrors of the residential school era. Rather, true reconciliation is a second chance at building a mutually respectful relationship."[58]

The words of the apologies will ring hollow if Canada's actions fail to produce the necessary social, cultural, political, and economic change that benefits Aboriginal peoples and all Canadians.

A just reconciliation requires more than simply talking about the need to heal the deep wounds of history. Words of apology alone are insufficient; concrete actions on both symbolic and material fronts are required. Reparations for historical injustices must include not only apology, financial redress, legal reform, and policy change, but also the rewriting of national history and public commemoration.

In every region of the country, Survivors and others have sent a strong message, as received by this Commission: for reconciliation to thrive in the coming years, Canada must move from apology to action.

Canada's apology

June 11, 2008, was an important day for the Aboriginal peoples of Canada, and for the country as a whole. It has come to be known as the "Day of the Apology," the day when Prime Minister Stephen Harper, and the leaders of all other federal political parties, formally apologized in the House of Commons for the harms caused by the residential school system. In their presentations to the TRC, many Survivors clearly recalled the day of the apology. They recalled where they were, who they were with, and, most importantly, how they felt. Many spoke of the intense emotions they had when they heard the prime minister acknowledge that it had been wrong for the government to have taken them away from their families for the purpose of "killing the Indian" in them. They talked of the tears that fell when they heard the words "We are sorry."

Survivors and their families needed to hear those words. They had lived with pain, fear, and anger for most of their lives, resulting from the abrupt separation from their families and their experiences at residential schools, and they wanted desperately to begin their healing. They needed to have validated their sense that what had been done to them was wrong. They wanted to believe that things would begin to change—not the schools, which had long been closed, but the attitude and behaviours that lay behind the existence of the schools. They wanted to believe that the government that had so long controlled their lives and abused its relationship with them now "saw the light." They wanted to believe that the future for their children and their grandchildren would be different from their own experiences; that their lives would be better. The apology gave them cause to think that their patience and perseverance through the trauma and negativity of their experiences in and beyond the residential schools had been worth the struggle. It gave them hope.

At the TRC's Saskatchewan National Event, National Chief of the Assembly of First Nations Shawn A-in-chut Atleo said,

> I think as was heard here, what I'm so grateful for is that there's a growing experience ... about the work of reconciliation.... How do communities reconcile? Well, it begins with each and every one of us. How fortunate I am as a young man to have spent time with my late grandmother. I held her hand. She was eighty-seven years old, still here. During that apology, she said, "Grandson, they're just starting to see us, they're just beginning to see us." That's what she said. And she found that encouraging, because it's the first step, actually seeing

> one another, having the silence broken and the stories starting to be told.... I think that's where it begins, isn't it? Between us as individuals sharing the stories from so many different perspectives so that we can understand.[59]

The report of the Royal Commission on Aboriginal Peoples noted that for some time after settler contact, the relationship between Aboriginal and non-Aboriginal peoples had been one of mutual support, co-operation, and respect. Despite incidents of conflict, Aboriginal peoples' acceptance of the arrival of Europeans, and their willingness to participate with the newcomers in their economic pursuits, to form alliances with them in their wars, and to enter into Treaty with them for a variety of purposes, showed a wish to coexist in a relationship of mutual trust and respect.[60] That aspect of the relationship was confirmed on the non-Aboriginal side by evidence such as the Royal Proclamation of 1763 and the Treaty of Niagara of 1764, as discussed earlier.

The trust and respect initially established ultimately were betrayed. Since Confederation in 1867, the approach of successive Canadian federal governments to the Crown's fiduciary obligation to provide education for Aboriginal peoples has been deeply flawed. Equally important, the consequences of this broken trust have serious implications well beyond residential schools. The trust relationship and Canada's particular obligation to uphold the honour of the Crown with regard to Aboriginal peoples goes to the very heart of the relationship itself.

As the original peoples who had occupied the lands and territories for thousands of years throughout the region that became Canada, Aboriginal peoples have unique legal and constitutional rights. These rights arose from their initial occupation and ownership of the land, and were affirmed in the Royal Proclamation of 1763, which also decreed that the Crown had a special duty to deal fairly with, and protect, Aboriginal peoples and their lands. Subsequently, the Dominion of Canada assumed this fiduciary obligation under Section 91(24) of the *Constitution Act, 1867*, which gave Parliament legislative authority over "Indians, and lands reserved for Indians." Section 35 of the *Constitution Act, 1982* also recognized and affirmed existing Aboriginal and Treaty rights.

In several key decisions, Canadian courts have said that the federal government must always uphold the honour of the Crown in its dealings with Aboriginal peoples. In *R. v. Sparrow* (1990), the Supreme Court ruled that "the Government has the responsibility to act in a fiduciary capacity with respect to aboriginal peoples. The relationship between the Government and aboriginals is trust-like, rather than adversarial ... the honour of the Crown is at stake in dealings with aboriginal peoples." In *Haida Nation v. British Columbia (Minister of Forests)* (2004), the Supreme Court ruled that "in all its dealings with Aboriginal peoples, from the assertion of sovereignty to the resolution of claims and the implementation of treaties, the Crown must act honourably," and that "the honour of the Crown ... is not a mere incantation, but rather a core precept that finds its application in concrete practices." In other words, the honour of the Crown is not merely an abstract principle, but one that must be applied with diligence.[61]

In *Manitoba Métis Nation Inc. v. Canada (Attorney General)* (2013), the Métis Nation argued that when the Métis peoples negotiated an agreement with the federal government that would enable Manitoba to enter Confederation, "they trusted Canada to act in their best interests ... [and] to treat them fairly."[62] The Supreme Court said that in 1870, the

> broad purpose of S. 31 of the *Manitoba Act* was to reconcile the Métis community with the sovereignty of the Crown and to permit the creation of the province of Manitoba. This reconciliation was to be accomplished by a more concrete measure—the prompt and equitable transfer of the allotted public lands to the Métis children. [para. 98]

Ruling in favour of the Manitoba Métis Nation, the court observed that their "submissions went beyond the argument that the honour of the Crown gave rise to a fiduciary duty, raising the broader issue of whether the government's conduct generally comported with the honour of the Crown" (para. 87). The court found that although Section 31 promised that land grants to Métis peoples would be implemented "in the most effectual and equitable manner," this did not happen. "Instead, the implementation was ineffectual and inequitable. This was not a matter of occasional negligence, but of repeated mistakes and inaction that persisted for more than a decade. A government sincerely intent on fulfilling the duty that its honour demanded could and should have done better" (para. 128).

For Treaty peoples or First Nations, the unilateral imposition of the *Indian Act,* including the residential school system, represents a fundamental breach of the Crown's Treaty obligations and fiduciary duty to deal with them honourably in both principle and practice.

The Crown's position as a fiduciary with regard to Aboriginal peoples is clearly a complicated and potentially conflicting area of legal obligation. As a fiduciary, the Crown, through the Government of Canada, has a legal obligation to act in the best interests of Aboriginal people to whom it owes a fiduciary obligation. This is the same case for the Bureau of Indian Affairs in the United States, which is commonly referred to as a "Trustee." As a trustee, the Bureau of Indian Affairs has a similar obligation to act in the best interests of Native Americans, and to ensure that other government departments do not act in a manner that contravenes tribal rights and interests or the government's lawful obligations. In the United States, the Solicitor's Opinions issued from time to time by the Department of the Interior, which has authority over the Bureau of Indian Affairs, are used to give direction to government generally as well as to explain and justify government action. In Canada, it must be recognized that the federal Department of Justice has two important, and potentially conflicting, roles when it comes to Aboriginal peoples:

1) The Department of Justice Canada provides legal opinions to the Department of Aboriginal Affairs and Northern Development Canada (AANDC) to guide the department in its policy development, legislative initiatives, and actions. Those opinions, and the actions based on them, invariably affect Aboriginal governments and the lives of Aboriginal people significantly. Often, those opinions are about the scope and extent of Aboriginal and Treaty rights, and often they form the basis upon which federal Aboriginal policy is developed and enacted.
2) Justice Canada also acts as the legal advocate for AANDC and the government in legal disputes between the government and Aboriginal people. In that capacity, it takes instruction from senior officials within the Department of Aboriginal Affairs when the department is implicated in legal actions concerning its responsibilities. It gives advice about the conduct of litigation, the legal position to be advanced, the implementation of legal strategy, and the decision whether to appeal a particular court ruling.

Upholding the honour of the Crown, and disputing a legal challenge to an official's or department's action or decision, can sometimes give rise to conflicting legal obligations.

In the Commission's view, those legal opinions should be available, as of right and upon request, to Aboriginal peoples, for whom the Crown is a fiduciary. Canadian governments and their law departments have a responsibility to discontinue acting as though they are in an adversarial relationship with Aboriginal peoples and to start acting as true fiduciaries. Canada's Department of Justice must be more transparent and accountable to Aboriginal peoples; this includes sharing their legal opinions on Aboriginal rights. As noted above, there is precedent for making this change. Not only has the United States Department of the Interior's Office of the Solicitor made public its legal opinions on a range of issues affecting Native Americans, but also these are now widely available online.[63]

Call to Action

51) We call upon the Government of Canada, as an obligation of its fiduciary responsibility, to develop a policy of transparency by publishing legal opinions it develops and upon which it acts or intends to act, in regard to the scope and extent of Aboriginal and Treaty rights.

One of the aspects of the Doctrine of Discovery that continues to assert itself to this day is the fact that court cases involving Aboriginal territorial claims have placed a heavy onus on Aboriginal claimants to prove that they were in occupation of land since first contact and that the rights claimed over the territory continued from then to the present. The Commission believes that there is good reason to question this requirement, particularly in view of the fact that much of the record upon which courts rely is documentary proof or oral testimony from acknowledged Elder experts. History shows that for many years after Confederation, Aboriginal claimants were precluded from accessing legal advice or the courts in order to assert their claims, and that many of their best Elder experts have passed on without having had an opportunity to record their evidence.

The Commission believes that it is manifestly unfair for Aboriginal claimants to be held to the requisite standard of proof throughout legal proceedings. However, it is reasonable to require that an Aboriginal claimant establish occupation of specified territory at the requisite period of time. That could be at the time of contact or at the time of Crown assertion of sovereignty. It is our view that once occupation has been proven, then the onus should shift to the other party to show that the claim no longer exists, either through extinguishment, surrender, or some other valid legal means.[64] Therefore, we conclude that Aboriginal claims of title and rights should be accepted on assertion, with the burden of proof placed on those who object to such claims.

Call to Action

52) We call upon the Government of Canada, provincial and territorial governments, and the courts to adopt the following legal principles:

  i. Aboriginal title claims are accepted once the Aboriginal claimant has established occupation over a particular territory at a particular point in time.

  ii. Once Aboriginal title has been established, the burden of proving any limitation on any rights arising from the existence of that title shifts to the party asserting such a limitation.

The report of the Royal Commission on Aboriginal Peoples emphasized that the restoration of civic trust is essential to reconciliation. It concluded that "the purpose of engaging in a transaction of acknowledgement and forgiveness is not to bind Aboriginal and non-Aboriginal people in a repeating drama of blame and guilt, but jointly to acknowledge the past so that both sides are freed to embrace a shared future with a measure of trust." The report added that "the restoration of trust is essential to the great enterprise of forging peaceful relations."[65] The Truth and Reconciliation Commission of Canada agrees with these findings.

For reconciliation to take root, Canada, as the party to the relationship that has breached that trust, has the primary obligation to do the work needed to regain the trust of Aboriginal peoples. It is our view that at the time of Confederation, and in subsequent Treaty negotiations, Aboriginal peoples placed a great deal of faith in the words of those speaking for the Crown that the new relationship would be a positive one for both of them. That faith was betrayed, however, by the imposition of the *Indian Act*, the development of the residential school system, and a series of other repressive measures.

Survivors have indicated that despite the Settlement Agreement and Canada's apology, trust has not yet been restored. The Truth and Reconciliation Commission's Indian Residential Schools Survivor Committee member Eugene Arcand said,

> I was there at the apology. I thought I was on my way to reconciliation when I heard the prime minister's words, in a way, when his voice trembled.... It would be remiss of me to the Survivors of Saskatchewan and Survivors across this country to not talk about what's happened since the apology. It's been difficult to talk on one side of my mouth about reconciliation and truth, and on the other side of my heart I have very intense feelings about the actions of the federal government, Prime Minister Harper who gave that apology, and the Ministry of Indian Affairs in the administration of this agreement and other acts of government that have been an assault on our people....
>
> [W]e as First Nations, Métis, and Inuit people, especially residential school Survivors, want to reconcile. We really, really want to. But it's difficult when we see and feel and read what's coming out of the House, provincially, federally, in regards to our well-being. First, with the cuts to the Aboriginal Healing Foundation and other cuts that have happened in regards to education, in regards to our livelihood.[66]

A government apology sends a powerful symbolic message to citizens that the state's actions were wrong.[67] As important as Canada's apology was, it did not simply mark a closure of the past. It also created an opening for Canadians to begin a national dialogue about restoring Aboriginal peoples to a just and rightful place within Canada. In their evaluation of where things stood in the years immediately following the apology, Aboriginal leaders identified a post-apology gap between the aspirational language of Canada's apology and Aboriginal peoples' continuing realities. Closing this gap is vital to reconciliation.

Speaking to the Senate on June 11, 2009, the first anniversary of Canada's apology, Assembly of First Nations National Chief Phil Fontaine, who is also a Survivor, said,

> In a post-apology era, the honour of the Crown must be a defining feature in the new relationship where legal obligations are vigilantly observed, where First Nations are diligently consulted and accommodated on all matters affecting our lives, and our right to free, prior and informed consent is respected.... Let it be clear that First Nations care deeply about our human rights—the human rights of the women in our communities, our children, our families and our communities.

> The principles of reconciliation, such as mutual respect, coexistence, fairness, meaningful dialogue, and mutual recognition, are not empty words. These principles are about action; that is, they give shape and expression to the material, political and legal elements of reconciliation. It has been an eventful year in Canadian and global politics, society and the economy since last June. First Nations have been affected by the decisions of the Government of Canada during this time.... Given the level of poverty among First Nations, our economies and communities are at an alarmingly high risk of sinking further into the bleakness and despair of poverty. We, as a society, must not let this happen....
>
> If this partnership between all founding peoples of the federation is to be meaningful, mutual responsibility and accountability must also define the relationship.... Reconciliation then, implies a solemn duty to act, a responsibility to engage, and an obligation to fulfill the promises inherent in an advanced democratic and ethical citizenship. That is, the Government of Canada—in fact, all, all members of Parliament in both houses—has a responsibility ... to bridge the past to a future in which the gap in the quality of life and well-being between Aboriginal and non-Aboriginal people vanishes, where First Nations poverty is eradicated, where our children have the same opportunities and life chances as other children, and the promises of our treaties are fulfilled.
>
> Reconciliation must mean real change for all of our people in all the places we choose to live, change that addresses the wrongs in a way that brings all of us closer together. Human rights, hope, opportunity and human flourishing are not the privilege of one group or one segment of Canadian society; they belong to all of us. Achieving an apology is not an end point.[68]

National reconciliation involves respecting differences and finding common ground to build a better future together. Whether Survivors' hopes on the day of Canada's apology will ultimately be realized rests on our ability to find that common ground.

Therefore, we believe that all levels of government must make a new commitment to reconciliation and accountability. The federal government, First Nations, Inuit, and Métis peoples, and all Canadians will benefit from the establishment of an oversight body that will have a number of objectives, including assisting discussions on reconciliation and making regular reports that evaluate progress on commitments to reconciliation. Progress on reconciliation at all other levels of government and civil society organizations also needs vigilant attention and measurement to determine improvements. In terms of public education, it will be important to ensure all Canadians have the educational resources and practical tools required to advance reconciliation.

Calls to Action

53) We call upon the Parliament of Canada, in consultation and collaboration with Aboriginal peoples, to enact legislation to establish a National Council for Reconciliation. The legislation would establish the council as an independent, national, oversight body with membership jointly appointed by the Government of Canada and national Aboriginal organizations, and consisting of Aboriginal and non-Aboriginal members. Its mandate would include, but not be limited to, the following:

    i. Monitor, evaluate, and report annually to Parliament and the people of Canada on the Government of Canada's post-apology progress on reconciliation to ensure that government accountability for reconciling the relationship between Aboriginal peoples and the Crown is maintained in the coming years.

    ii. Monitor, evaluate, and report to Parliament and the people of Canada on reconciliation progress across all levels and sectors of Canadian society, including the implementation of the Truth and Reconciliation Commission of Canada's Calls to Action.

    iii. Develop and implement a multi-year National Action Plan for Reconciliation, which includes research and policy development, public education programs, and resources.

    iv. Promote public dialogue, public/private partnerships, and public initiatives for reconciliation.

54) We call upon the Government of Canada to provide multi-year funding for the National Council for Reconciliation to ensure that it has the financial, human, and technical resources required to conduct its work, including the endowment of a National Reconciliation Trust to advance the cause of reconciliation.

55) We call upon all levels of government to provide annual reports or any current data requested by the National Council for Reconciliation so that it can report on the progress towards reconciliation. The reports or data would include, but not be limited to:

    i. The number of Aboriginal children—including Métis and Inuit children—in care, compared with non-Aboriginal children, the reasons for apprehension, and the total spending on preventive and care services by child-welfare agencies.

    ii. Comparative funding for the education of First Nations children on and off reserves.

iii. The educational and income attainments of Aboriginal peoples in Canada compared with non-Aboriginal people.

iv. Progress on closing the gaps between Aboriginal and non-Aboriginal communities in a number of health indicators such as: infant mortality, maternal health, suicide, mental health, addictions, life expectancy, birth rates, infant and child health issues, chronic diseases, illness and injury incidence, and the availability of appropriate health services.

v. Progress on eliminating the overrepresentation of Aboriginal children in youth custody over the next decade.

vi. Progress on reducing the rate of criminal victimization of Aboriginal people, including data related to homicide and family violence victimization and other crimes.

vii. Progress on reducing the overrepresentation of Aboriginal people in the justice and correctional systems.

56) We call upon the prime minister of Canada to formally respond to the report of the National Council for Reconciliation by issuing an annual "State of Aboriginal Peoples" report, which would outline the government's plans for advancing the cause of reconciliation.

These new frameworks and commitments will not succeed without more understanding and sensitivity among those who will administer them.

Call to Action:

57) We call upon federal, provincial, territorial, and municipal governments to provide education to public servants on the history of Aboriginal peoples, including the history and legacy of residential schools, the United Nations *Declaration on the Rights of Indigenous Peoples*, Treaties and Aboriginal rights, Indigenous law, and Aboriginal–Crown relations. This will require skills-based training in intercultural competency, conflict resolution, human rights, and anti-racism.

Church apologies

There is an old and well-accepted adage that states, "It takes a village to raise a child." The removal of Aboriginal children from their villages was seen as a necessary step in the achievement of assimilation. However, not only did the Government of Canada take the children from their homes, but it also then proceeded to destroy the cultural and functional integrity of the communities from which the children came and to which they would return.

Christian teachings were a fundamental aspect of residential schools. Aboriginal children were taught to reject the spiritual ways of their parents and ancestors in favour of the religions that predominated among settler societies. As their traditional ways of worshipping the Creator were disparaged and rejected, so too were the children devalued. They were not respected as human beings who were equally loved by the Creator just as they were, as First Nations, Inuit, or Métis peoples. Rather, their Christian teachers saw them as inferior humans in need of being 'raised up' through Christianity, and tried to mould them into models of Christianity according to the racist ideals that prevailed at the time. The impact of such treatment was amplified by federal laws and policies that banned traditional Indigenous spiritual practices in the children's home communities for much of the residential school era.

Spiritual violence occurs when

- a person is not permitted to follow her or his preferred spiritual or religious tradition;
- a different spiritual or religious path or practice is forced on a person;
- a person's spiritual or religious tradition, beliefs, or practices are demeaned or belittled; or
- a person is made to feel shame for practising his or her traditional or family beliefs.

There is plenty of evidence to support our conclusion that spiritual violence was common in residential schools.

The effects of this spiritual violence have been profound and did not end with the schools. At the Alberta National Event, Survivor Theodore (Ted) Fontaine could have spoken for many Survivors when he said, "I went through sexual abuse. I went through physical abuse, mental, spiritual. And I'll tell you ... the one thing that we suffered [from] the most is the mental and spiritual abuse that we carried for the rest of our lives."[69]

At the Saskatchewan National Event, Survivor and Elder Noel Starblanket, National Chief of the National Indian Brotherhood (later the Assembly of First Nations), talked about the intergenerational spiritual impacts of the residential schools. He said, "My great-grandfather ... was the first one to be abused by these churches and by these governments, and they forced his children into an Indian residential school and this began that legacy. They called him a pagan, a heathen ... and that was in the late 1800s. So I've been living with that in my family since then."[70]

That Christians in Canada, in the name of their religion, inflicted serious harms on Aboriginal children, their families, and communities was in fundamental contradiction to what they purported to be their core beliefs. For the churches to avoid repeating their failures of the past, understanding how and why they perverted Christian doctrine to justify their actions is a critical lesson to be learned from the residential school experience.

Between 1986 and 1998, all four Settlement Agreement churches offered apologies or statements of regret, in one form or another, for their attempts to destroy Indigenous cultures, languages, spirituality, and ways of life, and, more specifically, for their involvement in residential schools. The United, Anglican, and Presbyterian churches followed similar pathways: individuals or committees at the national level of each church became aware that there might be a need to apologize, a decision-making process was established at the highest levels of the church, and the apology was subsequently issued through the moderator or primate who spoke for the whole church.

Unlike the three Protestant denominations, the Roman Catholic Church in Canada does not have a single spokesperson with authority to represent all of its many dioceses and distinct religious orders. The issuing of apologies or statements of regret was left up to each of them individually. The result has been a patchwork of apologies or statements of regret that few Survivors or church members may even know exist. Roman Catholics in Canada and across the globe look to the Pope as their spiritual and moral leader. Therefore, it has been disappointing to Survivors and others that the Pope has not yet made a clear and emphatic public apology in Canada for the abuses perpetrated in Catholic-run residential schools throughout the country.

On April 29, 2009, National Chief of the Assembly of First Nations Phil Fontaine, four other Aboriginal leaders, and five leaders from the Roman Catholic community in Canada travelled to Rome for a private audience with Pope Benedict XVI. No recording of the private meeting was permitted, but the Vatican issued a communiqué describing what the Pope had said.

> Given the sufferings that some indigenous children experienced in the Canadian Residential School system, the Holy Father expressed his sorrow at the anguish caused by the deplorable conduct of some members of the Church and he offered his sympathy and prayerful solidarity. His Holiness emphasized that acts of abuse cannot be tolerated in society. He prayed that all those affected would experience healing, and he encouraged First Nations people to continue to move forward with renewed hope.[71]

The media reported that National Chief Fontaine and other Aboriginal leaders who had met with the Pope said that the statement was significant for all Survivors. Fontaine told *CBC News* that although it was not an official apology, he hoped that the Pope's statement of regret would bring closure to the issue for residential school survivors. "The fact that the word 'apology' was not used does not diminish this moment in any way," he said. "This experience gives me great comfort."[72]

The Pope's statement of regret was significant to those who were present, and was reported widely in the media, but it is unclear what, if any, impact it had on Survivors, and their families and communities, who were not able to hear the Pope's words themselves. Many Survivors raised the lack of a clear Catholic apology from the Vatican as evidence that the Catholic Church still has not come to terms with its own wrongdoing in residential schools, and has permitted many Catholic nuns and priests to maintain that the allegations against their colleagues are false. A statement of regret that children were harmed in the schools is a far cry from a full and proper apology that takes responsibility for the harms that occurred.

The Commission notes that in 2010, Pope Benedict XVI responded to the issue of the abuse of children in Ireland differently and more clearly when he issued a pastoral letter, a public statement that was distributed through the churches to all Catholics in Ireland. He acknowledged that the church had failed to address the issue of child abuse in Catholic institutions. He said:

> Only by examining carefully the many elements that gave rise to the present crisis can a clear-sighted diagnosis of its causes be undertaken and effective remedies be found. Certainly, among the contributing factors we can include: inadequate procedures for determining the suitability of candidates for the priesthood and the religious life; insufficient human, moral, intellectual and spiritual formation in seminaries and novitiates; a tendency in society to favour the clergy and other authority figures; and a misplaced concern for the reputation of the Church and the avoidance of scandal, resulting in failure to apply existing canonical penalties and to safeguard the dignity of every person. Urgent action is required to address these factors, which have had such tragic consequences in the lives of victims and their families.[73]

He directly addressed those who were abused as children by church clergy:

> You have suffered grievously and I am truly sorry. I know that nothing can undo the wrong you have endured. Your trust has been betrayed and your dignity has been violated. Many of you found that, when you were courageous enough to speak of what happened to you, no one would listen. Those of you who were abused in residential institutions must have felt that there was no escape for your sufferings. It is understandable that you find it hard to forgive or be reconciled with the Church. In her name, I openly express the shame and remorse that we all feel. At the same time, I ask you not to lose hope.... Speaking to you as a pastor concerned for the good of all God's children, I humbly ask you to consider what I have said ... [and that] you will be able to find reconciliation, deep inner healing and peace.[74]

In Canada, for more than a century, thousands of First Nations, Inuit, and Métis children were subjected to spiritual, emotional, physical, and sexual abuse in Catholic-run residential schools. Other than a small private audience with Pope Benedict XVI in 2009, the Vatican has remained silent on the Roman Catholic Church's involvement in the Canadian residential school system. During the Commission's hearings, many

Survivors told us that they knew that the Pope had apologized to Survivors of Catholic-run schools in Ireland. They wondered why no similar apology had been extended to them. They said: "I did not hear the Pope say to me, 'I am sorry.' Those words are very important to me ... but he didn't say that to the First Nations people."[75]

Call to Action

58) We call upon the Pope to issue an apology to Survivors, their families, and communities for the Roman Catholic Church's role in the spiritual, cultural, emotional, physical, and sexual abuse of First Nations, Inuit, and Métis children in Catholic-run residential schools. We call for that apology to be similar to the 2010 apology issued to Irish victims of abuse and to occur within one year of the issuing of this Report and to be delivered by the Pope in Canada.

Survivors' responses to church apologies

Survivors made many statements to the Commission about Canada's apology, but the same cannot be said for their response to church apologies. It is striking that although Survivors told us a great deal about how churches have affected their lives, and how, as adults, they may or may not practise Christianity, they seldom mentioned the churches' apologies or healing and reconciliation activities. This was the case even though they heard church representatives offer apologies at the TRC's National Events. Their engagement with the churches was often more informal and personal. Survivors who visited the churches' archival displays in the TRC's Learning Places picked up copies of the apologies and talked directly with church representatives. They also had conversations with church representatives in the Churches Listening Areas and in public Sharing Circles.[76]

When the late Alvin Dixon, Chair of the United Church of Canada's Indian Residential School Survivors Committee, spoke to the Commission at the Northern National Event in Inuvik in 2011, he expressed what many other Survivors may have thought about all of the churches' apologies. He said,

> The apologies don't come readily. They don't come easily. And when we heard the apology in 1986, those of us First Nations members of the United Church didn't accept the apology but we agreed to receive it and watch and wait and work with the United Church to put some flesh, to put some substance to that apology. And we all believed that apologies should be words of action, words of sincerity that should mean something.... Our task is to make sure that the United Church lives up to that apology in meaningful ways....

> You know, our work is just beginning and we're going to hold the church's feet to the fire, other churches and Canada to make sure that this whole exercise of healing goes on for as long as it takes for us to recover from the impacts of our experiences in those residential schools.
>
> The other issue that comes up that we are addressing is having our native spiritual practice condemned initially not just by the United Church but all churches ... well, we now have our church supporting Native spiritual gatherings and we're going to host a national Native spiritual gathering in Prince Rupert this summer.... So, we are very much holding the church's feet to the fire and making sure that there are real commitments to putting life to the apologies.[77]

What Alvin Dixon told us is consistent with what the Commission heard from Survivors about Canada's apology. Official apologies made on behalf of institutions or governments may be graciously received but are also understandably viewed with some skepticism. When trust has been so badly broken, it can be restored only over time as Survivors observe how the churches interact with them in daily life. He explained, in practical terms, how Survivors would continue to hold the churches accountable. Apologies mark only a beginning point on pathways of reconciliation; the proof of their authenticity lies in putting words into action. He emphasized how important it was to Survivors that the churches not only admit that condemning Indigenous spirituality was wrong, but also that they go one step further and actively support traditional spiritual gatherings. That action, however, calls for ongoing commitment to educate church congregations into the future on the need for such action.

Call to Action

59) We call upon church parties to the Settlement Agreement to develop ongoing education strategies to ensure that their respective congregations learn about their church's role in colonization, the history and legacy of residential schools, and why apologies to former residential school students, their families, and communities were necessary.

Honouring Indigenous spirituality

Many Survivors told the Commission that reconnecting with traditional Indigenous spiritual teachings and practices has been essential to their healing, with some going so far as to say "it saved my life." One Survivor said, "The Sun Dances and all the other teachings, the healing lodges, sweat lodges ... I know that's what helped me keep my sanity; to keep me from breaking down and being a total basket case. That's what has helped me—the teachings of our Aboriginal culture and language."[78] Losing the connections to their languages and cultures in the residential schools had devastating impacts on Survivors, their families, and communities. Land, language, culture, and identity are inseparable from spirituality; all are necessary elements of a whole way of being, of living on the land as Indigenous peoples. As Survivor and Anishinaabe Elder Fred Kelly has explained,

> To take the territorial lands away from a people whose very spirit is so intrinsically connected to Mother Earth was to actually dispossess them of their very soul and being; it was to destroy whole Indigenous nations. Weakened by disease and separated from their traditional foods and medicines, First Nations peoples had no defence against further government encroachments on their lives. Yet they continued to abide by the terms of the treaties trusting in the honour of the Crown to no avail. They were mortally wounded in mind, body, heart, and spirit that turned them into the walking dead. Recovery would take time, and fortunately they took their sacred traditions underground to be practised in secret until the day of revival that would surely come.... I am happy that my ancestors saw fit to bring their sacred beliefs underground when they were banned and persecuted. Because of them and the Creator, my people are alive and in them I have found my answers.[79]

Jennie Blackbird, who attended the Mohawk Institute in Brantford, Ontario, explained it this way:

> Our Elders taught us that language is the soul of the nation, and the sound of our language is its cement. Anishinaabemowin gives the ability to see into our future.... Anishinaabemowin gives us the ability to listen ... to what is going on around us and the ability to listen to what is happening inside of us. Through seeing and listening, we can harvest what we need to sustain ourselves, and to secure the properties that will heal us. Ever since I can remember as a child, speaking my language, it helped me to restore my inner harmony by maintaining my mental, emotional, physical, and spiritual well-being.[80]

Spiritual fear, confusion, and conflict are the direct consequences of the violence with which traditional beliefs were stripped away from Indigenous peoples. This turmoil gives particular urgency to understanding the role of Canada's churches in effecting reconciliation with Indigenous peoples. A number of Survivors spoke to us about the many contradictions they now see between their adult knowledge of Christian ethics and biblical teachings and how they were treated in the schools. These contradictions indicate the spiritual fear and confusion that so many Survivors have experienced. Children who returned home from the residential schools were unable to relate to families who still spoke their traditional languages and practised traditional spirituality. Survivors who wanted to learn the spiritual teachings of their ancestors were criticized and sometimes ostracized by their own family members who were Christian, and by the church. Survivors and their relatives reported that these tensions led to family breakdown—such is the depth of this spiritual conflict. The cumulative impact of the residential schools was to deny First Nations, Inuit, and Métis peoples their spiritual birthright and heritage. In our view, supporting the right of Indigenous peoples to self-determination in spiritual matters must be a high priority in the reconciliation process. To be consistent with the *United Nations Declaration*, Indigenous peoples, who were denied the right to practise and teach their own spiritual and religious beliefs and traditions, must now be able to do so freely and on their own terms.[81] For many, this is not easily done.

Many Survivors and their families continue to live in spiritual fear of their own traditions. Such fear is a direct result of the religious beliefs imposed on them by those who ran the residential schools. This long-internalized fear has spanned several generations and is difficult to shed. It is exacerbated by the fact that Christian doctrine today still fails to accord full and proper respect for Indigenous spiritual belief systems.

If it were the Survivors alone who faced this dilemma, one could argue that they should be able to resolve this for themselves in whatever way they can, including with the assistance of trusted church allies. However, the dilemma of spiritual conflict is more than a personal one to Survivors. It is one that extends to their children and their grandchildren, who, in these modern times, realize that there is much more to their personal histories than what they have inherited from residential schools and Canadian society. They realize that each Indigenous nation also has its own history and that such histories are part of who they are. Young First Nations, Inuit, and Métis people today are searching for their identities, which include their own languages and cultures.

Aboriginal parents want their children raised in a community environment that provides all of this. However, there is often conflict within communities when those who have been influenced by the doctrines of the churches believe that to teach Indigenous cultural beliefs to their children is to propagate evil. There are those who continue to actively speak out against Indigenous spiritual beliefs and to block or prohibit their practice.[82]

To have a right that you are afraid to exercise is to have no right at all. The *Declaration* asserts that governments (and other parties) now have an obligation to assist Indigenous communities to restore their own spiritual belief systems and faith practices, where these have been damaged or subjected to spiritual violence through past laws, policies, and practices. No one should be told who is, or how to worship, their Creator. That is an individual choice and, for Indigenous peoples, it is also a collective right. However, First Nations, Inuit, and Métis people need to be assured that they do indeed have the freedom to choose and that their choice will be respected.

All religious denominations in Canada must respect this right, but the United, Anglican, Presbyterian, and Catholic churches, as parties to the Settlement Agreement, bear a particular responsibility to formally recognize Indigenous spirituality as a valid form of worship that is equal to their own. It cannot be left up to individuals in the churches to speak out when such freedom to worship is denied. Rather, the churches, as religious institutions, must affirm Indigenous spirituality in its own right. Without such formal recognition, a full and robust reconciliation will be impossible. Healing and reconciliation have a spiritual dimension that must continue to be addressed by the churches in partnership with Indigenous spiritual leaders, Survivors, their families, and communities.

Many Indigenous peoples who no longer subscribe to Christian teachings have found the reclaiming of their Indigenous spirituality important to their healing and sense of identity. Some have no desire to integrate Indigenous spirituality into Christian religious institutions. Rather, they believe that Indigenous spirituality and Western religion should coexist on separate but parallel paths.

Elder Jim Dumont told the Commission about the importance of non-interference and mutual respect. He said that the

> abuse and the damage that has been done in residential schools, one of the primary sources of that is the church. And the church has to take ownership for that. But what bothers me about it is that the church continues to have a hold on our people.... Just get out of the way for awhile so that we can do what we need to do because as long as you are standing there thinking that you are supporting us, you are actually preventing us from getting to our own truth about this and our own healing about this. But I think the other thing that's being avoided by the church is their need to reconcile with the Spirit.... I think that the church has to reconcile with the Creator.... I'm not a Christian but I have a high regard for this Spirit ... who is called Jesus.... What I think is that when the church can reconcile with their God and their Saviour for what they have done, then maybe we can talk to them about reconciling amongst ourselves.[83]

In contrast, Aboriginal Christians who also practise Indigenous spirituality seek Indigenous and Christian spiritual and religious coexistence within the churches themselves. United Church Rev. Alf Dumont, the first speaker of the All Native Circle Conference, said,

> Respect is one of the greatest teachings that come from the original people of this land. Our ancestors followed that teaching when they met with their Christian brothers and sisters so many years ago. They saw a truth and a sacredness they could not deny in Christian teachings. Many were willing to embrace these teachings and leave their traditional teachings. Some were willing to embrace the teachings but still wanted to hold to their own. Some did not leave their own traditions, and when persecuted, went into hiding either deep in the mountains or deep inside themselves. Many were suspicious of the way the [Christian] teachings were presented and how they were lived. They were suspicious of the fact that they were asked to deny their own sacred teachings and ways and adopt

> *only* the new teachings they were given. Why could they not take what they needed from these new understandings and still live from their own? That was the understanding and teaching of holding respect for others' beliefs. It was the way of the first people.[84]

Presbyterian Rev. Margaret Mullin (Thundering Eagle Woman) put it this way:

> Can the Rev. Margaret Mullin/Thundering Eagle [W]oman from the Bear Clan be a strong Anishinaabe woman and a Christian simultaneously? Yes I can, because I do not have my feet in two different worlds, two different religions, or two different understandings of God. The two halves of me are one in the same Spirit. I can learn from my grandparents, European and Indigenous Canadian, who have all walked on the same path ahead of me. I can learn from Jesus and I can learn from my Elders.[85]

Each of the Settlement Agreement churches has wrestled with the theological challenges and necessary institutional reforms that arise with regard to Indigenous spiritual beliefs and practices. At the same time, Aboriginal church members have taken a leadership role to advocate for Indigenous perspectives and ensure that they are fully represented in the institutional structures, programs, and services of their respective churches.

The General Assembly of the Presbyterian Church of Canada in 2013 endorsed a report on the development of a theological framework for Aboriginal spirituality within the church. The report noted "the need for Aboriginal Christians to be true to both their *Indigenous identity* and to their [Christian] faith," and concluded, among other things, that "this conversation has the potential not simply to help us address our relationship as Presbyterians with Aboriginal people; it has the potential to contribute to the renewal of our church."[86]

The Anglican Church has developed a vision for a self-governing Indigenous church to coexist within the broader institutional structure of the church. In 2001, a strategic plan called "A New Agape" was formally adopted by the church's General Synod meeting. The plan set out the church's vision for a

> new relationship ... based on a partnership which focuses on the cultural, spiritual, social and economic independence of Indigenous communities. To give expression to this new relationship The Anglican Church of Canada will work primarily with ... Indigenous peoples for a truly Anglican Indigenous Church in Canada. It is an important step in the overall quest for self-governance.[87]

In 2007, the church appointed Rev. Mark MacDonald as its first Indigenous National Bishop.

The United Church has also examined its theological foundations. In a 2006 report, "Living Faithfully in the Midst of Empire: Report to the Thirty-ninth General Council

2006," the United Church responded to an earlier call from the World Council of Churches "to reflect on the question of power and empire from a biblical and theological perspective and take a firm faith stance against hegemonic powers because all power is accountable to God."[88] The report recommended that further work be done, and a follow-up report, "Reviewing Partnership in the Context of Empire," was issued in 2009. The report's theological reflection noted:

> Our development of the partnership model was an attempt to move beyond the paternalism and colonialism of 19th century missions. The current work to develop right relations with Aboriginal peoples is an attempt to move beyond a history of colonization and racism. This ongoing struggle to move beyond empire involves the recognition that our theology and biblical interpretation have often supported sexism, racism, colonialism, and the exploitation of creation.... Theologies of empire have understood God and men as separate from and superior to women, Indigenous peoples, and nature.[89]

In 2012, the Executive of the General Council reported on the follow-up to the 2006 and 2009 reports on how to re-envision the church's theological purpose and restructure its institutions by shifting from a theology of empire to a theology of partnership.[90]

The Commission asked all the Settlement Agreement churches to tell us their views on Indigenous spirituality and what steps were being taken within their respective institutions to respect Indigenous spiritual practices. In 2015, two of the Settlement Agreement churches responded to this call.

On January 29, 2015, the Presbyterian Church in Canada issued a "Statement on Aboriginal Spiritual Practices." Among other things, the church said:

> As part of the Churches' commitment to a journey of truth and reconciliation, the Presbyterian Church in Canada has learned that many facets of Aboriginal traditional spiritualities bring life and oneness with creation. Accepting this has sometimes been a challenge for the Presbyterian Church in Canada. We are now aware that there is a wide variety of Aboriginal spiritual practices and we acknowledge that it is for our church to continue in humility to learn the deep significance of these practices and to respect them and the Aboriginal elders who are the keepers of their traditional sacred truths....
>
> We acknowledge and respect both Aboriginal members of the Presbyterian Church in Canada who wish to bring traditional practices into their congregations and those Aboriginal members who are not comfortable or willing to do so. The church must be a community where all are valued and respected. It is not for the Presbyterian Church in Canada to validate or invalidate Aboriginal spiritualities and practices. Our church, however, is deeply respectful of these traditions.[91]

On February 18, 2015, the United Church of Canada issued a statement, "Affirming Other Spiritual Paths." The document sets out various statements and apologies made by the church with regard to Indigenous spirituality, including an expression of reconciliation at the TRC's Alberta National Event on March 27, 2014. Among other things, the church said:

> In humility, the Church acknowledges its complicity in the degradation of Aboriginal wisdom and spirituality, and offers the following statements from its recent history. In doing so, the Church recognizes with pain that this is a complex and sensitive issue for some within Aboriginal communities of faith, who as a result of our Christianizing work, and the legacy of colonialism, are on a journey to restore harmony and spiritual balance....
>
> We have learned that 'good intentions' are never enough, especially when wrapped in the misguided zeal of cultural and spiritual superiority. Thus, we have learned that we were wrong to reject, discredit, and yes, even outlaw traditional indigenous spiritual practice and ceremony; in amazing circles of grace, as we have begun to listen to the wisdom of the Elders, we have found our own faith enriched and deepened. And we are grateful. We know we have a long journey ahead of us. We are committed to make that journey in humility and partnership, engaging in the healing work of making "whole" our own spirituality, and acknowledging that holding both your spirituality and ours is possible through listening and learning with open hearts.[92]

Unlike the Protestant churches, in which theological reflection and institutional reform have been undertaken at the national level, the Roman Catholic Church in Canada's approach to Indigenous spirituality has emphasized decision making at the local diocesan level. However, in a submission to the Royal Commission on Aboriginal Peoples in 1993, the Canadian Conference of Catholic Bishops expressed its views on Indigenous spirituality:

> The Native spiritual voice is now finding greater resonance in the broader Christian and social worlds. Native Christianity today is marked by the development of a theology that comes from Native prayer, culture, and experience.... As bishops, we have encouraged Native Catholic leaders to take increasing responsibility for the faith life of their communities....
>
> We also recognize that for some Native Peoples, Christianity and Native spirituality are mutually exclusive. We are committed to responding to this belief in a spirit of dialogue and respect, and to encouraging Native Peoples to join in conversation between Christianity and Native spirituality.... We will continue to explore the possibility of establishing channels of communication between our own spiritual heritage and Aboriginal spiritualities.[93]

In terms of institutional reform, the Canadian Catholic Aboriginal Council, established in 1998, advises the Canadian Conference of Catholic Bishops on issues regarding Aboriginal peoples within the Catholic Church. The council's mandate is to study and analyze "issues related to Catholic Aboriginal spirituality and education"; encourage "Aboriginal leadership in the Christian community"; support and promote "reconciliation in the context of the Catholic reality"; and serve "as an important link between Aboriginal Catholics and non-Aboriginal Catholics."[94]

The Commission notes that all the Settlement Agreement churches have recognized the need to provide theological education and training for Aboriginal church members to take leadership positions within the churches and work in Aboriginal ministry programs. Beginning in 2007, the Churches' Council on Theological Education in Canada held a series of conferences that sought to encourage and deepen the exploration of questions with respect to Indigenous and Christian beliefs and the incorporation of Indigenous cultural and spiritual practices into Christian practices. Through these events, the council also sought to challenge post-secondary institutions to consider how best to prepare theological students for ministry in Canada, in consideration not only of Indigenous people, their culture and spirituality, but also of the need for churches to engage in healing and reconciliation between Aboriginal and non-Aboriginal peoples.

The Toronto School of Theology made a public commitment to giving the same academic respect to Indigenous knowledge, including traditional Indigenous spiritual teachings, "as [to] traditions of Greek philosophy and modern science."[95] This pledge was made at "The Meeting Place," an event co-sponsored by Council Fire Native Cultural Centre and the Toronto Conference of the United Church of Canada in June of 2012.

Yet, more remains to be done in education and training with regard to reconciling Indigenous spirituality and Christianity in ways that support Indigenous self-determination. Writing in 2009, the former Archdeacon for the Anglican Church and founding member of the Indian Ecumenical Conference, Rev. John A. (Ian) MacKenzie, said,

> Most urgently, churches need to consider opening a serious dialogue with Aboriginal theologians, doctors, and healers who represent ... the North American intellectual tradition.... [Aboriginal peoples] call for recognition of the truth of past injustices and respect for their civilizations. Most of all, this is a call for respect for their traditional religious thoughts and practices. The only legitimate North American intellectual tradition comes from the diverse tribal societies in our midst!...
>
> Sustainable reconciliation will only take place when every Canadian seminary includes a course on Aboriginal religious traditions; when every congregation ... reflect[s] on North American intellectual tradition by initiating and inviting Aboriginal religious leaders to lead such discussions ... when Aboriginal peoples achieve real self-government within their churches; and when Christian theology not only respects Aboriginal thought, but learns from it.[96]

Call to Action

60) We call upon leaders of the church parties to the Settlement Agreement and all other faiths, in collaboration with Indigenous spiritual leaders, Survivors, schools of theology, seminaries, and other religious training centres, to develop and teach curriculum for all student clergy, and all clergy and staff who work in Aboriginal communities, on the need to respect Indigenous spirituality in its own right, the history and legacy of residential schools and the roles of the church parties in that system, the history and legacy of religious conflict in Aboriginal families and communities, and the responsibility that churches have to mitigate such conflicts and prevent spiritual violence.

Church healing and reconciliation projects

Beginning in the 1990s, the four Settlement Agreement churches began allocating specific funds for community-based healing and reconciliation projects. This work continued under the terms of the Settlement Agreement. Each of the defendant churches agreed to provide and manage funds specifically dedicated to healing and reconciliation. All the churches established committees, including Aboriginal representatives, to review and approve projects. In broad terms, the reconciliation projects funded by the Settlement Agreement churches have had three primary purposes:

1) Healing. The Toronto Urban Native Ministry, funded by Anglican, United, and Roman Catholic churches, "reaches out to Aboriginal people on the street, in hospitals, in jails, shelters and hostels."[97] The ministry works with all Aboriginal people who are socially marginalized and impoverished, including Survivors and intergenerational family members who have been impacted by residential schools. Anamiewigumming Kenora Fellowship Centre, with funds from the Presbyterian Church in Canada, developed "A Step Up . . . tools for the soul," in partnership with local Aboriginal organizations. Under the program, a series of ten teaching events led by Aboriginal Elders, teachers, and professionals were held to support Survivors and family members on their healing journey, featuring education about culture and tradition, with the goal of fostering reconciliation.[98]

2) Language and culture revitalization. The Language Immersion Canoe Course in Tofino, British Columbia, funded by the United Church, focused on reconnecting Aboriginal youth to their homelands and cultures. For one month, young Aboriginal people from Vancouver Island, including the community of Ahousaht, where the United Church operated a school, were taken to a remote

and ancient Hesquiaht village site to learn the Hesquiah language through the art of canoe making.[99]

The Four Season Cultural Camps of the Serpent River First Nation in Ontario, funded by the Anglican Church, used traditional practices of harvesting, food storage, storytelling, and related ceremonies to promote language and culture.[100] The Anglicans also supported a wilderness retreat for young people at the Nibinamik First Nation at Summer Beaver, Ontario. It taught traditional life ways, while instilling a sense of self-confidence in the youth as they successfully completed the activities in the camp.[101]

3) Education and relationship building. The Anglican and Roman Catholic churches still have relatively large numbers of Aboriginal members, so many of their initiatives focused on bringing their own Aboriginal and non-Aboriginal members together. The Anglican Church has worked to help build understanding and counter stereotypes among its members through anti-racism training. The Roman Catholic entities were among the core funders of the Returning to Spirit: Residential School Healing and Reconciliation Program. The program brings Aboriginal and non-Aboriginal participants together to gain new insights into the residential school experience and develop new communication and relationship-building skills.[102]

The Settlement Agreement churches bear a special responsibility to continue to support the long-term healing needs of Survivors, their families, and communities who are still struggling with a range of health, social, and economic impacts. The closure of the national Aboriginal Healing Foundation in 2014 when government funding ended has left a significant gap in funding for community-based healing projects, at the very time that healing for many individuals and communities is still just beginning.[103] The churches must also continue to educate their own congregations and facilitate dialogue between Aboriginal and non-Aboriginal peoples. Much has been accomplished through the healing and reconciliation projects of the Settlement Agreement churches, but more remains to be done.

Call to Action

61) We call upon church parties to the Settlement Agreement, in collaboration with Survivors and representatives of Aboriginal organizations, to establish permanent funding to Aboriginal people for:

    i. Community-controlled healing and reconciliation projects.

    ii. Community-controlled culture- and language-revitalization projects.

    iii. Community-controlled education and relationship-building projects.

iv. Regional dialogues for Indigenous spiritual leaders and youth to discuss Indigenous spirituality, self-determination, and reconciliation.

Education for reconciliation

Much of the current state of troubled relations between Aboriginal and non-Aboriginal Canadians is attributable to educational institutions and what they have taught, or failed to teach, over many generations. Despite that history, or, perhaps more correctly, because of its potential, the Commission believes that education is also the key to reconciliation. Educating Canadians for reconciliation involves not only schools and post-secondary institutions, but also dialogue forums and public history institutions such as museums and archives. Education must remedy the gaps in historical knowledge that perpetuate ignorance and racism.

But education for reconciliation must do even more. Survivors told us that Canadians must learn about the history and legacy of residential schools in ways that change both minds *and* hearts. At the Manitoba National Event in Winnipeg, Allan Sutherland said,

> There are still a lot of emotions [that are] unresolved. People need to tell their stories.... We need the ability to move forward together but you have to understand how it all began [starting with] Christopher Columbus, from Christianization, then colonization, and then assimilation.... If we put our minds and hearts to it, we can [change] the status quo.[104]

At the Commission's Community Hearing in Thunder Bay, Ontario, in 2010, Esther Lachinette-Diabo said,

> I'm doing this interview in hope that we could use this as an educational tool to educate our youth about what happened.... Maybe one day the Ministry of Education can work with the TRC and develop some kind of curriculum for Native Studies, Indigenous learning. So that not only Aboriginal people can understand, you know, what we had to go through—the experiences of all the Anishinaabe people that attended—but for the Canadian people as well to understand that the residential schools did happen. And through this sharing, they can understand and hear stories from Survivors like me.[105]

In Lethbridge, Alberta, in 2013, Charlotte Marten said,

> I would like to see action taken as a result of the findings of this Commission. I would like to see the history of the residential school system be part of the school curriculum across Canada. I want my grandchildren and the future generations of our society to know the whole truth behind Canada's residential school policy and how it destroyed generations of our people. It is my hope that by sharing the

> truth that it will help the public gain a better understanding of the struggles we face as First Nations.[106]

Non-Aboriginal Canadians hear about the problems faced by Aboriginal communities, but they have almost no idea how those problems developed. There is little understanding of how the federal government contributed to that reality through residential schools and the policies and laws in place during their existence. Our education system, through omission or commission, has failed to teach this. It bears a large share of the responsibility for the current state of affairs. It became clear over the course of the Commission's work that most adult Canadians have been taught little or nothing about the residential schools. More typically, they were taught that the history of Canada began when the first European explorers set foot in the New World. Nation building has been the main theme of Canada's history curricula for a long time, and Aboriginal peoples, with a few notable exceptions, have been portrayed as bystanders, if not obstacles, to that enterprise.

Prior to 1970, school textbooks across the country depicted Aboriginal peoples as being either savage warriors or onlookers who were irrelevant to the more important history of Canada: the story of European settlement. Beginning in the 1980s, the history of Aboriginal people was sometimes cast in a more positive light, but the poverty and social dysfunction in Aboriginal communities were emphasized without any historical context to help students understand how or why these happened. This has left most Canadians with the view that Aboriginal people were and are to blame for the situations in which they find themselves, as though there were no external causes. Aboriginal peoples have therefore been characterized as a social and economic problem that must be solved.

By the 1990s, textbooks emphasized the role of Aboriginal peoples as protestors, advocating for rights. Most Canadians failed to understand or appreciate the significance of these rights, given the overriding perspective of Aboriginal assimilation in Canada's education system.

Although textbooks have become more inclusive of Aboriginal perspectives over the past three decades, the role of Aboriginal people in Canadian history during much of the twentieth century remains invisible. Students learn something about Aboriginal peoples prior to contact, and during the exploration, fur-trade, and settlement periods. They learn about Métis resistance in the 1880s, and the signing of Treaties. Then, Aboriginal peoples virtually disappear until the 1960s and 1970s, when they resurface as political and social justice activists. The defining period in between remains largely unmentioned.[107] So much of the story of Aboriginal peoples, as seen through their own eyes, is still missing from Canadian history.

In the Commission's view, all students—Aboriginal and non-Aboriginal—need to learn that the history of this country did not begin with the arrival of Jacques Cartier on the banks of the St. Lawrence River. They need to learn about the Indigenous nations the Europeans met, about their rich linguistic and cultural heritage, about what they felt and thought as they dealt with such historic figures as Champlain, La Vérendrye, and the representatives of the Hudson's Bay Company. Canadians need to learn why Indigenous nations negotiated the Treaties and to understand that they negotiated with integrity and in good faith. They need to learn about why Aboriginal leaders and Elders still fight so hard to defend those Treaties, what these agreements represent to them, and why they have been ignored by European settlers or governments. They need to learn about what it means to have inherent rights, what those are for Aboriginal peoples, and what the settler government's political and legal obligations are in those areas where Treaties were never negotiated. They need to learn why so many of these issues are ongoing. They need to learn about the Doctrine of Discovery—the politically and socially accepted basis for presumptive European claims to the land and riches of this country—and to understand that this same doctrine is now being repudiated around the world, most recently by the United Nations and the World Council of Churches.

Survivors have also said that knowing about these things is not enough. Our public education system also needs to influence behaviour by undertaking to teach our children—Aboriginal and non-Aboriginal—how to speak respectfully to, and about, each other in the future. Reconciliation is all about respect.

The Commission's 2012 *Interim Report* made three recommendations directed at provincial and territorial governments:

> Recommendation 4: The Commission recommends that each provincial and territorial government undertake a review of the curriculum materials currently in use in public schools to assess what, if anything, they teach about residential schools.
>
> Recommendation 5: The Commission recommends that provincial and territorial departments of education work in concert with the Commission to develop age-appropriate educational materials about residential schools for use in public schools.
>
> Recommendation 6: The Commission recommends that each provincial and territorial government work with the Commission to develop public education campaigns to inform the general public about the history and impact of residential schools in their respective jurisdictions.

At various times, the Commission met with provincial and territorial education ministers from across Canada. In July 2014, the Council of Ministers of Education, Canada (CMEC) gave us an update on the status of curriculum-development commitments across the country.[108] The Commission was encouraged to see that progress has been made. We note, however, that not all provinces and territories have yet made curriculum about residential schools mandatory, and not all courses cover the subject in depth.

The Northwest Territories and Nunavut have taken a leadership role in developing and implementing mandatory curriculum about residential schools for all high school students, in engaging Survivors directly in the development of new materials, and in ensuring that teachers receive appropriate training and support, including direct dialogues with Survivors. At the time of this writing, Yukon had begun the process of adapting the Northwest Territories and Nunavut materials for mandatory use in its territory. Among the provinces, Alberta publicly declared that it was launching its own initiative to develop mandatory curriculum on the Treaties and residential schools for all students.

These education initiatives are significant, but it will be essential to ensure that momentum is not lost in the years following the end of the Commission's mandate. To be successful over the long term, this and similar initiatives will require substantive and sustained support from provincial and territorial governments, educators, and local school districts. An ongoing commitment from ministers of education throughout the country is critical. The Commission notes that on July 9, 2014, the CMEC announced that education ministers

> agreed to additional pan-Canadian work in Aboriginal education to take place over the next two years, which will focus on four key directional ideas: support for Aboriginal students interested in pursuing teaching as a career; development of learning resources on Canadian history and the legacy of Indian Residential Schools that could be used by teacher training programs; sharing of promising practices in Aboriginal education; and ongoing promotion of learning about Indian Residential Schools in K–12 education systems.[109]

In regions where curriculum and teacher training on residential schools have been introduced, it will be necessary to build on these early successes and evaluate progress on an ongoing basis. Where education about residential schools is minimal, provincial and territorial governments can benefit from the lessons learned in jurisdictions that have made this material a mandatory requirement.

The Commission notes that throughout the residential school era, Catholic and Protestant religious schools taught students only about their own religions. Students were ill prepared to understand or respect other religious or spiritual perspectives, including those of Aboriginal peoples. In our view, no religious school receiving public funding should be allowed to teach one religion to the complete exclusion of all other religions. This is consistent with the Supreme Court of Canada decision in *S.L. v. Commission scolaire des Chênes* in 2012. At issue was whether Québec's mandatory Ethics and Religious Cultures Program, which was introduced in 2008 to replace Catholic and Protestant programs of religious and moral instruction with a comparative religions course taught from a neutral and objective perspective, violated charter rights of Catholic parents and children to be taught only Catholic religious beliefs.[110] However, the court ruled:

> Exposing children to a comprehensive presentation of various religions without forcing the children to join them does not constitute an indoctrination of students that would infringe the freedom of religion.... Furthermore, the early exposure of children to realities that differ from those in their immediate family environment is a fact of life in society. The suggestion that exposing children to a variety of religious facts in itself infringes on religious freedom or that of their parents amounts to a rejection of the multicultural reality of Canadian society and ignores the Quebec government's obligations with regard to public education.[111]

The Commission believes that religious diversity courses must be mandatory in all provinces and territories. Any religious school receiving public funding must be required to teach at least one course on comparative religious studies, which must include a segment on Aboriginal spiritual beliefs and practices.

Calls to Action

62) We call upon the federal, provincial, and territorial governments, in consultation and collaboration with Survivors, Aboriginal peoples, and educators, to:

i. Make age-appropriate curriculum on residential schools, Treaties, and Aboriginal peoples' historical and contemporary contributions to Canada a mandatory education requirement for Kindergarten to Grade Twelve students.

ii. Provide the necessary funding to post-secondary institutions to educate teachers on how to integrate Indigenous knowledge and teaching methods into classrooms.

iii. Provide the necessary funding to Aboriginal schools to utilize Indigenous knowledge and teaching methods in classrooms.

iv. Establish senior-level positions in government at the assistant deputy minister level or higher dedicated to Aboriginal content in education.

63) We call upon the Council of Ministers of Education, Canada to maintain an annual commitment to Aboriginal education issues, including:

i. Developing and implementing Kindergarten to Grade Twelve curriculum and learning resources on Aboriginal peoples in Canadian history, and the history and legacy of residential schools.

ii. Sharing information and best practices on teaching curriculum related to residential schools and Aboriginal history.

iii. Building student capacity for intercultural understanding, empathy, and mutual respect.

iv. Identifying teacher-training needs relating to the above.

64) We call upon all levels of government that provide public funds to denominational schools to require such schools to provide an education on comparative religious studies, which must include a segment on Aboriginal spiritual beliefs and practices developed in collaboration with Aboriginal Elders.

Transforming the education system: Creating respectful learning environments

The Commission believes that to be an effective force for reconciliation, curriculum about residential schools must be part of a broader history education that integrates First Nations, Inuit, and Métis voices, perspectives, and experiences; and builds common ground between Aboriginal and non-Aboriginal peoples. The education system itself must be transformed into one that rejects the racism embedded in colonial systems of education and treats Aboriginal and Euro-Canadian knowledge systems with equal respect.[112]

This is consistent with the *United Nations Declaration on the Rights of Indigenous Peoples,* which articulates the state's responsibility with regard to public education and the promotion of respectful relationships between citizens, as follows:

> Indigenous peoples have the right to the dignity and diversity of their cultures, traditions, histories and aspirations which shall be appropriately reflected in education and public information. [Article 15:1]
>
> States shall take effective measures, in consultation and cooperation with the indigenous peoples concerned, to combat prejudice and eliminate discrimination and to promote tolerance, understanding and good relations among indigenous peoples and all other segments of society. [Article 15:2]

Fully implementing this national education framework will take many years, but will ensure that Aboriginal children and youth see themselves and their cultures, languages, and histories respectfully reflected in the classroom. Non-Aboriginal learners will benefit, as well. Taught in this way, all students, both Aboriginal and non-Aboriginal, gain historical knowledge while also developing respect and empathy for each other. Both elements will be vital to supporting reconciliation in the coming years.

Developing respect for, and understanding of, the situation of others is an important but often ignored part of the reconciliation process. Survivors' testimonies compelled those who listened to think deeply about what justice really means in the face of mass human rights violations. Teaching and learning about the residential schools are difficult for educators and students alike. They can bring up feelings of anger, grief, shame, guilt, and denial. But they can also shift understanding and alter world views.[113] Education for reconciliation requires not only age-appropriate curriculum, but also ensuring that teachers have the necessary skills, supports, and resources to teach Canadian students about the residential school system in a manner that fosters constructive dialogue and mutual respect.

Educating the heart as well as the mind helps young people to become critical thinkers who are also engaged, compassionate citizens.[114] At the Alberta National Event, a youth delegation from Feathers of Hope, a project sponsored by Ontario's Provincial Advocate for Children and Youth, offered an expression of reconciliation. Samantha Crowe said,

> Feathers of Hope began as a First Nations youth forum but it quickly [became] a movement of hope, healing, and positive change within northern Ontario's First Nations communities. You spoke passionately about wanting to learn about the past, and said that First Nations and non-First Nations people alike need to understand our history, and the impacts it still has on everything around us.... First Nations and non-First Nations people need to understand how colonization, racism, that residential schools still continue to negatively impact the quality of life in our communities.
>
> Everyone, especially the young people ... need to learn of Canada's history, of our past, to truly try and understand our present. This needs to be taught in school, but it also needs to be heard first-hand from our family, our friends, and our other community members. This will begin the journey of healing together as a family or as a community because we can no longer live [with] a silence that hides our pain. So while youth want to know of their past, they are ready to move forward. They understand they need positive change, but they don't want to do this alone. We all need to come together so we can share, so we can grow, and then we can uplift one another, because that's what reconciliation is about.[115]

Learning *about* the residential schools history is crucial to reconciliation, but can be effective only if Canadians also learn *from* this history in terms of repairing broken trust, strengthening a sense of civic responsibility, and spurring remedial and constructive action.[116] In a digital world, where students have ready access to a barrage of information concerning Treaties, Aboriginal rights, or historical wrongs such as residential schools, they must know how to assess the credibility of these sources for themselves. As active citizens, they must be able to engage in debates on these issues, armed with real knowledge and deepened understanding about the past.

Understanding the ethical dimension of history is especially important. Students must be able to make ethical judgments about the actions of their ancestors while recognizing that the moral sensibilities of the past may be quite different from their own in present times. They must be able to make informed decisions about what responsibility today's society has to address historical injustices.[117] This will ensure that tomorrow's citizens are both knowledgeable and caring about the injustices of the past, as these relate to their own futures.

Gathering new knowledge: Research on reconciliation

For reconciliation to thrive in the coming years, it will also be necessary for federal, provincial, and territorial governments, universities, and funding agencies to invest in and support new research on reconciliation. Over the course of the Commission's work, a wide range of research projects across the country have examined the meaning, concepts, and practices of reconciliation. Yet, there remains much to learn about the circumstances and conditions in which reconciliation either fails or flourishes. Equally important, there are rich insights into healing and reconciliation that emerge from the research process itself. Two research projects sponsored by the Commission illustrate this point.

Through a TRC-sponsored project at the Centre for Youth & Society at the University of Victoria, seven Aboriginal youth researchers embarked on a digital storytelling project, "Residential Schools Resistance Narratives: Strategies and Significance for Indigenous Youth." The project enabled youth researchers to learn about the critical role that resistance and resilience played in the residential schools and beyond, but also allowed them to reflect on their own identities and roles within their families and communities. One youth researcher said that "what started as a research job turned into a personal hunt for knowledge of my own family's history with residential schools." Others noted the importance of respecting and incorporating ceremony and protocols in their digital storytelling projects. Asma Antoine, the project coordinator, reported that the group learned the importance of

> knowing that when speaking to a Survivor ... you have to hear their past before you can hear their understanding of resistance. This project allowed the group [to have] a learning process that weaves [together] traditional [Indigenous] and Western knowledge to build our stories of resistance.... This research project has ignited a fire that shows in each digital story. The passion of resistance that validates the survival and resiliency of First Nations people and communities provides hope for healing and reconciliation over the next seven generations.[118]

In 2012, a digital storytelling project was undertaken by Aboriginal women at the Prairie Women's Health Centre of Excellence: "Nitâpwewininân: Ongoing Effects of Residential Schools on Aboriginal Women—Towards Inter-Generational Reconciliation." Using ceremony and protocols throughout the project, the first workshop began with a pipe ceremony, followed by a Sharing Circle in which participants talked about their lives and the group discussed their individual and collective needs for support. They later moved on to making videos of their individual stories, which were screened in March 2012 at the University of Winnipeg.[119] One of the participants, Lorena Fontaine, said,

> Reconciliation is about stories and our ability to tell stories. I think the intellectual part of ourselves wants to start looking for words to define reconciliation. And then there is the heart knowledge that comes from our life experiences. It's challenging to connect the two and relate it to reconciliation.... Without even thinking of the term reconciliation, I'm reminded about the power of story.... [People who watched the videos] said that when they saw the faces of Aboriginal women and heard their voices in the videos they understood assimilation in a different way. They felt the impact of assimilation.... It's far more powerful to have Aboriginal peoples talk about the impact of assimilation and hope for reconciliation than having words written down in a report.[120]

Research is vital to reconciliation. It provides insights and practical examples of why and how educating Canadians about the diverse concepts, principles, and practices of reconciliation contributes to healing and transformative social change.

The benefits of research extend beyond addressing the legacy of residential schools. Research on the reconciliation process can inform how Canadian society can mitigate intercultural conflicts, strengthen civic trust, and build social capacity and practical skills for long-term reconciliation. First Nations, Inuit, and Métis peoples have an especially strong contribution to make to this work.

Research partnerships between universities and communities or organizations are fruitful collaborations and can provide the necessary structure to document, analyze, and report research findings on reconciliation to a broader audience.

Call to Action

65) We call upon the federal government, through the Social Sciences and Humanities Research Council, and in collaboration with Aboriginal peoples, post-secondary institutions and educators, and the National Centre for Truth and Reconciliation and its partner institutions, to establish a national research program with multi-year funding to advance understanding of reconciliation.

TRC public education forums: Education Days and Youth Dialogues

Education for reconciliation must happen not only in formal education settings such as elementary and secondary schools and post-secondary institutions, but in more informal places. One of the ways that the Commission fulfilled its public education mandate was through forums such as National Event Education Days and Youth Dialogues. The Commission believes that establishing a strong foundation for reconciliation depends on the achievement of individual self-respect and mutual respect between Aboriginal and non-Aboriginal Canadians. While this is true for adults, it is particularly urgent with regard to young people; they are the lifeblood of reconciliation into the future.

At the Saskatchewan National Event, Grade Eight student Brooklyn Rae, who attended the Education Day, said, "I think it's really important for youth to voice their opinions, to not only prove to themselves that they can, that their voice is important, but to prove to adults that they have a voice and that they have a strong opinion that is important in the world."[121] Elder Barney Williams, a member of the TRC's Survivor Committee and one of the panellists at the Education Day Youth Dialogue, said,

> I think more and more people are realizing that the engagement of youth is crucial. For me, as a Survivor, I'm really impressed with how much they knew. I was very impressed with the type of questions the audience asked. It tells me, as somebody who's carried this pain for over sixty-eight years, that there's hope. Finally there's hope on the horizon and it's coming from the right place. It's coming from the youth.[122]

The Commission agrees. We believe that children and youth must have a strong voice in developing reconciliation policy, programs, and practices into the future. It is therefore vital to develop appropriate public education strategies to support the ongoing involvement of children and youth in age-appropriate reconciliation initiatives and projects at community, regional, and national levels.

Through direct participation in the TRC's National Events, thousands of young people and their teachers across the country had the opportunity to learn about the residential schools and think about their own role and responsibility in reconciliation. The TRC's Education Days were designed specifically for elementary and high school students and their teachers. Young people had the opportunity to listen to, and interact with, Elders and Survivors. They attended interactive workshops where they learned about the residential school history, resilience, and healing through the arts—painting, carving, storytelling, music, and film. They visited the Learning Places to walk through the Legacy of Hope Foundation display, "One Hundred Years of Loss," and to see posters and archival photographs of the residential schools from their own region.

Education Days were well attended. For example, at the British Columbia National Event in Vancouver, approximately 5,000 elementary and high school students from across the province spent the day at the National Event. In advance of Education Day, teachers in each region were given orientation materials to help prepare their students and themselves. In total, close to 15,000 young people across the country have participated in such Education Days, most with a commitment to take what they learned and witnessed back to their home schools to share with thousands more of their fellow students.

Over the course of the TRC's mandate, the Commission worked in partnership with the International Center for Transitional Justice's (ICTJ) Children and Youth Program to host a series of small retreats and workshops. Youth Dialogues were also integrated into Education Day activities at National Events. Their purpose was to engage youth in dialogue and to support their efforts to make their own submissions to the TRC. For example, in October 2010, the Commission co-sponsored an Aboriginal/non-Aboriginal youth retreat near Vancouver, British Columbia. Young people came together to learn about the residential schools, talk with Elders, and share team-building activities. One young participant said that during the retreat, "we learn[ed] more about each other and the past. It's really important because it actually teaches us, the stories that we heard it touched us, and it inspired us to become better people."[123]

In June of 2011, Molly Tilden and Marlisa Brown, two young women who attended this retreat, produced their own video documentary, *Our Truth: The Youth Perspective on Residential Schools*. The production featured interviews with their classmates in Yellowknife about what they knew about the residential schools. They presented the video at the Northern National Event in Inuvik, Northwest Territories.[124] Virginie Ladisch, director of ICTJ's Children and Youth Program, summarized what the two young women found and the subsequent impact of the project.

> The answers are shocking: some students had no knowledge, or simply complete indifference; those are largely the non-Aboriginal youth interviewed. Other students talk about the enduring impact they see in terms of high rates of alcoholism, suicide, and teenage pregnancies.
>
> So there's a huge disconnect in terms of how the young people view the relevance of this legacy and what knowledge they have of it. When that video was shared with people involved in designing the secondary school curriculum for the Northwest Territories and Nunavut, they could not believe that their youth had such reactions.
>
> So the curriculum on residential schools, which was previously barely addressed in the classroom, was revised to be a mandatory 25 hours of instruction, of which Ms. Brown and Ms. Tilden's video is a critical component.[125]

In October of 2011, the TRC–ICTJ initiative prepared and supported a group of Mi'kmaq youth reporters at the Halifax National Event. They interviewed Survivors and documented the TRC event. At a follow-up retreat in the community, the young reporters discussed their experiences and produced a documentary called *Our Legacy, Our Hope*.[126] In 2012, the documentary was presented at the Youth Dialogue during the TRC's National Event in Saskatchewan.[127] Some of the youth also presented this documentary to international policymakers at the United Nations Permanent Forum on Indigenous Issues in 2012.[128]

The Commission's interactions with youth indicated that young people care deeply about the past. They understand that knowing the whole story about Canada's history is relevant for today and crucial for their future. This was evident, for example, in an expression of reconciliation made to the TRC at the Alberta National Event on March 27, 2014, by a group of Aboriginal and non-Aboriginal youth from the Centre for Global Education in Edmonton. One of the non-Aboriginal youth, Hanshi Liu, told us about the project. First, the group—made up of youth from First Nations reserves, the rural communities of High Prairie and Fort MacLeod, and the city of Edmonton—spent a month studying and talking about residential schools and their shared history. They then held a virtual town hall where over 300 students talked about their vision for reconciliation.

Emerald Blesse from Little River Cree Nation told us that "youth believe that reconciliation is the way to re-establish lost trust and open doors to positive and productive communications. When we affirm every culture's pride in their heritage, healing can take place...." Hayley Grier-Stewart, representing the Kainai, Siksika, Tsuu T'ina, and Stony First Nations, said that "the youth believe that within our communities, we need to teach and create awareness, cultural appreciation, as well as healing and restoration. If we introduce youth to the culture at a young age in our schools, through curriculum and the practice of restorative justice, it will teach the younger generation to be proactive instead of reactive." Métis youth Shelby Lachlan said that

> the youth of Alberta believe that in order to move forward, towards healing and reconciliation, it is important for action to be taken on a national and provincial level. First we must re-establish trust between these two [Aboriginal and non-Aboriginal] collectives, and through the honouring, acknowledgement, and respect of all Treaties and settlements, we believe this can be achieved.[129]

Youth Forums and Dialogues are a vital component of education for reconciliation. Non-profit organizations can play a key role in providing ongoing opportunities for Aboriginal and non-Aboriginal youth to participate in intercultural dialogue and work actively together to foster reconciliation.

Call to Action

66) We call upon the federal government to establish multi-year funding for community-based youth organizations to deliver programs on reconciliation, and establish a national network to share information and best practices.

Role of Canada's museums and archives in education for reconciliation

Museums and archives, as sites of public memory and national history, have a key role to play in national reconciliation. As publicly funded institutions, museums and archives in settler colonial states such as Canada, New Zealand, Australia, and the United States have interpreted the past in ways that have excluded or marginalized Aboriginal peoples' cultural perspectives and historical experience. Museums have traditionally been thought of as places where a nation's history is presented in neutral, objective terms. Yet, as history that had formerly been silenced was revealed, it became evident that Canada's museums had told only part of the story.[130] In a similar vein, archives have been part of the "architecture of imperialism"—institutions that held the historical documents of the state.[131] As Canada confronts its settler colonial past, museums and archives have been gradually transforming from institutions of colony and empire into more inclusive institutions that better reflect the full richness of Canadian history.

Political and legal developments on international and national fronts have contributed to this change. Around the globe, the adoption of the *United Nations Declaration on the Rights of Indigenous Peoples* has resulted in the growing recognition that Indigenous peoples have the right to be self-determining peoples and that the state has a duty to protect Indigenous traditional knowledge and cultural rights. The *Declaration* also establishes that actions by the state that affect Indigenous peoples require their free, prior, and informed consent. States have an obligation to take effective measures to protect the rights of Indigenous peoples or to make reparations where traditional knowledge or cultural rights have been violated. This has significant implications for national museums and archives and the public servants who work in them.[132]

The Commission emphasizes that several articles under the *United Nations Declaration* have particular relevance for national museums and archives in Canada. These include:

- Indigenous peoples have the right to practise and revitalize their cultural traditions and customs. This includes the right to maintain, protect and develop the past, present and future manifestations of their cultures, such as archaeological and historical sites, artefacts, designs, ceremonies, technologies and visual and performing arts and literature. [Article 11:1]
- States shall provide redress through effective mechanisms which may include restitution, developed in conjunction with indigenous peoples, with respect to their cultural, intellectual, religious and spiritual property taken without their

free, prior and informed consent or in violation of their laws, traditions and customs. [Article 11:2]

- Indigenous peoples have the right to manifest, practise, develop and teach their spiritual and religious traditions, customs and ceremonies; the right to maintain, protect and have access in privacy to their religious and cultural sites; the right to use and control of their ceremonial objects; and the right to the repatriation of their human remains. [Article 12:1]
- States shall seek to enable the access and/or repatriation of ceremonial objects and human remains in their possession through fair, transparent and effective mechanisms developed in conjunction with indigenous peoples concerned. [Article 12:2]

The *Declaration,* in conjunction with Section 35 of Canada's *Constitution Act, 1982,* which recognizes and affirms existing Aboriginal and Treaty rights, and various court rulings related to Aboriginal rights have fundamentally altered the landscape in Canada's public history institutions. In light of court decisions that have declared that the principle of the honour of the Crown must be upheld by the state in all its dealings with Aboriginal peoples and that Aboriginal peoples' oral history must be "placed on an equal footing" with written historical documents, national museums and archives have been compelled to respond accordingly.[133] The governance structures, policies, ethical codes, and daily operations of national museums and archives have had to adapt to accommodate the constitutional and legal realities of Canada's changing relationship with Aboriginal peoples.[134]

Canada's national museums

The 1996 *Report of the Royal Commission on Aboriginal Peoples* made a specific recommendation to Canada's museums.

a) Museums and cultural institutions [should] adopt ethical guidelines governing all aspects of collection, disposition, display and interpretation of artifacts related to Aboriginal culture and heritage, including the following:

b) Involving Aboriginal people in drafting, endorsing and implementing the guidelines;

c) Creating inventories of relevant holdings and making such inventories freely accessible to Aboriginal people;

d) Cataloguing and designating appropriate use and display of relevant holdings;

e) Repatriating, on request, objects that are sacred or integral to the history and continuity of particular nations and communities;

f) Returning human remains to the family, community or nation of origin, on request, or consulting with Aboriginal advisers on appropriate disposition, where remains cannot be associated with a particular nation;

g) Ensuring that Aboriginal people and communities have effective access to cultural education and training opportunities available through museums and cultural institutions. [Recommendation 3.6.4][135]

In the years following the Royal Commission's report, museums across the country have implemented many of its recommendations.[136] Many have worked with communities to repatriate human remains or cultural artifacts. For some institutions, consultation and collaborative partnerships with Aboriginal communities have become standard practice, and Aboriginal internships and other training opportunities have been established. Yet, more is still needed, even as museums are faced with significant challenges in obtaining adequate and stable multi-year funding to properly support these critical initiatives.[137]

Over the past three decades, Canadian museums that used to tell the story of the nation's past with little regard for the histories of First Nations, Inuit, and Métis peoples are slowly transforming. Although dialogue between museums and Aboriginal peoples has improved substantially since the 1980s, the broader debate continues over whose history is told and how it is interpreted. Here, we focus on two national museums, the Canadian Museum of History (formerly the Canadian Museum of Civilization)[138] and the Canadian Museum for Human Rights. As national public history institutions, they bear a particular responsibility to retell the story of Canada's past so that it reflects not only diverse cultures, history, and experiences of First Nations, Inuit, and Métis peoples, but also the collective violence and historical injustices that they have suffered at the hands of the state. It is instructive to examine how these two public history institutions plan to interpret the history of Aboriginal peoples and address historical injustices in the coming years.

Canadian Museum of History

Appearing before the House of Commons Standing Committee on Canadian Heritage in June 2013, Mark O'Neill, president and chief executive officer of the Canadian Museum of Civilization Corporation, acknowledged that many important aspects and milestones of Canadian history—including residential schools—have been missing from the museum.

> [P]erhaps the most egregious flaw in the Canada Hall is its starting point. If you've been there, you will know that its telling of our national story begins not with the arrival of First Peoples but with the arrival of Europeans in the eleventh

> century. Colonization as a term or concept is not mentioned in Canada Hall. This is something we intend to correct. Canadians made it very clear to us during the public engagement process that the voices and the experiences of First Peoples must have a place in any narrative of Canadian history.... Canadians want us to be comprehensive, frank and fair in our presentation of their history. They want us to examine both the good and the bad from our past. We were urged to foster a sense of national pride without ignoring our failings, mistakes and controversies.[139]

In July 2013, the Canadian Museum of Civilization and its partner, the Canadian War Museum, released a joint research strategy intended to guide the research activities at both institutions until 2023. "Memory and commemoration" is a key research theme; objectives include the presentation of competing and contentious historical narratives of Confederation and the two world wars, and the use of "selected commemorations to explore concepts of myth, memory, and nation." The museums intended to "present honestly, but respectfully, for public understanding issues of contention or debate ... [through] deliberate exploration of traumatic pasts (e.g. Africville or residential schools)."[140]

Drawing on research showing that Canadians valued their "personal and family connections to history," the Canadian Museum of History said that it intended to "explore the realities of contemporary life for Canada's First Peoples [including] cultural engagements with modernity, environmental change, and globalization, evolving concepts of tradition, political mobilization, and new avenues of social expression ... [and] the impact of rapid change in Canada's North, especially for Inuit."[141] Another key research theme is "First Peoples," with a particular focus on Aboriginal histories.

> The histories and cultures of Aboriginal peoples are central to all Canadians' understanding of their shared past. Respectful exploration of the interwoven, often difficult histories of Aboriginal and non-Aboriginal Peoples is a responsible, timely contribution to contemporary Canada, and to global understanding of Aboriginal Peoples.... There are four principal objectives in exploring and sharing Aboriginal narratives.... 1) Represent Aboriginal histories and cultures within broader Canadian narratives ... 2) Explore intercultural engagement and its continuing impacts ... 3) Broaden understanding of Aboriginal history before European contact ... [and] 4) Deepen efforts to support First Peoples' stewardship.[142]

We are encouraged to note that much of what the museum's research strategy emphasizes is consistent with our own findings: Canadians, including youth and teachers, think they should learn about the history and legacy of residential schools and Aboriginal history more broadly. We take particular note of the prominence given to presenting both the positive and negative aspects of Canada's history, demonstrating the relevance of the past to the present, including marginalized voices and perspectives, encouraging collaboration, and making connections between personal and public history.

The Canadian Museum for Human Rights

As a national public history institution, the new Canadian Museum for Human Rights (CMHR) in Winnipeg is mandated to "explore the subject of human rights, with special but not exclusive reference to Canada, in order to enhance the public's understanding of human rights, to promote respect for others, and to encourage reflection and dialogue."[143] Speaking at the TRC's Forum on the National Research Centre in Vancouver on March 3, 2011, CMHR President and Chief Executive Officer Stuart Murray talked about the museum's vision for, and role in, national reconciliation. He emphasized the prominent role of the CMHR's First Nations, Inuit, and Métis advisors, as well as the Elders Advisory Council, Aboriginal Youth Council, and the broader Aboriginal community, in the planning and programs developed by the museum.[144]

Given the deep controversies that exist regarding the history of the residential school system, it is perhaps not surprising that the CMHR was criticized by the Southern Chiefs Organization in Manitoba in June of 2013, after media reports that the museum would not "label human rights violations against First Nations as genocide." From the Southern Chiefs Organization's perspective, the museum was "sanitizing the true history of Canada's shameful treatment of First Nations."[145] Stuart Murray issued a statement on July 26, 2013, clarifying the museum's position.

> In the Museum, we will examine the gross and systemic human rights violation of Indigenous peoples. This will include information about the efforts of the Aboriginal community, and others, to gain recognition of these violations as genocide—and we will use that word. We will look at the ways this recognition can occur when people combat denial and work to break the silence surrounding such horrific abuses.... We have chosen, at present, not to use the word "genocide" in the title for one of the exhibits about this experience, but will be using the term in the exhibit itself when describing community efforts for this recognition. Historical fact and emerging information will be presented to help visitors reach their own conclusions. While a museum does not have the power to make declarations of genocide, we can certainly encourage—through ongoing partnership with the Indigenous community itself—an honest examination of Canada's human rights history, in hopes that respect and reconciliation will prevail.[146]

The museum signalled its intention to create opportunities for Canadians to engage in a much broader and long-overdue public dialogue about the issue of genocide as it relates to the residential school system. The CMHR envisioned creating a public education venue for teaching all Canadians to think more critically about the history of human rights violations against Aboriginal peoples.

Speaking about the forthcoming 2017 commemoration of Canada's Confederation, Murray observed that Canada's human rights record is not unblemished, and that

> for many Aboriginal communities, this is not necessarily an event that warrants celebration. But by looking honestly and openly at our past, by engaging a diversity of voices and perspectives, and by celebrating what has been accomplished to overcome these mistakes, we will serve to make our nation more united, more proud, and more just. We can use this anniversary to continue on a journey of reconciliation.[147]

The Commission believes that, as Canada's 150th anniversary approaches in 2017, national reconciliation is the most suitable framework to guide commemoration of this significant historical benchmark in Canada's history. This intended celebration can be an opportunity for Canadians to take stock of the past, celebrating the country's accomplishments without shirking responsibility for its failures. Fostering more inclusive public discourse about the past through a reconciliation lens would open up new and exciting possibilities for a future in which Aboriginal peoples take their rightful place in Canada's history as founding nations who have strong and unique contributions to make to this country.

In the Commission's view, there is an urgent need in Canada to develop historically literate citizens who understand why and how the past is relevant to their own lives and the future of the country. Museums have an ethical responsibility to foster national reconciliation, and not simply tell one party's version of the past. This can be accomplished by representing the history of residential schools and of Aboriginal peoples in ways that invite multiple, sometimes conflicting, perspectives, yet ultimately facilitate empathy, mutual respect, and a desire for reconciliation that is rooted in justice.

The Canadian Museum of History and the Canadian Museum for Human Rights, working collaboratively with Aboriginal peoples, regional and local museums, and the Canadian Museums Association, should take a leadership role in making reconciliation a central theme in the commemoration of the 150th anniversary of Canada's Confederation in 2017.

It must be noted that although we have focused on national museums here, regional and local museums also have a critical role to play in creating opportunities for Canadians to examine the historical injustices suffered by First Nations, Inuit, and Métis peoples, engage in public dialogue about what has been done and what remains to be done to remedy this, and reflect on the spirit and intent of reconciliation. Through their exhibits, education outreach, and research programs, all museums are well positioned to contribute to education for reconciliation.

Calls to Action

67) We call upon the federal government to provide funding to the Canadian Museums Association to undertake, in collaboration with Aboriginal peoples, a national review of museum policies and best practices to determine the level of compliance with the United Nations *Declaration on the Rights of Indigenous Peoples* and to make recommendations.

68) We call upon the federal government, in collaboration with Aboriginal peoples, and the Canadian Museums Association to mark the 150th anniversary of Canadian Confederation in 2017 by establishing a dedicated national funding program for commemoration projects on the theme of reconciliation.

Canada's national archives: Sharing Aboriginal history versus keeper of state records

As Canada's national archives, Library and Archives Canada (LAC) has a dual function with regard to its holdings on Aboriginal peoples. It is both a public history institution tasked with making documents relevant to Aboriginal history accessible to the public, and it is the custodian of federal government departmental historical records.

In 2005, LAC issued a "Collection Development Framework," which set out the principles and practices that would guide the institution's acquisitions and preservation of its holdings. The framework made specific commitments regarding materials related to Aboriginal peoples.

> LAC recognizes the contributions of Aboriginal peoples to the documentary heritage of Canada, and realizes that, in building its collection of materials, it must take into account the diversity of Aboriginal cultures, the relationship the Government of Canada has with Aboriginal peoples, and the unique needs and realities of Aboriginal communities. The development of a national strategy will be done in consultation and collaboration with Aboriginal communities and organizations, and will respect the ways in which indigenous knowledge and heritage is preserved or ought to be preserved and protected within or outside of Aboriginal communities.[148]

Library and Archives Canada has developed various guides and resources related to researching Aboriginal heritage.[149] But a fundamental tension exists between LAC's public education mandate to work collaboratively with Aboriginal peoples to document their cultural and social history versus its legal obligation to serve the state. This tension is most evident where archived documents are relevant to various historical injustices involving Aboriginal peoples. Historical records housed in LAC have been used extensively as evidence by both Aboriginal claimants and Crown defendants in litigation involving residential schools, Treaties, Aboriginal title and rights cases, and land claims.

In the case of documents related to residential schools, the problems associated with LAC's dual function became apparent during the litigation period prior to the Settlement Agreement. During this time, with regard to its public education mandate, LAC produced "Native Residential Schools in Canada: A Selective Bibliography" in 2002, and assisted Aboriginal people, academics, and other researchers who wished to access these holdings.[150] But, because the residential schools litigation put the federal government in the position of being the major defendant in the court cases, the overriding priority for LAC, as the custodian of federal government departmental records, was to meet its legal obligations to the Crown.

Librarian and Archivist Emeritus Dr. Ian Wilson, Canada's former national archivist, described this tension. He explained that, as the residential school litigation intensified,

> Lawyers besieged the archives. Archivists, caught between the vagaries of old informal recordkeeping practices in church schools across the country, legal demands for instant and full access and obligations to employer and profession, struggled to uphold their ideal of the honest stewardship of the records.... This process has tested the capacity of the archives and our professional ability to respond.[151]

These challenges did not end with the implementation of the 2007 Settlement Agreement. The TRC's own difficulties in gaining access to government records held in LAC demonstrated why state-controlled archives are not necessarily best suited to meet the needs of Survivors, their families, and communities.

By 2009, in terms of public education, LAC had partnered with the Legacy of Hope Foundation and the Aboriginal Healing Foundation on two exhibitions: *Where are the Children? Healing the Legacy of the Residential Schools*; and *"We were so far away ...": The Inuit experience of residential schools.*[152] Library and Archives Canada also produced an updated online version of the bibliography, "The Legacy of the Residential School System in Canada: A Selective Bibliography."[153] In 2010, LAC made an online finding aid available, "Conducting Research on Residential Schools: A Guide to the Records of the Indian and Inuit Affairs Program and Related Resources at Library and Archives Canada."[154]

In the spirit of reconciliation, LAC archivists (along with church archivists) brought binders of residential school photographs to the Learning Places at the TRC's National Events, where Survivors and others could see them and get copies of their class pictures and other school activities. For many Survivors, especially those who had no visual record of their own childhood or no pictures of siblings who have since passed away, this proved to be one of the most treasured aspects of the National Events experience. However, during this same time period, LAC's holdings and its role in complying with the federal government's legal obligations for document production, under the terms of the Settlement Agreement, became the focus of court proceedings between the TRC and the federal government.

The TRC seeks full access to LAC records

Schedule N to the Indian Residential Schools Settlement Agreement describes the mandate of the TRC as well as the obligations of the parties to the Agreement to assist the Commission in its work. There is a provision that deals with the obligation of the parties to provide relevant records to the Commission. It states:

> In order to ensure the efficacy of the truth and reconciliation process, Canada and the churches will provide all relevant documents in their possession or control to and for the use of the Truth and Reconciliation Commission, subject to the privacy interests of an individual as provided by applicable privacy legislation, and subject to and in compliance with applicable privacy and access to information legislation, and except for those documents for which solicitor-client privilege applies and is asserted.
>
> In cases where privacy interests of an individual exist, and subject to and in compliance with applicable privacy legislation and access to information legislation, researchers for the Commission shall have access to the documents, provided privacy is protected. In cases where solicitor-client privilege is asserted, the asserting party will provide a list of all documents for which the privilege is claimed.
>
> Canada and the churches are not required to give up possession of their original documents to the Commission. They are required to compile all relevant documents in an organized manner for review by the Commission and to provide access to their archives for the Commission to carry out its mandate. Provision of documents does not require provision of original documents. Originals or true copies may be provided or originals may be provided temporarily for copying purposes if the original documents are not to be housed with the Commission.
>
> Insofar as agreed to by the individuals affected and as permitted by process requirements, information from the Independent Assessment Process (IAP), existing litigation and Dispute Resolution processes may be transferred to the Commission for research and archiving purposes.[155]

Gaining access to archival government records about the administration of the residential school system has been an important part of the mandate of the Truth and Reconciliation Commission of Canada. Such access has been essential for our own understanding of the history of government policy and practice in relation to Aboriginal peoples in general and residential schools in particular. But it has also been necessary to fulfilling our mandate obligation to ensure ongoing public access to the records through the National Centre for Truth and Reconciliation. The Commission's attempts to obtain records were frustrated by a series of bureaucratic and legal roadblocks.

In April 2012, the Commission was compelled to file a "Request for Direction" in the Ontario Superior Court of Justice regarding access to relevant federal records housed in the national archives. At issue was the question of what Canada's obligations were under the Settlement Agreement with respect to providing to the TRC archived government documents housed at Library and Archives Canada. The Commission, Aboriginal Affairs and Northern Development Canada, the Department of Justice, and Library and Archives Canada had very different views as to how the TRC should acquire these records.

In LAC's view, its role was that of the neutral keeper of government records, whose task was to facilitate and empower federal government departments to canvass their own archival holdings.

Faced with the onerous task of conducting its own research through LAC's vast holdings, Canada's position was that its obligation was limited to searching and producing relevant documents from the active and semi-active files in various departments. The government's view became that departments need provide the TRC only with departmental researcher status to access their archived documents at LAC so that the Commission could conduct its own research.

The TRC's position was that Canada was obligated to produce all relevant documents, including those at LAC, and had an additional obligation to provide the Commission with access to LAC in order to conduct its own research. Although the TRC, in the spirit of co-operation, had agreed to obtain departmental researcher status, it maintained that this was unnecessary because the Settlement Agreement already gave the Commission unconditional access to the archives. The end result was that Canada had effectively shifted the onus of its responsibility to produce LAC documents onto the TRC.

In rendering his decision in favour of the Commission, Justice Stephen Goudge ruled:

> In my view, the first paragraph of section 11 sets out Canada's basic obligation concerning documents in its possession or control. The plain meaning of the language is straightforward. It is to provide all relevant documents to the TRC. The obligation is in unqualified language unlimited by where the documents are located within the government of Canada. Nor is the obligation limited to the documents assembled by Canada for production in the underlying litigation. [para. 69]

> I therefore conclude that given their meaning, the language in section 11 of Schedule N does not exclude documents archived at LAC from Canada's obligation to the TRC. The context in which the Settlement Agreement was created provides further important support for that conclusion in several ways. [para. 71]
>
> First, telling the history of Indian Residential Schools was clearly seen as a central aspect of the mandate of the TRC when the Settlement Agreement was made. Since Canada played a vital role in the IRS [Indian Residential School] system, Canada's documents wherever they were held, would have been understood as a very important historical resource for this purpose. [para. 72]
>
> Second, the Settlement Agreement charged the TRC with compiling an historical record of the IRS system to be accessible to the public in the future. Here too, Canada's documents, wherever housed, would have been seen to be vital to this task. [para. 73]
>
> Third, the story of the history and the historical record to be compiled cover over 100 years and dates back to the nineteenth century. In light of this time span, it would have been understood at the time of the Settlement Agreement that much of the relevant documentary record in Canada's possession would be archived in LAC and would no longer be in the active or semi-active files of the departments of the Government of Canada. [para. 74]
>
> Fourth, it would have been obvious that the experienced staff at LAC would have vastly more ability to identify and organize the relevant documents at LAC than would the newly hired staff of the newly formed TRC. It would have made little sense to give that task to the latter rather than the former, particularly given its importance to the TRC's mandate. [para. 75][156]

Although the difficulties the TRC encountered in obtaining LAC documents were specific to the Commission's mandate, they highlight broader questions concerning the role of state archives and archivists in providing documents that reveal the facts of why and how a targeted group of people have suffered harms on a massive scale. As part of a growing trend towards demanding better government accountability and transparency, and the evolution of new privacy and freedom of information legislation, archives have become more directly connected to struggles for human rights and justice.[157]

Archives and access to justice

Library and Archives Canada's federal government departmental records pertaining to Aboriginal peoples are vital to understanding how human rights violations occurred and their subsequent impacts. In 2005, the United Nations adopted the

Joinet-Orentlicher Principles, which set out remedial measures that states must undertake to satisfy their duty to guard against impunity from past human rights violations and prevent their reoccurrence. This includes victims' right to know the truth about what happened to them and their missing family members. Society at large also has the right to know the truth about what happened in the past and what circumstances led to mass human rights violations. The state has a duty to safeguard this knowledge and to ensure that proper documentation is preserved in archives and history books.

The *Joinet-Orentlicher Principles* state, "The full and effective exercise of the right to truth is ensured through preservation of archives." Equally important, ready access to the archives must be facilitated for victims and their relatives, and for the purposes of research (principles 5, 14, 15, 16).[158]

The Commission notes that in his August 2013 report to the United Nations Human Rights Council, Pablo de Greiff, Special Rapporteur on the Promotion of Truth, Justice, Reparation and Guarantees of Non-Recurrence, made specific reference to the importance of archives. He found that both a truth commission's own records and those housed in national, regional, and local archives extend the life and legacy of the truth commission's work. Archives can serve as permanent sites where post-commission accountability and the right to truth can be realized.[159] He further explained that archives "are a means of guaranteeing that the voices of victims will not be lost, and they contribute to a culture of memorialisation and remembrance. They also provide a safeguard against revisionism and denial—essential given the long duration and non-linearity of social reconciliation and integration processes."[160] He concluded that "truth commissions and national archives contribute in a substantial manner to realizing the right to truth and may further criminal prosecutions, reparations, and institutional and personnel reforms," and recommended that international archival standards be established.[161]

Although de Greiff does not reference Indigenous peoples specifically, we note that in many countries, including Canada, the access to, and protection of, historical records have been instrumental in advancing the rights of Indigenous peoples and documenting the state's wrongful actions. In the wake of the South African and other truth commissions, some archivists have come to see themselves not simply as neutral custodians of national history, but also as professionals who are responsible for ensuring that records documenting past injustices are preserved and used to strengthen government accountability and support justice.[162]

Calls to Action

69) We call upon Library and Archives Canada to:

i. Fully adopt and implement the *United Nations Declaration on the Rights of Indigenous Peoples* and the *United Nations Joinet-Orentlicher Principles*, as related to Aboriginal peoples' inalienable right to know the truth about what happened and why, with regard to human rights violations committed against them in the residential schools.

ii. Ensure that its record holdings related to residential schools are accessible to the public.

iii. Commit more resources to its public education materials and programming on residential schools.

70) We call upon the federal government to provide funding to the Canadian Association of Archivists to undertake, in collaboration with Aboriginal peoples, a national review of archival policies and best practices to:

i. Determine the level of compliance with the *United Nations Declaration on the Rights of Indigenous Peoples* and the *United Nations Joinet-Orentlicher Principles*, as related to Aboriginal peoples' inalienable right to know the truth about what happened and why, with regard to human rights violations committed against them in the residential schools.

ii. Produce a report with recommendations for full implementation of these international mechanisms as a reconciliation framework for Canadian archives.

Missing children, unmarked graves, and residential school cemeteries

Over the course of the Commission's work, many Aboriginal people spoke to us about the children who never came home from residential school. The question of what happened to their loved ones and where they were laid to rest has haunted families and communities. Throughout the history of Canada's residential school system, there was no effort to record across the entire system the number of students who died while attending the schools each year. The National Residential School Student Death Register, established by the Truth and Reconciliation Commission of Canada, represents the first national effort to record the names of the students who died at school. The register is far from complete: there are, for example, many relevant documents that have yet to be received, collected, and reviewed.

Some of these records have been located in provincial records. In June 2012, at their annual general meeting, the Chief Coroners and Medical Examiners of Canada approved a unanimous resolution to support the TRC's Missing Children Project by making available to the Commission their records on the deaths of Aboriginal children in the care of residential school authorities. The Office of the Chief Coroner of Ontario had already done some groundbreaking work in terms of screening and reviewing its records, and identifying 120 possible cases of death of an Aboriginal residential school student. The TRC subsequently contacted chief coroners across the country to request their assistance in locating records related to deaths at residential school. As of 2014, chief coroners' offices in Saskatchewan, Northwest Territories, Manitoba, and Nova Scotia had also responded to the Commission's request for records.

Other regional agencies also hold critical information in their records. The TRC contacted offices of provincial vital statistics across the country. At the Alberta National Event, Assistant Deputy Minister Peter Cunningham, from the Ministry of Aboriginal Relations and Reconciliation in British Columbia, offered a flash drive in a small, carved, bentwood box, as an expression of reconciliation. He said,

> I think it's incredibly important that all of the information comes out about what was a very deeply dark and disturbing event in Canadian history ... residential schools.... I'm here today to add to that body of knowledge on behalf of the government of British Columbia and the Vital Statistics Agency of BC.... The information on this flash drive is information about Aboriginal children between the ages of 4 and 19 years of age who died in British Columbia between the years 1870 and 1984.[163]

As of 2014, in addition to the office in British Columbia, vital statistics offices in Alberta, Nova Scotia, Ontario, Saskatchewan, Yukon, and Nunavut had responded to the Commission's request for records. To complete the work begun by the Commission on the National Residential School Student Death Register, it will be critical for the National Centre for Truth and Reconciliation to obtain all records related to the deaths of residential school students.

Call to Action

71) We call upon all chief coroners and provincial vital statistics agencies that have not provided to the Truth and Reconciliation Commission of Canada their records on the deaths of Aboriginal children in the care of residential school authorities to make these documents available to the National Centre for Truth and Reconciliation.

The completion and maintenance of the National Residential School Student Death Register will require ongoing financial support.

Call to Action

72) We call upon the federal government to allocate sufficient resources to the National Centre for Truth and Reconciliation to allow it to develop and maintain the National Residential School Student Death Register established by the Truth and Reconciliation Commission of Canada.

There is also a need for information sharing with the families of those who died at the schools. As the historical record indicates, families were not adequately informed of the health condition of their children. There is a need for the federal government to ensure that appropriate measures are undertaken to inform families of the fate of their children and to ensure that the children are commemorated in a way that is acceptable to their families.

Calls to Action

73) We call upon the federal government to work with churches, Aboriginal communities, and former residential school students to establish and maintain an online registry of residential school cemeteries, including, where possible, plot maps showing the location of deceased residential school children.

74) We call upon the federal government to work with the churches and Aboriginal community leaders to inform the families of children who died at residential schools of the child's burial location, and to respond to families' wishes for appropriate commemoration ceremonies and markers, and reburial in home communities where requested.

As Commissioners, we have been honoured to bear witness to commemoration ceremonies held by communities to remember and honour children who died in the residential schools. Such ceremonies have played an important role in the reconciliation process. At the Alberta National Event, the board members of the Remembering the Children Society offered an expression of reconciliation. They spoke about the process they undertook to identify children who had died while attending the Red Deer Industrial School. Richard Lightning said,

> My father, Albert Lightning, and his younger brother, David, from Samson First Nation, went to the Red Deer Industrial School, which was operated by the Methodist Church from 1893 to 1919. Albert Lightning survived this school experience, but David died of Spanish flu in 1918. In 1986, Albert visited the Red Deer and District Museum and Archives, saying to the staff person, Lyle Keewatin-Richards, "Oh, there you are. You're the one who is going to find my little brother." Lyle learned that along with three other students who had died at the same time, David was buried in the Red Deer City Cemetery. Lyle also became aware of the existence of the school cemetery beside Sylvan Creek.

Rev. Cecile Fausak[164] explained,

> Around 2004 ... people at Sunnybrook United Church began to ask themselves, "Is there anything we can do to build better relations with First Nations peoples in this area?" And Lyle, remembering back, suggested then, "There is this little project. The children who were buried at the long-neglected [residential] school

> cemetery and in this city need to be remembered." So the church formed a committee ... and over the next few years, we researched the site and the school records, personally visited the seven Cree and Stony communities and the Métis nation from which all the students had come. In September 2009, over thirty people from those concerned First Nations and Métis communities travelled to Red Deer, had stew and bannock at Sunnybrook United Church, and visited the school cemetery for the first time, where we were welcomed by the [current] landowner.

Muriel Stanley Venne, from the Sunnybrook United Church, continued,

> A working group was formed to organize the first [commemoration] feast, which was held at Fort Normandeau, on June 30, 2010. As the more than 325 names of students were read, a hush fell over the crowd.... Since then the collaboration [has] continued, with First Nations Treaty 6 and 7, Métis Nation of Alberta, United Church members, the Red Deer Museum and Art Gallery, the City and County [of Red Deer], the [Indian] Friendship Centre, and school boards. This led to the formation of the Remembering the Children Society in 2011.... Our society's objectives include: continued support for recovering Indian residential school cemeteries and histories in Alberta; educating the public about the same; honouring the Survivors, and those who died in the schools; as well as identifying the unmarked graves. Each year for the next three years, a commemorative feast was held. At the third gathering, many descendants shared stories of the impact on them, their parents, and grandparents, because they attended the Red Deer Industrial School.

Charles Wood then said,

> The Society has worked with the museum in developing a new standing exhibit and with the Waskasoo Park administration in the preparation of new interpretive signage at Fort Normandeau regarding the school history. We are grateful for the truth spoken of a painful shared history, the friendships we have formed, and the healing that has happened as a result of working together for over five years. We will continue to remember the children of the past and present. In the Bentwood Box, as symbols of our work together, we place a program of the first ceremony, a DVD from the museum display, flower and ribbon pins from the third feast, and a copy of guidelines we have published of our experience, for those who wish to undertake a similar recovery of a residential school cemetery.[165]

For the most part, the residential school cemeteries and burial sites that the Commission documented are abandoned, disused, and vulnerable to disturbance. While there have been community commemoration measures undertaken in some locations, there is an overall need for a national strategy for the documentation, maintenance, commemoration, and protection of residential school cemeteries. This work is complex and sensitive. Although former schools might be associated with specific Aboriginal communities, the cemeteries may contain the bodies of children from many communities. They may also contain the bodies of teachers (or their children) who died while working at the institutions. No one set of recommendations will serve all circumstances.

Call to Action

75) We call upon the federal government to work with provincial, territorial, and municipal governments, churches, Aboriginal communities, former residential school students, and current landowners to develop and implement strategies and procedures for the ongoing identification, documentation, maintenance, commemoration, and protection of residential school cemeteries or other sites at which residential school children were buried. This is to include the provision of appropriate memorial ceremonies and commemorative markers to honour the deceased children.

As infrastructure and resource development accelerates throughout Canada, the risk of damage to undocumented residential school cemeteries increases. Depending on the jurisdiction, environmental impact assessments, which include the assessment of heritage sites, are usually required prior to development. This generally involves a review of existing documentation, evaluation of the potential for heritage sites within the development zone, and also often a physical search. Such work is often done in phases, with preliminary review of centralized archives and databases to inform subsequent investigation. Local knowledge about residential cemeteries might not be readily accessible to non-local planners, resource managers, and impact assessors. Therefore, it is important that locally collected information is shared with agencies responsible for land-use planning, environmental impact assessment, and protection and regulation of cemeteries.

Such information sharing is hindered by limited documentation, unclear jurisdictional responsibility, and uncoordinated consolidation of information. These problems could be addressed through the establishment of a registry of residential school cemeteries that could be available online. At a minimum, such a registry should include the identification, duration, and affiliation of each cemetery; its legal description; current land ownership and condition; and its location coordinates.

The complex and sensitive work of documenting, maintaining, commemorating, and protecting residential school cemeteries must be undertaken according to a set of guiding principles that are based on community priorities and knowledge. Any physical investigation of the cemeteries must involve close consultation with interested communities, with identification of community-driven objectives, suitable methodologies, and attention to spiritual and emotional sensitivities.

The generally sparse written documentation must be combined with locally held knowledge. Often, this information will be unwritten, and held by Survivors, the families of Survivors, staff, or local residents. This locally held information can be used to verify, correct, and amplify archival information. This work might involve local initiatives to physically document a cemetery's extent and location, and also to identify individual graves within or around the cemetery area. When undertaking physical inspection and documentation of the cemeteries, the most cost-effective strategy involves collection and consolidation of both documentary and locally held knowledge prior to initiating fieldwork. This will improve efficiency of the physical search, and aid selection of the most effective field methodologies. It also enables researchers to determine community wishes regarding the most appropriate approaches to site investigation. This includes preferred protocols regarding prayers and ceremonial observance prior to a site visit.

Call to Action

76) We call upon the parties engaged in the work of documenting, maintaining, commemorating, and protecting residential school cemeteries to adopt strategies in accordance with the following principles:

   i. The Aboriginal community most affected shall lead the development of such strategies.

   ii. Information shall be sought from residential school Survivors and other Knowledge Keepers in the development of such strategies.

   iii. Aboriginal protocols shall be respected before any potentially invasive technical inspection and investigation of a cemetery site.

The Commission believes that assisting families to learn the fate of children who died in residential schools; locating unmarked graves; and maintaining, protecting, and commemorating residential school cemeteries are vital to healing and reconciliation. Archives and government departments and agencies have a crucial role to play in this process. Equally important, archival records can help Survivors, their families, and communities to reconstruct their family and community histories. Yet, accessing such holdings is not without problems.

The limitations of archives

We have outlined how Library and Archives Canada has dealt with its residential school records. Other records that are relevant to the history and legacy of the residential school system are scattered across the country in provincial, territorial, municipal, and local archives, as well as in government departments and agencies that were not parties to the Settlement Agreement. All this has made it extremely difficult for Survivors, their families, and communities to access the very records that hold such critical pieces of information about their own lives and the history of their communities.

The Settlement Agreement church archives, to varying degrees, have endeavoured to make their residential school records more accessible to Survivors, their families and communities, researchers, and the general public.[166] For example, the United Church of Canada has made all its residential school photographs and school histories available online to make them more accessible to Survivors and others, and "as a form of repatriation to First Nations communities."[167]

The National Centre for Truth and Reconciliation: An emerging model

Archives may be viewed with distrust by First Nations, Inuit, and Métis peoples. Many feel that much of their lives is contained in documents (most of which they have never seen) kept by the state in order to study and categorize them in a depersonalized way.[168] In various ways, existing archives have been ill suited to serve the needs of Survivors, their families, and communities. What Aboriginal peoples required was a centre of their own—a cultural space that would serve as both an archives and a museum to hold the collective memory of Survivors and others whose lives were touched by the history and legacy of the residential school system.

With this understanding, the TRC mandate called for the establishment of a new National Research Centre (NRC) to hold all the historical and newly created documents and oral statements related to residential schools, and to make them accessible for the future. This NRC, as created by the Truth and Reconciliation Commission of Canada, and now renamed the National Centre for Truth and Reconciliation (NCTR), is an evolving, Survivor-centred model of education for reconciliation. Implementing a new approach to public education, research, and record keeping, the centre will serve as a public memory "site of conscience," bearing permanent witness to Survivors' testimonies and the history and legacy of the residential school system.[169] Along with other museums and archives across the country, the centre will shape how the residential school era is understood and remembered.

The concept of the National Centre for Truth and Reconciliation has deep roots. For many years, Survivors and their supporters called for a centre that would be their lasting legacy to their own history and to Canada's national memory. In March 2011, the TRC hosted an international forum in Vancouver, "Sharing Truth: Creating a National Research Centre on Residential Schools," to study how records and other materials from truth and reconciliation commissions around the world have been archived.[170]

Several speakers talked about their vision for the NCTR. Georges Erasmus, former co-chair of the Royal Commission on Aboriginal Peoples, and then president of the Aboriginal Healing Foundation, said,

> Those who become the keepers of the archives become stewards of human stories and relationships, of what has been an endowment to what will be. Because no legacy is enriched by counterfeit; a nation is ill served by a history which is not genuine. This is a high calling indeed and it must be said that too often the promise and the potential of this stewardship has gone unrealized.... If the stories of our people are not accessible to the general public, it will be as if their experiences never occurred. And if their voices are rendered as museum pieces, it will be as if their experience is frozen in time. What we need are open, dynamic, interactive spaces and participatory forms of narrative, knowledge, and research. This would be a fitting way to step into the twenty-first century and into a new kind of relationship.... The National Research Centre ought to be a treasure valued by all sorts of people.[171]

The Commission subsequently issued an open invitation for organizations to submit proposals for the NCTR, based on specific criteria. In June 2013, the TRC announced that the University of Manitoba would house the new centre.

The National Centre for Truth and Reconciliation will play a key educational role in ensuring that historic harms, and Treaty, constitutional, and human rights violations, against Aboriginal peoples are not repeated. As a highly visible site of conscience, it will serve as an intervention in the country's public memory and national history. The centre is independent from government. It is guided by a Governing Circle, the majority of whose members must be Aboriginal and which includes Survivor representatives. Among its various responsibilities, this governing body will make decisions and provide advice on ceremonies and protocols, and establish a Survivors' Circle.[172]

The centre will house TRC records, including Survivors' oral history statements, artworks, expressions of reconciliation, and other materials gathered by the Commission, as well as government and church documents. It is intended to be a welcoming and safe place for Survivors, their families, and communities to have access to their own history. The centre has committed to creating a culturally rooted and healing environment where all Canadians can honour, learn from, and commemorate the history and legacy of the residential schools.

Once the centre is fully operational, it will be well positioned to take a leadership role in forging new directions in residential school- and Indigenous rights-based research, establishing new standards and benchmarks for archival and museum policy, management, and operations, based on Indigenous and Western principles and best practices.

The University of Manitoba and its partners[173] have emphasized that the centre recognizes the

> paramount importance of accessibility [for] the Aboriginal survivor, family member [or]researcher, [and is] committed to recognition of Aboriginal peoples as co-creators of the IRS records, through co-curation and participatory archiving; and committed to continuing the work of the TRC of statement-gathering, public education, engagement and outreach.[174]

The NCTR will incorporate an

> archival system and approach which is devoted to "reconciling records"; [it] will … support Indigenous frameworks of knowledge, memory and evidence, and reposition … Indigenous communities as co-creators of archival records that relate to them, including government archives. Such approaches acknowledge rights in records that extend beyond access to working in partnership with archival institutions to manage appraisal, description and accessibility of records relating to Indigenous communities.[175]

The centre is committed to "establish[ing] trust with Aboriginal communities by working with these communities to realize their own goals through participatory archiving.... The process of participatory archiving, interacting with as complete a record as possible, will be a powerful force for reconciliation and healing."[176] As well, the Centre for Truth and Reconciliation is also committed to

> personally supporting survivors, their families, and all researchers in navigating, using, and understanding the records, in a culturally sensitive environment. The support that the NRC will provide includes emotionally-sensitive support, acknowledging that accessing the NRC documents may be traumatic, difficult or otherwise emotional experiences for many users. An Elder will be present or on call (from a nearby building) most of the time the NRC is open to the public. LAC and other government departments have no mandate or capacity to offer these various supports, which are critical to relationship-building and overcoming the perception of archives as yet another mechanism of colonization, cultural appropriation by Western society and hyper-surveillance and objectification of Aboriginal peoples.[177]

On June 21, 2013, First Nations, Inuit, and Métis Survivors, Elders, the TRC, the University of Manitoba and its partner institutions, along with other dignitaries, gathered in Treaty 1 territory of the Anishinaabe peoples and homeland of the Métis Nation for a signing ceremony at the University of Manitoba.[178] The signing of a Trust Deed with the university marks the transfer of a sacred trust—a solemn promise that the Truth and Reconciliation Commission made to Survivors and all those affected by the residential schools as it travelled across the country, bearing witness to their testimonies.

The NCTR is committed to making all its holdings readily accessible to Survivors, their families, and communities, as well as to the public, educators, and researchers.[179] To support reconciliation at the local level, the Commission believes, it will be especially important to ensure that communities are able to access the centre's holdings and resources in order to produce histories of their own residential school experiences and their involvement in the truth, healing, and reconciliation process.

The centre will be a living legacy, a teaching and learning place for public education to promote understanding and reconciliation through ongoing statement gathering, new research, commemoration ceremonies, dialogues on reconciliation, and celebrations of Indigenous cultures, oral histories, and legal traditions.[180]

Calls to Action

77) We call upon provincial, territorial, municipal, and community archives to work collaboratively with the National Centre for Truth and Reconciliation to identify and collect copies of all records relevant to the history and legacy of the residential school system, and to provide these to the National Centre for Truth and Reconciliation.

78) We call upon the Government of Canada to commit to making a funding contribution of $10 million over seven years to the National Centre for Truth and Reconciliation, plus an additional amount to assist communities to research and produce histories of their own residential school experience and their involvement in truth, healing, and reconciliation.

Public memory: Dialogue, the arts, and commemoration

For Survivors who came forward at the TRC's National Events and Community Hearings, remembering their childhood often meant reliving horrific memories of abuse, hunger, and neglect. It meant dredging up painful feelings of loneliness, abandonment, and shame. Many still struggle to heal deep wounds of the past. Words fail to do justice to their courage in standing up and speaking out.

There were other memories too: of resilience; of lifetime friendships forged with classmates and teachers; of taking pride in art, music, or sports accomplishments; of becoming leaders in their communities and in the life of the nation. Survivors shared their memories with Canada and the world so that the truth could no longer be denied. Survivors also remembered so that other Canadians could learn from these hard lessons of the past. They want Canadians to know, to remember, to care, and to change.

One of the most significant harms to come out of the residential schools was the attack on Indigenous memory. The federal government's policy of assimilation sought to break the chain of memory that connected the hearts, minds, and spirits of Aboriginal children to their families, communities, and nations. Many, but not all,

Survivors have found ways to restore those connections. They believe that reconciliation with other Canadians calls for changing the country's collective, national history so that it is based on the truth about what happened to them as children, and to their families, communities, and nations.

Public memory is important. It is especially important to recognize that the transmission of that collective memory from generation to generation of First Nations, Inuit, and Métis individuals, families, and communities was impaired by the actions of those who ran residential schools.

As Commissioners, we are governed in our approach to reconciliation with this thought: the way that we all have been educated in this country—Aboriginal children in residential schools and Aboriginal and non-Aboriginal children in public and other schools—has brought us to where we are today: to a point where the psychological and emotional well-being of Aboriginal children has been harmed, and the relationship between Aboriginal and non-Aboriginal peoples has been seriously damaged. We believe that true reconciliation can take place only through a reshaping of a shared, national, collective memory: our understanding of who we are and what has come before. The youth of this country are taking up this challenge.

At the Alberta National Event in March 2014, Jessica Bolduc, an Indigenous youth representing the 4Rs Youth Movement, a national consortium of Indigenous and non-Indigenous youth-representing organizations, said:

> We have re-examined our thoughts and beliefs around colonialism, and have made a commitment to unpack our own baggage, and to enter into a new relationship with each other, using this momentum, to move our country forward, in light of the 150th anniversary of the Confederation of Canada in 2017.
>
> At this point in time, we ask ourselves, "What does that anniversary mean for us, as Indigenous youth and non-Indigenous youth, and how do we arrive at that day with something we can celebrate together?"... Our hope is that, one day, we will live together, as recognized nations, within a country we can all be proud of.[181]

Reshaping national history is a public process, one that happens through discussion, sharing, and commemoration. As Canadians gather in public spaces to share their memories, beliefs, and ideas about the past with others, our collective understanding of the present and future is formed.[182] As citizens, our ideas, world views, cultural identities, and values are shaped not only in classrooms and museums or by popular culture, but also in everyday social relationships and patterns of living that become our way of life.[183]

Public memory is dynamic—it changes over time as new understandings, dialogues, artistic expressions, and commemorations emerge. Public memory, much like national history, is often contentious. Although public memory can simply reinforce the colonial story of how Canada began with European settlement and became a nation, the process of remembering the past together also invites people to question this limited version of history.

Unlike some truth and reconciliation commissions that have focused on individual victims of human rights violations committed over a short period of time, this Commission has examined both the individual and collective harms perpetrated against Aboriginal families, communities, and nations for well over a century, as well as the preconditions that enabled such violence and oppression to occur. Of course, previously inaccessible archival documents are critically important to correcting the historical record, but we have given equal weight and greater voice to Indigenous oral-based history, legal traditions, and memory practices in our work and in this final report, since these represent the previously unheard and unrecorded versions of history, knowledge, and wisdom.[184] This has significantly informed our thinking about why repairing and revitalizing individual, family, and community memory are so crucial to the truth and reconciliation process.

Dialogue: Ceremony, testimony, and witnessing

Just as Survivors were involved in the long struggle to achieve a legally binding Settlement Agreement for the harms they have experienced, and an official apology, they have also continued to advise the Commission as it has implemented its mandate. Guided by Elders, Knowledge Keepers, and the members of the TRC Survivor Committee, the Commission has made Aboriginal oral history, legal traditions, and memory practices—ceremony, protocols, and the rituals of storytelling and testimonial witnessing—central to the TRC's National Events, Community Hearings, forums, and dialogues. The Commission's proceedings themselves constitute an oral history record, duly witnessed by all those in attendance. Working with local communities in each region, sacred ceremonies and protocols were performed and followed at all TRC events. Elders and traditional healers ensured that a safe environment was created for truth sharing, apology, healing, and acts of reconciliation.

The power of ceremony

Sacred ceremony has always been at the heart of Indigenous cultures, law, and political life. When ceremonies were outlawed by the federal government, they were hidden away until the law was repealed. Historically and, to a certain degree, even at present, Indigenous ceremonies that create community bonds, sanctify laws, and ratify Treaty making have been misunderstood, disrespected, and disregarded by

Canada. These ceremonies must now be recognized and honoured as an integral, vital, ongoing dimension of the truth and reconciliation process.

Ceremonies also reach across cultures to bridge the divide between Aboriginal and non-Aboriginal peoples. They are vital to reconciliation because of their sacred nature and because they connect people, preparing them to listen respectfully to each other in a difficult dialogue. Ceremonies are an affirmation of human dignity; they feed our spirits and comfort us even as they call on us to reimagine or envision finding common ground. Ceremonies validate and legitimize Treaties, family and kinship lines, and connections to the land. Ceremonies are also acts of memory sharing, mourning, healing, and renewal; they express the collective memory of families, communities, and nations.

Ceremonies enable us to set aside, however briefly, our cynicism, doubts, and disbelief, even as they console us, educate us, and inspire hope.[185] They have an intangible quality that moves us from our heads to our hearts. They teach us about ourselves, our histories, and our lives. Ceremony and ritual have played an important role in various conflict and peace-building settings across the globe, including North America, where Indigenous nations have their own long histories of diplomacy and peacemaking. Ceremonial rituals have three functions in the peacemaking process. First, they create a safe space for people to interact and learn as they take part in the ceremony. Second, they enable people to communicate non-verbally and process their emotions. Third, ceremonies create an environment where change is made possible; world views, identities, and relationships with others are transformed.[186]

Those in attendance at TRC events learned to acknowledge and respect Indigenous ceremonies and protocols by participating in them. The Commission intentionally made ceremonies the spiritual and ethical framework of our public education work, creating a safe space for sharing life stories and bearing testimonial witness to the past for the future.

The Commission's National Events were designed to inspire reconciliation and shape individual and collective memory by demonstrating the core values that lie at the heart of reconciliation: respect, courage, love, truth, humility, honesty, and wisdom. These values are known by many Aboriginal peoples as the "Seven Sacred Teachings." They are also in the ancient teachings of most world religions.[187] Each National Event focused on one of these teachings. Working closely with local Aboriginal communities and various regional organizations, representatives of the parties to the Settlement Agreement, and other government and community networks, the Commission took great care to ensure that the proper ceremonies and protocols were understood and followed throughout every National Event. Elders offered prayers and teachings at the opening and closing of each event. Smudges, sacred pipe and water ceremonies, cedar brushings, songs, and drumming occurred on a regular basis throughout. At each event, a sacred fire was lit and cared for by Elders and Fire Keepers. Water ceremonies were performed by the women who were recognized as the Protectors of the Waters. The sacred fire was also used for ongoing prayers and tobacco offerings, as well as to receive the tissues from the many tears shed during each event. The ashes from each of the sacred fires were then carried forward to the next National Event, to be added in turn to its sacred fire, thus gathering in sacred ceremony the tears of an entire country.

The Commission's mandate also instructed that there be a "ceremonial transfer of knowledge" at the National Events. Coast Salish artist Luke Marston was commissioned by the TRC to design and carve a Bentwood Box as a symbol of this transfer. The box was steamed and bent in the traditional way from a single piece of west-coast red cedar. Its intricately carved and beautifully painted wood panels represent First Nations, Inuit, and Métis cultures. The Bentwood Box is a lasting tribute to all residential school Survivors and their families, both those who are living and those who have passed on, including the artist's grandmother, who attended Kuper Island residential school. This ceremonial box travelled with the Commission to every one of its seven National Events, where offerings—public expressions of reconciliation—were made by governments, churches and other faith communities, educational institutions, the business sector, municipalities, youth groups, and various other groups and organizations. The Truth and Reconciliation Bentwood Box, along with the many other sacred items the TRC received, will be housed permanently in the National Centre for Truth and Reconciliation at the University of Manitoba in Winnipeg.[188]

Life stories, testimonies, and witnessing as teachings

Reconciliation is not possible without knowing the truth. In order to determine the truth and be able to tell the full and complete story of residential schools in this country, it was fundamentally important to the Commission's work to be able to hear the stories of Survivors and their families. It was also important to hear the stories of those who worked in the schools—the teachers, the administrators, the cooks, the janitors—as well as their family members. Canada's national history must reflect this complex truth so that 50 or 100 years from now, our children's children and their children will know what happened. They will inherit the responsibility of ensuring that it never happens again.

Regardless of the different individual experiences that children had as students in the schools, they shared the common experience of being exploited. They were victims of a system intent on destroying intergenerational links of memory to their families, communities, and nations. The process of assimilation also profoundly disrespected parents, grandparents, and Elders in their rightful roles as the carriers of memory, through which culture, language, and identity are transmitted from one generation to the next.[189]

In providing their testimonies to the TRC, Survivors reclaimed their rightful place as members of intergenerational communities of memory. They remembered so that their families could understand what happened. They remembered so that their cultures, histories, laws, and nations can once again thrive for the benefit of future generations. They remembered so that Canada will know the truth and never forget.

The residential school story is complicated. Stories of abuse stand in sharp contradiction to the happier memories of some Survivors. The statements of former residential school staff also varied. Some were remorseful while others were defensive. Some were proud of their students and their own efforts to support them while others were critical of their own school and government authorities for their lack of attention, care, and resources. The stories of government and church officials involved acknowledgement, apology, and promises not to repeat history. Some non-Aboriginal Canadians expressed outrage at what had happened in the schools and shared their feelings of guilt and shame that they had not known this. Others denied or minimized the destructive impacts of residential schools. These conflicting stories, based on different experiences, locations, time periods, and perspectives, all feed into a national historical narrative.

Developing this narrative through public dialogue can strengthen civic capacity for accountability and so do justice to victims, not just in the legal sense, but also in terms of restoring human dignity, nurturing mutual respect, and supporting healing. As citizens use ceremony and testimony to remember, witness, and commemorate, they learn how to put the principles of accountability, justice, and reconciliation into everyday practice. They become active agents in the truth and reconciliation process.

Participants at Commission events learned from the Survivors themselves by interacting directly with them. Survivors, whose memories are still alive, demonstrated in the most powerful and compelling terms that by sitting together in Sharing Circles, people gain a much deeper knowledge and understanding of what happened in the residential schools than can ever be acquired at a distance by studying books, reading newspapers, or watching television reports.

For Indigenous peoples, stories and teachings are rooted in relationships. Through stories, knowledge and understanding about what happened and why are acquired, validated, and shared with others. Writing about her work with Survivors from her own community, social work scholar Qwul'sih'yah'maht (Robina Anne Thomas) said,

> I never dreamed of learning to listen in such a powerful way. Storytelling, despite all the struggles, enabled me to respect and honour the Ancestors and the storytellers while at the same time sharing tragic, traumatic, inhumanely unbelievable truths that our people had lived. It was this level of integrity that was essential to storytelling.... When we make personal what we teach ... we touch people in a different and more profound way.[190]

At a Community Hearing in St. Paul, Alberta, in January 2011, Charles Cardinal explained that although he did not want to remember his residential school experiences, he came forward because "we've got to let other people hear our voices." When he was asked how, given the history of the residential schools, Canada could be a better place, he replied that we must "listen to the people."[191] When asked the same question in Beausejour, Manitoba, Laurie McDonald said that Canada must begin by "doing exactly what is happening now ... governments ... [have got to know] that they can never, ever, ever do this again."[192] In Ottawa, Survivor Victoria Grant-Boucher said,

> I'm telling my story ... for the education of the Canadian general public ... [so that they] can understand what stolen identity is, you know, how it affects people, how it affects an individual, how it affects family, how it affects community.... I think the non-Aboriginal person, Canadian, has to understand that a First Nations person has a culture.... And I think that we, as Aboriginal people, have so much to share if you just let us regain that knowledge.... And I also take to heart what Elders talk about ... we have to heal ourselves. We have to heal each other. And for Canada to heal, they have to allow us to heal before we can contribute. That's what reconciliation means to me.[193]

Survivors told the Commission that an important reason for breaking their silence was to educate their own children and grandchildren by publicly sharing their life stories with them. The effect of this on intergenerational Survivors was significant. At the Manitoba National Event, Desarae Eashappie said,

> I have sat through this week having the honour of listening to the stories from Survivors. And I just feel—I just really want to acknowledge everybody in this room, you know, all of our Elders, all of our Survivors, all of our intergenerational Survivors.... We are all sitting here in solidarity right now ... and we are all on our own journey, and [yet we are] sitting here together ... with so much strength in this room, it really is phenomenal. And I just want to acknowledge that and thank everybody here. And to be given this experience, this opportunity, you know, to sit here ... and to listen to other people and listen to their stories and their experiences, you know, it has really humbled me as a person in such a way that is indescribable.... And I can take this home with me now and I can take it into my own home. Because my dad is a residential school Survivor, I have lived the traumas, but I have lived the history without the context.[194]

Survivors' life stories are teachings rooted in personal experience; the human relationships of their childhoods were scarred by those who harmed them in the schools. Their stories teach us about what it means to lose family, culture, community, self-esteem, and human dignity. They also teach us about courage, resilience, and resistance to violence and oppression. An ethical response to Survivors' life stories requires the listener to respond in ways that recognize the teller's dignity and affirm that injustices were committed. Non-Indigenous witnesses must be willing to "risk interacting differently with Indigenous people—with vulnerability, humility, and a willingness to stay in the decolonizing struggle of our own discomfort ... [and] to embrace [residential school] stories as powerful teachings—disquieting moments [that] can change our beliefs, attitudes, and actions."[195]

A number of former residential school staff came to the Commission to speak not only about their perspectives on the time they spent at the schools, but also about their struggles to come to terms with their own past. Florence Kaefer, a former teacher, spoke at the Manitoba National Event.

> And from my English ancestors, I apologize today for what my people did to you. I taught in two residential schools. In 1954, I taught in Norway House United Church Residential School for three or four years, and then I taught in the Alberni United Church Indian Residential School in BC. I worked very hard to be the best teacher I could be, and I did not know about the violence and cruelty going on in the dormitories and in the playrooms. But I have found out through one of my former students, who was five years old when he came to Norway House, his name is Edward Gamblin, and Edward Gamblin and I have gone through a personal truth and reconciliation.[196]

In a media interview afterwards, Ms Kaefer said that she contacted Mr. Gamblin after

> hearing his song a few years ago describing the cultural, physical and sexual abuse he had suffered at Norway House school. She said, "I just cried. I told my sister that I can never think of teaching in the residential school in the same way again." She called Gamblin after hearing the song. He told her he had to hide his abuse from the good teachers for fear he would lose them if they found out what was happening and left. He invited Kaefer to a healing circle in 2006 and they became close friends. Kaefer said Gamblin taught her not to be embarrassed about her past, being part of a school where abuse took place. "I was 19 and you don't question your church and your government when you're 19, but I certainly question my church and my government today." ... Gamblin said Kaefer taught him how to forgive. "There are good people [teachers] who don't deserve to be labeled," he said.[197]

Some family members of former staff also came forward. At the Manitoba National Event, Jack Lee told the Commission,

> My parents were staff members of the Indian residential school in Norway House. I was born on a reserve in Ontario and I moved with my family to Norway House when I was about one or two years old, and started school in the Indian residential school system, basically, at the very start as a day student ... as a white boy.... My father agonized very much over his role.... But I just want everyone to know that my father tried his best, as many other staff members tried their best, but they were working with so limited resources, and many of them felt

> very bad about their role in it, but they chose to stay in the system because it was still better than nothing, it was still better than abandoning the system, and abandoning the students that were in it.[198]

At the Atlantic National Event, Mark DeWolf spoke to us about his father, the Reverend James Edward DeWolf, who was the principal at two residential schools: St. Paul's in Alberta and La Tuque in Québec. He said,

> I'm quite hesitant to speak here this morning ... I'm not here to defend my father so much, as to speak part of the truth about the kind of person my father was. I think he was an exemplary principal of an Indian residential school.... Part of the story will be about what I saw around me, what my parents tried to do, however effective that was, however well-intentioned that was, however beneficial or not beneficial it was, you will at least when you leave here today, have a bit more of the story and you may judge for yourselves. I hope you will judge with kindness, understanding, and generosity of spirit....
>
> [My father] did so many things, coached the teams, blew the whistle or shot off the starting pistol at the sports days. Twelve o'clock at midnight, on the coldest of winter days, he would be out on the rink that he had constructed behind the school, flooding it so that the children could skate. He devoted his life to the service of his church, his God, and those that he thought had been marginalized, oppressed.... It is a terrible shame there were not more like him. When we leave today, though, let's remember that when you have a system like the residential school, there are the individuals within the system, some of whom are good, decent, loving, caring people, and some of whom are blind, intolerant, predatory.... My father worked within the system trying to make it a better one.[199]

TRC Honorary Witnesses

The mandate of the Truth and Reconciliation Commission describes "reconciliation" as an ongoing individual and collective process involving all the people of Canada. To help ensure that reconciliation will indeed be ongoing, even after the TRC's own official work is done, the Commissioners decided early on a public education and advocacy strategy to engage high-profile supporters, each willing to foster the continuing work of public education and dialogue. We called upon more than seventy of them across the country and internationally, and inducted them as Honorary Witnesses in a public ceremony at each of the National Events. Together, they represent accomplished and influential leaders from all walks of life, now serving as ambassadors in educating the broader public about why reconciliation is necessary. Most of them, including some who had worked with Aboriginal people in the past, frankly admitted to their own prior gaps in knowledge and understanding of the residential schools system and its continuing legacy. They now encourage the broader Canadian public to do what they have done: to learn and to be transformed in understanding and in commitment to societal change.

Speaking at the Saskatchewan National Event, TRC Honorary Witness and a former member of parliament, the Honourable Tina Keeper, who is also a member of the Norway House Cree Nation, talked about the importance of honouring individual, family, and community relationships and memory, her own emotional involvement in the ratification of the Settlement Agreement, and the struggles surrounding Canada's apology. She underscored the strong contributions that Aboriginal peoples have to make to national healing and reconciliation.

> Yesterday was an incredible opportunity for me personally to let the tears flow, and they flowed all day long. And I didn't do that when I was in the House of Commons. I had the privilege of delivering the speech on behalf of the official opposition when the Agreement was tabled in the House, and during that speech I had to stop midway and breathe ... because I didn't think I could do it. I kept thinking of my family and my extended family and my grandparents and so many of the people in the communities.... [O]ur cultures, our languages, our values, and spiritual beliefs that have taken care of us at this gathering ... they will become tools for the healing of a nation.[200]

At the Québec National Event, TRC Honorary Witness and a former prime minister, the Right Honourable Paul Martin, reminded participants about the role that education played in the attempted destruction of Aboriginal families, communities, and nations, and the role it must play in repairing this damage. He said,

> I've talked to a number of the people here, some of the members of parliament are here ... and the question we asked ourselves is, "How come we didn't know what happened?" ... I still can't answer that.... [L]et us understand that what happened at the residential schools was the use of education for cultural genocide ... [let's] call a spade a spade. What that really means is that we've got to offer Aboriginal Canadians, without any shadow of a doubt, the best education system that is possible to have.[201]

Although some Honorary Witnesses already had significant knowledge of Aboriginal issues, including residential schools, through the act of witnessing Survivors' testimonies, they learned about this history in a different way. At the Saskatchewan National Event, a former prime minister, the Right Honourable Joe Clark, said that the Saskatchewan National Event gave him a better understanding of the intergenerational impacts of the residential schools, and a better sense of the challenges and opportunities for reconciliation with the rest of Canada.

> When I came to take my place this morning, I knew the storyline, if you will. I knew what had happened. I had some idea of the consequences it [the

> residential school system] involved, but I had no real idea because I had not been able to witness it before ... the multi-generational emotion that is involved in what has happened to so many of the victims of the residential schools.... [Today] I heard, "We are only as sick as our secrets." That is an incentive to all that have kept these emotions and this history too secret, too long, to show the courage that so many of you have shown, and let those facts be known....
>
> There are cross-cultural difficulties here as we seek reconciliation, the reconciliation of people who have not been part of this experience with those who have. We are going to deal with cultural differences, but no one wants to be torn away from their roots. And there are common grounds here by which consensus can be built.... Reconciliation means finding a way that brings together the legitimate concerns of the people in this room, and the apprehensions, call them fear ... that might exist elsewhere in the country.... Among the things we have to do is to ensure that not only the stories of abuse as they touch First Nations and Aboriginal people, but also the story of their contribution to Canada, and the values that are inherent in those communities is much better known.[202]

Joe Clark's observations reinforce this Commission's view that learning happens in a different manner when life stories are shared and witnessed in ways that connect knowledge, understanding, and human relationships. He pinpointed a key challenge to reconciliation: how to bridge the divides between those who have been part of the residential school experience and those who have not, and between those who have participated in the Truth and Reconciliation Commission's proceedings and those who have not.

The former minister of Indian Affairs and Northern Development, the late Honourable Andy Scott, was inducted as an Honorary Witness at the 2012 Atlantic National Event in Halifax. He then served to welcome new inductees to the Honorary Witness circle at the Saskatchewan National Event, and to reflect on his experience. His comments reinforce the Commission's conviction that relationship-based learning and ways of remembering lead to a deeper knowledge and understanding of the links between the Survivors' experiences and community memory and our collective responsibility and need to re-envision Canada's national history, identity, and future. He told us,

> When I was invited to become an Honorary Witness, I thought I was prepared, having been involved in the Settlement process and having already met and heard from Survivors. I was not. In Halifax, I heard about not knowing what it meant to be loved, not knowing how to love. I heard about simply wanting to be believed that it happened, 'just like I said.' ... We heard about a deliberate effort to disconnect young children from who they are. We heard about a sense of betrayal by authority—government, community, and church. We heard about

> severe punishment for speaking one's language, living one's spirituality, seeking out one's siblings. We heard about forced feeding, physical and sexual abuse. And we heard about deaths. We heard about forgiving as a way to move on and we heard from those who felt that they would never be able to forgive. I could not and cannot imagine being taken away to a strange place as a five- or a six-year-old, never knowing why or for how long. Perhaps I remember most poignantly Ruth, who said simply, "I never thought I'd talk about this, and now I don't think I'll ever stop. But Canada is big. I'll need some help."
>
> Reconciliation is about Survivors speaking about their experiences, being heard and being believed, but it's also about a national shared history. As Canadians, we must be part of reconciling what we have done collectively with who we believe we are. To do that with integrity and to restore our honour, we must all know the history so we can reunite these different Canadas. [203]

The Commission also heard from a variety of other Aboriginal and non-Aboriginal witnesses from many walks of life. Some were there on behalf of their institution or organization. Some had close personal or professional ties to Aboriginal people, and others had none. Many said that the experience opened their eyes and was powerfully transformative. They commented on how much they had learned by listening to Survivors' life stories. This was true for both non-Aboriginal witnesses and Aboriginal witnesses whose own families had been impacted by the schools but who may have had few opportunities to learn more about the residential schools themselves, especially in those many families where no one was yet willing or able to talk about it.

At the 2011 Northern National Event in Inuvik, Therese Boullard, then the director of the Northwest Territories Human Rights Commission, told us,

> We need to have an accurate record of history.... As long as there are some that are in denial of what really happened, as long as we don't have the full picture of what happened, we really can't move forward in that spirit of reconciliation.... I want to acknowledge these stories as gifts, a hand towards reconciliation. I think it's amazing that after all that has passed, after all that you've experienced, that you would be willing to share your pain with the rest of Canada in this spirit of openness and reconciliation and in this faith that the government of Canada and non-Aboriginal Canadians will receive them in a way that will lead to a better relationship in the future. That you have that faith to share your stories in that spirit is amazing and it's humbling and it's inspiring and I just want to thank Survivors for that.[204]

At the 2010 Manitoba National Event, Ginelle Giacomin, a high school history teacher from Winnipeg who served as a private statement gatherer at the event, said,

> I was talking to a few students before I came this week to do this, and they said, "Well, what do you mean there are Survivors? That was a long time ago. That was hundreds of years ago." To them, this is a page in a history book.... So, I'm

> so blessed to have spent the past week sitting down one-on-one with Survivors and listening to their stories. And I have heard horrific things and the emotions. It's been very hard to hear. But what every single person I've spoken to has said is that "we are strong." And the strength is one thing that I'll carry with me when I leave. You carry on, and that's something that I want to bring back to my classrooms, is the strength of everyone that I spoke to and their stories. And it is so important for high school students, and all students in Canada, to be talking about this a lot more than they are. I just want to thank everyone involved for doing this, for educating me. I have a history degree in Canadian history. I learned more in the past five days about Canada than I have in three years of that degree.[205]

The Commission's seven National Events, by all accounts, provided a respectful space for public dialogue. Over 150,000 Canadians came out to participate in them and in some 300 smaller-scale Community Events. One of the most common words used in describing them was "transformational." It will be up to others to determine their long-term effectiveness, and to judge this model's potential in terms of ongoing public education. However, as Commissioners of the Truth and Reconciliation Commission of Canada, we are both confident and convinced that public dialogue is critical to the reconciliation process.

The arts: Practising resistance, healing, and reconciliation

The reconciliation process is not easy. It asks those who have been harmed to revisit painful memories and those who have harmed others—either directly or indirectly—to be accountable for past wrongs. It asks us to mourn and commemorate the terrible loss of people, cultures, and languages, even as we celebrate their survival and revitalization. It asks us to envision a more just and inclusive future, even as we struggle with the living legacies of injustice. As the TRC has experienced in every region of the country, creative expression can play a vital role in this national reconciliation, providing alternative voices, vehicles, and venues for expressing historical truths and present hopes. Creative expression supports everyday practices of resistance, healing, and commemoration at individual, community, regional, and national levels.

Across the globe, the arts have provided a creative pathway to breaking silences, transforming conflicts, and mending the damaged relationships of violence, oppression, and exclusion. From war-ravaged countries to local communities struggling with everyday violence, poverty, and racism, the arts are widely used by educators, practitioners, and community leaders to deal with trauma and difficult emotions, and communicate across cultural divides.[206]

Art is active, and "participation in the arts is a guarantor of other human rights because the first thing that is taken away from vulnerable, unpopular or minority groups is the right to self-expression."[207] The arts help to restore human dignity and identity in the face of injustice. Properly structured, they can also invite people to explore their own world views, values, beliefs, and attitudes that may be barriers to healing, justice, and reconciliation.

Even prior to the establishment of the TRC, a growing body of work, including Survivors' memoirs and works of fiction by well-known Indigenous authors, as well as films and plays, have brought the residential school history and legacy to a wider Canadian public, enabling them to learn about the schools through the eyes of Survivors. This body of work includes memoirs such as Isabelle Knockwood's *Out of the Depths: The Experiences of Mi'kmaw Children at the Indian Residential School at Shubenacadie, Nova Scotia* (1992), to the more recent works of Agnes Grant's *Finding My Talk: How Fourteen Native Women Reclaimed Their Lives after Residential School* (2004); Alice Blondin's *My Heart Shook Like a Drum: What I Learned at the Indian Mission Schools, Northwest Territories* (2009); Theodore Fontaine's *Broken Circle: The Dark Legacy of Indian Residential Schools: A Memoir* (2010); Bev Sellars's *They Called Me Number One: Secrets and Survival at an Indian Residential School* (2013); and Edmund Metatawabin and Alexandra Shimo's *Up Ghost River: A Chief's Journey through the Turbulent Waters of Native History* (2014).

Works of fiction (sometimes drawn from the author's own life experiences), such as Tomson Highway's *Kiss of the Fur Queen* (1998), Robert Alexie's *Porcupines and China Dolls* (2009), or Richard Wagamese's *Indian Horse* (2012), tell stories about abuse, neglect, and loss that are also stories of healing, redemption, and hope. In 2012, the Aboriginal Healing Foundation published *Speaking My Truth: Reflections on Reconciliation and Residential Schools,* and invited book clubs across the country to read and discuss the book. Documentary films such as *Where the Spirit Lives* (1989), *Kuper Island: Return to the Healing Circle* (1997), and *Muffins for Granny* (2008), as well as docu-dramas such as *We Were Children* (2012), all serve to educate Canadians and the wider world about the residential school experience, using the power of sound and images. Intergenerational Survivor Georgina Lightning was the first Indigenous woman in North America to direct a full-length feature film, *Older Than America* (2008). Kevin Loring's stage play, *Where the Blood Mixes,* won the Governor General's award for literary drama in 2009. It combines drama and humour to tell the stories of three Survivors living in the aftermath of their residential school experiences.

Art can be powerful and provocative. Through their work, Indigenous artists seek to resist and challenge the cultural understandings of settler-dominated versions of Canada's past and its present reality. Sharing intercultural dialogue about history, responsibility, and transformation through the arts is potentially healing and transformative for both Aboriginal and non-Aboriginal peoples.[208] Yet, art does not always cross this cultural divide, and neither does it have to in order to have a high impact. Acts of resistance sometimes take place in "irreconcilable spaces" where artists choose to keep their residential school experiences private or share them only with other Aboriginal people.[209] This is also essential to individual and collective reclaiming of identity, culture, and community memory.

The Commission notes that the use of creative arts in community workshops promotes healing for Survivors, their families, and the whole community through the recovery of cultural traditions. In conducting surveys of 103 community-based healing projects, the Aboriginal Healing Foundation (AHF) found that 80% of those projects included cultural activities and traditional healing interventions. These included Elders' teachings, storytelling and traditional knowledge, language programs, land-based activities, feasts and powwows; and learning traditional art forms, harvesting medicines, and drumming, singing, and dancing. The AHF report observed,

> A notable component of successful healing programs was their diversity—interventions were blended and combined to create holistic programs that met the physical, emotional, cultural, and spiritual needs of participants. Not surprisingly, arts-based interventions were included in many cultural activities (drum making, beading, singing, and drumming) as well as in therapeutic healing (art therapy and psychodrama).[210]

The Aboriginal Healing Foundation's findings make clear that creative art practices are highly effective in reconnecting Survivors and their families to their cultures, languages, and communities. In our view, this confirms yet again that funding for community-based healing projects is an urgent priority for Aboriginal communities.

Art exhibits have played a particularly powerful role in the process of healing and reconciliation. In 2009, nationally acclaimed Anishinaabe artist Robert Houle, who attended the Sandy Bay residential school in Manitoba, created a series of twenty-four paintings to be housed permanently in the University of Manitoba's School of Art Gallery. In an interview with *CBC News* on September 24, 2013, he explained that "during the process memories came back that he had previously suppressed ... [but that] he found the whole experience cathartic. At the end, he felt a sigh of relief, a sigh of liberation."[211]

Over the course of the Commission's mandate, several major art exhibits ran concurrently with its National Events. During the British Columbia National Event in Vancouver, for example, three major exhibits opened, featuring well-known Aboriginal artists, some of whom were also Survivors or intergenerational Survivors. A number of non-Aboriginal artists were also featured. Their work explored themes of denial, complicity, apology, and government policy. Two of these exhibits were at the University of British Columbia: *Witnesses: Art and Canada's Indian Residential Schools* at the Morris and Helen Belkin Art Gallery, and the Museum of Anthropology's *Speaking to Memory: Images and Voices from the St. Michael's Residential School.* Both exhibits were collaborative efforts that also engaged Survivors, artists, and curatorial staff in related public education initiatives, including workshops, symposia, and public dialogues based on the exhibits.[212]

A significant number of the statements gathered by the Commission also came to us in artistic formats. Some Survivors said that although it hurt too much to tell their story in the usual way, they had been able to find their voice instead by writing a poem, a song, or a book. Some made a video or audio recording, offered photographs, or produced a theatre performance piece or a film. Others created traditional blankets, quilts, carvings, or paintings to depict residential school experiences, to celebrate those who survived them, or to commemorate those who did not. Lasting public memory of the schools has therefore been produced not only through oral testimonies, but also through this wide range of artistic expressions. The arts have opened up new and critical space for Survivors, artists, curators, and public audiences to explore the complexities of "truth," "healing," and "reconciliation."

The Commission funded or supported several arts-related projects. Early in its mandate, the TRC sponsored the "Living Healing Quilt Project," which was organized by Anishinaabe quilter Alice Williams from Curve Lake First Nation in Ontario. Women Survivors and intergenerational Survivors from across the country created individual quilt blocks depicting their memories of residential schools. These were then stitched together into three quilts, *Schools of Shame, Child Prisoners,* and *Crimes Against Humanity.*

The quilts tell a complex story of trauma, loss, isolation, recovery, healing, and hope through women's eyes. The sewing skills taught to young Aboriginal girls in the residential schools and passed along to their daughters and granddaughters are now used to stitch together a counter-narrative.[213] This project also inspired the "Healing Quilt Project," which linked education and art. At the Manitoba National Event, as an expression of reconciliation, the Women's and Gender Studies and Aboriginal Governance departments at the University of Winnipeg gave the TRC a quilt created by students and professors as part of their coursework. Through classroom readings, dialogue, and art, they created a space for learning about, and reflecting on, the residential school history and legacy in the context of reconciliation.[214]

A report commissioned by the TRC, "Practicing Reconciliation: A Collaborative Study of Aboriginal Art, Resistance and Cultural Politics," was based on the findings of a one-year research project. Working with Survivors, artists, and curators, a multidisciplinary team of researchers examined the general question of how artistic practice contributes to the reconciliation process. The research was done through a series of interviews, workshops, artist residencies, planning sessions, symposia, artistic incubations, publications, and online learning platforms. The report reveals the depth and potential of arts-based approaches to reconciliation.

> We should begin by echoing what many of our interview and artist subjects have repeatedly said: that the act of reconciliation is itself deeply complicated, and that success should not be measured by *achieving* a putative [commonly accepted or supposed] reconciliation, but by *movement* towards these lofty goals. Indeed, it could be proposed that full reconciliation is both mercurial and impossible, and that the efforts of theorists, artists, survivors, and the various publics engaged in this difficult process are best focused on working collaboratively for better understanding our histories, our traumas, and ourselves.[215]

These various projects indicate that the arts and artistic practices may serve to shape public memory in ways that are potentially transformative for individuals, communities, and national history.

Residential school commemoration projects

Commemoration should not put closure to the history and legacy of the residential schools. Rather, it must invite citizens into a dialogue about a contentious past and why this history still matters today. Commemorations and memorials at former school sites and cemeteries are visible reminders of Canada's shame and church complicity. They bear witness to the suffering and loss that generations of Aboriginal peoples have endured and overcome. The process of remembering the past together is an emotional journey of contradictory feelings: loss and resilience, anger and acceptance, denial and remorse, shame and pride, despair and hope. The Settlement Agreement identified the historic importance and reconciliation potential of such remembering by establishing a special fund for projects that would commemorate the residential school experience, and by assigning a role in the approval of these projects to the Truth and Reconciliation Commission of Canada.

As previously noted in this report's section about the Commission's activities, commemoration projects across the country were funded under the terms of the Settlement Agreement. Twenty million dollars were set aside for Aboriginal communities and various partners and organizations to undertake community-based, regional or national projects. The Commission evaluated and made recommendations to the Department of Aboriginal Affairs and Northern Development Canada, which was responsible for administering the funding for the commemoration projects.

Unlike more conventional state commemorations, which have tended to reinforce Canada's story as told through colonial eyes, residential school commemorative projects challenged and recast public memory and national history. Many First Nations, Inuit, and Métis communities partnered with regional or national Aboriginal organizations, and involved local churches, governments, and their non-Aboriginal neighbours. The scope, breadth, and creativity of the projects were truly impressive. Projects ranged from traditional and virtual quilts, monuments and memorials, traditional medicine gardens, totem pole and canoe carving, oral history, community ceremonies and feasts, land-based culture and language camps, cemetery restoration, film and digital storytelling, commemorative walking trails, and theatre or dance productions.[216]

The Commission, advised by the TRC Survivor Committee, identified three elements of the commemoration process that were seen as being essential to supporting long-term reconciliation. First, the projects were to be Survivor-driven; that is, their success was contingent upon the advice, recommendations, and active participation of Survivors. Second, commemoration projects would forge new connections that linked Aboriginal family and community memory to Canada's public memory and national history. Third, incorporating Indigenous oral history and memory practices into commemoration projects would ensure that the processes of remembering places, reclaiming identity, and revitalizing cultures were consistent with the principle of self-determination.

Commemorating the life stories of Survivors strengthens the bonds of family and community memory that have been disrupted but not destroyed. Families grieve for all that was lost and can never be recovered. The act of commemoration remembers and honours those who are no longer living and comforts those for whom a history of injustice and oppression is still very much alive. Commemorations can also symbolize hope, signifying cultural revitalization and the reclaiming of history and identity. Even as they grieve, families envision a better future for children and youth and for generations yet unborn.

The collective memory of Aboriginal peoples lives in places: in their traditional homelands and in the actual physical locations where residential schools once stood.[217] On March 24, 2014, the Grand Council of Treaty 3 brought together Survivors, Elders, and others in Kenora, Ontario, for a final ceremony to mark commemorations that were held earlier at each site of the five residential schools that were located in the territory. Monuments had been placed at each of the sites. Richard Green, who coordinated the two-year memorial project, said, "This is a commemoration for all the sites together. This meeting is about honouring all the children and is part of remembering the legacy. Lest we forget, as they say. We can probably forgive, but we can never forget our history." He explained that the monuments "have been a big success with plenty of positive feedback. Now we have a physical place where people can go and commemorate."[218]

Bearing witness to the child: Children's art from the Alberni residential school

The story of a small collection of children's art created at the Alberni residential school in the 1950s and 1960s demonstrates how recognizing and respecting Indigenous protocols and practices of ceremony, testimony, and witnessing can breathe life, healing, and transformation into public memory making through dialogue, the arts, and commemoration. The story has deep roots within the family histories of the Survivors and in the oral history and community memory of the Nuu-chah-nulth peoples.

The paintings from the Alberni residential school are part of a larger collection of Indigenous children's art donated to the University of Victoria in 2009 by the late artist Robert Aller. As a resident of Port Alberni, British Columbia, Aller initially volunteered his time to teach art classes to selected students outside of the regular curriculum at the residential school. He was hired by Indian Affairs to teach art between 1956 and 1987 at the Alberni school, and also at the McKay residential school in Dauphin, Manitoba, as well as in Aboriginal communities in several other provinces.

There are over 750 paintings in the collection, including 36 paintings from the Alberni residential school. Aller also donated to the university his private papers, and hundreds of photographs, slides, and archival documents that detail his teaching philosophy and approach to art. Aller did not agree with the philosophy behind the residential schools. He saw art as a way to free students from their everyday environment and as a way for them to express their creativity, through either traditionally inspired works, or paintings that used the theories and ideas of the contemporary art world. The paintings from the Alberni residential school portray images of landscapes, people, animals, masks, and traditional stories, as well as some images of the school itself. Most of the artists signed their paintings, putting their age next to their name. In this sense, the children stand out; the anonymity that depersonalizes so much of the residential school history is removed.

In 2010, University of Victoria's Dr. Andrea Walsh, who was in the early stages of a research project on the art collection, met with the Commissioners and we urged her to begin her research with ceremony. She turned to two Elders from the First Peoples House at the university to guide her in this process: Tousilum (Ron George), who is a residential school Survivor; and Sulsa'meeth (Deb George), his wife. They helped her to reach out to Survivors, Elders, and chiefs in Port Alberni in Nuu-chah-nulth territory when the group travelled there with the paintings. As community members leafed through the paintings drawn by children's hands so many years ago, memories were shared about the artists, the school, and the parents and communities they had left behind.

Working under the direction of these community members, and in collaboration with her colleague, Qwul'sih'yah'maht (Dr. Robina Thomas), and TRC staff, Walsh began preparations to bring the artwork to the Learning Place at the TRC's Victoria Regional Event in April 2012. In a powerfully moving ceremony, Nuu-chah-nulth Elders, Survivors, and Hereditary Chiefs drummed, sang, and danced the art into the Learning Place. In this way, each painting, carried with respect and love by a Nuu-chah-nulth woman dressed in button blanket regalia, was brought out to be shared with others.

The community later received commemoration project funding to hold a traditional feast on March 30, 2013, in Port Alberni to reunite artists and their families with the paintings. Robert Aller's family members were also invited to attend. They were visibly moved when they heard the stories of the paintings, and said that Aller would have been happy that the paintings were being returned. Paintings were returned to those who wished to have them; the remaining art was loaned to the University of Victoria, where it will be housed, cared for, and exhibited, based on agreed-upon protocols with Survivors and their families.[219]

In a media interview, Survivor and Hereditary Chief Lewis George said that the art classes probably saved him from being sexually abused by convicted pedophile Arthur Plint, who had taught at the Alberni residential school. He remembered the kindness shown to him by Aller as being in stark contrast to the harsh realities of life at the school, and he said, "I want my story kept alive." Wally Samuel, another Survivor of the Alberni school who helped co-ordinate the project, said everyone reacted differently when told about the paintings. "Some got really quiet and others looked forward to seeing them ... but they all remembered being in art class."[220]

In May of 2013, the Alberni residential school paintings were displayed in a special exhibit, *To Reunite, To Honour, To Witness*, at the Legacy Art Gallery at the University of Victoria. Survivors, Elders, and community members continue to work with Walsh and Qwul'sih'yah'maht to document the story of the creation and return of the children's paintings as part of reconnecting individual, family, and community memory, and educating the public about a previously unknown part of the history and legacy of the residential schools.

In September 2013, the paintings returned once again to the Learning Place at the TRC's British Columbia National Event in Vancouver, and the group made an expression of reconciliation by providing copies of the artwork to the Commission's Bentwood Box, to become part of the permanent record of the Commission's work.

Canada's public commemoration initiative

The Commission takes note of the federal government's own national commemoration initiative, which was described as an "expression of reconciliation" when it was publicly announced at the Atlantic National Event in 2011. It is a specially commissioned stained-glass window entitled *Giniigaaniimenaaning* or *Looking Ahead*, designed by Métis artist Christi Belcourt. Its two-sided imagery depicts the history of the residential schools, the cultural resilience of Aboriginal peoples, and hope for the future. The window was permanently installed in the Centre Block of the federal parliament buildings, and unveiled in a dedication ceremony on November 26, 2012.[221] Putting this window in such a prominent public place helps to make the history and legacy of residential schools more visible to the Canadian public and the world at large, while also acknowledging the federal government's responsibility in establishing the residential school system.

At the dedication ceremony, artist Christi Belcourt said that her inspiration for the window's design came from Survivors themselves. She said,

> The stories of residential school students were never told in this building, so I'm going to tell you one now.... I asked Lucille [Kelly-Davis] who is a residential school survivor what she wanted to see on the window. I had assisted her through the residential school settlement process, and like so many survivors, her story is horrific.... Despite her childhood, she married, had four children, and now has many grandchildren. She is a pipe carrier, attends traditional ceremonies, and helps younger people learn the traditions. She's a powerful Anishnabeg grandmother who is generous, loving and caring, and gives all she can to her community and her family. She is not a victim, but a survivor. When I asked her what to put on the window, she said, "Tell our side of the story."... She said, "Make it about hope."... It's about looking ahead, as the name of the window says, "giniigaaniimenaaning" looking to the future for those yet unborn....
>
> Because she told me to make it about hope, what I've tried to show in the design is all the positive things I've seen in my life. Despite residential schools, children, adults, and Elders dance in full regalia in celebration of who they are as Indigenous people. We see Métis youth learning fiddling and jigging with pride across the country. We see arenas full of Inuk Elders drum dancing, with little kids running around, speaking Inuktitut. We see whole communities come together in times of joy and in times of great grief. The lodges are growing, the traditional songs are being sung, the ceremonies are being taught, and the ceremonies are still practiced.
>
> I wish I could show the government that reconciliation has the potential to be so much more. I wish I could convince them that reconciliation is not an unattainable goal, if there's the will and the courage to discard old paternalistic ways of thinking and of behaviour. We need action, and where we need action,

> don't meet us with silence. Where we need support, don't accuse us of being a burden.... I wish I could speak to the hearts of MPs, whether Conservative, or NDP, or Liberal, and let them know that renewal and reconciliation can be found between Aboriginal peoples and the rest of Canada through the sustained wellness of generations of Aboriginal people to come.[222]

At Commission hearings, we heard from many Survivors about windows. We heard from those who looked out from the school windows, waiting and hoping to see their parents come for them; those who cried when no one came for them, especially when it was Christmas or another holiday. We heard from those who were told, sometimes being pulled away from the window by the hair, to "get away from that window," or "your parents are not coming for you anyway." We heard from those who simply looked out into the dark or into the distance, crying because they were so lonesome and homesick. Windows were also a beacon of hope. Survivors also told us how they smiled and laughed and couldn't contain their tears of joy when they looked out the window and saw their parents or grandparents coming to visit them or take them away from the school.[223] The windows of the residential schools evoked both good and bad memories for Survivors. Thus, a commemorative window seems a fitting monument to remember and honour the children who went to residential schools.

Commemorations in highly visible public spaces such as the parliament buildings create openings for dialogue about what happened, why, and what can be learned from this history. Through dialogue, citizens can strengthen their ability to "accommodate difference, acknowledge injustice, and demonstrate a willingness to share authority over the past."[224] In the context of national reconciliation, ongoing public commemoration has the potential to contribute to human rights education in the broadest sense.

Although Canada's commemorative window was a significant gesture of reconciliation, the Commission believes that the federal government must do more to ensure that national commemoration of the history and legacy of residential schools becomes an integral part of Canadian heritage and national history. Under the *Historic Sites and Monuments Act* (1985), the minister responsible for Parks Canada has the authority to designate historic sites of national significance and approve commemorative monuments or plaques.[225] The minister is advised by the Historic Sites and Monuments Board of Canada "on the commemoration of nationally significant aspects of Canada's past, including the designation of national historic sites, persons and events."[226] The board reviews and makes recommendations on submissions received from Canadian citizens who make nominations through the National Program of Historical Commemoration.[227] Heritage sites, monuments, and plaques that celebrate Canada's past are common, but commemorating those aspects of our national history that reveal cultural genocide, human rights violations, racism, and injustice are more problematic.

As we noted earlier, at the international level, the *Joinet-Orentlicher Principles* adopted by the United Nations have established that states have a responsibility to take measures to ensure that collective violence against a targeted group of people does not reoccur. In addition to providing compensation, making apologies, and undertaking educational reform, states also have a duty "to remember." Under Principle 2,

> A people's knowledge of the history of its oppression is part of its heritage and, as such, must be preserved by appropriate measures in fulfillment of the State's duty to remember.... On a collective basis, symbolic measures intended to provide moral reparation, such as formal public recognition by the State of its responsibility, or official declarations aimed at restoring victims' dignity, commemorative ceremonies, naming of public thoroughfares or the erection of monuments, help to discharge the duty of remembrance.[228]

In 2014, the UN Special Rapporteur in the field of Cultural Rights, Farida Shaheed, issued a report on memorialization processes in countries where victims and their families, working collaboratively with artists and various civic society groups, have commemorated their experiences in unofficial ways that may run counter to state-sanctioned versions of national history.[229] Shaheed observed that the commemorations of Indigenous peoples' experience—both their oppression and their positive contributions to society—that have occurred in many countries, including Canada, have not been state-driven initiatives. Rather, they have been initiated by Indigenous peoples themselves.

> In Canada, a memorial to indigenous veterans from the First World War was built at the request of indigenous peoples, integrating many elements of indigenous cultures. This recognition took place at a later stage in history, however, and in a different venue to the main memorial established for other Canadian soldiers. Commemoration projects are also taking place ... regarding the history of Indian residential schools.[230]

The report concluded that state authorities have a key role to play in the commemoration process. The state is responsible for managing public space and has the capacity to maintain monuments and develop long-term national commemoration policies and strategies.[231]

The Special Rapporteur further concluded that states should ensure that

> memorial policies contribute to, in particular ... providing symbolic reparation and public recognition to the victims in ways that respond to the needs of all victims oppressed in a recent or distant past and contribute to their healing ... the development of reconciliation policies between groups ... [and] promoting civic engagement, critical thinking and stimulating discussions on the representation of the past, as well as contemporary challenges of exclusion and violence.[232]

The report recommended that states and relevant stakeholders

> promote critical thinking on past events by ensuring that memorialisation processes are complemented by measures fostering historical awareness and support the implementation and outreach of high-quality research projects, cultural interventions that encourage people's direct engagement and educational activities.... States should ensure the availability of public spaces for a diversity of narratives conveyed in artistic expressions and multiply opportunities for such narratives to engage with each other.... [States must also] take into consideration the cultural dimension of memorial processes, including where repression has targeted indigenous peoples.[233]

The Commission concurs with these conclusions and recommendations. They are consistent with our own findings on the residential schools commemoration projects. These Survivor-driven, community-based initiatives revealed the importance of integrating Indigenous knowledge and revitalizing Indigenous memory practices in commemorating the history and legacy of residential schools. They demonstrated the critical role that artists play in healing and commemoration.

The Commission believes that Canada's national heritage network also has a vital role to play in reconciliation. Our views were further confirmed in a study of residential school commemorations in the context of Canada's national heritage and commemoration policy. The research documented the Assembly of First Nations' and the Aboriginal Healing Foundation's national commemoration project to create a heritage plaque program to place commemorative markers at all residential school sites across the country.[234] Faced with logistical challenges and based on input from Survivors and communities, "the project transformed from what ostensibly had been an IRS [Indian Residential School] site heritage plaque program to a community-oriented public monumental art project."[235] The commemorative markers were not placed at residential school sites, many of which are in remote locations or otherwise inaccessible. Instead, they were placed in Aboriginal communities where Survivors and their families could access them more easily, where ceremonies and community events could be held, and where there were opportunities for ongoing healing, commemoration, and education.[236]

The study revealed the fundamental tensions that exist between the goals of Aboriginal peoples and Canada with regard to the commemoration of residential schools. Under the existing policies of Parks Canada's Historic Sites and Monuments Board of Canada National Program of Historical Commemoration, residential school sites do not meet the program criteria for heritage designation, which is based on Western heritage values of conservation and preservation.[237] For Survivors, their families, and communities, commemorating their residential school experiences does not necessarily involve preserving the school buildings, but is intended instead to contribute to individual and collective healing. For example, a residential school located in Port Alberni, British Columbia, was demolished by Survivors and their families, who burned sage and cedar in ceremonies in order to "cleanse and allow the trapped spirits to finally be freed."[238] Where commemoration activities have involved the destruction of a residential school structure, such actions are in direct conflict with Canadian heritage goals.[239]

Ultimately, reconciliation requires a paradigm shift in Canada's national heritage values, policies, and practices that focus on conservation and continue to exclude Indigenous history, heritage values, and memory practices, which prioritize healing and the reclaiming of culture in public commemoration.[240] For this to happen, Parks Canada's heritage and commemoration policies and programs must change.

By shaping commemoration projects to meet their own needs, Survivors, their families, and communities have provided a wealth of information and best practices for commemorating the history and legacy of the residential school system. These can inform and enrich the National Program of Historical Commemoration and the work of the Historic Sites and Monuments Board of Canada to ensure that Canada's heritage and commemoration legislation, programs, policies, and practices contribute constructively to the reconciliation process in the years ahead.

Calls to Action

79) We call upon the federal government, in collaboration with Survivors, Aboriginal organizations, and the arts community, to develop a reconciliation framework for Canadian heritage and commemoration. This would include, but not be limited to:

    i. Amending the *Historic Sites and Monuments Act* to include First Nations, Inuit, and Métis representation on the Historic Sites and Monuments Board of Canada and its Secretariat.

    ii. Revising the policies, criteria, and practices of the National Program of Historical Commemoration to integrate Indigenous history, heritage values, and memory practices into Canada's national heritage and history.

    iii. Developing and implementing a national heritage plan and strategy for commemorating residential school sites, the history and legacy of residential schools, and the contributions of Aboriginal peoples to Canada's history.

80) We call upon the federal government, in collaboration with Aboriginal peoples, to establish, as a statutory holiday, a National Day for Truth and Reconciliation to honour Survivors, their families, and communities, and ensure that public commemoration of the history and legacy of residential schools remains a vital component of the reconciliation process.

81) We call upon the federal government, in collaboration with Survivors and their organizations, and other parties to the Settlement Agreement, to commission and install a publicly accessible, highly visible, Residential Schools National Monument in the city of Ottawa to honour Survivors and all the children who were lost to their families and communities.

82) We call upon provincial and territorial governments, in collaboration with Survivors and their organizations, and other parties to the Settlement Agreement, to commission and install a publicly accessible, highly visible, Residential Schools Monument in each capital city to honour Survivors and all the children who were lost to their families and communities.

83) We call upon the Canada Council for the Arts to establish, as a funding priority, a strategy for Indigenous and non-Indigenous artists to undertake collaborative projects and produce works that contribute to the reconciliation process.

Media and reconciliation

The media has a role to play in ensuring that public information both for and about Aboriginal peoples reflects their cultural diversity and provides fair and non-discriminatory reporting on Aboriginal issues. This is consistent with Article 16:2 of the *United Nations Declaration on the Rights of Indigenous Peoples*, which says, "States shall take effective measures to ensure that State-owned media duly reflect indigenous cultural diversity." Canada's *Broadcasting Act* (1991) sets out national broadcasting policy for all Canadian broadcasters with regard to Aboriginal peoples. The policy states the need to,

> through its programming and employment opportunities arising out of its operations, serve the needs and interests, and reflect the circumstances and aspirations of Canadian men, women, and children, including equal rights, the linguistic duality and multicultural and multiracial nature of Canadian society, and the special place of aboriginal peoples within that society. [S. 3.1.d.iii]

The Act then states a more controversial obligation, that "programming that reflects the aboriginal cultures of Canada should be provided within the Canadian broadcasting system as resources become available for the purpose" (S.3.1.o).[241]

A submission to the federal Task Force on Aboriginal Languages and Cultures in 2004 pointed out deficiencies in the *Broadcasting Act* related to these service provisions for Aboriginal peoples. It stated:

> The Act did not enshrine Aboriginal language broadcasting as a priority: instead it noted that ... [S. S. 3.1.d.iii] means that Aboriginal language programming

> is not recognized nor protected to the same extent as English and French programming ... [and that] the phrase "as resources become available for the purpose" [S.3.1.o] has become a stumbling block for many producers and programmers, linking the availability of Aboriginal language broadcasting to the political process.[242]

The report recommended that the *Broadcasting Act* be revised to address these gaps. As of 2014, these provisions of the Act remain unchanged.

As Canada's national public broadcaster, the Canadian Broadcasting Corporation (CBC/Radio-Canada) is responsible for fulfilling national broadcasting policy. For many years, it has been providing a minimum level of Aboriginal radio and television programming and news, in a few specific regions, including some Aboriginal-language programming, especially in northern Canada. In the Commission's view, the budget cuts to the CBC over the past decade have significantly reduced and further limited its capacity to provide Aboriginal programming and dedicated news coverage on Aboriginal issues, and to increase the number of Aboriginal people in staff and leadership positions. As of March 31, 2014, Aboriginal people made up 1.6% of the CBC workforce, well below the demographic makeup of Aboriginal people, who represent 4.3% of the total Canadian population.[243]

The Aboriginal Peoples Television Network (APTN), an independent, non-profit broadcaster, has taken a leadership role since the 1990s, in part to make up for the programming and scheduling limitations of CBC/Radio-Canada, to provide nationwide programming and news that reflects Aboriginal peoples' perspectives, concerns, and experiences. The APTN has provided an outlet for Aboriginal journalists, producers, directors, writers, artists, and musicians, and attracts a wide Aboriginal and non-Aboriginal Canadian and international audience.[244] As of 2014, over 75% of APTN employees were Aboriginal, and 28% of its programming was broadcast in various Aboriginal languages.[245] In the Commission's view, the APTN is well positioned to provide media leadership to support the reconciliation process.

National public and private broadcasters must provide comprehensive and timely information and services to Aboriginal peoples and the Canadian public.

Calls to Action

84) We call upon the federal government to restore and increase funding to the CBC/Radio-Canada, to enable Canada's national public broadcaster to support reconciliation, and be properly reflective of the diverse cultures, languages, and perspectives of Aboriginal peoples, including, but not limited to:

i. Increasing Aboriginal programming, including Aboriginal-language speakers.

ii. Increasing equitable access for Aboriginal peoples to jobs, leadership positions, and professional development opportunities within the organization.

iii. Continuing to provide dedicated news coverage and online public information resources on issues of concern to Aboriginal peoples and all Canadians, including the history and legacy of residential schools and the reconciliation process.

85) We call upon the Aboriginal Peoples Television Network, as an independent non-profit broadcaster with programming by, for, and about Aboriginal peoples, to support reconciliation, including but not limited to:

i. Continuing to provide leadership in programming and organizational culture that reflects the diverse cultures, languages, and perspectives of Aboriginal peoples.

ii. Continuing to develop media initiatives that inform and educate the Canadian public, and connect Aboriginal and non-Aboriginal Canadians.

Educating journalists for reconciliation

In a submission to the Royal Commission on Aboriginal Peoples (RCAP) in 1993, the Canadian Association of Journalists noted, "The country's large newspapers, TV and radio news shows often contain misinformation, sweeping generalizations, and galling stereotypes about Natives and Native affairs.... The result is that most Canadians have little real knowledge of the country's Native peoples, or the issues that affect them."[246] In 1996, the RCAP report had noted,

> Public opinion polls in the past few years have consistently shown broad sympathy for Aboriginal issues and concerns, but that support is not very deep. More recent events have brought a hardening of attitudes towards Aboriginal issues in many parts of the country.... This growing hostility can be traced in large part to recent negative publicity over land claims, Aboriginal hunting and fishing rights, and issues of taxation.[247]

More recent studies indicate that this historical pattern persists.[248] Media coverage of Aboriginal issues remains problematic; social media and online commentary are often inflammatory and racist in nature.

In August 2013, the Journalists for Human Rights[249] conducted a study of media coverage of Aboriginal issues in Ontario from June 1, 2010, to May 31, 2013. The study found that:

1) "the Aboriginal population is widely underrepresented in mainstream media";

2) "when Aboriginal people choose to protest or 'make more noise' the number of stories focused on the community increase"; and
3) "as coverage related to the protests and talks between Aboriginal people and government became more frequent, the proportion of stories with a negative tone correspondingly increased."[250]

Media coverage of residential schools was low. From June 1, 2011, to May 31, 2012, media coverage of Aboriginal issues in Ontario accounted for only 0.23% of all news stories, and, of these, only 3.0% focused on residential schools. From June 1, 2012, to May 31, 2013, news stories on Aboriginal issues amounted to 0.46% of all news stories, and, of these, 3.0% focused on deaths in residential schools.[251]

The report included expert opinions on its findings, including those of CBC journalist Duncan McCue, who observed that editorial opinions "are often rooted in century-old stereotypes rather than reality."[252] He pointed out:

> Yes, protests often meet the test of whether a story is 'newsworthy,' because they're unusual, dramatic, or involve conflict. Yes, Aboriginal activists, who understand the media's hunger for drama, also play a role by tailoring protests in ways that guarantee prominent headlines and lead stories. But, does today's front-page news of some traffic disruption in the name of Aboriginal land rights actually have its roots in a much older narrative—of violent and "uncivilized" Indians who represent a threat to 'progress' in Canada? Are attitudes of distrust and fear underlying our decisions to dispatch a crew to the latest Aboriginal blockade? Is there no iconic photo of reconciliation, because no one from the newsrooms believes harmony between Aboriginal peoples and settlers is 'newsworthy'?[253]

Historian J. R. Miller has observed that when conflicts between Aboriginal peoples and the state have occurred in places like Oka or Ipperwash Park, for example, "politicians, journalists and ordinary citizens understood neither how nor why the crisis of the moment had arisen, much less how its deep historical roots made it resistant to solutions.... [This] does not bode well for effective public debate or sensible policy-making."[254]

In the Commission's view, the media's role and responsibility in the reconciliation process require journalists to be well informed about the history of Aboriginal peoples and the issues that affect their lives. As we have seen, this is not necessarily the case. Studies of media coverage of conflicts involving Aboriginal peoples have borne this out. In the conflict between some of the descendants of members of the Stony Point Reserve and their supporters and the Ontario Provincial Police in Ipperwash Provincial Park in 1995, which resulted in the death of Dudley George, journalism professor John Miller concluded,

> Much of the opinion—and there was a lot of it—was based not on the facts of the Ipperwash occupation, but on crude generalizations about First Nations people that fit many of the racist stereotypes that ... have [been] identified.... Accurate, comprehensive coverage can promote understanding and resolution, just as inaccurate, incomplete and myopic coverage can exacerbate stereotypes and prolong confrontations.... Reporters are professionally trained to engage in a discipline of verification, a process that is often mistakenly referred to as "objectivity." But ... research shows that news is not selected randomly or objectively.[255]

Miller identified nine principles of journalism that journalists themselves have identified as essential to their work. Of those, he said,

> Journalism's first obligation is to the truth.... Journalism does not pursue truth in an absolute or philosophical sense, but it can—and must—pursue it in a practical sense.... Even in a world of expanding voices, accuracy is the foundation upon which everything else is built—context, interpretation, comment, criticism, analysis and debate. The truth, over time, emerges from this forum....
>
> Its practitioners must be allowed to exercise their personal conscience. Every journalist must have a personal sense of ethics and responsibility—a moral compass. Each of us must be willing, if fairness and accuracy require, to voice differences with our colleagues.... This stimulates the intellectual diversity necessary to understand and accurately cover an increasingly diverse society. It is this diversity of minds and voices, not just numbers, that matters.[256]

With respect to the history and legacy of residential schools, all the major radio and television networks and newspapers covered the events and activities of the Commission. The TRC provided regular information briefings to the media who attended the National Events. We discussed earlier how students must not only learn the truth about what happened in residential schools, but also understand the ethical dimensions of this history. So too must journalists. Many of the reporters who covered the National Events were themselves deeply affected by what they heard from Survivors and their families. Some required the assistance of health-support workers. Some told us in off-the-record conversations that their perspectives and understanding of the impacts of residential schools, and the need for healing and reconciliation, had changed, based on their observations and experiences at the National Events.

Call to Action

86) We call upon Canadian journalism programs and media schools to require education for all students on the history of Aboriginal peoples, including the history and legacy of residential schools, the *United Nations Declaration on the*

Rights of Indigenous Peoples, Treaties and Aboriginal rights, Indigenous law, and Aboriginal–Crown relations.

Sports: Inspiring lives, healthy communities

The Commission heard from Survivors that the opportunity to play sports at residential school made their lives more bearable and gave them a sense of identity, accomplishment, and pride. At the Alberta National Event, Survivor Theodore (Ted) Fontaine placed a bundle of mementoes into the Bentwood Box as expressions of reconciliation. It included a pair of baseball pants that he had worn at residential school. He said,

> These woollen baseball pants carry a story of their own ... these are the baseball pants that I wore in 1957–58, as a fifteen-year-old incarcerated boy at the Fort Alexander residential school.... Little did I know that my mom would treasure and keep them as a memento of her youngest boy. When I leave this land, they won't have anywhere else to go, so I hope the Bentwood Box keeps them well....
>
> When we were little boys at Fort Alexander residential school, our only chance to play hockey literally did save our lives. A lot of people here will attest to that. As a young man, playing hockey saved me.... And later, playing with the Sagkeeng Old-Timers saved me again.... I came back twenty years later, fifteen years later and started playing with an old-timers hockey team in Fort Alexander.... In 1983, we ended up winning the first World Cup by an Indigenous team, in Munich, Germany.... So I'm including in this bundle, a story of the old-timers, a battalion of Anishinaabe hockey players who saved themselves and their friends by winning, not only winning in Munich, Germany, but in three or four other hockey tournaments in Europe.... People ask me, "Why don't you just enjoy life now instead of working so hard on reconciliation and talking about residential schools? What do you expect to achieve?" The answer is "freedom." I am free.[257]

Later that same day, journalist Laura Robinson's expression of reconciliation was a copy of the documentary *FrontRunners*, which she produced for APTN, about some residential school athletes who had made history. She said,

> In 1967, ten teenage First Nations boys, all good students and great runners, ran with the 1967 Pan Am Games torch, from St. Paul, Minnesota, to Winnipeg, a distance of 800 kilometres, which they did successfully.... But the young men who delivered that torch to the stadium were turned away at the door. They were not allowed in to watch those games. They were not allowed to run that last 400 metres. One of them told me that he remembered being turned around, [and] put back on the bus to residential school.... In 1999, Winnipeg hosted the Pan Am Games again and the organizers realized what had happened. They tracked

> down the original runners, apologized, and thirty-two years later, as men in their fifties, those runners finished that 400 metres and brought the torch in....
>
> Sport is a place that we speak a universal language—a language of shared passion for moving our bodies through time and space, with strength and skill. This summer [2014], Regina will host the North American Indigenous Games.... Let us all hope, and commit to reconcile divisiveness, racism, and stereotypes through the world of sport and support each and every young person attending those games. Because they are the frontrunners of the future.[258]

Such stories are indicative of the need for the rich history of Aboriginal peoples' contributions to sport to become part of Canadian sport history.

On November 18, 2014, we attended an event hosted by the Law Society of Upper Canada to celebrate the first time an Aboriginal community—the Mississaugas of the New Credit First Nation—was to be the Host First Nation for the Pan-Parapan American Games, held in Toronto in July and August of 2015. The FrontRunners attended and were honoured in a traditional blanketing ceremony.[259]

Calls to Action

87) We call upon all levels of government, in collaboration with Aboriginal peoples, sports halls of fame, and other relevant organizations, to provide public education that tells the national story of Aboriginal athletes in history.

88) We call upon all levels of government to take action to ensure long-term Aboriginal athlete development and growth, and continued support for the North American Indigenous Games, including funding to host the games and for provincial and territorial team preparation and travel.

Aboriginal youth today face many barriers to leading active, healthy lives in their communities. They lack opportunities to pursue excellence in sports. There is little access to culturally relevant traditional sports activities that strengthen Aboriginal identity and instill a sense of pride and self-confidence. Lack of resources, sports facilities, and equipment limits their ability to play sports. Racism remains an issue. Aboriginal girls face the extra barrier of gender discrimination.[260] Despite the many achievements of individual Indigenous athletes, too many Aboriginal youth remain excluded from community-based sports activities and the pursuit of excellence in sport. The *Physical Activity and Sport Act* (2003) set out the federal government's sport policy regarding the full and fair participation of all Canadians in sport, and mandated the minister to "facilitate the participation of under-represented groups in the Canadian sport system" (S. 5.m). However, the Act made no specific reference to Aboriginal peoples.[261]

Call to Action

89) We call upon the federal government to amend the *Physical Activity and Sport Act* to support reconciliation by ensuring that policies to promote physical activity as a fundamental element of health and well-being, reduce barriers to sports participation, increase the pursuit of excellence in sport, and build capacity in the Canadian sport system, are inclusive of Aboriginal peoples.

In 2005, Sport Canada developed the Aboriginal Peoples' Participation in Sports Policy, which recognized the unique circumstances of Aboriginal peoples and the role of sport as a vehicle for individual and community health and cultural revitalization. It recognized that Aboriginal peoples have their own culturally diverse, traditional knowledge and cultural teachings of play, games, and sports.[262] However, no action plan was subsequently developed to implement the policy.[263] In 2011, in preparation for revising the 2002 Canadian Sport Policy (CSP), Sport Canada conducted a series of consultations across the country, including a roundtable on "Sport and Aboriginal Peoples." The roundtable summary report noted:

> Participants believe that the needs and issues of Aboriginal Peoples were not adequately reflected in the 2002 CSP.... The feeling among the participants was that the previous policy had "no teeth."... The new CSP should acknowledge the unique identity of Aboriginal Peoples, what Aboriginal Peoples can contribute to Canadian sport ... and make a clear commitment to action. The CSP can support sport for Aboriginal Peoples by reflecting Aboriginal culture and realities, cross-cultural issues between Aboriginal and non-Aboriginal Peoples, and an understanding of the motivation behind the interest of Aboriginal Peoples in sport.... If the new policy doesn't reflect the needs and issues of Aboriginal sport, then it will not be relevant to the Aboriginal population.... It would be important to recognize that the barriers to sport extend beyond a lack of resources and gaps and weaknesses in the sport system. Aboriginal peoples are also affected by issues of identity and historical trauma.[264]

Despite this roundtable report based on the 2011 consultation, the Commission notes that the subsequent Canadian Sport Policy released in 2012 contains no specific references to Aboriginal peoples.[265]

Call to Action

90) We call upon the federal government to ensure that national sports policies, programs, and initiatives are inclusive of Aboriginal peoples, including, but not limited to, establishing:

i. In collaboration with provincial and territorial governments, stable funding for, and access to, community sports programs that reflect the diverse cultures and traditional sporting activities of Aboriginal peoples.

ii. An elite athlete development program for Aboriginal athletes.

iii. Programs for coaches, trainers, and sports officials that are culturally relevant for Aboriginal peoples.

iv. Anti-racism awareness and training programs.

The 2010 Winter Olympics in Vancouver, British Columbia, were held on the traditional territories of the Squamish, Musqueam, Tsleil-Waututh, and Lil'wat peoples, and they were an integral part of the event. In the spirit of reconciliation, which aligns easily with the spirit of the games themselves, the Four Host First Nations and the Vancouver Olympic Committee formed a partnership that ensured that Indigenous peoples were full participants in the decision-making process—a first in Olympic history. At the opening ceremonies and throughout the games, territorial protocols were respected, and the Four Host First Nations and other Indigenous peoples from across the province were a highly visible presence at various Olympic venues.

91) We call upon the officials and host countries of international sporting events such as the Olympics, Pan Am, and Commonwealth games to ensure that Indigenous peoples' territorial protocols are respected, and local Indigenous communities are engaged in all aspects of planning and participating in such events.

Corporate sector: Land, sustainability, and economic development

Survivors and their family members told us that their hope for the future lies in reclaiming and regenerating their own cultures, spirituality, laws, and ways of life that are deeply connected to their homelands. Indigenous nations are already doing this work in their communities, despite the many challenges they face. At the TRC's Traditional Knowledge Keepers Forum, Elder Dave Courchene said,

> As people who have gained this recognition to be Knowledge Keepers for our people, we accept that work in the most humble way.... It's going to be the spirit of our ancestors, the spirit that's going to help us to reclaim our rightful place in our homeland. We do have a lot of work and there's certainly a lot of challenges, but with the help of the spirit we will overcome [these].... We've arrived in a time of great change and great opportunity ... we are the true leaders of our homeland and they cannot take that away from us and they never will because our Creator put us here. This is our homeland and we have a sacred responsibility to teach all those that have come to our homeland how to be proper human beings because

> we have all been given original instructions on how to be a human being. We have great responsibilities as people to take care of the Earth, to speak on behalf of Mother Earth. That is our responsibility and that's the kind of leadership that we must reflect as a people.[266]

That same day, Chief Ian Campbell of the Squamish Nation said,

> I want to acknowledge my grandparents and my mentors for their generosity in teaching us our connections to our lands and our territories. Right now we're preparing back home for a canoe journey as our young people are training to represent our people on their journey to Bella Bella in a couple of weeks.... A number of families are travelling all up and down the coast to celebrate the resurgence of our identity, of our culture.[267]

In the face of global warming, growing economic inequities, and conflicts over large-scale economic development projects, there is an emerging consensus that the land that sustains all of us must be protected for future generations. In the wake of the Supreme Court of Canada Tsilhqot'in decision, Aboriginal peoples, corporations, and governments must find new ways to work together. Speaking to local community leaders at the Union of British Columbia Municipalities convention in September 2014, Tsilhqot'in Chief Percy Guichon said,

> We do live side-by-side and we need to work on a relationship to create or promote a common understanding among all our constituents ... we need to find the best way forward to consult with each other, regardless of what legal obligations might exist. I mean, that's just neighbourly, right? ... We share a lot of common interests in areas like resource development. We need to find ways to work together, to support one another on these difficult topics.[268]

In 1977, the *Report of the Mackenzie Valley Pipeline Inquiry* recommended that a proposed natural gas pipeline down the Mackenzie Valley in the Northwest Territories not be built before Aboriginal land claims in the region were resolved and environmental concerns were addressed. Justice Thomas Berger, who led the inquiry, identified the potentially devastating consequences that building a pipeline through the North would have for Dene and Inuvialuit peoples and for the fragile ecosystems. His observations, made almost forty years ago, foreshadow similar controversies and conflicts over proposed pipelines still occurring in various regions of Canada as the TRC has prepared this final report.[269]

The political and legal landscape has shifted significantly since Justice Berger issued his report in 1977. As Canada maps its economic future in regions covered by historical Treaties, modern land-claims agreements, and unceded Aboriginal title, governments and industry must now recognize that accommodating the rights of Aboriginal peoples is paramount to Canada's long-term economic sustainability. Governments aim to secure the necessary economic stability and growth to ensure prosperity for all

Canadians. Corporations invest time and resources in developing large-scale projects that create jobs and aim to produce profits for their shareholders. Although the corporate sector is not a direct party to Treaty and land-claims agreement negotiations, industry and business play an extremely significant role in how the economic, social, and cultural aspects of reconciliation are addressed, including the extent to which opportunities and benefits are truly shared with Indigenous peoples and the environment of traditional homelands is safeguarded.

The 1996 *Report of the Royal Commission on Aboriginal Peoples* noted that, historically, land and resource development activities, such as hydroelectric dams, mines, and agricultural and urban development, have had many adverse impacts on Aboriginal communities. Communities were not consulted before they were relocated from their vast traditional territories to much smaller, more remote, and more crowded reserves to make way for government and industrial land and resource development projects. Even when they were not relocated, Aboriginal peoples were economically marginalized in their own homelands when irreversible environmental damage was done in the name of 'progress.' All too often, economic development has disrupted Indigenous peoples' cultural, spiritual, and economic ties to the land, resulting in the devastation of traditional economies and self-sufficiency, community trauma, public welfare dependency, and poor health and socio-political outcomes.[270]

In the post-RCAP period, the Supreme Court of Canada has developed a body of law on the federal, provincial, and territorial governments' duty to consult with Aboriginal peoples where land and resource development might infringe on their Aboriginal or Treaty rights.[271] The court has ruled that governments can still infringe on Aboriginal rights if it can demonstrate that it is in the broader public interest to do so. In the *Delgamuukw* case, the court described the nature of that public interest:

> [T]he development of agriculture, forestry, mining and hydroelectric power, the general economic development of the interior of British Columbia, protection of the environment or endangered species, the building of infrastructure and the settlement of foreign populations to support those aims, are the kinds of objectives that are consistent with this purpose and, in principle, can justify the infringement of aboriginal title.[272]

Governments must also demonstrate that any infringement of Aboriginal rights is consistent with the Crown's fiduciary duty towards Aboriginal peoples and upholds the honour of the Crown. To meet these legal obligations, governments in all jurisdictions have developed Aboriginal consultation policies.

Although the court has ruled that the duty to consult rests solely with governments, it has also said that "the Crown may delegate procedural aspects of consultation to industry proponents seeking a particular development."[273] On a practical level, the business risks associated with legal uncertainty created by the duty to consult have motivated industry proponents to negotiate with Aboriginal communities to establish a range of mechanisms designed to ensure that Aboriginal peoples benefit directly from economic development projects in their traditional territories. These may include, for example, joint venture business partnerships; impact and benefit agreements; revenue-sharing agreements; and education, training, and job opportunities.[274]

Between 2012 and 2014, several reports highlighted the fact that Canada is once again facing significant challenges and potential opportunities related to land and resource development. Economic reconciliation will require finding common ground that balances the respective rights, legal interests, and needs of Aboriginal peoples, governments, and industry in the face of climate change and competitive global markets. In addition to the concrete remedial measures required, these reports also emphasized the importance of so-called soft skills—establishing trust, engaging communities, resolving conflicts, and building mutually beneficial partnerships—to advance reconciliation.

In 2012, Canada's Public Policy Forum, a non-profit organization, held a series of six regional dialogues across the country, bringing together Aboriginal leaders; senior federal, provincial, and territorial government officials; and representatives from industry, business, and financial institutions. The purposes of the dialogues were to discuss issues, identify best practices, and make recommendations for action on how to ensure that Aboriginal communities benefit from large-scale resource development projects. The resulting report, "Building Authentic Partnerships: Aboriginal Participation in Major Resource Development Opportunities," identified five key opportunities for action: (1) developing authentic partnerships among Aboriginal communities, industry, governments, and academic institutions by building trust; (2) developing human capital by removing barriers to education, training, and skills development for Aboriginal entrepreneurs, workers, and leaders; (3) enhancing community control over decision making; (4) promoting entrepreneurship and business development; and (5) increasing financial participation.[275] The report concluded:

> Natural resource companies are recognizing that their operational success relies on strong, authentic community engagement. Private sector initiatives have already demonstrated positive examples in areas such as revenue sharing, skills training, and business development for Aboriginal communities. Now corporations and governments need to build on these successes to keep up with the rapid pace of development, moving beyond superficial consultations toward genuine engagement. Aboriginal communities must also play a leadership role to help forge these relationships, to develop local and adaptive solutions that will be essential to success.[276]

In November 2013, after eight months of consultations with representatives from Aboriginal communities, industry, and local and provincial governments in British Columbia and Alberta, Douglas Eyford, Canada's special representative on west-coast energy infrastructure, issued his report to the prime minister. "Forging Partnerships,

Building Relationships: Aboriginal Canadians and Energy Development" focused on Aboriginal–Crown relations in the context of proposed energy infrastructure projects in British Columbia. He noted that although there are many differences among Aboriginal representatives, there was general consensus that development projects must respect constitutionally protected Aboriginal rights, involve Aboriginal communities in decision making and project planning, and mitigate environmental risks.[277] Eyford made recommendations for taking action in three key areas: building trust, fostering inclusion, and advancing reconciliation. He noted in particular that "Aboriginal communities view natural resource development as linked to a broader reconciliation agenda."[278] This is consistent with the Commission's view that meaningful reconciliation cannot be limited to the residential school legacy, but must become the ongoing framework for resolving conflicts and building constructive partnerships with Aboriginal peoples.

In December 2013, a group of current and former high-profile leaders from Aboriginal communities, business, banking, environment organizations, and federal and provincial governments released a report, "Responsible Energy Development in Canada," summarizing the results of a year-long dialogue. They concluded that Canada is facing an "energy resource development gridlock." In their view, the potential economic and social benefits derived from the exploitation of Canada's rich natural resources must be weighed against the potential risks to Aboriginal communities and their traditional territories, and must also address broader environmental concerns associated with global warming.[279] They emphasized that there are significant barriers to reconciliation, including conflicting values, lack of trust, and differing views on how the benefits of resource development should be distributed and adverse effects be mitigated.[280] The report identified four principles for moving forward on responsible energy resource development: (1) forging and nurturing constructive relationships, (2) reducing cumulative social and environmental impacts, (3) ensuring the continuity of cultures and traditions, and (4) sharing the benefits fairly.[281]

Writing about the 2014 Supreme Court of Canada decision in *Tsilhqot'in Nation v. British Columbia*, Kenneth Coates, Canada Research Chair in Regional Innovation at the University of Saskatchewan, and Dwight Newman, law professor and Canada Research Chair in Indigenous Rights in Constitutional and International Law at the University of Saskatchewan, concluded that although many challenges and barriers to reconciliation remain,

> [w]hat the Supreme Court of Canada has highlighted at a fundamental level is that Aboriginal communities have a right to an equitable place at the table in relation to natural resource development in Canada. Their empowerment through *Tsilhqot'in* and earlier decisions has the potential to be immensely exciting as a means of further economic development in Aboriginal communities and prosperity for all.... [T]he time is now for governments,

> Aboriginal communities, and resource sector companies to work together to build partnerships for the future.... We need to keep building a national consensus that responsible resource development that takes account of sustainability issues and that respects Indigenous communities, contributes positively—very positively—to Canada and its future.[282]

Internationally, there is a growing awareness in the corporate sector that the *United Nations Declaration on the Rights of Indigenous Peoples* is an effective framework for industry and business to establish respectful relationships and work collaboratively with Indigenous peoples. In 2013, the United Nations Global Compact published a business guide that sets out practical actions that corporations and businesses can undertake in compliance with the *Declaration*. It notes:

> Business faces both challenges and opportunities when engaging with indigenous peoples. When businesses collaborate with indigenous peoples, they are often able to achieve sustainable economic growth, for example, by optimizing ecosystem services and harnessing local or traditional knowledge. Positive engagement with indigenous peoples can also contribute to the success of resource development initiatives—from granting and maintaining social licenses to actively participating in business ventures as owners, contractors and employees. Failing to respect the rights of indigenous peoples can put businesses at significant legal, financial and reputational risk.... Continuing dialogue between business and indigenous peoples can potentially strengthen indigenous peoples' confidence in partnering with business and building healthy relationships.[283]

In the Commission's view, sustainable reconciliation on the land involves realizing the economic potential of Indigenous communities in a fair, just, and equitable manner that respects their right to self-determination. Economic reconciliation involves working in partnership with Indigenous peoples to ensure that lands and resources within their traditional territories are developed in culturally respectful ways that fully recognize Treaty and Aboriginal rights and title.

Establishing constructive, mutually beneficial relationships and partnerships with Indigenous communities will contribute to their economic growth, improve community health and well-being, and ensure environmental sustainability that will ultimately benefit Indigenous peoples and all Canadians. Unlike with the residential schools of the past, where Aboriginal peoples had no say in the design of the system and no ability to protect their children from intrinsic harms, First Nations, Inuit, and Métis peoples today want to manage their own lives. In terms of the economy, that means participating in it on their own terms. They want to be part of the decision-making process. They want their communities to benefit if large-scale economic projects come into their territories. They want to establish and develop their own businesses in ways that are compatible with their identity, cultural values, and world views as Indigenous peoples. They want opportunities to work for companies that are proactively addressing systemic racism and inequity. Corporations can demonstrate leadership by using the *United Nations Declaration* as a reconciliation framework.

Call to Action

92) We call upon the corporate sector in Canada to adopt the *United Nations Declaration on the Rights of Indigenous Peoples* as a reconciliation framework and to apply its principles, norms, and standards to corporate policy and core operational activities involving Indigenous peoples and their lands and resources. This would include, but not be limited to, the following:

i. Commit to meaningful consultation, building respectful relationships, and obtaining the free, prior, and informed consent of Indigenous peoples before proceeding with economic development projects.

ii. Ensure that Aboriginal peoples have equitable access to jobs, training, and education opportunities in the corporate sector, and that Aboriginal communities gain long-term sustainable benefits from economic development projects.

iii. Provide education for management and staff on the history of Aboriginal peoples, including the history and legacy of residential schools, the *United Nations Declaration on the Rights of Indigenous Peoples*, Treaties and Aboriginal rights, Indigenous law, and Aboriginal–Crown relations. This will require skills-based training in intercultural competency, conflict resolution, human rights, and anti-racism.

We are all Treaty people: Communities, alliances, and hope

The Commission believes that reconciliation cannot be left up to governments, the courts, and churches alone. There must also be dialogue and action in communities across the country. Reconciliation must happen across all sectors of Canadian society. Canadians still have much to learn from each other. Past generations of newcomers faced injustices and prejudice similar to those experienced by residential school students and their families. More recent immigrants have struggled with racism and misconceptions as they come to take their place in the Canadian nation.

Despite the many barriers to reconciliation, this Commission remains cautiously optimistic. At the Alberta National Event in March 2014, TRC Honorary Witness Wab Kinew spoke about the changes that are already happening across this land that give rise to hope. He began by explaining that all day he had been carrying with him

> a ceremonial pipe, a sacred pipe, which when you bind the two sides together—the stem and the bowl—it offers us a model of reconciliation, of two forces coming together to be more powerful than they were otherwise. So it's important for me to come up here before you all and to speak Anishnaabemowin, and a little bit of Lakota, and to carry a pipe because it sends a message. It sends a message to those who designed the residential school system, that you have failed. We were abused. Our languages were assaulted. Our families were harmed, in some cases, irreparably. But we are still here. We are still here. So in honour of my late father, Tobasonakwut, a Survivor of St. Mary's residential school in Rat Portage, Ontario, I wanted to say that. I so wish that he could have seen this—the final event of the Truth and Reconciliation Commission—so that he could see how this country has changed. How when he was a child, he was told that he was a savage. He was told that he was nothing. He was assaulted, taken away from his family, taken away from his father's trapline. To see the change that has happened, where today in Canada, there are tens of thousands of people from all walks of life gathering together to set that right and to stand up for justice for Indigenous peoples.
>
> The world has changed in another way as well; the old dichotomy of white people versus Indians no longer applies. Look around at Canada today. There are the descendants of Europeans. There are the descendents of Indigenous peoples. But there are also the descendants of Arab nations, of Iran, of the Slavic nations, of Africa, of the Caribbean, Southeast Asian, Chinese, and Japanese peoples. The challenge of reconciliation may have begun between Indigenous peoples and Europeans, but now the project of reconciliation will be undertaken by the children of all those nations that I just mentioned. And though the world has changed, and Canada has changed, we still have a long way to go.... We are all in this together. Let us commit to removing the political, economic, and social barriers that prevent the full realization of that vision [of reconciliation] on these lands. Let us raise up the residential school Survivors, and their example of courage, grace, and compassion, in whose footsteps we walk towards that brighter day.[284]

At the community level, where contact between Aboriginal and non-Aboriginal peoples is often minimal or marred by distrust and racism, establishing respectful relationships involves learning to be good neighbours. This means being respectful—listening to, and learning from, each other; building understanding; and taking concrete action to improve relationships. At the Victoria Regional Event, intergenerational Survivor Victoria Wells said,

> I'll know that reconciliation is happening in Canadian society when Canadians, wherever they live, are able to say the names of the tribes with which they're neighbours; they're able to pronounce names from the community, or of people that they know, and they're able to say hello, goodbye, in the language of their

> neighbours.... That will show me manners. That will show me that they've invested in finding out the language of the land [on] which they live ... because the language comes from the land ... the language is very organic to where it comes from and the invitation to you is to learn that and to be enlightened by that and to be informed by [our] ways of thinking and knowing and seeing and understanding. So that, to me, is reconciliation.[285]

Former public school teacher Lynne Phillips cautioned that establishing trust will be one of the major challenges of the reconciliation process. She said,

> I really understand the reticence of some First Nations people about wanting to accept offers of friendship and possibilities of interaction. I understand why that is and I hope that in time we will be able to gain trust and some kind ways of interacting with one another that will be mutually beneficial.... I think we're moving.... I think civil society, non-governmental organizations, church organizations, Aboriginal organizations are moving in the direction of openness ... and I think we have a long ways to go.[286]

In July of 2013, at the Community Hearing in Maskwacis (formerly Hobbema, Alberta), at the former site of Ermineskin residential school, Professor Roger Epp said that over the years, his Cree students helped him to understand

> what it was that a fourth-generation grandson of settler people needed to know in order to live here ... with a sense of memory and care and obligation. For I too have ancestors buried on Treaty 6 land.... I learned from a student from Hobbema that we're all Treaty people here.... A Treaty is a relationship after all and we live here on the basis of an agreement signed in 1876, 1877; the first time, not very far from where my settler ancestors homesteaded.... While it is good for national leaders to make public apologies, the work of reconciliation is not just for governments. Actually, I don't think they're very good at it. The work of reconciliation is work for neighbours.... I think the words [of the apology] were sincere, but they were not enough. They did not change relationships, not enough.[287]

We also heard that day from Mayor Bill Elliot, from the nearby city of Wetaskiwin. He explained that prior to the TRC's Community Hearing, he, along with Grade Ten students and others from Hobbema and Wetaskiwin, had attended a workshop with Survivors. Listening to their residential school experiences helped those who attended to begin to understand how deeply the residential schools had scarred Survivors, their families, and the whole community. He said,

> I think it helped the people of Wetaskawin come to an understanding of some of the trials and tribulations that our neighbours to the south have been going through all their lives.... We are working on a healing journey between the City of Wetaskiwin and the Cree First Nations.... As you come into Wetaskiwin from the south, you will see that our [city] sign is in Cree syllabics as well—that welcomes

> you.... We still have a long way to go. We are taking baby steps in the healing process. But we are working together for better communities, to understand and respect the differences and similarities in our cultures.[288]

At the Alberta National Event in 2014, Mayor Elliot, who was also inducted as a TRC Honorary Witness, offered an expression of reconciliation:

> Our community is trying to learn more about the Survivors and the residential schools. Our schools, churches, and community have made cupcakes and birthday cards for the big birthday party tomorrow. Members of our community have been here for the last two days.... They are very, very supportive and they want to learn. We are trying to learn more about and understand the effects of residential schools and our friends from Maskwacis because we want to be good neighbours.[289]

The cities of Vancouver, Toronto, Edmonton, and Calgary have also issued proclamations declaring a year of reconciliation. In 2014, Vancouver went a step further, declaring that it was now a "City of Reconciliation," and it has established a long-term framework for partnership and relationship building with the Musqueam, Squamish, and Tsleil-Waututh nations and urban Aboriginal people.[290] At the British Columbia National Event, TRC Honorary Witness Mayor Gregor Robertson said,

> We are blessed to have so many different cultures in this place, and all of us who come from afar ... have been incredibly lucky to be able to come to this place. Many of us come from families, from clans, from cultures, that were wiped out, that had to leave. We were forced off our territories, and somehow we've managed to make a home here. That's largely because of those First Nations ancestors who welcomed us ... who made it possible for refugees, for people of broken cultures all over the world to settle here, to stay here, even though our predecessors and our ancestors turned it right around and terrible things have happened. I think the strength that is in Aboriginal peoples across Canada is something for the world to learn from, something that we can apply to the big decisions that we have to make in our governments, our communities, our cities.
>
> When I hear the strength in Survivors, when I hear the phrase "brave children," when I think about brave Elders, I think "brave culture"—that bravery and that determination to learn from this past and to make the best decisions about how we look after each other, how we take care of each other, and those that need that help the most.... That we lift each other up; that we take care of the land and the sea that we inherited for the generations to come.[291]

Intergenerational youth across cultures

At the British Columbia National Event, the Commission, in partnership with the Inspirit Foundation, hosted a Youth Panel, "Be the Change: Young People Healing the Past and Building the Future." In this cross-cultural dialogue, youth leaders described the intergenerational impacts of human rights violations such as the residential schools, the Holocaust, Canada's internment of Japanese Canadians during World War Two, and the head tax imposed on Chinese immigrants to Canada. They spoke about community and about turning reconciliation into action. Tsilhqot'in intergenerational Survivor Kim Harvey said,

> I encountered many uncomfortable moments trying to explain what happened to my people and why there is so much alcoholism and drug abuse. There is so much focus on all the negative things.... No one talked about the residential schools.... There are so many horrible stereotypes that our young people face every day. I struggle with issues of family, identity, and community every day.... Reconciliation to me comes down to truth, education, and knowledge sharing practices.... Reconciliation is about relationship. To reconcile, I really need to understand what happened to you, who you are, and what, as a community member, I can do to make our community better....
>
> Reconciliation is a shared experience.... The residential schools were done [to us] by an outside party ... when people ask "why don't you just get over it?" I find that frustrating because it takes the onus off the shared relationship [as if] somehow this entire country is not involved in the reconciliation process.... That, to me, is a disservice to this nation in terms of reconciliation.... It's everyone's responsibility to educate themselves about what happened.... With relationship comes respect.... What helps young people, Indigenous or not, is to find your role, have adult allies to help you find that role, fulfill your responsibilities within that role, and then be of service to the community.... If we all did that ... to me that would be reconciliation in action.... It's about finding out about your neighbour.[292]

Kevin Takahide Lee, an intergenerational Survivor of the internment of Japanese Canadians during the Second World War, said,

> I acknowledge that we are on Coast Salish lands. It was also on these very lands here at the PNE [Pacific National Exhibition fairgrounds] that my family was held during the war before being sent to the internment camp. It is my parents and grandparents who are Survivors.... [They] never talked about what happened in the internment camps ... even after the Japanese-Canadian redress happened ... hearing these stories from our Elders is very rare.... When I was four or five, I came here to the PNE as most families do.... When it came to going inside the barn here, just two doors away, my grandmother would not come in. That's because that livestock building was used to hold her and

> other women and children, during the war, for months.... When I was a child, I couldn't comprehend this, but as an adult, I understand.... This is what it means to me, as an intergenerational Survivor. People who I love and admire were wronged, humiliated, and forgotten, and unjustly imprisoned by the country I ... call home.... [The part of the Japanese redress program that worked best] was the investment in communities and culture ... [and the establishment of] the Canadian Race Relations Foundation ... to ensure that this never happened again.... Only when "you" and "me" become "us" and "we" can there be any reconciliation.[293]

Caroline Wong said that as an intergenerational Survivor of the Chinese head tax, which her grandfathers had to pay when they entered Canada from China,

> I grew up rejecting the stereotypical [identity] of the Chinese person because I wanted to be as 'white' as possible.... In terms of reconciliation, my grandmother is a warrior ... she's been fighting for head tax redress. In 2006, the federal government offered an apology and compensation for head tax survivors and their spouses, but very few were still living. It was a huge slap in the face for many Survivors like my grandmother and other first-generation Chinese Canadians who suffered the impacts of discrimination.... What is the price you can put on loss of life, loss of land, loss of family, and discrimination and abuse. You can't put a price on these things.... Compensation is only part of the answer.... Reconciliation is not just an apology but a two-way path of apology and forgiveness.... Education ... exposing the truth of what happened and making sure it's never forgotten.... Reconciliation starts with youth and building intercultural understanding...I hope this is the start of many other intercultural dialogues.... We need to understand about residential schools and also what other cultural groups have experienced. I challenge all of you to ask, "What does it mean to be Canadian?" Or, if you're from another place, "What is your role in this community?"[294]

Danny Richmond, an intergenerational Holocaust Survivor, said,

> My grandmother and grandfather lived through things in their twenties that I can't even begin to imagine ... for my people, this history is still an open wound ... what can I tell you that will give you understanding of this? ... It's always been part of my life.... Because the Holocaust was at such a widespread global level ... who is the perpetrator? Every day, people were implicated ... and there were systems and nations involved ... so there's no one person I can accept an apology from. The German government has apologized. It's about the reconciliation of trust in humanity that this kind of persecution won't happen again to the Jews or globally.... Reconciliation is about making sure that none of our communities suffer that persecution again ... for me it's about guarding our institutions to make sure they aren't continuing this kind of persecution ... we've had the apology from the government but how are we checking in to see how we're

> doing today? ... We need to create a National Day of Reconciliation that deals with these past human rights abuses, and educates [people] about what [what happens when we] dehumanize people. Canada was a safe haven for my family but it's also a nation with a lot of pain and warts in its background. We shouldn't be afraid to talk about that and to institutionalize the healing process at a national level.[295]

Newcomers to Canada

For new Canadians, many of whom carry their own traumatic memories of colonial violence, racism, and oppression, finding common ground as Treaty people involves learning about the history of Aboriginal peoples and finding ways to build stronger relationships of solidarity with them. The Commission believes there is an urgent need for more dialogue between Aboriginal peoples and new Canadians. At a forum, "From Remembrance to Reconciliation," co-sponsored by the Ontario Human Rights Commission, Colour of Poverty, Colour of Change, and the Metro Toronto Chinese and South-East Asian Legal Clinic, and attended by the TRC Commissioners, participants reflected on how their own histories shaped their understanding of violence, oppression, and racism, the stereotypes they learned about Aboriginal peoples in Canada, and the challenges and opportunities of building alliances together.

Akua Benjamin, who came from the Caribbean, with its history of slavery, said,

> How is it that our histories ... [have] so many similarities in terms of violence? The violence of slavery is the violence of destruction in Aboriginal communities.... These are societies that are shaped by violence.... My grandmother talked about working in the fields and being beaten ... my mother carried coal on her head as a child ... so we have a lot in common.... How do we reconcile? How do we have those difficult conversations that say that you are implicated in my struggle? You have privilege that I don't. You have an education that I was not privy to.... This is a safe place for us to really have those difficult conversations.[296]

Ali Kazimi said,

> I came [to Canada] from India thirty years ago.... One of the things that became apparent to me right away was that I came [here] with my own baggage of stereotypes [of Aboriginal peoples]. These were defined by what I had seen in Hollywood films and comic books.... I spent a lot of time in Toronto going to soup kitchens, hanging out with people, trying to understand what the current reality is of First Nations people in an urban centre like Toronto. It was an incredible learning experience. It really humbled me. It really opened my eyes.... I remember having those discussions with people who would challenge me, and

> those challenges were absolutely essential.... That led me to my own question.... How do I fit into this landscape?
>
> Many Canadians feel that Canadian identity and cultural identity is somehow defined by this universal humanism. On the flip side, we have Prime Minister Harper who says Canada has no history of colonialism. They do the same thing. They deny colonialism and racism and [attitudes of] white superiority ... whose legacy we continue to see today.... It's a very toxic legacy.... One of the truths about Canada is that it was created as a white man's country and this term was used over and over again.... Twenty years ago, I became a Canadian citizen and one of the things that wasn't made clear to me ... was that when we took that oath [of allegiance] we would become party to the Treaties that were signed.... We were given this very uplifting lecture on the rights of Canadian citizenship but what was excluded was [information] on our responsibility and obligations ... as now being parties to these Treaties.[297]

Winnie Ng said,

> I was born in Hong Kong and came to Canada in 1968.... I landed in Victoria, BC, the oldest Chinatown in the country.... It has been a journey for me as a person of colour, as a person of the non-Indigenous communities ... to learn about the history of this Native land and my own social location and privilege as a member of the newer arrival communities.... From the [Chinese] labour of the CPR, to the head tax and the *Chinese Exclusion Act* ... the Chinese, along with Indigenous children, were secluded in the education system for so many years ... there's been a constant narrative of systemic racism, exclusion, and exploitation.... I think [we need to talk about] remembrance, resistance, and reconciliation.[298]

Becoming citizens

In preparing to become Canadian citizens, all immigrants to Canada study a booklet called *Discover Canada*. It explains, "To understand what it means to be Canadian, it is important to know about our three founding peoples—**Aboriginal**, **French** and **British**." It says the following about Aboriginal peoples:

> The ancestors of Aboriginal peoples are believed to have migrated from Asia many thousands of years ago. They were well established here long before explorers from Europe first came to North America. Diverse, vibrant First Nations cultures were rooted in religious beliefs about their relationship to the Creator, the natural environment and each other. Aboriginal and treaty rights are in the Canadian Constitution. Territorial rights were first guaranteed through the Royal Proclamation of 1763 by King George III, and established the basis for negotiating treaties with the newcomers—treaties that were not always fully

> respected. From the 1800s until the 1980s, the federal government placed many Aboriginal children in residential schools to educate and assimilate them into mainstream Canadian culture. The schools were poorly funded and inflicted hardship on the students; some were physically abused. Aboriginal languages and cultural practices were mostly prohibited. In 2008, Ottawa formally apologized to the former students. In today's Canada, Aboriginal peoples enjoy renewed pride and confidence, and have made significant achievements in agriculture, the environment, business and the arts.[299]

The guide explains the rights and responsibilities of citizenship. In describing Canada's legal system, it states,

> Canadian law has several sources, including laws passed by Parliament and the provincial legislatures, English common law, the civil code of France and the unwritten constitution that we have inherited from Great Britain. Together, these secure for Canadians an 800-year-old tradition of ordered liberty, which dates back to the signing of the Magna Carta in 1215 in England.[300]

Discover Canada ignores Indigenous peoples as being a source of law for Canada, and says that Canada's tradition of an "ordered liberty" is due to England, and not at all to Canada's Aboriginal peoples, who welcomed the European explorers, helped them survive in this climate, guided them throughout the country, and entered into Treaties with them to share their land with the newcomers from Europe.

A new citizenship oath for Canada

The guide includes the Oath of Citizenship to the Queen that all new citizens must currently pledge: "In Canada, we profess our loyalty to a person who represents all Canadians and not to a document such as a constitution, a banner such as a flag, or a geopolitical entity such as a country." The current oath requires new Canadians to pledge as follows: "I swear (or affirm) that I will be faithful and bear true allegiance to Her Majesty Queen Elizabeth II, Queen of Canada, Her Heirs and Successors, and that I will faithfully observe the laws of Canada and fulfill my duties as a Canadian citizen."

Precisely because "we are all Treaty people," Canada's Oath of Citizenship must include a solemn promise to respect Aboriginal and Treaty rights.

Calls to Action

93) We call upon the federal government, in collaboration with the national Aboriginal organizations, to revise the information kit for newcomers to Canada and its citizenship test to reflect a more inclusive history of the diverse Aboriginal peoples

of Canada, including information about the Treaties and the history of residential schools.

94) We call upon the Government of Canada to replace the Oath of Citizenship with the following:

I swear (or affirm) that I will be faithful and bear true allegiance to Her Majesty Queen Elizabeth II, Queen of Canada, Her Heirs and Successors, and that I will faithfully observe the laws of Canada including Treaties with Indigenous Peoples, and fulfill my duties as a Canadian citizen.

Closing Words

On September 22, 2013, the day after the British Columbia National Event, the Commissioners joined 70,000 people gathered in the pouring rain to participate in a Walk for Reconciliation, organized by Reconciliation Canada, a non-profit organization. If one was looking down Georgia Street in downtown Vancouver, a sea of multicoloured umbrellas was visible as far as the eye could see. Traditional ceremonies and protocols began the walk. Chiefs in regalia, women wrapped in button blankets and cedar capes, and drumming, dancing, and singing accompanied Survivors, their families, and people from multiple faith traditions and all walks of life, who marched together in solidarity. We walked for Survivors and all that they have done to bring the long-hidden story of residential schools to the country's attention. We walked to remember the thousands of children who died in residential schools. We walked to honour all Indigenous peoples as they reclaim and restore their identity, equality, and dignity. We walked to stand up for the transformative social change that is so urgently needed in Canada. And, we walked for the uplifting solidarity of being united with tens of thousands of others, all joined together in a new community of common purpose. Residential school Survivor and Gwawaenuk Elder Chief Dr. Robert Joseph, speaking as Reconciliation Canada's ambassador, has said, "Reconciliation includes anyone with an open heart and an open mind, who is willing to look to the future in a new way. Let us find a way to belong to this time and place together. Our future, and the well-being of all our children, rests with the kind of relationships we build today."[301]

In November 2012, Elders from Indigenous nations and many other cultures gathered for two days in Musqueam territory in Vancouver, British Columbia, to talk about how reconciliation can help Canada move forward. In a statement afterwards, they said,

> As Canadians, we share a responsibility to look after each other and acknowledge the pain and suffering that our diverse societies have endured—a pain that has been handed down to the next generations. We need to right those

> wrongs, heal together, and create a new future that honours the unique gifts of our children and grandchildren.
>
> How do we do this? Through sharing our personal stories, legends and traditional teachings, we found that we are interconnected through the same mind and spirit. Our traditional teachings speak to acts such as holding one another up, walking together, balance, healing and unity. Our stories show how these teachings can heal their pain and restore dignity. We discovered that in all of our cultural traditions, there are teachings about reconciliation, forgiveness, unity, healing and balance.
>
> We invite you to search in your own traditions and beliefs, and those of your ancestors, to find these core values that create a peaceful harmonious society and a healthy earth.[302]

The work of the TRC has shown just how difficult the process of truth determination has been. Thousands of Survivors came forward and, in tears and with anger, shared their pain. They showed how humour, perseverance, and resilience got them through the hardest of times, and how life after the schools sometimes just got too hard. They came forward to share their stories, not just to ease their burden, but also to try to make things better for their children and their grandchildren.

Reconciliation is going to take hard work. People of all walks of life and at all levels of society will need to be willingly engaged.

Reconciliation calls for personal action. People need to get to know each other. They need to learn how to speak to, and about, each other respectfully. They need to learn how to speak knowledgeably about the history of this country. And they need to ensure that their children learn how to do so as well.

Reconciliation calls for group action. The 2012 Vancouver Olympics Organizing Committee recognized, paid tribute to, and honoured the Four Host First Nations at all public events it organized. Clubs, sports teams, artists, musicians, writers, teachers, doctors, lawyers, judges, and politicians need to learn from that example of how to be more inclusive and more respectful, and how to engage more fully in the dialogue about reconciliation.

Reconciliation calls for community action. The City of Vancouver, British Columbia, proclaimed itself the City of Reconciliation. The City of Halifax, Nova Scotia, holds an annual parade and procession commemorating the 1761 Treaty of Peace and Friendship. Speeches are delivered and everyone who attends is feasted. The City of Wetaskiwin, Alberta, erected a sign at its outskirts with the city's name written in Cree syllabics. Other communities can do similar things.

Reconciliation calls for federal, provincial, and territorial government action.

Reconciliation calls for national action.

The way we govern ourselves must change.

Laws must change.

Policies and programs must change.

The way we educate our children and ourselves must change.

The way we do business must change.

Thinking must change.

The way we talk to, and about, each other must change.

All Canadians must make a firm and lasting commitment to reconciliation to ensure that Canada is a country where our children and grandchildren can thrive.

Calls to Action

In order to redress the legacy of residential schools and advance the process of Canadian reconciliation, the Truth and Reconciliation Commission makes the following calls to action.

LEGACY

Child welfare

1) We call upon the federal, provincial, territorial, and Aboriginal governments to commit to reducing the number of Aboriginal children in care by:

    i. Monitoring and assessing neglect investigations.

    ii. Providing adequate resources to enable Aboriginal communities and child-welfare organizations to keep Aboriginal families together where it is safe to do so, and to keep children in culturally appropriate environments, regardless of where they reside.

    iii. Ensuring that social workers and others who conduct child-welfare investigations are properly educated and trained about the history and impacts of residential schools.

    iv. Ensuring that social workers and others who conduct child-welfare investigations are properly educated and trained about the potential for Aboriginal communities and families to provide more appropriate solutions to family healing.

    v. Requiring that all child-welfare decision makers consider the impact of the residential school experience on children and their caregivers.

2) We call upon the federal government, in collaboration with the provinces and territories, to prepare and publish annual reports on the number of Aboriginal children (First Nations, Inuit, and Métis) who are in care, compared with non-Aboriginal children,

as well as the reasons for apprehension, the total spending on preventive and care services by child-welfare agencies, and the effectiveness of various interventions.

3) We call upon all levels of government to fully implement Jordan's Principle.

4) We call upon the federal government to enact Aboriginal child-welfare legislation that establishes national standards for Aboriginal child apprehension and custody cases and includes principles that:

   i. Affirm the right of Aboriginal governments to establish and maintain their own child-welfare agencies.

   ii. Require all child-welfare agencies and courts to take the residential school legacy into account in their decision making.

   iii. Establish, as an important priority, a requirement that placements of Aboriginal children into temporary and permanent care be culturally appropriate.

5) We call upon the federal, provincial, territorial, and Aboriginal governments to develop culturally appropriate parenting programs for Aboriginal families.

Education

6) We call upon the Government of Canada to repeal Section 43 of the *Criminal Code* of Canada.

7) We call upon the federal government to develop with Aboriginal groups a joint strategy to eliminate educational and employment gaps between Aboriginal and non-Aboriginal Canadians.

8) We call upon the federal government to eliminate the discrepancy in federal education funding for First Nations children being educated on reserves and those First Nations children being educated off reserves.

9) We call upon the federal government to prepare and publish annual reports comparing funding for the education of First Nations children on and off reserves, as well as educational and income attainments of Aboriginal peoples in Canada compared with non-Aboriginal people.

10) We call on the federal government to draft new Aboriginal education legislation with the full participation and informed consent of Aboriginal peoples. The new legislation would include a commitment to sufficient funding and would incorporate the following principles:

   i. Providing sufficient funding to close identified educational achievement gaps within one generation.

ii. Improving education attainment levels and success rates.

iii. Developing culturally appropriate curricula.

iv. Protecting the right to Aboriginal languages, including the teaching of Aboriginal languages as credit courses.

v. Enabling parental and community responsibility, control, and accountability, similar to what parents enjoy in public school systems.

vi. Enabling parents to fully participate in the education of their children.

vii. Respecting and honouring Treaty relationships.

11) We call upon the federal government to provide adequate funding to end the backlog of First Nations students seeking a post-secondary education.

12) We call upon the federal, provincial, territorial, and Aboriginal governments to develop culturally appropriate early childhood education programs for Aboriginal families.

Language and culture

13) We call upon the federal government to acknowledge that Aboriginal rights include Aboriginal language rights.

14) We call upon the federal government to enact an Aboriginal Languages Act that incorporates the following principles:

i. Aboriginal languages are a fundamental and valued element of Canadian culture and society, and there is an urgency to preserve them.

ii. Aboriginal language rights are reinforced by the Treaties.

iii. The federal government has a responsibility to provide sufficient funds for Aboriginal-language revitalization and preservation.

iv. The preservation, revitalization, and strengthening of Aboriginal languages and cultures are best managed by Aboriginal people and communities.

v. Funding for Aboriginal language initiatives must reflect the diversity of Aboriginal languages.

15) We call upon the federal government to appoint, in consultation with Aboriginal groups, an Aboriginal Languages Commissioner. The commissioner should help promote Aboriginal languages and report on the adequacy of federal funding of Aboriginal-languages initiatives.

16) We call upon post-secondary institutions to create university and college degree and diploma programs in Aboriginal languages.

17) We call upon all levels of government to enable residential school Survivors and their families to reclaim names changed by the residential school system by waiving administrative costs for a period of five years for the name-change process and the revision of official identity documents, such as birth certificates, passports, driver's licenses, health cards, status cards, and social insurance numbers.

Health

18) We call upon the federal, provincial, territorial, and Aboriginal governments to acknowledge that the current state of Aboriginal health in Canada is a direct result of previous Canadian government policies, including residential schools, and to recognize and implement the health-care rights of Aboriginal people as identified in international law, constitutional law, and under the Treaties.

19) We call upon the federal government, in consultation with Aboriginal peoples, to establish measurable goals to identify and close the gaps in health outcomes between Aboriginal and non-Aboriginal communities, and to publish annual progress reports and assess long-term trends. Such efforts would focus on indicators such as: infant mortality, maternal health, suicide, mental health, addictions, life expectancy, birth rates, infant and child health issues, chronic diseases, illness and injury incidence, and the availability of appropriate health services.

20) In order to address the jurisdictional disputes concerning Aboriginal people who do not reside on reserves, we call upon the federal government to recognize, respect, and address the distinct health needs of the Métis, Inuit, and off-reserve Aboriginal peoples.

21) We call upon the federal government to provide sustainable funding for existing and new Aboriginal healing centres to address the physical, mental, emotional, and spiritual harms caused by residential schools, and to ensure that the funding of healing centres in Nunavut and the Northwest Territories is a priority.

22) We call upon those who can effect change within the Canadian health-care system to recognize the value of Aboriginal healing practices and use them in the treatment of Aboriginal patients in collaboration with Aboriginal healers and Elders where requested by Aboriginal patients.

23) We call upon all levels of government to:

    i. Increase the number of Aboriginal professionals working in the health-care field.

ii. Ensure the retention of Aboriginal health-care providers in Aboriginal communities.

iii. Provide cultural competency training for all health-care professionals.

24) We call upon medical and nursing schools in Canada to require all students to take a course dealing with Aboriginal health issues, including the history and legacy of residential schools, the *United Nations Declaration on the Rights of Indigenous Peoples*, Treaties and Aboriginal rights, and Indigenous teachings and practices. This will require skills-based training in intercultural competency, conflict resolution, human rights, and anti-racism.

Justice

25) We call upon the federal government to establish a written policy that reaffirms the independence of the Royal Canadian Mounted Police to investigate crimes in which the government has its own interest as a potential or real party in civil litigation.

26) We call upon the federal, provincial, and territorial governments to review and amend their respective statutes of limitations to ensure that they conform with the principle that governments and other entities cannot rely on limitation defences to defend legal actions of historical abuse brought by Aboriginal people.

27) We call upon the Federation of Law Societies of Canada to ensure that lawyers receive appropriate cultural competency training, which includes the history and legacy of residential schools, the *United Nations Declaration on the Rights of Indigenous Peoples*, Treaties and Aboriginal rights, Indigenous law, and Aboriginal–Crown relations. This will require skills-based training in intercultural competency, conflict resolution, human rights, and anti-racism.

28) We call upon law schools in Canada to require all law students to take a course in Aboriginal people and the law, which includes the history and legacy of residential schools, the *United Nations Declaration on the Rights of Indigenous Peoples*, Treaties and Aboriginal rights, Indigenous law, and Aboriginal–Crown relations. This will require skills-based training in intercultural competency, conflict resolution, human rights, and anti-racism.

29) We call upon the parties and, in particular, the federal government, to work collaboratively with plaintiffs not included in the Indian Residential Schools Settlement Agreement to have disputed legal issues determined expeditiously on an agreed set of facts.

30) We call upon federal, provincial, and territorial governments to commit to eliminating the overrepresentation of Aboriginal people in custody over the next decade, and to issue detailed annual reports that monitor and evaluate progress in doing so.

31) We call upon the federal, provincial, and territorial governments to provide sufficient and stable funding to implement and evaluate community sanctions that will provide realistic alternatives to imprisonment for Aboriginal offenders and respond to the underlying causes of offending.

32) We call upon the federal government to amend the *Criminal Code* to allow trial judges, upon giving reasons, to depart from mandatory minimum sentences and restrictions on the use of conditional sentences.

33) We call upon the federal, provincial, and territorial governments to recognize as a high priority the need to address and prevent Fetal Alcohol Spectrum Disorder (FASD), and to develop, in collaboration with Aboriginal people, FASD preventive programs that can be delivered in a culturally appropriate manner.

34) We call upon the governments of Canada, the provinces, and territories to undertake reforms to the criminal justice system to better address the needs of offenders with Fetal Alcohol Spectrum Disorder (FASD), including:

   i. Providing increased community resources and powers for courts to ensure that FASD is properly diagnosed, and that appropriate community supports are in place for those with FASD.

   ii. Enacting statutory exemptions from mandatory minimum sentences of imprisonment for offenders affected by FASD.

   iii. Providing community, correctional, and parole resources to maximize the ability of people with FASD to live in the community.

   iv. Adopting appropriate evaluation mechanisms to measure the effectiveness of such programs and ensure community safety.

35) We call upon the federal government to eliminate barriers to the creation of additional Aboriginal healing lodges within the federal correctional system.

36) We call upon the federal, provincial, and territorial governments to work with Aboriginal communities to provide culturally relevant services to inmates on issues such as substance abuse, family and domestic violence, and overcoming the experience of having been sexually abused.

37) We call upon the federal government to provide more supports for Aboriginal programming in halfway houses and parole services.

38) We call upon the federal, provincial, territorial, and Aboriginal governments to commit to eliminating the overrepresentation of Aboriginal youth in custody over the next decade.

39) We call upon the federal government to develop a national plan to collect and publish data on the criminal victimization of Aboriginal people, including data related to homicide and family violence victimization.

40) We call on all levels of government, in collaboration with Aboriginal people, to create adequately funded and accessible Aboriginal-specific victim programs and services with appropriate evaluation mechanisms.

41) We call upon the federal government, in consultation with Aboriginal organizations, to appoint a public inquiry into the causes of, and remedies for, the disproportionate victimization of Aboriginal women and girls. The inquiry's mandate would include:

  i. Investigation into missing and murdered Aboriginal women and girls.

  ii. Links to the intergenerational legacy of residential schools.

42) We call upon the federal, provincial, and territorial governments to commit to the recognition and implementation of Aboriginal justice systems in a manner consistent with the Treaty and Aboriginal rights of Aboriginal peoples, the *Constitution Act, 1982*, and the *United Nations Declaration on the Rights of Indigenous Peoples*, endorsed by Canada in November 2012.

RECONCILIATION

Canadian Governments and the *United Nations Declaration on the Rights of Indigenous People*

43) We call upon federal, provincial, territorial, and municipal governments to fully adopt and implement the *United Nations Declaration on the Rights of Indigenous Peoples* as the framework for reconciliation.

44) We call upon the Government of Canada to develop a national action plan, strategies, and other concrete measures to achieve the goals of the *United Nations Declaration on the Rights of Indigenous Peoples*.

Royal Proclamation and Covenant of Reconciliation

45) We call upon the Government of Canada, on behalf of all Canadians, to jointly develop with Aboriginal peoples a Royal Proclamation of Reconciliation to be issued by the Crown. The proclamation would build on the Royal Proclamation of 1763 and the Treaty of Niagara of 1764, and reaffirm the nation-to-nation relationship between Aboriginal peoples and the Crown. The proclamation would include, but not be limited to, the following commitments:

   i. Repudiate concepts used to justify European sovereignty over Indigenous lands and peoples such as the Doctrine of Discovery and *terra nullius*.

   ii. Adopt and implement the *United Nations Declaration on the Rights of Indigenous Peoples* as the framework for reconciliation.

   iii. Renew or establish Treaty relationships based on principles of mutual recognition, mutual respect, and shared responsibility for maintaining those relationships into the future.

   iv. Reconcile Aboriginal and Crown constitutional and legal orders to ensure that Aboriginal peoples are full partners in Confederation, including the recognition and integration of Indigenous laws and legal traditions in negotiation and implementation processes involving Treaties, land claims, and other constructive agreements.

46) We call upon the parties to the Indian Residential Schools Settlement Agreement to develop and sign a Covenant of Reconciliation that would identify principles for working collaboratively to advance reconciliation in Canadian society, and that would include, but not be limited to:

   i. Reaffirmation of the parties' commitment to reconciliation.

   ii. Repudiation of concepts used to justify European sovereignty over Indigenous lands and peoples, such as the Doctrine of Discovery and *terra nullius*, and the reformation of laws, governance structures, and policies within their respective institutions that continue to rely on such concepts.

   iii. Full adoption and implementation of the *United Nations Declaration on the Rights of Indigenous Peoples* as the framework for reconciliation.

   iv. Support for the renewal or establishment of Treaty relationships based on principles of mutual recognition, mutual respect, and shared responsibility for maintaining those relationships into the future.

   v. Enabling those excluded from the Settlement Agreement to sign onto the Covenant of Reconciliation.

   vi. Enabling additional parties to sign onto the Covenant of Reconciliation.

47) We call upon federal, provincial, territorial, and municipal governments to repudiate concepts used to justify European sovereignty over Indigenous peoples and lands, such as the Doctrine of Discovery and *terra nullius*, and to reform those laws, government policies, and litigation strategies that continue to rely on such concepts.

Settlement Agreement Parties and the United Nations *Declaration on the Rights of Indigenous People*

48) We call upon the church parties to the Settlement Agreement, and all other faith groups and interfaith social justice groups in Canada who have not already done so, to formally adopt and comply with the principles, norms, and standards of the *United Nations Declaration on the Rights of Indigenous Peoples* as a framework for reconciliation. This would include, but not be limited to, the following commitments:

   i. Ensuring that their institutions, policies, programs, and practices comply with the *United Nations Declaration on the Rights of Indigenous Peoples.*

   ii. Respecting Indigenous peoples' right to self-determination in spiritual matters, including the right to practise, develop, and teach their own spiritual and religious traditions, customs, and ceremonies, consistent with Article 12:1 of the *United Nations Declaration on the Rights of Indigenous Peoples.*

   iii. Engaging in ongoing public dialogue and actions to support the *United Nations Declaration on the Rights of Indigenous Peoples.*

   iv. Issuing a statement no later than March 31, 2016, from all religious denominations and faith groups, as to how they will implement the *United Nations Declaration on the Rights of Indigenous Peoples.*

49) We call upon all religious denominations and faith groups who have not already done so to repudiate concepts used to justify European sovereignty over Indigenous lands and peoples, such as the Doctrine of Discovery and *terra nullius.*

Equity for Aboriginal People in the Legal System

50) In keeping with the *United Nations Declaration on the Rights of Indigenous Peoples,* we call upon the federal government, in collaboration with Aboriginal organizations, to fund the establishment of Indigenous law institutes for the development, use, and understanding of Indigenous laws and access to justice in accordance with the unique cultures of Aboriginal peoples in Canada.

51) We call upon the Government of Canada, as an obligation of its fiduciary responsibility, to develop a policy of transparency by publishing legal opinions it develops and upon which it acts or intends to act, in regard to the scope and extent of Aboriginal and Treaty rights.

52) We call upon the Government of Canada, provincial and territorial governments, and the courts to adopt the following legal principles:

i. Aboriginal title claims are accepted once the Aboriginal claimant has established occupation over a particular territory at a particular point in time.

ii. Once Aboriginal title has been established, the burden of proving any limitation on any rights arising from the existence of that title shifts to the party asserting such a limitation.

National Council for Reconciliation

53) We call upon the Parliament of Canada, in consultation and collaboration with Aboriginal peoples, to enact legislation to establish a National Council for Reconciliation. The legislation would establish the council as an independent, national, oversight body with membership jointly appointed by the Government of Canada and national Aboriginal organizations, and consisting of Aboriginal and non-Aboriginal members. Its mandate would include, but not be limited to, the following:

i. Monitor, evaluate, and report annually to Parliament and the people of Canada on the Government of Canada's post-apology progress on reconciliation to ensure that government accountability for reconciling the relationship between Aboriginal peoples and the Crown is maintained in the coming years.

ii. Monitor, evaluate, and report to Parliament and the people of Canada on reconciliation progress across all levels and sectors of Canadian society, including the implementation of the Truth and Reconciliation Commission of Canada's Calls to Action.

iii. Develop and implement a multi-year National Action Plan for Reconciliation, which includes research and policy development, public education programs, and resources.

iv. Promote public dialogue, public/private partnerships, and public initiatives for reconciliation.

54) We call upon the Government of Canada to provide multi-year funding for the National Council for Reconciliation to ensure that it has the financial, human, and technical

resources required to conduct its work, including the endowment of a National Reconciliation Trust to advance the cause of reconciliation.

55) We call upon all levels of government to provide annual reports or any current data requested by the National Council for Reconciliation so that it can report on the progress towards reconciliation. The reports or data would include, but not be limited to:

i. The number of Aboriginal children—including Métis and Inuit children—in care, compared with non-Aboriginal children, the reasons for apprehension, and the total spending on preventive and care services by child-welfare agencies.

ii. Comparative funding for the education of First Nations children on and off reserves.

iii. The educational and income attainments of Aboriginal peoples in Canada compared with non-Aboriginal people.

iv. Progress on closing the gaps between Aboriginal and non-Aboriginal communities in a number of health indicators such as: infant mortality, maternal health, suicide, mental health, addictions, life expectancy, birth rates, infant and child health issues, chronic diseases, illness and injury incidence, and the availability of appropriate health services.

v. Progress on eliminating the overrepresentation of Aboriginal children in youth custody over the next decade.

vi. Progress on reducing the rate of criminal victimization of Aboriginal people, including data related to homicide and family violence victimization and other crimes.

vii. Progress on reducing the overrepresentation of Aboriginal people in the justice and correctional systems.

56) We call upon the prime minister of Canada to formally respond to the report of the National Council for Reconciliation by issuing an annual "State of Aboriginal Peoples" report, which would outline the government's plans for advancing the cause of reconciliation.

Professional Development and Training for Public Servants

57) We call upon federal, provincial, territorial, and municipal governments to provide education to public servants on the history of Aboriginal peoples, including the history and legacy of residential schools, the *United Nations Declaration on the Rights of Indigenous Peoples*, Treaties and Aboriginal rights, Indigenous law, and

Aboriginal–Crown relations. This will require skills-based training in intercultural competency, conflict resolution, human rights, and anti-racism.

Church Apologies and Reconciliation

58) We call upon the Pope to issue an apology to Survivors, their families, and communities for the Roman Catholic Church's role in the spiritual, cultural, emotional, physical, and sexual abuse of First Nations, Inuit, and Métis children in Catholic-run residential schools. We call for that apology to be similar to the 2010 apology issued to Irish victims of abuse and to occur within one year of the issuing of this Report and to be delivered by the Pope in Canada.

59) We call upon church parties to the Settlement Agreement to develop ongoing education strategies to ensure that their respective congregations learn about their church's role in colonization, the history and legacy of residential schools, and why apologies to former residential school students, their families, and communities were necessary.

60) We call upon leaders of the church parties to the Settlement Agreement and all other faiths, in collaboration with Indigenous spiritual leaders, Survivors, schools of theology, seminaries, and other religious training centres, to develop and teach curriculum for all student clergy, and all clergy and staff who work in Aboriginal communities, on the need to respect Indigenous spirituality in its own right, the history and legacy of residential schools and the roles of the church parties in that system, the history and legacy of religious conflict in Aboriginal families and communities, and the responsibility that churches have to mitigate such conflicts and prevent spiritual violence.

61) We call upon church parties to the Settlement Agreement, in collaboration with Survivors and representatives of Aboriginal organizations, to establish permanent funding to Aboriginal people for:

   i. Community-controlled healing and reconciliation projects.

   ii. Community-controlled culture- and language-revitalization projects.

   iii. Community-controlled education and relationship-building projects.

   iv. Regional dialogues for Indigenous spiritual leaders and youth to discuss Indigenous spirituality, self-determination, and reconciliation.

Education for reconciliation

62) We call upon the federal, provincial, and territorial governments, in consultation and collaboration with Survivors, Aboriginal peoples, and educators, to:

i. Make age-appropriate curriculum on residential schools, Treaties, and Aboriginal peoples' historical and contemporary contributions to Canada a mandatory education requirement for Kindergarten to Grade Twelve students.

ii. Provide the necessary funding to post-secondary institutions to educate teachers on how to integrate Indigenous knowledge and teaching methods into classrooms.

iii. Provide the necessary funding to Aboriginal schools to utilize Indigenous knowledge and teaching methods in classrooms.

iv. Establish senior-level positions in government at the assistant deputy minister level or higher dedicated to Aboriginal content in education.

63) We call upon the Council of Ministers of Education, Canada to maintain an annual commitment to Aboriginal education issues, including:

i. Developing and implementing Kindergarten to Grade Twelve curriculum and learning resources on Aboriginal peoples in Canadian history, and the history and legacy of residential schools.

ii. Sharing information and best practices on teaching curriculum related to residential schools and Aboriginal history.

iii. Building student capacity for intercultural understanding, empathy, and mutual respect.

iv. Identifying teacher-training needs relating to the above.

64) We call upon all levels of government that provide public funds to denominational schools to require such schools to provide an education on comparative religious studies, which must include a segment on Aboriginal spiritual beliefs and practices developed in collaboration with Aboriginal Elders.

65) We call upon the federal government, through the Social Sciences and Humanities Research Council, and in collaboration with Aboriginal peoples, post-secondary institutions and educators, and the National Centre for Truth and Reconciliation and its partner institutions, to establish a national research program with multi-year funding to advance understanding of reconciliation.

Youth Programs

66) We call upon the federal government to establish multi-year funding for community-based youth organizations to deliver programs on reconciliation, and establish a national network to share information and best practices.

Museums and Archives

67) We call upon the federal government to provide funding to the Canadian Museums Association to undertake, in collaboration with Aboriginal peoples, a national review of museum policies and best practices to determine the level of compliance with the *United Nations Declaration on the Rights of Indigenous Peoples* and to make recommendations.

68) We call upon the federal government, in collaboration with Aboriginal peoples, and the Canadian Museums Association to mark the 150th anniversary of Canadian Confederation in 2017 by establishing a dedicated national funding program for commemoration projects on the theme of reconciliation.

69) We call upon Library and Archives Canada to:

    i. Fully adopt and implement the *United Nations Declaration on the Rights of Indigenous Peoples* and the *United Nations Joinet-Orentlicher Principles*, as related to Aboriginal peoples' inalienable right to know the truth about what happened and why, with regard to human rights violations committed against them in the residential schools.

    ii. Ensure that its record holdings related to residential schools are accessible to the public.

    iii. Commit more resources to its public education materials and programming on residential schools.

70) We call upon the federal government to provide funding to the Canadian Association of Archivists to undertake, in collaboration with Aboriginal peoples, a national review of archival policies and best practices to:

    i. Determine the level of compliance with the *United Nations Declaration on the Rights of Indigenous Peoples* and the *United Nations Joinet-Orentlicher Principles*, as related to Aboriginal peoples' inalienable right to know the truth about what happened and why, with regard to human rights violations committed against them in the residential schools.

ii. Produce a report with recommendations for full implementation of these international mechanisms as a reconciliation framework for Canadian archives.

Missing Children and Burial Information

71) We call upon all chief coroners and provincial vital statistics agencies that have not provided to the Truth and Reconciliation Commission of Canada their records on the deaths of Aboriginal children in the care of residential school authorities to make these documents available to the National Centre for Truth and Reconciliation.

72) We call upon the federal government to allocate sufficient resources to the National Centre for Truth and Reconciliation to allow it to develop and maintain the National Residential School Student Death Register established by the Truth and Reconciliation Commission of Canada.

73) We call upon the federal government to work with churches, Aboriginal communities, and former residential school students to establish and maintain an online registry of residential school cemeteries, including, where possible, plot maps showing the location of deceased residential school children.

74) We call upon the federal government to work with the churches and Aboriginal community leaders to inform the families of children who died at residential schools of the child's burial location, and to respond to families' wishes for appropriate commemoration ceremonies and markers, and reburial in home communities where requested.

75) We call upon the federal government to work with provincial, territorial, and municipal governments, churches, Aboriginal communities, former residential school students, and current landowners to develop and implement strategies and procedures for the ongoing identification, documentation, maintenance, commemoration, and protection of residential school cemeteries or other sites at which residential school children were buried. This is to include the provision of appropriate memorial ceremonies and commemorative markers to honour the deceased children.

76) We call upon the parties engaged in the work of documenting, maintaining, commemorating, and protecting residential school cemeteries to adopt strategies in accordance with the following principles:

i. The Aboriginal community most affected shall lead the development of such strategies.

ii. Information shall be sought from residential school Survivors and other Knowledge Keepers in the development of such strategies.

iii. Aboriginal protocols shall be respected before any potentially invasive technical inspection and investigation of a cemetery site.

National Centre for Truth and Reconciliation

77) We call upon provincial, territorial, municipal, and community archives to work collaboratively with the National Centre for Truth and Reconciliation to identify and collect copies of all records relevant to the history and legacy of the residential school system, and to provide these to the National Centre for Truth and Reconciliation.

78) We call upon the Government of Canada to commit to making a funding contribution of $10 million over seven years to the National Centre for Truth and Reconciliation, plus an additional amount to assist communities to research and produce histories of their own residential school experience and their involvement in truth, healing, and reconciliation.

Commemoration

79) We call upon the federal government, in collaboration with Survivors, Aboriginal organizations, and the arts community, to develop a reconciliation framework for Canadian heritage and commemoration. This would include, but not be limited to:

   i. Amending the *Historic Sites and Monuments Act* to include First Nations, Inuit, and Métis representation on the Historic Sites and Monuments Board of Canada and its Secretariat.

   ii. Revising the policies, criteria, and practices of the National Program of Historical Commemoration to integrate Indigenous history, heritage values, and memory practices into Canada's national heritage and history.

   iii. Developing and implementing a national heritage plan and strategy for commemorating residential school sites, the history and legacy of residential schools, and the contributions of Aboriginal peoples to Canada's history.

80) We call upon the federal government, in collaboration with Aboriginal peoples, to establish, as a statutory holiday, a National Day for Truth and Reconciliation to honour Survivors, their families, and communities, and ensure that public commemoration of the history and legacy of residential schools remains a vital component of the reconciliation process.

81) We call upon the federal government, in collaboration with Survivors and their organizations, and other parties to the Settlement Agreement, to commission and install

a publicly accessible, highly visible, Residential Schools National Monument in the city of Ottawa to honour Survivors and all the children who were lost to their families and communities.

82) We call upon provincial and territorial governments, in collaboration with Survivors and their organizations, and other parties to the Settlement Agreement, to commission and install a publicly accessible, highly visible, Residential Schools Monument in each capital city to honour Survivors and all the children who were lost to their families and communities.

83) We call upon the Canada Council for the Arts to establish, as a funding priority, a strategy for Indigenous and non-Indigenous artists to undertake collaborative projects and produce works that contribute to the reconciliation process.

MEDIA AND RECONCILIATION

84) We call upon the federal government to restore and increase funding to the CBC/Radio-Canada, to enable Canada's national public broadcaster to support reconciliation, and be properly reflective of the diverse cultures, languages, and perspectives of Aboriginal peoples, including, but not limited to:

  i. Increasing Aboriginal programming, including Aboriginal-language speakers.

  ii. Increasing equitable access for Aboriginal peoples to jobs, leadership positions, and professional development opportunities within the organization.

  iii. Continuing to provide dedicated news coverage and online public information resources on issues of concern to Aboriginal peoples and all Canadians, including the history and legacy of residential schools and the reconciliation process.

85) We call upon the Aboriginal Peoples Television Network, as an independent non-profit broadcaster with programming by, for, and about Aboriginal peoples, to support reconciliation, including but not limited to:

  i. Continuing to provide leadership in programming and organizational culture that reflects the diverse cultures, languages, and perspectives of Aboriginal peoples.

  ii. Continuing to develop media initiatives that inform and educate the Canadian public, and connect Aboriginal and non-Aboriginal Canadians.

86) We call upon Canadian journalism programs and media schools to require education for all students on the history of Aboriginal peoples, including the history and legacy of residential schools, the *United Nations Declaration on the Rights of Indigenous Peoples*, Treaties and Aboriginal rights, Indigenous law, and Aboriginal–Crown relations.

Sports and Reconciliation

87) We call upon all levels of government, in collaboration with Aboriginal peoples, sports halls of fame, and other relevant organizations, to provide public education that tells the national story of Aboriginal athletes in history.

88) We call upon all levels of government to take action to ensure long-term Aboriginal athlete development and growth, and continued support for the North American Indigenous Games, including funding to host the games and for provincial and territorial team preparation and travel.

89) We call upon the federal government to amend the *Physical Activity and Sport Act* to support reconciliation by ensuring that policies to promote physical activity as a fundamental element of health and well-being, reduce barriers to sports participation, increase the pursuit of excellence in sport, and build capacity in the Canadian sport system, are inclusive of Aboriginal peoples.

90) We call upon the federal government to ensure that national sports policies, programs, and initiatives are inclusive of Aboriginal peoples, including, but not limited to, establishing:

i. In collaboration with provincial and territorial governments, stable funding for, and access to, community sports programs that reflect the diverse cultures and traditional sporting activities of Aboriginal peoples.

ii. An elite athlete development program for Aboriginal athletes.

iii. Programs for coaches, trainers, and sports officials that are culturally relevant for Aboriginal peoples.

iv. Anti-racism awareness and training programs.

91) We call upon the officials and host countries of international sporting events such as the Olympics, Pan Am, and Commonwealth games to ensure that Indigenous peoples' territorial protocols are respected, and local Indigenous communities are engaged in all aspects of planning and participating in such events.

Business and Reconciliation

92) We call upon the corporate sector in Canada to adopt the *United Nations Declaration on the Rights of Indigenous Peoples* as a reconciliation framework and to apply its principles, norms, and standards to corporate policy and core operational activities involving Indigenous peoples and their lands and resources. This would include, but not be limited to, the following:

i. Commit to meaningful consultation, building respectful relationships, and obtaining the free, prior, and informed consent of Indigenous peoples before proceeding with economic development projects.

ii. Ensure that Aboriginal peoples have equitable access to jobs, training, and education opportunities in the corporate sector, and that Aboriginal communities gain long-term sustainable benefits from economic development projects.

iii. Provide education for management and staff on the history of Aboriginal peoples, including the history and legacy of residential schools, the *United Nations Declaration on the Rights of Indigenous Peoples*, Treaties and Aboriginal rights, Indigenous law, and Aboriginal–Crown relations. This will require skills-based training in intercultural competency, conflict resolution, human rights, and anti-racism.

Newcomers to Canada

93) We call upon the federal government, in collaboration with the national Aboriginal organizations, to revise the information kit for newcomers to Canada and its citizenship test to reflect a more inclusive history of the diverse Aboriginal peoples of Canada, including information about the Treaties and the history of residential schools.

94) We call upon the Government of Canada to replace the Oath of Citizenship with the following:

I swear (or affirm) that I will be faithful and bear true allegiance to Her Majesty Queen Elizabeth II, Queen of Canada, Her Heirs and Successors, and that I will faithfully observe the laws of Canada including Treaties with Indigenous Peoples, and fulfill my duties as a Canadian citizen.

Appendix 1
The Mandate of the Truth and Reconciliation Commission

Schedule N of the Indian Residential Schools Settlement Agreement

There is an emerging and compelling desire to put the events of the past behind us so that we can work towards a stronger and healthier future. The truth telling and reconciliation process as part of an overall holistic and comprehensive response to the Indian Residential School legacy is a sincere indication and acknowledgement of the injustices and harms experienced by Aboriginal people and the need for continued healing. This is a profound commitment to establishing new relationships embedded in mutual recognition and respect that will forge a brighter future. The truth of our common experiences will help set our spirits free and pave the way to reconciliation.

Principles

Through the Agreement, the Parties have agreed that an historic Truth and Reconciliation Commission will be established to contribute to truth, healing and reconciliation.

The Truth and Reconciliation Commission will build upon the "Statement of Reconciliation" dated January 7, 1998 and the principles developed by the Working Group on Truth and Reconciliation and of the Exploratory Dialogues (1998-1999). These principles are as follows: accessible; victim-centered; confidentiality (if required by the former student); do no harm; health and safety of participants; representative; public/transparent; accountable; open and honourable process; comprehensive; inclusive, educational, holistic, just and fair; respectful; voluntary; flexible; and forward looking in terms of rebuilding and renewing Aboriginal relationships and the relationship between Aboriginal and non-Aboriginal Canadians.

Reconciliation is an ongoing individual and collective process, and will require commitment from all those affected including First Nations, Inuit and Métis former

Indian Residential School (IRS) students, their families, communities, religious entities, former school employees, government and the people of Canada. Reconciliation may occur between any of the above groups.

Terms of Reference

1. Goals

The goals of the Commission shall be to:

(a) Acknowledge Residential School experiences, impacts and consequences;

(b) Provide a holistic, culturally appropriate and safe setting for former students, their families and communities as they come forward to the Commission;

(c) Witness[1], support, promote and facilitate truth and reconciliation events at both the national and community levels;

(d) Promote awareness and public education of Canadians about the IRS system and its impacts;

(e) Identify sources and create as complete an historical record as possible of the IRS system and legacy. The record shall be preserved and made accessible to the public for future study and use;

(f) Produce and submit to the Parties of the Agreement[2] a report including recommendations[3] to the Government of Canada concerning the IRS system and experience including: the history, purpose, operation and supervision of the IRS system, the effect and consequences of IRS (including systemic harms, intergenerational consequences and the impact on human dignity) and the ongoing legacy of the residential schools;

(g) Support commemoration of former Indian Residential School students and their families in accordance with the Commemoration Policy Directive (Schedule "X" of the Agreement).

2. Establishment, Powers, Duties and Procedures of the Commission

The Truth and Reconciliation Commission shall be established by the appointment of "the Commissioners" by the Federal Government through an Order in Council, pursuant to special appointment regulations.

Pursuant to the Court-approved final settlement agreement and the class action judgments, the Commissioners:

(a) in fulfilling their Truth and Reconciliation Mandate, are authorized to receive statements and documents from former students, their families, community and all other interested participants, and, subject to (f), (g) and (h) below, make use of all documents and materials produced by the parties. Further, the Commissioners are authorized and required in the public interest to archive all such documents, materials, and transcripts or recordings of statements received, in a manner that will ensure their preservation and accessibility to the public and in accordance with access and privacy legislation, and any other applicable legislation;

(b) shall not hold formal hearings, nor act as a public inquiry, nor conduct a formal legal process;

(c) shall not possess subpoena powers, and do not have powers to compel attendance or participation in any of its activities or events. Participation in all Commission events and activities is entirely voluntary;

(d) may adopt any informal procedures or methods they may consider expedient for the proper conduct of the Commission events and activities, so long as they remain consistent with the goals and provisions set out in the Commission's mandate statement;

(e) may, at its discretion, hold sessions in camera, or require that sessions be held in camera;

(f) shall perform their duties in holding events, in activities, in public meetings, in consultations, in making public statements, and in making their report and recommendations without making any findings or expressing any conclusion or recommendation, regarding the misconduct of any person, unless such findings or information has already been established through legal proceedings, by admission, or by public disclosure by the individual. Further, the Commission shall not make any reference in any of its activities or in its report or recommendations to the possible civil or criminal liability of any person or organization, unless such findings or information about the individual or institution has already been established through legal proceedings;

(g) shall not, except as required by law, use or permit access to statements made by individuals during any of the Commissions events, activities or processes, except with the express consent of the individual and only for the sole purpose and extent for which the consent is granted;

(h) shall not name names in their events, activities, public statements, report or recommendations, or make use of personal information or of statements made which identify a person, without the express consent of that individual, unless that information and/or the identity of the person so identified has already been established through legal proceedings, by admission, or by public disclosure by that individual. Other information that could be used to identify individuals shall be anonymized to the extent possible;

(i) notwithstanding (e), shall require in camera proceedings for the taking of any statement that contains names or other identifying information of persons alleged by the person making the statement of some wrong doing, unless the person named or identified has been convicted for the alleged wrong doing. The Commissioners shall not record the names of persons so identified, unless the person named or identified has been convicted for the alleged wrong doing. Other information that could be used to identify said individuals shall be anonymized to the extent possible;

(j) shall not, except as required by law, provide to any other proceeding, or for any other use, any personal information, statement made by the individual or any information identifying any person, without that individual's express consent;

(k) shall ensure that the conduct of the Commission and its activities do not jeopardize any legal proceeding;

(l) may refer to the NAC for determination of disputes involving document production, document disposal and archiving, contents of the Commission's Report and Recommendations and Commission decisions regarding the scope of its research and issues to be examined. The Commission shall make best efforts to resolve the matter itself before referring it to the NAC.

3. Responsibilities

In keeping with the powers and duties of the Commission, as enumerated in section 2 above, the Commission shall have the following responsibilities:

(a) to employ interdisciplinary, social sciences, historical, oral traditional and archival methodologies for statement-taking, historical fact-finding and analysis, report-writing, knowledge management and archiving;

(b) to adopt methods and procedures which it deems necessary to achieve its goals;

(c) to engage the services of such persons including experts, which it deems necessary to achieve its goals;

(d) to establish a research centre and ensure the preservation of its archives;

(e) to have available the use of such facilities and equipment as is required, within the limits of appropriate guidelines and rules;

(f) to hold such events and give such notices as appropriate. This shall include such significant ceremonies as the Commission sees fit during and at the conclusion of the 5 year process;

(g) to prepare a report;

(h) to have the report translated in the two official languages of Canada and all or parts of the report in such Aboriginal languages as determined by the Commissioners;

(i) to evaluate commemoration proposals in line with the Commemoration Policy Directive (Schedule "J" of the Agreement).

4. Exercise of Duties

As the Commission is not to act as a public inquiry or to conduct a formal legal process, it will, therefore, not duplicate in whole or in part the function of criminal investigations, the Independent Assessment Process, court actions, or make recommendations on matters already covered in the Agreement. In the exercise of its powers the Commission shall recognize:

(a) the unique experiences of First Nations, Inuit and Métis former IRS students, and will conduct its activities, hold its events, and prepare its Report and Recommendations in a manner that reflects and recognizes the unique experiences of all former IRS students;

(b) that the truth and reconciliation process is committed to the principle of voluntariness with respect to individuals' participation;

(c) that it will build upon the work of past and existing processes, archival records, resources and documentation, including the work and records of the Royal Commission on Aboriginal Peoples of 1996;

(d) the significance of Aboriginal oral and legal traditions in its activities;

(e) that as part of the overall holistic approach to reconciliation and healing, the Commission should reasonably coordinate with other initiatives under the Agreement and shall acknowledge links to other aspects of the Agreement such that the overall goals of reconciliation will be promoted;

(f) that all individual statements are of equal importance, even if these statements are delivered after the completion of the report;

(g) that there shall be an emphasis on both information collection/storage and information analysis.

5. Membership

The Commission shall consist of an appointed Chairperson and two Commissioners, who shall be persons of recognized integrity, stature and respect.

(a) Consideration should be given to at least one of the three members being an Aboriginal person;

(b) Appointments shall be made out of a pool of candidates nominated by former students, Aboriginal organizations, churches and government;

(c) The Assembly of First Nations (AFN) shall be consulted in making the final decision as to the appointment of the Commissioners.

6. Secretariat

The Commission shall operate through a central Secretariat.

(a) There shall be an Executive Director in charge of the operation of the Commission who shall select and engage staff and regional liaisons;

(b) The Executive Director and the Secretariat shall be subject to the direction and control of the Commissioners;

(c) The Secretariat shall be responsible for the activities of the Commission such as:

(i) research;

(ii) event organization;

(iii) statement taking/truth-sharing;

(iv) obtaining documents;

(v) information management of the Commission's documents;

(vi) production of the report;

(vii) ensuring the preservation of its records;

(viii) evaluation of the Commemoration Policy Directive proposals.

(d) The Executive Director and Commissioners shall consult with the Indian Residential School Survivor Committee on the appointment of the Regional Liaisons.

(e) Regional liaisons shall:

   (i) act as knowledge conduits and promote sharing of knowledge among communities, individuals and the Commission;

   (ii) provide a link between the national body and communities for the purpose of coordinating national and community events;

   (iii) provide information to and assist communities as they plan truth and reconciliation events, coordinate statement-taking/truth-sharing and event-recording, and facilitate information flow from the communities to the Commission.

7. Indian Residential School Survivor Committee (IRSSC)

The Commission shall be assisted by an Indian Residential School Survivor Committee (IRSSC).

(a) The Committee shall be composed of 10 representatives drawn from various Aboriginal organizations and survivor groups. Representation shall be regional, reflecting the population distribution of Indian Residential Schools (as defined in the Agreement). The majority of the representatives shall be former residential school students;

(b) Members of the Committee shall be selected by the Federal Government, in consultation with the AFN, from a pool of eligible candidates developed by the stakeholders;

(c) Committee members are responsible for providing advice to the Commissioners on:

   (i) the characteristics of a "community" for the purposes of participation in the Commission processes;

   (ii) the criteria for the community and national processes;

   (iii) the evaluation of Commemoration Policy Directive proposals;

   (iv) such other issues as are required by the Commissioners.

8. Timeframe

The Commission shall complete its work within five years. Within that five year span, there are two timelines:

Two Year Timeline

(a) Preparation of a budget within three months from being launched, under the budgetary cap provision in the Agreement;

(b) Completion of all national events, and research and production of the report on historic findings and recommendations, within two years of the launch of the Commission, with the possibility of a 6 month extension, which shall be at the discretion of the Commissioners.

Five Year Timeline

(a) Completion of the community truth and reconciliation events, statement taking/truth sharing, reporting to the Commission from communities, and closing ceremonies;

(b) Establishment of a research centre.

9. Research

The Commission shall conduct such research, receive and take such statements and consider such documents as it deems necessary for the purpose of achieving its goals.

10. Events

There are three essential event components to the Truth and Reconciliation Commission: National Events, Community Events and Individual Statement-Taking/Truth Sharing. The Truth and Reconciliation process will be concluded with a final Closing Ceremony.

(A) National Events

The national events are a mechanism through which the truth and reconciliation process will engage the Canadian public and provide education about the IRS system, the experience of former students and their families, and the ongoing legacies of the institutions.

The Commission shall fund and host seven national events in different regions across the country for the purpose of:

(a) sharing information with/from the communities;

(b) supporting and facilitating the self empowerment of former IRS students and those affected by the IRS legacy;

(c) providing a context and meaning for the Common Experience Payment;

(d) engaging and educating the public through mass communications;

(e) otherwise achieving its goals.

The Commission shall, in designing the events, include in its consideration the history and demographics of the IRS system.

National events should inclu de the following common components:

(f) an opportunity for a sample number of former students and families to share their experiences;

(g) an opportunity for some communities in the regions to share their experiences as they relate to the impacts on communities and to share insights from their community reconciliation processes;

(h) an opportunity for participation and sharing of information and knowledge among former students, their families, communities, experts, church and government officials, institutions and the Canadian public;

(i) ceremonial transfer of knowledge through the passing of individual statement transcripts or community reports/statements. The Commission shall recognize that ownership over IRS experiences rests with those affected by the Indian Residential School legacy;

(j) analysis of the short and long term legacy of the IRS system on individuals, communities, groups, institutions and Canadian society including the intergenerational impacts of the IRS system;

(k) participation of high level government and church officials;

(l) health supports and trauma experts during and after the ceremony for all participants.

(B) Community Events

It is intended that the community events will be designed by communities and respond to the needs of the former students, their families and those affected by the IRS legacy including the special needs of those communities where Indian Residential Schools were located.

The community events are for the purpose of:

(a) acknowledging the capacity of communities to develop reconciliation practices;

(b) developing collective community narratives about the impact of the IRS system on former students, families and communities;

(c) involving church, former school employees and government officials in the reconciliation process, if requested by communities;

(d) creating a record or statement of community narratives–including truths, insights and recommendations–for use in the historical research and report, national events, and for inclusion in the research centre;

(e) educating the public and fostering better relationships with local communities;

(f) allowing for the participation from high level government and church officials, if requested by communities;

(g) respecting the goal of witnessing in accordance with Aboriginal principles.

The Commission, during the first stages of the process in consultation with the IRSSC, shall develop the core criteria and values consistent with the Commission's mandate that will guide the community processes.

Within these parameters communities may submit plans for reconciliation processes to the Commission and receive funding for the processes within the limits of the Commission's budgetary capacity.

(C) Individual Statement-Taking/Truth Sharing

The Commission shall coordinate the collection of individual statements by written, electronic or other appropriate means. Notwithstanding the five year mandate, anyone affected by the IRS legacy will be permitted to file a personal statement in the research centre with no time limitation.

The Commission shall provide a safe, supportive and sensitive environment for individual statement-taking/truth sharing.

The Commission shall not use or permit access to an individual's statement made in any Commission processes, except with the express consent of the individual.

(D) Closing Ceremony

The Commission shall hold a closing ceremony at the end of its mandate to recognize the significance of all events over the life of the Commission. The closing ceremony shall have the participation of high level church and government officials.

11. Access to Relevant Information

In order to ensure the efficacy of the truth and reconciliation process, Canada and the churches will provide all relevant documents in their possession or control to and for the use of the Truth and Reconciliation Commission, subject to the privacy interests of an individual as provided by applicable privacy legislation, and subject to and in compliance with applicable privacy and access to information legislation, and except for those documents for which solicitor-client privilege applies and is asserted.

In cases where privacy interests of an individual exist, and subject to and in compliance with applicable privacy legislation and access to information legislation, researchers for the Commission shall have access to the documents, provided privacy is protected. In cases where solicitor-client privilege is asserted, the asserting party will provide a list of all documents for which the privilege is claimed.

Canada and the churches are not required to give up possession of their original documents to the Commission. They are required to compile all relevant documents in an organized manner for review by the Commission and to provide access to their archives for the Commission to carry out its mandate. Provision of documents does not require provision of original documents. Originals or true copies may be provided or originals may be provided temporarily for copying purposes if the original documents are not to be housed with the Commission.

Insofar as agreed to by the individuals affected and as permitted by process requirements, information from the Independent Assessment Process (IAP), existing litigation and Dispute Resolution processes may be transferred to the Commission for research and archiving purposes.

12. National Research Centre

A research centre shall be established, in a manner and to the extent that the Commission's budget makes possible. It shall be accessible to former students, their families and communities, the general public, researchers and educators who wish to include this historic material in curricula.

For the duration of the term of its mandate, the Commission shall ensure that all materials created or received pursuant to this mandate shall be preserved and archived with a purpose and tradition in keeping with the objectives and spirit of the Commission's work.

The Commission shall use such methods and engage in such partnerships with experts, such as Library and Archives Canada, as are necessary to preserve and maintain the materials and documents. To the extent feasible and taking into account the relevant law and any recommendations by the Commission concerning the continued confidentiality of records, all materials collected through this process should be accessible to the public.

13. Privacy

The Commission shall respect privacy laws, and the confidentiality concerns of participants. For greater certainty:

(a) any involvement in public events shall be voluntary;

(b) notwithstanding 2(i), the national events shall be public or in special circumstances, at the discretion of the Commissioners, information may be taken in camera;

(c) the community events shall be private or public, depending upon the design provided by the community;

(d) if an individual requests that a statement be taken privately, the Commission shall accommodate;

(e) documents shall be archived in accordance with legislation.

14. Budget and Resources

The Commission shall prepare a budget within the first three months of its mandate and submit it to the Minister of Indian Residential Schools Resolution Canada for approval. Upon approval of its budget, it will have full authority to make decisions on spending, within the limits of, and in accordance with, its Mandate, its establishing Order in Council, Treasury Board policies, available funds, and its budgetary capacity.

The Commission shall ensure that there are sufficient resources allocated to the community events over the five year period. The Commission shall also ensure that a portion of the budget is set aside for individual statement-taking/truth sharing and to archive the Commission's records and information.

Institutional parties shall bear the cost of participation and attendance in Commission events and community events, as well as provision of documents. If requested by the party providing the documents, the costs of copying, scanning, digitalizing, or otherwise reproducing the documents will be borne by the Commission.

Appendix 2
Canada's Residential Schools

The Indian Residential Schools Settlement Agreement (IRSSA) provides the most comprehensive listing of Canadian residential schools for Aboriginal people. At the time of approval, the Settlement Agreement listed 130 residential schools and residences. The Settlement Agreement also outlined a process by which additional schools could be added to the list of approved institutions. At the time of writing, nine institutions had been added to the list.[1]

The IRSSA list of approved schools has a number of limits.

- It was developed in the early twenty-first century as part of a process through which individuals were compensated for their experiences at residential schools that they attended. Therefore, the list did not include schools that closed in the late nineteenth and early twentieth centuries.
- The original list did not include the dates of operation for the schools. Due to limitations in the records, there are difficulties in determining opening and closing dates. Some schools, for example, might informally open when a missionary began boarding one or more students in his home. Continuity in the operation of schools could be interrupted. For example, schools that burned down might not reopen for several years. The precise date of closure might be difficult to pinpoint: the Blue Quills school, for example, is still in operation as a post-secondary educational facility.
- There were several anomalies in the list. The Methodist school at Red Deer, Alberta, which closed in 1919, and the Methodist school in Edmonton, which opened in 1924, are listed as one school. Similarly, the Anglican school at The Pas, Manitoba, which closed in 1933, and the Anglican school in Dauphin, Manitoba, which opened in 1957, are listed as one school (in part because both were known as the "McKay school"). There are separate listings for Roman Catholic schools at Fort Pelly and Kamsack, Saskatchewan, although these appear to refer to the same institution.[2]
- It was not uncommon for schools to be known by a variety of names: one might relate to its geographic name, one might refer to a Christian saint, and another

might refer to the region in which the school was located. The industrial school at Lebret, for example, was referred to as the "Lebret school," the "Qu'Appelle school," and the "St. Paul's school"—all at the same time. It later became known as the "Whitecalf school." There is also duplication in names: there were three St. Marys, four St. Pauls, and at least eight St. Josephs.

- The question of religious affiliation is not always straightforward. At first, most of the schools were quite clearly the initiatives of Catholic and Protestant missionary organizations. That affiliation formally ended in 1969. However, for a number of years after that, church-appointed principals remained in offices, and the religious denomination that had been previously associated with the school continued to provide pastoral care.
- All these issues combine to complicate any attempt to list the schools on the Settlement Agreement with their opening and closing dates, location, and religious affiliation.

Appendix 2.1 presents the schools listed on the Settlement Agreement by province (in alphabetical order). Because of the number of schools with the same name, the schools are listed by location. (When more than one school was located in a single location, there are multiple entries for that location.) Appendix 2.1 also addresses the anomalies that appeared in the Settlement Agreement list: separate listings have been created for schools that were combined on the Settlement Agreement list, such as those at Edmonton and Red Deer. The Kamsack and Fort Pelly Roman Catholic schools have been combined, as have the Roman Catholic schools at Cross Lake, Norway House, Notre Dame, and Jack River, which appear to have been part of a linked administrative structure. Where possible, the opening and closing dates are based on archival documents. Where this was not possible, secondary sources were consulted. In most cases, the dates represent only the opening and closing, and do not reflect periods when the school might have been temporarily closed. The Truth and Reconciliation Commission of Canada attempted to be as comprehensive as possible. For this reason, the dates may not correspond to those used in assessing claims under the Common Experience Payment program and the Independent Assessment Process, which employ criteria relating to the degree of federal involvement in the operation of the facility.

Appendix 2.2 lists residential schools that were funded by Indian Affairs in the late nineteenth and early twentieth centuries, but were not included in the Settlement Agreement. The information on these schools comes from the Indian Affairs annual reports, particularly the table of schools published annually.

Appendix 2.1.

Residential schools and residences included in the Indian Residential Schools Settlement Agreement

Alberta

Assumption
Our Lady Assumption, Assumption, Hay Lakes
Roman Catholic
Opening: 1951[3]
Closing: 1973[4]

Brocket
Sacred Heart, Brocket
Roman Catholic
Opening: 1887[5]
Closing: 1961[6]

Brocket
St. Cyprian's, Queen Victoria's Jubilee Home, Peigan
Anglican
Opening: 1890[7]
Closing: 1961[8]

Calais
Sturgeon Lake, Calais, St. Francis Xavier
Roman Catholic
Opening: 1907[9]
Closing: 1961[10]

Cardston
St. Mary's, Blood, Immaculate Conception
Roman Catholic
Opening: 1898[11]
Closing: 1988[12]

Cardston
St. Paul's, Blood
Anglican
Opening: 1891[13]
Closing: 1975[14]

Cluny
Crowfoot, St. Joseph's, St. Trinité
Roman Catholic
Opening: 1900[15]
Closing: 1968[16]

Desmarais-Wabasca
Desmarais (Wabisca Lake, St. Martins, Wabisca Roman Catholic)
Roman Catholic
Opening: 1901[17]
Closing: 1973[18]

Edmonton (St. Albert)
Edmonton (Poundmaker)
Methodist, later United Church of Canada
Opening: 1924[19]
Closing: 1968[20]

Fort Chipewyan
Holy Angels, Fort Chipewyan, École des Saints-Anges
Roman Catholic
Opening: 1874[21]
Closing: 1974[22]

Fort Vermilion
Fort Vermilion, St. Henry's
Roman Catholic
Opening: 1900[23]
Closing: 1968[24]

Gleichen
Old Sun (Old Sun's)
Anglican
Opening: 1886[25]
Closing: 1971[26]

Grouard
St. Bernard's, Grouard, Lesser Slave Lake
Roman Catholic
Opening: 1886[27]
Closing: 1961[28]

High River
St. Joseph's, High River, Dunbow
Roman Catholic
Opening: 1884[29]
Closing: 1922[30]

Hobbema
Ermineskin
Roman Catholic
Opening: 1895[31]
Closing: 1975[32]

Joussard
Joussard, St. Bruno's
Roman Catholic
Opening: 1913[33]
Closing: 1969[34]

Lac La Biche
Lac La Biche, Notre Dame des Victoires
Roman Catholic
Opening: 1863[35]
Closing: 1898[36]

Lesser Slave Lake
Lesser Slave Lake, St. Peter's
Anglican
Opening: 1894[37]
Closing: 1932[38]

Morley
Morley, Stony
Methodist, later United Church of Canada
Opening: 1922[39]
Closing: 1969[40]

Red Deer
Red Deer
Methodist
Opening: 1893[41]
Closing: 1919[42]

Saddle Lake (later St. Paul)
Blue Quills, Saddle Lake, Sacred Heart
Roman Catholic
Opening: 1898[43]
Closing: 1990[44]

St. Albert
St. Albert, Youville
Roman Catholic
Opening: 1863[45]
Closing: 1948[46]

Smoky River
St. Augustine, Smoky River
Roman Catholic
Opening: 1898[47]
Closing: 1908[48]

T'suu Tina
Sarcee, St. Barnabas
Anglican
Opening: 1892[49]
Closing: 1922[50]

Wabasca
Wabasca Anglican, St. John's, John's Mission Wapuskaw
Anglican
Opening: 1894[51]
Closing: 1966[52]

Whitefish Lake
St. Andrews, Whitefish Lake
Anglican
Opening: 1903[53]
Closing: 1950[54]

British Columbia

Ahousat
Ahousat, Ahousaht
Presbyterian, later United Church
Opening: 1904[55]
Closing: 1940[56]

Alert Bay
St. Michael's, Alert Bay Girls' Home, Alert Bay Boys' Home
Anglican
Opening: 1894[57]
Closing: 1974[58]

Anahim
Anahim Lake
Non-denominational
Opening: 1968[59]
Closing: 1977[60]

Chilliwack/Sardis
Coqualeetza
Methodist, later United Church
Opening: 1894[61]
Closing: 1940[62]

Cranbrook
Cranbrook, St. Eugene's, Kootenay
Roman Catholic
Opening: 1890[63]
Closing: 1970[64]

Fraser Lake
Lejac, Fraser Lake
Roman Catholic
Opening: 1922[65]
Closing: 1976[66]

Kamloops
Kamloops
Roman Catholic
Opening: 1890[67]
Closing: 1978[68]

Kitamaat/Kitimaat
Kitamaat (Elizabeth Long Memorial Home for Girls)
Methodist, United Church after 1925
Opening: 1905[69]
Closing: 1941[70]

Kuper Island
Kuper Island
Roman Catholic
Opening: 1890[71]
Closing: 1975[72]

Lower Post
Lower Post
Roman Catholic
Opening: 1951[73]
Closing: 1975[74]

Lytton
St. George's, Lytton
Anglican
Opening: 1902[75]
Closing: 1979[76]

Meares Island/Christie/Tofino
Christie, Clayoquot, Kakawis
Roman Catholic
Opening: 1900[77]
Closing: 1983[78]

Mission
St. Mary's, Mission
Roman Catholic
Opening: 1863[79]
Closing: 1984[80]

North Vancouver/Squamish
St. Paul's, Squamish, North Vancouver
Roman Catholic
Opening: 1899[81]
Closing: 1959[82]

Port Alberni
Alberni
Presbyterian, United Church after 1925
Opening: 1893[83]
Closing: 1973[84]

Port Simpson/Fort Simpson
Port Simpson, Crosby Home for Girls
Methodist, later United Church
Opening: 1879[85]
Closing: 1948[86]

Sechelt
Sechelt
Roman Catholic
Opening: 1904[87]
Closing: 1975[88]

Williams Lake
Cariboo, St. Joseph's, Williams Lake
Roman Catholic
Opening: 1891[89]
Closing: 1981[90]

Manitoba

Birtle
Birtle
Presbyterian
Opening: 1888[91]
Closing: 1970[92]

Brandon
Brandon
Methodist, United Church after 1925 (1929?), Roman Catholic (1970–1972)
Opening: 1895[93]
Closing: 1972[94]

Churchill
Churchill Vocational Centre
Non-denominational
Opening: 1964[95]
Closing: 1973[96]

Cross Lake
Cross Lake, St. Joseph's, Norway House, Notre Dame Hostel, Jack River Hostel
Roman Catholic
Opening: 1912[97]
Closing: 1969[98]

Dauphin
McKay
Anglican
Opening: 1957[99]
Closing: 1988[100]

Elkhorn
Elkhorn, Washakada
Anglican
Opening: 1889[101]
Closing: 1918[102]
Reopening: 1923[103]
Closing: 1949[104]

Norway House
Norway House
Methodist, later United Church
Opening: 1898[105]
Closing: 1969[106]

Pine Creek
Pine Creek, Camperville
Roman Catholic
Opening: 1890[107]
Closing: 1969[108]

Pine Falls
Fort Alexander
Roman Catholic
Opening: 1905[109]
Closing: 1969[110]

Portage la Prairie
Portage la Prairie
Presbyterian, later United Church
Opening: 1891[111]
Closing: 1975[112]

Sandy Bay
Sandy Bay
Roman Catholic
Opening: 1905[113]
Closing: 1970[114]

The Pas
McKay
Anglican
Opening: 1915[115]
Closing: 1933[116]

The Pas/Clearwater Lake
Clearwater, Guy Hill, Clearwater Lake
Roman Catholic
Opening: 1952[117]
Closing: 1979[118]

Winnipeg
Assiniboia
Roman Catholic
Opening: 1958[119]
Closing: 1973[120]

Northwest Territories

Aklavik
Aklavik, Immaculate Conception
Roman Catholic
Opening: 1926[121]
Closing: 1959[122]

Aklavik
Aklavik, All Saints
Anglican
Opening: 1936[123]
Closing: 1959[124]

Fort Franklin
Fort Franklin Hostel
Non-denominational
Opening: 1967[125]
Closing: 1972[126]

Fort McPherson
Fleming Hall
Anglican
Opening: 1958[127]
Closing: 1976[128]

Fort Providence
Fort Providence Boarding Home (Sacred Heart)
Roman Catholic
Opening: 1867[129]
Closing: 1960[130]

Fort Resolution
Roman Catholic
Fort Resolution Residence (St. Joseph's)
Opening: 1903[131]
Closing: 1957[132]

Fort Simpson
Bompas Hall
Anglican
Opening: 1960[133]
Closing: 1975[134]

Fort Simpson
Lapointe Hall
Roman Catholic
Opening: 1960[135]
Closing: 1973[136]

Fort Simpson
Lapointe Hall, Deh Cho Hall
Roman Catholic/Non-denominational
Opening: 1974[137]
Closing: 1986[138]

Fort Smith
Breynat Hall
Roman Catholic
Opening: 1958[139]
Closing: 1975[140]

Fort Smith
Grandin College
Roman Catholic
Opening: 1964[141]
Closing: 1985[142]

Hay River
St. Peter's
Anglican
Opening: 1895[143]
Closing: 1937[144]

Inuvik
Grollier Hall
Roman Catholic
Opening: 1959[145]
Closing: 1997[146]

Inuvik
Stringer Hall
Anglican
Opening: 1959[147]
Closing: 1975[148]

Yellowknife
Akaitcho Hall
Non-denominational
Opening: 1958[149]
Closing: 1994[150]

Nova Scotia

Shubenacadie
Shubenacadie, St. Anne's
Roman Catholic
Opening: 1930[151]
Closing: 1967[152]

Nunavut

Arviat
Federal Hostel at Eskimo Point/Arviat
Arviat (Eskimo Point)
Non-denominational
Opening: 1962[153]
Closing: 1967[154]

Cambridge Bay
Federal Hostel at Cambridge Bay
Non-denominational
Opening: 1964[155]
Closing: 1996[156]

Chesterfield Inlet
Chesterfield Inlet, Turquetil Hall
Roman Catholic
Opening: 1955[157]
Closing: 1969[158]

Coppermine
Coppermine Tent Hostel
Coppermine
Anglican
Opening: 1955[159]
Closing: 1959[160]

Igloolik/Iglulik
Federal Hostel at Igloolik/Iglulik
Non-denominational
Opening: 1962[161]
Closing: 1969[162]

Iqaluit
Federal Hostel at Frobisher Bay (Ukkivik)
Frobisher Bay
Non-denominational
Opening: 1971[163]
Closing: 1997[164]

Kimmirut
Federal Hostel at Lake Harbour
Non-denominational
Opening: 1964[165]
Closing: 1968[166]

Kinngait
Federal Hostel at Cape Dorset/Kinngait
Cape Dorset
Non-denominational
Opening: 1962[167]
Closing: 1965[168]

Mittimatalik
Federal Hostel at Pond Inlet/Mittimatalik
Non-denominational
Opening: 1962[169]
Closing: 1970[170]

Pangnirtung/Panniqtuuq
Federal Hostel at Pangnirtung (Pangnirtang)
Non-denominational
Opening: 1964[171]
Closing: 1967[172]

Qamani'tuaq/Qamanittuaq
Federal Hostel at Baker Lake/Qamani'tuaq
Baker Lake
Non-denominational
Opening: 1961[173]
Closing: 1967[174]

Qikiqtarjuaq
Federal Hostel at Broughton Island/Qikiqtarjuaq
Broughton Island
Non-denominational
Opening: 1962[175]
Closing: 1966[176]

Sanikiluaq
Federal Hostel at Belcher Islands
Belcher Islands
Non-denominational
Opening: 1963[177]
Closing: 1964[178]

Ontario

Brantford
Mohawk Institute
Anglican
Opening: 1832[179]
Closing: 1970[180]

Chapleau
Chapleau, St. John's
Anglican
Opening: 1907[181]
Closing: 1948[182]

Cristal Lake
Cristal Lake
Northern Light Gospel Mission
Opening: 1976[183]
Closing: 1986[184]

Fort Albany
St. Anne's, Fort Albany
Roman Catholic
Opening: 1902[185]
Closing: 1976[186]

Fort Frances
Fort Frances, St. Margaret's
Roman Catholic
Opening: 1905[187]
Closing: 1974[188]

Fort William
Fort William, St. Joseph's
Roman Catholic
Opening: 1870[189]
Closing: 1968[190]

Kenora
St. Mary's, Kenora
Roman Catholic
Opening: 1897[191]
Closing: 1972[192]

Kenora/Shoal Lake
Cecilia Jeffrey, Kenora, Shoal Lake
Presbyterian, United Church briefly, Presbyterian
Opening: 1902[193]
Closing: 1976[194]

McIntosh
McIntosh
Roman Catholic
Opening: 1925[195]
Closing: 1969[196]

Moose Factory Island
Bishop Horden Hall, Moose Fort, Moose Factory
Anglican
Opening: 1855[197]
Closing: 1976[198]

Muncey (Munceytown)
Mount Elgin, Muncey, St. Thomas
Methodist, later United Church
Opening: 1851[199]
Closing: 1946[200]

Poplar Hill
Poplar Hill Development School
Northern Light Gospel Mission
Opening: 1962[201]
Closing: 1989[202]

Sault Ste. Marie
Shingwauk Home
Anglican
Opening: 1873[203]
Closing: 1970[204]

Sault Ste. Marie
Wawanosh Home
Anglican
Opening: 1879[205]
Closing: 1894[206]

Sioux Lookout
Pelican Lake, Pelican Falls
Anglican
Opening: 1926[207]
Closing: 1978[208]

Spanish
Spanish Boys' School, Charles Garnier, St. Joseph's
Roman Catholic
Opening: 1913[209]
Closing: 1958[210]

Spanish
Spanish Girls' School, St. Joseph's, St. Peter's, St. Anne's
Roman Catholic
Opening: 1913[211]
Closing: 1962[212]

Stirland Lake
Stirland Lake, Wahbon Bay Academy
Northern Light Gospel Mission
Opening: 1973[213]
Closing: 1991[214]

Québec

Amos
Amos, Amos Student Residence, St-Marc Residence, St-Marc-de-Figuery
Roman Catholic
Opening: 1955[215]
Closing: 1973[216]

Fort George
Fort George, St. Phillip's
Anglican
Opening: 1932[217]
Closing: 1975[218]

Fort George
Fort George, St. Joseph's Mission, Residence Couture, Sainte-Thérèse-de-l'Enfant-Jésus
Roman Catholic
Opening: 1931[219]
Closing: 1978[220]

Fort George
Fort George Hostels
Non-denominational
Opening: 1975[221]
Closing: 1978[222]

Inukjuak
Federal Hostel at Port Harrison, Inoucdjouac, Inoucdouac
Non-denominational
Opening: 1960[223]
Closing: 1971[224]

Kangirsualujjuaq/Fort George
Federal Hostel at George River
Non-denominational
Opening: 1960[225]
Closing: 1960[226]

Kangirsuk
Federal Hostel at Payne Bay, Bellin
Non-denominational
Opening: 1960[227]
Closing: 1962[228]

Kuujjuaraapik/Whapmagoostui
Federal Hostel at Great Whale River, Poste-de-la-Baleine, Kuujjuaraapik
Non-denominational
Opening: 1960[229]
Closing: 1970[230]

La Tuque
La Tuque
Anglican
Opening: 1963[231]
Closing: 1978[232]

Mistassini
Mistassini Hostels
Non-denominational
Opening: 1971[233]
Closing: 1978[234]

Pointe Bleue
Pointe Bleue
Roman Catholic
Opening: 1960[235]
Closing: 1991[236]

Sept-Îles
Sept-Îles, Seven Islands, Notre Dame, Maliotenam
Roman Catholic
Opening: 1952[237]
Closing: 1971[238]

Saskatchewan

Balcarres
File Hills
Presbyterian, later United Church
Opening: 1889[239]
Closing: 1949[240]

Battleford
Battleford
Anglican
Opening: 1883[241]
Closing: 1914[242]

Beauval
Beauval, Lac la Plonge, Île-à-la-Crosse
Roman Catholic
Opening: 1860[243]
Closing: 1995[244]

Delmas
Thunderchild, Delmas, St. Henri
Roman Catholic
Opening: 1901[245]
Closing: 1948[246]

Duck Lake
St. Michael's, Duck Lake
Roman Catholic
Opening: 1894[247]
Closing: 1996[248]

Gordon's Reserve, Punnichy
Gordon's, Punnichy
Anglican
Opening: 1888[249]
Closing: 1996[250]

Grayson
Marieval, Cowessess, Crooked Lake
Roman Catholic
Opening: 1898[251]
Closing: 1997[252]

Kamsack
Cote Improved Federal Day School
United Church
Opening: 1928[253]
Closing: 1940[254]

Kamsack
Crowstand
Presbyterian
Opening: 1889[255]
Closing: 1915[256]

Kamsack/Fort Pelly
Kamsack, St. Phillips
Roman Catholic
Opening: 1928[257]
Closing: 1969[258]

Lac La Ronge
All Saints School, Lac La Ronge
Anglican
Opening: 1906[259]
Closing: 1947[260]

Lebret/Qu'Appelle
Lebret, Qu'Appelle, St. Paul's, Whitecalf
Roman Catholic
Opening: 1884[261]
Closing: 1998[262]

Muscowequan
Lestock, Muscowequan, Muskowekwan, Touchwood
Roman Catholic
Opening: 1889[263]
Closing: 1997[264]

Onion Lake
St. Barnabas, Onion Lake
Anglican
Opening: 1893[265]
Closing: 1943[266]

Onion Lake
St. Anthony's, Onion Lake, Sacred Heart
Roman Catholic
Opening: 1892[267]
Closing: 1974[268]

Prince Albert
Prince Albert, St. Alban's, All Saints, St. Barnabas, Lac La Ronge
Anglican
Opening: 1951[269]
Closing: 1997[270]

Prince Albert
Saint Alban's
Anglican
Opening: 1944[271]
Closing: 1951[272]

Regina
Regina
Presbyterian
Opening: 1891[273]
Closing: 1910[274]

Round Lake
Round Lake
Presbyterian, later United Church
Opening: 1884[275]
Closing: 1950[276]

Sturgeon Landing
Sturgeon Landing
Roman Catholic
Opening: 1927[277]
Closing: 1952[278]

Yukon

Carcross
Carcross IRS (Chooulta)
Anglican
Opening: 1903[279]
Closing: 1969[280]

Dawson City
St. Paul's Hostel
Anglican
Opening: 1920[281]
Closing: 1953[282]

Shingle Point
Shingle Point
Anglican
Opening: 1929[283]
Closing: 1936[284]

Whitehorse
Coudert Hall
Roman Catholic
Opening: 1960[285]
Closing: 1971[286]

Whitehorse
Whitehorse Baptist Mission (Baptist Indian School)
Baptist
Opening: 1947[287]
Closing: 1959[288]

Whitehorse
Yukon Hall
Non-denominational/Protestant
Opening: 1960[289]
Closing: 1985[290]

Appendix 2.2.
Residential schools identified in Indian Affairs annual reports that were not included in the Indian Residential Schools Settlement Agreement.

Alberta

Calgary
St. Dunstan
Anglican
Opening: 1896
Closing: 1907

Morley
McDougall Orphanage
Methodist
Opening: 1886
Closing: 1908

Stony Plains
Stony Plains
Presbyterian
Opening: 1892
Closing: 1894

Vermilion Lake
Irene Training Institute at Vermilion Lake
Anglican
Opening: 1885
Closing: 1894

British Columbia

Fort St. James
Fort St. James (Stuart Lake)
Roman Catholic
Opening: 1917
Closing: 1922

Metlakatla
Metlakatla
Anglican
Opening: 1872
Closing: 1908

Yale
All Hallows School
Anglican
Opening: 1884
Closing: 1918

Manitoba

Middlechurch
St. Paul's, Middlechurch (Rupert's Land)
Anglican
Opening: 1890
Closing: 1906

St. Boniface
St. Boniface
Roman Catholic
Opening: 1890
Closing: 1905

Water Hen
Water Hen
Roman Catholic
Opening: 1890
Closing: 1900

Ontario

Wikwemikong
Wikwemikong (Manitoulin Island)
Roman Catholic
Opening: 1868
Closing: 1911

Saskatchewan

Muscowpetung
Muscowpetung Agency Boarding School
Presbyterian
Opening: 1888
Closing: 1894

Muskeg Lake
Roman Catholic
Opening: 1892
Closing: 1892

Prince Albert
Emmanuel College
Anglican
Opening: 1879
Closing: 1909

Standing Buffalo
Standing Buffalo
Presbyterian
Opening: 1889
Closing: 1893

Northwest Territories

Fort Resolution
Fort Resolution
Anglican
Opening: 1891
Closing: 1892

Appendix 3

Persons Found Guilty of Abusing Residential School Students

The following list of individuals convicted of abusing residential school students was compiled by the Truth and Reconciliation Commission of Canada through a review of documents provided by parties to the Settlement Agreement, government archives, and court records, and searches of online legal and non-legal databases. There are a number of limitations to this list. Because document production has been an ongoing process throughout the operation of the Commission, it has not been possible to review all documents provided to the Commission. The Commission has not had the time or resources to review the various court and police records for information on prosecutions and convictions relating to the abuse of students.

School	Offender	Conviction	Sentence
Alberta			
Edmonton	James Ludford	gross indecency (1960)	1 year's suspended sentence; report to provincial mental hospital and not participate in activities with individuals under age 21[1]
Morley	Robert G. Pooley	indecent assault (1963)	1 year's suspended sentence, to be served at a provincial mental institute[2]
British Columbia			
Alert Bay	Harry Joseph	indecent assault (1970)	suspended sentence[3]
Kamloops and Mission	Gerald Moran	12 counts sexual abuse (2004)	3 years' incarceration[4]

School	Offender	Conviction	Sentence
Kuper Island and Williams Lake	Glenn Doughty	4 counts gross indecency, Williams Lake (1991)	1 year's incarceration[5]
		6 counts, including indecent assault and gross indecency, Kuper Island (1995)	4 additional months' incarceration[6]
		36 counts (sex related), Williams Lake and Kuper Island (2000)	3 additional years' incarceration[7]
Lower Post, BC, and Grollier Hall, NWT	George Maczynski	sexual assault (molesting boys), Lower Post (1973)	2 years' incarceration (served 10 months)[8]
		11 counts indecent assault, 6 counts buggery, 1 count attempted buggery, 9 counts gross indecency, and 1 count attempted gross indecency, Lower Post (1995)	16 years' incarceration[9]
		5 counts, including indecent assault, gross indecency, and buggery, Grollier Hall (1997)	4 years' incarceration, to be served consecutively after completion of 16-year sentence (for the 1995 conviction)[10]
Lytton	Derek Clarke	8 counts buggery and 6 counts indecent assault (1988)[11]	12 years' incarceration[12]
		4 additional counts (1996)	2 additional years' incarceration[13]
Port Alberni	Bruce Donald Haddock	4 counts indecent assault (2004)	23 months' incarceration[14]
	Arthur Plint	18 counts indecent assault (1995)	11 years' incarceration[15]
		17 counts (1997)	11 years' incarceration, concurrent with above-noted sentence[16]

School	Offender	Conviction	Sentence
Williams Lake	Harold McIntee	17 counts sexual assault (13 related to Williams Lake) (1989)	2 years' incarceration on each count concurrently, with 3 years' probation to follow; ordered to meet families of his victims and hear their stories face-to-face[17]
Manitoba			
Dauphin McKay	Ernest Constant	1 count indecent assault (2005)	2 years less a day, conditional sentence[18]
Northwest Territories			
Flewming Hall	William Hamilton	sexual assault (1964)	3 years' incarceration[19]
	Donald Perdue	contributing to the delinquency of juveniles (1964)[20]	unknown
Grollier Hall	Joseph Louis Comeau	2 counts indecent assault (1998)	1 year's incarceration on each count, to be served concurrently[21]
	Martin Houston	buggery, gross sexual indecency (1962) 1 count sodomy and 2 counts indecent assault (2004)	indefinite sentence; declared a dangerous sex offender (spent 10 years in jail)[22] 3 years' probation[23]
Grollier Hall, NWT, and Beauval, SK	Paul Leroux	1 count sexual assault (1979)	4 months' incarceration[24] (later received a pardon and conviction was removed from criminal record)
		1 count attempted buggery, 1 count attempted indecent assault, 3 counts indecent assault, 4 counts gross indecency, Grollier Hall (1998)	10 years' incarceration (paroled after serving less than 4 years of his sentence)[25]
		10 counts indecent assault, Beauval, SK (2013)	3 years' incarceration[26]
Ontario			
Fort Albany	Jane Belanger	assault (1998)[27]	unknown
	Marcel Blais	1 count indecent assault (1997)	unknown[28]
	Claude Lambert	1 count indecent assault (1997)	8 months' incarceration[29]

School	Offender	Conviction	Sentence
	John Rodrique	5 counts indecent assault (1997)	18 months' incarceration[30]
	Anna Wesley	3 counts administering a noxious substance and 2 counts simple assault (1999)	conditional sentence[31]
Sioux Lookout	Leonard Hands	19 counts indecent assault (1996)	4 years' incarceration[32]
Saskatchewan			
Gordon's	[No first name given] Courtney	unknown	incarcerated[33]
	Henry Cyr	touching a person under the age of 14 for sexual purposes and setting traps to cause bodily harm (1989)	$300 fine on both counts[34]
	Ewald Holfeld[35]	common assault (1945)	$20 fine plus costs[36]
		2 counts buggery and 1 count attempted buggery (1945)	2 years' incarceration on each count, to be served concurrently[37]
	William McNab	1 count sodomy (1947)	6 months' incarceration[38]
	Kenneth McNabb	unknown (c. 1955)	fined[39]
	William Penniston Starr	10 counts sexual assault (1993)	4.5 years' incarceration[40]
Kamsack	R. Jubinville	3 counts assault causing bodily harm (1994)	fined $300 on each count[41]
Prince Albert	George Zimmerman	9 counts indecent assault, 1 count attempted sexual intercourse, and 1 count sexual intercourse (1995)	5 years' incarceration[42]
Yukon			
Coudert Hall	Claude Frappier	13 counts indecent assault (1990)	5 years' incarceration[43]

Appendix 4
Apologies

This Appendix includes the full texts of apologies and statements concerning residential schools made by parties to the Indian Residential Schools Settlement Agreement, and by others who played direct roles in the residential school system.

Apologies in the House of Commons, 2008

In addition to the Government of Canada's June 11, 2008 apology, the Commission has included the statements made by the leaders of other elected members of Parliament with respect to residential schools in the House of Commons on June 11, 2008.

Statement of Apology – to former students of Indian Residential Schools on behalf of the Government of Canada by The Right Honourable Stephen Harper, Prime Minister of Canada

June 11, 2008

The treatment of children in Indian Residential Schools is a sad chapter in our history.

For more than a century, Indian Residential Schools separated over 150,000 Aboriginal children from their families and communities. In the 1870s, the federal government, partly in order to meet its obligation to educate Aboriginal children, began to play a role in the development and administration of these schools. Two primary objectives of the Residential Schools system were to remove and isolate children from the influence of their homes, families, traditions and cultures, and to assimilate them into the dominant culture. These objectives were based on the assumption Aboriginal cultures and spiritual beliefs were inferior and unequal. Indeed, some sought, as it was infamously said, "to kill the Indian in the child." Today, we recognize that this policy of assimilation was wrong, has caused great harm, and has no place in our country.

One hundred and thirty-two federally-supported schools were located in every province and territory, except Newfoundland, New Brunswick and Prince Edward Island. Most schools were operated as "joint ventures" with Anglican, Catholic, Presbyterian or United Churches. The Government of Canada built an educational system in which very young children were often forcibly removed from their homes, often taken far from their communities. Many were inadequately fed, clothed and housed. All were deprived of the care and nurturing of their parents, grandparents and communities.

First Nations, Inuit and Métis languages and cultural practices were prohibited in these schools. Tragically, some of these children died while attending residential schools and others never returned home.

The government now recognizes that the consequences of the Indian Residential Schools policy were profoundly negative and that this policy has had a lasting and damaging impact on Aboriginal culture, heritage and language. While some former students have spoken positively about their experiences at residential schools, these stories are far overshadowed by tragic accounts of the emotional, physical and sexual abuse and neglect of helpless children, and their separation from powerless families and communities.

The legacy of Indian Residential Schools has contributed to social problems that continue to exist in many communities today.

It has taken extraordinary courage for the thousands of survivors that have come forward to speak publicly about the abuse they suffered. It is a testament to their resilience as individuals and to the strength of their cultures. Regrettably, many former students are not with us today and died never having received a full apology from the Government of Canada.

The government recognizes that the absence of an apology has been an impediment to healing and reconciliation. Therefore, on behalf of the Government of Canada and all Canadians, I stand before you, in this Chamber so central to our life as a country, to apologize to Aboriginal peoples for Canada's role in the Indian Residential Schools system.

To the approximately 80,000 living former students, and all family members and communities, the Government of Canada now recognizes that it was wrong to forcibly remove children from their homes and we apologize for having done this. We now recognize that it was wrong to separate children from rich and vibrant cultures and traditions, that it created a void in many lives and communities, and we apologize for having done this. We now recognize that, in separating children from their families, we undermined the ability of many to adequately parent their own children and sowed the seeds for generations to follow, and we apologize for having done this. We now recognize that, far too often, these institutions gave rise to abuse or neglect and were inadequately controlled, and we apologize for failing to protect you. Not only did you suffer these abuses as children, but as you became parents, you were powerless to protect your own children from suffering the same experience, and for this we are sorry.

The burden of this experience has been on your shoulders for far too long. The burden is properly ours as a Government, and as a country. There is no place in Canada for the attitudes that inspired the Indian Residential Schools system to ever again prevail. You have been working on recovering from this experience for a long time and in a very real sense, we are now joining you on this journey.

The Government of Canada sincerely apologizes and asks the forgiveness of the Aboriginal peoples of this country for failing them so profoundly.

In moving towards healing, reconciliation and resolution of the sad legacy of Indian Residential Schools, implementation of the Indian Residential Schools Settlement Agreement began on September 19, 2007. Years of work by survivors, communities, and Aboriginal organizations culminated in an agreement that gives us a new beginning and an opportunity to move forward together in partnership. A cornerstone of the Settlement Agreement is the Indian Residential Schools Truth and Reconciliation Commission. This Commission presents a unique opportunity to educate all Canadians on the Indian Residential Schools system. It will be a positive step in forging a new relationship between Aboriginal peoples and other Canadians, a relationship based on the knowledge of our shared history, a respect for each other and a desire to move forward together with a renewed understanding that strong families, strong communities and vibrant cultures and traditions will contribute to a stronger Canada for all of us.

God bless all of you. God bless our land.

Statement by The Honourable Stéphane Dion, M.P.

Leader of the Opposition
House of Commons, June 11, 2008

Mr. Speaker, today, Canada comes face to face with some of the darkest chapters of its history.

Forced assimilation of Aboriginal peoples was carried out through the residential school system, a system, sadly, older than Confederation itself: schools aimed at "killing the Indian in the child" and eradicating Aboriginal identity; schools built on the removal of children from their families and communities; schools designed to rip out of children their Aboriginal identity, culture, beliefs and language. It was a dehumanizing system that resulted in the worst kinds of abuse.

Government policy destroyed the fabric of family in First Nations, Métis and Inuit communities. Parents and children were made to feel worthless. Parents and grandparents were given no choice. Their children were stolen from them. And only today are we starting to measure the devastating costs of these terrible policies.

Today we live in a reality created by the residential schools system, a present that is haunted by this tragic and painful heritage from those First Nations, Métis and Inuit children, from their families and their communities, a dark and painful heritage that all Canadians must accept as a part of our history.

For too long, Canadian governments chose denial over truth, and when confronted with the weight of truth, chose silence. For too long, Canadian governments refused to acknowledge their direct role in creating the residential schools system and perpetrating their dark and insidious goal of wiping out Aboriginal identity and culture. For too long, Canadian governments chose to ignore the consequences of this tragedy instead of trying to understand them so that the suffering of First Nations, Métis and Inuit communities continues to this day.

Let me quote the damning verdict of the 1996 Royal Commission on Aboriginal Peoples: "With very few exceptions, neither senior departmental officials nor churchmen no r members of Parliament raised their voices against the assumptions that underlay the [residential schools] system or its abusive character. And, of course, the memory did not and has not faded. It has persisted, festered and become a sorrowful monument."

Today, we lay the first stone in building a new monument, a monument dedicated to truth, reconciliation and a better future.

Today, we representatives of the Canadian people, apologize to those who survived residential schools and to those who died as a result of laws enacted by previous governments and parliaments. By speaking directly to survivors and victims today on the floor of the House of Commons, we apologize to those who died waiting for these words to be spoken and these wrongs acknowledged.

Successive Canadian governments and various churches were complicit in the mental, physical and sexual abuse of thousands of Aboriginal children through the residential schools system. As the leader of the Liberal Party of Canada, a party that was in government for more than seventy years in the twentieth century, I acknowledge our role and our shared responsibility in this tragedy. I am deeply sorry. I apologize.

I am sorry that Canada attempted to eradicate your identity and culture by taking you away from your families when you were children and by building a system to punish you for who you were. To First Nations, Inuit and Métis, mothers and fathers, I am so very sorry we took away your children. I am sorry we did not value you as parents. I am sorry we did not trust and respect you.

Today's apology is about a past that should have been completely different. But it must be also about the future. It must be about collective reconciliation and fundamental changes. It must be about moving forward together, Aboriginal and non-Aboriginal, into a future based on respect. It is about trying to find in each of us some of the immense courage that we see in the eyes of those who have survived. It is about being inspired by the determination of survivors like National Chief Phil Fontaine and Willie Blackwater who had the courage to speak out and pursue justice. It is about building on the work of former First Nations member of Parliament Gary Merasty, whose motion calling on the government to apologize to survivors of residential schools was unanimously adopted by members of Parliament on May 1, 2007.

If we are to succeed, we need to be firmly committed to the work of the Truth and Reconciliation Commission, chaired by Justice Harry LaForme, which is responsible for investigating all aspects of the residential school system in Canada.

This means that we will have to listen to testimony from victims of physical, emotional and sexual abuse. This means that we will have to understand why and how Canada let residential schools cause deaths and spread illness, tuberculosis and pneumonia. This also means that we will have to get to the bottom of what really happened to the many children who disappeared into unmarked graves.

This means giving a voice to those who were silenced by Canada. This means giving a name to those whose identities were erased. This means showing our respect to those we humiliated. This means understanding the pain of the parents and families who were abandoned and, as a result of our actions, destroyed forever.

We must listen carefully to the victims who testify before the Truth and Reconciliation Commission, and we must be prepared to hear the Commission recount a very shameful collective past. We must together, as a nation, face the truth to ensure that never again do we have to apologize to another generation, and that never again is such a tragedy allowed to happen.

I say this as I think of the survivors I met last night. One woman remembers clearly her early days growing up in an isolated community with her family. At age seven, her father took her by canoe to a residential school. She has great memories of life with her parents and siblings up to that day. Yet, she has no memory of the two years she spent at the residential school. She survived by erasing all memory of the harsh treatment she endured.

Another survivor, Marion Ironquill-Meadmore, talked about the ten years she spent in a church-run institution. The first lesson she was taught was that her parents were not worthy. After ten years, she left the school feeling lost in both the Aboriginal and non-Aboriginal worlds, ill-equipped to return to the traditional lifestyle of her community, and yet never feeling at home elsewhere.

Reconciliation will require a commitment from Canadian society for action. This means ensuring that all Aboriginal Canadians, First Nations, Inuit and Métis alike, share in the bounty and opportunity of this country. This means ensuring that we hear the voices of First Nations, Métis and Inuit people in their own languages, and that these Aboriginal voices and languages continue to enrich the cultural heritage of the world.

We cannot be intimidated by the scale of the challenge or discouraged by the failures of the past. We owe it to all our children to pass along an even better country than we inherited from our parents and we will not do so as long as Aboriginal peoples continue to be left behind.

Four years after the conclusion of the five year Truth and Reconciliation Commission of Canada, Canada will mark the one hundred and fiftieth anniversary of Confederation. On that anniversary, it is my sincere hope that Aboriginal and non-Aboriginal peoples in this country will fulfill the dream voiced in the very building sixty years ago by decorated Aboriginal veteran Thomas Prince, a dream of First Nations, Inuit and Métis people and non-Aboriginal Canadians forging a new and lasting relationship. He said in his own words, "so that they can trust each other and . . . can walk side by side and face this world having faith and confidence in one another."

Until that day, we humbly offer our apology as the first step on the path to reconciliation and healing.

Merci. Thank you. Meegwetch. Ekosi. Nakurmiik.

Statement by The Honourable Gilles Duceppe, M.P.

Leader of the Bloc Québécois
House of Commons, June 11, 2008

Mr. Speaker, I am very pleased to be here to witness—at last—the Canadian government's apology to the First Nations, Métis and Inuit people who were victims of federally funded residential schools.

Nearly 150,000 people have waited their whole lives for this day of truth and reconciliation; 90,000 of them are still with us. These 90,000 are true survivors. Over one hundred years ago, the Bryce report revealed that the mortality rate in residential schools was close to twenty-five per cent. In the Old Sun's residential school in Alberta, the death rate was as high as forty-seven per cent. That is why I consider these former students to be survivors.

These 150,000 people were abducted from their mothers and fathers. They were separated from their sisters and brothers. They were forcibly uprooted from their communities and their traditional cultures.

For those who cannot imagine the impact that residential schools had on Aboriginal peoples, picture a small village, a small community. Now picture all of its children, gone. No more children between seven and sixteen playing in the lanes or the woods, filling the hearts of their elders with their laughter and joy. Imagine the ever-present fear of watching their children disappear when they reached school age.

Rumours abounded about what happened to the children. All these years later, it is still horrifying to think of these things. Children were torn from their parents' arms to be assimilated. They were taken away and raised by people who had but one goal: to "kill the Indian in the child." Forced to unlearn their languages, these children could no longer communicate with their own parents. All of these things really happened, and they are a part of our collective history.

Between 1934 and 1962, six residential schools were established in Quebec: two in Cree territory, one in Algonquin territory, one in Attikamek territory and two in Innu territory. Just like residential schools everywhere, these ones left wounds caused by abuse, ill treatment and neglect.

Roméo Saganash, himself a survivor of residential schools, told me the story of his brother, who died within a year of entering the school. His family never found out why he died, and it took forty years—forty long years—for his mother to find the place where he had been buried. It is impossible to erase these indelible scars, impossible to heal the souls shattered by these memories.

Yet this apology is necessary. It is necessary but not sufficient. As Roméo Saganash says, "An apology, once made, is only as good as the actions that come after it." For those who lost their childhood in the residential schools, the best apology consists of real action that will allow their children and grandchildren to hope in the future. This means that the government must take real action now.

For example, the government is not spending enough to help Aboriginal children reach their full potential. For example, when problems occur that affect children, the government recommends that the children be taken out of their community for their own protection. In a way, the government is repeating the mistakes of the past.

For more than a year, we and the First Nations of Quebec have been calling for more money for First Nations so that children can remain in their communities. Does the government not think that enough Aboriginal children were removed from their communities in the past?

Here is another example: the Assembly of First Nations of Quebec and Labrador has been waiting for over a year and a half for a response from the government so that it can implement its "10,000 possibilities" project. This ten-year plan is aimed at building 10,000 housing units, helping 10,000 young people graduate from high school, and creating 10,000 jobs.

If the Prime Minister's apology is sincere, let him take real action. We will support him.

Finally, there is this disgrace: the government's refusal to endorse the United Nations Declaration on the Rights of Indigenous Peoples. I am very proud that the Bloc Québécois has given clear support to this draft declaration. By agreeing to endorse the declaration, the Prime Minister can send a clear message to Aboriginal peoples that he has learned from past mistakes and is making a solemn promise to the victims that their children and grandchildren will have respect and dignity.

I am speaking to you, the Aboriginal representatives present on the floor of the House and watching from the gallery. All the members of the Bloc Québécois join me in reaching out to you so that, together, we can build a better future for our children and grandchildren. That requires a relationship of mutual respect that can only be forged between nations.

On behalf of the Bloc Québécois, I extend a sincere apology for the past, and I invite us to build the future together, as nations.

Statement by The Honourable Jack Layton, M.P.

Leader of the New Democratic Party
House of Commons, June 11, 2008

Mr. Speaker, today, I rise in this House to add the voice of the New Democratic Party to the profound apology being offered humbly to First Nations, Métis and Inuit on behalf of the Canadian people.

I wish to acknowledge and honour the Elders who are with us here today and are participating in this ceremony, the length and breadth of this land at this very moment.

I wish to pay tribute to the First Nations, Métis and Inuit leaders who are here with us and to all of those who are guiding their communities through this difficult, emotional, momentous and hope-filled day.

I wish to recognize the children, here in this chamber today and watching at home in gatherings across the land, who also bear witness to the legacy of the residential schools.

Most importantly, I want to say to the survivors of the residential schools, some of whom have joined us here today, we are sorry for what has taken place.

Today we mark a very significant moment for Canada. It is the moment when we, as a Parliament, as a country, take responsibility for one of the most shameful periods in our history. It is the moment for us to finally apologize. It is the moment when we will start to build a shared future, a future based on equality and built on mutual respect and truth.

It was this Parliament that enacted, 151 years ago, the racist legislation that established the residential schools. This Parliament chose to treat First Nations, Métis and Inuit people as not equally human. It set out to kill the Indian in the child. That choice was horribly wrong. It led to incredible suffering. It denied First Nations, Métis and Inuit the basic freedom to choose how to live their lives. For those wrongs that we have committed, we are truly sorry.

Our choice denied their children the love and nurturing of their own families and communities. It denied children the pride and self-esteem that come from learning one's heritage, language, culture and traditions. In addition to these wounds, they experienced our neglect, inadequate health care, mistreatment and sexual abuse, all of which harmed so many children and even killed some. Because of Canada's policies, those who survived learned to be ashamed of who they are. For these terrible actions, we are sorry.

The legacy of residential schools casts a shadow over our country. It tore apart families and communities for generations, and this continues to be felt, and felt very personally.

Nearly every First Nations person of my age that I have met is a survivor. Many are also the children of survivors. One of those children told me about her mother, a Cree from northern Quebec, who had 12 of her 14 children taken from her. Her brother died in a residential school, but their mother was never told why or how. She was never told where her son was buried. She did not have the right to pay tribute to his life or his death. She could not mourn or say her final goodbyes to her child, as every mother should.

Many years later, her daughter was working in northern Ontario and she happened to mention the story of her brother to a local. He said, "I know where your brother is buried." They went to the graveyard and he pointed to a spot beside a headstone, and said, "Your brother is buried here, unmarked."

The pain inflicted by the residential schools is deeply felt by these children, who were forced to attend, and by the parents who had their children stolen from them. It is still felt in First Nations, Métis and Inuit communities across the country. The destruction of family and community ties, the psychological wounds, the loss of language and culture, and substandard education all led to widespread poverty, which remains rampant in First Nations, Métis and Inuit communities today. The horrors of the residential schools continue to harm even those who never experienced them personally.

There can be no equivocation. The laws consciously enacted in this House put the residential schools into place and kept them going for many years. It is in this House that we must start the process of reconciliation. That is why we are here together today and why we are here together to say we are sorry. This is a crucial first step.

However, reconciliation must be built through positive steps that show respect and restore trust. This apology must not be an end; it must be a beginning.

What is needed is a commitment to never again allow such a travesty of justice and transgression against equality to occur. It begins with officially recognizing the rights and cultures of First Nations, Métis and Inuit peoples by signing the UN Declaration on the Rights of Indigenous Peoples.

But reconciliation also means that, as a Parliament and as a country, we must take action to address the terrible inequality faced by First Nations, Métis and Inuit communities. We can start by restoring the nation-to-nation relationship between the Government of Canada and First Nations, Métis and the Inuit. Even as we speak here today, thousands of Aboriginal children are without proper schools or clean water, adequate food, their own bed, good health care, safety, comfort, land and rights.

We can no longer throw up our hands and say, "There's nothing we can do." Taking responsibility and working toward reconciliation means saying, "We must act together to resolve this."

Let us reverse the horrific and shameful statistics afflicting Aboriginal populations, now: the high rates of poverty, suicide, the poor or having no education, overcrowding, crumbling housing, and unsafe drinking water. Let us make sure that all survivors of the residential schools receive the recognition that is due to them.

We must make a serious, collective commitment. All of us together—First Nations, Métis and Inuit, Canadians who have been here for generations and new Canadians as well—must build a future based on fairness, equality and respect.

Meegwetch. Ekosi. Nakurmiik.

Church Apologies, 1986–2015

In this section the Commission includes the institutional apologies from the church parties to the IRSSA. Of the several Roman Catholic statements, including a number from bishops and groups of bishops, the Commission chose to include those of the Catholic religious orders whose members worked in the schools. Schools run by the Mennonite or Anabaptist community of churches were added to the Settlement Agreement after it came into force. A statement by Anabaptist church leaders therefore is also included.

Apologies made on behalf of The United Church of Canada

Apology to First Nations Peoples
The Right Reverend Robert Smith, Moderator
The United Church of Canada, 1986

Long before my people journeyed to this land your people were here, and you received from your Elders an understanding of creation and of the Mystery that surrounds us all that was deep, and rich, and to be treasured.

We did not hear you when you shared your vision. In our zeal to tell you of the good news of Jesus Christ we were closed to the value of your spirituality.

We confused Western ways and culture with the depth and breadth and length and height of the gospel of Christ.

We imposed our civilization as a condition for accepting the gospel.

We tried to make you be like us and in so doing we helped to destroy the vision that made you what you were. As a result you, and we, are poorer and the image of the Creator in us is twisted, blurred, and we are not what we are meant by God to be.

We ask you to forgive us and to walk together with us in the Spirit of Christ so that our peoples may be blessed and God's creation healed.

Apology to Former Students of United Church Indian Residential Schools, and to Their Families and Communities

The Right Reverend Bill Phipps, Moderator
The United Church of Canada, 1998

From the deepest reaches of your memories, you have shared with us your stories of suffering from our church's involvement in the operation of Indian Residential Schools. You have shared the personal and historic pain that you still bear, and you have been vulnerable yet again. You have also shared with us your strength and wisdom born of the life-giving dignity of your communities and traditions and your stories of survival.

In response to our church's commitment to repentance, I spoke these words of apology on behalf of the General Council Executive on Tuesday, October 27, 1998:

"As Moderator of The United Church of Canada, I wish to speak the words that many people have wanted to hear for a very long time. On behalf of The United Church of Canada, I apologize for the pain and suffering that our church's involvement in the Indian Residential School system has caused. We are aware of some of the damage that this cruel and ill-conceived system of assimilation has perpetrated on Canada's First Nations peoples. For this we are truly and most humbly sorry.

"To those individuals who were physically, sexually, and mentally abused as students of the Indian Residential Schools in which The United Church of Canada was involved, I offer you our most sincere apology. You did nothing wrong. You were and are the victims of evil acts that cannot under any circumstances be justified or excused.

"We know that many within our church will still not understand why each of us must bear the scar, the blame for this horrendous period in Canadian history. But the truth is, we are the bearers of many blessings from our ancestors, and therefore, we must also bear their burdens."

Our burdens include dishonouring the depths of the struggles of First Nations peoples and the richness of your gifts. We seek God's forgiveness and healing grace as we take steps toward building respectful, compassionate, and loving relationships with First Nations peoples.

We are in the midst of a long and painful journey as we reflect on the cries that we did not or would not hear, and how we have behaved as a church. As we travel this difficult road of repentance, reconciliation, and healing, we commit ourselves to work toward ensuring that we will never again use our power as a church to hurt others with attitudes of racial and spiritual superiority.

We pray that you will hear the sincerity of our words today and that you will witness the living out of our apology in our actions in the future.[1]

Apology of the Anglican Church of Canada

A message from the Primate, Archbishop Michael Peers, to the National Native Convocation, Minaki, Ontario, August 6, 1993

My Brothers and Sisters:

Together here with you I have listened as you have told your stories of the residential schools.

I have heard the voices that have spoken of pain and hurt experienced in the schools, and of the scars which endure to this day.

I have felt shame and humiliation as I have heard of suffering inflicted by my people, and as I think of the part our church played in that suffering.

I am deeply conscious of the sacredness of the stories that you have told and I hold in the highest honour those who have told them.

I have heard with admiration the stories of people and communities who have worked at healing, and I am aware of how much healing is needed.

I also know that I am in need of healing, and my own people are in need of healing, and our church is in need of healing. Without that healing, we will continue the same attitudes that have done such damage in the past.

I also know that healing takes a long time, both for people and for communities.

I also know that it is God who heals, and that God can begin to heal when we open ourselves, our wounds, our failures and our shame to God. I want to take one step along that path here and now.

I accept and I confess before God and you, our failures in the residential schools. We failed you. We failed ourselves. We failed God.

I am sorry, more than I can say, that we were part of a system which took you and your children from home and family.

I am sorry, more than I can say, that we tried to remake you in our image, taking from you your language and the signs of your identity.

I am sorry, more than I can say, that in our schools so many were abused physically, sexually, culturally and emotionally.

On behalf of the Anglican Church of Canada, I present our apology.

I do this at the desire of those in the Church like the National Executive Council, who know some of your stories and have asked me to apologize.

I do this in the name of many who do not know these stories.

And I do this even though there are those in the church who cannot accept the fact that these things were done in our name.

As soon as I am home, I shall tell all the bishops what I have said, and ask them to co-operate with me and with the National Executive Council in helping this healing at the local level. Some bishops have already begun this work.

I know how often you have heard words which have been empty because they have not been accompanied by actions. I pledge to you my best efforts, and the efforts of our church at the national level, to walk with you along the path of God's healing.

The work of the Residential Schools Working Group, the video, the commitment and the effort of the Special Assistants to the Primate for this work, the grants available for healing conferences, are some signs of that pledge, and we shall work for others.

This is Friday, the day of Jesus' suffering and death. It is the anniversary of the first atomic bomb at Hiroshima, one of the most terrible injuries ever inflicted by one people on another.

But even atomic bombs and Good Friday are not the last word. God raised Jesus from the dead as a sign that life and wholeness are the everlasting and unquenchable purpose of God.

Thank you for listening to me.

Statements of The Presbyterian Church in Canada

The Confession of The Presbyterian Church in Canada as adopted by the General Assembly, June 9, 1994

The Holy Spirit, speaking in and through Scripture, calls The Presbyterian Church in Canada to confession. This confession is our response to the word of God. We understand our mission and ministry in new ways in part because of the testimony of Aboriginal peoples.

1) We, the 120th General Assembly of The Presbyterian Church in Canada, seeking the guidance of the Spirit of God, and aware of our own sin and shortcomings, are called to speak to the Church we love. We do this, out of new understandings of our past not out of any sense of being superior to those who have gone before us, nor out of any sense that we would have done things differently in the same context. It is with humility and in great sorrow that we come before God and our Aboriginal brothers and sisters with our confession.

2) We acknowledge that the stated policy of the Government of Canada was to assimilate Aboriginal peoples to the dominant culture, and that The Presbyterian Church in Canada co-operated in this policy. We acknowledge

that the roots of the harm we have done are found in the attitudes and values of western European colonialism, and the assumption that what was not yet moulded in our image was to be discovered and exploited. As part of that policy we, with other churches, encouraged the government to ban some important spiritual practices through which Aboriginal peoples experienced the presence of the creator God. For the Church's complicity in this policy we ask forgiveness.

3) We recognize that there were many members of The Presbyterian Church in Canada who, in good faith, gave unstintingly of themselves in love and compassion for their Aboriginal brothers and sisters. We acknowledge their devotion and commend them for their work. We recognize that there were some who, with prophetic insight, were aware of the damage that was being done and protested, but their efforts were thwarted. We acknowledge their insight. For the times we did not support them adequately nor hear their cries for justice, we ask forgiveness.

4) We confess that The Presbyterian Church in Canada presumed to know better than Aboriginal peoples what was needed for life. The Church said of our Aboriginal brothers and sisters, "If they could be like us, if they could think like us, talk like us, worship like us, sing like us, and work like us, they would know God and therefore would have life abundant." In our cultural arrogance we have been blind to the ways in which our own understanding of the Gospel has been culturally conditioned, and because of our insensitivity to Aboriginal cultures, we have demanded more of the Aboriginal people than the Gospel requires, and have thus misrepresented Jesus Christ who loves all peoples with compassionate, suffering love that all may come to God through him. For the Church's presumption we ask forgiveness.

5) We confess that, with the encouragement and assistance of the Government of Canada, The Presbyterian Church in Canada agreed to take the children of Aboriginal peoples from their own homes and place them in residential schools. In these schools, children were deprived of their traditional ways, which were replaced with Euro-Canadian customs that were helpful in the process of assimilation. To carry out this process, The Presbyterian Church in Canada used disciplinary practices which were foreign to Aboriginal peoples, and open to exploitation in physical and psychological punishment beyond any Christian maxim of care and discipline. In a setting of obedience and acquiescence there was opportunity for sexual abuse, and some were so abused. The effect of all this, for Aboriginal peoples, was the loss of cultural identity and the loss of a secure sense of self. For the Church's insensitivity we ask forgiveness.

6) We regret that there are those whose lives have been deeply scarred by the effects of the mission and ministry of The Presbyterian Church in Canada. For our Church we ask forgiveness of God. It is our prayer that God, who is merciful, will guide us in compassionate ways towards helping them to heal.

7) We ask, also, for forgiveness from Aboriginal peoples. What we have heard we acknowledge. It is our hope that those whom we have wronged with a hurt too deep for telling will accept what we have to say. With God's guidance our Church will seek opportunities to walk with Aboriginal peoples to find healing and wholeness together as God's people.

Statement on Aboriginal Spiritual Practices, The Presbyterian Church in Canada, 2015

First Nations, Inuit and Métis peoples, before any encounter with Christianity, found meaning, spiritual benefit and the presence of the creator through life-giving Indigenous spiritual practices that have deeply rooted traditions.

Through the churches' participation in the residential school system, The Presbyterian Church in Canada contributed to the banning of those traditions. The Presbyterian Church in Canada presumed to know better and in our cultural arrogance tried to suppress practices whose value we were then incapable of perceiving. We acknowledge in a spirit of repentance our role in failing to recognize and respect these spiritual traditions and practices. The church believes that faith and devotion, reverence for life, truth and goodness coexist both in and outside of our own Christian experience.

As part of the churches' commitment to a journey of truth and reconciliation, The Presbyterian Church in Canada has learned that many facets of Aboriginal traditional spiritualities bring life and oneness with creation. Accepting this has sometimes been a challenge for The Presbyterian Church in Canada. We are now aware that there is a wide variety of Aboriginal spiritual practices and we acknowledge that it is for our church to continue in humility to learn the deep significance of these practices and to respect them and the Aboriginal elders who are the keepers of their traditional sacred truths.

Some of our congregations have been blessed with experiencing various traditional Aboriginal practices when Aboriginal elders, Aboriginal members of our church and Indigenous people visited our congregations as guests, and graciously shared some of these practices and the traditions that give rise to them.

These practices are received as gifts and serve to enrich our congregations. Ceremonies and traditions such as smudging, the circle/medicine wheel, drum songs and drumming, and Indigenous wisdom teachings have been some of the practices our church has experienced as gifts from Aboriginal brothers and sisters. We acknowledge and respect both Aboriginal members of The Presbyterian Church in Canada who wish to bring traditional practices into their congregations and those Aboriginal members who are not comfortable or willing to do so. The church must be a community where all are valued and respected.

It is not for The Presbyterian Church in Canada to validate or invalidate Aboriginal spiritualities and practices. Our church, however, is deeply respectful of these traditions. We acknowledge them as important spiritual practices through which Aboriginal peoples experience the presence of the creator God. In this spirit The Presbyterian Church in Canada is committed to walking with Aboriginal people in seeking shared truth that will lead to restoring right relations.

Statements from Roman Catholic orders of men and women religious who worked in residential schools

An Apology to the First Nations of Canada by the Oblate Conference of Canada
Reverend Doug Crosby, Oblates of Mary Immaculate, President of the Oblate Conference of Canada on behalf of the 1200 Missionary Oblates of Mary Immaculate living and ministering in Canada, July 24, 1991.

The Missionary Oblates of Mary Immaculate in Canada wish, after one hundred and fifty years of being with and ministering to the Native people of Canada, to offer an apology for certain aspects of that presence and ministry.

A number of historical circumstances make this moment in history most opportune for this.

First, there is a symbolic reason. Next year, 1992, marks the five hundredth anniversary of the arrival of Europeans on the shores of America. As large scale celebrations are being prepared to mark this occasion, the Oblates of Canada wish, through this apology, to show solidarity with many Native people in Canada whose history has been adversely affected by this event. Anthropological and sociological insights of the late 20th century have shown how deep, unchallenged, and damaging was the naïve cultural, ethnic, linguistic, and religious superiority complex of Christian Europe when its peoples met and interrelated with the Aboriginal people of North America.

As well, recent criticisms of Indian residential schools and the exposure of instances of physical and sexual abuse within these schools call for such an apology.

Given this history, Native peoples and other groups alike are realizing that a certain healing needs to take place before a new and more truly cooperative phase of history can occur. This healing cannot however happen until some very complex, long-standing, and deep historical issues have been addressed.

It is in this context, and with a renewed pledge to be in solidarity with Native peoples in a common struggle for justice that we, the Oblates of Canada, offer this apology:

We apologize for the part we played in the cultural, ethnic, linguistic, and religious imperialism that was part of the mentality with which the peoples of Europe first met the Aboriginal peoples and which consistently has lurked behind the way the Native peoples of Canada have been treated by civil governments and by the churches. We were, naively, part of this mentality and were, in fact, often a key player in its implementation. We recognize that this mentality has, from the beginning, and ever since, continually threatened the cultural, linguistic, and religious traditions of the Native peoples.

We recognize that many of the problems that beset Native communities today—high unemployment, alcoholism, family breakdown, domestic violence, spiraling suicide rates, lack of healthy self-esteem—are not so much the result of personal failure as they are the result of centuries of systemic imperialism. Any people stripped of its traditions as well as of its pride falls victim to precisely these social ills. For the part that we played, however inadvertent and naïve that participation might have been, in the setting up and maintaining of a system that stripped others of not only their lands but also of their cultural, linguistic, and religious traditions we sincerely apologize.

Beyond this regret for having been part of a system which, because of its historical privilege and assumed superiority did great damage to the Native peoples of Canada, we wish to apologize more specifically for the following:

In sympathy with recent criticisms of Native Residential Schools, we wish to apologize for the part we played in the setting up and the maintaining of those schools. We apologize for the existence of the schools themselves, recognizing that the biggest abuse was not what happened in the schools, but that the schools themselves happened—that the primal bond inherent within families was violated as a matter of policy, that children were usurped from their natural communities, and that, implicitly and explicitly, these schools operated out of the premise that European languages, traditions, and religious practices were superior to Native languages, traditions, and religious practices. The residential schools were an attempt to assimilate Aboriginal peoples and we played an important role in the unfolding of this design. For this we sincerely apologize.

We wish to apologize in a very particular way for the instances of physical and sexual abuse that occurred in those schools. We reiterate that the bigger issue of abuse was the existence of the schools themselves but we wish to publicly acknowledge that there were instances of individual physical and sexual abuse. Far from attempting to defend or rationalize these cases of abuse in any way, we wish to state publicly that we acknowledge that they were inexcusable, intolerable, and a betrayal of trust in one of its most serious forms. We deeply, and very specifically, apologize to every victim of such abuse and we seek help in searching for means to bring about healing.

Finally, we wish to apologize as well for our past dismissal of many of the riches of Native religious tradition. We broke some of your peace pipes and we considered some of your sacred practices as pagan and superstitious. This, too, had its origins in the colonial mentality, our European superiority complex which was grounded in a particular view of history. We apologize for this blindness and disrespect.

One qualification is, however, in order. As we publicly acknowledge a certain blindness in our past, we wish, too, to publicly point to some of the salient reasons for this. We do this, not as a way of subtly excusing ourselves or of rationalizing in any way so as to denigrate this apology, but as a way of more fully exposing the reasons for our past blindness and, especially, as a way of honouring, despite their mistakes, those many men and women, Native and white alike, who gave their lives and their very blood in a dedication that was most sincere and heroic.

Hindsight makes for 20-20 vision and judging the past from the insights of the present is an exact and often cruel science. When Christopher Columbus set sail for the Americas, with the blessing of the Christian Church, Western civilization lacked the insights it needed to appreciate what Columbus met upon the shores of America. The cultural, linguistic, and ethical traditions of Europe were caught up in the naïve belief that they were inherently superior to those found in other parts of the world. Without excusing this superiority complex, it is necessary to name it. Sincerity alone does not set people above their place in history. Thousands of persons operated out of this mentality and gave their lives in dedication to an ideal that, while sincere in its intent, was, at one point, naively linked to a certain cultural, religious, linguistic, and ethnic superiority complex. These men and women sincerely believed that their vocations and actions were serving both God and the best interests of the Native peoples to whom they were ministering. History has, partially, rendered a cruel judgment on their efforts, showing how, despite much sincerity and genuine dedication, their actions were sometimes naïve and disrespectful in that they violated the sacred and cherished traditions of others. Hence, even as we apologize for some of the effects of their actions, we want at the same time to affirm their sincerity, the goodness of their intent, and the goodness, in many cases, of their actions.

Recognizing that within every sincere apology there is implicit the promise of conversion to a new way of acting, we, the Oblates of Canada, wish to pledge ourselves to a renewed relationship with Native peoples which, while very much in line with the sincerity and intent of our past relationship, seeks to move beyond past mistakes to a new level of respect and mutuality. Hence . . .

We renew the commitment we made 150 years ago to work with and for Native peoples. In the spirit of our founder, Blessed Eugene De Mazenod, and the many dedicated missionaries who have served in Native communities during these 150 years, we again pledge to Native peoples our service. We ask help in more judiciously discerning what forms that service might take today.

More specifically, we pledge ourselves to the following:

- We want to support an effective process of disclosure vis-à-vis Residential Schools. We offer to collaborate in any way we can so that the full story of the Indian Residential Schools may be written, that their positive and negative features may be recognized, and that an effective healing process might take place.
- We want to proclaim as inviolable the natural rights of Indian families, parents and children, so that never again will Indian communities and Indian parents see their children forcibly removed from them by other authorities.
- We want to denounce imperialism in all its forms and, concomitantly, pledge ourselves to work with Native peoples in their efforts to recover their lands, their languages, their sacred traditions, and their rightful pride.
- We want, as Oblates, to meet with Native peoples and together help forge a template for a renewed covenant of solidarity. Despite past mistakes and many present tensions, the Oblates have felt all along as if the Native peoples and we belonged to the same family. As members of the same family it is imperative that we come again to that deep trust and solidarity that constitutes family. We recognize that the road beyond past hurt may be long and steep but we pledge ourselves anew to journey with Native peoples on that road.

An Apology to the First Nations of Canada by the Missionary Oblates of Canada

Ken Forster, Oblates of Mary Immaculate, Provincial of the Oblates of Mary Immaculate, Lacombe Canada, March 29th 2014

In 1991, on the eve of the 500th anniversary of the colonization of the Americas, the Missionary Oblates of Mary Immaculate made a public apology to the Native Peoples of Canada. Today in the context of this final National Truth and Reconciliation event, the Oblates of Lacombe Province would like to renew this apology and pledge once more our desire to journey in solidarity and mutual respect with all the First Peoples of Canada.

Through the first centuries of contact, the relationship of non-native to First Nations People was deeply wounded by the settlers' attitude of cultural and religious superiority and the imposition of colonial power.

For the last many decades the Indian Residential Schools have come to epitomize the harm of that colonial relationship. The good that came out of the Schools came at an unbearable cost to the First Nations. The primal bond inherent within families was violated as a matter of policy, as children were separated from their natural communities. These schools operated out of the premise that European languages, traditions, and religious practices were superior to those of First Nations and as such contributed to the domination of aboriginal culture, language and the integrity of the family itself. We missionaries played a significant role in the implementation of this flawed policy. For this we sincerely apologize.

The residential environment made children very vulnerable. We wish to apologize for failing to protect the children in our care, and for the times when we placed the reputation of the institution above the well-being of the students. The significant number of incidents of abuse has shocked society and the church. These acts are inexcusable, intolerable, and a profound betrayal of trust. We deeply, and very specifically, apologize to every victim of such abuse.

As missionaries, with a desire to serve, we commit ourselves to that deeper service Jesus Christ modeled for all Christians when he washed the feet of his disciples. Our hope for the journey forward is that we may serve not from a place of 'above' or 'below', but from a place of friendship, of equality, and of respect.

As a gesture of reconciliation, we, Missionaries Oblates of Mary Immaculate, would like to place a copy of these words along with the Apology of 1991 into your care.

Statement on behalf of Congregations of Women Religious involved in the Indian Residential Schools of Canada

Sister Marie Zarowny, Sisters of Saint Ann, at the General House of Oblates of Mary Immaculate, Rome, April 30, 2009. The statement was delivered by Marie Zarowny, on behalf of the Congregations of Women Religious involved in the Indian Residential Schools of Canada, to a delegation of Aboriginal leaders, residential school Survivors, and Roman Catholic officials in Rome on April 30, 2009.

Father Guillermo Steckling and Members of the Oblate General Council, thank you for welcoming us to your home and for providing me with this opportunity to say a few words. National Chief Phil Fontaine, Elders, Chiefs and Representatives of Canada's First Nations, Inuit and Métis, especially those of you who are former residents of the schools; Archbishop Pettipas and other representatives of the Catholic Entities; Ambassador Anne Leahy; other distinguished guests.

As I begin, I want to say, as I did earlier today, what an honour it has been for me to have shared the profound experiences of these last few days with you. I will carry this experience with me for as long as I live and will speak of its various meanings, some already spoken today and others yet to be discovered as we continue to contemplate and ponder its significance.

As we draw to a close the formal part of these days together, it is a privilege for me to speak on behalf of the Congregations of Women Religious that provided, over a long period of time, hundreds of their members to teach and care for children in the Residential Schools.

Some of these institutions, especially in the far north were started to care for orphans when almost all the adults of entire villages died as a result of various flu epidemics. We were invited to help the children, at least, survive. In these instances and in the schools themselves in other parts of the country, we were motivated by a sincere desire to further the education, health and Christian formation of the Aboriginal peoples in such a way that they would be able to achieve their rightful place in an evolving Canadian society. We wanted them to grow into personal fullness, to be proud of themselves and of their giftedness and to be able to live with a sense of innate dignity. For many students, however, this was far from their experience. How could our good intentions have had such tragic consequences!

We were products of the times in which we lived, with the teaching methods, cultural misunderstandings, social attitudes and theology of those times. As well, some of our members suffered from emotional problems that they took out on the children.

We now know that the residential school system itself, initiated by the federal government and in which we participated, was racist and discriminatory, bringing about a form of cultural oppression and personal shame that has had a lasting effect not only on those who attended the schools but also on subsequent generations. We carry immense sorrow for having contributed to this tragedy, a sorrow that is not momentary but that stays within our hearts.

We also now know that many children in our care suffered unspeakable abuse and mistreatment. Some Sisters have been accused of actual abuse; many others have been accused of not protecting those in their care. We are deeply grieved by all these revelations. Good intentions and genuine love on the part of many of our Sisters for the children in our care were not enough and in fact were often not experienced as such.

At the same time, many of our members formed lasting friendships with the children in their care; we have all been enriched by these relationships and are grateful for them.

Our priorities in working on the settlement agreement were that suffering be acknowledged, justice be done through adequate compensation and that there be a way for us as women religious to both contribute to and to enter into a process of healing and reconciliation with you.

Throughout the last 150 years or so, our involvement in the schools has not been our only ministry with First Nations. We have served as pastoral workers and counselors on reserves and other First Nations communities: teaching, providing health care, visiting families, helping with religious education, supporting those in leadership of various kinds, and participating in community events. Although our numbers are small now and we have withdrawn from several communities, to the extent we are able and at your invitation, we commit ourselves to continue to live and serve in your midst.

Institutionally we commit ourselves to use what influence we have to continue to support your efforts to achieve justice within Canada, including adequate housing, education, health care, healing programs and land rights. We also commit ourselves to enhance our efforts to foster awareness and understanding between Aboriginal and non-Aboriginal Canadians and to diminish in some way persistent attitudes of racism and superiority.

Personally, I commit myself, to the extent I am able, to assist the continuing process of creating a new future in Canada and the Church, one in which all peoples are appreciated and live with dignity and mutual respect.

And now a more personal word to National Chief, Phil Fontaine: *You have been a brother to us, Phil, working with us each step of the way to first help us understand the depths of hurt experienced by you and your people and then to walk with us to new understandings. This has not been an easy journey for you or for us but we have travelled it together. As a result our bonds with you and your people have deepened. You have also consistently expressed the desire of many of your people that we continue to be in relationship with you, and you have helped that to happen. We thank you for all the ways you have assisted in this process and we pray our Creator's abundant blessing upon you.*

In closing, I return to an earlier comment. Each of our involvements, whether educational, political, spiritual or other, has resulted in deep and lasting friendships between our Sisters and many First Nations people. We treasure these friendships and look forward to them deepening in the years to come.

Statement of Reconciliation, The Jesuits in English Canada

Delivered by Father Winston Rye, S.J., at the Truth and Reconciliation Commission of Canada's Québec National Event, Montreal, April 25, 2013

Let me begin today by first acknowledging all Survivors of the Residential Schools and their families, the Elders present, the Commissioners, Church and community leaders and members of the wider communities. We thank you sincerely for the invitation to share in this important event.

The Jesuits in English Canada want to take this special occasion to honour the Survivors. It has taken great courage, strength and generosity for you to come forward and to share your story with all of us here, a story of loss, grief, hardship, but also of resistance and healing.

We also greet the children and grandchildren of the Survivors, who suffered in turn from their parent's trauma in the Residential Schools and learned from their character and bravery.

We come today to pay tribute to the individuals who attended the Spanish Residential School; both boys and girls. We recognize and embrace the students who attended the St. Peter Claver Residential School for Boys, St. Charles Garnier Collegiate and St. Joseph's School for Girls, some of whom are with us today in the audience.

This gathering is a symbol of hope and a reminder to all of us that such abuse must never happen again.

I stand here on behalf of the Jesuits to say that we are truly, deep within our hearts, sorry for what we did to injure individuals, families and communities by participating in the Canadian Residential School system.

When the Jesuits first met with First Nations peoples 400 years ago, we recognized the greatness of your traditional spiritual beliefs. That openness was lost in the 20th Century.

The legacy of the Residential Schools is a terrible cloud on our legacy of friendship. Today, we are relearning how to trust each other in a deeper understanding of our own faith through the lessons that your Elders have taught us.

It has been a struggle for the Jesuits to recognize that we became an active part of a system aimed at the assimilation of your traditional culture. It was not until it was much too late that we realized the harm that we had done.

The Jesuits are proud to still count many of our former students as friends and colleagues. We are grateful for the forgiveness and understanding that you have extended to us over the years. We humbly thank you for sticking with us and continuing to welcome us in your homes and communities.

We come to celebrate the achievements of our students. We recognize that what they achieved as professionals, athletes and community leaders was *not* because of our efforts at the school—but through their own strength of character and love of knowledge.

We also come to acknowledge the students who were brave enough to confront us about our role in the Residential School system some thirty years ago. We treated you as dissenters and malcontents rather than listening to what you had to tell us.

Through litigation and lawsuits, we learned about harsh conditions, poor food, brutal punishment and horrible incidents of sexual molestation. You turned to the courts because the Jesuits turned away from you.

As educators, we have been shocked by stories of bullying, inadequate clothing, strapping and beatings for minor offences. Our school harbored individuals who molested or abused students. Bed wetters were tormented by older students and staff alike. The food was not fit for the needs of growing boys and girls.

Children who were much too young were taken from the love of their families and placed under the guidance of men and women who had little training and less compassion.

Most of all, we have heard stories of the inherent unfairness of the system. Students were given the strap for things that they did not do. Bullies were rewarded and victims punished. Abuse was not disclosed because there was no one who would hear a student's cry for help.

We are still struggling with how it could possibly have happened. We realize that the abuse might have been uncovered and punished many years ago, if there had been someone that the students could turn to. We failed in putting the needs and interests of the Jesuit priests and brothers ahead of the welfare of our students.

We vow that this will never be "the way things are" ever again.

Amongst the heartache, we have delighted in stories about how students outwitted their teachers and kept their spirit alive through practical jokes and ingenuity. Our students understood their instructors and their human frailties so much better than their teachers understood them. They fought against the unfairness of the system with humor and good nature.

We have heard of brave students who were resourceful enough to set out for their home communities. We are ashamed of the harsh punishments that they received when they were brought back by the authorities.

We offer a sincere prayer of thankfulness that no young lives were lost at our school because students ran away.

We have learned from these harsh lessons and have become stronger from your example. To the students who have defended us and taken our part, we are truly grateful. We will strive to prove ourselves worthy of the respect and love that you have shown your teachers.

We are deeply grateful to the communities that have continued to welcome us as pastors and as friends in the years since the Spanish Residential Schools closed. We are humbled by your love and forgiveness. We have never had to beg for reconciliation; you have offered it to us freely for so many years by your example.

We ask for your forgiveness for any role that our school may have played in sowing distrust and division between Catholic and Protestant families. It is not enough to decry the narrow mindedness of the times. By teaching intolerance in our schools, we sowed division where it had never existed.

Many of you have asked when the reconciliation between the churches will occur. We desire and pray that it is happening today as we move together in healing with our friends in the Ecumenical Working Group.

Finally, we have learned of the terrible inequality that continues to exist between the educational opportunities for white students and students from First Nations in Canada. Young people are still being transported to white communities, to obtain an education in an environment that is foreign to them. This is exactly what happened in the past and we seem to be reliving it again.

We share Shannen Koostachin's dream that in our lifetime we will see equal opportunities for education in the home community of every Canadian. We will do everything in our power and influence to ensure that this comes to pass and the injustices of the past are not perpetuated.

You had the courage to stand up and speak out about the past. You can help us all to open our minds and our hearts to understand and to stop the destruction now and not have to go through this all over again.

Today we stand before you to pledge our support in the rebuilding of your language and culture. We cannot undo the things that are done, but we can take positive and meaningful steps to rebuild.

We have opened our Archives so that the whole picture of the Residential Schools can be seen. We will unlock the doors to the ancient books that preserved the languages of the First Nations and make copies available to people in their own communities. These precious resources will never again be the exclusive property of white scholars and academics.

We thank the Commissioners for challenging us to undertake this journey of self-examination and reflection with them. We will work hand in hand with our students past and present to bring all these things to pass.

May the Creator God who sees all and knows what is truly in our hearts, bring us together. May the Blessed Kateri Tekakwitha guide us that we can learn from each other, for she is a model for us all.

May we come once again to call each other "friend."

Statement of Anabaptist Church Leaders

Presented to the Truth and Reconciliation Commission of Canada at the Alberta National Event, Edmonton, March 2014

Signed by Tim Dyck, General Secretary, Evangelical Mennonite Conference, Douglas P. Sider Jr., Canadian Director, Brethren in Christ Canada, Willard Metzger, Executive Director, Mennonite Church Canada, Willy Reimer, Executive Director, Canadian Conference of Mennonite Brethren Churches, and Donald Peters, Executive Director, Mennonite Central Committee Canada.

We are leaders of a group of Canadian Christian churches known as Anabaptist denominations. Our delegation includes Mennonite Church Canada, the Evangelical Mennonite Conference, the Canadian Conference of Mennonite Brethren Churches, the Brethren in Christ Church of Canada, and Mennonite Central Committee

Canada. Many people from our churches have come to the Truth and Reconciliation Commission events, including this one, to volunteer, to listen, to learn.

We acknowledge that we are all treaty people and that we are meeting on Treaty 6 territory, on land that is part of an historic agreement between First Nations people and newcomers, an agreement involving mutuality and respect.

Throughout the period of the Truth and Reconciliation Commission events across the country, we have watched and listened with respect, as residential school survivors have told stories with graciousness and courage, sharing experiences of the Residential School Legacy from its beginning. We are humbled to witness this Truth and Reconciliation Commission event.

As we have listened to your stories, we've added our tears to the countless tears that you have shed. We acknowledge that there was, and is, much hurt and much suffering.

We have learned much and we have much to learn.

We heard the wise words of Justice Sinclair encouraging us to acknowledge that all of us, in one way or another, have been affected by the Residential School experience. We recognize that being part of a dominant culture, our attitudes and perspectives made the Residential School experience possible and that these attitudes and perspectives became entrenched in our relationships and in our culture.

We regret our part in the assimilation practice that took away language use and cultural practice, separating child from parent, parent from child, and Indigenous peoples from their culture.

We regret that, at times, the Christian faith was used, wrongly, as an instrument of power, not as an invitation to see how God was already at work before we came. We regret that some leaders within the Church abused their power and those under their authority.

We acknowledge the paternalism and racism of the past. As leaders of Mennonite and Brethren in Christ church communities, we acknowledge that we have work to do in addressing paternalism and racism both within our communities and in the broader public.

We repent of our denominational encounters with Indigenous peoples that at times may have been motivated more by cultural biases than by the unconditional love of Jesus Christ. We repent of our failure to advocate for marginalized Indigenous peoples as our faith would instruct us to.

We are aware that we have a long path to walk. We hope to build relationships with First Nations communities so that we can continue this learning journey and walk this path together.

We are followers of Jesus Christ, the great reconciler. We are aware that words without actions are not only ineffective but may also be harmful. We commit ourselves to take your challenges to us very seriously. We will seek to model the reconciling life and work of Jesus in seeking reconciliation with you. We will encourage our churches to reach out in practical and loving ways, including dialogue and expressions of hospitality.

We commit ourselves to walk with you, listening and learning together as we journey to a healthier and more just tomorrow.

The Apology of The Royal Canadian Mounted Police (RCMP) with respect to the Indian Residential School legacy, May 2004

Giuliano Zaccardelli, Commissioner Royal Canadian Mounted Police

Many Aboriginal people have found the courage to step outside of that legacy of this terrible chapter in Canadian history to share their stories. You heard one of those stories today. To those of you who suffered tragedies at residential schools we are very sorry for your experience. Healing has begun in many communities as you heard today, a testament that is a testament to the strength and tenacity of Aboriginal people and Aboriginal communities.

Canadians can never forget what happened and they never should. The RCMP is optimistic that we can all work together to learn from this residential school system experience and ensure that it never happens again.

The RCMP is committed to working with Aboriginal people to continue the healing process. Your communities deserve better choices and better chances. Knowing the past, we must all turn to the future and build a brighter future for all our children.

We, I , as Commissioner of the RCMP, am truly sorry for what role we played in the residential school system and the abuse that took place in that system.

Appendix 5
Honorary Witnesses

One of the goals set out in the Truth and Reconciliation Commission of Canada's mandate was to "witness, support, promote and facilitate truth and reconciliation events at both the national and community levels." Witnessing in this context refers to the traditional and continuing Aboriginal practice of calling forth witnesses to validate moments of great historic significance. Their role is to recall, remember, and care for the history witnessed and experienced, to share it more widely once they are back home, and to carry the knowledge of it with others into the future. In its work, the Commission has called upon a number of prominent Canadian and international individuals, as well as a number of institutions, to serve as TRC Honorary Witnesses. It is in this spirit that those named in the list below have accepted the sacred trust of bearing witness to the truths of residential school Survivors, and of contributing to the goal of ongoing reconciliation between the Indigenous and Non-Indigenous peoples of Canada, beginning with sharing what they have heard and learned.

Individuals

Dr. Evan Adams
Her Excellency Madame Justice Louise Arbour
Dr. Cindy Blackstock
Joseph Boyden
Charles-Mathieu Brunelle
Éloge Butera
Francisco Cali Tzay
The Right Honourable Joe Clark
His Honour Charles Cunliffe Barnett
Renée Dupuis
His Worship Bill Elliot
Grand Chief Phil Fontaine
Dr. Sheila Fraser (honoris causa)
Patsy George
Jim Gladstone
The Honourable Judith Guichon
Barbara Hall
Clara Hughes
The Honourable Justice Frank Iacobucci
His Worship Don Iveson
Her Excellency the Right Honourable Michaëlle Jean
Grand Chief Edward John
His Excellency David Johnston
Her Excellency Sharon Johnston
Chief Dr. Robert Joseph (honoris causa)
Joé Juneau
Tina Keeper

Marc Kielburger
Wab Kinew
David Langtry
The Honourable Philip S. Lee
Dr. Stephen Lewis (honoris causa)
The Right Honourable Paul Martin
Sir Sidney Mead
Jane Middleton-Moz
Nick Noorani
Dr. Alanis Obomsawin (honoris causa)
The Honourable David C. Onley
Dr. Daniel Pauly
Gwendolyn Point
The Honourable Stephen Point
His Worship Gregor Robertson
Dr. Shelagh Rogers (honoris causa)
Dr. Buffy Sainte-Marie (honoris causa)
Jonathan Sas
His Worship James V. "Jim" Scarrow
The Honourable Andy Scott
Dr. Mary Simon
Sylvia Smith
Her Honour Corrine E. Sparks
The Honourable Chuck Strahl
Naty Atz Sunuc
Imam Michael Abdur Rashid Taylor
David Tuccaro
Robert Waisman
Dr. Andrea Walsh
Dr. Cynthia Wesley-Esquimaux
Charlotte Wolfrey
David Wong
Victor Wong

Organizations

Association des Femmes Autochtones du Québec—Quebec Native Women's Association (AFAQ-QNWA)
Canadians for a New Partnership (CFNP)
Connecting Home Ltd., Australia
International Center for Transitional Justice (ICTJ)
Maine Wabanaki State Child Welfare Truth and Reconciliation Commission

Appendix 6
Commission Staff and Contractors

The Truth and Reconciliation Commission of Canada (TRC) was established by Order-in-Council in June 2008. The initial Commission consisted of Justice Harry LaForme as chair, Claudette Dumont-Smith, and Jane Brewin Morley. Justice LaForme resigned in October 2008, while Commissioners Dumont-Smith and Brewin Morley resigned in January 2009. The parties to the Settlement Agreement then selected three new Commissioners: Justice Murray Sinclair as chair, Chief Wilton Littlechild, and Dr. Marie Wilson. Their appointments took effect on July 1, 2009: the following is a listing of individuals and organizations that worked for or were contracted by the new Commission.

Commissioners

Justice Murray Sinclair, Chair
Chief Wilton Littlechild
Dr. Marie Wilson

Commissioners' Spiritual Advisors

James Dumont
Rick Lighting
Jerry Saddleback
Peter Short

Survivors Committee

Eugene Arcand
Raymond Arcand (until Nov/09)
John Banksland
Madeleine Basile
Terri Brown
Lottie Mae Johnson
Barney Williams
Gordon Williams
Rebekah Williams
Doris Young

Special Advisors

Mario Dion
Robert Joseph
Brenda Reynolds

Executive Director

Kimberly Murray

Legal Counsel

Tom McMahon
Seetal Sunga
Don Worme

Corporate Services

Maryanne Boulton, Director
Kongkham Ackharath
Jackie Angeconeb
Justin Beauchamp
Dianne Bechard
Enza Bongiorno
Teresa Buckshot
Loretta Carroll
Myles Chalmers
Anna Côté
Judy Courchene
Lyne Cousineau
Brenda Edmondson
Brian Flamand
Sharon Fletcher
Tamara Genaille
Beverley Greisman
Susan (Bobbi) Herrera
Marie Ladouceur
Emily Lank
Karen Leclerc
Shelly Longbottom
Brandon Mitchell
Melissa Nepinak
Tim O'Loan
Roberta Pescitelli
Geneviève Rankin
Sherri Rollins
Laver Simard
Sean Stiff
Jason Su
Rick Valcourt
Carolyn Ward
Wendy Webber
Anne Wildcat
Mary Wilson
Stanley Wood

Communications

James Bardach, Director
Rod Carleton
Jeanette Doucet
Heather Frayne
Guy Freedman
Denis Guertin
Wendy Johnson
Jane Luhtassari
Colleen Patterson
Nancy Pine
Stacey Stone
Viola Thomas
Mandy Wesley

Events

Shannon-Lee Barry
Jacqueline Black
Leo Dufault
Marie-Anick Elie
Jeff Erbach
Kyle Irving
Melissa Knapp
Lisa Meeches
Janell Melenchuk
Kim Rey
Joanne Soldier

Gloria Spence
Sam Vint

Inuit Sub-Commission

Jennifer Hunt-Poitras, Co-director
Robert Watt, Co-director
Siku Allooloo
Cristine Bayly
Jeannie Maniapik
Lucy Ann Yakeleya

Regional Liaison Officers

Darlene Auger
Alvin Fiddler
Frank Hope
Samaya Jardey
Richard Kistabish
Ida Moore
Kimberly Quinney

Research

Alison Biely
Kristina Bowie
Tara Flynn
Helen Harrison
Maggie Hodgson
Brenda Ireland
Alex Maass
Natasha Mallal
Laurie Messer
Andrea Migone
John Milloy
Dipa Patel
Brock Pitawanakwat
Lori Ransom
Paulette Regan
Simon Solomon
Doug Smith
Eldon Yellowhorn
Greg Younging

Students and Co-op Placements

Saba Ahmed
Eden Alexander
Andrea Briggs
Regan Burles
Stephanie Clark
Chris Durrant
Charles Dumais
Sarah Ens
Niki Ferland
Kim Haiste
Jayme Herschkopf
Julie Hunter
Antonio Ingram
Jessica Iveson
Emma Jarvis
Nathalie Kalina
Celina Kilgallen-Asencio
Tala Khoury
Judith Lê
Lana Mccrea
Josh Mentanko
Darren Modzelewski
Alexandra Olshefsky
Cassandra Porter
Gajan Sathananthan
John Simpson
Stephanie Wade
Bobbi Whiteman
Harsh Zaran

Statement Gathering

Ry Moran, Director
Barb Cameron
Brad Crawford
Kim-Marie Cormier
Sylvia Genaille
Roxanne Greene
Rose Hart
Kaila Johnston
Ken Letander
Sonja Matthies
Trina McKellep
Lisa Michell
Stephanie Scott
Bryan Verot

Archives and Document Collection

Graham Constant
Marta Dabros
Sarah Gauntlett
Crystal Dawn Greene
Peter Houston
Francine Jebb
Jordan Molaro
Margaret Anne Lindsay
Amanda Linden
Kezia Malabanan-Abugal
Marianne McLean
Lisa Muswagon
Billy Nepinak
Terry Reilly
Josephine Sallis
Reagan Swanson

Statement Gathering Field Personnel

Janice Acoose
Eden Alexander
Yves Martin Allard
Gloria Alvernaz Mulcahy
Lill Anderson
Bernadette Apples
Darlene Auger
Kevin Bacon
Nicole Badry
Sharon Baptiste
BJ Barnes
Jonathan Bartlett
Brenda Bear
Melanie Bernard
Saghar Birjandian
Marie Blackduck
Trina Bolan
Amy Bombay
Laura Boucher
Ramona Laura Boucher
Trinity Bruce
Marie Burke
Kevin Lee Burton
Rhonda Cameron
Tobie Caplette
Leona Cardinal
Kristina Chand
Mona Chartrand
Nora Cochrane
Myles Courchene
Dolly Creighton
Leslie Crowley
Marta Dabros
Jeannie Daniels
Desiree Desnomie
Eileen Doerksen
Aiden Duffy

Damian Eagle Bear
Desarae Eashappie
Serena Ehrmantraut
Kim Erickson
Cheryl Fontaine
Suzanne Ford
Cheryl Fraehlich
Sara Fryer
Sylvia Genaille
Ginelle Giacomin
Delores Gladue
Julie Goertzen
Annie Goose
Sylvia Gopher
Joanne M. Grandboin
Irene Sarah Green
Roxanne Greene
Helga Hamilton
Jo-Anne Hansen
Helen Harrison
Lisa Hinks
Maggie Hodgson
Dustin Hollings
Marge Hudson
Beverly Hunter
Heather Iqlohionte
Angie Ironstar
Katelyn Ironstar
Ingrid Isaac
Edwin Jebb
Marie Johnston
Amber Jones
Austin Kaye
Roisin Kenny
Celina Kilgallen
Michelle Klippenstein
Louis Knott
Judi Kochon
Liberty Kreutzer
J.E. Lafreniere
Melanie Lameboy
Linda Lamirande
Adelaide Lathlin
Janis Libby
Len Lindstrom
Krista Loughton
Heather MacAndrew
Donna Marion
Jaimee Marks
Ann Martin
Marie Mason
Joseph Maud
Priscilla Maud
Sheila Mazhari
Loren McGinnis
Celina McIntyre
Kim McKay
Germaine Mckenzie
Rian Mercer
Ruth Mercredi
Linda Migwans
Courtney Montour
Philip Morin
Robyn Morin
Sheila M. Moss Sr.
Barbara Nepinak
Reg Nepinak
Jasmine Netsena
Langford Ogemah
Laura Orchard
Caitlyn Pantherbone
Sean Parenteau
Bernice Perkins
Tara Petti
Stella Piercey
Morgan Phillips
Simon Paul Ptashnick
James Queskekapaw
Bernadette Rabesca-Apples
Wilma Ratt

Lynn Rear
Kimberly Redlac
Julian Robbins
Julia Robson
Zach Romano
Jack Saddleback
Stephen St. Laurent
April Seenie
Lindi Shade
Geraldine Shingoose
Oliver Shouting
Melanie Simon
Kristi Lane Sinclair
Vanessa Stevens
Trudy Stewart
Yvonne Still
Jennifer Storm
Isabella Tatar
Carla Taunton
Sarah Tautuagjuk
Viola Thomas
Harvey Tootoosis
Shirley Tsetta
Bertha Twin
Carla Ulrich
Steve Upton
Tina Vassiliou
Pamela Vernaus
Jaysen Villeneuve
Kanapaush Vollant
Lashawn Wahpooseyan
Howard Walker
Martha Walls
Barb Wapoose
Jeff Ward
Cybil Williams
Janine Windolph
Amber Wood
Faith Woodruff
Lucy Yakeleya
Brandy Yanchyk

Contract service providers

All Nation Print Ltd.
AMR Planning and Consulting Inc.
Anishinabe Printing
Anish Corporation
Artopex Inc.
Associated Marketing Partners Inc.
Attendance Marketing
Glenn Bergen
John Borrows
Boyle Street Community Services
Broadview Networks
Bronson Consulting Group
Bruce and Boivin Consulting Group Inc.
Canadian Human Rights Commission Financial Services
Fred Cattroll
Colourblind Graphics Design
Competitive Edge Media Group
Barbara Czarnecki
Tamara Dionne Stout
Doowah Design Inc.
Égale Canada Human Rights Trust
Jacqueline Esmonde
Earnscliffe Strategy Group
Elm Printing
Excel Human Resources Ottawa Inc.
Falconer LLP
Flat Out Pictures
Freeman Audio Visual
Alvin Finkel
Gerald Friesen
Jean Friesen
Gamut Productions
Genesis Integration Inc.
Dick Gordon
R. E. Gilmore Investments Corp.
Heidi Harms
The Harris Consulting Corporation
Higgins International Inc.

The History Group
Anne Holloway
Hunter-Courchene Consulting
Insight Canada
Institute on Governance
John A. Tyler and Associates
Mirjana Jurcevic
Kisik Inc.
Allen Kraut
Kromar Printing Ltd.
Legacy of Hope Foundation
Amanda Le Rougetel
MacGillivray & Associates
Margaret Anne Lindsay
Manitoulin Transport Inc.
MediaStyle
Meltwater News Canada Inc.
Nashel Management Inc.
Nation Media and Design
A Northern Micro Aboriginal Partner
Oswald Productions Inc.
Pido Productions Ltd.
Polar Bear Productions
Project of Heart
Printers Xclusive
RAS Creative
Ed Reed
RESOLVE
Kent Roach
Wendy Robbins
Patricia Sanders
Roberta Stout
Spirit Creative Advertising and Promotion Inc.
Sussex Circle
Jesse Todres
TOTEM Offisource
Agnes Vanya
Voice Capture Digital Recording

Research Contracts

Aboriginal Legal Services of Toronto
ArtsLink
Aulneau Renewal Centre
Justin Tolly Bradford
Peter Bush
Sue Campbell
Contentworks Inc.
Centre for Youth and Society, University of Victoria
Julian Falconer
Steven Fick
First Nations Child & Family Caring Society of Canada
Brian Gettler
Philip Goldring
Susan Gray
Brenda Gunn
Evan Habkirk
Norma Hall
Scott Hamilton
Matthew James
David MacDonald
Natasha Mallal
Maraya Cultural Projects Society
McGill University, Faculty of Law, Centre for Human Rights and Legal Pluralism
Celeste McKay
Laurie Meijer-Drees
David Milward
Alison Norman
Carlos Quinonez
Prairie Women's Health Centre of Excellence
Jeffrey Rosenthal
Arthur Schafer
Thompson Rivers University
Andrew Woolford

Pro bono assistance

Laurel Fletcher
Keith Denny
Jennifer Henderson
Kenneth Osborne
Michael Moffatt
Gustaaf Sevenhuysen

Bibliography

Primary Sources

1. Truth and Reconciliation Commission Databases

The endnotes of this report often commence with the abbreviation TRC, followed by one of the following abbreviations: ASAGR, AVS, CAR, IRSSA, NRA, RBS, and LAC. The documents so cited are located in the Truth and Reconciliation Commission of Canada's database. At the end of each of these endnotes, in square brackets, is the document identification number for each of these documents. The following is a brief description of each database.

Active and Semi-Active Government Records (ASAGR) Database: The Active and Semi-Active Government Records database contains active and semi-active records collected from federal governmental departments that potentially intersected with the administration and management of the residential school system. Documents that were relevant to the history and/or legacy of the system were disclosed to the Truth and Reconciliation Commission of Canada (TRC) in keeping with the federal government's obligations in relation to the Indian Residential Schools Settlement Agreement (IRSSA). Some of the other federal government departments included, but were not limited to, the Department of Justice, Health Canada, the Royal Canadian Mounted Police, and National Defence. Aboriginal Affairs and Northern Development Canada undertook the responsibility of centrally collecting and producing the records from these other federal departments to the TRC.

Audio/Video Statement (AVS) Database: The Audio/Video Statement database contains video and audio statements provided to the trc at community hearings and regional and national events held by the trc, as well as at other special events attended by the trc.

Church Archival Records (CAR) Database: The Church Archival Records database contains records collected from the different church/religious entities that were involved in administration and management of residential schools. The church/religious entities primarily included, but were not limited to, entities associated with the Roman Catholic Church, the Anglican Church of Canada, the Presbyterian Church in Canada, and the United Church of Canada. The records were collected as part of the trc's mandate, as set out in the Indian Residential Schools Settlement Agreement, to "identify sources and create as complete an historical record as possible of the irs system and legacy."

Indian Residential Schools School Authority (IRSSA) Database: The Indian Residential Schools School Authority database is comprised of individual records related to each residential school, as set out by the IRSSA.

National Research and Analysis (NRA) Database: The National Research and Analysis database contains records collected by the National Research and Analysis Directorate, Aboriginal Affairs and Northern Development Canada, formerly Indian Residential Schools Resolution Canada (IRSRC). The records in the database were originally collected for the purpose of research into a variety of allegations, such as abuse in residential schools, and primarily resulted from court processes such as civil and criminal litigation, and later the Indian Residential Schools Settlement Agreement (IRSSA), as well as from out-of-court processes such as Alternative Dispute Resolution. A majority of the records were collected from Aboriginal Affairs and Northern Development Canada. The collection also contains records from other federal departments and religious entities. In the case of some records in the database that were provided by outside entities, the information in the database is incomplete. In those instances, the endnotes in the report reads, "No document location, no document file source."

Red, Black and School Series (RBS) Database: The Red, Black and School Series database contains records provided by Library and Archives Canada to the TRC. These three sub-series contain records that were originally part of the "Headquarters Central Registry System," or records management system, for departments that preceded the current federal department of Aboriginal Affairs and Northern Development Canada. The archival records are currently related to the Department of Indian Affairs and Northern Development fonds and are held as part of Library and Archives Canada's collection.

Library and Archives Canada (LACAR) Archival Records Container and Document Databases – The LAC Records Container (and Document databases contain records collected from Library and Archives Canada (LAC). The archival records of federal governmental departments that potentially intersected with the administration and management of Indian Residential Schools were held as part of Library and Archives Canada's collection. Documents that were relevant to the history and/or legacy of the Indian Residential School system were initially collected by the Truth and Reconciliation Commission, in conjunction with Aboriginal Affairs and Northern Development Canada, as part of their mandate, as set out in the Indian Residential School Settlement Agreement. The collection of records was later continued by Aboriginal Affairs and Northern Development Canada, based on federal government's obligation to disclose documents in relation to the Indian Residential Schools Settlement Agreement.

2. Indian Affairs Annual Reports, 1864–1997

Within this report, *Annual Report of the Department of Indian Affairs* denotes the published annual reports created by the Government of Canada, and relating to Indian Affairs over the period from 1864 to 1997.

The Department of Indian Affairs and Northern Development was created in 1966. In 2011, it was renamed Aboriginal Affairs and Northern Development. Before 1966, different departments were responsible for the portfolios of Indian Affairs and Northern Affairs.

The departments responsible for Indian Affairs were (in chronological order):

- The Department of the Secretary of State of Canada (to 1869)
- The Department of the Secretary of State for the Provinces (1869–1873)
- The Department of the Interior (1873–1880)
- The Department of Indian Affairs (1880–1936)
- The Department of Mines and Resources (1936–1950)
- The Department of Citizenship and Immigration (1950–1965)
- The Department of Northern Affairs and National Resources (1966)
- The Department of Indian Affairs and Northern Development (1966 to the present)

The exact titles of Indian Affairs annual reports changed over time, and were named for the department.

3. Library and Archives Canada

RG10 (Indian Affairs Records Group) The records of RG10 at Library and Archives Canada are currently part of the R216, Department of Indian Affairs and Northern Development fonds. For clarity and brevity, in footnotes throughout this report, records belonging to the RG10 Records Group have been identified simply with their RG10 information. Where a copy of an RG10 document held in a TRC database was used, the TRC database holding that copy is clearly identified, along with the RG10 information connected with the original document.

4. Other Archives

Provincial Archives of British Columbia.

United Church of Canada Archives.

5. Government Publications

Audette, L. A. *Report on The Commission, under Part II of the Inquiries Act, to investigate and report the circumstances in connection with the alleged flogging of Indian pupils recently at Shubenacadie, in The Province of Nova Scotia, 17 September 1934.*

Australia. Department of the Prime Minister and Cabinet. "Closing the Gap – The Prime Minister's Report 2015." http://www.dpmc.gov.au/pmc-indigenous-affairs/publication/closing-gap-prime-ministers-report-2015.

Berger, Thomas R. *Northern Frontier, Northern Homeland: The Report of the Mackenzie Valley Pipeline Inquiry, Volume 1.* Ottawa: Supply and Services Canada, 1977.

Brennan, Shannon. "Violent victimization of Aboriginal women in the Canadian provinces, 2009." *Juristat*, 17 May 2011. Catalogue no. 85-002-x. Ottawa: Statistics Canada, 2011. http://www.statcan.gc.ca/pub/85-002-x/2011001/article/11439-eng.pdf.

British Columbia. Ministry of Justice, Corrections Branch, Aboriginal Programs and Relationships. *Inclusivity: Strategic Plan 2012–2016.* http://www.pssg.gov.bc.ca/corrections/docs/AboriginalStratPlan.pdf.

British Columbia. Office of the Provincial Health Officer. "Health, Crime and Doing Time: Potential Impacts of the *Safe Streets and Communities Act (Former Bill C-10)* on the Health and Well-Being of Aboriginal People in B.C." Vancouver: Office of the Provincial Health Officer, 2013. http://www.health.gov.bc.ca/pho/pdf/health-crime-2013.pdf.

Bryce, P. H. *Report on the Indian Schools of Manitoba and the North-West Territories.* Ottawa: Government Printing Bureau, 1907.

Brzozowski, Jodi-Anne, Andrea Taylor-Butts, and Sara Johnson. "Victimization and offending among the Aboriginal population in Canada." *Juristat* 26, no. 3 (2006). Catalogue no. 85-002-XIE. Ottawa: Statistics Canada, 2006. http://www.statcan.gc.ca/pub/85-002-x/85-002-x2006003-eng.pdf

Canada. Aboriginal Affairs and Northern Development Canada. "Canada's Endorsement of the United Nations Declaration on the Rights of Indigenous Peoples." http://www.aadnc-aandc.gc.ca/eng/1309374807748/1309374897928.

Canada. Aboriginal Affairs and Northern Development Canada. "Commemoration 2011–2012 – Project Descriptions." http://www.aadnc-aandc.gc.ca/eng/1370974213551/1370974338097.

Canada. Aboriginal Affairs and Northern Development Canada. "Commemoration 2012–2013 – Project Descriptions." http://www.aadnc-aandc.gc.ca/eng/1370974253896/1370974471675.

Canada. Aboriginal Affairs and Northern Development Canada. "Remembering the Past: A Window to the Future." http://www.aadnc-aandc.gc.ca/eng/1332859355145/1332859433503.

Canada. Aboriginal Affairs and Northern Development. "Canada's Statement of Support on the United Nations Declaration on the Rights of Indigenous Peoples." 12 November 2010. http://www.aadnc-aandc.gc.ca/eng/1309374239861/1309374546142.

Canada. Aboriginal Affairs and Northern Development. "Jordan's Principle." http://www.aadnc-aandc.gc.ca/eng/1334329827982/1334329861879. (accessed 3 January 2014).

Canada. Auditor General of Canada. *2011 Status Report of the Office of the Auditor General of Canada to the House of Commons. Chapter Four: Programs for First Nations on Reserves.* Ottawa: Office of the Auditor General of Canada, 2011. http://www.oag-bvg.gc.ca/internet/docs/parl_oag_201106_04_e.pdf.

Canada. Canadian Human Rights Commission. *Report on Equality Rights of Aboriginal People.* Ottawa: Government of Canada, 2013.

Canada. Department of Canadian Heritage. *2012–2013 Report on Plans and Priorities.* Ottawa: Canadian Heritage, 2012.

Canada. Department of Justice. Youth Justice Research, *A One-Day Snapshot of Aboriginal Youth in Custody Across Canada: Phase II.* Ottawa: Department of Justice, February 2004. http://www.justice.gc.ca/eng/rp-pr/cj-jp/yj-jj/yj2-jj2/yj2.pdf.

Canada. Governor General David Johnson. Speech delivered at the Symposium in Honour of the Royal Proclamation of 1763. Gatineau, Quebec. 7 October 2013. http://www.gg.ca/document.aspx?id=15345&lan=eng (accessed 5 December 2014).

Canada. Indian Residential Schools Adjudication Secretariat. "Adjudication Secretariat Statistics, from September 19, 2007 to January 31, 2015." http://iap-pei.ca/information/stats-eng.php (accessed 20 February 2015).

Canada. Indian Residential Schools Settlement Agreement. Schedule N. http://www.residential-schoolsettlement.ca/settlement.html (accessed 5 March 2015).

Canada. Law Commission of Canada. *Restoring Dignity: Responding to Child Abuse in Canadian Institutions.* Ottawa: Public Works and Government Services Canada, 2000.

Canada. Library and Archives Canada. "Aboriginal Heritage." http://www.bac-lac.gc.ca/eng/discover/aboriginal-heritage/Pages/introduction.aspx#d.

Canada. Library and Archives Canada. "Collection Development Framework." 30 March 2005. http://www.collectionscanada.gc.ca/obj/003024/f2/003024-e.pdf.

Canada. Library and Archives Canada. "Conducting Research on Residential Schools: A Guide to the Records of the Indian and Inuit Affairs Program and Related Resources at Library and Archives Canada." http://www.collectionscanada.gc.ca/obj/020008/f2/020008-2000-e.pdf.

Canada. Library and Archives Canada. "Native Residential Schools: A Selective Bibliography." http://www.collectionscanada.gc.ca/native-residential/index-e.html.

Canada. Library and Archives Canada. "The Legacy of the Residential School System in Canada: A Selective Bibliography." August 2009. http://www.bac-lac.gc.ca/eng/archives/archives-en/aboriginal-heritage/Pages/residential-schools-bibliography-2009.aspx.

Canada. Library and Archives Canada. Media release. "New Exhibition Reflecting the Uniqueness of the Inuit Experience of Residential Schools Launched at Library and Archives Canada." 4 March 2009. http://www.collectionscanada.gc.ca/013/013-380-e.html.

Canada. Minister of Citizenship and Immigration Canada. *Discover Canada: The Rights and Responsibilities of Citizenship.* 2012. http://www.cic.gc.ca/english/resources/publications/discover/index.asp (accessed 26 March 2015).

Canada. Parks Canada. "Historic Sites and Monuments Board of Canada." http://www.pc.gc.ca/clmhc-hsmbc/comm-board/Transparence-Transparency.aspx.

Canada. Parliament. *House of Commons Debates,* 2 November 2006 (Bev Oda, Minister of Canadian Heritage and Status of Women). http://www.parl.gc.ca/HousePublications/Publication.aspx?Language=E&Mode=1&Parl=39&Ses=1&DocId=2463069.

Canada. Parliament. House of Commons. Standing Committee on Canadian Heritage. 41st Parliament, 1st Session, 5 June 2013. http://www.parl.gc.ca/HousePublications/Publication.aspx?DocId=6209352&Language=E&Mode=1&Parl=41&Ses=1.

Canada. Parliament. Senate. *Debates,* 11 June 2009. http://www.parl.gc.ca/Content/Sen/Chamber/402/Debates/045db_2009-06-11-e.htm#3.

Canada. Parliament. Senate. Standing Senate Committee on Aboriginal Peoples. *Reforming First Nations Education: From Crisis to Hope.* Ottawa: Queen's Printer, 2011.

Canada. Parliament. Senate. Standing Senate Committee on Legal and Constitutional Affairs. *Language Rights in Canada's North: Nunavut's New Official Languages Act: Final Report*. Ottawa: Senate Committees Directorate, June 2009.

Canada. Parliament. Special Joint Committee of the Senate and the House of Commons appointed to examine and consider the Indian Act. Minutes of Proceedings and Evidence, 1946–1948.

Canada. Permanent Mission of Canada to the United Nations. "Canada's Statement on the World Conference on Indigenous Peoples Outcome Document." New York, 22 September 2014. http://www.canadainternational.gc.ca/prmny-mponu/canada_un-canada_onu/statements-declarations/other-autres/2014-09-22_WCIPD-PADD.aspx?lang=eng (accessed 17 March 2015).

Canada. Prime Minister Stephen Harper. "Statement of Apology – to former students of Indian Residential Schools." 11 June 2008. http://www.aadnc-aandc.gc.ca/eng/1100100015644/1100100015649.

Canada. Public Safety Canada, Aboriginal Corrections Policy Unit. *Fetal Alcohol Spectrum Disorder and the Criminal Justice System*. 2010. http://www.publicsafety.gc.ca/cnt/rsrcs/pblctns/ftl-lchl-spctrm/ftl-lchl-spctrm-eng.pdf.

Canada. Royal Canadian Mounted Police. *Missing and Murdered Aboriginal Women: A National Operational Overview*. Cat. no.: PS64-115/2014E-PDF, 2014. http://www.rcmp-grc.gc.ca/pubs/mmaw-faapd-eng.pdf (accessed 31 December 2014).

Canada. Royal Commission on Aboriginal Peoples. *Highlights from the report of the Royal Commission on Aboriginal Peoples: People to People, Nation to Nation*. Ottawa: Minister of Supply and Services Canada, 1996. http://www.aadnc-aandc.gc.ca/eng/1100100014597/1100100014637.

Canada. Royal Commission on Aboriginal Peoples. *Report of the Royal Commission on Aboriginal Peoples*. Ottawa: Minister of Supply and Services Canada, 1996.

Canada. *Statement of the Government of Canada on Indian Policy*. Presented to the first session of the 28th Parliament by the Honourable Jean Chrétien, Minister of Indian Affairs and Northern Development. Ottawa: Queen's Printer, 1969.

Canada. Statistics Canada. "2006 Census Inuit Tables." Catalogue no. 89-636-x. http://www.statcan.gc.ca/pub/89-636-x/89-636-x2008001-eng.htm.

Canada. Statistics Canada. "Aboriginal People in Canada: First Nations People, Metis and Inuit." National Household Survey, 2011. Catalogue no. 99-011-X2011001. Ottawa: Ministry of Industry, 2013. http://www12.statcan.gc.ca/nhs-enm/2011/as-sa/99-011-x/99-011-x2011001-eng.pdf.

Canada. Statistics Canada. "Aboriginal Peoples and Language." National Household Survey (NHS), 2011. Catalogue no. 99-011-X2011003. http://www12.statcan.gc.ca/nhs-enm/2011/as-sa/99-011-x/99-011-x2011003_1-eng.cfm.

Canada. Statistics Canada. "Fact Sheet – 2011 National Household Survey Aboriginal Demographics, Educational Attainment and Labour Market Outcomes." 15 August 2013. https://www.aadnc-aandc.gc.ca/eng/1376329205785/1376329233875.

Canada. Statistics Canada. "Mortality rates among children and teenagers living in Inuit Nunangat, 1994 to 2008." Ottawa: Statistics Canada, 2012. http://www.statcan.gc.ca/pub/82-003-x/2012003/article/11695-eng.htm

Canada. Statistics Canada. "Population reporting an Aboriginal identity, by mother tongue, by province and territory (2006 Census)." 16 January 2008. http://www.statcan.gc.ca/tables-tableaux/sum-som/l01/cst01/demo38a-eng.htm.

Canada. Statistics Canada. "Select health indicators of First Nations people living off reserve, Métis and Inuit, 2007 to 2010." 29 January 2013. http://www.statcan.gc.ca/daily-quotidien/130129/dq130129b-eng.htm.

Canada. Statistics Canada. "The Educational Attainment of Aboriginal People in Canada." *National Household Survey, 2011*. Catalogue no. 99-012-X2011003. https://www12.statcan.gc.ca/nhs-enm/2011/as-sa/99-012-x/99-012-x2011003_3-eng.cfm.

Canada. Statistics Canada. "Youth Court Statistics 2011/2012." *The Daily,* 13 June 2013. http://www.statcan.gc.ca/daily-quotidien/130613/dq130613d-eng.pdf.

Canada. Statistics Canada. *Educational Portrait of Canada, Census Year 2006.* Catalogue no. 97-560-XIE2006001. Ottawa: Statistics Canada, 2006.

Canadian Museum of Civilization and the Canadian War Museum. "Research Strategy." 15 July 2013. http://www.civilization.ca/research-and-collections/files/2013/07/research-strategy.pdf.

Council of Ministers of Education. "Education Ministers Signal Transformation Key to the Future." Press Release. 9 July 2014. http://cmec.ca/278/Press-Releases/Education-Ministers-Signal-Transformation-Key-to-the-Future.html?id_article=826.

Davin, Nicholas Flood. *Report on Industrial Schools for Indians and Half-Breeds.* Report produced for the Minister of the Interior. Ottawa: 1879.

Eyford, Douglas R. "Forging Partnerships, Building Relationships: Aboriginal Canadians and Energy Development." Report to the Prime Minister, November 2013. https://www.nrcan.gc.ca/sites/www.nrcan.gc.ca/files/www/pdf/publications/ForgPart-Online-e.pdf (accessed 26 March 2015).

Fraser, R. D. "Section B: Vital Statistics and Health." In *Historical Statistics of Canada,* edited by F. H. Leachy. Second edition. Ottawa: Statistics Canada, 1983. http://www.statcan.gc.ca/pub/11-516-x/sectionb/4147437-eng.htm.

Indian and Métis Conference, Committee of the Community Welfare Planning Council. *Survey of Canadian History Textbooks.* Winnipeg: Submission to the Curriculum Revision Committee, Manitoba Department of Education, 1964.

LeBeuf, Marcel-Eugène. *The Role of the RCMP during the Indian Residential School System.* Ottawa: Royal Canadian Mounted Police, 2011.

MacPherson, Patricia, and Albert Chudley. *Fetal Alcohol Spectrum Disorder (FASD) in a correctional population: Prevalence, screening, and characteristics.* Ottawa: Correctional Service of Canada, 2011. http://www.publicsafety.gc.ca/lbrr/archives/cn21451-eng.pdf.

Maire, Sinha, editor. "Measuring Violence Against Women: Statistical Trends." Catalogue no. 85-002-X . Ottawa: Statistics Canada, 2013.

Mitten, H. Rae. "Section 9: Fetal Alcohol Spectrum Disorders and the Justice System." The First Nations and Métis Justice Reform Commission Final Report, Volume II. January 2004. http://www.justicereformcomm.sk.ca/volume2/12section9.pdf.

Munch, Christopher. "Youth correctional statistics in Canada, 2010/2011." *Juristat.* Catalogue no. 85-002-X. Ottawa: Statistics Canada, 2012. http://www.statcan.gc.ca/pub/85-002-x/2012001/article/11716-eng.pdf.

Norris, Mary Jane. "Aboriginal Languages in Canada: Emerging Trends and Perspectives on Second Language Acquisition." Catalogue No. 11-008. Ottawa: Statistics Canada, 2007.

Perreault, Samuel. "*Admissions to Youth Correctional Services in Canada 2011–2012." Juristat,* 2014. Catalogue no. 85-002-x. Ottawa : Statisitics Canada, 2014. http://www.statcan.gc.ca/pub/85-002-x/2014001/article/11917-eng.htm#a5.

Perreault, Samuel. "Adult Correctional Services in Canada 2011-2012." *Juristat.* Catalogue no. 85-002-x. Ottawa: Statisitics Canada, 2014. http://www.statcan.gc.ca/pub/85-002-x/2014001/article/11918-eng.htm#a5.

Perreault, Samuel. "Violent victimization of Aboriginal people in the Canadian provinces, 2009." *Juristat*. Catalogue no. 85-002-X. Ottawa: Statistics Canada, 2011. http://www.statcan.gc.ca/pub/85-002-x/2011001/article/11415-eng.pdf.

Quebec. *Rapport de la Commission royale d'enquête sur l'enseignement dans la province de Québec.* Quebec: Government of Quebec, 1966. http://classiques.uqac.ca/contemporains/quebec_commission_parent/rapport_parent_4/rapport_parent_vol_4.pdf (accessed 7 August 2012).

Reed, Micheline, and Peter Morrison. "Adult Correctional Services in Canada 1995–96." *Juristat* 17, no. 4. Catalogue no. 85-002-XPE. Ottawa: Statisitics Canada, 1997. http://www.statcan.gc.ca/pub/85-002-x/85-002-x1997004-eng.pdf.

Rosenthal, Jeffrey S. "Statistical Analysis of Deaths at Residential Schools: Conducted on behalf of the Truth and Reconciliation Commission of Canada." January 2015.

Ryerson, Egerton. "Report on Industrial Schools, 26 May 1847." In *Statistics Respecting Indian Schools*. Ottawa: Government Printing Bureau, 1898.

Ryerson, Egerton. *Report on a System for Public Elementary Instruction for Upper Canada*. Printed by order of the Legislative Assembly of Upper Canada. Montreal: Lovell & Gibson, 1847.

Truth and Reconciliation Commission of Canada and the University of Manitoba. Centre for Truth and Reconciliation Trust Deed, 21 June 2013. http://umanitoba.ca/admin/indigenous_connect/media/IND-00-013-NRCAS-TrustDeed.pdf.

Truth and Reconciliation Commission of Canada. "Atlantic National Event Concept Paper." Halifax, Nova Scotia, 26–29 October 2011. http://www.myrobust.com/websites/atlantic/File/Concept%20Paper%20atlantic%20august%2010%20km_cp%20_3_.pdf.

Truth and Reconciliation Commission of Canada. "Centre for Truth and Reconciliation Administrative Agreement." http://chrr.info/images/stories/Centre_For_Truth_and_Reconciliation_Administrative_Agreement.pdf.

Truth and Reconciliation Commission of Canada. *Educating our Youth* (video). 19 September 2013. http://www.trc.ca/websites/trcinstitution/index.php?p=3 (accessed 10 February 2014).

Truth and Reconciliation Commission of Canada. *Truth and Reconciliation Commission: Interim Report.* Winnipeg: Truth and Reconciliation Commission of Canada, 2012.

United States. Board of Indian Commissioners. *Eighteenth Annual Report of the Board of Indian Commissioners, 1886*. Washington: Government Printing Office, 1887.

United States. Department of the Interior, Office of the Solicitor. Solicitor's Opinions on Native American Issues. http://www.doi.gov/solicitor/opinions.html.

Ziestsma, Danielle. "Aboriginal People Living Off-reserve and the Labour Market: Estimates from the Labour Force Survey, 2008–2009." Catalogue no. 710588-X, no. 2. Ottawa: Statistics Canada, 2010. http://www.statcan.gc.ca/pub/71-588-x/71-588-x2010001-eng.pdf.

6. Legislation

Act to amend the Museums Act in order to establish the Canadian Museum of History, Statutes of Canada, 2013, chapter 38.

An Act respecting Indians [*Indian Act*], *Statutes of Canada* 1951, chapter 29, sections 113–122, 169–172.

Broadcasting Act, Statutes of Canada 1991, chapter 11.

Corrections and Conditional Release Act, Statutes of Canada 1992, chapter 20.

Criminal Code, Statutes of Canada, 1985, chapter C-46.

Great Britain. *Rupert's Land and North-Western Territory Order* (Order of Her Majesty in Council Admitting Rupert's Land and the North-Western Territory into the Union), 23 June 1870. Schedule A, *Rupert's Land Act* 1868, 31–32 Vict., chapter 105 (U.K.). http://www.justice.gc.ca/eng/rp-pr/csj-sjc/constitution/lawreg-loireg/p1t32.html.

Historic Sites and Monuments Act, Statutes of Canada 1985, chapter H4.

Museums Act, Statutes of Canada 1990, chapter 3, section 3.

Physical Activity and Sport Act, Statutes of Canada 2003, chapter 2.

Public Schools Act, Statutes of Manitoba 1954, chapter 215, pages 923–1,114.

Safe Streets and Communities Act, Statutes of Canada 2012, chapter 1.

Youth Criminal Justice Act, Statutes of Canada 2002, chapter 1, section 38(1).

7. Legal Cases

Cloud v. Canada (Attorney General) [2004] OJ 4924, 247 DLR (4th) 667.

Delgamuukw v. British Columbia [1997] 3 SCR 1010.

Fontaine v. Canada (Attorney General) [2011] ONSC 4938.

Fontaine v. Canada (Attorney General) [2013] ONSC 684.

Grassy Narrows First Nation v. Ontario (Natural Resources) [2014] SCC 48.

Guerin v. R. [1984] 2 SCR.

Haida Nation v. British Columbia (Minister of Forests) [2004] 3 SCR 511.

Manitoba Métis Nation Inc. v. Canada (Attorney General) [2013] SCC 14.

Mikisew Cree First Nation v. Canada (Minister of Canadian Heritage) [2005] 3 SCR 388, [2005] SCC 69.

Pictou Landing Band Council v. Canada (Attorney General) [2013] FC 342.

R. v. Comeau [1998] NWTJ 34 (NTSC).

R. v. Constant [2005] Man. QB (Dauphin) (CR03-05-00069).

R. v. Frappier [1990] YJ 163 (Terr. Ct.).

R. v. Gladue [1999] 1 SCR 688.

R. v. Hands [1996] OJ 264.

R. v. Harris [2002] BCCA 152.

R. v. Ipeelee [2012] 1 SCR 433, [2012] SCC 13.

R. v. Leroux [1998] NWTJ 139 (SC).

R. v. Plint [1995] BCJ 3060 (BCSC).

R. v. Smickle [2012] ONSC 602.

R. v. Sparrow [1990] 1 SCR 1075.

R. v. Vanderpeet [1996] 2 SCR 507.

R. v. Maczynski [1997] CanLII 2491 (BCCA) (appeal of sentence).

Rio Tinto Alcan Inc. v. Carrier Sekani Tribal Council [2010] SCC 43, [2010] 2 SCR 650.

S. L. v. Commission scolaire des Chênes [2012] SCC 7.

Tsilhqot'in Nation v. British Columbia [2014] SCC 44.

8. Other Sources

de Greiff, Pablo. *Report of the Special Rapporteur on the promotion of truth, justice, reparations and guarantees on non-recurrence*. New York: United Nations General Assembly, Human Rights Council, 2012. http://www.ohchr.org/Documents/HRBodies/HRCouncil/RegularSession/Session21/A-HRC-21-46_en.pdf.

United Nations General Assembly. "Outcome Document of the high-level plenary meeting of the General Assembly know as the World Conference on Indigenous Peoples." 25 September 2014. http://www.un.org/en/ga/search/view_doc.asp?symbol=A/RES/69/2 (accessed 15 March 2015).

United Nations General Assembly. "Report of the Special Rapporteur on the rights of indigenous peoples, James Anaya, The Situation of Indigenous Peoples in Canada." http://unsr.jamesanaya.org/docs/countries/2014-report-canada-a-hrc-27-52-add-2-en.pdf.

United Nations General Assembly. "United Nations Declaration on the Rights of Indigenous Peoples." Adopted by the General Assembly, 2 October 2007. http://www.un.org/esa/socdev/unpfii/documents/DRIPS_en.pdf (accessed 15 March 2015).

United Nations General Assembly. Human Rights Council. UN Expert Mechanism of the Rights of Indigenous Peoples. "Access to justice in the promotion and protection of the rights of indigenous peoples." 29 April 2013. http://www.ohchr.org/Documents/Issues/IPeoples/EMRIP/Session6/A-HRC-EMRIP-2013-2_en.pdf (accessed 21 March 2015).

United Nations Global Compact. "A Business Reference Guide: United Nations Declaration on the Rights of Indigenous Peoples." New York: UN Global Compact, 2013. https://www.unglobalcompact.org/docs/issues_doc/human_rights/IndigenousPeoples/BusinessGuide.pdf (accessed 26 March 2015).

United Nations. Committee on the Rights of the Child. "Concluding observations on the combined third and fourth periodic report of Canada, adopted by the Committee at its sixty-first session (17 September–5 October 2012)." http://www.unicef.ca/sites/default/files/imce_uploads/TAKE%20ACTION/ADVOCATE/DOCS/uncrc_concluding_observations_for_canada_december_2012.pdf.

United Nations. Economic and Social Council. Permanent Forum on Indigenous Issues. "Study on the impacts of the Doctrine of Discovery on indigenous peoples, including mechanisms, processes, and instruments of redress." Thirteen Session, New York, 12–23 May 2014. http://daccess-dds-ny.un.org/doc/UNDOC/GEN/N14/241/84/PDF/N1424184.pdf (accessed 14 March 2015).

United Nations. Human Rights Council. "Report of the Special Rapporteur in the field of cultural rights, Farida Shaheed. Memorialization processes." 23 January 2014. http://www.ohchr.org/EN/HRBodies/HRC/RegularSessions/Session25/Pages/ListReports.aspx.

United Nations. Office of the High Commissioner for Human Rights. *International Covenant on Civil and Political Rights*, article 27. http://www.ohchr.org/en/professionalinterest/pages/ccpr.aspx.

United Nations. Permanent Forum on Indigenous Issues. "Study on the impacts of the Doctrine of Discovery on indigenous peoples, including mechanisms, processes and instruments of redress." New York, 24 February 2014. http://daccess-dds-ny.un.org/doc/UNDOC/GEN/N14/241/84/PDF/N1424184.pdf?OpenElement (accessed 14 March 2015).

United Nations. Permanent Forum on Indigenous Issues. Joint Statement of the Assembly of First Nations, Chiefs of Ontario, Grand Council of the Crees (Eeyou Istchee), Amnesty International, and the Canadian Friends Service Committee (Quakers), KAIROS: Canadian Ecumenical Justice Initiatives to 11th session of the Permanent Forum on Indigenous Issues, New York, 7–18 May 2012. http://www.afn.ca/uploads/files/pfii_2012_-_doctrine_of_discovery_-_joint_statement_fe.pdf (accessed 20 March 2015).

United Nations. Permanent Observer Mission of the Holy See. Statement to Economic and Social Council, 9th session of the Permanent Forum on Indigenous Issues on Agenda item 7: Discussion on the reports "Impact on Indigenous Peoples of the International Legal construct known as the Doctrine of Discovery, which has served as the Foundation of the Violation of the Human Rights" and "Indigenous Peoples and Boarding Schools: A Comparative Study." New York, 27 April 2010. http://www.ailanyc.org/wp-content/uploads/2010/09/Holy-See.pdf (accessed 20 January 2015).

United Nations. UN Permanent Observer Mission of the Holy See. "A Short History of the Diplomacy of the Holy See." http://www.holyseemission.org/about/history-of-diplomacy-of-the-holy-see.aspx.

Vatican. Communiqué of the Holy See Press Office. 29 April 2009. http://www.vatican.va/resources/resources_canada-first-nations-apr2009_en.html (accessed 22 March 2015).

Vatican. Pastoral Letter of His Holiness Pope Benedict XVI to the Catholics of Ireland, 19 March 2010. http://www.vatican.va/holy_father/benedict_xvi/letters/2010/documents/hf_ben-xvi_let_20100319_church-ireland_en.html (accessed 27 November 2014).

Secondary Sources

1. Books and Published Reports

Aboriginal Peoples' Television Network. *Annual Report*. 2013. http://aptn.ca/corporate/PDFs/APTN_2013_AnnualReport_ENG.pdf.

Ahenakew, Edward. *Voices of the Plains Cree*. Edited by Ruth M. Buck. Toronto: McClelland and Stewart, 1973.

Alfred, Gerald (Taiaiake). *Heeding the Voices of Our Ancestors: Kahnawake Mohawk Politics and the Rise of Native Nationalism*. Toronto: Oxford University Press, 1995.

Amagoalik, John. *Changing the Face of Canada: The Life Story of John Amagoalik*. Edited by Louis McComber. Life Stories of Northern Leaders 2. Iqaluit: Nunavut Arctic College, 2007.

Anderson, Mark Cronlund, and Carmen L. Robertson. *Seeing Red: A History of Natives in Canadian Newspapers*. Winnipeg: University of Manitoba Press, 2011.

Archibald, Linda, with Jonathan Dewar, Carrie Reid, and Vanessa Stevens. *Dancing, Singing, Painting, and Speaking the Healing Story: Healing through Creative Arts*. Ottawa: Aboriginal Healing Foundation, 2012.

Armitage, David. *The Ideological Origins of the British Empire*. Cambridge: Cambridge University Press, 2000.

Assembly of First Nations. "IndigenACTION: Phase One: Roundtable Report." 2012. http://www.afn.ca/uploads/files/indigenaction/indigenactionroundtablereport.pdf.

Assembly of First Nations. *Assembly of First Nations Report on Canada's Dispute Resolution Plan to Compensate for Abuses in Indian Residential Schools*. Ottawa: Assembly of First Nations, 2004.

Assembly of First Nations. *Breaking the Silence: An Interpretive Study of Residential School Impact and Healing as Illustrated by the Stories of First Nation Individuals*. Ottawa: Assembly of First Nations, 1994.

Assembly of First Nations. National Panel on First Nation Elementary and Secondary Education for Students on Reserve. *Nurturing the Learning Spirit of First Nation Students*. National Assembly of First Nations, 2012. http://www.afn.ca/uploads/files/education2/national-panel.pdf.

Assembly of First Nations. *Royal Commission Aboriginal Peoples at 10 Years: A Report Card.* Ottawa: Assembly of First Nations, 2006.

Auger, Donald J. *Indian Residential Schools in Ontario.* Ontario: Nishnawbe Aski Nation, 2005.

Axtell, James. *The Invasion Within: The Contest of Cultures in Colonial North America.* New York: Oxford University Press, 1985.

Baker, Simon. *Khot-La-Cha: The Autobiography of Chief Simon Baker.* Compiled and edited by Verna J. Kirkness. Vancouver: Douglas and McIntyre, 1994.

Banner, Stuart. *How the Indians Lost Their Land: Law and Power on the Frontier.* Cambridge, Massachusetts: The Belknap Press of Harvard University Press, 2005.

Barkan, Elazar, and Alexander Karn, eds. *Taking Wrongs Seriously: Apologies and Reconciliation.* Stanford, California: Stanford University Press, 2006.

Barron, Laurie F. *Walking in Indian Moccasins: The Native Policies of Tommy Douglas and the CCF.* Vancouver: University of British Columbia Press, 1997.

Bartels, Dennis A., and Alice L. Bartels. *When the North was Red.* Montreal and Kingston: McGill-Queen's University Press, 1995.

Battiste, Marie. *Decolonizing Education: Nourishing the Learning Spirit.* Saskatoon: Purich Publishing, 2013.

Bayly, C. A. *The Birth of the Modern World: 1780–1914.* Oxford: Blackwell Publishing, 2004.

Blackstock, C., T. Prakash, J. Loxley, F. Wien. *Wen:de: We are Coming to the Light of Day.* Ottawa: First Nations Child and Family Caring Society of Canada, 2005.

Bloch, Alexia. *Red Ties and Residential Schools: Indigenous Siberians in a Post-Soviet State.* Philadelphia: University of Pennsylvania Press, 2004.

Blue Quills First Nations College. *Pimohteskanaw, 1971–2001: Blue Quills First Nations College.* St. Paul, Alberta: Blue Quills First Nations College, 2002.

Bodnar, John. *Remaking America: Public Memory, Commemoration and Patriotism in the Twentieth Century.* Princeton: Princeton University Press, 1992.

Bolt, Clarence. *Thomas Crosby and the Tsimshian: Small Shoes for Feet Too Large.* Vancouver: University of British Columbia Press, 1992.

Booth, W. James. *Communities of Memory: On Witness, Identity, and Justice.* Ithaca, New York: Cornell University Press, 2006.

Borrows, John. *Canada's Indigenous Constitution.* Toronto: University of Toronto Press, 2010.

Borrows, John. *Recovering Canada: The Resurgence of Indigenous Law.* Toronto: University of Toronto Press, 2002.

Brass, Eleanor. *I Walk in Two Worlds.* Calgary: Glenbow Museum, 1987.

Bruno-Jofre, Rosa. *The Missionary Oblate Sisters: Vision and Mission.* Montreal and Kingston: McGill-Queen's University Press, 2005.

Bryce, P. H. *The Story of a National Crime: Being an Appeal for Justice to the Indians of Canada; the Wards of the Nation, Our Allies in the Revolutionary War, Our Brothers-in-Arms in the Great War.* Ottawa: James Hope and Sons, 1922.

Buck, Ruth Matheson. *The Doctor Rode Side-Saddle.* Toronto: McClelland and Stewart, 1974.

Bush, Peter. *Western Challenge: The Presbyterian Church in Canada's Mission on the Prairies and North, 1885–1925.* Winnipeg: Watson and Dwyer Publishing, 2000.

Butcher, Margaret. *The Letters of Margaret Butcher: Missionary-Imperialism on the North Pacific Coast.* Edited by Mary-Ellen Kelm. Calgary: University of Calgary Press, 2006.

Campbell, Sue. *Our Faithfulness to the Past: The Ethics and Politics of Memory.* Edited by Christine M. Koggel and Rockney Jacobsen. New York: Oxford University Press, 2014.

Canadian Bar Association. *Submission on Bill C-10: Safe Streets and Communities Act*. Ottawa: Canadian Bar Association, October 2011. http://www.cba.org/cba/submissions/PDF/11-45-eng.pdf.

Canadian Welfare Council. *Indian Residential Schools: A Research Study of the Child Care Programs of Nine Residential Schools in Saskatchewan*. Prepared for the Department of Indian Affairs and Northern Development. Ottawa: Canadian Welfare Council, 1967.

Canadien, Albert. *From Lishamie*. Penticton: Theytus Books, Limited, 2010.

Carter, Sarah. *Lost Harvests: Prairie Indian Reserve Farmers and Government Policy*. Montreal and Kingston: McGill-Queen's University Press, 1990.

CBC-Radio Canada. "Going the Distance: Annual Report 2013–2014." http://www.cbc.radio-canada.ca/_files/cbcrc/documents/annual-report/2013-2014/cbc-radio-canada-annual-report-2013-2014.pdf.

Centre for Youth and Society. "Residential Schools Resistance Narratives: Strategies and Significance for Indigenous Youth." University of Victoria, 27 March 2012. Research report prepared for the Truth and Reconciliation Commission of Canada.

Chamberlin, J. Edward. *If This is Your Land, Where are Your Stories? Finding Common Ground*. Toronto: Alfred A. Knopf Canada, 2003.

Chansonneuve, Deborah. *Addictive Behaviours Among Aboriginal People in Canada*. Ottawa: Aboriginal Healing Foundation, 2007.

Charrette on Energy, Environment and Aboriginal Issues, The. "Responsible Energy Resource Development in Canada: Summary of the Dialogue of the Charrette on Energy, Environment and Aboriginal Issues." December 2013. http://www.boldon.org/pdf/EnergyCharrette.pdf.

Chartrand, Larry N., Tricia E. Logan, and Judy D. Daniels. *Métis History and Experience and Residential Schools in Canada*. Ottawa: Aboriginal Healing Foundation, 2006.

Choquette, Robert. *Canada's Religions: An Historical Introduction*. Ottawa: University of Ottawa Press, 2004.

Choquette, Robert. *The Oblate Assault on Canada's Northwest*. Ottawa: University of Ottawa Press, 1995.

Coates, Kenneth, and Dwight Newman. "The End is Not Nigh: Reason over Alarmism in Analysing the *Tsilhqot'in* Decision." Ottawa: MacDonald Laurier Institute, September 2014. http://www.macdonaldlaurier.ca/files/pdf/MLITheEndIsNotNigh.pdf.

Coates, Kenneth. *A Global History of Indigenous Peoples: Struggle and Survival*. Basingstoke, England: Palgrave Macmillan, 2004.

Coccola, Nicolas. *They Call Me Father: Memoirs of Father Nicolas Coccola*. Edited by Margaret Whitehead. Vancouver: University of British Columbia Press, 1988.

Cohen, Cynthia E., Roberto Gutiérrez Varea, and Polly O. Walker, editors. *Acting Together: Performance and the Creative Transformation of Conflict*. Volumes 1 and 2. Oakland, California: New Village Press, 2011.

Cole, Douglas, and Ira Chaikin. *An Iron Hand Upon the People: The Law Against the Potlatch on the Northwest Coast*. Vancouver: Douglas and McIntyre, 1990.

Cronin, Kay. *Cross in the Wilderness*. Vancouver: Mitchell Press, 1960.

Daschuk, James. *Clearing the Plains: Disease, Politics of Starvation and the Loss of Aboriginal Life*. Regina: University of Regina Press, 2013.

David, Jennifer. "Aboriginal Languages Broadcasting in Canada: An Overview and Recommendations to the Task Force on Aboriginal Languages and Cultures." Report for Aboriginal Peoples

Television Network. 2004. http://aptn.ca/corporate/PDFs/Aboriginal_Language_and_Broadcasting_2004.pdf.

Dewar, Jonathan, David Gaertner, Ayumi Goto, Ashok Mathur, and Sophie McCall. "Practicing Reconciliation: a collaborative study of Aboriginal art, resistance and cultural politics." Report commissioned by the Truth and Reconciliation Commission on Indian Residential Schools, 2013.

Diffie, Bailey W., and George D. Winius. *Foundations of the Portuguese Empire, 1415–1580*. Minneapolis: University of Minnesota Press, 1978.

Dion, Joseph F. *My Tribe the Crees*. Edited and with an introduction by Hugh Dempsey. Second edition. Calgary: Glenbow Museum, 1996.

Duchaussois, J. R. *The Grey Nuns in the Far North (1867–1917)*. Toronto: McClelland and Stewart, 1919.

Elliott, John H. *Empires of the Atlantic World: Britain and Spain in America, 1492–1830*. New Haven, Connecticut: Yale University Press, 2007.

Erasmus, Peter. *Buffalo Days and Nights*. Calgary: Fifth House Publishers, 1999. First published 1976 by Glenbow-Alberta Institute.

Fear-Segal, Jacqueline. *White Man's Club: Schools, Race, and the Struggle of Indian Acculturation*. Lincoln: University of Nebraska, 2007.

First Nations Centre. *First Nations Regional Longitudinal Health Survey (RHS) 2002/03*. Ottawa: First Nations Centre, 2005.

First Nations Education Council (FNEC), Quebec, Nishnawbe Aski Nation (NAN), Federation of Saskatchewan Indian Nations (FSIN). *Report on Priority Actions in View of Improving First Nations Education*. November 2011. http://www.fsin.com/index.php/downloads-education/708-report-on-priority-actions-in-view-of-improving-first-nations-education.

First Nations Education Council. *Funding Formula for First Nation Schools: The Instrument of a Detrimental Policy*. 2009. http://www.cepn-fnec.com/PDF/etudes_documents/fiche_complete_eng.pdf.

Fisher, Robin. *Contact and Conflict: Indian-European Relations in British Columbia, 1774–1890*. Second edition. Vancouver: University of British Columbia Press, 1992.

Fisher, Robin. *Contact and Conflict: Indian–European Relations in British Columbia, 1774–1890*. Vancouver: University of British Columbia Press, 1992.

Fontaine, Theodore. *Broken Circle: The Dark Legacy of Indian Residential Schools*. Vancouver: Heritage House, 2010.

French, Alice. *My Name Is Masak*. Winnipeg: Peguis Publishers, 1976.

Frichner, Tonya Gonnella. *Preliminary Study of the Impact on Indigenous Peoples of the International Legal Construct Known as the Doctrine of Discovery*. New York: United Nations, Permanent Forum on Indigenous Issues, 2010.

Gagan, Rosemary R. *A Sensitive Independence: Canadian Methodist Women Missionaries in Canada and the Orient, 1881–1925*. Montreal and Kingston: McGill-Queen's University Press, 1992.

Getty, A. L., and Antoine S. Lussier. *As Long as the Sun Shines and Water Flows: A Reader in Canadian Native Studies*. Vancouver: University of British Columbia Press, 1983.

Goodwill, Jean, and Norma Sluman. *John Tootoosis*. Winnipeg: Pemmican Publications, 1984.

Gordon, Mary. *Roots of Empathy: Changing the World Child by Child*. New York: The Experiment, 2009.

Graham, Elizabeth. *The Mush Hole: Life at Two Indian Residential Schools*. Waterloo: Heffle Publishing, 1997.

Hamilton, W. D. *The Federal Indian Day Schools of the Maritimes*. Fredericton, New Brunswick: Micmac-Maliseet Institute, University of New Brunswick, 1986.

Head, Edmund Walker, Froome Talfourd, Thomas Worthington, and Richard T. Pennefather. *Report of the Special Commissioners appointed on the 8th of September 1856, to Investigate Indian Affairs in Canada*. Toronto: Stewart Derbishire and George Desbarats, 1858.

Hobsbawm, E. J. *On Empire: America, War and Global Supremacy*. New York: Pantheon Books, 2008.

Hodgson-Smith, Kathy. *The State of Métis Nation Learning*. Canadian Council on Learning, 2005. http://www.ccl-cca.ca/pdfs/AbLKC/StateOfMetisNationLearning.pdf.

Howe, Stephen. *Empire: A Very Short Introduction*. Oxford: Oxford University Press, 2002.

Huel, Raymond J. A. *Proclaiming the Gospel to the Indians and Métis*. Edmonton: University of Alberta Press, 1996.

Hughes, Kenneth James, and Jackson Beardy. *Jackson Beardy, Life and Art*. Winnipeg: Canadian Dimension Publishers, 1979.

Hyam, Ronald. *Britain's Imperial Century, 1815–1914: A Study of Empire and Expansion*. Third edition. Basingstoke, England: Palgrave Macmillan, 2002.

Indian Chiefs of Alberta. *Citizens Plus*. 1970. Reprinted in *Aboriginal Policy Studies* 1, no. 2 (2011): 188–281.

Istvanffy, Jay. *Gladue Primer*. Vancouver: Legal Services Society, BC, 2001. http://resources.lss.bc.ca/pdfs/pubs/Gladue-Primer-eng.pdf.

Jaenen, Cornelius. *Friend and Foe Aspects of French-Amerindian Cultural Contact in the Sixteenth and Seventeenth Centuries*. Toronto: McClelland and Stewart, 1976.

Johnston, Sheila M. F. *Buckskin & Broadcloth: A Celebration of E. Pauline Johnson Tekahionwake, 1861–1913*. Toronto: Natural Heritage/Natural History, 1997.

Journalists for Human Rights. "Buried Voices: Media Coverage of Aboriginal Issues in Ontario – Media Monitoring Report, 2010-2013." August 2013. http://www.documentcloud.org/documents/784473-media-coverage-of-aboriginal-issues.html#document/p1.

Kino-nda-niimi Collective. *The Winter We Danced: Voices from the Past, the Future, and the Idle No More Movement.* Winnipeg: Arbeiter Ring Publishing, 2014.

Kirkness, Verna J. *Creating Space: My Life and Work in Indigenous Education*. Winnipeg: University of Manitoba Press, 2013.

Kirmayer, Laurence, Gregory Brass, Tara Holton, Ken Paul, Cori Simpson, Caroline Tait. *Suicide Among Aboriginal People in Canada.* Ottawa: Aboriginal Healing Foundation, 2007.

LaViolette, Forrest. *The Struggle for Survival: Indian Cultures and the Protestant Ethic in British Columbia*, Toronto: University of Toronto Press, 1961.

Loxley, John, Linda DeRiviere, Tara Prakash, Cindy Blackstock, Fred Wien, and Shelley Thomas Prokop. *Wen:de: The Journey Continues.* Ottawa: First Nations Child and Family Caring Society of Canada, 2005.

Lux, Maureen K. *Medicine that Walks: Disease, Medicine and Canadian Plains Native People, 1880–1940*. Toronto: University of Toronto Press, 2001.

MacDonald, David, and Daniel Wilson. *Poverty or Prosperity: Indigenous Children in Canada.* Ottawa: Canadian Centre for Policy Alternatives, 2013.

MacGregor, Roy. *Chief: The Fearless Vision of Billy Diamond*. Toronto: Viking, 1989.

Magnuson, Roger. *Education in New France*. Montreal, Kingston: McGill-Queen's University Press, 1992.

Marks, Don. *They Call Me Chief: Warriors on Ice*. Winnipeg: J. Gordon Shillingford, 2008.

McCarthy, Martha. *From the Great River to the Ends of the Earth: Oblate Missions to the Dene, 1847–1921.* Edmonton: University of Alberta Press; Western Canadian Publishers, 1995.

McGregor, Heather E. *Inuit Education and Schools in the Eastern Arctic.* Vancouver: University of British Columbia Press, 2010.

McMillan, Alan D., and Eldon Yellowhorn. *First Peoples in Canada.* Vancouver and Toronto: Douglas & McIntyre, 2004.

McNally, Vincent J. *The Lord's Distant Vineyard: A History of the Oblates and the Catholic Community in British Columbia.* Edmonton: University of Alberta Press, 2000.

McNally, Vincent J. *The Lord's Distant Vineyard: A History of the Oblates and the Catholic Community in British Columbia.* Edmonton: University of Alberta Press, 2000.

Miller, J. R. *Compact, Contract, Covenant: Aboriginal Treaty Making in Canada.* Toronto: University of Toronto Press, 2009.

Miller, J. R. *Lethal Legacy: Current Native Controversies in Canada.* Toronto: McClelland and Stewart, 2004.

Miller, J. R. *Skyscrapers Hide the Heavens: A History of Indian-White Relations in Canada.* Second edition. Toronto: University of Toronto Press, 2000.

Miller, Robert J. et al. *Discovering Indigenous Lands: The Doctrine of Discovery in the English Colonies.* Oxford, New York: Oxford University Press, 2012.

Moine, Louise. *My Life in a Residential School.* Saskatchewan: Provincial Chapter Imperial Order of Daughters of the Empire, Saskatchewan, in Cooperation with the Provincial Library of Saskatchewan, 1975.

Montour, Enos. *Brown Tom's Schooldays.* Edited by Elizabeth Graham. Waterloo, Ontario: The Author, 1985.

Moorhouse, Geoffrey. *The Missionaries.* Philadelphia and New York: J. B. Lippincott Company, 1973.

Moran, Bridget. *Stoney Creek Woman: The Story of Mary John.* Vancouver: Arsenal Pulp Press, 1997.

Morley, Alan. *Roar of the Breakers: A biography of Peter Kelly.* Toronto: Ryerson Press, 1967.

Morris, Alexander. *The treaties of Canada with the Indians of Manitoba and the North-West Territories, Including the Negotiations on which they were Based, and Other Information Relating thereto.* Saskatoon: Fifth House Publishers, 1991. First published, Toronto: Belfords, Clarke and Company, 1880.

Moseley, Christopher; Nicolas, Alexandre; UNESCO. *Atlas of the World's Languages in Danger* 3rd ed. Paris: UNESCO Publishing, 2010.

National Collaborating Centre for Aboriginal Health, *Child and Youth Health: Child Welfare Services in Canada: Aboriginal and Mainstream.* Prince George: National Collaborating Centre for Aboriginal Health, 2009.

National Collaborating Centre for Aboriginal Health. *Looking for Aboriginal Health in Legislation and Policies, 1970 to 2008: The Policy Synthesis Project.* Prince George: National Collaborating Centre for Aboriginal Health, 2011.

National Committee on Inuit Education. *First Canadians, Canadians First: National Strategy on Inuit Education.* National Committee on Inuit Education, 2011. https://www.itk.ca/sites/default/files/National-Strategy-on-Inuit-Education-2011_0.pdf.

National Indian Brotherhood. *Indian Control of Indian Education: Policy Paper Presented to the Minister of Indian Affairs and Northern Development.* Ottawa: National Indian Brotherhood, 1972.

Native Women's Association of Canada. *Voices of Our Sisters in Spirit: A Report to Families and Communities.* Second edition. March 2009. http://www.nwac.ca/sites/default/files/download/admin/NWAC_VoicesofOurSistersInSpiritII_March2009FINAL.pdf.

Newcomb, Steven T. *Pagans in the Promised Land: Decoding the Doctrine of Christian Discovery.* Golden, Colorado: Fulcrum Publishing, 2008.

Newman, Dwight. *The Rule and Role of Law: The Duty to Consult, Aboriginal Communities, and the Canadian Natural Resource Sector.* Ottawa: MacDonald-Laurier Institute, May 2014. http://www.macdonaldlaurier.ca/files/pdf/DutyToConsult-Final.pdf.

Newman, Morton. *Indians of the Saddle Lake Reserve.* Edmonton: Human Resources and Development Council, 1967.

Ngugi wa Thiong'o. *Dreams in a Time of War A Childhood Memoir.* London: Vintage Books, 2011.

Nobles, Melissa. *The Politics of Official Apologies.* Cambridge: Cambridge University Press, 2008.

Ontario Provincial Advocate for Children and Youth. *Feathers of Hope: A First Nations Youth Action Plan.* 2014. http://www.inspiritfoundation.org/files/6114/0656/0111/Feathers-of-Hope_report.pdf.

Opp, James, and John C. Walsh. *Placing Memory and Remembering Place in Canada.* Vancouver: University of British Columbia Press, 2010.

Ospina, Maria, and Liz Dennett. *Systematic Review on the Prevalence of Fetal Alcohol Spectrum Disorders.* Edmonton: Institute of Health Economics, 2013.

Pagden, Anthony. *Peoples and Empires: A Short History of European Migration and Conquest from Greece to the Present.* New York: Modern Library, 2001.

Pagden, Anthony. *Spanish Imperialism and the Political Imagination: Studies in European and Spanish-American Social and Political Theory, 1513–1830.* New Haven, Connecticut: Yale University Press, 1990.

Pagden, Anthony. *The Lords of All the World: Ideologies of Empire in Spain, Britain and France c. 1500–c. 1800.* New Haven, Connecticut: Yale University Press, 1995.

Paquette, Jerry, and Gérald Fallon. *First Nations Education Policy in Canada: Progress or Gridlock.* Toronto: University of Toronto Press, 2010.

Parker, R. A. *Uprooted: The Shipment of Poor Children to Canada, 1867–1917.* Bristol, UK: Policy Press, 2010.

Peake, Frank A. *The Bishop Who Ate His Boots: A Biography of Isaac O. Stringer.* Toronto: Anglican Church of Canada, 1966.

Pertusati, Linda. In Defense of Mohawk Land: *Ethnopolitical Conflict in Native North America.* Albany, NY: SUNY Press, 1997.

Pettipas, Katherine. *Severing the Ties that Bind: Government Repression of Indigenous Ceremonies on the Prairies.* Winnipeg: University of Manitoba Press, 1994.

Prairie Women's Health Centre of Excellence. *Nitâpwewininân: Ongoing Effects of Residential Schools on Aboriginal Women—Towards Inter-Generational Reconciliation.* Final Report to the Truth and Reconciliation Commission of Canada. March 2012.

Presbyterian Church in Canada. *Acts and Proceedings of the 137th General Assembly of The Presbyterian Church in Canada.* 2011.

Primrose, A. P. (5th Earl of Rosebery). *Australian speechlets, 1883–84.*

Public Policy Forum. *Building Authentic Partnerships: Aboriginal Participation in Major Resource Development Opportunities.* Ottawa: Public Policy Forum, 2012. http://www.ppforum.ca/sites/default/files/Aboriginal%20Participation%20in%20Major%20Resource%20Development_ENG_3.pdf.

Quassa, Paul. *We Need to Know Who We Are: The Life Story of Paul Quassa*. Edited by Louis McComber. Translated by Letia Qiatsuk. Life Stories of Northern Leaders, Volume 3. Iqaluit: Nunavut Arctic College, 2008.

Quiring, David M. *CCF Colonialism in Northern Saskatchewan: Battling Parish Priests, Bootleggers and Fur Sharks*. Vancouver: University of British Columbia Press, 2004.

Ray, Arthur J. *An Illustrated History of Canada's Native People: I have lived here since the world began*. Toronto: Key Porter, 2010.

Ray, Arthur J., Jim Miller and Frank Tough. Bounty and Benevolence: *A History of Saskatchewan Treaties.* Montreal and Kingston: McGill-Queens University Press, 2000.

Regan, Paulette. *Unsettling the Settler Within: Indian Residential Schools, Truth Telling and Reconciliation in Canada*. Vancouver: University of British Columbia Press, 2010.

Richards, John, Jennifer Hove, and Kemi Afolabi. *Understanding the Aboriginal/Non-Aboriginal Gap in Student Performance: Lessons from British Columbia*. Toronto: CD Howe Institute, 2008. http://www.cdhowe.org/pdf/commentary_276.pdf.

Rompkey, William. *The Story of Labrador*. Montreal and Kingston: McGill-Queen's University Press, 2003.

Schirch, Lisa. *Ritual and Symbol in Peacebuilding*. Bloomfield, CT: Kumarian Press, 2005.

Seed, Patricia. *Ceremonies of Possession in Europe's Conquest of the New World, 1492–1640*. Cambridge, Massachusetts: Cambridge University Press, 1995.

Seixas, Peter, and Jill Colyer. "A Report on the National Meeting of the Historical Thinking Project." 15–17 January 2013. http://historicalthinking.ca/sites/default/files/files/docs/HTP2013Report.pdf (accessed 15 April 2015).

Shanahan, David F. *The Jesuit Residential School at Spanish: "More than Mere Talent."* Toronto: Canadian Institute of Jesuit Studies, 2004.

Sharpe, Andrew, Jean-François Arsenault, Simon Lapointe and Fraser Cowan. *The Effect of Increasing Aboriginal Educational Attainment on the Labour Force, Output and the Fiscal Imbalance.* Ottawa: Centre for the Study of Living Standards, 2009.

Shea, Goldie. *Institutional Child Abuse in Canada: Criminal Cases*. Ottawa: Law Commission of Canada, 1999.

Simpson, Leanne, and Kiera L. Ladner, editors. *This is an Honour Song: Twenty Years Since the Blockades, An Anthology of Writing on the Oka Crisis.* Winnipeg: Arbeiter Ring, 2010.

Simpson, Leanne. *Dancing on Our Turtle's Back: Stories of Nishnaabeg Re-Creation, Resurgence and a New Emergence.* Winnipeg: Arbeiter Ring Publishing, 2011.

Sinha, Vandna, and Nico Trocmé, Barbara Fallon, Bruce MacLaurin, Elizabeth Fast, Shelley Thomas Prokop, et al. *Kiskisik Awasisak: Remember the Children: Understanding the Overrepresentation of First Nations Children in the Child Welfare System*. Ontario: Assembly of First Nations, 2011.

Snow, John. *These Mountains are our Sacred Places: The Story of the Stoney Indians*. Toronto: Samuel Stevens, 1977.

Sport Canada. "Canadian Sport Policy Renewal, Round Table on Sport and Aboriginal Peoples, Summary Report." 15 July 2011. https://sirc.ca/sites/default/files/content/docs/pdf/aboriginal.pdf.

Sprague, D. N. *Canada's Treaties with Aboriginal People*. Winnipeg: University of Manitoba, Faculty of law, Canadian Legal History Project, 1991.

Standing Bear, Luther. *My People the Sioux*, Boston: Houghton Mifflin Company, 1928.

Stocken, H. W. Gibbon. *Among the Blackfoot and Sarcee*. Introduction by Georgeen Barrass. Calgary: Glenbow Museum, 1976.

Sutherland, Neil. *Children in English-Canadian Society: Framing the Twentieth-Century Consensus*. Waterloo: Wilfrid Laurier University Press, 2000.

Tait, Caroline L. *Fetal Alcohol Syndrome among Aboriginal People in Canada: Review and Analysis of the Intergenerational Links to Residential Schools*. Ottawa: Aboriginal Healing Foundation, 2003.

Tavuchis, Nicholas. *Mea Culpa: A Sociology of Apology and Reconciliation*. Stanford: Stanford University Press, 1991.

Treaty 7 Tribal Council, Walter Hildebrandt, Sarah Carter and Dorothy First Rider. *The True Spirit and Original Intent of Treaty 7*. Montreal and Kingston: McGill-Queens University Press, 1996.

Trudel, Marcel. *The Beginnings of New France: 1524–1663*. Toronto: McClelland and Stewart, 1973.

Usher, Jean. *William Duncan of Metlakatla: A Victorian Missionary in British Columbia*. Publications in History 9. Ottawa: National Museums of Canada, 1974.

Vanderburgh, Rosamond M. *The Canadian Indian in Ontario's School Texts: A study of Social Studies textbooks, Grade 1 through 8*. Port Credit, Ontario: University Women's Club of Port Credit, Study Group on the Canadian Indian Eskimo, 1968.

Venne, Sharon H., editor. *Indian Acts and Amendments 1868–1975, An Indexed Collection*. Saskatoon: University of Saskatchewan, Native Law Centre, 1981.

Waldram, James B. *The Way of the Pipe: Aboriginal Spirituality and Symbolic Healing in Canadian Prisons*. Peterborough, ON: Broadview Press, 1997.

Waldram, James, D. Ann Herring, and T. Kue Young. *Aboriginal Health in Canada: Historical, Cultural, and Epidemiological Perspectives*. Second edition. Toronto: University of Toronto Press, 2006.

Weaver, Sally M. *Making Canadian Indian Policy: The Hidden Agenda, 1968–70*. Toronto: University of Toronto Press, 1981.

Wherrett, George Jasper. *The Miracle of the Empty Beds: A History of Tuberculosis in Canada*. Toronto: University of Toronto Press, 1977.

Williams Jr., Robert A. *Savage Anxieties: The Invention of Western Civilization*. New York: Palgrave MacMillan, 2012.

Williams Jr., Robert A. *The American Indian in Western Legal Thought: The Discourses of Conquest*. New York: Oxford University Press, 1990.

Wilson, Daniel, and David Macdonald. *The Income Gap Between Aboriginal Peoples and the Rest of Canada*. Ottawa: Canadian Centre for Policy Alternatives, 2010.

Wilson, E. F. *Missionary work among the Ojebway Indians*. London, 1886.

Wood, Ellen Meiksins. *Empire of Capital*. New York: Verso Books, 2003.

Wood, Ellen Meiksins. *The Origin of Capitalism: A Longer View*. London: Verso Books, 2002.

2. Book Chapters and Articles

Adams, Ian. "The Indians: An Abandoned and Dispossessed People." *Weekend Magazine* 15, no. 31 (31 July 1965).

Alfred, Taiaiake, and Lana Lowe, "Warrior Societies in Contemporary Indigenous Communities." Research paper for the Ipperwash Inquiry, 2007. http://www.attorneygeneral.jus.gov.on.ca/

inquiries/ipperwash/policy_part/research/pdf/Alfred_and_Lowe.pdf (accessed 22 February 2015).

Anaya, S. James. "The Right of Indigenous Peoples to Self-Determination in the Post-Declaration Era." In *Making the Declaration Work: The United Nations Declaration on the Rights of Indigenous Peoples*, edited by Claire Charters and Rodolfo Stavenhagen, 184–198. Copenhagen: International Work Group for Indigenous Affairs, 2009.

Atwood, Barbara. "The Voice of the Indian Child: Strengthening the Indian Child Welfare Act Through Children's Participation." *Arizona Law Review* 50, no.1 (2008): 127–156

Banner, Stuart. "Why Terra Nullius? Anthropology and Property Law in Early Australia." *Law and History Review 23, no. 1 (*Spring 2005): *95–132.*

Barron, F. Laurie. "The Indian Pass System in the Canadian West, 1882–1935." *Prairie Forum* 13, no. 1 (Spring 1988): 25–42.

Blondin-Andrew, Ethel. "New Ways of Looking for Leadership." In *Leading in an Upside-Down World: New Canadian Perspectives on Leadership*, edited by J. Patrick Boyer, 59–70. Toronto: Dundurn Press, 2003.

Boler, Megan, and Michalinos Zembylas. "Discomforting Truths: The Emotional Terrain of Understanding Difference." In *Pedagogies of Difference: Rethinking Education for Social Change*, edited by Peter Pericles Trifonas, 110–136. New York: Routledge Falmer, 2003.

Bolton, Stephanie. "Museums Taken to Task: Representing First Peoples at the McCord Museum of Canadian History." In *First Nations, First Thoughts: The Impact of Indigenous Thought in Canada*, edited by Annis May Timpson, 145–169. Vancouver: University of British Columbia Press, 2009.

Bonta, J., Carol LaPrairie, and S. Wallace-Capretta. "Risk Prediction and Re-offending: Aboriginal and non-Aboriginal Offenders." *Canadian Journal of Criminology* 39, no. 2 (1997): 127–144.

Borrows, John. "Wampum at Niagara: The Royal Proclamation, Canadian Legal History, and Self-Government." In *Aboriginal and Treaty Rights in Canada: Essays on Law, Equality and Respect for Difference*, edited by Michael Asch, 155–172. Vancouver: University of British Columbia Press, 1997.

Bougie, Evelyne, and Sacha Senecal. "Registered Indian Children's School Success and Intergenerational Effects of Residential Schooling in Canada." *International Indigenous Policy Journal* 1, no. 1 (2010). http://ir.lib.uwo.ca/iipj/vol1/iss1/5.

Boyer, Yvonne. "Aboriginal Health: A Constitutional Rights Analysis." National Aboriginal Health Organization, Discussion Paper Series in Aboriginal Health: Legal Issues. No. 1. Saskatoon: Native Law Centre. Ottawa: National Aboriginal Health Organization. 2003.

Brown, Judith. "Economic Organization and the Position of Women among the Iroquois." *Ethnohistory* 17 (1970): 151–167.

Buchanan, Rachel. "Decolonizing the Archives: The Work of New Zealand's Waitangi Tribunal." *Public History Review* 14 (2007): 44–63.

Bush, Peter. "How Have the Churches Lived Out Their Apologies." Research report prepared for Truth and Reconciliation Commission of Canada, 2012.

Campbell, Sue. "Remembering for the Future: Memory as a Lens on the Indian Residential School Truth and Reconciliation Commission." Discussion paper prepared for the Truth and Reconciliation Commission of Canada, April 2008.

Canadian Medical Association. "Aboriginal health programming under siege, critics charge." *Canadian Medical Association Journal* 184, no. 14 (2012).

Carney, Robert. "The Grey Nuns and the Children of Holy Angels: Fort Chipewyan, 1874–1924." In *Proceedings of the Fort Chipewyan and Fort Vermilion Bicentennial Conference*, edited by P. A.

McCormack and R. Geoffrey Ironside. Edmonton: Boreal Institute for Northern Studies, University of Alberta, 1990.

Castellano, Marlene Brant, Linda Archibald, and Mike DeGagné. "Introduction: Aboriginal Truths in the Narrative of Canada." In *From Truth to Reconciliation: Transforming the Legacy of Residential Schools*, edited by Marlene Brant Castellano, Linda Archibald, and Mike DeGagne, 1–8. Ottawa: Aboriginal Healing Foundation, 2008.

Chartrand, Larry N. "Métis Residential School Participation: A Literature Review." In *Métis History and Experience and Residential Schools in Canada*, by Larry N. Chartrand, Tricia E. Logan, and Judy D. Daniels, 5–55. Ottawa: Aboriginal Healing Foundation, 2006.

Clark, Penney. "Representations of Aboriginal People in English Canadian History Textbooks: Toward Reconciliation." In *Teaching the Violent Past: History Education and Reconciliation*, edited by Elizabeth A. Cole, 81–120. Lanham, Maryland: Rowman and Littlefield, 2007.

Cook, Terry. "Evidence, memory, identity, and community: four shifting archival paradigms." *Archival Science: International Journal on Recorded Information* 13, nos. 2–3 (2013): 95–120.

Corntassel, Jeff, et al., "Indigenous story-telling, truth-telling and community approaches to reconciliation." *ESC: English Studies in Canada* 35, no. 1 (2009): 137–159.

Côté, M. M. "*St. Albert, Cradle of the Catholic Church in Alberta.*" *Canadian Catholic Historical Association Report* 32 (1965): 29–35.

Cradock, Gerald. "Extraordinary Costs and Jurisdictional Disputes." In *Wen: De: We are Coming to the Light of Day*, 178–207. *Ottawa:* First Nations Child and Family Caring Society of Canada, 2005.

Crutcher, Nicole, and Shelley Trevethan. "An Examination of Healing Lodges for Aboriginal Offenders in Canada." *Forum on Corrections Research* 14, no. 3 (2002): 52–54.

Cuthand, Stan. "The Native Peoples of the Prairie Provinces in the 1920s and 1930s." In *Sweet Promises: A Reader on Indian-White Relations in Canada*, edited by J. R. Miller, 381–392. Toronto: University of Toronto Press, 1991.

de Greiff, Pablo. "The Role of Apologies in National Reconciliation Processes: On Making Trustworthy Institutions Trustworthy." In *The Age of Apology: Facing Up to the Past*, edited by Mark Gibney, Rhoda E. Howard-Hassmann, Jean-Marc Coicaud, and Niklaus Steiner, 120–136. Philadelphia: University of Pennsylvania Press, 2008.

Driver, Felix. "Discipline Without Frontiers? Representations of the Mettray Reformatory Colony in Britain, 1840–1880." *Journal of Historical Sociology* 3 (September 1990): 272–93.

Dumont, Alf, and Roger Hutchinson. "United Church Mission Goals and First Nations Peoples," in *The United Church of Canada: A History*, edited by Don Schweitzer, 221–238. Waterloo: Wilfred Laurier University Press, 2011.

Elias, Lillian. "Lillian Elias." In *We Were So Far Away: The Inuit Experience of Residential Schools*, 47–62. Ottawa: Legacy of Hope, 2010.

Erickson, Lesley. "'Bury Our Sorrows in the Sacred Heart': Gender and the Métis Response to Colonialism—the Case of Sara and Louis Riel, 1848–83." In *Unsettled Pasts: Reconceiving the West through Women's History*, edited by Sarah Carter, Lesley Erickson, Patricia Roome, and Char Smith, 17–46. Calgary: University of Calgary Press, 2005.

Fingard, Judith. "The New England Company and the New Brunswick Indians, 1786–1826: A Comment on Colonial Perversion British Benevolence." *Acadiensis* 1, no. 2 (Spring 1972): 29–42.

First Nations Education Council. "Paper on First Nations Education Funding." Wendake, Quebec: First Nations Education Council, 2009.

Fiske, Jo-Anne. "Fishing Is Women's Business: Changing Economic Roles of Carrier Women and Men." In *Native Peoples, Native Lands: Canadian Indians, Inuit and Metis*, edited by Bruce Cox, 186–198. Ottawa: Carleton University Press, 1987.

Fletcher, Matthew. "The Origins of the Indian Child Welfare Act: A Survey of the Legislative History." Michigan State University College of Law, Indigenous Law and Policy Center Occasional Paper 2009-04. 10 April 2009.

Friesen, Jean. "Magnificent Gifts: The Treaties of Canada with the Indians of the Northwest 1869–1876." In *The Spirit of the Alberta Indian Treaties*, edited by Richard T. Price, 203–13. Edmonton: University of Alberta Press, 1999.

Garneau, David. "Imaginary Spaces of Conciliation and Reconciliation." *West Coast Line* 74 (Summer 2012): 28–38.

Grant, John W. "Two-Thirds of the Revenue: Presbyterian Women and Native Indian Missions." In *Changing Roles of Women within the Christian Church in Canad*a, edited by E. G. Muir and M. F. Whiteley, 99–116. Toronto: University of Toronto Press, 1995.

Gresko, Jacqueline. "Everyday Life at Qu'Appelle Industrial School." In *Western Oblate Studies 2*, edited by Raymond Huel, 71–94. Lewiston, New York: Edwin Mellon Press, 1992.

Hare, Jan, and Barman, Jean. "Good Intentions Gone Awry: From Protection to Confinement in Emma Crosby's Home for Aboriginal Girls." In *With Good Intentions: EuroCanadian and Aboriginal Relations in Colonial Canada*, edited by D. Nock and C. Haig-Brown, 179–198. Vancouver: University of British Columbia Press, 2006.

Harris, Verne, "The Archival Sliver: Power, Memory, and Archives in South Africa." *Archival Science* 2, nos. 1–2 (2002): 63–86.

Hepburn, D. W. "Northern Education: Facade for Failure." *Variables: The Journal of the Sociology Club* (University of Alberta) 2, no. 1 (February 1963): 16–21.

Immordino-Yang, M.H., and Antonio Damasio. "We feel, therefore we learn: The relevance of affective and social neuroscience to education." *Mind, Brain, and Education* 1 (2007): 3–10.

Jaenen, Cornelius J. "Education for Francization: The Case of New France in the Seventeenth Century." In *Indian Education in Canada. Volume 1, The Legacy*, edited by Jean Barman, Yvonne Hebert, and Don McCaskill, 45–63. Vancouver: University of British Columbia Press, 1986.

James, Matt. "Wrestling with the Past: Apologies, Quasi-Apologies, and Non-Apologies in Canada." In *The Age of Apology: Facing Up to the Past*, edited by Mark Gibney, Rhoda E. Howard-Hassmann, Jean-Marc Coicaud, and Niklaus Steiner, 137–153. Philadelphia: University of Pennsylvania Press, 2008.

Jimerson, Randall C. "Archives for All: Professional Responsibility and Social Justice." *American Archivist* 70 (2007): 252–281.

Johns, Robert. "A History of St Peter's Mission and of Education in Hay River, NWT Prior to 1950." *Musk Ox* 13 (1973): 22–32.

Johnston, Darlene. "Aboriginal Traditions of Tolerance and Reparation: Introducing Canadian Colonialism." In *Le Devoir de Memoire et les Politiques du Pardon*, edited by Micheline Labelle, Rachad Antoinius, and Georges Leroux, 141–159. Quebec: Presses de l'Universite de Quebec, 2005.

Kelly, Fred. "Confession of a Born Again Pagan." In *From Truth to Reconciliation: Transforming the Legacy of Residential Schools*, edited by Marlene Brant Castellano, Linda Archibald and Mike DeGagne, 13–40. Ottawa: Aboriginal Healing Foundation, 2008.

Kelm, Mary-Ellen. "Introduction." In *The Letters of Margaret Butcher: Missionary-Imperialism on the North Pacific Coast*, by Margaret Butcher, xi–xxxi. Edited by Mary-Ellen Kelm. Calgary: University of Calgary Press, 2006.

Klein, Laura. "Mother as Clanswoman: Rank and Gender in Tlingit Society." In *Women and Power in Native North America*, edited by Laura Klein and Lillian Ackerman, 28–45. Norman: University of Oklahoma Press, 1995

Krech, Shepard, III. "Nutritional Evaluation of a Mission Residential School Diet: The Accuracy of Informant Recall." *Human Organization* 37 (1978): 186–190.

Kulchyski, Peter. "'A Considerable Unrest': F. O. Loft and the League of Indians." *Native Studies Review* 4, nos. 1–2 (1988): 95–117.

Lleweyn, Jennifer. "Dealing with the Legacy of Native Residential School Abuse in Canada: Litigation, ADR and Restorative Justice." *University of Toronto Law Journal* 52 (2002): 253–300.

MacKenzie, Ian. "For Everything There is a Season." In *Response, Responsibility, and Renewal: Canada's Truth and Reconciliation Journey*, edited by Gregory Younging, Jonathan Dewar, and Mike DeGagne, 87–96. Ottawa: Aboriginal Healing Foundation, 2009.

Mandryk, Murray. "Uneasy Neighbours: White-Aboriginal relations and agricultural decline." In *Writing Off the Rural West: Globalization, Governments and the Transformation of Rural Communities*, edited by Roger Epp and Dave Whitson, 205–221. Edmonton: University of Albert Press with the Parkland Institute, 2001.

Sison, Marites N. "Primate's Commission begins work." *Anglican Journal*, 2 May 2014. http://www.anglicanjournal.com/articles/primate-s-commission-begins-work.

Mason, Courtney, and Joshua Koehli. "Barriers to Physical Activity for Aboriginal Youth: Implications for Community Health, Policy and Culture." *Pimatisiwin: A Journal of Aboriginal and Indigenous Community Health* 10, no. 1 (2012): 97–107.

McCue, Harvey. "First Nations 2nd and 3rd Level Education Services: A Discussion Paper for the Joint Working Group INAC-AFN." 2006. http://www.afn.ca/uploads/files/education/9._2006_april_harvey_mccue_first_nations_2nd_&_3rd_level_services_paper.pdf.

McKay, Stan. "Expanding the Dialogue on Truth and Reconciliation—In a good way." In *From Truth to Reconciliation: Transforming the Legacy of Residential Schools*, edited by Marlene Brant Castellano, Linda Archibald and Mike DeGagne, 103–115. Ottawa: Aboriginal Healing Foundation, 2008.

McKay, Stan. "Expanding the Dialogue on Truth and Reconciliation—In a good way." In *From Truth to Reconciliation: Transforming the Legacy of Residential Schools*, edited by Marlene Brant Castellano, Linda Archibald, and Mike DeGagne, 103–115. Ottawa: Aboriginal Healing Foundation, 2008.

McKenzie, Brad, and Pete Hudson. "Native Children, Child Welfare, and the Colonization of Native People." In *The Challenge of Child Welfare*, edited by Ken Levitt and Brian Wharf, 125–141. Vancouver: University of British Columbia Press, 1985.

Miller, John. "Ipperwash and the Media: A critical analysis of how the story was covered." Report prepared for Aboriginal Legal Services of Toronto, October 2005. http://www.attorneygeneral.jus.gov.on.ca/inquiries/ipperwash/policy_part/projects/pdf/ALST_Ipperwash_and_media.pdf (accessed 28 February 2015).

Morse, Bradford W. "Indigenous human rights and knowledge in archives, museums and libraries: Some International Perspectives with specific reference to New Zealand and Canada." *Archival Science* 12, no. 2 (2012): 113–140.

Nielson, Marianne O. "Canadian Aboriginal Healing Lodges: A Model for the United States?" *Prison Journal* 83, no. 1 (March 2003): 67–89.

Penny, Chris. "Formal Educational Attainment of Inuit in Canada, 1981–2006." In *Aboriginal Education: Current Crisis and Future Alternatives,* edited by Jerry P. White, et. al., 33–47. Toronto: Thompson Educational Publishing, 2009.

Perry, Adele. "Metropolitan Knowledge, Colonial Practice, and Indigenous Womenhood." In *Contact Zones: Aboriginal and Settler Women in Canada's Colonial Past,* edited by Myra Rutherdale and Katie Pickles. Vancouver: University of British Columbia Press, 2005.

Qwul'sih'yah'maht (Robina Anne Thomas). "Honouring the Oral Traditions of My Ancestors through Storytelling." In *Research as Resistance: Critical, Indigenous, and Anti-Oppressive Approaches,* edited by Leslie Brown and Susan Strega, 237–254. Toronto: Canadian Scholars Press/ Women's Press, 2005.

Reid, Jennifer. "The Roman Catholic Foundations of Land Claims in Canada." *Historical Papers 2009: Canadian Society of Church History* (2009): 5–19. http://pi.library.yorku.ca/ojs/index.php/historicalpapers/article/viewFile/39133/35490.

Renaud, André. "Indian education today." *Anthropologica* (1958): 1–49.

Robertson, Kirsty. "Threads of Hope: The Living Healing Quilt Project," *ESC: English Studies in Canada* 35, no. 1 (March 2009): 85–107.

Ruben, Abraham. "Abraham Ruben." In *We Were So Far Away: The Inuit Experience of Residential Schools,* edited by Heather L. Igloliorte. Ottawa: Legacy of Hope Foundation, 2010.

Ruiz-Casares, M., et al. "Supervisory neglect and risk of harm. Evidence from the Canadian Child Welfare System." *Child Abuse and Neglect* 36, no. 6 (2012): 471–480.

Sadowski, Edward G. "Preliminary report on the investigation into missing school files for the Shingwauk Indian Residential School." Algoma University College, Shingwauk Project Archives, November 2006.

Schonert-Reichl, K. A., and S. Hymel. "Educating the heart as well as the mind: Social and emotional learning for school and life success." *Education Canada* 47, 2 (2007): 20–25.

Sheppard, Maia G. "Creating a Caring Classroom in which to Teach Difficult Histories." *The History Teacher* 43, no. 3 (May 2010): 411–426.

Simon, Roger. "Towards a Hopeful Practice of Worrying: The Problematics of Listening and the Educative Responsibilities of Canada's Truth and Reconciliation Commission." In *Reconciling Canada: Critical Perspectives on the Culture of Redress,* edited by Jennifer Henderson and Pauline Wakeham, 129–142. Toronto: University of Toronto Press, 2013.

Sinha, V., and A. Kozlowski. "The Structure of Aboriginal Child Welfare in Canada." *International Indigenous Policy Journal* 4 no. 2 (2013): article 2. http://ir.lib.uwo.ca/iipj/vol4/iss2/2.

Sluman, Norma. "The Text Book Indian." *Toronto Education Quarterly* 5, no. 3 (1967).

Smylie, J. "A Review of Aboriginal Infant Mortality Rates in Canada: Striking and Persistent Aboriginal/Non-Aboriginal Inequities." *Canadian Journal of Public Health* 101 no. 2 (2010): 143–148.

Stanley, George F. G. "Alberta's Half-Breed Reserve Saint-Paul-des Métis, 1896–1909." In *The Other Natives: The Metis, vol. 2,* edited by A. S. Lussier and D. B. Sealey, 75–107. Winnipeg: Manitoba Metis Federation Press, 1978.

Stanton, Kim. "Canada's Truth and Reconciliation Commission: Settling the Past?" *International Indigenous Policy Journal* 2, issue 3 (2011): 1–18. http://ir.lib.uwo.ca/cgi/viewcontent.cgi?article=1034&context=iipj.

Stevenson, Winona. "The Red River Indian Mission School and John West's 'Little Charges' 1820–1833." *Native Studies Review* 4, nos. 1–2 (1988): 129–65.

Stonechild, Blair. "The Indian View of the 1885 Uprising." In *Sweet Promises: A reader on Indian-White Relations in Canada*, edited by J. R. Miller, 259–76. Toronto: University of Toronto Press, 1991.

Taylor, J. Garth. "Northern Algonquians on the Frontiers of 'New Ontario,' 1890–1945." In *Aboriginal Ontario: Historical Perspectives on the First Nations*, edited by Edward S. Rogers and Donald B. Smith. Toronto: Dundurn Press, 1994.

Taylor, John Leonard. "Canada's Northwest Indian Policy in the 1870s: Traditional Premises and Necessary Innovations." In *The Spirit of the Alberta Indian Treaties*, edited by Richard T. Price, 3–7. Edmonton: University of Alberta Press, 1999.

Te Hiwi, Braden P. "'What is the Spirit of this Gathering?' Indigenous Sport Policy-Makers and Self-Determination in Canada." *International Indigenous Policy Journal* 5, issue 4 (October 2014): 1–16.

Thomas, Robina Anne (Qwul'sih'yah'maht). "Honouring the Oral Traditions of My Ancestors through Storytelling." In *Research as Resistance: Critical, Indigenous, and Anti-Oppressive Approaches*, edited by Leslie Brown and Susan Strega, 237–54. Toronto: Canadian Scholars Press/ Women's Press, 2005.

Tobias, John L. "Protection, Civilization, Assimilation: An Outline History of Canada's Indian Policy." In *Sweet Promises: A Reader on Indian-White Relations in Canada*, edited by J. R. Miller. Toronto: University of Toronto Press, 1991.

Upton, L. F. S. "The Origins of Canadian Indian Policy." *Journal of Canadian Studies* 8, no. 4 (November 1973): 51–60.

Valaskakis, Gail Guthrie. "Rights and Warriors: Media Memories and Oka." In *Indian Country: Essays on Contemporary Native Culture*, edited by Gail Guthrie Valaskakis, 35–65. Waterloo: Wilfred Laurier University Press, 2005.

Van Camp, Rosa. "Bishop Paul Piché." *Arctic Profiles* 42, no. 2 (1989): 168–170.

van Erven, Eugene, and Kate Gardner. "Performing Cross-Cultural Conversations: Creating New Kinships through Community Theatre." In *Acting Together: Performance and the Creative Transformation of Conflict. Vol. 2: Building Just and Inclusive Communities*, edited by Cynthia E. Cohen, Roberto Gutierrez Varea, and Polly O. Walker, 9–41. Oakland, California: New Village Press, 2011.

Wien, Fred, Cindy Blackstock, John Loxley, and Nico Trocmè. "Keeping First Nations Children at Home: A Few Federal Policy Changes could make a Big Difference." *First Peoples Child and Family Review* 3, no. 1 (2007): 10–14.

Wilk, Piotr, Jerry P. White, and Éric Guimond. "Métis Educational Attainment." In *Aboriginal Education: Current Crisis and Future Alternatives*, edited by Jerry P. White, et al., 49–67. Toronto: Thompson Educational Publishing, 2009.

Wilson, Ian E. "Peace, Order and Good Government: Archives in Society." *Archival Science: International Journal on Recorded Information* 12, issue 2 (2012): 235–244.

Wolfe, Patrick. "Settler Colonialism and the Elimination of the Native." *Journal of Genocide Research* 8, no. 4 (2006): 387–409.

3. Newspapers and Broadcast Media

Aboriginal Peoples' Television Network. "Cree Community Bans FNs Spirituality." 17 January 2011. http://aptn.ca/news/2011/01/17/crees-ban-sweat-lodges-fns-spirituality-from-community/.

Adams, Ian. "The Lonely Death of Charlie Wenjack." *Maclean's* (February 1967): 30–44.

BasicNews.ca. "Two-Row Wampum Centers Idle No More Toronto Rally, Not the Royal Proclamation." 9 October 2013. http://basicsnews.ca/2013/10/two-row-wampum-centers-idle-no-more-toronto-rally-not-the-royal-proclamation/.

Brantford Expositor. "Damages for Plaintiff in Miller vs. Ashton Case." 1 April 1914.

Brean, Joseph. "'Reconciliation' with First Nations, Not the Charter of Rights & Freedoms, Will Define the Supreme Court in Coming years, Chief Justice Says." *National Post*, 13 March 2014. http://news.nationalpost.com/2014/03/13/reconciliation-with-first-nations-not-the-charter-of-rights-freedoms-will-define-the-supreme-court-in-coming-years-chief-justice-says/

Brent Jang. "Gas Exports from B.C. Seen as Key to Reviving Pipeline. *Globe and Mail,* 2 February 2014. http://www.theglobeandmail.com/report-on-business/industry-news/energy-and-resources/gas-exports-from-bc-said-key-to-reviving-pipeline/article16657138/

CBC News, Manitoba. "Teacher Seeks Healing Through Truth Commission." 18 June 2010. http://www.cbc.ca/news/canada/manitoba/story/2010/06/18/mb-truth-reconciliation-healing-teachers-winnipeg.html.

CBC News. "6 Landmark Rulings on Native Rights." 8 January 2013. http://www.cbc.ca/news/canada/6-landmark-rulings-on-native-rights-1.1316961.

CBC News. "Civilization Museum Now the Canadian Museum of History." 12 December 2013. http://www.cbc.ca/news/canada/ottawa/civilization-museum-now-the-canadian-museum-of-history-1.2461738.

CBC News. "Ex-residential school worker convicted of abusing boys." 5 November 2013. http://www.cbc.ca/news/canada/saskatchewan/ex-residential-school-worker-convicted-of-abusing-boys-1.2415810.

CBC News. "Murdered and Missing Aboriginal Women Deserve Inquiry, Rights Group Says." 12 January 2015. http://www.cbc.ca/news/politics/murdered-and-missing-aboriginal-women-deserve-inquiry-rights-group-says-1.2897707.

CBC News. "Nun guilty in residential school assaults." 28 December 1998. http://www.cbc.ca/news/canada/nun-guilty-in-residential-school-assaults-1.166827.

CBC News. "Paul Leroux gets 3 years for residential school abuse." 12 December 2013. http://www.cbc.ca/news/canada/saskatoon/paul-leroux-gets-3-years-for-residential-school-abuse-1.2461629.

CBC News. "Pope Expresses 'Sorrow' for Abuse at Residential Schools." 29 April 2009. http://www.cbc.ca/news/world/pope-expresses-sorrow-for-abuse-at-residential-schools-1.778019.

CBC News. "Residential School Day Scholars Launch Class-action Lawsuit." 16 August 2012. http://www.cbc.ca/news/canada/british-columbia/residential-school-day-scholars-launch-class-action-lawsuit-1.1146607.

CBC News. "Sixties Scoop Case Moves Forward as Class-action Lawsuit." 3 December 2014. http://www.cbc.ca/news/canada/thunder-bay/sixties-scoop-case-moves-forward-as-class-action-lawsuit-1.2859332.

CBC News. "Women's Memorial March in Vancouver Attracts Hundreds." 14 February 2015. http://www.cbc.ca/news/canada/british-columbia/womens-memorial-march-in-vancouver-attracts-hundreds-1.2957930.

Coates, Ken S. "Aboriginal Women Deserve Much More than an Inquiry." *National Post*, 16 February 2015. http://news.nationalpost.com/2015/02/16/ken-s-coates-aboriginal-women-deserve-much-more-than-an-inquiry/.

Daily News (Halifax). "Bernard's Lawsuit helped natives nationwide." 30 December 2007. http://www.canada.com/story_print.html?id=983a8b88-a8ac-4e09-9e5c-b2c0e207ac3d.

Edmiston, Jake. "Indian Residential Schools or Settler Colonial Genocide? Native Group Slams Human Rights Museum Over Exhibit Wording." *National Post*, 8 June 2013. http://news.nationalpost.com/news/canada/indian-residential-schools-or-settler-colonial-genocide.

Edmonton Journal. "Deaths of Alberta Aboriginal Children in Care no 'Fluke of Statistics.'" 8 January 2014. http://www.edmontonjournal.com/life/Deaths+Alberta+aboriginal+children+care+-fluke+statistics/9212384/story.html.

Edmonton Journal. "Demolition of former residential school called for to put bad memories to rest." 13 August 1998.

Edmonton Journal. "Indians will operate Blue Quills School." 1 August 1970.

Edmonton Journal. "Nun forced native students to eat their own vomit." 25 June 1999.

Edwards, Peter. "'This is about reuniting a family, even in death.'" *Toronto Star*, 4 March 2011. http://www.thestar.com/news/gta/2011/03/04/this_is_about_reuniting_a_family_even_in_death.html.

Edwards, Peter. "Star gets action: Charlie Hunter headed home." *Toronto Star*, 24 March 2011. http://www.thestar.com/news/gta/2011/03/24/star_gets_action_charlie_hunter_headed_home.html.

Gazette: Law Society of Upper Canada. "Law Society Throws Support Behind Reconciliation Initiatives." 11 December 2014. http://www.lawsocietygazette.ca/news/law-society-throws-support-behind-reconciliation-initiatives/.

Gleeson, Richard. "Four years for sex assault." Northern News Services, 8 August 1997. http://www.nnsl.com/frames/newspapers/1997-08/aug8_97jail.html.

Hale, Alan S. "Treaty 3 Holds Commemoration Ceremony for Survivors of District Residential School System." *Kenora Daily Miner and News*, 25 March 2014.

Hunter, Carrie. "Education Centre set to re-open." *Prince Albert Herald*, 15 October 1997.

Indian Country Today Media Network. "Christian Crees Tear Down Sweat Lodge." 7 February 2011. http://indiancountrytodaymedianetwork.com/2011/02/07/christian-crees-tear-down-sweat-lodge-15500.

Kenora Miner and News. "2 boys died from exposure." 18 December 1970.

Kenora Miner and News. "Inquest hears tragic tale of runaway boy." 18 November 1966.

Kinew, Wab. "It's the Same Great Spirit." *Winnipeg Free Press*, 22 October 2012. http://www.winnipegfreepress.com/local/its-the-same—great-spirit-175193351.html.

LaRose, Stephen. "Wrecker's ball claims White Calf Collegiate." *Saskatchewan Sage* 3, issue 8 (1999). http://www.ammsa.com/publications/saskatchewan-sage/wreckers-ball-claims-white-calf-collegiate-0.

Lavoie, Judith. "Paintings Bear Witness to Residential Schools' Harsh Life." *Victoria Times-Colonist*, 31 March 2013.

Lee, Jeff. "Tsilhqot'in Nation Strikes Conciliatory Note with Municipalities." *Vancouver Sun*, 24 September 2014.

Lewis, Jeff. "Northwest Territories Eyes Revival of Mackenzie Valley Pipeline Project." *Financial Post*, 11 June 2013. http://business.financialpost.com/2013/06/11/northwest-territories-eyes-revival-of-mackenzie-valley-pipeline-project/?__lsa=c5d4-608a.

Lewis, Jeff. "TransCanada CEO Says Canada Needs to Resolve Conflicts over Pipelines." *Globe and Mail*, 4 February 2015. http://www.theglobeandmail.com/report-on-business/economy/transcanada-ceo-says-canada-needs-to-resolve-conflicts-over-pipelines/article22798276/.

MacDonald, Michael. "Shale Gas Conflict in New Brunswick Underscores Historical Grievances, Rights of First Nations." *Toronto Star*, 25 December 2013. http://www.thestar.com/news/canada/2013/12/25/shale_gas_conflict_in_new_brunswick_underscores_historic_grievances_rights_of_first_nations.html.

Mehta, Diana. "'Sixties Scoop' Class-action Lawsuit to Proceed." Canadian Press, 4 December 2014. http://www.ctvnews.ca/canada/60s-scoop-class-action-lawsuit-to-proceed-1.2132317.

Moore, Dene. "Federal Appeal Court Gives Ok on Hearing First Nations' Day-school Suit." Canadian Press, 4 March 2014. http://www.ctvnews.ca/canada/federal-appeal-court-gives-ok-on-hearing-first-nations-day-school-suit-1.1713809.

Ostrem, Dawn. "Back to court: Paul Leroux challenges convictions, sentence." Northern News Services, 26 June 1997. http://www.nnsl.com/frames/newspapers/2000-06/jun26_00back.html.

Pigott, Catherine. "The Leadership Factory: Grandin College never turned out a priest or a nun, but it produced an elite North of 60." *National Post*, 4 December 1999.

Porter, Jody. "Remains Found Near Residential School Are 'Non-human.'" CBC News, 12 July 2012. http://www.cbc.ca/news/canada/thunder-bay/remains-found-near-residential-school-are-non-human-1.1249599.

Ratuski, Andrea. "Residential School Art Series Awarded to U of M." CBC News, 24 September 2013. http://www.cbc.ca/news/canada/manitoba/scene/residential-school-art-series-awarded-to-u-of-m-1.1865994.

Raven, Andrew. "Grollier Hall supervisor sentenced." Northern News Services, 20 August 2004. http://www.nnsl.com/frames/newspapers/2004-08/aug20_04crt.html.

Rees, Ann. "Priest's victims admit sexual abuse." *The Province* (Vancouver), 19 July 1989.

Rennie, Steve. "Idle No More Protestors Mark 25th Anniversary of Royal Proclamation." Canadian Press, 7 October 2013. http://www.thestar.com/news/canada/2013/10/07/idle_no_more_protesters_mark_250th_anniversary_of_royal_proclamation.html.

Salinas, Eva. "Four-year hunt ends in arrest." *Globe and Mail*, 3 August 2006. http://www.theglobeandmail.com/news/national/four-year-hunt-ends-in-arrest/article713735/.

Saskatoon Star-Phoenix. "Former Students File Suit Over Sexual, Physical Abuse." 26 November 1996.

Schwartz, Daniel, and Mark Gollom. "NB Fracking Protests and the Fight for Aboriginal Rights." CBC News, 19 October 2013. http://www.cbc.ca/news/canada/n-b-fracking-protests-and-the-fight-for-aboriginal-rights-1.2126515.

Steel, Debora. "Alberni Residential Students Reunited With Childhood Art." *Ha-Shilth-Sa*, 2 April 2013. http://www.hashilthsa.com/news/2013-04-03/alberni-indian-residential-students-reunited-childhood-art.

Struzik, Ed. "Priest's sordid past shocks parish: Father Houston was declared dangerous sex offender, sent to prison in 1962." *Edmonton Journal*, 6 June 2002.

Taylor, Glenn. "Arrest in Grollier Hall sex case: Former boys supervisor faces 32 counts of sexual assault on his student." Northern News Services, 16 June 1997. http://www.nnsl.com/frames/newspapers/1997-06/jun16_97sex.html.

Taylor, Glenn. "Grollier man pleads not guilty to sex offences." Northern News Services. 28 November 1997. http://www.nnsl.com/frames/newspapers/1997-11/nov28_97sex.html.

Thompson, Roxanna. "Dehcho Hall to close its doors." Northern News Services online, 26 January 2009. http://www.nnsl.com/frames/newspapers/2009-01/jan26_09h.html.

University of Manitoba. "Historic Agreement Signed on National Aboriginal Day." 21 June 2013. http://umanitoba.ca/news/blogs/blog/2013/06/21/historic-agreement-signed-on-national-aboriginal-day/.

University of Winnipeg. "UWinnipeg Healing Quilt Gifted to TRC Commissioners." 17 June 2010. http://www.uwinnipeg.ca/index/uw-news-action/story.364/title.uwinnipeg-healing-quilt-gifted-to-trc-commissioners-.

Vancouver Province. "Historic Children's Paintings on Display at the BC National Event Learning Centre." 15 September 2013. http://www.theprovince.com/entertainment/Historic+children+paintings/8914210/story.html.

Vancouver Sun. "School sex assaults bring jail." 4 October 1996.

Victoria Times-Colonist. "Former employee of residential school jailed for sex abuses." 24 January 2004.

Windspeaker. "Man sentenced to five years for sexually assaulting Native girls." Volume 12, Issue 20 (1995). http://www.ammsa.com/publications/windspeaker/man-sentenced-five-years-sexually-assaulting-native-girls.

Winnipeg Free Press. "Find Body of Indian Girl, Long Missing." 17 April 1930.

Winnipeg Free Press. "Missing Birtle Girl Is Not Yet Found." 28 March 1930.

4. Online Sources

Amnesty International Canada, et al. "Canada uses World Conference to continue indefensible attack on UN Declaration on the Rights of Indigenous Peoples." 24 September 2014. http://www.fns.bc.ca/pdf/Joint_Public_Statement_re_Canada_attack_on_UNDRIP_Sept_24_2014.pdf (accessed 17 March 2015).

Anglican Church of Canada. "A Message to the Church Concerning the Primate's Commission on Discovery, Reconciliation and Justice." http://www.anglican.ca/primate/communications/commission-on-discovery-reconciliation-justice/ (accessed 20 March 2015).

Anglican Church of Canada. "A New Agape: Plan of Anglican work in support of a new partnership between Indigenous and non-Indigenous Anglicans." http://www.anglican.ca/about/ccc/acip/a-new-agape/ (accessed 22 March 2015).

Anglican Church of Canada. "Learning to call one another friends: The Primate's Commission on Discovery, Justice and Reconciliation." June 2014. http://www.anglican.ca/primate/files/2014/06/PCDRJ_June2014_Update.pdf (acccessed 20 March 2015).

Anglican Church of Canada. General Synod. "Bishop Horden Memorial School, Moose Factory Island, ON." 2008. http://www.anglican.ca/relationships/histories/bishop-horden (accessed 4 April 2015).

Anglican Church of Canada. General Synod. "Resolution A086 R1: Repudiate the Doctrine of Discovery." 2010. http://archive.anglican.ca/gs2010/resolutions/a086/ (accessed 19 March 2015).

Anglican Church of Canada. Mission and Justice Relationships. "Truth and Reconciliation." http://www.anglican.ca/relationships/trc.

Belcourt, Christi. Speech at dedication ceremony for the stained glass window on Parliament Hill. Ottawa, Ontario. 26 November 2012. https://www.aadnc-aandc.gc.ca/eng/1370613921985/1370613942308.

Benedictine Sisters of Mount Angel. "About Us: A Brief History of the Benedictine Sisters of Mt. Angel." http://www.benedictine-srs.org/history.html (accessed 12 June 2014).

Canadian Catholic Aboriginal Council. "Mandate." http://www.cccb.ca/site/eng/commissions-committees-and-aboriginal-council/aboriginal-council/canadian-catholic-aboriginal-council (accessed 22 March 2015).

Canadian Conference of Catholic Bishops. "Let Justice Flow Like a Mighty River: Brief to the Royal Commission on Aboriginal Peoples." 8 November 1993. http://www.cccb.ca/site/images/stories/pdf/let_justice_flow_like_a_mighty_river.pdf (accessed 22 March 2015).

Canadian Museum for Human Rights. President and CEO Stuart Murray. Speech delivered at "2017 Starts Now " Forum. 3 May 2013. https://humanrights.ca/about-museum/news/speech-delivered-cmhr-president-and-ceo-stuart-murray-2017-starts-nowdebute (accessed 15 April 2015).

Canadian Museum for Human Rights. President and CEO Stuart Murray. "Use of 'Genocide' in relation to treatment of Indigenous peoples in Canada." 26 July 2013. http://museumforhumanrights.ca/about-museum/news/statement-president-and-ceo-use-genocide-relation-treatment-indigenous-peoples.

Canadian Museum for Human Rights. President and CEO Stuart Murray. Speech to the Truth and Reconciliation Commission of Canada's National Research Centre Forum. Vancouver, BC. 3 March 2011. https://humanrights.ca/about-museum/news/speech-delivered-president-and-ceo-stuart-murray-truth-and-reconciliation.

City of Vancouver. "Framework for City of Reconciliation." Report from City Manager to Vancouver City Council, 18 September 2014. http://former.vancouver.ca/ctyclerk/cclerk/20141028/documents/rr1.pdf.

Fast, Vera K. "Amelia Le Sueur (Yeomans)." In *Dictionary of Canadian Biography* Online. http://www.biographi.ca/009004-119.01-e.php?BioId=41653 (accessed 26 May 2013).

First Nations Summit. "Royal Proclamation still relevant on 250th Anniversary." 2013. http://www.fns.bc.ca/pdf/FNS_Op-ed_re_250th_anniver_of_Royal_Proclamation_10_07_13.pdf (accessed 5 December 2014).

Gresko, Jacqueline. "Paul Durieu." In *Dictionary of Canadian Biography* Online. http://www.biographi.ca/en/bio/durieu_paul_12E.html (accessed 31 August 2014).

Hiltz, Fred. "A Step Along the Path: Apology by Archbishop Fred Hiltz." 6 August 1993. http://www.anglican.ca/relationships/files/2011/06/Apology-English.pdf (accessed 27 October 2014).

Institute for Women's and Gender Studies, University of Winnipeg. "TRC Quilting Project: Education and Art." http://www.iwgs.ca/projects-a-publications/projects/118-healing-quilt-project-winter-2010.

International Center for Transitional Justice. "Our Legacy, Our Hope" (video). 20 June 2012. http://www.youtube.com/watch?v=Xz2SUV0vFCI.

International Center for Transitional Justice. "Youth Reporters Tell the Story of Residential Schools." 18 November 2011. http://ictj.org/news/youth-reporters-tell-story-residential-schools.

International Centre for Transitional Justice. "Canada TRC Youth Retreat" (video). http://vimeo.com/26397248 (accessed 2 March 2015).

International Centre for Transitional Justice. "ICTJ Program Report: Children and Youth." 2 August 2013. http://www.ictj.org/news/ictj-program-report-children-and-youth.

International Centre for Transitional Justice. "Strengthening Indigenous Rights through Truth Commissions: A Practitioner's Resource." 2012. https://www.ictj.org/sites/default/files/ICTJ-Truth-Seeking-Indigenous-Rights-2012-English.pdf.

International Coalition of Sites of Conscience. http://www.sitesofconscience.org/.

Littlechild, Commissioner Wilton. Speech at Dedication Ceremony for the Stained Glass Window on Parliament Hill. Ottawa. 26 November 2012. https://www.aadnc-aandc.gc.ca/eng/1370615213241/1370615618980.

Manitoba Historical Society. "Memorable Manitobans: Robert Alexander Hoey (1883–1965)." http://www.mhs.mb.ca/docs/people/hoey_ra.shtml (accessed 21 December 2013).

McCullough, Alan B. "Peyasiw-awasis (Thunderchild, also known as Kapitikow, meaning 'the one who makes the sound')." In *Dictionary of Canadian Biography* Online. http://www.biographi.ca/en/bio/peyasiw_awasis_15E.html (accessed 19 February 2015).

Missionary Oblates of Mary Immaculate. "An Apology to the First Nations of Canada by the Oblate Conference of Canada." 24 July 1991. http://www.cccb.ca/site/images/stories/pdf/oblate_apology_english.pdf (accessed 27 October 2014).

Mullin, Rev. Margaret (Thundering Eagle Woman). "We are One in the Spirit." In *The Presbyterian Church in Canada, We are One in the Spirit: Liturgical Resources*, 28. 2010. http://presbyterian.ca/?wpdmdl=89&.

Onondaga Nation. "Oren Lyons Presents at U.N. 5/15/14." http://www.onondaganation.org/news/2014/oren-lyons-presents-at-u-n-51514/ (accessed 21 March 2015).

Presbyterian Church in Canada. "Indian Residential Schools. Photographs from The Presbyterian Church in Canada Archives." http://www.presbyterianarchives.ca/RS%20-%20Home%20Page.html.

Presbyterian Church in Canada. "Presbyterian Statement on Aboriginal Spiritual Practices." https://ecumenism.net/2015/01/presbyterian-statement-on-aboriginal-spiritual-practices.htm (accessed 17 March 2015).

Presbyterian Church in Canada. *The Confession of the Presbyterian Church in Canada as Adopted by the General Assembly*. 9 June 1994. http://presbyterian.ca/?wpdmdl=92& (accessed 27 October 2014).

Presbyterian Church of Canada. "Aboriginal Spirituality—A Theological Framework For." General Assembly Referral. 2013. http://presbyterian.ca/?wpdmdl=779&&ind=16 (accessed 22 March 2015).

Reconciliation Canada. "Bernice King's Speech at the Walk for Reconciliation" (video). September 2013. http://reconciliationcanada.ca/2013/09/.

Reconciliation Canada. "City of Vancouver Council Unanimously Support City of Reconciliation Framework." http://reconciliationcanada.ca/city-of-vancouver-council-unanimously-support-city-of-reconciliation-framework/.

Reconciliation Canada. "Elders' Statement. A Shared Tomorrow." http://reconciliationcanada.ca/explore/elders-statement/.

Smith, Reverend Robert. "Apology to First Nations People." United Church of Canada, 31st General Council, 1986. http://www.united-church.ca/beliefs/policies/1986/a651 (accessed 23 October 2014).

Treaty Relations Commission of Manitoba. "Public Education/Learning Centre." http://www.trcm.ca/public-education/learning-centre/.

United Church of Canada. "Affirming Other Spiritual Paths." http://www.united-church.ca/files/aboriginal/schools/affirming-other-spiritual-paths.pdf (accessed 17 March 2015).

United Church of Canada. "Apology to Former Students of United Church Indian Residential Schools, and to Their Families and Communities." October 1998. http://www.united-church.ca/beliefs/policies/1998/a623 (accessed 27 October 2014).

United Church of Canada. "Living Faithfully in the Midst of Empire: Report to the 39th General Council." 2006. http://www.united-church.ca/files/economic/globalization/report.pdf (accessed 22 March 2015).

United Church of Canada. "Residential Schools Update, January 2012." http://develop.united-church.ca/files/communications/newsletters/residential-schools-update_120101.pdf (accessed 15 April 2015).

United Church of Canada. "Reviewing Partnership in the Context of Empire." 2009. http://www.gc41.ca/sites/default/files/pcpmm_empire.pdf (accessed 22 March 2015).

United Church of Canada. "The Executive of the General Council, 24–26 March 2012." Addendum H: Covenanting for Life. http://www.united-church.ca/files/general-council/gc40/addenda_2012-03-2426_executive.pdf (accessed 22 March 2015).

United Church of Canada. Executive of the General Council. "Meeting Summary." 24–26 March 2013. http://www.united-church.ca/files/general-council/gc40/gce_1203_highlights.pdf (accessed 20 March 2015).

United Church of Canada. Residential School Archive Project. "The Children Remembered." http://thechildrenremembered.ca/.

Wiebe, Rudy. "Mistahimaskwa." In *Dictionary of Canadian Biography* Online. http://www.biographi.ca/en/bio/mistahimaskwa_11E.html (accessed 14 July 2014).

World Council of Churches. "Statement on the doctrine of discovery and its enduring impact on Indigenous Peoples." 14–17 February 2012, Bossey, Switzerland. http://www.oikoumene.org/en/resources/documents/executive-committee/bossey-february-2012/statement-on-the-doctrine-of-discovery-and-its-enduring-impact-on-indigenous-peoples.

5. Theses and Dissertations

Brandak, George Michael. "A Study of Missionary Activity in the Diocese of Athabasca, 1884–1903." MA thesis, Waterloo Lutheran University, 1972.

Braun, Connie. "Colonization, Destruction, and Renewal: Stories from Aboriginal Men at the Pe' Sakastew Centre." MA thesis, Department of Sociology, University of Saskatchewan, 1998.

Callahan, Ann B. "On Our Way to Healing: Stories from the Oldest Living Generation of the File Hills Indian Residential School." MA thesis, University of Manitoba, 2002.

Carney, Robert. "Relations in Education Between the Federal and Territorial Governments and the Roman Catholic Church in the Mackenzie District, Northwest Territories, 1867–1961." PhD dissertation, University of Alberta, 1971.

Cooper-Bolam, Trina. "Healing Heritage: New Approaches to Commemorating Canada's Indian Residential School System." MA thesis, Carleton University, 2014

Foran, Timothy Paul. "'Les Gens de cette place': Oblates and the Evolving Concept of Métis at Île-à-la-Crosse, 1845–1898." PhD dissertation, University of Ottawa, 2011.

Gresko, Jacqueline Kennedy. "Gender and Mission: The Founding Generations of the Sisters of Saint Ann and the Oblates of Mary Immaculate in British Columbia 1858–1914." PhD dissertation, University of British Columbia, 1999.

Gull, Norman Andrew. "The 'Indian Policy' of the Anglican Church of Canada from 1945 to the 1970s." MA thesis, Trent University, 1992.

Kennedy, Jacqueline. "Qu'Appelle Industrial School. White 'Rites' for the Indians of the Old North-West." MA thesis, Carleton University, 1970.

Persson, Diane Iona. "Blue Quills: A Case Study of Indian Residential Schooling." PhD dissertation, University of Alberta, 1980.

Pettit, Jennifer Lorretta. "'To Christianize and Civilize': Native Industrial Schools in Canada." PhD dissertation, University of Calgary, 1997.

Wasylow, Walter Julian. "History of Battleford Industrial School for Indians." Masters of Education thesis, University of Saskatchewan, 1972.

Endnotes

Introduction

1. For coercion, see: Ray, *Illustrated History*, 151–152. For fraud, see: Upton, "Origins of Canadian Indian Policy," 56. For failure to implement Treaties, see: Sprague, *Canada's Treaties with Aboriginal People*, 13. For taking land without Treaty, see Fisher, *Contact and Conflict*.
2. For examples from Saskatchewan, see: Miller, *Skyscrapers Hide the Heavens*, 222; Stonechild, "Indian View," 263; Wiebe, "Mistahimaskwa," http://www.biographi.ca/en/bio/mistahimaskwa_11E.html (accessed 14 July 2014).
3. Barron, "Indian Pass System."
4. For an example, see: *An Act to amend and consolidate the laws respecting Indians*, Statutes of Canada 1880, chapter 28, section 72, reproduced in Venne, *Indian Acts*, 75.
5. For examples, see Brown. "Economic Organization and the Position of Women;" Fiske, "Fishing Is Women's Business;" Klein, "Mother as Clanswoman."
6. *An Act for the gradual enfranchisement of Indians*, Statutes of Canada 1869, chapter 42, reproduced in Venne, *Indian Acts*, 11.
7. For an example, see: *An Act further to amend "The Indian Act, 1880*," Statutes of Canada 1884, chapter 27, section 3, reproduced in Venne, *Indian Acts*, 93.
8. Canada, House of Commons Debates (9 May 1883), 1107–1108.
9. Library and Archives Canada, RG10, volume 6810, file 470-2-3, volume 7, Evidence of D. C. Scott to the Special Committee of the House of Commons Investigating the Indian Act amendments of 1920, (L-2)(N-3).
10. Canada, "Statement of the Government of Canada on Indian Policy," page 20 of 24-page portable document format file.
11. Canada, *Annual Report of the Department of Indian Affairs, 1931*, 60.
12. Indian Residential Schools Settlement – Official Court Website, http://www.residentialschoolsettlement.ca/schools.html (accessed 5 February 2015).
13. Prime Minister Stephen Harper, Statement of Apology – to former students of Indian Residential Schools, 11 June 2008, http://www.aadnc-aandc.gc.ca/eng/1100100015644/1100100015649.
14. TRC, NRA, Library and Archives Canada, RG10, volume 7936, file 32-104, J. W. House to G. H. Gooderham, 26 January 1942. [OLD-004156-0001]
15. Canada, Special Joint Committee, 1947, 1474.
16. Canada, Special Joint Committee, 1947, 1508–1509.
17. TRC, NRA, The Presbyterian Church in Canada Archives, Toronto, ON, Acc. 1988-7004, box 46, file 1, "Cecilia Jeffrey Indian Residential School," J. C. E. Andrews, 1953, 36. [NCA-009046]
18. TRC, NRA, INAC – Resolution Sector – IRS Historical Files Collection – Ottawa, GRS Files, box 1A, file 43, Albert Southard, 8 March 1957. [IRC-040039]
19. Renaud, "Indian Education Today," 30.
20. TRC, AVS, Alma Mann Scott, Statement to the Truth and Reconciliation Commission of Canada, Winnipeg, Manitoba, 17 June 2010, Statement Number: 02-MB-16JU10-016.
21. For further information on these issues, see the Legacy section below.
22. Media coverage on the call for an inquiry on missing and murdered Aboriginal women has been extensive. See, for example: "Women's Memorial March in Vancouver Attracts Hundreds," *CBC*

News, 14 February 2015, http://www.cbc.ca/news/canada/british-columbia/womens-memorial-march-in-vancouver-attracts-hundreds-1.2957930; "Murdered and Missing Aboriginal Women Deserve Inquiry, Rights Group Says," *CBC News*, 12 January 2015, http://www.cbc.ca/news/politics/murdered-and-missing-aboriginal-women-deserve-inquiry-rights-group-says-1.2897707; Ken S. Coates, "Aboriginal Women Deserve Much More than an Inquiry," *National Post*, 16 February 2015, http://news.nationalpost.com/2015/02/16/ken-s-coates-aboriginal-women-deserve-much-more-than-an-inquiry/.

On economic development issues, see, for example: Jeff Lewis, "TransCanada CEO Says Canada Needs to Resolve Conflicts over Pipelines," *Globe and Mail*, 4 February 2015, http://www.theglobeandmail.com/report-on-business/economy/transcanada-ceo-says-canada-needs-to-resolve-conflicts-over-pipelines/article22798276/; Daniel Schwartz and Mark Gollom, "NB Fracking Protests and the Fight for Aboriginal Rights," *CBC News Canada*, 19 October 2013, http://www.cbc.ca/news/canada/n-b-fracking-protests-and-the-fight-for-aboriginal-rights-1.2126515; Michael MacDonald, "Shale Gas Conflict in New Brunswick Underscores Historical Grievances, Rights of First Nations," *Toronto Star*, 25 December 2013, http://www.thestar.com/news/canada/2013/12/25/shale_gas_conflict_in_new_brunswick_underscores_historic_grievances_rights_of_first_nations.html.

23. On the role of the courts in Aboriginal rights and reconciliation, see: Joseph Brean, "'Reconciliation' with First Nations, Not the Charter of Rights & Freedoms, Will Define the Supreme Court in Coming years, Chief Justice Says," *National Post*, 13 March 2014, http://news.nationalpost.com/2014/03/13/reconciliation-with-first-nations-not-the-charter-of-rights-freedoms-will-define-the-supreme-court-in-coming-years-chief-justice-says/.

    On Aboriginal rights cases, see, for example: "6 Landmark Rulings on Native Rights," *CBC News*, 8 January 2013, http://www.cbc.ca/news/canada/6-landmark-rulings-on-native-rights-1.1316961. On day schools litigation, see, for example: "Residential School Day Scholars Launch Class-action Lawsuit," *CBC News*, 16 August 2012, http://www.cbc.ca/news/canada/british-columbia/residential-school-day-scholars-launch-class-action-lawsuit-1.1146607;

    Dene Moore, "Federal Appeal Court Gives Ok on Hearing First Nations' Day-school Suit," *Canadian Press*, 4 March 2014, http://www.ctvnews.ca/canada/federal-appeal-court-gives-ok-on-hearing-first-nations-day-school-suit-1.1713809. On Sixties Scoop legislation, see, for example: "Sixties Scoop Case Moves Forward as Class-action Lawsuit," *CBC News*, 3 December 2014, http://www.cbc.ca/news/canada/thunder-bay/sixties-scoop-case-moves-forward-as-class-action-lawsuit-1.2859332; Diana Mehta, "'Sixties Scoop' Class-action Lawsuit to Proceed," *Canadian Press*, 4 December 2014, http://www.ctvnews.ca/canada/60s-scoop-class-action-lawsuit-to-proceed-1.2132317.
24. Miller, *Lethal Legacy*, vi.
25. TRC, AVS, Mary Deleary, Statement to the Truth and Reconciliation Commission of Canada, Winnipeg, Manitoba, 26 June 2014, Statement Number: SE049.
26. TRC, AVS, Archie Little. Statement to the Truth and Reconciliation Commission of Canada, Victoria, British Columbia, 13 April 2012, Statement Number: SP135.
27. McKay, "Expanding the Dialogue," 107. McKay was the first Aboriginal moderator of the United Church of Canada (1992 to 1994).
28. TRC, AVS, Jessica Bolduc, Statement to the Truth and Reconciliation Commission of Canada, Edmonton, Alberta, 30 March 2014, Statement Number: ABNE401.
29. *Educating our Youth*, video, Truth and Reconciliation Commission of Canada, 19 September 2013, http://www.trc.ca/websites/trcinstitution/index.php?p=3 (accessed 10 February 2014).

30. TRC, AVS, Patsy George, Statement to the Truth and Reconciliation Commission of Canada, Vancouver, British Columbia, 21 September 2013, Statement Number: BCNE404.
31. TRC, AVS, Dave Courchene, Statement to the Truth and Reconciliation Commission of Canada, Winnipeg, Manitoba, 25 June 2014, Statement Number: SE048.
32. The mandate of the Truth and Reconciliation Commission is listed under Schedule N of the Indian Residential Schools Settlement Agreement, http://www.residentialschoolsettlement.ca/settlement.html (accessed 5 March 2015). In accordance with the TRC's mandate, the Commission was required to recognize "the significance of Aboriginal oral and legal traditions in its activities," Schedule N, 4(d); and "witness, support, promote and facilitate truth and reconciliation events at both the national and community levels," Schedule N, 1(c). The term *witness* "refers to the Aboriginal principle of 'witnessing,'" Indian Residential Schools Settlement Agreement, Schedule N, 1(c), n1.

    Aboriginal oral history, legal traditions, and the principle of witnessing have deep historical roots and contemporary relevance for reconciliation. Indigenous law was used to resolve family and community conflict, to establish Treaties among various Indigenous nations, and to negotiate nation-to-nation treaties with the Crown. For a comprehensive history of Aboriginal–Crown Treaty making from contact to the present, see: Miller, *Compact, Contract, Covenant*. The term *witness* is in reference to the Aboriginal principle of witnessing, which varies among First Nations, Métis, and Inuit peoples. Generally speaking, witnesses are called to be the keepers of history when an event of historic significance occurs. Through witnessing, the event or work that is undertaken is validated and provided legitimacy. The work could not take place without honoured and respected guests to witness it. Witnesses are asked to store and care for the history they witness and to share it with their own people when they return home. For Aboriginal peoples, the act of witnessing these events comes with a great responsibility to remember all the details and be able to recount them accurately as the foundation of oral histories. See: Thomas, "Honouring the Oral Traditions," 243–244.
33. TRC, AVS, Jim Dumont, Statement to the Truth and Reconciliation Commission of Canada, Winnipeg, Manitoba, 26 June 2014, Statement Number: SE049.
34. TRC, AVS, Wilfred Whitehawk, Statement to the Truth and Reconciliation Commission of Canada, Key First Nation, Saskatchewan, 21 January 2012, Statement Number: SP039.
35. TRC, AVS, Vitaline Elsie Jenner, Statement to the Truth and Reconciliation Commission of Canada. Winnipeg, Manitoba, 16 June 2010, Statement Number: 02-MB-16JU10-131.
36. TRC, AVS, Daniel Elliot, Statement to the Truth and Reconciliation Commission of Canada, Victoria, British Columbia, 13 April 2012, Statement Number: SP135.
37. TRC, AVS, Clement Chartier, Statement to the Truth and Reconciliation Commission of Canada, Saskatoon, Saskatchewan, 22 June 2013, Statement Number: SNE202.
38. TRC, AVS, Steven Point, Statement to the Truth and Reconciliation Commission of Canada, Vancouver, British Columbia, 20 September 2013, Statement Number: BCNE304.
39. TRC, AVS, Merle Nisley, Statement to the Truth and Reconciliation Commission of Canada, Thunder Bay, Ontario, 14 December 2011, Statement Number: 2011-4199.
40. TRC, AVS, Tom Cavanaugh, Statement to the Truth and Reconciliation Commission of Canada, Victoria, British Columbia, 14 April 2012, Statement Number: SP137.
41. TRC, AVS, Ina Seitcher, Statement to the Truth and Reconciliation Commission of Canada, Victoria, British Columbia, 14 April 2012, Statement Number: SP136.
42. TRC, AVS, Evelyn Brockwood, Statement to the Truth and Reconciliation Commission of Canada, Winnipeg, Manitoba, 18 June 2010, Statement Number: SC110.

43. Indian Residential Schools Settlement Agreement, Schedule N, Principles, 1, http://www.residentialschoolsettlement.ca/settlement.html (accessed 5 March 2015).
44. Johnston, "Aboriginal Traditions," 141–159.
45. TRC, AVS, Barney Williams, Statement to the Truth and Reconciliation Commission of Canada, Winnipeg, Manitoba, 26 June 2014, Statement Number: SE049.
46. TRC, AVS, Stephen Augustine, Statement to the Truth and Reconciliation Commission of Canada, Winnipeg, Manitoba, 25 June 2014, Statement Number: SE048.
47. TRC, AVS, Reg Crowshoe, Statement to the Truth and Reconciliation Commission of Canada, Winnipeg, Manitoba, 26 June 2014, Statement Number: SE049.
48. TRC, AVS, Kirby Littletent, Statement to the Truth and Reconciliation Commission of Canada, Regina, Saskatchewan, 16 January 2012, Statement Number: SP035.
49. TRC, AVS, Simone (last name not provided), Statement to the Truth and Reconciliation Commission of Canada, Inuvik, Northwest Territories, 1 July 2011, Statement Number: SC092.
50. TRC, AVS, Patrick Etherington, Statement to the Truth and Reconciliation Commission of Canada, Winnipeg, Manitoba, 17 June 2010, Statement Number: SC108.
51. TRC, AVS, Maxine Lacorne, Statement to the Truth and Reconciliation Commission of Canada, Inuvik, Northwest Territories, 29 June 2011, Statement Number: SC090.
52. TRC, AVS, Barney Williams, Statement to the Truth and Reconciliation Commission of Canada, Vancouver, British Columbia, 21 September 2013, Statement Number: BCNE404.
53. TRC, AVS, Hon. Chuck Strahl, Statement to the Truth and Reconciliation Commission of Canada, Winnipeg, Manitoba, 16 June 2010, Statement Number: SC093.
54. TRC, AVS, Archbishop Fred Hiltz, Statement to the Truth and Reconciliation Commission of Canada, Inuvik, Northwest Territories, 1 July 2011, Statement Number: NNE402.
55. TRC, AVS, Anonymous, Statement to the Truth and Reconciliation Commission of Canada, Regina, Saskatchewan, 17 January 2012, Statement Number: SP036.

Commission activities

1. In this context, the Commission defines a "visit" as one person attending one day of one National Event. The Commission made daily attendance estimates of its National Events but did not attempt to track those individuals who attended more than one day of any single National Event.
2. Schedule N to the Settlement Agreement provides at section 1(e) that one of the goals of the Commission is to "identify sources and create as complete an historical record as possible of the IRS system and legacy." In addition, section 11 of Schedule N provides that "Canada and the churches will provide all relevant documents in their possession or control to and for the use of the Truth and Reconciliation Commission" and that Canada and the churches are required to "compile all relevant documents in an organized manner for review by the Commission and to provide access to their archives for the Commission to carry out its mandate."
3. *Fontaine v. Canada (Attorney General)*, 2013 ONSC 684 at para 69.
4. *Fontaine v. Canada (Attorney General)*, 2014 ONSC 283 (CanLII) at paras. 24–25.
5. *Fontaine v. Canada (Attorney General)*, 2014 ONSC 283 (CanLII) at paras. 24–25.
6. *Fontaine v. Canada (Attorney General)*, 2014 ONSC 283 (CanLII) at para 191.
7. *Fontaine v. Canada (Attorney General)*, 2014 ONSC 283 (CanLII) at para 192.
8. *Fontaine v. Canada (Attorney General)*, 2014 ONSC 4585 (CanLII) at para 19.
9. The Catholic entities filed main appeals and the Commission and the National Centre filed cross

appeals. Based on preliminary documents filed by the Catholic entities, it appears that they intend to argue that no notice period should be ordered and that the IAP documents cannot be archived without the consent of alleged perpetrators and other persons of interest. The Commission intends to appear before the Court of Appeal of Ontario to argue that the IAP documents cannot be destroyed without consulting IAP claimants.

10. The Commission's engagement with the United Nations included participation at the Permanent Forum on Indigenous Issues, the Expert Panel on Indigenous Issues, an Expert Seminar on Truth Commissions and Access to Justice, and a Human Rights Council Special Panel on Education and Teaching History.
11. A complete list of projects funded is available on the website of Aboriginal Affairs and Northern Development Canada at http://www.aadnc-aandc.gc.ca/eng/1100100015635/1100100015636.

The History

1. TRC, AVS, Frederick Ernest Koe, Statement to the Truth and Reconciliation Commission of Canada, Inuvik, Northwest Territories, 30 June 2011, Statement Number: SC091.
2. TRC, AVS, Marlene Kayseas, Statement to the Truth and Reconciliation Commission of Canada, Regina, Saskatchewan, 16 January 2012, Statement Number: SP035.
3. TRC, AVS, Larry Beardy, Statement to the Truth and Reconciliation Commission of Canada, Thompson, Manitoba, 25 September 2012, Statement Number: SP082.
4. TRC, AVS, Florence Horassi, Statement to the Truth and Reconciliation Commission of Canada, Tulita, Northwest Territories, 10 May 2011, Statement Number: 2011-0394.
5. TRC, AVS, Lily Bruce, Statement to the Truth and Reconciliation Commission of Canada, Alert Bay, British Columbia, 4 August 2011, Statement Number: 2011-3285.
6. TRC, AVS, Vitaline Elsie Jenner, Statement to the Truth and Reconciliation Commission of Canada, Winnipeg, Manitoba, 16 June 2010, Statement Number: 02-MB-16JU10-131. (Translated words confirmed by Translation Bureau, Public Works and Government Services Canada [8817169_TG_Kinugus_EN_CP].)
7. TRC, AVS, Nellie Ningewance, Statement to the Truth and Reconciliation Commission of Canada, Sault Ste. Marie, Ontario, 1 July 2011, Statement Number: 2011-0305.
8. TRC, AVS, Bernice Jacks, Statement to the Truth and Reconciliation Commission of Canada, Victoria, British Columbia, 13 April 2012, Statement Number: 2011-3971.
9. TRC, AVS, Marthe Basile-Coocoo, Statement to the Truth and Reconciliation Commission of Canada (translated from French), Montréal, Québec, 26 April 2013, Statement Number: 2011-6103.
10. TRC, AVS, Pauline St-Onge, Statement to the Truth and Reconciliation Commission of Canada (translated from French), Montréal, Québec, 25 April 2013, Statement Number: 2011-6134.
11. TRC, AVS, Campbell Papequash, Statement to the Truth and Reconciliation Commission of Canada, Key First Nation, Saskatchewan, 20 January 2012, Statement Number: SP038.
12. TRC, AVS, Roy Denny, Statement to the Truth and Reconciliation Commission of Canada, Eskasoni First Nation, Nova Scotia, 14 October 2011, Statement Number: 2011-2678.
13. TRC, AVS, Calvin Myerion, Statement to the Truth and Reconciliation Commission of Canada, Winnipeg, Manitoba, 16 June 2010, Statement Number: 02-MB-16JU10-122.
14. TRC, AVS, Archie Hyacinthe, Statement to the Truth and Reconciliation Commission of Canada, Kenora, Ontario, 15 March 2011, Statement Number: 2011-0279.
15. TRC, AVS, Margo Wylde, Statement to the Truth and Reconciliation Commission of Canada, Val

d'Or, Québec, 5 February 2012, Statement Number: SP100.

16. TRC, AVS, Murray Crowe, Statement to the Truth and Reconciliation Commission of Canada, Sault Ste. Marie, Ontario, 1 July 2011, Statement Number: 2011-0306.
17. TRC, AVS, Wilbur Abrahams, Statement to the Truth and Reconciliation Commission of Canada, Terrace, British Columbia, 30 November 2011, Statement Number: 2011-3301.
18. TRC, AVS, Martin Nicholas, Statement to the Truth and Reconciliation Commission of Canada, Grand Rapids, Manitoba, 24 February 2010, Statement Number: 07-MB-24FB10-001.
19. TRC, AVS, Lorna Morgan, Statement to the Truth and Reconciliation Commission of Canada, Winnipeg, Manitoba, 17 June 2010, Statement Number: 02-MB-16JU10-041.
20. TRC, AVS, Gilles Petiquay, Statement to the Truth and Reconciliation Commission of Canada (translated from French), La Tuque, Québec, 6 March 2013, Statement Number: 2011-6001.
21. TRC, AVS, Wilbur Abrahams, Statement to the Truth and Reconciliation Commission of Canada, Terrace, British Columbia, 30 November 2011, Statement Number: 2011-3301.
22. TRC, AVS, Peter Ross, Statement to the Truth and Reconciliation Commission of Canada, Tsiigehtchic, Northwest Territories, 8 September 2011, Statement Number: 2011-0340.
23. TRC, AVS, Daniel Nanooch, Statement to the Truth and Reconciliation Commission of Canada, High Level, Alberta, 4 July 2013, Statement Number: 2011-1868.
24. TRC, AVS, Bernice Jacks, Statement to the Truth and Reconciliation Commission of Canada, Victoria, British Columbia, 13 April 2012, Statement Number: 2011-3971.
25. TRC, AVS, Helen Kakekayash, Statement to the Truth and Reconciliation Commission of Canada, Ottawa, Ontario, 5 February 2011, Statement Number: 01-ON-05FE11-002.
26. TRC, AVS, Bernard Catcheway, Statement to the Truth and Reconciliation Commission of Canada, Skownan First Nation, Manitoba, 12 October 2011, Statement Number: 2011-2510.
27. TRC, AVS, Julianna Alexander, Statement to the Truth and Reconciliation Commission of Canada, Enderby, British Columbia, 12 October 2011, Statement Number: 2011-3286.
28. TRC, AVS, William Herney, Statement to the Truth and Reconciliation Commission of Canada, Halifax, Nova Scotia, 29 October 2011, Statement Number: 2011-2923.
29. TRC, AVS, Raymond Cutknife, Statement to the Truth and Reconciliation Commission of Canada, Hobbema, Alberta, 25 July 2013, Statement Number: SP125.
30. TRC, AVS, Timothy Henderson, Statement to the Truth and Reconciliation Commission of Canada, Winnipeg, Manitoba, 28 June 2011, Statement Number: 2011-0291.
31. TRC, AVS, Shirley Waskewitch, Statement to the Truth and Reconciliation Commission of Canada, Saskatoon, Saskatchewan, 24 June 2012, Statement Number: 2011-3521.
32. TRC, AVS, Patrick Bruyere, Statement to the Truth and Reconciliation Commission of Canada, Winnipeg, Manitoba, 16 June 2010, Statement Number: 02-MB-16JU10-157.
33. TRC, AVS, Ernest Barkman, Statement to the Truth and Reconciliation Commission of Canada, Garden Hill First Nation, Manitoba, 30 March 2011, Statement Number: 2011-0123. (Translated from Oji-Cree to English by Translation Bureau, Public Works and Government Services Canada, 8956124.)
34. TRC, AVS, Paul Dixon, Statement to the Truth and Reconciliation Commission of Canada, Val d'Or, Québec, 6 February 2012, Statement Number: SP101.
35. TRC, AVS, Betsy Annahatak, Statement to the Truth and Reconciliation Commission of Canada, Halifax, Nova Scotia, 28 October 2011, Statement Number: 2011-2896.
36. TRC, AVS, Rick Gilbert, Statement to the Truth and Reconciliation Commission of Canada, Vancouver, British Columbia, 20 September 2013, Statement Number: 2011-2389.
37. TRC, AVS, Nick Sibbeston, Statement to the Truth and Reconciliation Commission of Canada,

Inuvik, Northwest Territories, 30 June 2011, Statement Number: NNE202.
38. TRC, AVS, [Name redacted], Statement to the Truth and Reconciliation Commission of Canada, Prince Albert, Saskatchewan, 1 February 2012, Statement Number: 2011-3879. (Translated from Woodland Cree to English by Translation Bureau, Public Works and Government Services Canada, 8956130.)
39. TRC, AVS, Jack Anawak, Statement to the Truth and Reconciliation Commission of Canada, Inuvik, Northwest Territories, 30 June 2011, Statement Number: NNE202.
40. TRC, AVS, Lydia Ross, Statement to the Truth and Reconciliation Commission of Canada, Winnipeg, Manitoba, 16 June 2010, Statement Number: 02-MB-16JU10-029.
41. TRC, AVS, Stephen Kakfwi, Statement to the Truth and Reconciliation Commission of Canada, Inuvik, Northwest Territories, 30 June 2011, Statement Number: NNE202.
42. TRC, AVS, Victoria McIntosh, Statement to the Truth and Reconciliation Commission of Canada, Winnipeg, Manitoba, 16 June 2010, Statement Number: 02-MB-16JU10-123.
43. TRC, AVS, Shirley Flowers, Statement to the Truth and Reconciliation Commission of Canada, Goose Bay, Newfoundland and Labrador, 20 September 2011, Statement Number: SP025.
44. Howe, *Empire*, 21–22.
45. Howe, *Empire*, 57.
46. For East Africa, see: Thiong'o, *Dreams in a Time of War*. For Australia, see: Australia, "'Bringing Them Home,' National Inquiry," www.humanrights.gov.au/sites/default/files/content/pdf/social_justice/bringing_them_home_report.pdf [25]. For Siberia, see: Bartels and Bartels, *When the North Was Red*, 12; Bloch, *Red Ties*, 38.
47. Diffie and Winnius, *Foundations*, 78–83; Pagden, *Peoples and Empires*, 56.
48. Howe, *Empire*, 62–63.
49. Hobsbawm, *On Empire*, 67.
50. Wood, *Empire of Capital*, 74–87.
51. Wolfe, "Settler Colonialism," 388.
52. Wolfe, "Settler Colonialism," 388, 391, 399.
53. Address of C. C. Painter to the 1886 Lake Mohonk Conference, "Proceedings of the Lake Mohonk Conference," in *Eighteenth Annual Report of the Board of Indian Commissioners, 1886*, 61–62.
54. Howe, *Empire*, 80–81.
55. Howe, *Empire*, 62.
56. Wood, *Empire of Capital*, 40–41.
57. For examples, see: Diffie and Winius, *Foundations*, 65–66, 94–95; Pagden, *Peoples and Empires*, 54; Williams, *American Indian*, 72–73.
58. Elliott, *Empires of the Atlantic*, 11, 23; Pagden, *Spanish Imperialism*, 14.
59. Pagden, *Lords of All the World*, 47.
60. Elliott, *Empires of the Atlantic*, 11–12; Frichner, "Preliminary Study," 11; Seed, *Ceremonies of Possession*, 17–18.
61. H. Verelst, "Some Observations on the Right of the Crown of Great Britain to the North West Continent of America," PRC co 5/283, f. 5, quoted in Armitage, *Ideological Origins*, 192.
62. Banner, "Why Terra Nullius," 95. The court case is referred to as *Mabo v. Queensland (No. 2)*.
63. Wood, *Origin of Capitalism*, 111.
64. Howe, *Empire*, 86–87.
65. Speech quoted in: *Archibald Philip Primrose* (*5th earl of Rosebery*) ... *Australian speechlets, 1883–84 [by A. P. Primrose*], http://books.google.ca/books?id=CncIAAAAQAAJ&printsec=frontcover&dq=Australian+speechlets,+1883-84+[by+A.P.+Primrose.].&hl=en&sa=X&ei=zN2IUuGdMOTA2g-

W0vIHYDA&ved=0CDkQ6AEwAA#v=onepage&q=Australian%20speechlets%2C%201883-84%20 [by%20A.P.%20Primrose.].&f=false (accessed 17 November 2013).

66. Canada, *Annual Report of the Department of Indian Affairs, 1884,* 154.
67. Usher, *William Duncan*, 41. See also: Choquette, *Oblate Assault*; Huel, *Proclaiming the Gospel*; Hyam, *Britain's Imperial Century*.
68. Howe, *Empire*, 85.
69. Howe, *Empire*, 90; Perry, "Metropolitan Knowledge," 109–111.
70. Huel, *Proclaiming the Gospel*, 1–6; Choquette, *Oblate Assault*, 1–20; Choquette, *Canada's Religions*, 173–176.
71. For example, see: Usher, *William Duncan*, 8, 11.
72. Moorhouse, *Missionaries*, 274.
73. Moorhouse, *Missionaries*, 33; Rompkey, *Story of Labrador*, 34, 36–39.
74. For Canada, see, for example: McMillan and Yellowhorn, *First Peoples*. For a global perspective, see: Coates, *A Global History*.
75. Jaenen, "Education for Francization," 54–55; Trudel, *Beginnings of New France*, 134–135.
76. Jaenen, *Friend and Foe Aspects*, 96, 163, 166.
77. Magnuson, *Education in New France*, 47–50; Trudel, *Beginnings of New France*, 231; Axtell, *Invasion Within*, 56–58; Jaenen, "Education for Francization," 56; Jaenen, *Friend and Foe Aspects*, 95, 168.
78. Hamilton, *Federal Indian Day Schools*, 4–5; Fingard, "New England Company," 30–32.
79. Stevenson, "Red River Indian Mission School," 141.
80. Graham, *Mush Hole*, 7.
81. TRC, NRA, Library and Archives Canada, RG10, Acc. 1984-85/112, box 47, file 451/25-1, Newspaper article, "Mohawk Institute May Close after 139 Years," no date; [TAY-001133] TRC, NRA, Diocese of Huron Archives, Anglican Church of Canada, Huron University College, London, ON, Luxton Papers, box 27, Indian Reserves, Richard Isaac, Six Nations Council To Whom It May Concern, 13 March 1970; [TAY-001432] TRC, NRA, INAC – Resolution Sector – IRS Historical Files Collection – Ottawa, file 479/25-13-001, volume 3, G. D. Cromb to Deputy Minister, 20 March 1970. [TAY-003053-0001]
82. Ryerson, "Report on Industrial Schools," 76.
83. Ryerson, "Report on Industrial Schools," 73.
84. *Report of the Special Commissioners 1858*, n.p.
85. TRC, NRA, Library and Archives Canada, RG10, volume 6210, file 468-10, part 5, Samuel Devlin to Indian Affairs, 20 May 1946. [MER-003806-0001]
86. Gresko, "Paul Durieu," http://www.biographi.ca/en/bio/durieu_paul_12E.html (accessed 31 August 2014). McNally gives the opening as 1862: McNally, *Lord's Distant Vineyard*, 67.
87. McCarthy, *From the Great River*, 160; Carney, "Grey Nuns and Children," 291; Duchaussois, *Grey Nuns*, 148.
88. Miller, *Compact, Contract, Covenant*, 156; Davin, *Report on Industrial Schools*, 10. Population figures for this period are only estimates. James Miller cites 12,000 mixed-blood people in 1870, and, in his 1879 report, Nicholas Flood Davin stated that 28,000 people were under Treaty. Miller, *Compact, Contract, Covenant*, 199; Davin, *Report on Industrial Schools*, 10.
89. Great Britain, *Rupert's Land and North-Western Territory Order* (Schedule A), 23 June 1870, http://www.justice.gc.ca/eng/rp-pr/csj-sjc/constitution/lawreg-loireg/p1t32.html.
90. Getty and Lussier, *Long as the Sun Shines*, 35.
91. Banner, *How Indians Lost Their Land*, 85.

92. Tobias, "Protection, Civilization, Assimilation," 128.
93. Miller, *Compact, Contract, Covenant*, 156.
94. Miller, *Compact, Contract, Covenant*, 154.
95. Friesen, "Magnificent Gifts," 205, 212.
96. Erasmus, *Buffalo Days*, 250.
97. Ray, *Illustrated History*, 212; Taylor, "Canada's Northwest Indian Policy," 3.
98. Sprague, *Canada's Treaties with Aboriginal People*, 13.
99. For an example of a request for a day school on a reserve, see: McCullough, "Peyasiw-awasis," http://www.biographi.ca/en/bio/peyasiw_awasis_15E.html (accessed 6 June 2014).
100. Miller, *Compact, Contract, Covenant*, 164–165.
101. Morris, *Treaties of Canada*, 202.
102. In Canada, the *Indian Act* had been preceded by the 1868 *Act to provide for the organization of the Department of the Secretary of State of Canada and for the Administration of the Affairs of the Indians,* and the 1869 *An Act for the gradual enfranchisement of Indians.*
103. *An Act to amend and consolidate the laws respecting Indians*, Statutes of Canada 1876, chapter 18.
104. Miller, *Skyscrapers Hide the Heavens*, 255.
105. Library and Archives Canada, RG10, volume 6810, file 470-2-3, volume 7, Evidence of D. C. Scott to the Special Committee of the House of Commons Investigating the Indian Act amendments of 1920, (L-2)(N-3).
106. For the banning of the Potlatch, see: LaViolette, Struggle for Survival, 41–42; Cole and Chaikin, *Iron Hand*, 16–17, 95. For the banning of the Thirst Dance, see: Pettipas, *Severing the Ties*, 53–54, 95–96.
107. For examples, see: LaViolette, *Struggle for Survival*, 41–42; Cole and Chaikin, *Iron Hand*, 16–17, 95; TRC, NRA, Library and Archives Canada, RG10, volume 3825, file 60511-1, J. Hugonard to Indian Commissioner, 23 November 1903. [RCA-011007-0001]
108. Canada, Sessional Papers 1885, number 116. F., 95–96, J. S. Dennis to Sir John A. Macdonald, 20 December 1878.
109. Davin, *Report on Industrial Schools*, 14.
110. Driver, "Discipline Without Frontiers?," 282.
111. Parker, *Uprooted*, 190.
112. Sutherland, *Children in English-Canadian Society*, 100.
113. Sutherland, *Children in English-Canadian Society*, 138.
114. Fear-Segal, *White Man's Club*, 186; Standing Bear, *My People the Sioux*, 123–133.
115. Canada, *Annual Report of the Department of Indian Affairs, 1884* (for High River, 76; for Battleford, 154; for Qu'Appelle, 161).
116. Canada, House of Commons Debates (22 May 1883), 1376.
117. Library and Archives Canada, RG10, volume 3647, file 8128, Andsell Macrae, 18 December 1886.
118. Canada, *Annual Report of the Department of Indian Affairs, 1910*, 273.
119. Canada, *Annual Report of the Department of Indian Affairs, 1883*, 104.
120. Library and Archives Canada, RG10, volume 3924, file 116823, L. Vankoughnet to Sir John A. Macdonald, 15 March 1886.
121. TRC, NRA, Library and Archives Canada, RG10, volume 6001, file 1-1-1, part 1, Privy Council Order Number 1278, 7 June 1888; [PLD-007312] Library and Archives Canada, RG10, volume 3819, file 58418, J. Hugonnard to Hayter Reed, 11 May 1889; [PLD-009475] Library and Archives Canada, RG10, volume 3675, file 11422-4, J. Hugonnard to E. Dewdney, 5 May 1891. [PLD-009435]
122. TRC, NRA, Library and Archives Canada, RG10, volume 3879, file 91833, Order-in-Council, 22 October 1892. [RIS-000354]

123. For the admission of infected children, see: TRC, NRA, Library and Archives Canada, RG10, volume 4037, file 317021, T. Ferrier to the editor, 23 November 1907. [RCA-000315]
124. For details, see: Canada, *Annual Report of the Department of Indian Affairs, 1904*, xxvii–xxviii; TRC, NRA, Library and Archives Canada, MG17, B2, Class 'G' C.1/P.2, Church Missionary Society, "Resolutions Regarding the Administration of the North-West Canada Missions," 7 April 1903; [PAR-003622] Blake, *Don't you hear*; TRC, NRA, Library and Archives Canada, RG10, volume 3928, file 117004-1, "Report on Indian Missions and Schools," Presented to the Diocesan Synod, Diocese of Calgary, J. W. Tims, August 1908; [OLD-008159] The United Church of Canada Archives, Toronto, Acc. No. 1979.199C, box 5, file 68, "Report of the Synod's Commission on Indian Affairs," 5 December 1904; [RIS-000246] TRC, NRA, Library and Archives Canada, RG10, volume 6039, file 160-1, part 1, Frank Pedley to Reverend and dear sirs, 21 March 1908; [AEMR-120155] TRC, NRA, Anglican Church of Canada, General Synod Archives, ACC-MSCC-GS 75-103, series 3:1, box 48, file 3, Frank Pedley to Norman Tucker, 26 March 1909; [AAC-090228] Archives of Saskatchewan, MacKay Papers, Frank Oliver, "Letter to S. H. Blake, 28 January, 1908," quoted in Wasylow, "History of Battleford Industrial School," 225–226; Anglican Church General Synod Archives, 75-103, series 2-14, Frank Oliver to A. G. G., 28 January 1908, quoted in Gull, "'Indian Policy,'" 15; TRC, NRA, Anglican Church of Canada, General Synod Archives, ACC-MSCC-GS 75-103, series 3:1, box 48, file 3, Letter signed by S. H. Blake, Andrew Baird, Hamilton Cassels, T. Ferrier, R. F. MacKay, 22 May 1908; [AAC-090192] TRC, NRA, Library and Archives Canada, RG10, volume 6039, file 160-1, part 1, Frank Pedley to Frank Oliver, 9 April 1908; [AEMR-120157] TRC, NRA, Anglican Church of Canada, General Synod Archives, ACC-MSCC-GS 75-103, series 3:1, box 48, file 3, "Report of the Sub-Committee of the Advisory Board On Indian Education," n.d.; [AAC-090231] TRC, NRA, Library and Archives Canada, RG10, volume 3919, file 116751-1A, J. B. Magnan to D. Laird, 12 December 1902; [SBR-003409] TRC, NRA, Library and Archives Canada, RG10, volume 3919, file 116751-1A, Clifford Sifton to Governor General in Council, 23 December 1903; [FAR-000095] TRC, NRA, Library and Archives Canada, RG10, volume 6039, file 160-1, part 1, Frank Pedley to Mr. Oliver, 30 May 1908; [120.00294] TRC, NRA, Library and Archives Canada, RG10, volume 6327, file 660-1, part 1, J. Hugonnard to Frank Oliver, 28 March 1908; [PLD-007334] TRC, NRA, Library and Archives Canada, RG10, volume 6039, file 160-1, part 1, Superintendent General of Indian Affairs to T. Ferrier, 18 July 1908; [AEMR-016328] TRC, NRA, Library and Archives Canada, RG10, volume 6039, file 160-1, part 1, Heron to Frank Oliver, 16 February 1909; [AEMR-120164] TRC, NRA, Library and Archives Canada, RG10, volume 6039, file 160-4, part 1, Association of Indian Workers to Frank Oliver, 19 February 1909; [AEMR-016332] TRC, NRA, Library and Archives Canada, RG10, FA 10-17, volume 6041, file 160-5, part 1, 1905–1934, Emile Legal to Frank Pedley, 20 July 1908; [AEMR-254243] TRC, NRA, Anglican Church of Canada, General Synod Archives, ACC-MSCC-GS 75-103, series 3:1, box 48, file 3, Arthur Barner to S. H. Blake, 16 February 1909. [AAC-090206]
125. For the initial improvement, see: TRC, NRA, Library and Archives Canada, RG10, volume 6032, file 150-40A, part 1, Headquarters – Compulsory Attendance of Pupils – Indian Schools, 1904–1933, Microfilm reel C-8149, FA 10-17, "Re: Per Capita Grants at Indian Residential Schools," Russell Ferrier, 5 April 1932. [120.18050] For an example of the impact of inflation, see: TRC, NRA, Library and Archives Canada, RG10, volume 6468, file 890-1, part 1, J. Welch to D. C. Scott, 28 July 1916. [MIS-001473] For cuts in the 1930s, see: TRC, NRA, Anglican Church of Canada, General Synod Archives, ACC-MSCC-GS 75-103, series 2.15, box 27, file 1, The Joint Delegation and Interview with the Prime Minister, 20 December 1934; [AAC-087280] TRC, NRA, Library and Archives Canada, RG10, volume 7185, file 1/25-1-7-1, part 1, Harold McGill to Church Officers, Principals of Indian Residential Schools, 22 February 1933. [AEMR-255373]

126. TRC, NRA, Library and Archives Canada, RG10, volume 7185, file 1/25-1-7-?, part 1, R. A. Hoey to Dr. McGill, 4 November 1938. [AEMR-120432]
127. For staffing, see: Canada, *Annual Report of the Department of Indian Affairs, 1955*, 51; Canada, *Annual Report of the Department of Indian Affairs, 1957*, 56. As an experiment in 1949, Indian Affairs had taken on responsibility for directly employing the teaching staff in schools at Shubenacadie, the Mohawk Institute, and Port Alberni. TRC, NRA, DIAND HQ, file 1/25-1-5-2, volume 1, 1952–1969, Laval Fortier to J. P. Mulvihill, 26 October 1953. [AEMR-120563] For diet, see: TRC, NRA, Library and Archives Canada, RG55, FA 55-19, volume 20784, Treasury Board Submission 559690, Req. Authority for the Recommendation and Establishment of Domestic Staff, Laval Fortier to Secretary, Treasury Board, 22 January 1960. [120.04620]
128. TRC, NRA, Canadian Welfare Council and Caldwell 1967, 89. [AEMR-019759]
129. TRC, NRA, Canadian Welfare Council and Caldwell 1967, 92. [AEMR-019759]
130. TRC, NRA, Library and Archives Canada, RG10, volume 6032, file 150-40A, part 1, Regulations Relating to the Education of Indian Children, Ottawa: Government Printing Bureau, 1894. [AGA-001516-0000]
131. For example, see: TRC, NRA, Library and Archives of Canada, RG10, volume 6374, file 764-10, part 1, S. H. Middleton to J. E. Pugh, 26 April 1940. [PUL-071183]
132. TRC, NRA, Library and Archives Canada – Burnaby, RG10, FA 10-136, volume 11466, 987/18-24, part 1, Truancy, 1952–1969, NAC, Burnaby, R. Sedgewick to Acting Deputy Superintendent General Indian Affairs, 11 October 1891; [SQU-001298-0001] RG10, volume 1575, C-14851, 1898–1899, NAC, Application for Admission, 30 November 1898. [BQL-008267-0001]
133. TRC, NRA, Library and Archives Canada, RG10, FA 10-379, 1999-01431-6, box 405, 987/25-1-018, part 1, Indian Education – Squamish Students Residence, Fraser District, 1950–1969, NAC, Ottawa, P. Phelan to Legal Adviser, 17 November 1952; [SQU-000595] Burnaby, RG10, FA 10-136, volume 11466, 987/18-24, part 1, Truancy, 1952–1969, NAC, Burnaby, P. Phelan to W. S. Arneil, 22 November 1952. [SQU-001297] For an example of a father who successfully went to court to have his children, who had been voluntarily enrolled in a residential school, returned to him, see: Library and Archives Canada, RG10, volume 2552, file 112-220-1, Martin Benson to Deputy Superintendent General of Indian Affairs, 25 September 1903.
134. TRC, NRA, Library and Archives Canada, RG10, volume 7184, file 1/25-1-5-7, part 1, W. M. Graham to Secretary, 19 February 1926. [NCA-014626]
135. Canada, Annual Report of the Department of Indian Affairs, 1945, 168, 183.
136. TRC, NRA, Library and Archives Canada, RG10, volume 6039, file 160-1, part 1, Martin Benson, Memorandum, 13, 15 July 1897. [100.00108]
137. For *Indian Act*, see: *An Act respecting Indians*, Statutes of Canada 1951, chapter 29, sections 113–122, 169–172. For regulations, see: TRC, NRA, INAC – Resolution Sector – IRS Historical Files Collection – Ottawa, file 1/25-1-5-2, volume 1, "Regulations With Respect to Teaching, Education, Inspection, and Discipline for Indian Residential Schools, Made and Established for the Superintendent General of Indian Affairs Pursuant to Paragraph (a) of Section 114 of the Indian Act," 20 January 1953. [PAR-001203-0001]
138. The *Public Schools Act*, Revised Statutes of Manitoba 1954, chapter 215, 923–1,114.
139. *The Manitoba Gazette*, April 9, 1955, 509–510.
140. TRC, NRA, Library and Archives Canada, RG10, volume 6032, file 150-40A, part 1, Headquarters – Compulsory Attendance of Pupils – Indian Schools, 1904–1933, Microfilm reel C-8149, FA 10-17, Indian Agent, Hagersville to Secretary, Indian Affairs, 20 February 1922; [AEMR-255312] *An Act respecting Indians*, Statutes of Canada 1919–1920, chapter 50, section 1, amending Revised Statutes

of Canada 1906, chapter 81, section 10, reproduced in Venne, *Indian Acts*, 178–179.

141. TRC, NRA, Library and Archives Canada, RG10, volume 6309, file 654-1, part 1, J. K. Irwin to Indian Affairs, 22 October 1926. [GDC-006528]
142. TRC, NRA, Library and Archives Canada, RG10, volume 6309, file 654-1, part 1, J. D. McLean to J. K. Irwin, 29 October 1926. [GDC-006529]
143. TRC, NRA, DIAND HQ, file 1/25-1, volume 19, 1968, J. A. MacDonald to the Minister, 9 October 1968. [AEMR-121636]
144. Canada, *Annual Report of the Department of Indian Affairs, 1956*, 76–77; TRC, ASAGR, Department of Northern Affairs and National Resources, *Annual Report Fiscal Year 1957–1958*, 115. [AAN-DC-452773]
145. Canada, *Annual Report of the Department of Indian Affairs, 1931*, 60.
146. TRC, NRA, Anglican Church of Canada, General Synod Archives, ACC-MSCC-GS 75-103, series 3:2, box 55, file 6, S. Gould to D. C. Scott, Ottawa, 18 December 1931; [AAC-090271] TRC, NRA, Anglican Church of Canada, General Synod Archives, Triennial Report of the Board of Management to the Board of Missions, M.S.C.C. 07/1934, Accession GS 75-2A, Archibald [Fleming], Bishop of the Arctic, "The Arctic," in S. Gould, General Secretary, Board of Management, M.S.C.C., "Triennial Report of the Board of Management, M.S.C.C.," 4 July 1934, 353. [AGS-000185]
147. TRC, NRA, Library and Archives Canada, RG10, volume 6112, file 350-10, part 1, W. L. Tyrer to Sutherland, 8 February 1934. [FGA-001100] Although no trace of the decision to award funds to the Catholic school has been found in the archives, by April 1937, the Oblates had begun submitting official Indian Affairs paperwork with regard to the student population at St. Joseph's. See, for example: TRC, NRA, Library and Archives Canada, RG10, volume 6113, file 351-10, part 1, D. Couture, "Application for Admission to the Ste. Theresa Fort George Catholic Residential School for Louise Jolly," 1 April 1937. [FTG-003180-0000]
148. For the Carcross, Yukon, fire, see: Canada, *Annual Report of the Department of Indian Affairs, 1940*, 186. For the Ahousaht, British Columbia, fire, see: Canada, *Annual Report of the Department of Indian Affairs, 1940*, 186. For the Alberni, British Columbia, fire, see: Canada, *Annual Report of the Department of Indian Affairs, 1941*, 166. For the File Hills, Saskatchewan, fire, see: TRC, NRA, Library and Archives Canada, volume 6303, file 653-5, part 6, E. S. Jones to The Secretary, Indian Affairs Branch, Department of Mines and Resources, 10 April 1943; [FHR-000252] Canada, *Annual Report of the Department of Indian Affairs, 1942*, 136. For the Fort George, Québec (the Anglican school), fire, see: TRC, NRA, Library and Archives Canada, RG10, volume 6112, file 350-5, part 1, Thomas Orford to Secretary, Indian Affairs, 3 February 1943. [FGA-001026] For the Onion Lake, Saskatchewan (the Anglican school), fire, see: Canada, *Annual Report of the Department of Indian Affairs, 1944*, 155. For the Wabasca, Alberta, fire, see: TRC, NRA, Library and Archives Canada, RG10, volume 6378, file 767-5, part 3, H. A. Alderwood to R. A. Hoey, 3 January 1945; [JON-003675] Canada, Annual Report of the Department of Indian Affairs, *1945*, 169. For the Norway House, Manitoba, fire, see: TRC, NRA, Library and Archives Canada, RG10, volume 6268, file 581-1, part 2, R. A. Hoey to Acting Deputy Minister, 29 May 1946. [NHU-000117] For the Lac La Ronge, Saskatchewan, fire, see: TRC, NRA, Provincial Archives of Alberta, Anglican Diocese of Athabasca Fonds, Edmonton, AB, Acc. PR1970.0387/1641, box 41, Anglican Diocese of Athabasca Fonds, file A320/572, Indian Schools – General, Official Correspondence of Bishop Sovereign, 1941–1947, Report of Fire at All Saints' School, Lac la Ronge, Sask., 2 February 1947. [PAR-123539] For the Delmas, Saskatchewan, fire, see: TRC, NRA, Library and Archives Canada, RG10, volume 8756, file 671/25-1-010, J. P. B. Ostrander to Indian Affairs Branch, 19 January 1948. [THR-000266-0001]
149. See, for example: TRC, NRA, Library and Archives Canada, RG85, volume 229, file 630/158-9, part

1, Government Hostel – Chesterfield Inlet, 1929–1953, Extracts from S. J. Bailey's Report, Eastern Arctic Patrol, 27 July 1948. [CIU-000189]

150. See, for example: Davin, *Report on Industrial Schools*, 9.
151. For an example of Métis children at a church-run boarding school, see: Erickson, "'Bury Our Sorrows in the Sacred Heart,'" 34–35.
152. For an example of the Métis being viewed as 'dangerous,' see: Library and Archives Canada, RG10, volume 6031, "Extract from a letter dated the 19th July, 1899, from the Rev. Father Hugonard."
153. For an example, see: TRC, NRA, Library and Archives Canada, R776-0-5 (RG55), volume 562, T.B. #252440, Clifford Sifton to Mr. Smart, 18 October 1899. [NPC-523981c]
154. For an early example of this view, see: Canada, Sessional Papers 1885, number 116, 81, Memo: Hugh Richardson, 1 December 1879.
155. For an example, see: Library and Archives Canada, RG10, volume 6323, file 658-10, part 3, W. M. Graham to the Secretary of the Department of Indian Affairs, 5 December 1929.
156. For example, it was estimated in 1936 that 80% of Métis children in Alberta received no education. Chartrand, "Métis Residential School Participation," 41.
157. Quiring, *CCF Colonialism in Northern Saskatchewan*; Barron, *Walking in Indian Moccasins*.
158. For detailed treatment of the issue, see: Chartrand, Logan, and Daniels, *Métis History and Experience*.
159. For examples, see: TRC, NRA, National Capital Regional Service Centre – LAC – Ottawa, volume 2, file 600-1, locator #062-94, Education of Eskimos (1949–1957), Department of Northern Affairs and National Resources to Northern Administration and Lands Branch, 8 April 1958; [NCA-016925] TRC, NRA, Library and Archives Canada – Ottawa, RG85, volume 1506, file 600-1-1, part 2A, J. G. Wright to Mr. Gibson, 19 November 1946. [NCA-005728]
160. For a 1940 assessment of building conditions, see: TRC, NRA, Library and Archives Canada, RG10, volume 6012, file 1-1-5A, part 2, R. A. Hoey to Dr. McGill, 31 May 1940. [BIR-000248]
161. Canada, Special Joint Committee, 1946, 3, 15.
162. Canada, *Annual Report of the Department of Indian Affairs, 1945*, 168, 183; Canada, *Annual Report of the Department of Indian Affairs, 1955*, 70, 76–78.
163. Canada, *Annual Report of the Department of Indian Affairs, 1949*, 199.
164. *An Act respecting Indians*, Statutes of Canada 1951, chapter 29, section 113, reproduced in Venne, *Indian Acts*, 350.
165. Canada, *Annual Report of the Department of Indian Affairs, 1961*, 57.
166. Canada, *Annual Report of the Department of Indian Affairs, 1961*, 63.
167. See, for example: TRC, NRA, No document location, no document file source, The Canadian Catholic Conference, "A Brief to the Parliamentary Committee on Indian Affairs," May 1960, 8. [GMA-001642-0000]
168. Newman, *Indians of the Saddle Lake Reserve*, 81–87.
169. For a discussion that places both child welfare and residential schools in the context of the ongoing colonization of Aboriginal people, see: McKenzie and Hudson, "Native Children."
170. For an example of this assessment, see: TRC, NRA, Canadian Welfare Council and Caldwell 1967, 89. [AEMR-019759]
171. For examples of the link between the closure of residential schools and the increase in children in care, see: TRC, NRA, Library and Archives Canada, RG10, box 98, Acc., 1999-01431-6, file 274/25-1-010, part 1, P. L. McGillvray to Indian Affairs Branch, 17 November 1964; [NCA-010544] TRC, NRA, INAC – Resolution Sector – IRS Historical Files Collection – Ottawa, file 211/6-1-010, volume 6, R. F. Davey to Michael Kearney, 12 June 1967; [SRS-000175] TRC, NRA, Library and Archives Canada,

RG10, Acc. 1984-85/112, box 47, file 451/25-1, Newspaper article, "Mohawk Institute May Close after 139 Years," no date; [TAY-001133] TRC, NRA, Diocese of Huron Archives, Anglican Church of Canada, Huron University College, London, ON, Luxton Papers, box 27, Indian Reserves, Richard Isaac, Six Nations Council To Whom It May Concern, 13 March 1970; [TAY-001432] TRC, NRA, INAC – Resolution Sector – IRS Historical Files Collection – Ottawa, file 479/25-13-001, volume 3, G. D. Cromb to Deputy Minister, 20 March 1970; [TAY-003053-0001] TRC, NRA, National Capital Regional Service Centre – LAC – Ottawa, file 671/6-2-025, volume 4, Onion Lake Band Council Resolution, 31 July 1974. [ORC-008733-0002]

172. McKenzie and Hudson, "Native Children," 126.
173. See, for example: TRC, NRA, INAC – Resolution Sector – IRS Historical Files Collection – Ottawa, RCAP [89-22], file E4974-2031, St. Mary's Student Residence, BC Region, part 1, 1981–1989, B, "Benefit to Children," undated notes from 1982. [MIS-008062-0001]
174. TRC, NRA, DIAND, file 1/25-13, volume 13, R. F. Battle to Deputy Minister, 2 February 1968; [AEMR-014646] TRC, NRA, INAC – Resolution Sector – IRS Historical Files Collection – Ottawa, 1/25-13, 01/68–07/68, volume 13, R. F. Davey to Regional Superintendent of Schools, 13 June 1968. [LOW-016591]
175. Canada, *Annual Report of the Department of Indian Affairs, 1969–1970*, 128.
176. TRC, NRA, DIAND HQ, file 1/25-13-2, volume 2, 06/1968–03/1969, J. A. MacDonald to J. J. Carson, 8 November 1968. [AEMR-121640]
177. TRC, NRA, Government of Northwest Territories – Education, Culture and Employment, Miscellaneous Hostel Reports RIMS ID# 1209, box 9, "Student Residences (Hostels)," undated. [RCN-007183]
178. Canada, *Annual Report of the Department of Indian Affairs, 1968–1969*, 139; Canada, *Annual Report of the Department of Indian Affairs, 1970–1971*, 19.
179. Canada, "Statement of the Government of Canada on Indian Policy," 1969, pages 7, 8, and 22 of 24-page portable document format file.
180. Canada, "Statement of the Government of Canada on Indian Policy," 1969, pages 8 and 20 of 24-page portable document format file.
181. National Indian Brotherhood, "Statement on the Proposed New Indian Policy," Ottawa, 26 June 1969, quoted in Weaver, *Making Canadian Indian Policy*, 174.
182. Indian Chiefs of Alberta 1970, page 16 of 95-page portable document file. [Citizens plus red paper]
183. Weaver, *Making Canadian Indian Policy*, 187.
184. For an example of local dissatisfaction, see: TRC, NRA, No document location, no document file source, Jos Houle to G.-M. Latour, 24 July 1966. [OGP-417032]
185. TRC, NRA, INAC – Resolution Sector – IRS Historical Files Collection – Ottawa, file 779/25-2-009, volume 1 (Ctrl #55-4), Dennis Bell, "Indian School," CP [Canadian Press], 15 September 1970. [NCA-007310-0001]
186. "Indians Will Operate Blue Quills School," *Edmonton Journal*, 1 August 1970. [Blue Quills clippings.pdf]
187. TRC, NRA, Library and Archives Canada – Burnaby, file 951/6-1-030, volume 9, New Christie Student Residence, 1974–1977, FA 10-138, Archival Acc. V1985-86/397, Archival box 2, R. C. Telford to L. E. Wight, 6 May 1974; [CST-001710-0000] INAC – Main Records Office – Ottawa 901/16-2, volume 5, Audit Reports – B.C. Regional Office, 07/1974–06/1978, locator #L362, DIAND – Ottawa Central Registry, [illegible] for R. C. Pankhurst to Director, Finance and Management, 29 January 1975. [CST-009455]
188. All these schools were in Saskatchewan. The Beauval school closed in 1995, see: TRC, NRA, INAC

– Resolution Sector – IRS Historical Files Collection – Ottawa, file E4965-2013, volume 3, Beauval Residential School, box 1, file 1-5, Memorandum of Understanding and Agreement Re: The Beauval Indian Education Centre, 6 June 1995. [BVL-001306] The Duck Lake and the Gordon's residences both closed in 1996, see: TRC, NRA, INAC – Resolution Sector – IRS Historical Files Collection – Ottawa, file E4974-10474, volume 2, Ray Gamracy to Dana Commercial Credit Canada, 6 June 1996; [SMD-000651-0000] Gordon's School, Anglican Indian and Eskimo Residential Schools, Anglican Church of Canada, www.anglican.ca/relationships/histories/gordons-school-punnichy (accessed 5 May 2014). The Lestock, Marieval, and Prince Albert residences all closed in 1997, see: TRC, NRA, INAC – Resolution Sector – IRS Historical Files Collection – Ottawa, Muskowekwan Residential School, box 67, file 1, Muskowekwan Education Centre Board of Directors, Minutes 16 July 1997; [MDD-007310-0001] INAC – Resolution Sector – IRS Historical Files Collection – Ottawa, file E4971-361, volume 3, Myler Savill to Lionel Sparvier, 21 July 1997; [MRS-000002-0001] INAC – Resolution Sector – IRS Historical Files Collection – Ottawa, file E4974-1355, volume 8, "Education Centre Set to Re-open," *Prince Albert Herald*, Carrie Hunter, 15 October 1997 [PAR-003103-0001]

189. Canada, *Annual Report of the Department of Indian Affairs, 1984–1985*, 54.
190. Thompson, "Dehcho Hall to Close its Doors," *Northern News Services online*, 26 January 2009, http://www.nnsl.com/frames/newspapers/2009-01/jan26_09h.html.
191. TRC, NRA, No document location, no document file source, B. Pusharenko, Inuvik, NWT, "Demolition of Former Residential School Called for to Put Bad Memories to Rest," *Edmonton Journal*, 13 August 1998. [GNN-000298-0026]
192. TRC, NRA, Library and Archives Canada, RG10, volume 6040, file 160-4, part 1, R. B. Heron to Regina Presbytery, April 1923. [AEMR-016371]
193. Canada, *Annual Report of the Department of Indian Affairs, 1941*, 189; Canada, *Annual Report of the Department of Indian Affairs, 1942*, 154; Canada, *Annual Report of the Department of Indian Affairs, 1943*, 168; Canada, *Annual Report of the Department of Indian Affairs, 1944*, 177; Canada, *Annual Report of the Department of Indian Affairs, 1945*, 190; Canada, *Annual Report of the Department of Indian Affairs, 1946*, 231; Canada, *Annual Report of the Department of Indian Affairs, 1947*, 236; Canada, *Annual Report of the Department of Indian Affairs, 1948*, 234; Canada, *Annual Report of the Department of Indian Affairs, 1949*, 215, 234; Canada, *Annual Report of the Department of Indian Affairs, 1950*, 86–87; Canada, *Annual Report of the Department of Indian Affairs, 1951*, 34–35; Canada, *Annual Report of the Department of Indian Affairs, 1952*, 74–75; Canada, *Annual Report of the Department of Indian Affairs, 1953*, 82–83; Canada, *Annual Report of the Department of Indian Affairs, 1954*, 88–89; Canada, *Annual Report of the Department of Indian Affairs, 1955*, 78–79; Canada, *Annual Report of the Department of Indian Affairs, 1956*, 76–77; Canada, *Annual Report of the Department of Indian Affairs, 1956–57*, 88–89; Canada, *Annual Report of the Department of Indian Affairs, 1958*, 90–91; Canada, *Annual Report of the Department of Indian Affairs, 1959*, 94; Canada, *Annual Report of the Department of Indian Affairs, 1960*, 94; Canada, *Annual Report of the Department of Indian Affairs, 1961*, 103.
194. Canada, *Annual Report of the Department of Indian Affairs, 1942*, 154; Canada, *Annual Report of the Department of Indian Affairs, 1943*, 168; Canada, Annual Report of the Department of Indian Affairs, 1944, 177; Canada, Annual Report of the Department of Indian Affairs, 1945, 190; Canada, *Annual Report of the Department of Indian Affairs, 1946*, 231; Canada, *Annual Report of the Department of Indian Affairs, 1947*, 236; Canada, *Annual Report of the Department of Indian Affairs, 1948*, 234; Canada, *Annual Report of the Department of Indian Affairs, 1949*, 215; Canada, *Annual Report of the Department of Indian Affairs, 1950*, 86–87; Canada, *Annual Report of the Department of Indian Affairs, 1951*, 34–35; Canada, *Annual Report of the Department of Indian Affairs, 1952*,

74–75; Canada, *Annual Report of the Department of Indian Affairs, 1953*, 82–83; Canada, *Annual Report of the Department of Indian Affairs, 1954*, 88–89; Canada, *Annual Report of the Department of Indian Affairs, 1955*, 78–79; Canada, *Annual Report of the Department of Indian Affairs, 1956*, 76–77; Canada, *Annual Report of the Department of Indian Affairs, 1956–57*, 88–89; Canada, *Annual Report of the Department of Indian Affairs, 1958*, 91; Canada, *Annual Report of the Department of Indian Affairs, 1959*, 94; Canada, *Annual Report of the Department of Indian Affairs, 1960*, 94; Canada, *Annual Report of the Department of Indian Affairs, 1961*, 102; Canada, *Annual Report of the Department of Indian Affairs, 1962*, 73; Canada, *Annual Report of the Department of Indian Affairs, 1963*, 62.

195. Canada, *Annual Report of the Department of Indian Affairs, 1883*, 96.
196. TRC, NRA, Library and Archives Canada, RG10, volume 6323, file 658-6, part 1, Department of Indian Affairs Inspector's Report for the St. Barnabas, Indian Residential school, D. Hicks, 25 September 1928. [PAR-003233]
197. Library and Archives Canada, RG10, volume 6205, file 468-1, part 2, S. R. McVitty to Secretary, Indian Affairs, 30 January 1928. [McVittie to Secretary, Jan 30 1928]
198. TRC, NRA, Library and Archives Canada, RG10, volume 6342, file 750-1, part 1, Microfilm reel C-8699, J. D. McLean to Reverend E. Ruaux, 21 June 1915. [MRY-001517] For a similar report from the Battleford, Saskatchewan, school, see: Canada, *Annual Report of the Department of Indian Affairs, 1909*, 349–350. For a Manitoba example, see: TRC, NRA, Library and Archives Canada, RG10, volume 6267, file 580-5, part 4, Joseph Hamilton Inspection Report, not dated. [DRS-000570]
199. TRC, NRA, INAC – Resolution Sector – IRS Historical Files Collection – Ottawa, file 673/23-5-038, volume 1, H. L. Winter to Indian Affairs, 9 September 1932. [MRS-000138-0001]
200. TRC, NRA, Library and Archives Canada, RG10, volume 6327, file 660-1, part 1, J. D. McLean to Rev. J. Hugonard, 30 May 1911. [PLD-007442]
201. TRC, NRA, Library and Archives Canada, RG10, volume 6422, file 869-1, part 2, R. H. Cairns, inspector to J. D. McLean, 5 January 1915. [COQ-000390]
202. TRC, NRA, Library and Archives Canada, RG10, volume 6431, file 877-1, part 2, "Extract from Report of Mr. Inspector Cairns dated September 5th and 6th, 1928 on the Alberni Indian Residential School." [ABR-001591]
203. TRC, NRA, Library and Archives Canada, RG10, volume 6001, file 1-1-1, part 3, "Department of Indian Affairs, Schools Branch," 31 March 1935. [SRS-000279]
204. For a British Columbia example, see: TRC, NRA, Library and Archives Canada, RG10, volume 6431, file 877-1, part 1, A. W. Neill to A. W. Vowell, 8 July 1909. [ABR-007011-0001] For a Manitoba example, see: TRC, NRA, Library and Archives Canada, RG10, volume 6262, file 578-1, part 4, W. M. Graham to Secretary, Indian Affairs, 4 February 1922. [ELK-000299]
205. For example, a 1936 United Church document on First Nations education policy stated that the staff of all United Church schools should be composed of people who had a "Christian motive, or, in other words, a missionary purpose coupled with skill in some particular field to teach his specialty to the Indians." Staff members were expected to be "closely related to and actively interested in the work of the nearest United Church," and be acquainted with, and sympathetic to, "the religious education programme of the United Church." Having laid out these fairly specific requirements, the policy document added that "some minimum educational qualifications for staff members should be outlined." TRC, NRA, United Church Archives, Acc. 83.050C, box 144-21, "Statement of Policy Re Indian Residential Schools," June 1936. [UCC-050004]
206. For an example of the link between low pay and unqualified teachers, see: TRC, NRA, Library and Archives Canada, RG10, volume 6039, file 160-1, part 1, Martin Benson, Memorandum, 15 July

1897, 4, 25. [100.00108]

207. TRC, NRA, Library and Archives Canada, RG10, volume 4041, file 334503, F. H. Paget to Frank Pedley, 25 November 1908, 55. [RCA-000298]
208. TRC, NRA, Library and Archives Canada, RG10, volume 6431, file 877-1, part 1, A. W. Vowell to Secretary, Indian Affairs, 14 July 1909. [ABR-007011-0000]
209. Canada, *Annual Report of the Department of Indian Affairs, 1955*, 51.
210. TRC, NRA, DIAND, file 1/25-1, volume 22, R. F. Davey to Bergevin, 15 September 1959, 3. [AEMR-019616]
211. Canada, *Annual Report of the Department of Indian Affairs, 1903*, 342–343. For other examples of the emphasis on religious training in the schools, see: Canada, Annual Report of the Department of Indian Affairs, 1887, 27–28; Canada, *Annual Report of the Department of Indian Affairs, 1910*, 433–434; Canada, *Annual Report of the Department of Indian Affairs, 1890*, 119; Canada, *Annual Report of the Department of Indian Affairs, 1900*, 323. Canada, *Annual Report of the Department of Indian Affairs, 1901*, 317, 320.
212. Moine, *My Life in a Residential School*, n.p.
213. TRC, NRA, The Presbyterian Church in Canada Archives, Toronto, ON, Tyler Bjornson File, 'Presbyterian Research,' "Presbyterian Indian Residential School Staff Handbook," 1. [IRC-041206]
214. For Kelly, see: Morley, *Roar of the Breakers*, 57, 158. For Ahenakew, see: Ahenakew, *Voices of the Plains Cree*, 14–24. For Kennedy, see: Canada, *Annual Report of the Department of Indian Affairs, 1902*, 194. For Dion, see: Dion, *My Tribe the Crees*, 156–163. For Johnson, see: Johnston, *Buckskin & Broadcloth*, 46. For Lickers, see: "Norman Lickers First Ontario Indian Lawyer," *Brantford Expositor*, November 18, 1938, quoted in Briggs, "Legal Professionalism," 2.
215. Canada, Special Joint Committee, 1947, 747.
216. TRC, AVS, David Charleson, Statement to the Truth and Reconciliation Commission of Canada, Deroche, British Columbia, 20 January 2010, Statement Number: 2011-5043.
217. TRC, AVS, Isabelle Whitford, Statement to the Truth and Reconciliation Commission of Canada, Keeseekoowenin First Nation, Manitoba, 28 May 2010, Statement Number: S-KFN-MB-01-004.
218. TRC, AVS, Betsy Olson, Statement to the Truth and Reconciliation Commission of Canada, Saskatoon, Saskatchewan, 21 June 2012, Statement Number: 2011-4378.
219. TRC, AVS, Leona Agawa, Statement to the Truth and Reconciliation Commission of Canada, Sault Ste. Marie, Ontario, 6 November 2010, Statement Number: 01-ON-4-6NOV10-006.
220. Canada, *Annual Report of the Department of Indian Affairs, 1921*, 28.
221. TRC, NRA, Library and Archives Canada, RG10, volume 6014, file 1-1-6 MAN, part 1, Duncan Campbell Scott to Mr. Meighen, 1 June 1920. [NCA-002403]
222. Canada, Special Joint Committee, *Minutes of Evidence*, D. F. Brown Presiding, 15 April 1947, 483–484.
223. Canada, Special Joint Committee, *Minutes of Evidence*, D .F. Brown Presiding, 17 April 1947, 505.
224. TRC, NRA, Library and Archives Canada, RG85, volume 1338, file 600-1-1, part 19, D. W. Hepburn, "Northern Education: Facade for Failure," *Variables: the Journal of the Sociology Club* (University of Alberta) 2, no. 1 (February 1963): 16. [NCA-005960]
225. TRC, NRA, Library and Archives Canada, RG85, volume 1338, file 600-1-1, part 19, D. W. Hepburn, "Northern Education: Facade for Failure." *Variables: the Journal of the Sociology Club* (University of Alberta) 2, no. 1 (February 1963): 17. [NCA-005960]
226. TRC, NRA, Library and Archives Canada, RG85, volume 1338, file 600-1-1, part 19, D. W. Hepburn, "Northern Education: Facade for Failure." *Variables: the Journal of the Sociology Club* (University of Alberta) 2, no. 1 (February 1963): 18. [NCA-005960]

227. TRC, NRA, National Archives of Canada, RG10, volume 8760, file 901/25-1, part 2, R. F. Davey to Director, 14 March 1956, 4. [AEMR-120651]
228. See, for example: TRC, NRA, DIAND, file 1/25-1 (E.10), "Report on Textbooks," 6–9; [AEMR-019193A] Commission Parent, *Rapport de la Commission royale d'enquête sur l'enseignement dans la province de Québec*, volume 3, *L'administration de l'enseignement*, part B, "Diversité religieuse, culturelle, et unité de l'administration," http://classiques.uqac.ca/contemporains/quebec_commission_parent/rapport_parent_4/rapport_parent_vol_4.pdf, paragraph 210 (accessed 7 August 2012); TRC, NRA, DIAND, file 1/25-1 (E.10), "Report on Textbooks," 6–9; [AEMR-019193A] Vanderburgh, The Canadian Indian.
229. TRC, NRA, DIAND, file 1/25-1 (E.10), "Report on Textbooks," 1–6. [AEMR-019193A]
230. TRC, AVS, Mary Courchene, Statement to the Truth and Reconciliation Commission of Canada, Pine Creek First Nation, Manitoba, 28 November 2011, Statement Number: 2011-2515.
231. TRC, AVS, Lorna Cochrane, Statement to the Truth and Reconciliation Commission of Canada, Winnipeg, Manitoba, 18 June 2010, Statement Number: SC110.
232. Elias, "Lillian Elias," 51.
233. See, for example: TRC, AVS, Victoria McIntosh, Statement to the Truth and Reconciliation Commission of Canada, Winnipeg, Manitoba, 16 June 2010, Statement Number: 02-MB-16JU10-123.
234. TRC, AVS, Walter Jones, Statement to the Truth and Reconciliation Commission of Canada, Victoria, British Columbia, 14 April 2012, Statement Number: 2011-4008.
235. Pigott, "The Leadership Factory," B3.
236. Blondin-Andrew, "New Ways of Looking for Leadership," 64.
237. John Amagoalik, quoted in McGregor, *Inuit Education*, 110.
238. Amagoalik, *Changing the Face of Canada*, 43–46.
239. TRC, AVS, David Simailak, Statement to the Truth and Reconciliation Commission of Canada, Baker Lake, Nunavut, 15 November 2011, Statement Number: SP032.
240. TRC, AVS, Roddy Soosay, Statement to the Truth and Reconciliation Commission of Canada, Hobbema, Alberta, 25 July 2013, Statement Number: 2011-2379.
241. TRC, AVS, Martha Loon, Statement to the Truth and Reconciliation Commission of Canada, Thunder Bay, Ontario, 25 November 2010, Statement Number: 01-ON-24NOV10-021.
242. TRC, AVS, Frederick Ernest Koe, Statement to the Truth and Reconciliation Commission of Canada, Inuvik, Northwest Territories, 30 June 2011, Statement Number: SC091.
243. TRC, AVS, Madeleine Dion Stout, Statement to the Truth and Reconciliation Commission of Canada, Winnipeg, Manitoba, 18 June 2010, Statement Number: 02-MB-18JU10-059.
244. TRC, NRA, Library and Archives Canada, RG10, volume 6191, file 462-1, part 1, Russell T. Ferrier to George Prewer, 8 February 1922. [CRS-001015]
245. Canada, *Annual Report of the Department of Indian Affairs, 1887*, 126.
246. Canada, *Annual Report of the Department of Indian Affairs, 1884*, 155.
247. Canada, *Annual Report of the Department of Indian Affairs, 1886*, 139.
248. Library and Archives Canada, RG10, volume 3930, file 117377-1 A, H. Reed to Bishop of Rupert's Land, 31 May 1893.
249. Wasylow, "History of Battleford Industrial School," 467.
250. Elias, "Lillian Elias," 54–55.
251. For laundry example, see: TRC, NRA, Library and Archives Canada, RG10, volume 6207, file 468-5, part 6, S. R. McVitty to Secretary Indian Affairs, 3 January 1929. [MER-000751] For kitchen example, see: TRC, NRA, Library and Archives Canada, RG10, volume 6058, file 265-13, part 1, J. P. Mackey to A. F. MacKenzie, 20 May 1930. [SRS-000252] For workshop example, see: TRC, NRA, Library

and Archives Canada, RG10, volume 6219, file 471-13, part 1, Russell T. Ferrier to J. Howitt, 13 June 1932. [AGA-000069]

252. For an example, see: TRC, NRA, Library and Archives Canada, RG10, volume 6327, file 660-1, part 3, A. F. MacKenzie to G. Leonard, 6 May 1936. [PLD-006119]
253. TRC, NRA, Library and Archives Canada, RG10, volume 6327, file 660-1, part 3, A. F. MacKenzie to William Hall, 18 May 1936. [PLD-000750]
254. TRC, NRA, Library and Archives Canada, RG10, volume 6327, file 660-1, part 3, William Hall to Indian Affairs, 30 April 1936. [PLD-000746]
255. TRC, NRA, Library and Archives Canada, RG10, volume 6255, file 576-1, part 4, R. T. Chapin to A. G. Hamilton, 10 September 1941. [BRS-000461-0001] For the boy's age, see: TRC, NRA, Library and Archives Canada, RG10, volume 6258, file 576-10, part 8, "Application for Admission," Kenneth Smith, 1 July 1938. [BRS-002184-0007]
256. TRC, NRA, Library and Archives Canada, RG10, volume 6259, file 576-23, part 1, G. C. Elwyn to RCMP, 20 April 1949. [BRS-000332]
257. TRC, NRA, Library and Archives Canada, RG10, volume 6352, file 753-23, part 1, 1935–1944, Microfilm reel C-8709, Acting Director to J. T. Faunt, 18 December 1944. [EDM-003369]
258. TRC, NRA, Library and Archives Canada, RG10, volume 6251, file 575-1, part 3, R. A. Hoey to A. G. Smith, 24 September 1942. [BIR-000272]
259. For ending of half-day system, see: TRC, NRA, INAC – Resolution Sector – IRS Historical Files Collection – Ottawa, file 1/25-1-5-2, volume 1, Superintendent General DIAND, "Regulations with respect to teaching, education, inspection, and discipline for Indian Residential Schools, Made and Established by the Superintendent General of Indian Affairs Pursuant to Paragraph (a) of Section 114 of the Indian Act," 20 January 1953; [PAR-001203-0001] H. M. Jones to Deputy Minister. [PAR-001203-0000]
260. TRC, NRA, INAC – Resolution Sector – IRS Historical Files Collection – Ottawa, file 128/25-2-575, volume 1, J. R. Bell to R. D. Ragan, 17 February 1959. [IRC-041312]
261. TRC, NRA, Library and Archives Canada, RG10, volume 3674, file 11422, E. Dewdney to Thomas Clarke, 31 July 1883. [120.06668]
262. TRC, NRA, Library and Archives Canada, RG10, volume 6452, file 884-1, part 1, Microfilm reel 8773, "Rules and Regulations, Kootenay Industrial School." [AEMR-011621A]
263. Library and Archives Canada, RG10, volume 3836, file 68557, H. Reed, Suggestions for the Government of Indian schools, 27 January 1890.
264. Canada, *Annual Report of the Department of Indian Affairs, 1894*, 248–249.
265. Canada, *Annual Report of the Department of Indian Affairs, 1887*, 128.
266. Canada, *Annual Report of the Department of Indian Affairs, 1898*, 345.
267. Canada, *Annual Report of the Department of Indian Affairs, 1898*, 355.
268. Canada, *Annual Report of the Department of Indian Affairs, 1898*, 302.
269. Canada, *Annual Report of the Department of Indian Affairs, 1903*, 457.
270. TRC, NRA, St. Paul's Archives, Acts of Canonical Visitation, 1883–1966, Stacks 2L, Acte Général de Visite des Missions Indiennes du Nord-Ouest Canadien par le T.R.P. Théodore Labouré, O.M.I., Supérieur Géneral, Rome Maison Générale, 45. [OMI-034614]
271. Wasylow, "History of Battleford Industrial School," 449.
272. Moran, *Stoney Creek Woman*, 58.
273. Callahan, "On Our Way to Healing," 68.
274. Graham, *Mush Hole*, 368.
275. Provincial Archives of British Columbia, Transcript Disc #182, Mary Englund, interviewed by Mar-

garet Whitehead, 31 July 1980, PABC No. 3868.

276. Graham, *Mush Hole*, 449.
277. TRC, AVS, Arthur Ron McKay, Statement to the Truth and Reconciliation Commission of Canada, Winnipeg, Manitoba, 18 June 2010, Statement Number: 02-MB-18JU10-044.
278. TRC, AVS, Peter Nakogee, Statement to the Truth and Reconciliation Commission of Canada, Timmins, Ontario, 9 November 2010, Statement Number: 01-ON-4-6NOV10-023. (Translated from Swampy Cree to English by Translation Bureau, Public Works and Government Services Canada, 8961944_002.)
279. TRC, AVS, Meeka Alivaktuk (translated from Inuktitut), Statement to the Truth and Reconciliation Commission of Canada, Pangnirtung, Nunavut, 13 February 2012, Statement Number: SP045.
280. TRC, AVS, Sam Kautainuk (translated from Inuktitut), Statement to the Truth and Reconciliation Commission of Canada, Pond Inlet, Nunavut, 7 February 2012, Statement Number: SP044.
281. TRC, AVS, Greg Rainville, Statement to the Truth and Reconciliation Commission of Canada, Saskatoon, Saskatchewan, 22 June 2012, Statement Number: 2011-1752.
282. TRC, AVS, William Herney, Statement to the Truth and Reconciliation Commission of Canada, Halifax, Nova Scotia, 29 October 2011, Statement Number: 2011-2923.
283. TRC, AVS, Alphonsine McNeely, Statement to the Truth and Reconciliation Commission of Canada, Fort Good Hope, Northwest Territories, 13 July 2010, Statement Number: 01-NWT-JY10-002.
284. TRC, AVS, Pierrette Benjamin, Statement to the Truth and Reconciliation Commission of Canada, La Tuque, Québec, 6 March 2013, Statement Number: SP105.
285. TRC, AVS, John Kistabish (translated from French), Statement to the Truth and Reconciliation Commission of Canada, Montréal, Québec, 26 April 2013, Statement Number: 2011-6135.
286. Snow, *These Mountains Are Our Sacred Places*, 110.
287. TRC, AVS, Andrew Bull Calf, Statement to the Truth and Reconciliation Commission of Canada, Lethbridge, Alberta, 10 October 2013, Statement Number: 2011-0273.
288. TRC, AVS, Evelyn Kelman, Statement to the Truth and Reconciliation Commission of Canada, Lethbridge, Alberta, 10 October 2013, Statement Number: SP128.
289. TRC, AVS, Marilyn Buffalo, Statement to the Truth and Reconciliation Commission of Canada, Hobbema, Alberta, 25 July 2013, Statement Number: SP125.
290. TRC, AVS, Sarah McLeod, Statement to the Truth and Reconciliation Commission of Canada, Kamloops, British Columbia, 8 August 2009, Statement Number: 2011-5009.
291. TRC, NRA, Library and Archives Canada, RG10, volume 7936, file 32-104, J. W. House to G. H. Gooderham, 26 January 1942. [OLD-004156-0001]
292. TRC, NRA, Library and Archives Canada, 875-1, part 4, volume 6426, 1937–1947, NAC, F. E. Anfield to Ex-Pupils & Graduates of the Kwawkewlth Agency, 6 April 1943. [MIK-002742-0001]
293. Thaddee Andre (translated from French), Statement to the Truth and Reconciliation Commission of Canada, Montréal, Québec, 25 April 2013, Statement Number: 2011-6068.
294. See, for example, the brief that the Canadian Catholic Conference submitted to the Joint Committee of the Senate and House of Commons on Indian Affairs in 1960. TRC, NRA, No document source, no document location, "CCC Brief on Indian Welfare and Education," *Indian Record*, June 1960, 3. [BVT-001818]
295. TRC, AVS, Alex Alikashuak, Statement to the Truth and Reconciliation Commission of Canada, Winnipeg, Manitoba, 16 June 2010, Statement Number: 02-MB-16JU10-137.
296. Canadian Welfare Council, *Indian Residential Schools*, 100.
297. TRC, NRA, Provincial Archives of Alberta, PAA 71.220 B56 2429, J. Weitz, "Report on the use of the language, history and customs of the Blood Indians in the classes of Level I, during the school year

1968–69," 30 June 1969. [OGP-023347]

298. For an example from British Columbia, see: TRC, NRA, No document location, no document file source, 958/25-13, volume 3, J. A. Andrews to R. F. Davey, 28 June 1966. [ABR-000402]
299. Canada, *Annual Report of the Department of Indian Affairs, 1974–1975*, 32–33.
300. TRC, AVS, Rose Dorothy Charlie, Statement to the Truth and Reconciliation Commission of Canada, Whitehorse, Yukon, 27 May 2011, Statement Number: 2011-1134.
301. TRC, AVS, Joline Huskey, Statement to the Truth and Reconciliation Commission of Canada, Behchoko, Northwest Territories, 15 April 2011, Statement Number: 2011-0231.
302. TRC, AVS, Bruce R. Dumont, Statement to the Truth and Reconciliation Commission of Canada, Batoche, Saskatchewan, 23 July 2010, Statement Number: 01-SK-18-25JY10-013.
303. Canada, House of Commons Debates (22 May 1888), 1681.
304. Library and Archives Canada, RG10, volume 6816, file 486-2-5, part 1, H. Reed to J. Hugonnard, 13 June 1890.
305. Canada, *Annual Report of the Department of Indian Affairs, 1896*, xxxviii.
306. See, for examples: Canada, *Annual Report of the Department of Indian Affairs, 1894*, 151; Canada, *Annual Report of the Department of Indian Affairs, 1894*, 193–194; Canada, *Annual Report of the Department of Indian Affairs, 1897*, 284.
307. TRC, NRA, Library and Archives Canada, RG10, volume 1347, Microfilm reel C-13916, P. Claessen to W. R. Robertson, 17 August 1909. [KUP-004235]
308. Canada, *Annual Report of the Department of Indian Affairs, 1909*, 420.
309. Library and Archives Canada, RG10, volume 3881, file 934189, M. Begg to A. Forget, 23 February 1895.
310. TRC, NRA, Library and Archives Canada, RG10, volume 6318, file 657-1, part 1, A. E. Forget to Indian Agent, Touchwood Hills, 31 January 1896. [MDD-000851]
311. TRC, NRA, Library and Archives Canada, RG10, volume 6326, file 659-10, part 1, J. E. Pratt to Philip Phelan, 15 June 1936. [ORC-006021]
312. Library and Archives Canada, RG10, volume 6816, file 486-2-5, part 1, Extract Presbytery of Winnipeg, Committee on Indian Work, R. J. MacPherson, 9 September 1922.
313. Montour, *Brown Tom's School Days*, 26.
314. Brass, *I Walk in Two Worlds*, 25.
315. Brass, *I Walk in Two Worlds*, 25–26.
316. Moran, *Stoney Creek Woman*, 53–54.
317. Quoted in Krech, "Nutritional Evaluation," 186.
318. Quoted in Krech, "Nutritional Evaluation," 186.
319. Canada, *Annual Report of the Department of Indian Affairs, 1895*, 114.
320. TRC, NRA, Library and Archives Canada, RG10, volume 3918, file 116659-1, John F. Smith to Assistant Deputy and Secretary, Indian Affairs, 29 March 1918. [AEMR-255360]
321. TRC, NRA, Library and Archives Canada, RG10, FA 10-13, volume 3918, Microfilm reel C-10161, file 116.659-1, 1892–1920, Spec. Claims Kamloops Agency: General Correspondence Pertaining to Kamloops Industrial School, F. V. Agnew to Indian Affairs, 4 June 1918. [KAM-009763]
322. TRC, NRA, Library and Archives Canada, RG10, volume 6039, file 160-1, part 1, Martin Benson, to J. D. McLean, 15 July 1897. [100.00109]
323. TRC, NRA, Library and Archives Canada, RG10, volume 6187, file 461-1, part 3, Frank Edwards to the Secretary, Indian Affairs Branch, 26 June 1939. [IRC-048013]
324. For examples just from the 1920s, see: TRC, NRA, Library and Archives Canada, RG10, volume 3933, file 117657-1, Microfilm reel C-10164, W. M. Graham to Duncan C. Scott, 1 October 1914;

[AEMR-013533] TRC, NRA, Library and Archives Canada, RG10, volume 6348, file 752-1, part 1, 1894–1936, Microfilm reel 8705, "Extract from Nurse Ramage's report, November 1921"; [CFT-000156-0001] TRC, NRA, Library and Archives Canada, RG10, volume 6348, file 752-1, part 1, 1894–1936, Microfilm reel 8705, "Extract of report of G. H. Gooderham, for month of October 1921"; [CFT-000148] TRC, NRA, Library and Archives Canada, RG10, volume 6337, file 663-1, part 1, Russell T. Ferrier to Reverend A. Watelle, 31 January 1922; [THR-000149] TRC, NRA, Library and Archives Canada, RG10, volume 6337, file 663-1, part 1, Russell T. Ferrier to Reverend A. Watelle, 16 February 1922; [THR-000151] TRC, NRA, Library and Archives Canada, RG10, volume 6327, file 660-1, part 2, "Memorandum for File," Russell T. Ferrier, 17 March 1922; [PLD-007242] TRC, NRA, Library and Archives Canada, RG10, volume 6444, file 881-5, part 2, 1922–1924, Microfilm reel C-8767, "Extract from Inspector's Report on the Fraser Lake Residential School, dated April 23rd and 24th, 1923"; [LEJ-003751] TRC, NRA, Library and Archives Canada, RG10, volume 6443, file 881-1, part 1, N. Coccola to J. D. McLean, 22 June 1923; [LEJ-001012] TRC, NRA, Library and Archives Canada, RG10, volume 6318, file 657-1, part 1, A. F. MacKenzie to J. B. Hardinge, 21 September 1923; [MDD-000731] TRC, NRA, Library and Archives Canada, RG10, volume 6324, file 659-5, part 2, "Onion Lake R.C. Boarding School," 1926; [ORC-000346-0001] TRC, NRA, Library and Archives Canada, RG10, volume 6252, file 575-5, part 2, A. G. Hamilton to Mr. Graham, 23 June 1927; [BIR-000079] TRC, NRA, Library and Archives Canada, RG10, volume 6252, file 575-5, part 2, W. Murison to W. Graham, 17 November 1927; [BIR-000093] TRC, NRA, Library and Archives Canada, RG10, volume 6268, file 580-14, part 1, A. F. MacKenzie to J. W. Waddy, 25 April 1927; [DRS-000574] TRC, NRA, Library and Archives Canada, volume 6268, file 580-14, part 1, J. W. Waddy to Assistant Deputy and Secretary, 6 May 1927; [DRS-000575] TRC, NRA, Library and Archives Canada, RG10, volume 6267, file 580-1, part 2, J. Waddy to Indian Affairs, 24 November 1928; [DRS-000564] TRC, NRA, Library and Archives Canada, RG10, volume 6267, file 580-1, part 2, Inspection report, 31 October 1929. [DRS-000566]

325. TRC, NRA, No document location, no document file source, T. M. Kennedy to Reverend Father Provincial, 2 December 1937. [OKM-000248]
326. TRC, NRA, Library and Archives Canada, RG10, volume 6455, file 884-14, part 1, Microfilm reel C-8777, "Extract from report of Inspector Cairns, Dated Nov. 9, 1922, on the Kuper Island Industrial School." [KUP-003836-0000]
327. TRC, NRA, Library and Archives Canada, RG10, volume 6262, file 578-1, part 4, W. Murison to Indian Affairs, 2 June 1925. [ELK-000330]
328. Health Canada, Food and Nutrition, Canada's Food Guides from 1942 to 1992, http://www.hc-sc.gc.ca/fn-an/food-guide-aliment/context/fg_history-histoire_ga-eng.php#fnb9 (accessed 14 December 2013).
329. TRC, NRA, Library and Archives Canada, RG10, volume 6306, file 652-5, part 6, L. B. Pett to P. E. Moore, 8 December 1947. [SMD-001897-0000]
330. TRC, NRA, Library and Archives Canada, RG10, 8796, file 1/25-13, part 4, L. B. Pett to H. M. Jones, 21 March 1958. [NPC-400776]
331. TRC, NRA, Headquarters, 1/25-1-4-1, Indian Education – Dietary Scale, Residential Schools, K. A. Feyrer, G. C. Butler, 22 December 1966. [LOW-002326-0004]
332. TRC, NRA, Unknown document location, file 901/25-13, Gerald Michaud, 1 April 1969. [120.08100C]
333. TRC, NRA, Library and Archives Canada, RG29, volume 2990, file 851-6-4, part 5a, L. Leclerc to A/Regional Director, Manitoba Region, 26 November 1970. [NPC-605542]
334. TRC, AVS, Daisy Diamond, Statement to the Truth and Reconciliation Commission of Canada,

Winnipeg, Manitoba, 18 June 2010, Statement Number: SC110.

335. TRC, AVS, Dora Fraser, Statement to the Truth and Reconciliation Commission of Canada, Winnipeg, Manitoba, 19 June 2010, Statement Number: 02-MB-19JU10-012.

336. TRC, AVS, Ellen Okimaw, Statement to the Truth and Reconciliation Commission of Canada, Timmins, Ontario, 8 November 2010, Statement Number: 01-ON-4-6NOV10-022.

337. TRC, AVS, Bernard Catcheway, Statement to the Truth and Reconciliation Commission of Canada, Skownan First Nation, Manitoba, 12 October 2011, Statement Number: 2011-2510.

338. TRC, AVS, Bernard Sutherland, Statement to the Truth and Reconciliation Commission of Canada, Fort Albany, Ontario, 29 January 2013, Statement Number: 2011-3180. (Translated from Cree to English by Translation Bureau, Public Works and Government Services Canada, 8961944_003.)

339. "Nun Forced Native Students to Eat Their Own Vomit," *Edmonton Journal*, 25 June 1999.

340. TRC, AVS, Simon Awashish, Statement to the Truth and Reconciliation Commission of Canada, La Tuque, Québec, 5 March 2013, Statement Number: SP104.

341. TRC, AVS, Woodie Elias, Statement to the Truth and Reconciliation Commission of Canada, Fort McPherson, Northwest Territories, 12 September 2012, Statement Number: 2011-0343.

342. TRC, AVS, Dorothy Nolie, Statement to the Truth and Reconciliation Commission of Canada, Alert Bay, British Columbia, 20 October 2011, Statement Number: 2011-3294.

343. TRC, AVS, Nellie Trapper, Statement to the Truth and Reconciliation Commission of Canada, Winnipeg, Manitoba, 18 June 2010, Statement Number: 02-MB-16JU10-086.

344. TRC, AVS, Inez Dieter, Statement to the Truth and Reconciliation Commission of Canada, Regina, Saskatchewan, 16 January 2012, Statement Number: SP035.

345. TRC, AVS, Gladys Prince, Statement to the Truth and Reconciliation Commission of Canada, Brandon, Manitoba, 13 October 2011, Statement Number: 2011-2498. (Translated from Ojibway to English by Translation Bureau, Public Works and Government Services Canada, 8956132.)

346. TRC, AVS, Frances Tait, Statement to the Truth and Reconciliation Commission of Canada, Victoria, British Columbia, 13 April 2012, Statement Number: 2011-3974.

347. TRC, AVS, Hazel Bitternose, Statement to the Truth and Reconciliation Commission of Canada, Regina, Saskatchewan, 17 January 2012, Statement Number: SP036.

348. Sadowski, "Preliminary Report on the Investigation," 7–8.

349. TRC, LACAR, Library and Archives Canada, Ottawa, RG29, Department of Health fonds, Medical Services sous-fonds, Medical Services Branch Central Registry File series, Administrative Records from Blocks 800 to 849 sub-series, finding aid 29-143, Perm. volume 2622, file 800-4-9, file volume 1, file dates 09/1952 to 11/1976, file name "Records Retirement," *Indian and Northern Health Services Administrative Circular 57-66*, Destruction and Retention of Documents, P. E. Moore, 7 August 1957. [46a-c000301-d0008-001]

350. For an example, see: Canada, *Annual Report of the Department of Indian Affairs, 1893*, 91–97.

351. TRC, NRA, Library and Archives Canada, RG10, volume 6016, file 1-1-23, part 1, A. F. MacKenzie to Indian Agents, Principals of Indian Residential Schools, 17 April 1935. [SBR-001147-0000] Under this policy, the principal was to inform the Indian agent of the death of a student. The agent was then to convene and chair a three-person board of inquiry. The two other members of the board were to be the principal and the physician who attended the student. The board was to complete a form provided by Indian Affairs that requested information on the cause of death and the treatment provided to the child. Parents were to be notified of the inquiry and given the right to attend or have a representative attend the inquiry to make a statement. However, an inquiry was not to be delayed for more than seventy-two hours to accommodate parents. TRC, NRA, Library and Archives Canada, RG10, volume 6016, file 1-1-23, part 1, Indian Affairs Memorandum, 17 April

1935. [SBR-001147-0001]

352. See, for examples: TRC, NRA, Anglican Church of Canada, General Synod Archives, Anglican Church of Canada, GS-75-103, B17, Minutes of meeting of Indian and Eskimo Commission Held on Tuesday, January 11th, 1927, 11; [AAC-083001] St. Boniface Historical Society, Archives Deschâtelets, L 541 M27L 266, Brachet to père provincial, 20 October 1928.
353. TRC, NRA, Library and Archives Canada, RG10, volume 6302, file 650-23, part 2, Inspector, Commanding Prince Albert Sub-Division to The Officer in Charge, RCMP, Regina, Saskatchewan, 10 September 1942. [BVL-000822]
354. For discussions of the health conditions on the Prairies and the federal government's failure to meet its Treaty commitments, see: Carter, *Lost Harvests*; Daschuk, *Clearing the Plains*; and Lux, *Medicine that Walks*. For food and Treaties, see: Miller, *Skyscrapers Hide the Heavens*, 228–230.
355. TRC, NRA, Library and Archives Canada, RG10, volume 6039, file 160-1, part 1, Martin Benson, to J. D. McLean, 15 July 1897. [100.00109]
356. Canada, *Annual Report of the Department of Indian Affairs, 1904*, 204.
357. TRC, NRA, Library and Archives Canada, RG10, volume 6012, file 1-1-5A, part 2, R. A. Hoey to Dr. McGill, 31 May 1940. [BIR-000248] For date of Hoey's appointment, see: Manitoba Historical Society, Memorable Manitobans: Robert Alexander Hoey (1883–1965), http://www.mhs.mb.ca/docs/people/hoey_ra.shtml (accessed 21 December 2013).
358. TRC, NRA, INAC – Resolution Sector – IRS Historical Files Collection – Ottawa, file 6-21-1, volume 4, control 25-2, The National Association of Principals and Administrators of Indian Residences Brief Presented to the Department of Indian Affairs and Northern Development as requested by Mr. E. A. Cote, Deputy Minister, prepared in 1967, presented 15 January 1968. [NCA-011495]
359. TRC, NRA, Library and Archives Canada, RG10, volume 13033, file 401/25-13, volume 1, R. F. Davey to H. B. Rodine, 5 February 1968. [AEMR-014634]
360. For Beauval fire, see: TRC, NRA, Library and Archives Canada, RG10, volume 6300, file 650-1, part 1, Louis Mederic Adam to Indian Affairs, 22 September 1927. [BVL-000879] For Cross Lake fire, see: TRC, NRA, Library and Archives Canada, RG10, volume 6260, file 577-1, part 1, J. L. Fuller to A. MacNamara, 8 March 1930; [CLD-000933-0000] TRC, NRA, Library and Archives Canada, RG10, volume 6260, file 577-1, part 1, William Gordon to Assistant Deputy and Secretary, Indian Affairs, 10 March 1930. [CLD-000934]
361. For deaths, see: Stanley, "Alberta's Half-Breed Reserve," 96–98; Library and Archives Canada, RG10, volume 6300, file 650-1, part 1, O. Charlebois to Duncan Scott, 21 September 1927; [BVL-000874] Louis Mederic Adam to Indian Affairs, 22 September 1927; [BVL-000879] TRC, NRA, Library and Archives Canada, RG10, volume 6260, file 577-1, part 1, J. L. Fuller to A. McNamara, 8 March 1930; [CLD-000933-0000] William Gordon to Assistant Deputy and Secretary, Indian Affairs, 10 March 1930; [CLD-000934] TRC, NRA, INAC – Resolution Sector – IRS Historical Files Collection – Ottawa, file 675/6-2-018, volume 2, D. Greyeyes to Indian Affairs, 22 June 1968. [GDC-005571]
362. Canada, *Annual Report of the Department of Indian Affairs, 1906*, 274–275.
363. Bryce, *Report on the Indian Schools*, 18.
364. Bryce, *Report on the Indian Schools*, 17.
365. Bryce, *Report on the Indian Schools*, 18.
366. For details, see: Canada, *Annual Report of the Department of Indian Affairs, 1904*, xxvii–xxviii; TRC, NRA, Library and Archives Canada, MG17, B2, Class 'G' C.1/P.2, Church Missionary Society, "Resolutions Regarding the Administration of the North-West Canada Missions," 7 April 1903; [PAR-003622] Blake, *Don't you hear*; TRC, NRA, Library and Archives Canada, RG10, volume 3928, file 117004-1, "Report on Indian Missions and Schools," Presented to the Diocesan Synod,

Diocese of Calgary, J. W. Tims, August 1908; [OLD-008159] The United Church of Canada Archives, Toronto, Acc. No. 1979.199C, box 5, file 68, "Report of the Synod's Commission on Indian Affairs," 5 December 1904; [RIS-000246] TRC, NRA, Library and Archives Canada, RG10, volume 6039, file 160-1, part 1, Frank Pedley to Reverend and dear sirs, 21 March 1908; [AEMR-120155] TRC, NRA, Anglican Church of Canada, General Synod Archives, ACC-MSCC-GS 75-103, series 3:1, box 48, file 3, Frank Pedley to Norman Tucker, 26 March 1909; [AAC-090228] Archives of Saskatchewan, MacKay Papers, Frank Oliver, "Letter to S. H. Blake, 28 January, 1908," quoted in Wasylow, "History of Battleford Industrial School," 225–226; Anglican Church General Synod Archives, 75-103, series 2-14, Frank Oliver to A. G. G., 28 January 1908, quoted in Gull, "'Indian Policy,'" 15; TRC, NRA, Anglican Church of Canada, General Synod Archives, ACC-MSCC-GS 75-103, series 3:1, box 48, file 3, Letter signed by S. H. Blake, Andrew Baird, Hamilton Cassels, T. Ferrier, R. F. MacKay, 22 May 1908; [AAC-090192] TRC, NRA, Library and Archives Canada, RG10, volume 6039, file 160-1, part 1, Frank Pedley to Frank Oliver, 9 April 1908; [AEMR-120157] TRC, NRA, Anglican Church of Canada, General Synod Archives, ACC-MSCC-GS 75-103, series 3:1, box 48, file 3, "Report of the Sub-Committee of the Advisory Board On Indian Education," n.d.; [AAC-090231] TRC, NRA, Library and Archives Canada, RG10, volume 3919, file 116751-1A, J. B. Magnan to D. Laird, 12 December 1902; [SBR-003409] TRC, NRA, Library and Archives Canada, RG10, volume 3919, file 116751-1A, Clifford Sifton to Governor General in Council, 23 December 1903; [FAR-000095] TRC, NRA, Library and Archives Canada, RG10, volume 6039, file 160-1, part 1, Frank Pedley to Mr. Oliver, 30 May 1908; [120.00294] TRC, NRA, Library and Archives Canada, RG10, volume 6327, file 660-1, part 1, J. Hugonnard to Frank Oliver, 28 March 1908; [PLD-007334] TRC, NRA, Library and Archives Canada, RG10, volume 6039, file 160-1, part 1, Superintendent General of Indian Affairs to T. Ferrier, 18 July 1908; [AEMR-016328] TRC, NRA, Library and Archives Canada, RG10, volume 6039, file 160-1, part 1, Heron to Frank Oliver, 16 February 1909; [AEMR-120164] TRC, NRA, Library and Archives Canada, RG10, volume 6039, file 160-4, part 1, Association of Indian Workers to Frank Oliver, 19 February 1909; [AEMR-016332] TRC, NRA, Library and Archives Canada, RG10, FA 10-17, volume 6041, file 160-5, part 1, 1905–1934, Emile Legal to Frank Pedley, 20 July 1908; [AEMR-254243] TRC, NRA, Anglican Church of Canada, General Synod Archives, ACC-MSCC-GS 75-103, series 3:1, box 48, file 3, Arthur Barner to S. H. Blake, 16 February 1909. [AAC-090206]

367. Library and Archives Canada, RG10, volume 6039, file 160-1, part 1, *Correspondence and Agreement Relating to the Maintenance and Management of Indian Boarding Schools* (Ottawa: Government Printing Bureau, 1911). [AEMR-120208A]
368. For examples, see: TRC, NRA, Library and Archives Canada, RG10, volume 6113, file 350-23, part 1, H. A. Alderwood to Percy Moore, 25 January 1946; [FGA-001121] TRC, NRA, No document location, no file source, 988/23-9, p. 2, 1947–48, R. H. Moore to Indian Affairs Branch, 30 June 1948; [KUP-001240] TRC, NRA, Library and Archives Canada, RG10, volume 6279, file 584-10, part 4, R. S. Davies to Indian Affairs, 3 October 1951; [SBR-004545-0000] TRC, NRA, Library and Archives Canada, RG10, volume 6445, file 881-10, part 5, P. E. Moore to Superintendent, Welfare and Training Division, 23 December 1940. [LEJ-002117]
369. Canada, *Annual Report of the Department of Indian Affairs, 1893*, 173.
370. Library and Archives Canada, RG10, volume 3674, file 11422-5, H. Reed to Deputy Superintendent General of Indian Affairs, 13 May 1891.
371. TRC, NRA, Library and Archives Canada, RG10, volume 3920, file 116818, H. J. Denovan, 1 May 1901. [EDM-009805]
372. For Regina, see: TRC, NRA, Library and Archives Canada, RG10, volume 3927, file 116836-1A, J. A. Graham to J. A. Sinclair, 2 February 1904. [RIS-000075] For Onion Lake, see: TRC, NRA, Library

and Archives Canada, RG29, volume 2915, file 851-1-A671, part 1a, Lang Turner to Secretary, Indian Affairs, 31 October 1921. [NPC-602633] For Mission, see: TRC, NRA, Library and Archives Canada, RG10, volume 6470, file 890-5, part 2, A. O'N. Daunt, 18 December 1924. [MIS-004992] For Muncey, see: TRC, NRA, Library and Archives Canada, RG10, volume 6207, file 468-5, part 7, A. F. MacKenzie to K. J. Beaton, 9 July 1935. [MER-000845]

373. TRC, NRA, Library and Archives Canada, RG10, volume 6305, file 652-1, part 1, J. McArthur to Secretary, Indian Affairs, 5 July 1909; [SMD-001186] 6 July 1909. [SMD-001187]
374. TRC, NRA, Library and Archives Canada, RG10, volume 3921, file 116818-1B, J. F. Woodsworth to Secretary, Indian Affairs, 25 November 1918. [EDM-000956]
375. TRC, NRA, Library and Archives Canada, RG10, volume 6041, file 160-5, part 1, "Memorandum of the Convention of the Catholic Principals of Indian Residential Schools held at Lebret, Saskatchewan, August 28 and 29, 1924." [200.4.00016]
376. For an example from the Sarcee Reserve school, see: TRC, NRA, Library and Archives Canada, RG29, volume 3403, file 823-1-A772, T. J. Fleetham to Secretary, Indian Affairs, 4 March 1915. [NPC-604045a] For an example from the High River school, see: Provincial Archives of Alberta, Oblates of Mary Immaculate, école Dunbow, Boîte 80, #3381, Journal quotidien de l'école Dunbow, 18 January 1916, quoted in Pettit, "'To Christianize and Civilize,'" 254.
377. For concerns about hospitals from the 1940s, see: TRC, NRA, Library and Archives Canada, RG29, volume 2905, file 851-1-A486, part 1, P. E. Moore to B. T. McGhie, 19 February 1942. [NPC-620532] For overall concerns regarding care in British Columbia school infirmaries in 1960, see: TRC, NRA, Library and Archives Canada – Ottawa, RG10, volume 8697, file 957/6-1, part 3, P. E. Moore to H. M. Jones, 22 July 1960. [MIS-000240]
378. For complaints from the Winnipeg, Manitoba, school, see: TRC, NRA, Library and Archives Canada, RG10, volume 8797, file 1/25-13, part 10, André Renaud to R. F. Davey, 10 August 1959. [NRD-300276] For complaints from the Roman Catholic school in The Pas, Manitoba, see: TRC, NRA, Library and Archives Canada, RG29, volume 2915, file 851-1-A578, part 3, P. E. Moore to Regional Superintendent, Central Region, INHS, 15 May 1961. [NPC-602638] For complaints from the La Tuque, Québec, school, see: TRC, NRA, Quebec Regional Service Centre – LAC – Québec City, Acc. 81-116, box 303441, file 377/17-1, J. E. DeWolf to R. L. Boulanger, 21 January 1965. [LTR-001513-0005] For concerns from the Roman Catholic school in Cardston, Alberta, see: TRC, NRA, Provincial Archives – Alberta, PAA 71.220 B161 2419, J. E. Y. Levaque to Mr. Tully, 19 November 1967. [OGP-023087]
379. Waldram, Herring, and Young, *Aboriginal Health in Canada*, 188–198; Wherrett, *Miracle of the Empty Beds*, 109–110.
380. Library and Archives Canada, Canadian Tuberculosis Association, quoted in Wherrett, *Miracle of the Empty Beds*, 111.
381. Library and Archives Canada, RG10, volume 3940, file 121698-13, Summary of statements made at meeting attached to correspondence, H. R. Halpin to Secretary, Indian Affairs, 16 November 1897. For Kah-pah-pah-mah-am-wa-ko-we-ko-chin's name and his being deposed from office, see: Library and Archives Canada, RG10, volume 3940, file 121698-13, Extract of a report of a Committee of the Honourable Privy Council Approved his Excellency on the 20 September 1897.
382. Moine, *My Life in a Residential School.*
383. Dion, *My Tribe the Crees*, 129.
384. Baker, *Khot-La-Cha*, 46.
385. TRC, AVS, Ray Silver, Statement to the Truth and Reconciliation Commission of Canada, Mission, British Columbia, 17 May 2011, Statement Number: 2011-3467.

386. TRC, AVS, [Name redacted], Statement to the Truth and Reconciliation Commission of Canada, Deline, Northwest Territories, 2 March 2010, Statement Number: 07-NWT-02MR1-002.
387. Canada, *Annual Report of the Department of Indian Affairs, 1888*, xiv.
388. Fraser River Heritage Park, The OMI Cemetery, http://www.heritagepark-mission.ca/omicemetery.html (accessed 4 November 2014).
389. Father Allard's diary, quoted in Cronin, Cross in the Wilderness, 219.
390. TRC, NRA, Library and Archives Canada, RG10, volume 3921, file 116818-1B, J. F. Woodsworth to Secretary, Indian Affairs, 25 November 1918. [EDM-000956]
391. Shanahan, *Jesuit Residential School at Spanish*, 4.
392. TRC, NRA, Library and Archives Canada, RG10, volume 6016, file 1-1-12, part 1, "Burial Expenses," J. D. McLean, no date. [PAR-008816]
393. For examples from the Spanish, Ontario, school, see: Library and Archives Canada, RG10, volume 6217, file 471-1, part 1, N. Dugas to Dear Sir, 25 August 1913; [Story no 1.1.jpg] Library and Archives Canada, RG10, volume 6217, file 471-1, part 1, N. Dugas to Secretary, Indian Affairs, 2 September 1913. [Story no 1.1.6.jpg]
394. Brass, *I Walk in Two Worlds*, 26.
395. TRC, LACAR, Department of Indian Affairs and Northern Development, Indian and Inuit Affairs Program, 133619, Yukon Regional Office, Accession 89-476 VFRC, box 7, file volume 1, file number 29-3, J. H. Gordon to Superintendent, Indian Affairs, Yukon, 16 July 1958; [46b-c009024-d0015-001] TRC, LACAR, Department of Indian Affairs and Northern Development, Indian and Inuit Affairs Program, 133619, Yukon Regional Office, Accession 89-476 VFRC, box 7, file volume 1, file number 29-3, M. Matas to Gordon Harris, 16 April 1958; [46a-c001040-d0010-005] TRC, LACAR, Department of Indian Affairs and Northern Development, Indian and Inuit Affairs Program, 133619, Yukon Regional Office, Accession 89-476 VFRC, box 7, file volume 1, file number 29-3, M. Matas to W. L. Falconer, 22 July 1958; [46a-c001040-d0010-002] TRC, LACAR, Department of Indian Affairs and Northern Development, Indian and Inuit Affairs Program, 133619, Yukon Regional Office, Accession 89-476 VFRC, box 7, file volume 1, file number 29-3, W. L. Falconer to Director, Indian and Northern Health Services, 24 July 1958; [46a-c001040-d0010-001] TRC, LACAR, Department of Indian Affairs and Northern Development, Indian and Inuit Affairs Program, 133619, Yukon Regional Office, Accession 89-476 VFRC, box 7, file volume 1, file number 29-3, M. G. Jutras to Indian Commissioner, British Columbia, 26 August 1958. [46b-c009024-d0010-001]
396. TRC, NRA, The Presbyterian Church in Canada Archives, Toronto, ON, Acc. 1988-7004, box 17, file 4, Colin Wasacase to Giollo Kelly, 17 November 1966. [CJC-007910] For Wenjack's age, see: Adam, "The Lonely Death of Charlie Wenjack," 30.
397. TRC, NRA, National Capital Regional Service Centre – LAC – Ottawa, file 486/18-2, volume 2, box V-24-83, 06/26/1946–09/23/1975, M. J. Pierce to Indian Affairs, 23 October 1974; [FTA-001096] Edwards, "This Is about Reuniting a Family, Even in Death," *Toronto Star*, 4 March 2011, http://www.thestar.com/news/gta/2011/03/04/this_is_about_reuniting_a_family_even_in_death.html; Edwards, "Star Gets Action: Charlie Hunter Headed Home," *Toronto Star*, 24 March 2011, http://www.thestar.com/news/gta/2011/03/24/star_gets_action_charlie_hunter_headed_home.html.
398. Wasylow, "History of Battleford Industrial School," 268.
399. TRC, NRA, Library and Archives Canada, RG10, volume 3920, file 116818, D. L. Clink to Indian Commissioner, June 4 1895. [EDM-003380]
400. TRC, NRA, Library and Archives Canada, RG10, volume 3920, file 116818, H. Reed to Assistant Commissioner, 28 June 1895. [EDM-003376]
401. TRC, NRA, Library and Archives Canada, RG10, volume 6358, file 758-1, part 1, Reverend Canon

Gould to Duncan Campbell Scott, 26 January 1920. [IRC-041334]

402. TRC, NRA, Library and Archives Canada, RG10, volume 8542, file 51/25-1, part 2, Philip Phelan, 14 April 1953. [FAR-000067]
403. Library and Archives Canada, RG10, volume 3558, file 64, part 39, David Laird to Superintendent of Indian Affairs, 13 March 1899.
404. TRC, NRA, Library and Archives Canada, RG10, volume 1346, Microfilm reel C-13916, G. Donckele to W. H. Lomas, 29 December 1896. [KUP-004264]
405. Audette, "Report on the Commission," 2–7.
406. Library and Archives Canada, RG10, volume 3880, file 92499, Memorandum, Hayter Reed, undated; T. Clarke, "Report of Discharged Pupils," in Canada, Sessional Papers 1894, Paper 13, 103.
407. TRC, NRA, Library and Archives Canada, RG10 (Red), volume 2771, file 154845, part 1, J. G. Ramsden to J. D. McLean, 23 December 1907. [TAY-003542]
408. "Damages for Plaintiff in Miller Vs. Ashton Case," *Brantford Expositor*, 1 April 1914.
409. TRC, NRA, Anglican Church of Canada, General Synod Archives, Accession GS 75-403, series 2:15[a], box 16, [Illegible] Chairman, Indian and Eskimo Commission, Westgate, T. B. R., Field Secretary, Indian and Eskimo Commission, "Minutes of the Meeting of the Indian Residential School Commission held on March 18th, 1921." [AGS-000014]
410. TRC, NRA, Library and Archives Canada, RG10, School Files, volume 6358, file 758-1, part 1, 20 August 1919 [OLD-000497]; TRC, NRA, Library and Archives Canada, RG10, volume 6358, file 758-1, part 1, "Statement taken by Constable Wright, RNWMP, 27 November 1919"; [IRC-041330] TRC, NRA, Library and Archives Canada, RG10, School Files, volume 6358, file 758-1, part 1, 20 August 1919; [OLD-000497] TRC, NRA, Library and Archives Canada, RG10, volume 6358, file 758-1, part 1, Thomas Graham to W. M. Graham, 1 December 1919; [IRC-041328] TRC, NRA, Library and Archives Canada, RG10, volume 6358, file 758-1, part 1, P. H. Gentleman to Canon Gould, 12 January 1920. [IRC-041335]
411. TRC, NRA, Library and Archives Canada, RG10, volume 6436, file 878-1, part 1, Microfilm reel C-8762, 1890–1912, Statement of Johnny Sticks, 28 February 1902. [JOE-060004]
412. TRC, NRA, Library and Archives Canada, RG10, volume 6267, file 580-1, part 2, J. W. Waddy to W. M. Graham, 5 October 1925. [DRS-000543-0001]
413. TRC, AVS, Isabelle Whitford, Statement to the Truth and Reconciliation Commission of Canada, Keeseekoowenin First Nation, Manitoba, 28 May 2010, Statement Number: S-KFN-MB-01-004.
414. TRC, AVS, Rachel Chakasim, Statement to the Truth and Reconciliation Commission of Canada, Timmins, Ontario, 9 November 2010, Statement Number: 01-ON-4-6NOV10-019.
415. TRC, AVS, Fred Brass, Statement to the Truth and Reconciliation Commission of Canada, Key First Nation, Saskatchewan, 21 January 2012, Statement Number: SP039.
416. TRC, AVS, Geraldine Bob, Statement to the Truth and Reconciliation Commission of Canada, Fort Simpson, Northwest Territories, 23 November 2011, Statement Number: 2011-2685.
417. TRC, AVS, William Antoine, Statement to the Truth and Reconciliation Commission of Canada, Little Current, Ontario, 12 May 2011, Statement Number: 2011-2002.
418. TRC, AVS, Eva Simpson, Statement to the Truth and Reconciliation Commission of Canada, Norway House First Nation, Manitoba, 10 May 2011, Statement Number: 2011-0290.
419. TRC, AVS, Dorothy Ross, Statement to the Truth and Reconciliation Commission of Canada, Thunder Bay, Ontario, 25 November 2010, Statement Number: 01-ON-24NOV10-014.
420. TRC, AVS, Archie Hyacinthe, Statement to the Truth and Reconciliation Commission of Canada, Kenora, Ontario, 15 March 2011, Statement Number: 2011-0279.
421. TRC, AVS, Jonas Grandjambe, Statement to the Truth and Reconciliation Commission of Canada,

Fort Good Hope, Northwest Territories, 15 July 2010, Statement Number: 01-NWT-JY10-024.

422. TRC, AVS, Delores Adolph, Statement to the Truth and Reconciliation Commission of Canada, Mission, British Columbia, 19 May 2011, Statement Number: 2011-3458.
423. TRC, AVS, Joseph Wabano, Statement to the Truth and Reconciliation Commission of Canada, Fort Albany, Ontario, 29 January 2013, Statement Number: SP099.
424. TRC, AVS, Noel Starblanket, Statement to the Truth and Reconciliation Commission of Canada, Regina, Saskatchewan, 16 January 2012, Statement Number: 2011-3314.
425. TRC, AVS, Mervin Mirasty, Statement to the Truth and Reconciliation Commission of Canada, Saskatoon, Saskatchewan, 21 June 2012, Statement Number: 2011-4391.
426. TRC, AVS, Nellie Trapper, Statement to the Truth and Reconciliation Commission of Canada, Winnipeg, Manitoba, 18 June 2010, Statement Number: 02-MB-16JU10-086.
427. TRC, AVS, Wendy Lafond, Statement to the Truth and Reconciliation Commission of Canada, Batoche, Saskatchewan, 24 July 2010, Statement Number: 01-SK-18-25JY10-015.
428. TRC, AVS, Don Willie, Statement to the Truth and Reconciliation Commission of Canada, Alert Bay, British Columbia, 3 August 2011, Statement Number: 2011-3284.
429. Adams, "The Indians."
430. TRC, NRA, Library and Archives Canada, "Native Mission School Shut Down over Discipline Controversy," by Margaret Loewen Reimer, *Mennonite Reporter*, Volume 19, Number 22, 13 November 1989. [PHD-000143]
431. TRC, NRA, INAC – Resolution Sector – IRS Historical Files Collection – Ottawa, file 372/25-13-024, volume 1, C. T. Blouin and L. Poulin, to A. R. Jolicoeur, 13 October 1970. [LTR-001178-0001]
432. TRC, NRA, INAC – Resolution Sector – IRS Historical Files Collection – Ottawa, GRS Files, box R2, [Name redacted], Ronald J. Pratt and Herman Blind to [Name redacted], 8 December 1993. [IRC-047202-0002]
433. Library and Archives Canada, Hayter Reed Papers MG29, E 106, volume 18, Personnel H-L, J. W. Tims to Indian Commissioner, October 27, 1891.
434. Library and Archives Canada, Hayter Reed Papers MG29, E 106, volume 18, Personnel H-L, L. Vankoughnet to H. Reed, 7 December 1891.
435. For example, see: Library and Archives Canada, Sifton Papers, volume 19, 12129-39; 12123, J. H. Fairlie to A. Forget, 23 August 1897; A. Forget to Sifton, 30 October 1897; TRC, NRA, Library and Archives Canada, RG10, volume 6211, file 469-1, part 3, Duncan C. Scott to B. P. Fuller, 16 November 1916. [SWK-001406]
436. TRC, NRA, Library and Archives Canada, RG10, volume 13356, "Investigation – Kuper Island School 1939, Police report regarding runaways from Kuper Island School," 10 January 1939; [IRC-040001] TRC, NRA, Library and Archives Canada, RG10, volume 13356, "Investigation – Kuper Island School 1939," D. M. MacKay to Secretary, Indian Affairs Branch, Ottawa, 12 January 1939; [IRC-040007-0001] TRC, NRA, Library and Archives Canada, RG10, volume 13356, "Investigation – Kuper Island School 1939, Cpl S. Service, 13 January 1939; [IRC-040003] TRC, NRA, Library and Archives Canada, RG10, volume 13356, "Investigation – Kuper Island School 1939, Confidential Notes," Gerald H. Barry, 13 January 1939. [IRC-040010]
437. TRC, NRA, Library and Archives Canada, RG10, volume 13356, "Investigation – Kuper Island School 1939," G. H. Barry to Major D. M. MacKay, 17 January 1939; [IRC-040014] TRC, NRA, Library and Archives Canada, RG10, volume 13356, "Investigation – Kuper Island School 1939," Harold McGill to Major D. M. MacKay, 27 January 1939. [IRC-040021]
438. For example, see: TRC, NRA, INAC – Archival Unit – Ottawa, file 772/3-1, volume 2, 10/11–05/66, C. Pant Schmidt to Harold McGill, 17 August 1944; [IRC-047003] T. R. L. MacInnes to Director, In-

dian Affairs, 25 August 1944; [IRC-047005] Sarah Elizabeth Brown, "Ex-residential School Student Files Suit," *Whitehorse Star*, 21 April 2003; Elizabeth Asp, Jackie McLaren, Jim Sheldon, Michelle Tochacek, and Ruby Van Bibber, "Bishop's comments invalided any apology," Letter to the Editor, *Whitehorse Star*, 11 August 1999.

439. TRC, NRA, Library and Archives Canada, RG10, volume 6309, file 645-1, part 3, R. S. Davis, excerpt from Quarterly Report Ending March, 1945, on Touchwood Agency. [IRC-047128]
440. TRC, NRA, INAC – Resolution Sector – IRS Historical Files Collection – Ottawa, GRS Files, box 1A, file 22, Head Teacher [Illegible] to My Lord Bishop, 10 January 1956. [IRC-040120]
441. For examples, see: TRC, NRA, Library and Archives Canada, 709/25-1-001, 1951–1961, part 2, L. C. Hunter to R. F. Davey, 30 November 1960; [IRC-040054] TRC, NRA, United Church of Canada/Victoria University Archives, Acc. No. 8 [Illegible].050C, box 112, file 17, Edmonton IRS – Correspondence 1958–60/UCC Docs Toronto, Dwight Powell to E. E. M. Joblin, 25 November 1960. [UCA-080215] It was not until 1968 that Indian Affairs began requiring school schools superintendents to submit the names of all who had been dismissed because they had "created problems." TRC, NRA, National Archives of Canada, Acc. E1996-97/312, Vol. 2, File 672/25-1, R.F. Davey to All School Superintendents, 7 May 1968; [120.07885] TRC, NRA, Library and Archives Canada – Burnaby Vol. 11500, File 901/1-13, pt. 1, School Establishment, 1968-1972, FA 10-138, A. H. Friesen to All District School Superintendents, 1 June 1968. [120.07891]
442. TRC, NRA, Library and Archives Canada – Burnaby Vol. 11500, File 901/1-13, pt. 1, School Establishment, 1968-1972, FA 10-138, A. H. Friesen to All District School Superintendents, 1 June 1968. [120.07891]
443. The details of these convictions will be outlined in a forthcoming TRC report.
444. Indian Residential Schools Adjudication Secretariat, Adjudication Secretariat Statistics, from September 19, 2007, to January 31, 2015, http://iap-pei.ca/information/stats-eng.php (accessed 20 February 2015).
445. Joseph Jean Louis Comeau worked there from 1959 to 1965, *R. v. Comeau*, 1988 CanLII 3839 (AB QB). Martin Houston worked there from 1960 to 1962, TRC, ASAGR, Aboriginal Affairs and Northern Development Canada, Walter Rudnicki to Director, Indian Affairs, 17 August 1962; [AANDC-234696] Aboriginal Affairs and Northern Development Canada, Royal Canadian Mounted Police Report, Western Arctic Division, Division file number 628-626-1, code 0559, re: Martin Houston, 29 August 1962. [AANDC-234684] George Maczynski worked there from 1966 to 1967, TRC, NRA, Beaufort-Delta Education Council Warehouse, Inuvik, NWT, Payroll, 1959 to 1966 [box 1], M. Ruyant to Department of Northern Affairs and National Resources, Payroll list of employees at the hostel for September 1966, September 1966; [GHU-002427] Beaufort-Delta Education Council Warehouse, Inuvik, NWT, Payroll, 1967 to 1970 [box 1], Department of Northern Affairs and National Resources, Northern Administration: Paylist – Hostel, May 1967. [GHU-002435] Paul Leroux worked there from 1967 to 1979, TRC, ASAGR, Glenn Taylor, "Grollier Man Pleads Not Guilty to Sex Offences," Northern News Services, 28 November 1997, http://www.nnsl.com/frames/newspapers/1997-11/nov28_97sex.html.
446. Mandryk, "Uneasy Neighbours," 210.
447. TRC, NRA, Library and Archives Canada, RG10, volume 8798, file 371/25-13-019, part 2, R. F. Davey to William Starr, 19 July 1962; [FGA-001179] TRC, NRA, Anglican Church of Canada, General Synod Archives, ACC-MSCC-GS 75-103, series 2:15, box 24, file 3, Extract from Report on Visit of Major-General G. R. Turner to St. Paul's Anglican Indian Residential School, Cardston, Alberta, 6–8, 1958. [AAC-090593]
448. Mandryk, "Uneasy Neighbours," 210.

449. *R. v. Plint*, [1995] B.C.J. No. 3060 (B.C. S.C.); "Former Employee of Residential School Jailed for Sex Abuses," Victoria *Times-Colonist*, January 24, 2004.
450. TRC, AVS, Jean Pierre Bellemare, Statement to the Truth and Reconciliation Commission of Canada, La Tuque, Québec, 5 March 2013, Statement Number: SP104.
451. TRC, AVS, Andrew Yellowback, Statement to the Truth and Reconciliation Commission of Canada, Kamloops, British Columbia, 9 August 2009, Statement Number: 2011-5015.
452. See, for example: TRC, AVS, [Name redacted], Statement to the Truth and Reconciliation Commission of Canada, Winnipeg, Manitoba, 18 June 2010, Statement Number: 02-MB-18JU10-055; TRC, AVS, Myrna Kaminawaish, Statement to the Truth and Reconciliation Commission of Canada, Thunder Bay, Ontario, 7 January 2011, Statement Number: 01-ON-06JA11-004; TRC, AVS, Percy Tuesday, Statement to the Truth and Reconciliation Commission of Canada, Winnipeg, Manitoba, 18 June 2010, Statement Number: 02-MB-18JU10-083; TRC, AVS, Isaac Daniels, Statement to the Truth and Reconciliation Commission of Canada, Saskatoon, Saskatchewan, 22 June 2012, Statement Number: 2011-1779.
453. TRC, AVS, Marlene Kayseas, Statement to the Truth and Reconciliation Commission of Canada, Regina, Saskatchewan, 16 January 2012, Statement Number: SP035. For gifts of candy, see: TRC, AVS, Elaine Durocher, Statement to the Truth and Reconciliation Commission of Canada, Winnipeg, Manitoba, 16 June 2010, Statement Number: 02-MB-16JU10-059; TRC, AVS, John B. Custer, Statement to the Truth and Reconciliation Commission of Canada, Winnipeg, Manitoba, 19 June 2010, Statement Number: 02-MB-19JU10-057; TRC, AVS, Louise Large, Statement to the Truth and Reconciliation Commission of Canada, St. Paul, Alberta, 7 January 2011, Statement Number: 01-AB-06JA11-012. For field trips, see: TRC, AVS, Ben Pratt, Statement to the Truth and Reconciliation Commission of Canada, Regina, Saskatchewan, 18 January 2012, Statement Number: 2011-3318.
454. See, for example: TRC, AVS, [Name redacted], Statement to the Truth and Reconciliation Commission of Canada, Winnipeg, Manitoba, 18 June 2010, Statement Number: 02-MB-18JU10-055; TRC, AVS, Leona Bird, Statement to the Truth and Reconciliation Commission of Canada, Saskatoon, Saskatchewan, 21 June 2012, Statement Number: 2011-4415; TRC, AVS, Barbara Ann Pahpasay Skead, Statement to the Truth and Reconciliation Commission of Canada, Winnipeg, Manitoba, 17 June 2010, Statement Number: 02-MB-16JU10-159.
455. TRC, AVS, Josephine Sutherland, Statement to the Truth and Reconciliation Commission of Canada, Timmins, Ontario, 8 November 2010, Statement Number: 01-ON4-6NOV10-013.
456. TRC, AVS, Marie Therese Kistabish, Statement to the Truth and Reconciliation Commission of Canada, Val d'Or, Québec, 6 February 2012, Statement Number: SP101.
457. TRC, AVS, Richard Morrison, Statement to the Truth and Reconciliation Commission of Canada, Winnipeg, Manitoba, 17 June 2010, Statement Number: 02-MB-17JU10-080.
458. For shower, see: TRC, AVS, Leonard Peter Alexcee, Statement to the Truth and Reconciliation Commission of Canada, Vancouver, British Columbia, 18 September 2013, Statement Number: 2011-3228. For lunch pail, see: TRC, AVS, Mervin Mirasty, Statement to the Truth and Reconciliation Commission of Canada, Saskatoon, Saskatchewan, 21 June 2012, Statement Number: 2011-4391.
459. TRC, AVS, Donna Antoine, Statement to the Truth and Reconciliation Commission of Canada, Enderby, British Columbia, 13 October 2011, Statement Number: 2011-3287.
460. TRC, AVS, Helen Harry, Statement to the Truth and Reconciliation Commission of Canada, Vancouver, British Columbia, 20 September 2013, Statement Number: 2011-3203.
461. TRC, AVS, Bernard Catcheway, Statement to the Truth and Reconciliation Commission of Canada,

Skownan First Nation, Manitoba, 12 October 2011, Statement Number: 2011-2510; TRC, AVS, Doris Judy McKay, Statement to the Truth and Reconciliation Commission of Canada, Rolling River First Nation, Manitoba, 23 November 2011, Statement Number: 2011-2514.

462. TRC, AVS, Timothy Henderson, Statement to the Truth and Reconciliation Commission of Canada, Winnipeg, Manitoba, 28 June 2011, Statement Number: 2011-0291.
463. TRC, AVS, Nellie Ningewance, Statement to the Truth and Reconciliation Commission of Canada, Sault Ste. Marie, Ontario, 1 July 2011, Statement Number: 2011-0305.
464. TRC, AVS, Flora Northwest, Statement to the Truth and Reconciliation Commission of Canada, Hobbema, Alberta, 24 July 2013, Statement Number: SP124.
465. For examples, see: TRC, AVS, Hazel Mary Anderson, Statement to the Truth and Reconciliation Commission of Canada, Winnipeg, Manitoba, 18 June 2010, Statement Number: 02-MB-18JU10-034; TRC, AVS, Peter Ross, Statement to the Truth and Reconciliation Commission of Canada, Tsiigehtchic, Northwest Territories, 8 September 2011, Statement Number: 2011-0340.
466. TRC, AVS, Eric Robinson, Statement to the Truth and Reconciliation Commission of Canada, Winnipeg, Manitoba, 16 June 2010, Statement Number: SC093.
467. TRC, AVS, Lynda Pahpasay McDonald, Statement to the Truth and Reconciliation Commission of Canada, Winnipeg, Manitoba, 16 June 2010, Statement Number: 02-MB-16JU10-130.
468. For examples, see: TRC, AVS, Larry Roger Listener, Statement to the Truth and Reconciliation Commission of Canada, Hobbema, Alberta, 25 July 2013, Statement Number: SP125; TRC, AVS, Mary Vivier, Statement to the Truth and Reconciliation Commission of Canada, Winnipeg, Manitoba, 18 June 2010, Statement Number: SC110.
469. TRC, AVS, Louisa Papatie, Statement to the Truth and Reconciliation Commission of Canada, Val d'Or, Québec, 6 February 2012, Statement Number: SP101. For an example of abuse stopping as students became older, see: Fontaine, *Broken Circle*, 18–19.
470. For examples, see: TRC, AVS, Ken A. Littledeer, Statement to the Truth and Reconciliation Commission of Canada, Thunder Bay, Ontario, 26 November 2010, Statement Number: 01-ON-24-NOV10-028; TRC, AVS, Sphenia Jones, Statement to the Truth and Reconciliation Commission of Canada, Terrace, British Columbia, 29 November 2011, Statement Number: 2011-3300.
471. TRC, AVS, Lawrence Waquan, Statement to the Truth and Reconciliation Commission of Canada, Winnipeg, Manitoba, 18 June 2010, Statement Number: SC111.
472. TRC, AVS, Hazel Mary Anderson, Statement to the Truth and Reconciliation Commission of Canada, Winnipeg, Manitoba, 18 June 2010, Statement Number: 02-MB-18JU10-034.
473. TRC, AVS, Wayne Reindeer, Statement to the Truth and Reconciliation Commission of Canada, Hobbema, Alberta, 25 July 2013, Statement Number: SP125.
474. TRC, AVS, Michael Muskego, Statement to the Truth and Reconciliation Commission of Canada, Winnipeg, Manitoba, 18 June 2010, Statement Number: 02-MB-18JU10-045.
475. TRC, AVS, Josephine Sutherland, Statement to the Truth and Reconciliation Commission of Canada, Timmins, Ontario, 8 November 2010, Statement Number: 01-ON4-6NOV10-013.
476. TRC, AVS, Norman Courchene, Statement to the Truth and Reconciliation Commission of Canada, Winnipeg, Manitoba, 16 June 2010, Statement Number: 02-MB-16JU10-065.
477. For examples, see: TRC, AVS, Ben Pratt, Statement to the Truth and Reconciliation Commission of Canada, Regina, Saskatchewan, 18 January 2012, Statement Number: 2011-3318; TRC, AVS, Amelia Galligos-Thomas, Statement to the Truth and Reconciliation Commission of Canada, Victoria, British Columbia, 13 April 2012, Statement Number: 2011-3975.
478. TRC, AVS, Violet Rupp Cook, Statement to the Truth and Reconciliation Commission of Canada, Bloodvein First Nation, Manitoba, 25 January 2012, Statement Number: 2011-2565.

479. For examples, see: TRC, AVS, Ivan George, Statement to the Truth and Reconciliation Commission of Canada, Mission, British Columbia, 18 May 2011, Statement Number: 2011-3472; TRC, AVS, Dorothy Jane Beaulieu, Statement to the Truth and Reconciliation Commission of Canada, Fort Resolution, Northwest Territories, 28 April 2011, Statement Number: 2011-0379; TRC, AVS, Lorna Morgan, Statement to the Truth and Reconciliation Commission of Canada, Winnipeg, Manitoba, 17 June 2010, Statement Number: 02-MB-16JU10-041.
480. Ruben, "Abraham Ruben," 136.
481. For examples, see: TRC, AVS, Stella Marie Tookate, Statement to the Truth and Reconciliation Commission of Canada, Timmins, Ontario, 9 November 2010, Statement Number: 01-ON-8-10NOV10-003; TRC, AVS, Richard Hall, Statement to the Truth and Reconciliation Commission of Canada, Vancouver, British Columbia, 18 September 2013, Statement Number: 2011-1852.
482. TRC, AVS, William Garson, Statement to the Truth and Reconciliation Commission of Canada, Split Lake First Nation, Manitoba, 24 March 2011, Statement Number: 2011-0122.
483. TRC, AVS, Percy Thompson, Statement to the Truth and Reconciliation Commission of Canada, Hobbema, Alberta, 25 July 2013, Statement Number: SP125.
484. TRC, AVS, Alice Ruperthouse, Statement to the Truth and Reconciliation Commission of Canada, Val d'Or, Québec, 5 February 2012, Statement Number: SP100.
485. TRC, AVS, Albert Elias, Statement to the Truth and Reconciliation Commission of Canada, Inuvik, Northwest Territories, 1 July 2011, Statement Number: SC092.
486. TRC, AVS, Denis Morrison, Statement to the Truth and Reconciliation Commission of Canada, Winnipeg, Manitoba, 17 June 2010, Statement Number: 02-MB-17JU10-028.
487. TRC, AVS, Bob Baxter, Statement to the Truth and Reconciliation Commission of Canada, Thunder Bay, Ontario, 24 November 2010, Statement Number: 01-ON-24NOV10-012.
488. TRC, AVS, Clara Quisess, Statement to the Truth and Reconciliation Commission of Canada, Winnipeg, Manitoba, 17 June 2010, Statement Number: 02-MB-17JU10-032.
489. TRC, AVS, Louisa Birote, Statement to the Truth and Reconciliation Commission of Canada, La Tuque, Québec, 5 March 2013, Statement Number: SP104.
490. See, for example: TRC, AVS, Ruth Chapman, Statement to the Truth and Reconciliation Commission of Canada, Winnipeg, Manitoba, 16 June 2010, Statement Number: 02-MB-16JU10-118; TRC, AVS, Gordon James Pemmican, Statement to the Truth and Reconciliation Commission of Canada, Winnipeg, Manitoba, 18 June 2010, Statement Number: 02-MB-18JU10-0069; TRC, AVS, Mary Vivier, Statement to the Truth and Reconciliation Commission of Canada, Winnipeg, Manitoba, 18 June 2010, Statement Number: 02-MB-18JU10-082; TRC, AVS, Roy Johnson, Statement to the Truth and Reconciliation Commission of Canada, Dawson City, Yukon, 24 May 2011, Statement Number: 2011-0203; TRC, AVS, Ken Lacquette, Statement to the Truth and Reconciliation Commission of Canada, Winnipeg, Manitoba, 18 June 2010, Statement Number: 02-MB-18JU10-052.
491. TRC, AVS, Agnes Moses, Statement to the Truth and Reconciliation Commission of Canada, Inuvik, Northwest Territories, 29 June 2011, Statement Number: SC090.
492. TRC, AVS, Don Willie, Statement to the Truth and Reconciliation Commission of Canada, Alert Bay, British Columbia, 3 August 2011, Statement Number: 2011-3284.
493. TRC, AVS, Christina Kimball, Statement to the Truth and Reconciliation Commission of Canada, Winnipeg, Manitoba, 17 January 2011, Statement Number: 03-001-10-020.
494. TRC, AVS, Noel Starblanket, Statement to the Truth and Reconciliation Commission of Canada, Regina, Saskatchewan, 16 January 2012, Statement Number: 2011-3314.
495. TRC, AVS, Geraldine Shingoose, Statement to the Truth and Reconciliation Commission of Canada, Winnipeg, Manitoba, 19 June 2010, Statement Number: 02-MB-19JU10-033.

496. TRC, AVS, Paul Andrew, Statement to the Truth and Reconciliation Commission of Canada, Inuvik, Northwest Territories, 30 June 2011, Statement Number: NNE202.
497. TRC, NRA, National Archives of Canada - Burnaby, FA 10-138, 07/1956, Perm. volume 13528, C. G. Brown, G. J. Buck, B. O. Filteau, "Report of the Educational Survey Commission on the Educational Facilities and Requirements of the Indians of Canada," July 1956, 10. [120.18398]
498. TRC, NRA, Library and Archives Canada - Ottawa, RG10, volume 8703, file 962/6-1, part 7, NAC - Ottawa, L. K. Poupore to H. M. Jones, 14 October 1957. [JOE-063234]
499. TRC, NRA, INAC - Departmental Library - Ottawa, "St. Michael's Indian School Wins Service Club Trophy," The Indian Record, April 1946. [SMD-002822]
500. TRC, NRA, Library and Archives Canada, RG10, volume 8610, file 652/1-13, part 1, George Roussel to B. F. Neary, 25 March 1949. [SMD-001575-0001]
501. TRC, NRA, Library and Archives Canada, RG10, volume 8610, file 652/1-13, part 1, Geo.-L. Roussel to B. F. Neary, 25 March 1949. [SMD-001575-0001]
502. Marks, *They Call Me Chief*, 31. Sasakamoose played with the Chicago Blackhawks in the 1952–53 season. He was born on the Sandy Lake, Saskatchewan, reserve in 1933. TRC, NRA, INAC - Departmental Library - Ottawa, "Saskatchewan Midget Hockey Champions," Indian Record, Volume 12, Number 5, May 1949. [SMD-002829]
503. TRC, NRA, Library and Archives Canada, RG29, volume 792, file 344, Pratt, Gerry. "Little Indians Are Big Fighters," in the *Vancouver Sun Magazine Supplement*, 31 March 1951. [NPC-600625]
504. TRC, NRA, INAC - Departmental Library - Ottawa, "First Winner of the Tom Longboat Trophy," *The Indian Missionary Record*, Volume 15, Number 3, March 1952, 3. [IMR-000400]
505. Hughes, *Jackson Beardy*, 6–7.
506. MacGregor, *Chief*, 34–35.
507. Canadien, *From Lishamie*, 253–254.
508. Canadien, *From Lishamie*, 264–265.
509. For an example from the Presbyterian school at Shoal Lake, see: TRC, NRA, Library and Archives Canada, RG10, volume 6187, file 461-1, part 1, "Report of Inspector Semmens on the Cecilia Jaffrey [sic] Boarding School," 22 January 1917. [IRC-048048]
510. Library and Archives Canada, RG10, volume 4041, file 334503, Duncan Campbell Scott to Frank Pedley, 19 February 1912, cited in Wasylow, "History of Battleford Industrial School," 261–263. For Battleford capacity, see: Canada, *Annual Report of the Department of Indian Affairs, 1907*, 341.
511. Canada, *Annual Report of the Department of Indian Affairs, 1915*, xxvi.
512. Canada, *Annual Report of the Department of Indian Affairs, 1898*, 297; Canada, *Annual Report of the Department of Indian Affairs, 1910*, 474; TRC, NRA, Provincial Archives of Alberta, PAA 71.220 B16 668, unsigned letter to J. T. McNally, 22 February 1922. [OGP-090011]
513. Canada, *Annual Report of the Department of Indian Affairs 1906*, 191; Canada, *Annual Report of the Department of Indian Affairs, 1907*, xxxiii.
514. For St. Boniface closing, see: Canada, *Annual Report of the Department of Indian Affairs, 1905*, xxxiii; Canada, *Annual Report of the Department of Indian Affairs, 1906*, 191. For difficulty in recruiting, see: Canada, *Annual Report of the Department of Indian Affairs, 1896*, 362. For Calgary closing, see: Canada, *Annual Report of the Department of Indian Affairs, 1908*, 197. For Calgary recruiting problem, see: Canada, *Annual Report of the Department of Indian Affairs, 1904*, 375. For Regina closing, see: Canada, *Annual Report of the Department of Indian Affairs, 1910*, 364. For evidence of Indian Affairs' dissatisfaction with the management of the Regina school, see: TRC, NRA, Library and Archives Canada, RG10, volume 6332, file 661-1, part 1, W. M. Graham to Secretary, Indian Affairs, 17 November 1910. [RLS-000027] For the Elkhorn school, see: TRC, NRA, Library

and Archives Canada, RG10, volume 3925, file 116823-1A, Clerk of the Privy Council to Superintendent General, Indian Affairs, 18 February 1918. [ELK-000248] For the Red Deer school, see: TRC, NRA, Library and Archives Canada, RG10, volume 6350, file 753-1, part 1, J. F. Woodsworth to James Endicott, 5 June 1919. [EDM-000242]

515. The government actually closed day schools in an effort to force parents to send their children to residential schools. Canada, *Annual Report of the Department of Indian Affairs, 1895,* xxi–xii.
516. For examples of the withholding of rations, see: TRC, NRA, Library and Archives Canada, RG10, volume 1629, A. J. McNeill to D. Laird, 10 December 1901; [SAR-000404] TRC, NRA, Library and Archives Canada, RG10, volume 6320, file 658-1, part 1, David Laird to Secretary, Indian Affairs, 3 April 1906; [PAR-000980-0000] TRC, NRA, Library and Archives Canada, RG10, volume 6320, file 658-1, part 1, Microfilm reel C-9802, M. Benson to Deputy Superintendent General, Indian Affairs, 21 February 1907. [120.00284]
517. TRC, NRA, Library and Archives Canada, RG10, volume 6475, file 918-1, part 1, [Illegible], Office of the General Superintendent, Oblate Catholic Indian Missions to Philip Phelan, 21 October 1941. [FPU-000133]
518. TRC, NRA, Library and Archives Canada, RG10, School Files, volume 6352, file 753-10, part 1, Microfilm reel C-8708, P. Phelan to J. F. Woodsworth, 22 January 1941; [EDM-003580]
519. TRC, NRA, Library and Archives Canada, RG10, volume 1346, Microfilm reel C-13916, G. Donckele to W. R. Robertson, 23 July 1906. [KUP-004276]
520. TRC, NRA, English Language Summary of the Fort Resolution Chronicles, Volume 1, 1903–1942, 3. [GNN-000077-0001]
521. TRC, NRA, Library and Archives Canada, RG10, Perm. volume 6451, file 883-1, part 1, Bella Coola Agency – Kitamaat Boarding School – General Administration, 1906–1932, FA 10-17, Microfilm reel C-8773; [KMT-095676-0001] TRC, NRA, Library and Archives Canada, "Royal Canadian Mounted Police Report, Re: Kitimat Indian Reserve, Re: Hanna Grant, Deceased, 15 June 1922," I. Fougner to Secretary, Indian Affairs, 15 June 1922. [KMT-095674]
522. TRC, NRA, INAC – Resolution Sector – IRS Historical Files Collection – Ottawa, 773/25-1-003, 05/36–09/70, volume 1, RCAP, R. D. Ragan, "Extract from minutes of Blood Indian Council Meeting March 15, 1948." [MRY-000302] For Charron's initials, see: TRC, NRA, National Archives of Canada, RG29, volume 974, file 388-6-4, part 1, 02/1948–07/1949, B. F. Neary to P. A. Charron, 21 July 1948. [120.03363]
523. TRC, NRA, Library and Archives Canada, RG10, volume 6262, file 578-1, part 4, A. Ogletree to Deputy Secretary, Department of Indian Affairs, 23 July 1926. [ELK-000331]
524. TRC, NRA, Library and Archives Canada, RG10, volume 6371, file 764-1, part 1, M. Christianson to W. M. Graham, 28 October 1927. [PUL-001008]
525. TRC, NRA, Library and Archives Canada, RG10, volume 6445, file 881-10, part 5, Agent's Report on Stuart Lake Agency for September, Robert Howe, 2 October 1940. [LEJ-002079]
526. For examples from British Columbia, see: TRC, NRA, Library and Archives Canada, RG10, volume 6445, file 881-10, part 6, Report of Corporal L. F. Fielder, 14 October 1943; [LEJ-001389] TRC, NRA, Library and Archives Canada – Ottawa, RG10, volume 6443, file 881-1, part 2, R. Howe to Indian Affairs Branch, 12 September 1946; [LEJ-000855] TRC, NRA, Library and Archives Canada, RG10, volume 6445, file 881-10, part 7, R. Howe to Indian Affairs, 7 October 1946. [LEJ-001830] For Manitoba example, see: TRC, NRA, Library and Archives Canada, INAC – Resolution Sector – IRS Historical Files Collection – Ottawa, file 501/25-1-076, volume 1, A. G. Hamilton to Indian Affairs, 4 November 1943. [SBR-000408] For Saskatchewan examples, see: TRC, NRA, Library and Archives Canada, RG10, volume 6302, file 650-10, part 3, R. A. Hoey to J. P. B. Ostrander, 11 September 1942;

[BVL-000433] TRC, NRA, Library and Archives Canada, RG10, volume 9148, file 309-11 ACE, John Baptiste, Peter King, and Alex Sapp to Indian Agent, Battleford, 31 August 1945. [PAR-000897-0002] For Alberta examples, see: TRC, NRA, National Capital Regional Service Centre - LAC - Ottawa, file 1/18-24, volume 1 (locator #X-46-4), Rev. L. C. Schmidt to Harold McGill, 2 July 1943; [NCA-014258] TRC, NRA, Library and Archives Canada, RG10, volume 6374, file 764-10, part 2, PARC, H. A. R. Gagnon to Director, Indian Affairs Branch, 12 October 1945; [PUL-009517-0000] TRC, NRA, Library and Archives Canada, RG10, volume 6355, file 757-1, part 2, 1928–1948, John E. Pugh to Indian Affairs, 8 October 1947; [MOR-005548] TRC, NRA, Provincial Archives - Alberta, PAA 71.220 B94 3972, Principal Ermineskin Indian Residential School to Indian Affairs Branch, 31 March 1948; [OGP-032546] TRC, NRA, Library and Archives Canada, RG10, volume 6374, file 764-10, part 2, PARC, J. E. Pugh to Indian Affairs Branch, 7 March 1946; [PUL-009511] TRC, NRA, Library and Archives Canada - Edmonton, 103/6-1-764, volume 1, 09/44–12/54, C. A. F. Clark to Superintendent of Education, 9 November 1949; [IRC-048180] TRC, NRA, INAC - Resolution Sector - IRS Historical Files Collection - Ottawa, file 773/25-1-003, volume 1, 10/36–09/70, "Minutes of the Blood Band Council Held in The Indian Agency Office," 22 November 1949, annotated by C. A. F. Clark. [IRC-041373]

527. TRC, NRA, Library and Archives Canada, RG10, volume 6467, file 889-1, part 1, 12/1894–11/1933, Vancouver Agency - Squamish Residential School - General Administration, FA 10-17, Microfilm reel C-8785, NAC, Ottawa, A. W. Vowell to the Secretary, Department of Indian Affairs, 5 April 1905. [SQU-000423]
528. TRC, NRA, Library and Archives Canada, RG10, volume 6270, file 582-1, part 1, "Extract from report on meeting Chief of Pine Creek Band," A. Ogletree, Indian Agent, 16 June 1917. [PCR-010082]
529. For an example from Morley, Alberta, see: TRC, NRA, Library and Archives Canada, NAC - Ottawa, 772/3-6, volume 1, dates 1940–1954, Minutes from the council meeting for the Stony Indian Agency, 15 October 1946, 3. [MOR-006118] For an example from Lestock, Saskatchewan, see: TRC, NRA, Library and Archives Canada, RG10, volume 8756, file 673/25-1-003, 25 August 1949. [MRS-046113-0001]
530. TRC, NRA, Library and Archives Canada, RG10, volume 8756, file 673/25-1-003, J. P. B. Ostrander to Neary, 24 January 1950. [MRS-046113-0005]
531. For an example from the Presbyterian school at Shoal Lake, Ontario, see: TRC, NRA, Library and Archives Canada, RG10, volume 6187, file 461-1, part 1, Chief Kesik, Chief Redsky, and three others to McKenzie, 28 March 1917. [CJC-000006-0002]
532. TRC, NRA, Library and Archives Canada, RG10, volume 6187, file 461, part 1, "Report of the Commission of Presbytery appointed to investigate conditions at 'Cecilia Jeffries [sic] Boarding School,'" 26 February 1918. [CJC-000847-0001]
533. TRC, NRA, Library and Archives Canada, RG10, volume 6187, file 461-1, part 1, "Report of the Commission of Presbytery appointed to investigate conditions at 'Cecilia Jeffries [sic] Boarding School,'" 26 February 1918. [CJC-000847-0001]
534. TRC, NRA, Library and Archives Canada, volume 6332, file 661-1, part 2, petition from parents to Crooked Lakes Agency, 25 July 1949. [IRC-041159] Although Indian Affairs official J. P. B. Ostrander opposed replacing the teacher, he did report that she kept a strap on display in her class. He said, "If she does not use it for punishment, at least she keeps it on display as a threat of punishment, which does not promote harmony in the classroom." TRC, NRA, Library and Archives Canada, volume 6332, file 661-1, part 2, J. P. B. Ostrander to Indian Affairs Branch, Department of Mines and Resources, 12 August 1949. [RLS-000512-0000]
535. TRC, NRA, Library and Archives Canada, RG10, volume 6187, file 461-1, part 2, Mr. Paget to Mr.

Ferrier, 21 August 1928. [CJC-001354]

536. TRC, NRA, Library and Archives Canada, RG10, volume 6254, file 575-10, part 1, A. G. Smith to Secretary, Indian Affairs, 29 December 1936. [BIR-002631]

537. For an example of a request for an investigation into a death, see: TRC, NRA, Library and Archives Canada, RG10, volume 6332, file 661-1, part 2, Garnet Neff to T. G. Murphy, 26 January 1935; [RLS-000366-0001] TRC, NRA, Library and Archives Canada, RG29, volume 2917, file 851-1-A673, part 1, Memorandum to Mr. McLean, 13 January 1914. [NPC-603178] For an example of a complaint regarding discipline, see: TRC, NRA, Library and Archives Canada, RG10, volume 6200, file 466-1, part 3, H. H. Craig to H. A. Snell, 29 July 1937. [MSC-000080-0001] For an example of working on behalf of an injured student, see: TRC, NRA, Library and Archives Canada, RG10, volume 6327, file 660-1, part 3, William Hall to Indian Affairs, 30 April 1936. [PLD-000746] For an example of seeking a discharge, see: TRC, NRA, Library and Archives Canada, volume 12333, box 19, part 1, 1936–1939, NAC, J. D. Caldwell to [Severed], 16 March 1939. [KUP-004496]

538. TRC, NRA, Library and Archives Canada – Ottawa, RG85, volume 1505, file 600-1-1, part 1, N.W.T. – General Policy File – Education and Schools, 1905–1944, Extract From Act. Sgt. G. T. Makinson's Report-Resolution, N.W.T., 3 July 1937. [FRU-010059]

539. Cuthand, "Native Peoples," 382–383; Kulchyski, "Considerable Unrest," 100.

540. Goodwill and Sluman, *John Tootoosis*, 155.

541. Goodwill and Sluman, *John Tootoosis,* 156.

542. Both the 1905 fire at the Saint-Paul-des-Métis, Alberta, school and the 1930 fire at the Cross Lake, Manitoba, school were set by students. The Saint-Paul fire resulted in one death; the Cross Lake fire, in thirteen deaths. For the Saint-Paul fire, see: Stanley, "Alberta's Half-Breed Reserve," 96–98. For the Cross Lake fire, see: TRC, NRA, Library and Archives Canada, RG10, volume 6260, file 577-1, part 1, J. L. Fuller to A. McNamara, 8 March 1930; [CLD-000933-0000] William Gordon to Assistant Deputy and Secretary, Indian Affairs, 10 March 1930. [CLD-000934]

543. Wilson, *Missionary work*, 167–170.

544. TRC, NRA, Library and Archives Canada, RG10, volume 6032, file 150-40A, part 1, "Regulations Relating to the Education of Indian Children" (Ottawa: Government Printing Bureau, 1894). [AGA-001516-0000]

545. See, for examples: Canada, *Annual Report of the Department of Indian Affairs, 1893*, 104; Canada, *Annual Report of the Department of Indian Affairs, 1902*, 423.

546. See, for example: TRC, NRA, Library and Archives Canada, RG10, volume 6258, file 576-10, part 9, "Royal Canadian Mounted Police Report, Re: Thomas 'Tommy' Linklater et al.," 23 September 1936; [BRS-000240-0006] TRC, NRA, Library and Archives Canada, RG10, volume 6258, file 576-10, part 9, "Royal Canadian Mounted Police Report Re: Thomas 'Tommy' Linklater et al.," 20 October 1936; [BRS-000240-0005] TRC, NRA, Library and Archives Canada, RG10, volume 6209, file 468-10, part 2, "Royal Canadian Mounted Police Report, Re: Abner Elliott and Leonard Beeswax, truants," 13 October 1938. [MER-001043-0001] TRC, NRA, Library and Archives Canada, RG10, volume 6209, file 468-10, part 2, "Royal Canadian Mounted Police Report, Re: Abner Elliott and Leonard Beeswax, truants," 11 January 1939. [MER-001048-0001]

547. For Duncan Sticks, see: TRC, NRA, Library and Archives Canada, RG10, volume 6436, file 878-1, part 1, Statement of Reverend Henry Boening, 3 March 1902; [IRC-047093] Statement of Joseph Fahey, 3 March 1903; [IRC-047092] TRC, NRA, Library and Archives Canada, RG10, volume 6436, file 878-1, part 1, Statement of Antonio Boitano, 1 March 1902. [IRC-047086] For William Cardinal, see: TRC, NRA, Library and Archives Canada, RG10, volume 3921, file 116818-1B, J. F. Woodsworth to Secretary, Indian Affairs, 25 November 1918. [EDM-000956] For unnamed boy from The Pas,

Manitoba, school, see: TRC, NRA, Anglican Church of Canada, General Synod Archives Anglican Church of Canada GS 75-103, B17, "Minutes of meeting of Indian and Eskimo Commission, M.S.C.C., Held on Tuesday, January 11th, 1927," 11. [AAC-083001] For three unnamed boys from the Fort Alexander, Manitoba, school, see: St. Boniface Historical Society, Archives Deschâtelets, L 541 M27L 266, Brachet to père provincial, 20 October 1928. For Agnes Ben, see: "Find Body of Indian Girl, Long Missing," *Winnipeg Free Press*, 17 April 1930. For Percy Ochapowace, see: TRC, NRA, Library and Archives Canada, RG10, volume 6332, file 661-1, part 2, Royal Canadian Mounted Police Report, "Re: Percy Ochapowace - Death of, Ochapowace Indian Reserve, Saskatchewan," H. S. Casswell, 19 January 1935; [RLS-000365-0003] J. P. B. Ostrander to Secretary, Indian Affairs, 19 January 1935. [RLS-000365-0001] For Allen Patrick, Andrew Paul, Justa Maurice, and John Jack, see: TRC, NRA, Library and Archives Canada, RG10, volume 6446, file 881-23, part 1, R. H. Moore to Secretary, Indian Affairs, 6 January 1937. [LEJ-004083-0000] For Andrew Gordon, see: TRC, NRA, Library and Archives Canada, RG10, volume 9151, file 312-11 ACE, "Royal Mounted Police Report, Re Andrew Gordon (Juvenile), Deceased," 16 March 1939. [GDC-009280-0001] For John Kioki, Michael Sutherland, and Michael Matinas, see: TRC, NRA, Library and Archives Canada, RG10, volume 6186, file 460-23, part 1, Paul Langlois to Constable Dexter, 14 June 1941. [FTA-000105-0001] For Leonard Major, Ambrose Alexander, and Alec Francis, see: TRC, NRA, Library and Archives Canada - Ottawa, file 882-2, part 8, Kamloops Agency - Kamloops Residential School - Quarterly Returns, 1947–1952, FA 10-17, volume 6447, Microfilm reel C-8770, Library and Archives Canada - Ottawa, Indian Residential School Quarterly Return for Kamloops Indian Residential School, 30 September 1947, pages 8, 9, and 10 of 20-page portable document file; [KAM-002274] TRC, ASAGR, RCMP-564517, Royal Canadian Mounted Police, E-Div NIRS task force Final Report, M. W. Pacholuk, "Final Report of the Native Indian Residential School Task Force, Project E-NIRS," Royal Canadian Mounted Police, 49. [AGCA-564517] For Albert Nepinak, see: TRC, NRA, Library and Archives Canada, RG10, volume 6272, file 582-23, part 1, Royal Canadian Mounted Police Report, 9 April 1951. [PCR-000190] For Tom and Charles Ombash, see: TRC, NRA, National Capital Regional Service Centre - LAC - Ottawa, file 494/3-3-3, volume 1, "Provincial Police Report," G. A. McMonagle, 19 December 1956. [PLK-001205-0001] For Beverly Joseph and Patricia Joseph, see: TRC, NRA, INAC - Resolution Sector - IRS Historical Files Collection - Ottawa, file 961/25-2, volume 15, Admissions and Discharges - Kuper Island Residence, Cowichan Agency, B.C., 01/08/1958–02/07/1966, Control No. 34-15 IRSRC - Historical Files, J. V. Boys to Indian Commissioner for B.C., 29 January 1959. [KUP-200601] For Mabel Crane Bear and Belinda Raw Eater, see: TRC, NRA, Library and Archives Canada - Edmonton, 772/25-1, volume 1, 04/60–06/70, N. Goater to A. H. Murray, 10 March 1962. [OLD-007287-0005] For Alfred Whitehawk, see: TRC, NRA, Library and Archives Canada - Edmonton, RG10, Acc. E1996-97/415, box 36, file 25-2-662, 1964–1966, E. Turenne to K. Kerr, 6 June 1965. [SPR-006307] For Charles Wenjack, see: TRC, NRA, The Presbyterian Church in Canada Archives, Toronto, On., Acc. 1988-7004, box 17, file 4, "Inquest Hears Tragic Tale of Runaway Boy," *Kenora Miner and News*, 18 November 1966; Coroner's Statement Upon Issuing His Warrant for Holding an Inquest in the Case of Charles Wenjack, R. Glenn Davidson, 4 November 1966; Report of Post-Mortem Examination, A-258, Charles Wenjack, 23 October 1966, Dr. Peter Pan; Adams, "The Lonely Death," 30–44. [CJC-007909] For Joseph Commanda, see: TRC, NRA, INAC - Resolution Sector - IRS Historical Files Collection - Ottawa, file 451/25-2-004, volume 2, "Report on the Death of Joseph Commanda," H. B. Rodine, 6 September 1968. [TAY-001114-0001] For Philip Swain and Roderick Keesick, see: TRC, NRA, INAC, file 487/18-2, volume 1, "2 Boys Died from Exposure," *Kenora Miner and News*, 18 December 1970; [KNR-003158-0002] P. J. Hare to Indian Affairs, 7 December 1970. [KNR-003168] For Jack Elanik and Dennis Dick, see:

TRC, NRA, Anglican Church of Canada, Diocese of the Arctic, General Synod Archives, file 110-09, Stringer Hall, Accession M96-7, series 2:1, Notice of missing boys, 1972; [AGS-000341] TRC, NRA, Government of Northwest Territories Archives Confidential, Hostels, 1971–1974, Archival box 8-24, Archival Acc. G1995-004, Leonard Holman to J. Coady, 14 July 1972. [SHU-000486]

548. For examples of cases where criticism was directed against school authorities for the handling of runaways, including cases that led to fatalities, see: TRC, NRA, Library and Archives Canada, RG10, volume 6436, file 878-1, part 1, Statement of Reverend Henry Boening, 3 March 1902; [IRC-047093] TRC, NRA, Library and Archives Canada, RG10, volume 6436, file 878-1, part 1, Statement of Reverend Henry Boening, Statement of Joseph Fahey, 3 March 1903; [IRC-047092] TRC, NRA, Library and Archives Canada, RG10, volume 6267, file 580-1, part 2, W. G. Tweddell to W. M. Graham, 6 May 1931; [DRS-000588] TRC, NRA, Library and Archives Canada, RG10, volume 6332, file 661-1, part 2, Royal Canadian Mounted Police Report, “Re: Percy Ochapowace - Death of, Ochapowace Indian Reserve, Saskatchewan,” H. S. Casswell, 19 January 1935; [RLS-000365-0003] TRC, NRA, Library and Archives Canada, RG10, volume 6332, file 661-1, part 2, J. P. B. Ostrander to Secretary, Indian Affairs, 19 January 1935; [RLS-000365-0001] TRC, NRA, Library and Archives Canada, RG10, volume 6446, file 881-23, part 1, R. H. Moore to Secretary, Indian Affairs, 6 January 1937; [LEJ-004083-0000] TRC, NRA, Library and Archives Canada, RG10, volume 6309, file 654-1, part 2, “Memorandum of an inquiry into the cause and circumstances of the death of Andrew Gordon,” R. W. Frayling, 11 March 1939; [GDC-028479] TRC, NRA, Library and Archives Canada, RG10, volume 11553, file 312-11, “Indian Boy Frozen on Bush Trail,” *Regina Leader-Post*, 16 March 1939; [GDC-009281] TRC, NRA, Library and Archives Canada, RG10, volume 9151, file 312-11 ACE, “Royal Mounted Police Report, Re Andrew Gordon (Juvenile), Deceased,” 16 March 1939; [GDC-009280-0001] TRC, NRA, Library and Archives Canada, RG10, volume 6278, file 584-10, part 2, Police Report, G. N. McRae, 23 April 1940; [SBR-110686-0001] TRC, NRA, Library and Archives Canada, RG10, volume 6278, file 584-10, part 2, Police Report, G. L. Tisdale, 30 April 1940; [SBR-110686-0002] TRC, NRA, Library and Archives Canada, RG10, volume 6186, file 460-23, part 1, Paul Langlois to Constable Dexter, 14 June 1941; [FTA-000105-0001] TRC, NRA, Library and Archives Canada, RG10, volume 6186, file 460-23, part 1, “Statement of Charles Kioki,” 22 June 1942; [FTA-000116-0013] TRC, NRA, Library and Archives Canada, RG10, volume 6320, file 657-10, part 2, Royal Canadian Mounted Police Report, J. P. Douglas, 7 October 1944; [MDD-001704] TRC, NRA, Library and Archives Canada, RG10, volume 6320, file 657-10, part 2, Royal Canadian Mounted Police Report, T. H. Playford, 10 October 1944; [MDD-002258] TRC, NRA, Library and Archives Canada, RG10, volume 6272, file 582-23, part 1, Royal Canadian Mounted Police Report, 9 April 1951; [PCR-000190] TRC, NRA, National Capital Regional Service Centre - LAC - Ottawa, file 487/18-24, volume 1, L. A. Marshall to Indian Affairs, 20 December 1954; [KNR-001380-0003] TRC, NRA, INAC - Resolution Sector - IRS Historical Files Collection - Ottawa, file 961/25-2, volume 15, Admissions and Discharges - Kuper Island Residence, Cowichan Agency, B.C., 01/08/1958–02/07/1966, Control no. 34-15 IRSRC - Historical Files, J. V. Boys to Indian Commissioner for B.C., 29 January 1959; [KUP-200601] TRC, NRA, Library and Archives Canada - Edmonton, 772/25-1, volume 1, 04/60–06/70, N. Goater to A. H. Murray, 10 March 1962; [OLD-007287-0005] TRC, NRA, INAC, file 487/18-2, volume 1, “2 Boys Died from Exposure,” *Kenora Miner and News*, 18 December 1970; [KNR-003158-0002] TRC, NRA, INAC, file 487/18-2, volume 1, P. J. Hare to Indian Affairs, 7 December 1970. [KNR-003168]

549. For the reporting to the Ontario Provincial Police, see: TRC, NRA, National Capital Regional Service Centre - LAC - Ottawa, file 494/3-3-3, volume 1, “Provincial Police Report,” G. A. McMonagle, 19 December 1956. [PLK-001205-0001] For the reporting to Indian Affairs, see: TRC, NRA, Library

and Archives Canada, RG10, volume 8275, file 494/6-1-014, part 5, R. F. Davey to G. Swartman, 13 November 1956. [PLK-000488]

550. Porter, "Remains Found Near Residential School Are 'Non-human,'" *CBC News*, 12 July 2012, http://www.cbc.ca/news/canada/thunder-bay/remains-found-near-residential-school-are-non-human-1.1249599.
551. TRC, NRA, INAC – Resolution Sector – IRS Historical Files Collection – Ottawa, file 1/25-1-5-2, volume 1, "Regulations With Respect to Teaching, Education, Inspection, and Discipline for Indian Residential Schools, Made and Established for the Superintendent General of Indian Affairs Pursuant to Paragraph (a) of Section 114 of the Indian Act," 20 January 1953. [PAR-001203-0001]
552. TRC, NRA, INAC – Resolution Sector – IRS Historical Files Collection – Ottawa, file 901/25-13, volume 4 (locator 156-2), J. B. Bergevin to H. B. Cotnam, 1 March 1971. [NCA-012545-0000]
553. For an example from Chilliwack, British Columbia, see: TRC, NRA, Library and Archives Canada, RG10, volume 6422, file 869-1, part 1, Microfilm reel C-8754, J. Hall to F. Devlin, 19 January 1900. [COQ-000345]
554. TRC, NRA, Library and Archives Canada, RG10, volume 6308, file 653-10, part 1, "Royal Canadian Mounted Police Report Re: Douglas Shingoose and Donald Stevenson," 23 February 1935. [FHR-001050-0001]
555. See, for examples: North-West Mounted Police, *Annual Report, 1894*, 52–53; TRC, NRA, Library and Archives Canada, RG10, volume 3920, file 116818, C. E. Somerset to Indian Commissioner, 6 October 1896; [EDM-009788] TRC, NRA, Library and Archives Canada, RG10, volume 2771, file 154845, part 1, Mohawk Institute to Hayter Reed, 18 March 1896; [TAY-003510] TRC, NRA, Library and Archives Canada, RG10, volume 6278, file 584-10, part 1, "RCMP Report regarding [Name redacted]," 16 October 1933. [SBR-110565-0001]
556. Sutherland, *Children in English-Canadian Society*, 122. For examples of prosecutions, see: TRC, NRA, Library and Archives Canada, RG10, volume 6278, file 584-10, part 1, A. H. L. Mellor to Deputy Superintendent General, Indian Affairs, 19 September 1935; [SBR-110607-0000] TRC, NRA, Library and Archives Canada, RG10, volume 6209, file 468-10, part 1, "Royal Canadian Mounted Police report, Re: [Names redacted]," 21 November 1937; [MER-000580-0001] TRC, NRA, Library and Archives Canada, RG10, volume 6193, file 462-10, part 3, A. D. Moore to Secretary, Indian Affairs, 16 September 1940. [CRS-000507-0000]
557. For examples of the Royal Canadian Mounted Police's being used to return students to school, see: TRC, NRA, Library and Archives Canada, RG10, volume 6330, file 660-10, part 1, R. W. Greatwood to Indian Affairs, 11 April 1930; [PLD-003278-0001] TRC, NRA, Library and Archives Canada, RG10, volume 6330, file 660-10, part 2, H. E. P. Mann to Commissioner, RCMP, 6 February 1934; [PLD-003316-0001] TRC, NRA, Library and Archives Canada, RG10, volume 6193, file 462-10, part 1, page 1/1, "Royal Canadian Mounted Police Report," 11 February 1935, C. Graham; [CRS-001237-0001] TRC, NRA, Library and Archives Canada, RG10, volume 6275, file 583-10, part 1, "Royal Canadian Mounted Police Report, Re: Frank Puckina or Edwards," 15 September 1939; [PLP-000374] TRC, NRA, Library and Archives Canada, RG10, volume 6304, file 651-10, part 1, Constable G. J. Mitchell, 9 September 1931. [MRS-045402-0001]
558. TRC, NRA, Untitled document, purportedly Chronologie Dépuis Leur Foundations, École Blue Quills (Daily Journal from their Founding, Grey Nuns at Blue Quills) 1931–1936, entry for 1 May 1932. [GNA-000404]
559. TRC, NRA, Library and Archives Canada, RG10, volume 6278, file 584-10, part 1, "RCMP's Report on Truant," Constable R. D. Toews, 23 October 1936; [SBR-110630-0001] TRC, NRA, Library and Archives Canada, RG10, volume 6278, file 584-10, part 1, Constable R. D. Toews, 8 May 1937. [SBR-

110645-0001]

560. TRC, NRA, Library and Archives Canada, RG10, volume 6258, file 576-10, part 9, "Royal Canadian Mounted Police Report Re: Wallace Hahawahi, Delinquent," 28 October 1936. [BRS-000240-0004]
561. TRC, NRA, Library and Archives Canada, RG10, volume 6258, file 576-10, part 9, "Royal Canadian Mounted Police Report Re: Kenneth Thompson, Runaway Boy," 28 October 1936. [BRS-000240-0001]
562. TRC, NRA, Library and Archives Canada, RG10, volume 6258, file 576-10, part 9, "Royal Canadian Mounted Police Report Re: Peter Ryder Runaway Boy," 28 October 1936. [BRS-000240-0002]
563. TRC, NRA, Library and Archives Canada, RG10, volume 6267, file 580-1, part 2, J. Waddy, 24 November 1928. [DRS-000564]
564. TRC, NRA, Library and Archives Canada, RG10, volume 6253, file 575-5, part 5, A. G. Hamilton to Indian Affairs, November 4, 1935. [BIR-000208]
565. TRC, NRA, Library and Archives Canada, RG10, volume 6057, file 265-10, part 1, J. P. Mackey to Secretary, Indian Affairs, 16 July 1937; [SRS-006077] J. P. Mackey to Secretary, Indian Affairs, 27 July 1937. [SRS-006079]
566. TRC, NRA, Library and Archives Canada, RG10, volume 6057, file 265-10, part 2, "Royal Canadian Mounted Police Report Re: Steven LaBobe," 15 October 1938. [SRS-006090-0001]
567. TRC, NRA, Library and Archives Canada, RG10, volume 6053, file 260-10, part 1, J. P. Mackey to W. J. Cameron, 21 March 1939; [SRS-007977] TRC, NRA, Library and Archives Canada, RG10, volume 6053, file 260-10, part 1, J. P. Mackey to Secretary, Indian Affairs, 14 April 1939. [SRS-007980]
568. TRC, AVS, Ken Lacquette, Statement to the Truth and Reconciliation Commission of Canada, Winnipeg, Manitoba, 18 June 2010, Statement Number: 02-MB-18JU10-052.
569. TRC, AVS, Anthony Wilson, Statement to the Truth and Reconciliation Commission of Canada, Terrace, British Columbia, 30 November 2011, Statement Number: 2011-3303.
570. TRC, AVS, Arthur Ron McKay, Statement to the Truth and Reconciliation Commission of Canada, Winnipeg, Manitoba, 18 June 2010, Statement Number: 02-MB-18JU10-044.
571. TRC, AVS, Ivan George, Statement to the Truth and Reconciliation Commission of Canada, Mission, British Columbia, 18 May 2011, Statement Number: 2011-3472.
572. TRC, AVS, Muriel Morrisseau, Statement to the Truth and Reconciliation Commission of Canada, Winnipeg, Manitoba, 18 June 2010, Statement Number: 02-MB-18JU10-057.
573. TRC, AVS, Isaac Daniels, Statement to the Truth and Reconciliation Commission of Canada, Saskatoon, Saskatchewan, 22 June 2012, Statement Number: 2011-1779.
574. TRC, AVS, Dora Necan, Statement to the Truth and Reconciliation Commission of Canada, Ignace, Ontario, 3 June 2011, Statement Number: 2011-1503.
575. TRC, AVS, Nellie Cournoyea, Statement to the Truth and Reconciliation Commission of Canada, Inuvik, Northwest Territories, 28 June 2011, Statement Number: NNE105. Cournoyea later went on to lead the negotiation of the first comprehensive land rights agreement in the Northwest Territories for her Inuvialuit people, and later became the first Aboriginal and female premier in Canada.
576. TRC, AVS, Lawrence Waquan, Statement to the Truth and Reconciliation Commission of Canada, Winnipeg, Manitoba, 18 June 2010, Statement Number: SC111.
577. TRC, AVS, Beverley Anne Machelle, Statement to the Truth and Reconciliation Commission of Canada, Whitehorse, Yukon, 27 May 2011, Statement Number: 2011-1133.
578. TRC, NRA, INAC, file 494/18-28, volume 1, G. Swartman to Indian Affairs Branch, 12 May 1955. [PLK-002025]
579. TRC, AVS, Mel H. Buffalo, Statement to the Truth and Reconciliation Commission of Canada, Hobbema, Alberta, 24 July 2013, Statement Number: SP124.

580. Canada, *Annual Report of the Department of Indian Affairs, 1907*, 189.
581. United Church of Canada Archives, Toronto, Archive accession information: Fonds, 3282: John Chantler McDougall Fonds, 1986.291C, box 1, file 8, Mrs. J. McDougall, "Founding of the McDougall Orphanage and Training School," Historical Sketch, no date.
582. Coccola, *They Call Me Father*, 89.
583. Stocken, *Among the Blackfoot*, 1–2.
584. Kelm, "Introduction" to Butcher, *Letters of Margaret Butcher*, xi, xxvi.
585. Butcher, *Letters of Margaret Butcher*, 5.
586. TRC, AVS, Lorraine Arbez, Statement to the Truth and Reconciliation Commission of Canada, Winnipeg, Manitoba, 18 June 2010, Statement Number: 02-MB-18JU10-007.
587. TRC, AVS, Noreen Fischbuch, Statement to the Truth and Reconciliation Commission of Canada, Beaver Mines, Alberta, 3 August 2011, Statement Number: 2011-1692.
588. TRC, AVS, George Takashima, Statement to the Truth and Reconciliation Commission of Canada, Lethbridge, Alberta, 3 August 2011, Statement Number: 2011-1700.
589. TRC, NRA, Library and Archives Canada, RG10, volume 3938, file 121607, Deputy Superintendent General of Indian Affairs to A. E. Forget, Assistant Commissioner of Indian Affairs, NWT, 18 January 1895. [RIS-000385-0000]
590. Library and Archives Canada, RG10, volume 2100, file 17960, part 2, A. Sutherland to Superintendent General of Indian Affairs, 31 March 1887.
591. TRC, NRA, Library and Archives Canada, RG10, volume 8843, file 709/16-2-001, part 1, C. H. Birdsall to Dr. Dorey, 2 June 1948. [EDM-000371]
592. TRC, NRA, No document location, no document file source, H. F. Dunlop to P. Phelan, 4 November 1948. [SEC-000063]
593. TRC, NRA, No document location, no document file source, A. Noonan to L. K. Poupore, 27 November 1960. [CIS-000553]
594. TRC, NRA, Library and Archives Canada, file 883-1, part 1, Bella Coola Agency - Kitamaat Boarding School - General Administration, 1906–1932, FA 10-17, Perm. volume 6451, Microfilm reel C-8773, Library and Archives Canada, L. Spotton to C. G. Young, 28 February 1930. [KMT-095721]
595. TRC, NRA, Library and Archives Canada, RG10, volume 6377, file 767-1, part 1, M. Christianson to H. W. McGill, 2 August 1933. [JON-000073]
596. Fast, "Amelia Le Soeur (Yeomans)," http://www.biographi.ca/009004-119.01-e.php?BioId=41653 (accessed 26 May 2013); Canada, *Annual Report of the Department of Indian Affairs, 1900*, 109; Canada, *Annual Report of the Department of Indian Affairs, 1901*, 80. (Charlotte Amelia's name is mistakenly given as Annie in the annual report.)
597. TRC, AVS, Theresa Reid, Statement to the Truth and Reconciliation Commission of Canada, Powell River, British Columbia, 28 September 2011, Statement Number: 2011-0263.
598. TRC, AVS, George Takashima, Statement to the Truth and Reconciliation Commission of Canada, Lethbridge, Alberta, 3 August 2011, Statement Number: 2011-1700.
599. TRC, AVS, Olive Saunders, Statement to the Truth and Reconciliation Commission of Canada, Thunder Bay, Ontario, 7 and 8 March 2011, Statement Number: 2011-0042.
600. TRC, NRA, Provincial Archives Alberta, PAA 71.220 B161 2357, E. O. Drouin to Chief Shot on Both Sides and Blood Band Council, Indian Agency, Cardston, 27 December 1966. [OGP-022362]
601. Regina principal A. J. McLeod (1900), TRC, NRA, The United Church of Canada Archives, Toronto, Acc. No. 1979.199C, box 2, file 20, Alex Skene to Mr. McKay, 1 December 1900; [RIS-000436] Muncey, Ontario, principal W. W. Shepherd (died after a horse-drawn cart accident in 1903), TRC, NRA, Library and Archives Canada, RG10, volume 6205, file 468-1, part 1, R. G. Howes to Deputy

Superintendent General, 25 May 1903; [MER-000331] Regina principal J. A. Sinclair (1905), TRC, NRA, Library and Archives Canada, RG10, volume 3927, file 116836-1A, Frank Pedley to W. M. Graham, 16 January 1905; [RIS-000090] Mission, British Columbia, principal Charles Marchal (diphtheria, 1906), TRC, NRA, Library and Archives Canada, RG10, volume 6468, file 890-1, part 1, Microfilm reel C-8786, A. W. Vowell to Secretary, Indian Affairs, 10 October 1906; [MIS-004766] Onion Lake, Saskatchewan, Anglican school principal John Matheson (1916), TRC, NRA, Library and Archives Canada, RG10, volume 6320, file 658-1, part 1, W. Sibbald to Secretary, Indian Affairs, 28 August 1916; [PAR-003569] Qu'Appelle, Saskatchewan, principal Joseph Hugonnard (1917), RG10, volume 6327, file 660-1, part 1, M. Kalmes to Duncan C. Scott, 13 February 1917; [PLD-000005] Shoal Lake, Ontario, principal Mr. Mathews (influenza, 1918), TRC, NRA, RG10, volume 6187, file 461-1, part 1, R. S. McKenzie to Assistant Deputy and Secretary, 23 October 1918; [CJC-000870] High River, Alberta, principal George Nordmann (influenza, 1918), Library and Archives Canada, RG10, volume 3933, file 117657-1, A. Naessens to Secretary, Indian Affairs, 7 January 1919; Gordon's, Saskatchewan, principal H. W. Atwater (1925), TRC, NRA, INAC – Resolution Sector – IRS Historical Files Collection – Ottawa, file E4974-02016, volume 4, T. J. Davies to Mr. Moore, 25 November 1925; [GDC-002528] Beauval, Saskatchewan, principal Mederic Adam (typhoid, 1930), TRC, NRA, Library and Archives Canada, RG10, volume 6300, file 650-1, part 1, O. Charlebois to Duncan Scott, 28 October 1930; [BVL-000005] Grayson, Saskatchewan, principal J. Carriere (1933), TRC, NRA, Library and Archives Canada, RG10, volume 6303, file 651-1, part 1, A. F. MacKenzie to J. P. B. Ostrander, 3 July 1933; [MRS-001401] Kamsack, Saskatchewan, principal C. Brouillet (1935), TRC, NRA, Library and Archives Canada, RG10, volume 6334, file 662-1, part 2, A. F. MacKenzie to W. Murison, 14 February 1935. [SPR-000465]

602. TRC, NRA, Library and Archives Canada, RG10, volume 1346, Microfilm reel C-13916, G. Donckele to W. R. Robertson, 1 January 1907; [KUP-004280] RG10, FA 10-1, volume 1346, Microfilm reel C-13916, Cowichan Agency – Incoming Correspondence re Kuper Island Industrial School, 1891–1907, P. Claessen to W. R. Robertson, 5 June 1907. [KUP-022198] For A. J. McLeod's initials, see: Canada, *Annual Report of the Department of Indian Affairs, 1900*, 383.

603. TRC, NRA, Anglican Church of Canada Archives, Diocese of the Arctic, M96-7, box 188, "File 8, Collected Material – Bessie Quirt, Articles written by Bessie re: Shingle Point and Fort George" "RE: First Eskimo Residential School (Anglican) – Shingle Point. Story One – Fifty Years Ago – August 1929–1979"; Library and Archives Canada, RG919-10, part 1, Fort Norman Agency – Aklavik Church of England Residential School – Admissions and Discharges, 1936–1946, FA 10-17, Perm. volume 6477, Microfilm reel C-8792, H. S. Shepherd to Philip Phelan, 30 March 1939; [ASU-001138] RG29, volume 2906, file 851-1-A486, part 3, H. S. Shepherd to P. E. Moore, 14 January 1948; [NPC-603247] RG10, volume 10728, file 484/25-2-467, part 1, H. S. Shepherd to J. L. Whitey, 17 November 1952; [MFI-001074] Anglican Church of Canada, General Synod Archives, ACC-MSCC-GS 75-103, series 2.15, box 22, file 2, "Minutes of a Meeting of the Sub-Executive Committee MSCC," 8th September 1954; [AAC-090761]Anglican Church of Canada, General Synod Archives GS 75-103, series 2-15, box 22, "Report of the Superintendent, Indian School Administration, to the M.S.C.C. Board of Management, Toronto, November 16th, 1954." [GDC-007201]

604. TRC, NRA, Library and Archives Canada, RG10, volume 6430, file 876-1, part 1, West Coast Agency – Ahousaht Residential School – General Administration, 1901–1931, FA 10-17, Microfilm reel C-8759, W. R. Woods to Dr. Young, 5 November 1929. [AST-200068-0001]

605. Methodist Church of Canada, British Columbia Conference, Port Simpson District, Ministerial Sessions, 1893, 188, quoted in Bolt, *Thomas Crosby*, 63.

606. TRC, NRA, Library and Archives Canada – Ottawa, RG10, volume 8803, file 959/25-13, part 2, Hen-

ry Cook to Frank Howard, 29 March 1960. [MIK-002122]

607. TRC, NRA, O.M.I. House - Vancouver, box 39, Fort St. John–Kakawis Family Development, folder 20, Kakawis Correspondence 1942–1979, Series One Plus Finding Aid, B.C./Yukon Local Community of O.M.I. Lacombe Canada Province [formerly St. Paul's Province], Mary Gemma to M. Kearney, 3 February 1958. [CST-800117] For background on the Benedictine Sisters of Mount Angel, see: The Benedictine Sisters of Mount Angel, "About Us, A Brief History of the Benedictine Sisters of Mt. Angel," http://www.benedictine-srs.org/history.html (accessed 12 June 2014).
608. TRC, NRA, Library and Archives Canada, RG55, FA 55-22, Acc. 1980-81/069, box 118, file 1105, part 2, Rates of Pay & Conditions of Employment of Teachers, 1964–1965, R. F. Davey to Peter Fillipoff, 25 May 1965. [AEMR-150636]
609. Bruno-Jofre, *Missionary Oblate Sisters,* 4–12, 132–139; Choquette, *Canada's Religions,* 83–84, 201; McCarthy, *From the Great River,* 156; Gresko, "Gender and Mission," 9; Huel, *Proclaiming the Gospel,* 165–166, 171; Shanahan, *Jesuit Residential School,* 5; TRC, NRA, Provincial Archives - Alberta, Acc. 78.204/5, Vital Grandin to Mother Ste. Marie, 27 September 1890; [ORC-000775] No document location, no document file source, Victor Rassier to Gerald Murphy, 15 September 1930; [BVT-000239] No document location, no document file source, M. Agatha, to Gerald Murray, 26 May 1931; [BVT-000260] TRC, NRA, Library and Archives Canada, RG10, volume 6276, file 584-3, part 1, H. B. Rayner to W. M. Graham, 26 August 1931. [SBR-000879-0001]
610. TRC, CAR, United Church Archives, Presbyterian Church in Canada, Board of Foreign Missions, Records Pertaining to Missions to Aboriginal People in Manitoba and the North West, 79.199C, box 3, file 29, (C0990), Austin McKitrick to Dr. R. P. MacKay, 30 September 1901, quoted in Hildebrand, "Staff Perspectives," 170. [13d-c000990-d0017-001]
611. Gagan, *Sensitive Independence,* 201.
612. Canada, *Annual Report of the Department of Indian Affairs, 1906,* 2:52–56.
613. Grant, "Two-Thirds of the Revenue," 108–109.
614. For an example, see: Canada, *Annual Report of the Department of Indian Affairs, 1893,* 172.
615. TRC, NRA, Library and Archives Canada, file 886-24, part 1, Skeena River Agency - Crosby Girls Residential School [Port Simpson] - Audit Reports 1935–1948, FA 10-17, Perm. volume 6458, Microfilm reel C-8779; Library and Archives Canada - Ottawa, "Crosby Girls' Home, United Church of Canada, Cost of Operations for Fiscal Year 1934–35." [PSM-200049-0003]
616. TRC, NRA, Library and Archives Canada, RG10, volume 8845, file 963/16-2, part 1, July 3, 1936, Re: Kamloops Residential School, Roman Catholic. [KAM-002000]
617. TRC, NRA, Anglican Diocese of Cariboo Archives Section #205, St. George Indian Residential School, Card D.C. 2C11, Lytton-St.-George's School, #88.44, "All Saints Indian Residential School Staff Manual 2nd Revision, 1967, Mr. A. W. Harding, Vice-Principal," 26–27. [AEMR-177341]
618. Canada, *Annual Report of the Department of Indian Affairs, 1896,* 366.
619. TRC, NRA, Anglican Church of Canada, General Synod Archives, ACC-MSCC-GS 75-103, series 9:08, box 131, file 5-3, "The Indian Residential School Commission of the Mission Society of the Church of England in Canada, An Outline of the Duties of Those Who Occupy Positions on the Staff at the Society's Indian Residential Schools, No. III, The Teacher." [AAC-090142]
620. TRC, NRA, Library and Archives Canada, RG10, volume 6462, file 888-1, part 1, H, EGN-007951, F. J. C. Ball to D. C. Scott, 5 May 1921. [GRG-022150-0000]
621. TRC, NRA, Library and Archives Canada, RG10, volume 6028, file 118-7-1, part 1, E. B. Glass to Dr. Sutherland, 4 September 1896. [WFL-000648-0002]
622. Hare and Barman, "Good Intentions," 168, 205, 206, 216.
623. Buck, *Doctor Rode Side-Saddle,* 114, 133.

624. Buck, *Doctor Rode Side-Saddle,* 92.
625. Brandon, Manitoba, principal T. Ferrier in 1903; Mount Elgin, Ontario, principal S. R. McVitty in 1913; and Kuper Island, British Columbia, principal W. Lemmens in 1915—all used the word "evil" in describing tendencies in Aboriginal culture. Canada, *Annual Report of the Department of Indian Affairs, 1903,* 342–343; TRC, NRA, Library and Archives Canada, RG10, volume 6205, file 468-1, part 1, Public Archives Canada, S. R. McVitty, "Helping the Indian: How it Is Done at Mount Elgin Industrial Institute," *The Christian Guardian,* 31 May 1913; [MER-0376] RG10, volume 1347, Microfilm reel C-13916, W. Lemmens to W. R. Robertson, 10 February 1915. [KUP-004240]
626. See, for example, *Algoma Missionary News* (April 1877): 14, quoted in Wilson, "Note on Shingwauk Industrial Home," 69; Butcher, *Letters of Margaret Butcher,* 26.
627. TRC, NRA, Library and Archives Canada, RG10, volume 6057, file 265-10, part 1, J. P. Mackey to Father MacNeil, 5 October 1936. [SRS-000280-0003]
628. Bush, *Western Challenge,* 27.
629. Fisher, *Contact and Conflict,* 185–188; Usher, *William Duncan,* 126.
630. TRC, NRA, Anglican Church of Canada, General Synod Archives, MSCC, GS 75-103, series 2-15, box 29, file 10, Anglican document no. 52.63, Victoria Ketcheson and Patricia Watson, 29 November 1952. [PAR-001992]
631. TRC, NRA, Document location to be determined, Hance/Aleck/Michell – Anglican Church of Canada and Anglican Church of Cariboo List of Documents, Helen Clafton to Bishop Dean, 5 March 1957. [ANG-063238]
632. Canada, *Annual Report of the Department of Indian Affairs, 1930,* 17.
633. TRC, NRA, Library and Archives Canada, RG10, volume 6200, file 466-1, part 2, "Successful Graduates." [TAY-004294-0002]
634. TRC, NRA, Library and Archives Canada, RG10, volume 2006, file 7825-1A, "Report on the Mohawk Institute and Six Nations Board School," 30 August 1895, 43. [TAY-003821-0000]
635. TRC, NRA, Library and Archives Canada, RG10, volume 6200, file 466-1, part 2, A. F. MacKenzie to H. W. Snell, 7 May 1936. [TAY-003085-0002]
636. Canada, *Annual Report of the Department of Indian Affairs, 1903,* 402.
637. TRC, NRA, United Church of Canada Archives, Acc. No. 1979.199C, box 5, file 60, J. A. Sinclair to R. P. MacKay, 26 April 1904. [RIS-000306]
638. TRC, NRA, Library and Archives Canada, RG10, volume 6255, file 576-1, part 2, J. Doyle to Secretary, Indian Affairs, 14 September 1932. [BRS-000234]
639. Canada, *Annual Report of the Department of Indian Affairs, 1960,* 56.
640. TRC, AVS, Stanley McKay, Statement to the Truth and Reconciliation Commission of Canada, Winnipeg, Manitoba, 13 July 2011, Statement Number: 2011-0269
641. Kirkness, *Creating Space,* 3–12, 29–40.
642. Kirkness, *Creating Space,* 29–30.
643. TRC, NRA, Library and Archives Canada, RG10, file 494/1-13-014, volume 1, T. B. Jones to R. F. Davey, 21 June 1963. [PLK-001867] For Spence as a residential school student, see: Canada, Special Joint Committee, 1947, 1066–1067.
644. TRC, NRA, INAC – Resolution Sector – IRS Historical Files Collection – Ottawa, file 494/25-1-014, volume 2, "The Anglican Indian Residential School, Sioux Lookout, Ontario," 10 June 1965. [PLK-000304-0001]
645. TRC, NRA, INAC – Resolution Sector – IRS Historical Files Collection – Ottawa, file 487/25-1-014, R. F. Davey to Giollo Kelly, 10 June 1966. [CJC-000308]
646. TRC, NRA, The Presbyterian Church in Canada Archives, Toronto, ON, Acc. 1988-7004, box 43, file

4, Giollo Kelly to Mrs. Colin Wasacase, 8 July 1966. [NCA-009161-0002]

647. For Mission, see: TRC, NRA, "Historic Transfer of Authority," *Fraser Valley Record*, 5 September 1973. [OMS-000307] For Kamloops, see: TRC, NRA, Library and Archives Canada - Burnaby, RG10, FA 10-138, Acc. v85-86/353, file 963/1-13, Perm. volume 6 [502372], part 1, Student Residence Establishment, 1969–78, NAC - Burnaby, A. H. Friesen to A. H. Noonan, 18 April 1973. [KAM-008144] For Blue Quills, Alberta, see: TRC, NRA, INAC - Resolution Sector - IRS Historical Files Collection - Ottawa, file 779/25-2-009, volume 1 (Ctrl #55-4), "Confidential: Notes: Re Blue Quills," undated. [NCA-007302] For Prince Albert, see: TRC, NRA, INAC - Resolution Sector - IRS Historical Files Collection - Ottawa, file 601/25-13-1, J. B. Freeman to James A. Roberts, 2 April 1973. [PAR-019374] For Duck Lake, see: TRC, NRA, INAC - Resolution Sector - IRS Historical Files Collection - Ottawa, GRS Files, box 8A, file 15, D. Seesequasis to H. Kolakowski, 3 February 1982. [GDC-014654-0004] For Qu'Appelle, see: LaRose, "Wrecker's ball Claims White Calf Collegiate," http://www.ammsa.com/publications/saskatchewan-sage/wreckers-ball-claims-white-calf-collegiate-0. For Fort George, see: TRC, NRA, INAC - Resolution Sector - IRS Historical Files Collection - Ottawa, file 371/25-1-019, volume 2, Right Rev. James A. Watton to A. Gill, 7 September 1971. [FGA-000225-0001] TRC, NRA, INAC - Resolution Sector - IRS Historical Files Collection - Ottawa, NCR-E4974-1 (Encl 1), volume 3, (Ctrl #446-19), Saskatchewan Region, Student Residences: An Issue Management Discussion Paper, 8 February 1994. [NCA-016023-0002]

648. TRC, NRA, INAC - Resolution Sector - IRS Historical Files Collection - Ottawa, NCR-E4974-1 (Encl 1), volume 3, (Ctrl #446-19), Saskatchewan Region, Student Residences: An Issue Management Discussion Paper, 8 February 1994. [NCA-016023-0002]

649. TRC, NRA, Anglican Church of Canada, General Synod Archives, file 1, Visit Reports of the Superintendent 02/54–12/54, pg. 004126-004227, Accession GS 75-103, series 2:15, box 24, "Superintendent's Visit to Chooutla School, Carcross, Y.T., December 3th–6th, 1954." [DYK-201620]

650. TRC, CAR, General Synod of the Anglican Church of Canada Archives, Archive accession information: MSSC Indian School Administration, Visit Reports, 1954–62, file 2 (1955–56), "Superintendent's Visit to St. John's Residential School, Wabasca, Alberta, 26th August, 1956." [13a-c000034-d0002-022]

651. General Synod of the Anglican Church of Canada Archives, Missionary Society of the Church of England in Canada, Indian School Administration - Visit Reports, Committees, Textual Records, 1903–1968, Indian and Eskimo Residential Schools and Indian School Administration, 1921–1977, GS75-103, box 23, file 10, "Superintendent's Visit to St. Philip's School, Fort George - March 24–25," 1953. [13a-c000032-d0025-001]

652. TRC, CAR, The General Synod of the Anglican Church of Canada Archives, ACC-MSCC-GS 75-103, series 2:15, box 24, file 2, Superintendent's Visit to St. Philip's School, Fort George, P.Q., January 16 and 17, 1956. [13a-c000034-d0002-004]

653. TRC, AVS, Jeanne Rioux, Statement to the Truth and Reconciliation Commission of Canada, Vancouver, British Columbia, 18 September 2013, Statement Number: 2011-3207.

654. TRC, AVS, Mary Chapman, Statement to the Truth and Reconciliation Commission of Canada, Vancouver, British Columbia, 4 October 2011, Statement Number: 2011-1529.

655. Vitaline Elsie Jenner, Statement to the Truth and Reconciliation Commission of Canada, Winnipeg, Manitoba, 16 June 2010, Statement Number: 02-MB-16JU10-131.

656. Coates, *A Global History of Indigenous Peoples*, 244–245.

657. United Nations, *United Nations Declaration on the Rights of Indigenous Peoples*; Coates, *A Global History of Indigenous Peoples*, 244–245.

658. Smith, *Apology to First Nations People*, http://www.united-church.ca/beliefs/policies/1986/a651

(accessed 23 October 2014).
659. The Missionary Oblates of Mary Immaculate, *An Apology to the First Nations of Canada by the Oblate Conference of Canada*, http://www.cccb.ca/site/images/stories/pdf/oblate_apology_english.pdf (accessed 27 October 2014)
660. For the Anglican apology, see: Hiltz, *A Step Along the Path: Apology by Archbishop Fred Hiltz*, http://www.anglican.ca/relationships/files/2011/06/Apology-English.pdf (accessed 27 October 2014). For the Presbyterian apology, see: Presbyterian Church in Canada, *The Confession of the Presbyterian Church in Canada as Adopted by the General Assembly*, http://presbyterian.ca/?wpdmdl=92& (accessed 27 October 2014); The United Church of Canada, *Apology to Former Students of United Church Indian Residential Schools, and to Their Families and Communities*, http://www.united-church.ca/beliefs/policies/1998/a623 (accessed 27 October 2014).
661. "Bernard's Lawsuit Helped Natives Nationwide," *The Daily News*, http://www.canada.com/story_print.html?id=983a8b88-a8ac-4e09-9e5c-b2c0e207ac3d.
662. Canadian Broadcasting Corporation, *The Journal*, Barbara Frum interview with Phil Fontaine, 30 October 1990, http://archives.cbc.ca/society/education/clips//11177.
663. Lleweyn, "Dealing with the Legacy," 253 at 261.
664. Assembly of First Nations, *Assembly of First Nations Report*, 11.
665. *Cloud v. Canada (Attorney General)* 2004 CanLII 45444 (ON CA).
666. Canada, House of Commons Debates (11 June 2008), 6850.
667. Canada, House of Commons Debates (11 June 2008), 6851.
668. Canada, House of Commons Debates (11 June 2008), 6852.
669. Canada, House of Commons Debates (11 June 2008), 6853.
670. Canada, House of Commons Debates (11 June 2008), 6855.
671. Canada, House of Commons Debates (11 June 2008), 6855.
672. Canada, House of Commons Debates (11 June 2008), 6855.
673. Canada, House of Commons Debates (11 June 2008), 6856.
674. Canada, House of Commons Debates (11 June 2008), 6856.

The legacy

1. TRC, AVS, Johanne Coutu-Autut, Statement to the Truth and Reconciliation Commission of Canada, Rankin Inlet, Nunavut, 21 March 2011, Statement Number: 2011- 0160.
2. TRC, AVS, Joseph Martin Larocque, Statement to the Truth and Reconciliation Commission of Canada, Saskatoon, Saskatchewan, 21 June 2012, Statement Number: 2011-4386.
3. TRC, AVS, Mervin Mirasty, Statement to the Truth and Reconciliation Commission of Canada, Saskatoon, Saskatchewan, 21 June 2012, Statement Number: 2011-4391.
4. TRC, AVS, Genine Paul-Dimitracopoulos, Statement to the Truth and Reconciliation Commission of Canada, Halifax, Nova Scotia, 27 October 2011, Statement Number: 2011-2862.
5. TRC, AVS, Alma Scott, Statement to the Truth and Reconciliation of Canada, Winnipeg, Manitoba, 17 June 2010, Statement Number: 02-MB-16JU10-016.
6. Canada, Truth and Reconciliation Commission of Canada, *Interim Report*, Recommendation 15, 29.
7. Canada, Aboriginal Affairs and Northern Development Canada, *Canada's Statement of Support*, http://www.aadnc-aandc.gc.ca/eng/1309374239861/1309374546142.

8. TRC, NRA, INAC - Resolution Sector - IRS Historical Files Collection - Ottawa, file 6-21-1, volume 2 (Ctrl #27-6), H. M. Jones to Deputy Minister, 13 December 1956. [NCA-001989-0001]
9. For a discussion that places both child welfare and residential schools in the context of the ongoing colonization of Aboriginal people, see: McKenzie and Hudson, "Native Children."
10. Royal Commission on Aboriginal Peoples, as cited in Sinha and Kozlowski, "Structure of Aboriginal Child Welfare," 4.
11. Canada, Statistics Canada, *Aboriginal People in Canada,* 19.
12. TRC, AVS, Norma Kassi, Statement to the Truth and Reconciliation Commission of Canada, Inuvik, Northwest Territories, 29 June 2011, Statement Number: NNE203.
13. United Nations, Convention on the Rights of the Child, *Concluding observations,* 12–13.
14. United Nations, Convention on the Rights of the Child, *Concluding observations,* 7.
15. Vandna et al., *Kiskisik Awasisak,* x–xi.
16. Vandna et al., *Kiskisik Awasisak,* xi. The authors concluded that there was not enough data on Métis and Inuit children, and excluded them from the study. Vandna et al., *Kiskisik Awasisak,* ix.
17. Vandna et al., *Kiskisik Awasisak,* 83–87.
18. Vandna et al., *Kiskisik Awasisak,* xviii.
19. Vandna et al., *Kiskisik Awasisak,* xii.
20. Ruiz-Casares et al., "Supervisory Neglect," 478.
21. TRC, AVS, [Name redacted], Statement to the Truth and Reconciliation Commission of Canada, Winnipeg, Manitoba, 19 June 2010, Statement Number: 02-MB-19JU10-048.
22. TRC, AVS, Linda Clarke, Statement to the Truth and Reconciliation Commission of Canada, St. Albert, Alberta, 12 June 2011, Statement Number: 2011-0013.
23. Information about ethnicity was available for 94 of the 145 children who have died in foster care since 1999. Of that number, 74 were Aboriginal. "Deaths of Alberta Aboriginal Children in Care No 'Fluke of Statistics,'" *Edmonton Journal,* 8 January 2014, http://www.edmontonjournal.com/life/Deaths+Alberta+aboriginal+children+care+fluke+statistics/9212384/story.html (accessed 18 February 2014).
24. Sinha and Kozlowski, "Structure of Aboriginal Child Welfare," 3; "Deaths of Alberta Aboriginal Children in Care No 'Fluke of Statistics,'" *Edmonton Journal,* 8 January 2014, http://www.edmontonjournal.com/life/Deaths+Alberta+aboriginal+children+care+fluke+statistics/9212384/story.html (accessed 18 February 2014).
25. Sinha and Kozlowski, "Structure of Aboriginal Child Welfare," 4.
26. Canada, Aboriginal Affairs and Northern Development Canada, Program Expenditures/Statistics, First Nations Child and Family Services Program Statistics, First Nations children ordinarily resident on reserve in care, https://www.aadnc-aandc.gc.ca/eng/1382549135936/1382549233428 (accessed 1 May 2015).
27. National Collaborating Centre for Aboriginal Health, *Child and Youth Health,* 3.
28. Wien et al., "Keeping First Nations Children at Home," 13.
29. Blackstock et al., *Wen: de: We Are Coming,* 38.
30. Blackstock et al., *Wen: de: We Are Coming,* 89–90.
31. Cradock, "Extraordinary Costs," 179.
32. Canada, Aboriginal Affairs and Northern Development Canada, "Jordan's Principle," http://www.aadnc-aandc.gc.ca/eng/1334329827982/1334329861879 (accessed 3 January 2014).
33. *Pictou Landing Band Council v. Canada (Attorney General),* 2013 FC 342 (CanLII), para. 82.
34. *Pictou Landing Band Council v. Canada (Attorney General),* 2013 FC 342 (CanLII), para. 82.
35. Fletcher, "Origins of the Indian Child Welfare Act," 1, 4.

36. Atwood, "Voice of the Indian Child," 128.
37. TRC, AVS, Doris Young, Statement to the Truth and Reconciliation Commission of Canada, Saskatoon, Saskatchewan, 22 June 2012, Statement Number: 2011-3517.
38. Canada, *Annual Report of the Department of Indian Affairs, 1942,* 154; Canada, *Annual Report of the Department of Indian Affairs, 1943,* 168; Canada, *Annual Report of the Department of Indian Affairs, 1944,* 177; Canada, *Annual Report of the Department of Indian Affairs, 1945,* 190; Canada, *Annual Report of the Department of Indian Affairs, 1946,* 231; Canada, *Annual Report of the Department of Indian Affairs, 1947,* 236; Canada, *Annual Report of the Department of Indian Affairs, 1948,* 234; Canada, *Annual Report of the Department of Indian Affairs, 1949,* 215; Canada, *Annual Report of the Department of Indian Affairs, 1950,* 86–87; Canada, *Annual Report of the Department of Indian Affairs, 1951,* 34–35; Canada, *Annual Report of the Department of Indian Affairs, 1952,* 74–75; Canada, *Annual Report of the Department of Indian Affairs, 1953,* 82–83; Canada, *Annual Report of the Department of Indian Affairs, 1954,* 88–89; Canada, *Annual Report of the Department of Indian Affairs, 1955,* 78–79; Canada, *Annual Report of the Department of Indian Affairs, 1956,* 76–77; Canada, *Annual Report of the Department of Indian Affairs, 1956–57,* 88–89; Canada, *Annual Report of the Department of Indian Affairs, 1958,* 91; Canada, *Annual Report of the Department of Indian Affairs, 1959,* 94; Canada, *Annual Report of the Department of Indian Affairs, 1960,* 94; Canada, *Annual Report of the Department of Indian Affairs, 1961,* 102; Canada, *Annual Report of the Department of Indian Affairs, 1962,* 73; Canada, *Annual Report of the Department of Indian Affairs, 1963,* 62.
39. United Nations, *Declaration on the Rights of Indigenous Peoples,* Article 14:1, http://www.un.org/esa/socdev/unpfii/documents/DRIPS_en.pdf.
40. Bougie and Senecal, "Registered Indian Children's School Success," 21.
41. Bougie and Senecal, "Registered Indian Children's School Success," 21.
42. Canada, Statistics Canada, *Educational Portrait of Canada, Census Year 2006,* 6, 19.
43. Canada, Statistics Canada Fact Sheet, *2011 National Household Survey Aboriginal Demographics,* https://www.aadnc-aandc.gc.ca/eng/1376329205785/1376329233875.
44. National Committee on Inuit Education, *First Canadians, Canadians First,* https://www.itk.ca/sites/default/files/National-Strategy-on-Inuit-Education-2011_0.pdf, 7; Penny, "Formal Educational Attainment," 33; Canada, Statistics Canada, *Educational attainment of Aboriginal peoples,* http://www12.statcan.gc.ca/nhs-enm/2011/as-sa/99-012-x/99-012-x2011003_3-eng.pdf.
45. Richards et al., *Understanding the Aboriginal/Non-Aboriginal Gap,* 1; Wilk et al., "Métis Educational Attainment," 51–52.
46. Canadian Human Rights Commission, "Report on Equality Rights," 3, 12, 32.
47. Canada, Statistics Canada, *Aboriginal People Living Off-reserve,* 15.
48. Canada, Statistics Canada, "Census Inuit Table: 89-636-x," http://www.statcan.gc.ca/pub/89-636-x/89-636-x2008001-eng.htm.
49. Joe Friesen, "Ottawa Failing to Include First Nations in Key Employment Data," *Globe and Mail,* 23 January 2015, http://www.theglobeandmail.com/news/politics/unemployment-stats-missing-in-areas-where-job-training-is-a-priority/article22598523 (accessed 1 May 2015).
50. Wilson and Macdonald, *Income Gap,* 8.
51. Wilson and Macdonald, *Income Gap,* 4.
52. Macdonald and Wilson, *Poverty or Prosperity,* 6.
53. Wilson and Macdonald, *Income Gap,* 14.
54. Canadian Human Rights Commission, *Report on Equality Rights of Aboriginal People,* 17. The poverty line is measured by the 2009 SLID Low-Income Measure (LIM).

55. Canadian Human Rights Commission, *Report on Equality Rights of Aboriginal People*, 18–19.
56. Canada, Standing Senate Committee on Aboriginal Peoples, *Reforming First Nations Education,* 9.
57. Canada, Department of Indian and Northern Affairs, "Indian Education Paper: Phase 1," 1982, as cited in Paquette and Fallon, *First Nations Education Policy,* 80.
58. Canada, Standing Senate Committee on Aboriginal Peoples, *Reforming First Nations Education,* 56.
59. McCue, *First Nations 2nd and 3rd Level Education Services,* 52, http://www.afn.ca/uploads/files/education/9._2006_april_harvey_mccue_first_nations_2nd_&_3rd_level_services_paper.pdf.
60. Canada, Standing Senate Committee on Aboriginal Peoples, *Reforming First Nations Education,* 11; First Nations Education Council, *Funding Formula for First Nation Schools,* http://www.cepn-fnec.com/PDF/etudes_documents/fiche_complete_eng.pdf.
61. Canada, Standing Senate Committee on Aboriginal Peoples, *Reforming First Nations Education,* 11, 31.
62. First Nations Education Council, *Funding Formula for First Nation Schools,* 1, http://www.cepn-fnec.com/PDF/etudes_documents/fiche_complete_eng.pdf.
63. Canada, Standing Senate Committee on Aboriginal Peoples, *Reforming First Nations Education,* 35.
64. Canada, Standing Senate Committee on Aboriginal Peoples, *Reforming First Nations Education;* Assembly of First Nations, National Panel on First Nation Elementary and Secondary Education for Students on Reserve, *Nurturing the Learning Spirit,* http://www.afn.ca/uploads/files/education2/national-panel.pdf; First Nations Education Council et al., *Report on Priority Actions,* http://www.cepnfnec.com/PDF/accueil/Report%20on%20Priority%20Actions%20in%20View%20of%20Improving%20First%20Nations%20Education%20-%20November%202011_eng_website%20version_.pdf.
65. TRC, AVS, Albert Marshall, Statement to the Truth and Reconciliation Commission of Canada, Winnipeg, Manitoba, 17 June 2010, Statement Number: 02-MB-17JU10-050.
66. Assembly of First Nations, National Panel on First Nation Elementary and Secondary Education for Students on Reserve, *Nurturing the Learning Spirit,* 14, http://www.afn.ca/uploads/files/education2/national-panel.pdf.
67. Hodgson-Smith, *State of Métis Nation Learning,* 4, 26, http://www.ccl-cca.ca/pdfs/AbLKC/StateOfMetisNationLearning.pdf.
68. Hodgson-Smith, *State of Métis Nation Learning,* 4, 17, 82, http://www.ccl-cca.ca/pdfs/AbLKC/StateOfMetisNationLearning.pdf.
69. National Committee on Inuit Education, *First Canadians, Canadians First,* 7–9, 76–79.
70. National Committee on Inuit Education, *First Canadians, Canadians First,* 80.
71. Canada, Statistics Canada, *The Educational Attainment of Aboriginal People,* Table 2, https://www12.statcan.gc.ca/nhs-enm/2011/as-sa/99-012-x/99-012-x2011003_3-eng.cfm.
72. Canada, Auditor General of Canada, *Status Report,* 13, http://www.oag-bvg.gc.ca/internet/docs/parl_oag_201106_04_e.pdf.
73. TRC, AVS, Geraldine Bob, Statement to the Truth and Reconciliation Commission of Canada, Fort Simpson, Northwest Territories, 23 November 2011, Statement Number: 2011-2685.
74. Assembly of First Nations, "Financial Support for First Nation Students in College and University: The Cost of Implementing the Recommendations of the Standing Committee of the House of Commons on Aboriginal Affairs and Northern Development," as cited in First Nations Education Council, *Paper on First Nations Education Funding,* 35.

75. Assembly of First Nations, Chiefs Assembly on Education, *Early Childhood Education,* http://www.afn.ca/uploads/files/events/fact_sheet-ccoe-5.pdf.
76. Assembly of First Nations, *Breaking the Silence*, 25–26.
77. Royal Commission on Aboriginal Peoples, *Gathering Strength*, 3:612–613.
78. TRC, AVS, Michael Sillett, Statement to the Truth and Reconciliation Commission of Canada, Halifax, Nova Scotia, 27 October 2011, Statement Number: 2011-2870.
79. TRC, NRA, INAC – Resolution Sector – IRS Historical Files Collection – Ottawa, file 81/25-1 (Ctrl #240-13), R. Morris to Chiefs, Petahbun [Pehtabun] Area, 9 February 1979, 2–3. [NCA-001721]
80. TRC, AVS, Conrad Burns, Statement to the Truth and Reconciliation Commission of Canada, Regina, Saskatchewan, 17 January 2012, Statement Number: SP036.
81. United Nations, *International Covenant,* Article 27.
82. United Nations, *Declaration of the Rights of Indigenous Peoples*, articles 8, 13, 14, and 16.
83. TRC, AVS, Agnes Mills, Statement to the Truth and Reconciliation Commission of Canada, Inuvik, Northwest Territories, 29 June 2011, Statement Number: SC090.
84. TRC, AVS, Mary Courchene, Statement to the Truth and Reconciliation Commission of Canada, Pine Creek First Nation, Manitoba, 28 November 2011, Statement Number: 2011-2515.
85. Canada, Statistics Canada, *Aboriginal Peoples and Language,* http://www12.statcan.gc.ca/nhs-enm/2011/as-sa/99-011-x/99-011-x2011003_1-eng.cfm.
86. Canada, Statistics Canada, *Aboriginal Peoples and Language,* http://www12.statcan.gc.ca/nhs-enm/2011/as-sa/99-011-x/99-011-x2011003_1-eng.cfm; Canada, Statistics Canada, *Population reporting an Aboriginal identity,* http://www.statcan.gc.ca/tables-tableaux/sum-som/l01/cst01/demo38a-eng.htm; Canada, Statistics Canada, *Aboriginal Languages in Canada.* http://www.statcan.gc.ca/pub/11-008-x/2007001/9628-eng.htm.
87. Moseley and Nicolas, *Atlas of the World's Languages,* 117.
88. *R. v. Van der Peet,* 1996 CanLII 216 (SCC).
89. Assembly of First Nations, *Royal Commission on Aboriginal Peoples at 10 Years,* 18.
90. Canada, House of Commons Debates (2 November 2006), 1010.
91. TRC, AVS, Michael Sillett, Statement to the Truth and Reconciliation Commission of Canada, Halifax, Nova Scotia, 27 October 2011, Statement Number: 2011-2870.
92. Email from Glenn Morrisson, Policy Manager of the Aboriginal Affairs Directorate in the Citizenship Participation Branch, to the Truth and Reconciliation Commission (July 9, 2012).
93. Canada, Department of Canadian Heritage, *2012–2013 Report on Plans and Priorities,* 26.
94. Canada, Standing Senate Committee on Legal and Constitutional Affairs, *Language Rights in Canada's North,* 19–20.
95. TRC, AVS, Sabrina Williams, Statement to the Truth and Reconciliation Commission of Canada, Victoria, British Columbia, 13 April 2012, Statement Number: 2011-3982.
96. French, *My Name Is Masak,* 19.
97. Gresko, "Everyday Life at Qu'Appelle Industrial School," 80.
98. TRC, AVS, Ruby Firth, Statement to the Truth and Reconciliation Commission of Canada, Inuvik, Northwest Territories, 22 July 2011, Statement Number: 2011-0326.
99. TRC, AVS, Sonia Wuttunee-Byrd, Statement to the Truth and Reconciliation Commission of Canada, Winnipeg, Manitoba, 16 June 2010, Statement Number: SC093.
100. TRC, AVS, Katherine Copenace, Statement to the Truth and Reconciliation Commission of Canada, Winnipeg, Manitoba, 16 June 2010, Statement Number: 02-MB-16JU10-129.
101. United Nations, *Declaration on the Rights of Indigenous Peoples,* articles 7, 21, 22, 24.
102. United Nations, *Declaration on the Rights of Indigenous Peoples,* Article 23.

103. United Nations, *Declaration on the Rights of Indigenous Peoples,* articles 24, 31.
104. National Collaborating Centre for Aboriginal Health, *Looking for Aboriginal Health,* 43–50.
105. Canada, Report of an Interdepartmental Working Group to the Committee of Deputy Ministers on Justice and Legal Affairs, Fiduciary Relationship of the Crown with Aboriginal Peoples: Implementation and Management Issues – A Guide for Managers (Ottawa, 1995), 13, as cited in Boyer, *No. 1 Aboriginal Health,* 5, 20–21.
106. Boyer, *No. 1 Aboriginal Health,* 19–21, 23.
107. Boyer, *No. 1 Aboriginal Health,* 19.
108. Smylie, "Review of Aboriginal Infant Mortality Rates, 147.
109. Canada, Statistics Canada, *Mortality rates among children and teenagers,* http://www.statcan.gc.ca/pub/82-003-x/2012003/article/11695-eng.htm.
110. Canada, Statistics Canada, *Select health indicators of First Nations people,* http://www.statcan.gc.ca/daily-quotidien/130129/dq130129b-eng.htm.
111. First Nations Centre, *First Nations Regional Longitudinal Health Survey,* 114.
112. Kirmayer et al., *Suicide Among Aboriginal People,* xv, 22.
113. Australia, Department of the Prime Minister and Cabinet, *Closing the Gap,* http://www.dpmc.gov.au/pmc-indigenous-affairs/publication/closing-gap-prime-ministers-report-2015.
114. Canadian Medical Association, "Aboriginal Health Programming under Siege," E740.
115. TRC, AVS, Trudy King, Statement to the Truth and Reconciliation Commission of Canada, Fort Resolution, Northwest Territories, 28 April 2011, Statement Number: 2011-0381.
116. TRC, AVS, M. R. E. Linklater, Statement to the Truth and Reconciliation Commission of Canada, Winnipeg, Manitoba, 18 June 2010, Statement Number: 02-MB-18JU10-055.
117. Chansonneuve, *Addictive Behaviours,* 42–46.
118. TRC, ASAGR, Royal Canadian Mounted Police, M. W. Pacholuk, Final Report of the Native Indian Residential School Task Force, Project E-NIRS, Royal Canadian Mounted Police, no date, 20, 21, 28, 45. [RCMP-564517]
119. TRC, ASGAR, Stephen N. S. Thatcher, Affidavit in Supreme Court of BC, no date, 25–35. [RCMP-564327]
120. TRC, ASAGR, Royal Canadian Mounted Police, M. W. Pacholuk, Final Report of the Native Indian Residential School Task Force, Project E-NIRS, Royal Canadian Mounted Police, no date, 27, 32, 45. [RCMP-564517]
121. TRC, ASAGR, Royal Canadian Mounted Police, M. W. Pacholuk, Final Report of the Native Indian Residential School Task Force, Project E-NIRS, Royal Canadian Mounted Police, no date, 40. [RCMP-564517]
122. *Criminal Code, 1985,* chapter C-46, section 274.
123. Canada, Indian Residential Schools Adjudication Secretariat, Adjudication Secretariat Statistics, from September 19, 2007, January 31, 2015, http://iap-pei.ca/information/stats-eng.php (accessed 20 February 2015).
124. TRC, ASAGR, Royal Canadian Mounted Police, M. W. Pacholuk, Final Report of the Native Indian Residential School Task Force, Project E-NIRS, Royal Canadian Mounted Police, no date, 45. [RCMP-564517]
125. Canada, Law Commission of Canada, *Restoring Dignity,* 151, 178.
126. Indian Residential Schools Settlement Agreement, http://www.residentialschoolsettlement.ca/IRS%20Settlement%20Agreement-%20ENGLISH.pdf.
127. TRC, AVS, Bernard Catcheway, Statement to the Truth and Reconciliation Commission of Canada, Skownan First Nation, Manitoba, 12 October 2011, Statement Number: 2011-2510.

128. TRC, AVS, Amelia Galligos-Thomas, Statement to the Truth and Reconciliation Commission of Canada, Victoria, British Columbia, 14 April 2012, Statement Number: 2011-3975.
129. Canada, Statistics Canada, *Adult Correctional Services in Canada 1995–1996,* http://www.statcan.gc.ca/pub/85-002-x/85-002-x1997004-eng.pdf; Canada, Statistics Canada, *Adult Correctional Services in Canada 2011–2012,* http://www.statcan.gc.ca/pub/85-002-x/2014001/article/11918-eng.htm#a5.
130. Canada, Statistics Canada, *Adult Correctional Services in Canada, 2011–2012,* http://www.statcan.gc.ca/pub/85-002-x/2014001/article/11918-eng.htm#a5.
131. Canada, Statistics Canada, *Adult Correctional Services in Canada, 2011–2012,* http://www.statcan.gc.ca/pub/85-002-x/2014001/article/11918-eng.htm#a5.
132. TRC, AVS, [Name redacted], Statement to the Truth and Reconciliation Commission of Canada, Long Plain First Nation, Manitoba, 27 July 2010, Statement Number: 01-MB-26JY10-011.
133. TRC, AVS, Daniel Andre, Statement to the Truth and Reconciliation Commission of Canada, Whitehorse, Yukon, 23 May 2011, Statement Number: 2011-0202.
134. TRC, AVS, Grace Campbell, Statement to the Truth and Reconciliation Commission of Canada, Winnipeg, Manitoba, 16 June 2010, Statement Number: 02-MB-16JU10-136.
135. *Criminal Code,* 1985, chapter C-46, section 718.2(e).
136. *R. v. Gladue,* 1999 CanLII 679 (SCC), para. 58–65.
137. *R. v. Gladue,* 1999 CanLII 679 (SCC), para. 64.
138. For a description of the process of preparing Gladue reports, see: Istvanffy, *Gladue Primer.*
139. *R. v. Ipeelee,* 2012 SCC 13 (CanLII), para. 81, 84.
140. *Safe Streets and Communities Act,* 2012, chapter 1.
141. There have been some recent cases in which courts have made decisions counter to the mandatory minimum provisions. See, for example: *R. v. Smickle,* 2012, ONSC 602 (CanLII).
142. Canada, Public Safety Canada, *Fetal Alcohol Spectrum Disorder,* 5, http://www.publicsafety.gc.ca/cnt/rsrcs/pblctns/ftl-lchl-spctrm/ftl-lchl-spctrm-eng.pdf.
143. Tait, *Fetal Alcohol Syndrome.*
144. Tait, *Fetal Alcohol Syndrome,* xviii.
145. Ospina and Dennett, *Systematic Review,* iii.
146. Canada, Correctional Service of Canada, *Fetal Alcohol Spectrum Disorder(FASD),* iv, http://www.publicsafety.gc.ca/lbrr/archives/cn21451-eng.pdf.
147. *R. v. Harris,* 2002 BCCA 152 (CanLII), para. 18–20.
148. Mitten, "Fetal Alcohol Spectrum Disorders," http://www.justicereformcomm.sk.ca/volume2/12section9.pdf.
149. For a study that involved interviews with inmates in a minimum security institution designed specifically for Aboriginal inmates, see: Braun, *Colonization, Destruction, and Renewal.* See also: Waldram, *The Way of the Pipe,* 129–150; Crutcher and Trevethan, *Examination of Healing Lodges,* 52.
150. Nielson, "Canadian Aboriginal Healing Lodges."
151. British Columbia, Ministry of Justice, Corrections Branch, Aboriginal Programs and Relationships, *Inclusivity,* http://www.pssg.gov.bc.ca/corrections/docs/AboriginalStratPlan.pdf.
152. TRC, AVS, Chris Gargan, Statement to the Truth and Reconciliation Commission of Canada, Yellowknife, Northwest Territories, 30 October 2012, Statement Number: 2011-0430.
153. *Corrections and Conditional Release Act,* SC 1992, chapter 20, http://canlii.ca/t/52db0.
154. Bonta et al., "Risk Prediction," 127.

155. Canada, Statistics Canada, *Youth Correctional Services in Canada 2011–2012,* http://www.statcan.gc.ca/pub/85-002-x/2014001/article/11917-eng.htm#a5; Canada, Department of Justice, Youth Justice Research, "A One-Day Snapshot," 3. These figures do not include Saskatchewan, which has a high rate of Aboriginal youth incarceration
156. *Youth Criminal Justice Act,* SC 2002, chapter 1, section 38(1).
157. Canada, Statistics Canada, "Youth Court Statistics 2011/2012," http://www.statcan.gc.ca/daily-quotidien/130613/dq130613d-eng.pdf); Canada, Statistics Canada, *Youth Correctional Statistics in Canada, 2010/2011*; Canadian Bar Association, *Submission on Bill C-10,* 8, http://www.cba.org/cba/submissions/PDF/11-45-eng.pdf. Not all provinces and territories have seen a decrease in youth in correctional services. In fact, since 2005–06, rates have increased in Manitoba, Yukon, and Alberta. Canada, Statistics Canada, *Youth Correctional Statistics in Canada, 2010/2011,* 5.
158. Canada, Statistics Canada, *Youth Correctional Statistics in Canada, 2010/2011,* 7.
159. British Columbia, Office of the Provincial Health Officer, "Health, Crime and Doing Time," http://www.health.gov.bc.ca/pho/pdf/health-crime-2013.pdf.
160. Canada, Indian Residential Schools Adjudication Secretariat, Adjudication Secretariat Statistics, from September 19, 2007, January 31, 2015, http://iap-pei.ca/information/stats-eng.php (accessed 20 February 2015).
161. TRC, AVS, Ruby Firth, Statement to the Truth and Reconciliation Commission of Canada, Inuvik, Northwest Territories, 22 July 2011, Statement Number: 2011-0326.
162. Canada, Statistics Canada, *Violent Victimization of Aboriginal People,* http://wgc.ca/pub/85-002-x/2011001/article/11415-eng.pdf.
163. Canada, Statistics Canada, *Violent Victimization of Aboriginal Women,* http://www.statcan.gc.ca/pub/85-002-x/2011001/article/11439-eng.pdf.
164. Canada, Statistics Canada, *Violent Victimization of Aboriginal People,* 15, http://wgc.ca/pub/85-002-x/2011001/article/11415-eng.pdf; Canada, Statistics Canada, *Measuring Violence Against Women,* 67; Native Women's Association of Canada, *Voices of Our Sisters in Spirit,* 6, http://www.nwac.ca/sites/default/files/download/admin/NWAC_VoicesofOurSistersInSpiritII_March2009FINAL.pdf.
165. Canada, Statistics Canada, *Victimization and Offending,* http://www.statcan.gc.ca/pub/85-002-x/85-002-x2006003-eng.pdf.
166. Canada, Statistics Canada, *Measuring Violence Against Women,* 9, 19; Native Women's Association of Canada, *Voices of Our Sisters in Spirit,* 94–95, http://www.nwac.ca/sites/default/files/download/admin/NWAC_VoicesofOurSistersInSpiritII_March2009FINAL.pdf.
167. TRC, AVS, Velma Jackson, Statement to the Truth and Reconciliation Commission of Canada, St. Paul, Alberta, 6 January 2011, Statement Number: 01-AB-06JA11-003.
168. Royal Canadian Mounted Police, *Missing and Murdered Aboriginal Women,* 3, http://www.rcmp-grc.gc.ca/pubs/mmaw-faapd-eng.pdf.

The challenge of reconciliation

1. TRC, AVS, Ian Campbell, Statement to the Truth and Reconciliation Commission of Canada, Winnipeg, Manitoba, 25 June 2014, Statement Number: SE048.
2. Canada, Debates of the Senate, 40th Parliament, 2nd session (11 June 2009), volume 146, issue 45.
3. Miller, *Lethal Legacy,* 165.

4. For various perspectives on the events at Oka, see, for example: Alfred, *Heeding the Voices*; Pertusati, *In Defense of Mohawk Land*; Miller, *Lethal Legacy*; Simpson and Ladner, *This is an Honour Song*.
5. On the place of media in shaping popular opinion on the role of warriors in conflicts with the state, see: Valaskakis, *Indian Country*. On warriors and warrior societies in contemporary Indigenous communities, see: Alfred and Lowe, "Warrior Societies,"
6. Letters from Prime Minister Brian Mulroney to Tony Penikett, Government Leader, Government of the Yukon Territory, 15 November 1990, and Dennis Patterson, Government Leader, Government of the Northwest Territories, 15 November 1990, PCO 2150-1, Ident. No. 34788, TRC Document Number TRC3379.
7. Canada, Royal Commission on Aboriginal Peoples, *Report*, 1:675–697.
8. United Nations, *Declaration on the Rights of Indigenous Peoples,* Article 43, http://www.un.org/esa/socdev/unpfii/documents/DRIPS_en.pdf.
9. Anaya, "Right of Indigenous Peoples," 196.
10. Canada, Aboriginal Affairs and Northern Development Canada, "Canada's Endorsement," http://www.aadnc-aandc.gc.ca/eng/1309374807748/1309374897928 (accessed 15 March 2015).
11. Canada, Aboriginal Affairs and Northern Development Canada, "Canada's Endorsement," http://www.aadnc-aandc.gc.ca/eng/1309374807748/1309374897928 (accessed 15 March 2015).
12. United Nations General Assembly, "Outcome Document," A/RES/69/2, 25 September 2014, http://www.un.org/en/ga/search/view_doc.asp?symbol=A/RES/69/2.
13. Canada, Permanent Mission of Canada to the United Nations, "Canada's Statement on the World Conference," http://www.canadainternational.gc.ca/prmny-mponu/canada_un-canada_onu/statements-declarations/other-autres/2014-09-22_WCIPD-PADD.aspx?lang=eng.
14. Amnesty International Canada et al., "Canada Uses World Conference," http://www.fns.bc.ca/pdf/Joint_Public_Statement_re_Canada_attack_on_UNDRIP_Sept_24_2014.pdf.
15. John, "Survival, Dignity, Well-Being," 58. Grand Chief John, an executive member of the First Nations Summit Task Group in British Columbia, participated in the development of the *Declaration*. He is a former co-chair of the North American Indigenous Peoples Caucus and will serve as a North American Representative to the United Nations Permanent Forum on Indigenous Issues until 2016. See: First Nations Summit, http://www.fns.bc.ca/about/e_john.htm.
16. *Tsilhqot'in Nation v. British Columbia,* 2014 CanLII 44 (SCC), para. 73.
17. *Tsilhqot'in Nation v. British Columbia,* 2014 CanLII 44 (SCC), para. 97.
18. TRC, AVS, Sol Sanderson, Statement to the Truth and Reconciliation Commission of Canada, Winnipeg, Manitoba, 17 June 2010, Statement Number: SC108.
19. Reid, "Roman Catholic Foundations," 5.
20. The Permanent Observer Mission of the Holy See explains its role and function at the United Nations as follows: "The Holy See ... is the central government of the Roman Catholic Church. As such, the Holy See is an institution, which under international law and in practice, has a legal personality that allows it to enter into treaties as the juridical equal of a State.... The Holy See maintains full diplomatic relations with one hundred seventy-seven (177) countries out of the one hundred ninety-three (193) member countries of the UN.... The Holy See enjoys *by its own choice* the status of Permanent Observer at the United Nations, rather than of a full Member. This is due primarily to the desire of the Holy See to obtain absolute neutrality in specific political problems." See: UN Permanent Observer Mission of the Holy See, "A Short History," http://www.holyseemission.org/about/history-of-diplomacy-of-the-holy-see.aspx (accessed 19 February 2015).

21. UN Permanent Observer Mission of the Holy See, Statement to Economic and Social Council, Discussion on the reports, "Impact on Indigenous Peoples," http://www.ailanyc.org/wp-content/uploads/2010/09/Holy-See.pdf (accessed 20 January 2015).
22. For example, in a study of how the doctrine was used to justify colonization, American legal scholar Robert A. Williams Jr. observed that the United States Supreme Court decision issued by Chief Justice John Marshall in 1823 in the case of *Johnson v. McIntosh* 21 U.S. 543 (1823), "represents the most influential legal opinion on indigenous peoples' human rights ever issued by a court of law in the Western world. All the major English-language-speaking settler states adopted Marshall's understanding of the Doctrine of Discovery and its principle that the first European discoverer of lands occupied by non-Christian tribal savages could claim a superior right to those lands under the European Law of Nations. Canada, Australia, and New Zealand all followed Marshall's opinion as a precedent for their domestic law on indigenous peoples' inferior rights to property and control over their ancestral lands." See: Williams, *Savage Anxieties*, 224. See also: Williams, *American Indian*; Miller et al., *Discovering Indigenous Lands;* Newcomb, *Pagans in the Promised Land*, 2008.
23. United Nations Economic and Social Council, Permanent Forum on Indigenous Issues, "Study on the Impacts of the Doctrine," http://daccess-dds-ny.un.org/doc/UNDOC/GEN/N14/241/84/PDF/N1424184.pdf?OpenElement.
24. Anglican Church of Canada, General Synod 2010, Resolution A086 R1, http://archive.anglican.ca/gs2010/resolutions/a086/.
25. Sison, "Primate's Commission." See also: Anglican Church of Canada, "Message to the Church," http://www.anglican.ca/primate/communications/commission-on-discovery-reconciliation-justice. See also: Anglican Church of Canada, "Learning to Call One Another Friends," http://www.anglican.ca/primate/files/2014/06/PCDRJ_June2014_Update.pdf.
26. World Council of Churches, *What Is the World Council of Churches?*, http://www.oikoumene.org/en/about-us (accessed 15 April 2015). Settlement Agreement signatories the Anglican Church of Canada, the Presbyterian Church in Canada, and the United Church of Canada are members of the WCC.
27. World Council of Churches, *Statement on the doctrine of discovery,* http://www.oikoumene.org/en/resources/documents/executive-committee/bossey-february-2012/statement-on-the-doctrine-of-discovery-and-its-enduring-impact-on-indigenous-peoples (accessed 20 March 2015).
28. Executive of the General Council of the United Church of Canada, *Meeting Summary, March 24–26, 2013,* http://www.united-church.ca/files/general-council/gc40/gce_1203_highlights.pdf (accessed 20 March 2015).
29. United Nations Permanent Forum on Indigenous Issues, "Joint Statement," http://www.afn.ca/uploads/files/pfii_2012_-_doctrine_of_discovery_-_joint_statement_fe.pdf (accessed 20 March 2015).
30. United Nations Permanent Forum on Indigenous Issues, "Study on the Impacts of the Doctrine," para. 13, http://daccess-dds-ny.un.org/doc/UNDOC/GEN/N14/241/84/PDF/N1424184.pdf?OpenElement (accessed 14 March 2015). For the views of the court on the need for reconciliation, John cited *Haida Nation v. British Columbia (Minister of Forests),* 2004 SCC 73 (CanLII), para. 20. For the judicial notice on colonialism, John cited *R. v. Ipeelee,* 2012 SCC 13 (CanLII), para. 60.
31. Onondaga Nation, "Oren Lyons Presents," http://www.onondaganation.org/news/2014/oren-lyons-presents-at-u-n-51514/ (accessed 21 March 2015). Article 7, paragraph 2 of the *Declaration* affirms that "Indigenous peoples have the collective right to live in freedom, peace and security as distinct peoples and shall not be subjected to any act of genocide or any other act of violence, including forcibly removing children of the group to another group."

32. Kelly, "Confessions of a Born Again Pagan," 22–23.
33. See, for example: Treaty 7 Tribal Council et al., *True Spirit and Original Intent*; Miller, *Compact, Contract, Covenant*; Ray, Miller, and Tough, *Bounty and Benevolence*.
34. The Treaty commissions in Ontario, Saskatchewan, and Manitoba have developed public education programs and materials designed to teach Canadians, particularly children and youth, about the Treaties. See, for example: Treaty Relations Commission of Manitoba, Public Education/Learning Centre, http://www.trcm.ca/public-education/learning-centre/ (accessed 15 April 2015).
35. Borrows, "Wampum at Niagara," 160–161.
36. Miller, *Compact, Contract, Covenant*, 72.
37. Capt. Thomas G. Anderson, "Report on the Affairs of the Indians of Canada, Section III," Appendix No. 95 in Appt T of the *Journals of the Legislative Assembly of Canada*, vol. 6 (1818), cited in Borrows, "Wampum at Niagara," 166.
38. Capt. Thomas G. Anderson, "Report on the Affairs of the Indians of Canada, Section III," Appendix No. 95 in Appt T of the *Journals of the Legislative Assembly of Canada*, vol. 6 (1818), cited in Borrows, "Wampum at Niagara," 167–168.
39. The Governor General of Canada, his Excellency the Right Honourable David Johnston, Speech delivered at the Symposium in Honour of the 250th Anniversary of the Royal Proclamation of 1763, Gatineau, Que., October 7, 2013, http://www.gg.ca/document.aspx?id=15345&lan=eng.
40. First Nations Summit, "Royal Proclamation Still Relevant," http://www.fns.bc.ca/pdf/FNS_Op-ed_re_250th_anniver_of_Royal_Proclamation_10_07_13.pdf (accessed 5 December 2014).
41. Steve Rennie, "Idle No More Protestors Mark 25th Anniversary of Royal Proclamation," *Canadian Press*, October 7, 2013, http://www.thestar.com/news/canada/2013/10/07/idle_no_more_protesters_mark_250th_anniversary_of_royal_proclamation.html. For more on the Idle No More movement, see: The Kino-nda-niimi Collective, *The Winter We Danced*.
42. Legal scholar Robert A. Williams Jr. explains the Gus-Wen-Tah or Two-Row Wampum as "a sacred treaty belt ... comprised of a bed of white wampum shell beads symbolizing the sacredness and purity of the treaty agreement between the two sides. Two parallel rows of purple wampum beads that extend down the length of the belt represent the separate paths travelled by the two sides on the same river. Each side travels in its own vessel: the Indians in a birch bark canoe, representing their laws, customs, and ways, and the whites in a ship, representing their laws, customs, and ways." See: Williams Jr., *Linking Arms Together*, 12–13.
43. "Two-Row Wampum Centers Idle No More Toronto Rally, Not the Royal Proclamation," October 9, 2013, *BasicNews.ca*, http://basicsnews.ca/two-row-wampum-centers-idle-no-more-toronto-rally-not-the-royal-proclamation/.
44. United Nations, *Declaration on the Rights of Indigenous Peoples*, Article 40, http://www.un.org/esa/socdev/unpfii/documents/DRIPS_en.pdf.
45. United Nations General Assembly, Human Rights Council, UN Expert Mechanism on the Rights of Indigenous Peoples, "Access to Justice," 23, http://www.ohchr.org/Documents/Issues/IPeoples/EMRIP/Session6/A-HRC-EMRIP-2013-2_en.pdf.
46. United Nations General Assembly, Human Rights Council, UN Expert Mechanism on the Rights of Indigenous Peoples, "Access to Justice," 6, 8, 22–24, http://www.ohchr.org/Documents/Issues/IPeoples/EMRIP/Session6/A-HRC-EMRIP-2013-2_en.pdf.
47. United Nations General Assembly, "Report of the Special Rapporteur," 13, 20.
48. See, for example: Borrows, *Canada's Indigenous Constitution*.
49. Canada, Royal Commission on Aboriginal Peoples, *Highlights from the Report*, http://www.aadnc-aandc.gc.ca/eng/1100100014597/1100100014637.

50. TRC, AVS, Stephen Augustine, Statement to the Truth and Reconciliation Commission of Canada, Winnipeg, Manitoba, 26 June 2014, Statement Number: SE049.
51. Friedland, "IBA Accessing Justice and Reconciliation," 18, quoting Chief White, Snuneymuxw First Nation, 16 November 2012, http://indigenousbar.ca/indigenouslaw/wp-content/uploads/2013/04/iba_ajr_final_report.pdf (accessed 15 April 2015). Funding for the AJR project was provided by the Ontario Law Foundation. The Academic Lead for the project was Professor Val Napoleon, Law Foundation Professor of Aboriginal Justice and Governance, University of Victoria, Faculty of Law. The project coordinator was Hadley Friedland, PhD candidate, Vanier Scholar, University of Alberta, Faculty of Law.
52. On the importance of recognizing that victims of violence are also holders of rights, see: de Greiff, "Report of the Special Rapporteur," 2012, 10, para. 29, http://www.ohchr.org/Documents/HRBodies/HRCouncil/RegularSession/Session21/A-HRC-21-46_en.pdf.
53. Simpson, *Dancing on Our Turtle's Back*, 22.
54. TRC, AVS, Honourable Steven Point, Statement to the Truth and Reconciliation Commission of Canada, Vancouver, British Columbia, 20 September 2013, Statement Number: BCNE304.
55. Stanton, "Canada's Truth and Reconciliation Commission," 4.
56. Castellano, Archibald, and DeGagné, "Introduction," in Castellano, Archibald, and DeGagné, *From Truth to Reconciliation*, 2–3.
57. de Greiff, "Report of the Special Rapporteur," 2012, 10–12, http://www.ohchr.org/Documents/HRBodies/HRCouncil/RegularSession/Session21/A-HRC-21-46_en.pdf.
58. Wab Kinew, "It's the Same Great Spirit," *Winnipeg Free Press*, October 22, 2012.
59. TRC, AVS, Shawn A-in-chut Atleo, Statement to the Truth and Reconciliation Commission of Canada, Saskatoon, Saskatchewan, 22 June 2012, Statement Number: SNE202.
60. Canada, Royal Commission on Aboriginal Peoples, *Report*, 1:38.
61. *R. v. Sparrow*, 1990 CanLII 104 (SCC). See also: *Guerin v. R.*, 1984 CanLII 25 (SCC); *Delgamuukw v. BC*, 1997 CanLII 302 (SCC); *Haida Nation v. British Columbia (Minister of Forests)*, 2004 SCC 73 (CanLII).
62. *Manitoba Métis Federation Inc. v. Canada (Attorney General)*, 2013 SCC 14 (CanLII), Appellants Factum, para. 94, citing Manitoba Court of Appeal ruling *Manitoba Métis Federations Inc. v. Canada (Attorney General) et al.*, 2010 MBCA 71, paras. 533, 534.
63. The Solicitor's Opinions on Native American issues can be found at: http://www.doi.gov/solicitor/opinions.html (accessed 25 March 2015).
64. On the unfair burden of proof placed on Aboriginal peoples and the need to shift the onus onto the Crown, see, for example: Borrows, *Recovering Canada*, 101.
65. Canada, Royal Commission on Aboriginal Peoples, *Report*, 1:8. The Commission adopts the definition of "civic trust" put forward by justice scholar Pablo de Greiff as it relates to the role of apologies in reconciliation processes: "Trust involves an expectation of ... commitment to the norms and values we share ... not the thick form of trust characteristic of relations between intimates, but rather 'civic' trust ... that can develop among citizens who are strangers to one another, but who are members of the same political community.... Trusting an institution, then, amounts to knowing that its constitutive rules, values, and norms are shared by participants and that they regard them as binding.... Reconciliation, minimally, is the condition under which citizens can trust one another as citizens again (or anew).... It presupposes that both institutions and persons can become *trustworthy*, and this is not something that is merely granted but *earned*." See: de Greiff, "Role of Apologies," 125–127.

66. TRC, AVS, Eugene Arcand, Statement to the Truth and Reconciliation Commission of Canada, Saskatoon, Saskatchewan, 22 June 2012, Statement Number: SNE202.
67. On the role of official apologies in reparations and reconciliation, see, for example: Barkan and Karn, *Taking Wrongs Seriously*; de Greiff, "Role of Apologies"; James, "Wrestling with the Past"; Nobles, *Politics of Official Apologies*; Tavuchis, *Mea Culpa*.
68. Canada, Debates of the Senate, 40th Parliament, 2nd session (11 June 2009), volume 146, issue 45. Other speakers included National President Mary Simon, Inuit Tapiriit Kanatami; Métis National Council President Clément Chartier; and Kevin Daniels, Interim National Chief, Congress of Aboriginal Peoples.
69. TRC, AVS, Theodore Fontaine, Statement to the Truth and Reconciliation Commission of Canada, Edmonton, Alberta, 28 March 2014, Statement Number: SP203.
70. TRC, AVS, Noel Starblanket, Statement to the Truth and Reconciliation Commission of Canada, Regina, Saskatchewan, 16 January 2012, Statement Number: SP035.
71. Vatican, Communiqué of the Holy See Press Office, April 29, 2009, http://www.vatican.va/resources/resources_canada-first-nations-apr2009_en.html.
72. "Pope Expresses 'Sorrow' for Abuse at Residential Schools," *CBC News*, April 29, 2009, http://www.cbc.ca/news/world/pope-expresses-sorrow-for-abuse-at-residential-schools-1.778019.
73. Pastoral Letter of His Holiness Pope Benedict XVI to the Catholics of Ireland, March 19, 2010, http://www.vatican.va/holy_father/benedict_xvi/letters/2010/documents/hf_ben-xvi_let_20100319_church-ireland_en.html.
74. Pastoral Letter of His Holiness Pope Benedict XVI to the Catholics of Ireland, March 19, 2010, http://www.vatican.va/holy_father/benedict_xvi/letters/2010/documents/hf_ben-xvi_let_20100319_church-ireland_en.html.
75. TRC, AVS, Commissioner Wilton Littlechild, speaking at Oblates of St. Mary Immaculate gathering in St. Albert, Alberta, 2 May 2011, Statement Number: SC012.
76. In the Learning Places at National Events, there were information posters on the schools in the region, the Legacy of Hope Foundation exhibit, an information booth on the Missing Children Project, interactive maps, and a writing wall where people could offer their personal reflections. At each event in or near the Learning Place, the Settlement Agreement churches also organized a Churches Listening Area. The intent was to provide an opportunity for those Survivors who wished to do so to speak personally with a church representative about their residential school experience. When requested, church representatives also offered apologies to Survivors.
77. TRC, AVS, Alvin Dixon, Statement to the Truth and Reconciliation Commission of Canada, Inuvik, Northwest Territories, 30 June 2011, Statement Number: NNE302.
78. TRC, AVS, Anonymous, Statement to the Truth and Reconciliation Commission of Canada, Winnipeg, Manitoba, 18 June 2010, Statement Number: 02-MB-18JU10-055.
79. Kelly, "Confession of a Born Again Pagan," 20–21, 39.
80. TRC, AVS, Jennie Blackbird, Statement to the Truth and Reconciliation Commission of Canada, Muncey, Ontario, 16 September 2011, Statement Number: 2011-4188.
81. The right of Indigenous peoples to observe traditional spiritual practices is upheld by the United Nations. Article 12:1 of the *United Nations Declaration on the Rights of Indigenous Peoples* says, "Indigenous peoples have the right to manifest, practice, develop and teach their spiritual and religious traditions, customs and ceremonies; the right to maintain, protect, and have access in privacy to their religious and cultural sites; the right to use and control of their ceremonial objects; and the right to the repatriation of their human remains." See: United Nations, *Declaration on the Rights of Indigenous Peoples*, http://www.un.org/esa/socdev/unpfii/documents/DRIPS_en.pdf.

82. See, for example, the case of a Christian Cree community that passed a resolution denying some of its community members the right to construct a sweat lodge and to teach youth about Cree spirituality: http://aptn.ca/news/2011/01/17/crees-ban-sweat-lodges-fns-spirituality-from-community/; http://indiancountrytodaymedianetwork.com/2011/02/07/christian-crees-tear-down-sweat-lodge-15500.
83. TRC, AVS, Jim Dumont, Statement to the Truth and Reconciliation Commission of Canada, Winnipeg, Manitoba, 26 June 2014, Statement Number: SE049.
84. Dumont and Hutchinson, "United Church Mission Goals," 226–227.
85. Mullin (Thundering Eagle Woman), "We Are One in the Spirit," 28, http://presbyterian.ca/healing/ (accessed 22 March 2015).
86. Presbyterian Church of Canada, 2013 General Assembly Referral, *Aboriginal Spirituality,* 2, 6, http://presbyterian.ca/gao/2013referrals/ (accessed 22 March 2015).
87. Anglican Church of Canada, "A New Agape," http://www.anglican.ca/about/ccc/acip/a-new-agape/ (accessed 22 March 2015).
88. United Church of Canada, "Living Faithfully," 2, http://www.united-church.ca/files/economic/globalization/report.pdf (accessed 22 March 2015).
89. United Church of Canada, "Reviewing Partnership," 26, http://www.gc41.ca/sites/default/files/pcpmm_empire.pdf (accessed 22 March 2015).
90. United Church of Canada, The Executive of the General Council, March 24–26, 2012, Addendum H: Covenanting for Life, http://www.united-church.ca/files/general-council/gc40/addenda_2012-03-2426_executive.pdf (accessed 22 March 2015).
91. Presbyterian Church in Canada, "Presbyterian Statement," https://ecumenism.net/2015/01/presbyterian-statement-on-aboriginal-spiritual-practices.htm (accessed 17 March 2015).
92. United Church of Canada, "Affirming Other Spiritual Paths," http://www.united-church.ca/files/aboriginal/schools/affirming-other-spiritual-paths.pdf (accessed 17 March 2015).
93. Canadian Conference of Catholic Bishops, "Let Justice Flow," 24–25, http://www.cccb.ca/site/images/stories/pdf/let_justice_flow_like_a_mighty_river.pdf (accessed 22 March 2015).
94. Canadian Catholic Aboriginal Council, Mandate, http://www.cccb.ca/site/eng/commissions-committees-and-aboriginal-council/aboriginal-council/canadian-catholic-aboriginal-council (accessed 22 March 2015).
95. TRC, AVS, Dr. Alan L. Hayes, Statement to the Truth and Reconciliation Commission of Canada, Toronto, Ontario, 2 June 2012, Statement Number: SE020.
96. MacKenzie, "For Everything There Is a Season," 89.
97. "Toronto Urban Native Ministry," cited in Bush, "How Have the Churches Lived out Their Apologies," 16.
98. Presbyterian Church in Canada, *Acts and Proceedings of the 137th General Assembly,* 368.
99. Healing Fund, Anglican Church, 2008, cited in Bush, "How Have the Churches Lived out Their Apologies," 24–25.
100. Healing Fund, Anglican Church, 2008, cited in Bush, "How Have the Churches Lived out Their Apologies," 24–25.
101. Healing Fund, Anglican Church, 2000, cited in Bush, "How Have the Churches Lived out Their Apologies," 19.
102. Bush, "How Have the Churches Lived out Their Apologies," 18.
103. The Aboriginal Healing Foundation (AHF) was mandated to provide funding and support for Aboriginal community-based healing projects. For more on the history of the AHF and the circum-

stances surrounding the closure, see: Spear, "Full Circle," http://www.ahf.ca/downloads/full-circle-2.pdf (accessed 28 April 2015).

104. TRC, AVS, Allan Sutherland, Statement to the Truth and Reconciliation Commission of Canada, Winnipeg, Manitoba, 16 June 2010, Statement Number: 02-MB-16JU10-067.

105. TRC, AVS, Esther Lachinette-Diabo, Statement to the Truth and Reconciliation Commission of Canada, Thunder Bay, Ontario, 24 November 2010, Statement Number: 01-ON-24Nov10-020.

106. TRC, AVS, Charlotte Marten, Statement to the Truth and Reconciliation Commission of Canada, Lethbridge, Alberta, 9 October 2013, Statement Number: SP127.

107. Education scholar Penney Clark's study identifies how Aboriginal peoples have been portrayed in Canadian history textbooks and how gaps in the history impact students. See: Clark, "Representations of Aboriginal People," 96–98, 103–111.

108. Council of Ministers of Education, "Developments on Indian Residential Schools by Jurisdiction," July 2014, email correspondence from Christy Bressette, Coordinator, Aboriginal Education, Council of Ministers of Education, Canada to Truth and Reconciliation Commission of Canada, 18 July 2014, TRC Document Number TRC3353.

109. Council of Ministers of Education, "Education Ministers Signal Transformation Key," http://cmec.ca/278/Press-Releases/Education-Ministers-Signal-Transformation-Key-to-the-Future.html?id_article=826.

110. Freedom of conscience and religion is protected under Section 2 of the Canadian Charter of Rights and Freedoms, and Section 3 of Québec's Charter of Human Rights and Freedoms.

111. *S.L. v. Commission scolaire des Chênes,* 2012 SCC 7 (CanLII), p. 237.

112. Educator and scholar Marie Battiste's work on decolonizing and transforming the education system has informed the Commission's thinking on this issue. See: Battiste, *Decolonizing Education,* 175–191.

113. Education scholars Megan Boler and Michalinas Zembylas describe this way of teaching as a "pedagogy of discomfort" that requires both educators and students to "move outside their comfort zones" in constructive ways that can "radically alter their worldviews." See: Boler and Zembylas, "Discomforting Truths," 111. See also: Sheppard, "Creating a Caring Classroom."

114. See, for example, studies by education scholars: Immordino-Yang and Domasio, "We Feel, Therefore We Learn"; Schonert-Reichl and Hymel, "Educating the Heart." See also: Mary Gordon's initiative, Roots of Empathy, "an evidence-based classroom program that has shown significant effect in reducing levels of aggression among school children while raising social/emotional competence and increasing empathy," http://www.rootsofempathy.org/ (accessed 15 April 2015). See also: Gordon, *Roots of Empathy.*

115. TRC, AVS, Samantha Crowe, Statement to the Truth and Reconciliation Commission of Canada, Edmonton, Alberta, 30 March 2014. Statement Number: ABNE401. For more information on the project, see: Ontario Provincial Advocate for Children and Youth, "Feathers of Hope: A First Nations Youth Action Plan, 2014," http://www.inspiritfoundation.org/files/6114/0656/0111/Feathers-of-Hope_report.pdf (accessed 15 April 2015).

116. Cultural theorist Roger Simon makes this point in an essay on the pedagogical practice of public history in the context of the Commission's public education mandate. See: Simon, "Towards a Hopeful Practice," 135–136.

117. The 2013 annual report of the Historical Thinking Project makes a similar point, arguing that the education system must produce historically literate citizens. See: Seixas and Colyer, "Report on the National Meeting," 3, http://historicalthinking.ca/sites/default/files/files/docs/HTP2013Report.pdf (accessed 15 April 2015). The purpose of the Historical Thinking Project was to provide history

education resources for teachers to train students how to think critically and effectively about history. See: Seixas and Colver, "Report on the National Meeting," 2, http://historicalthinking.ca/sites/default/files/files/docs/HTP2013Report.pdf (accessed 15 April 2015).

118. Centre for Youth & Society, "Residential Schools Resistance Narratives." Videos available online at: http://youth.society.uvic.ca/TRC (accessed 15 April 2015).
119. Prairie Women's Health Centre of Excellence, "Nitâpwewininân," 3–7.
120. Prairie Women's Health Centre of Excellence, "Nitâpwewininân," 14–16.
121. Brooklyn Rae, Saskatchewan National Event Education Day, Saskatoon, Saskatchewan, 23 June 2013, video, Statement Number: SNE502, https://vimeo.com/48143907.
122. Barney Williams, Saskatchewan National Event Education Day, Saskatoon, Saskatchewan, 23 June 2013, video, Statement Number: SNE502, https://vimeo.com/48143907.
123. ICTJ/Canada TRC Youth Retreat, http://vimeo.com/26397248.
124. ICTJ/Canada TRC Youth Retreat, http://vimeo.com/26128253.
125. International Center for Transitional Justice, "ICTJ Program Report," http://www.ictj.org/news/ictj-program-report-children-and-youth.
126. International Center for Transitional Justice, "Youth Reporters Tell the Story," http://ictj.org/news/youth-reporters-tell-story-residential-schools.
127. International Center for Transitional Justice, "Our Legacy, Our Hope," press release, 20 June 2012. Video, *Our Legacy, Our Hope,* at: http://www.youtube.com/watch?v=Xz2SUV0vFCI.
128. International Center for Transitional Justice, "ICTJ Program Report," http://www.ictj.org/news/ictj-program-report-children-and-youth.
129. TRC, AVS, Centre for Global Citizenship Education and Research, Statement to the Truth and Reconciliation Commission of Canada, Edmonton, Alberta, 27 March 2014, Statement Number: ABNE102.
130. Bolton, "Museums Taken to Task," 146–147.
131. Buchanan, "Decolonizing the Archives," 44.
132. Morse, "Indigenous Human Rights," 2, 10.
133. The decisions state that "the laws of evidence must be adapted in order that this type of evidence be accommodated and placed on an equal footing with the types of historic evidence that courts are familiar with, which largely consists of historical documents." See: Reasons for Decision, *Delgamuukw v. British Columbia,* 1997 CanLII 302 (SCC), para. 87. On the honour of the Crown, see, for example: *R. v. Sparrow,* 1990 CanLII 104 (SCC); *Haida Nation v. British Columbia Minister of Forests,* 2004 CanLII 73 (SCC); *Delgamuukw v. British Columbia,* 1997 CanLII 302 (SCC).
134. Legal scholar Bradford W. Morse makes this point. See: Morse, "Indigenous Human Rights," 12, 26.
135. Canada, Royal Commission on Aboriginal Peoples, *Report,* 5:232–233.
136. They have done so in accordance with their legislated mandate. Canada's *Museums Act (1990)* provides the legislative framework for museums. See: *Museums Act (1990),* chapter 3, section 3, http://laws-lois.justice.gc.ca/PDF/M-13.4.pdf. The Act was amended in 2008 to include the Canadian Museum for Human Rights.
137. Bolton, "Museums Taken to Task," 151.
138. On December 12, 2013, Bill C-7, *An Act to amend the Museums Act in order to establish the Canadian Museum of History,* received Royal Assent, thus officially establishing the legislative authority to "rebrand" the Canadian Museum of Civilization. Neither the original *Museums Act* nor the amendment made specific reference to Aboriginal peoples. See: http://www.parl.gc.ca/LegisInfo/BillDetails.aspx?Language=E&Mode=1&billId=6263562&View=3. See also: "Civilization Museum

Now the Canadian Museum of History," *CBC News,* December 12, 2013, http://www.cbc.ca/news/canada/ottawa/civilization-museum-now-the-canadian-museum-of-history-1.2461738.

139. House of Commons Standing Committee on Canadian Heritage, 41st Parliament, 1st session, June 5, 2013, http://www.parl.gc.ca/HousePublications/Publication.aspx?DocId=6209352&Language=E&Mode=1&Parl=41&Ses=1 (accessed 12 January 2014).
140. The Canadian Museum of Civilization and the Canadian War Museum, Research Strategy, July 15, 2013, 7, http://www.civilization.ca/research-and-collections/files/2013/07/research-strategy.pdf.
141. The Canadian Museum of Civilization and the Canadian War Museum, Research Strategy, July 15, 2013, 8–9, http://www.civilization.ca/research-and-collections/files/2013/07/research-strategy.pdf.
142. The Canadian Museum of Civilization and the Canadian War Museum, Research Strategy, July 15, 2013, 10, http://www.civilization.ca/research-and-collections/files/2013/07/research-strategy.pdf.
143. Canadian Museum for Human Rights, https://humanrights.ca/about (accessed 15 April 2015).
144. President and CEO, Stuart Murray, Canadian Museum for Human Rights, Speech to the Truth and Reconciliation Commission of Canada's National Research Centre Forum, March 3, 2011, Vancouver, BC, https://humanrights.ca/about-museum/news/speech-delivered-president-and-ceo-stuart-murray-truth-and-reconciliation (accessed 15 April 2015).
145. Jake Edmiston, "Indian Residential Schools or Settler Colonial Genocide? Native Group Slams Human Rights Museum over Exhibit Wording," *National Post,* June 8, 2013, http://news.nationalpost.com/news/canada/indian-residential-schools-or-settler-colonial-genocide.
146. Canadian Museum for Human Rights, Statement from the President and CEO: Use of "Genocide" in relation to treatment of Indigenous peoples in Canada, July 26, 2013, http://museumforhumanrights.ca/about-museum/news/statement-president-and-ceo-use-genocide-relation-treatment-indigenous-peoples.
147. Canadian Museum for Human Rights, President and CEO Stuart Murray, speech delivered at "2017 Starts Now" forum, May 3, 2013, https://humanrights.ca/about-museum/news/speech-delivered-cmhr-president-and-ceo-stuart-murray-2017-starts-nowdebute.
148. Library and Archives Canada, "Collection Development Framework," March 30, 2005, 7–8, http://www.collectionscanada.gc.ca/obj/003024/f2/003024-e.pdf.
149. Library and Archives Canada, "Aboriginal Heritage," http://www.bac-lac.gc.ca/eng/discover/aboriginal-heritage/Pages/introduction.aspx#d.
150. Library and Archives Canada, "Native Residential Schools in Canada," http://www.collectionscanada.gc.ca/native-residential/index-e.html (accessed 15 April 2015).
151. Wilson, "Peace, Order and Good Government," 239.
152. "New Exhibition Reflecting the Uniqueness of the Inuit Experience of Residential Schools Launched at Library and Archives Canada," media release, March 4, 2009, http://www.collectionscanada.gc.ca/013/013-380-e.html. See also: Legacy of Hope Foundation, http://wherearethechildren.ca/en; Legacy of Hope Foundation, http://weweresofaraway.ca/ (accessed 15 April 2015).
153. Library and Archives Canada, "Legacy of the Residential School System," http://www.bac-lac.gc.ca/eng/archives/archives-en/aboriginal-heritage/Pages/residential-schools-bibliography-2009.aspx (accessed 15 April 2015).
154. Library and Archives Canada, "Conducting Research on Residential Schools," http://www.collectionscanada.gc.ca/obj/020008/f2/020008-2000-e.pdf (accessed 15 April 2015).
155. Indian Residential Schools Settlement Agreement, Truth and Reconciliation Commission of Canada, Mandate, Schedule N, 11, http://www.trc.ca/websites/trcinstitution/File/pdfs/SCHEDULE_N_EN.pdf.

156. *Fontaine v. Canada (Attorney General),* 2013 ONSC 684 (CanLII).
157. Professor Terry Cook, University of Manitoba, long-time archivist at the National Archives, Fellow of the Association of Canadian Archivists, and a Fellow of the Royal Society of Canada, makes this point. See: Cook, "Evidence, Memory, Identity," 111.
158. United Nations Commission on Human Rights, Sub-Commission on the Prevention of Discrimination and Protection of Minorities, *The Administration of Justice and the Human Rights of Detainees: Question of the Impunity of Perpetrators of Human Rights Violations (Civil and Political)* (revised final report prepared by Mr. Joinet to the Sub-commission decision 1996/199) UN Doc. E/CN.4/Sub,2/1997/20/Rev.1, 1997-10-02; updated by UN DocE/CN.4/2005/102 (18 February 2005), and UN Doc E/CN.4/2005/102/Add.1 (8 February 2005), cited in *Fontaine v. Canada (Attorney General),* 2013 ONSC 684 (CanLII), University of Manitoba brief, Written Argument. December 13, 2012, note 35, 14, http://chrr.info/images/stories/Materials_filed_by_UM_2_.pdf.
159. de Greiff, "Report of the Special Rapporteur," 2013, 22, http://daccess-dds-ny.un.org/doc/UNDOC/GEN/G13/165/05/PDF/G1316505.pdf?OpenElement (accessed 28 April 2015).
160. de Greiff, "Report of the Special Rapporteur," 2013, 23, http://daccess-dds-ny.un.org/doc/UNDOC/GEN/G13/165/05/PDF/G1316505.pdf?OpenElement (accessed 28 April 2015).
161. de Greiff, "Report of the Special Rapporteur," 2013, 29, http://daccess-dds-ny.un.org/doc/UNDOC/GEN/G13/165/05/PDF/G1316505.pdf?OpenElement (accessed 28 April 2015).
162. Several prominent archivists have noted this trend. See, for example: Cook, "Evidence, Memory, Identity"; Wilson, "Peace, Order and Good Government"; Harris, "Archival Sliver"; Jimerson, "Archives for All."
163. TRC, AVS, Peter Cunningham, Statement to the Truth and Reconciliation Commission of Canada, Edmonton, Alberta, 28 March 2014, Statement Number: ABNE201.
164. Rev. Fausak is also General Council Liaison Minister, Indigenous Justice and Residential Schools, United Church of Canada.
165. TRC, AVS, Remembering the Children Society, Statement to the Truth and Reconciliation Commission of Canada, Edmonton, Alberta, 29 March 2014, Statement Number: ABNE302. Based on their experience, United Church of Canada staff, in collaboration with the Remembering the Children Society, developed an educational resource with guidelines for other communities wishing to develop their own commemoration projects for residential school cemeteries and unmarked burials. See: United Church of Canada, Residential Schools Update, January 2012, http://develop.united-church.ca/files/communications/newsletters/residential-schools-update_120101.pdf (accessed 16 April 2015).
166. The United Church of Canada's online resources are available at: http://thechildrenremembered.ca/. Anglican Church online resources and school histories are available at: http://www.anglican.ca/relationships/trc. Presbyterian Church of Canada's online resources are available at: http://www.presbyterianarchives.ca/RS%20-%20Home%20Page.html (accessed 15 April 2015).
167. United Church of Canada, Residential School Archive Project, "The Children Remembered," http://thechildrenremembered.ca/about/ (accessed 15 April 2015).
168. Ian Wilson makes this point. See: Wilson, "Peace, Order and Good Government," 238.
169. This is based on the concept and philosophy of "sites of conscience," as described by the International Coalition of Sites of Conscience, which is "a global network of historic sites, museums and memory initiatives connecting past struggles to today's movements for human rights and social justice," See: International Coalition of Sites of Conscience, http://www.sitesofconscience.org/ (accessed 15 April 2015).

170. Truth and Reconciliation Commission of Canada, "Sharing Truth: Creating a National Research Centre on Residential Schools," Forum, Vancouver, British Columbia, March 1–4, 2011. Videos of the forum can be viewed at: http://www.trc.ca/websites/trcinstitution/index.php?p=513.
171. Georges Erasmus, Truth and Reconciliation Commission of Canada, "Sharing Truth: Creating a National Research Centre on Residential Schools," Forum, Vancouver, British Columbia, 2 March 2011, https://vimeo.com/207788339.
172. Centre for Truth and Reconciliation Administrative Agreement, clauses 9 (c), (d), 11 (a), (e), http://chrr.info/images/stories/Centre_For_Truth_and_Reconciliation_Administrative_Agreement.pdf.
173. As of April 2015, existing partners included: The National Association of Friendship Centres, Legacy of Hope Foundation, Canadian Museum for Human Rights, University of British Columbia, Lakehead University, University College of the North, University of Winnipeg, Red River College, Archives of Manitoba, University College of the North, L'Université de Saint-Boniface, St. John's College, St. Paul's College, Manitoba Museum, Centre for Indigenous Environmental Resources, and the Sandy-Saulteaux Spiritual Centre. It is anticipated that more partners will be added as the centre develops. See: National Centre for Truth and Reconciliation, Our Partners, http://umanitoba.ca/centres/nctr/partners.html (accessed 15 April 2015).
174. *Fontaine v. Canada (Attorney General),* 2013 ONSC 684 (CanLII), University of Manitoba brief, Written Argument, December 13, 2012, 6–7, http://chrr.info/images/stories/Materials_filed_by_UM_2_.pdf.
175. Sue McKemmish, Shannon Faulkhead, and Lynette Russell, "Distrust in the Archive: Reconciling Records," *Archival Science* 11 (2011): 212, cited in *Fontaine v. Canada (Attorney General),* 2013 ONSC 684 (CanLII), University of Manitoba brief, Written Argument, December 13, 2011, 11, http://chrr.info/images/stories/Materials_filed_by_UM_2_.pdf.
176. *Fontaine v. Canada (Attorney General),* 2013 ONSC 684 (CanLII), University of Manitoba brief, Written Argument, December 13, 2012, 11–12, http://chrr.info/images/stories/Materials_filed_by_UM_2_.pdf.
177. *Fontaine v. Canada (Attorney General),* 2013 ONSC 684 (CanLII), University of Manitoba brief, Written Argument, December 13, 2012, 12–13, http://chrr.info/images/stories/Materials_filed_by_UM_2_.pdf.
178. University of Manitoba, "Historic Agreement Signed on National Aboriginal Day," 21 June 2013, http://umanitoba.ca/news/blogs/blog/2013/06/21/historic-agreement-signed-on-national-aboriginal-day/.
179. Such access will be "subject to privacy law and culturally appropriate protocols," Truth and Reconciliation Commission of Canada and the University of Manitoba, Centre for Truth and Reconciliation Trust Deed, 21 June 2013, 3–4, http://umanitoba.ca/admin/indigenous_connect/media/IND-00-013-NRCAS-TrustDeed.pdf.
180. Centre for Truth and Reconciliation, http://umanitoba.ca/centres/nctr/reconciliation.html (accessed 16 April 2015). See also: Centre for Truth and Reconciliation Administrative Agreement, http://chrr.info/images/stories/Centre_For_Truth_and_Reconciliation_Administrative_Agreement.pdf.
181. TRC, AVS, Jessica Bolduc, Statement to the Truth and Reconciliation Commission of Canada, Edmonton, Alberta, 30 March 2014, Statement Number: ABNE401.
182. The Commission's definition of "public memory" is based on the work of historians who study public memory. For example, James Opp and John C. Walsh define "public memory" as "memories that are made, experienced, and circulated in public spaces and that are intended to be com-

municated and shared," See: Opp and Walsh, *Placing Memory*, 9. John Bodnar says that "public memory" is "a body of beliefs and ideas about the past that help [sic] a public or society understand both [sic] its past, present, and by implication, its future," See: Bodnar, *Remaking America*, 15.

183. Historian W. James Booth makes this important point in his study of how communities of memory are established, maintained, or disrupted through everyday habits and practices. See: Booth, *Communities of Memory*, 45.
184. In its report "Strengthening Indigenous Rights through Truth Commissions: A Practitioner's Resource," the International Center for Transitional Justice identifies four thematic areas where commissions must rethink widely held assumptions in the field of transitional justice in order to become more responsive to Indigenous rights. These include: a) moving beyond a state-centric approach; b) moving beyond an individualistic form of analysis; c) moving beyond a focus only on recent violations; and d) moving beyond an overreliance on archival and written sources. See: International Center for Transitional Justice, "Strengthening Indigenous Rights," 3–5, https://www.ictj.org/sites/default/files/ICTJ-Truth-Seeking-Indigenous-Rights-2012-English.pdf.
185. Chamberlin, *If This Is Your Land*, 238–239.
186. Schirch, *Ritual and Symbol*, 1–2.
187. Truth and Reconciliation Commission of Canada, "Atlantic National Event Concept Paper," 4, http://www.myrobust.com/websites/atlantic/File/Concept%20Paper%20atlantic%20august%2010%20km_cp%20_3_.pdf.
188. In 2015, the Bentwood Box was on temporary loan to the Canadian Museum for Human Rights, where it was part of a public exhibit.
189. Campbell, "Remembering for the Future," 30. See also: Campbell, *Our Faithfulness to the Past.*
190. Qwul'sih'yah'maht (Thomas), "Honouring the Oral Traditions," 253.
191. TRC, AVS, Charles Cardinal, Statement to the Truth and Reconciliation Commission of Canada, St. Paul, Alberta, 7 January 2011, Statement Number: 01-AB-06JA11-005.
192. TRC, AVS, Laurie McDonald, Statement to the Truth and Reconciliation Commission of Canada, Beausejour, Manitoba, 4 September 2010, Statement Number: 01-MB-3-6SE10-005.
193. TRC, AVS, Victoria Grant-Boucher, Statement to the Truth and Reconciliation Commission of Canada, Ottawa, Ontario, 25 February 2011, Statement Number: 01-ON-05-FE11-004.
194. TRC, AVS, Desarae Eashappie, Statement to the Truth and Reconciliation Commission of Canada, Winnipeg, Manitoba, 19 June 2010, Statement Number: SC112.
195. Regan, *Unsettling the Settler Within*, 13.
196. TRC, AVS, Florence Kaefer, Statement to Truth and Reconciliation Commission of Canada, Winnipeg, Manitoba, 18 June 2010, Statement Number: SC111.
197. "Teacher Seeks Healing through Truth Commission," *CBC News, Manitoba,* June 18, 2010, http://www.cbc.ca/news/canada/manitoba/story/2010/06/18/mb-truth-reconciliation-healing-teachers-winnipeg.html.
198. TRC, AVS, Jack Lee, Statement to the Truth and Reconciliation Commission of Canada, Winnipeg, Manitoba, 18 June 2010, Statement Number: SC111.
199. TRC, AVS, Mark DeWolf, Statement to the Truth and Reconciliation Commission of Canada, Halifax, Nova Scotia, 28 October 2011, Statement Number: SC075.
200. TRC, AVS, Tina Keeper, Statement to the Truth and Reconciliation Commission of Canada, Saskatoon, Saskatchewan, 24 June 2013, Statement Number: SNE403.
201. TRC, AVS, the Right Honourable Paul Martin, Statement to the Truth and Reconciliation Commission of Canada, Montreal, Québec, 26 April 2013, Statement Number: QNE303.

202. TRC, AVS, the Right Honourable Joe Clark, Statement to Truth and Reconciliation Commission of Canada, Saskatoon, Saskatchewan, 23 June 2012, Statement Number: SNE301.
203. TRC, AVS, Andy Scott, Statement to the Truth and Reconciliation Commission of Canada, Saskatoon, Saskatchewan, 22 June 2012, Statement Number: SNE203.
204. TRC, AVS, Therese Boullard, Statement to the Truth and Reconciliation Commission of Canada, Inuvik, Northwest Territories, 28 June 2011, Statement Number: NNE103.
205. TRC, AVS, Ginelle Giacomin, Statement to the Truth and Reconciliation Commission of Canada, Winnipeg, Manitoba, 19 June 2010, Statement Number: SC112.
206. See, for example: Cohen, Varea, and Walker, *Acting Together*.
207. van Erven and Gardner, "Performing Cross-Cultural Conversations," 41. Quote from Francois Matarraso in correspondence with van Erven, March 19, 2008.
208. David Garneau, artist, writer, curator, and professor of visual arts, makes this critical point. See: Garneau, "Imaginary Spaces," 38.
209. Garneau, "Imaginary Spaces," 33–34.
210. Archibald et al., *Dancing, Singing, Painting*, 18.
211. Andrea Ratuski, "Residential School Art Series Awarded to U of M," *CBC News*, September 24, 2013, http://www.cbc.ca/news/canada/manitoba/scene/residential-school-art-series-awarded-to-u-of-m-1.1865994.
212. Morris and Helen Belkin Art Gallery, http://www.belkin.ubc.ca/past/witnesses (accessed 16 April 2015); University of British Columbia Museum of Anthropology, http://moa.ubc.ca/portfolio_page/speaking-to-memory/ (accessed 16 April 2015).
213. Robertson, "Threads of Hope," 87, 99–101.
214. University of Winnipeg, "UWinnipeg Healing Quilt Gifted to TRC Commissioners," 17 June 2010, http://www.uwinnipeg.ca/index/uw-news-action/story.364/title.uwinnipeg-healing-quilt-gifted-to-trc-commissioner.
215. Dewar et al., "Practicing Reconciliation," 5–6.
216. Full descriptions of the 2011–12 commemoration projects can be found online at: http://www.aadnc-aandc.gc.ca/eng/1370974213551/1370974338097 (accessed 15 April 2015). For 2012–13 commemoration projects, see: http://www.aadnc-aandc.gc.ca/eng/1370974253896/1370974471675 (accessed 15 April 2015).
217. Hague defines place as "a geographic space that is defined by meanings, sentiments and stories rather than by a set of co-ordinates." See: Cliff Hague, "Planning and Place Identity," in Cliff Hague and Paul Jenkins, eds., *Place Identity, Participation and Planning* (New York, 2005), 4, cited in Opp and Walsh, *Placing Memory*, 5.
218. Alan S. Hale, "Treaty 3 Holds Commemoration Ceremony for Survivors of District Residential School System," *Kenora Daily Miner and News*, March 25, 2014, http://www.kenoradailyminerandnews.com/2014/03/25/treaty-3-holds-commemoration-ceremony-for-survivors-of-district-residential-school-system.
219. Debora Steel, "Alberni Residential Students Reunited with Childhood Art," *Ha-Shilth-Sa*, 2 April 2013, http://www.hashilthsa.com/news/2013-04-03/alberni-indian-residential-students-reunited-childhood-art.
220. Judith Lavoie, "Paintings Bear Witness to B.C. Residential Schools' Harsh Life," *Victoria Times-Colonist*, March 31, 2013, http://www.timescolonist.com/news/local/paintings-bear-witness-to-b-c-residential-schools-harsh-life-1.101179.
221. Canada, Aboriginal Affairs and Northern Development Canada, "Remembering the Past," http://www.aadnc-aandc.gc.ca/eng/1332859355145/1332859433503.

222. Christi Belcourt, Speech at dedication ceremony for the stained-glass window on Parliament Hill, November 26, 2012, Ottawa, Ontario, Canada, Aboriginal Affairs and Northern Development Canada, https://www.aadnc-aandc.gc.ca/eng/1370613921985/1370613942308. A detailed description of the window is available at: Canada, Aboriginal Affairs and Northern Development Canada, https://www.aadnc-aandc.gc.ca/eng/1353338933878/1353338974873 (accessed 30 March 2015).
223. Commissioner Wilton Littlechild, Speech at dedication ceremony for the stained-glass window on Parliament Hill, November 26, 2012, Ottawa, Ontario, Canada, Aboriginal Affairs and Northern Development Canada, https://www.aadnc-aandc.gc.ca/eng/1370615213241/1370615618980.
224. Opp and Walsh, *Placing Memory*, 15–16.
225. *Historic Sites and Monuments Act,* Revised Statutes of Canada 1985, chapter H-4, http://laws-lois.justice.gc.ca/PDF/H-4.pdf (accessed 15 April 2015).
226. Parks Canada, Historic Sites and Monuments Board of Canada, http://www.pc.gc.ca/clmhc-hsmbc/comm-board/Transparence-Transparency.aspx (accessed 15 April 2015).
227. Parks Canada, Historic Sites and Monuments Board of Canada, National Program of Historical Commemoration, http://www.pc.gc.ca/clmhc-hsmbc/ncp-pcn.aspx (accessed 15 April 2015).
228. *Joinet-Orentlicher Principles,* cited in United Nations Human Rights Council, "Report of the Special Rapporteur," 8, http://www.ohchr.org/EN/HRBodies/HRC/RegularSessions/Session25/Pages/ListReports.aspx.
229. United Nations Human Rights Council, "Report of the Special Rapporteur," 14, http://www.ohchr.org/EN/HRBodies/HRC/RegularSessions/Session25/Pages/ListReports.aspx.
230. United Nations Human Rights Council, "Report of the Special Rapporteur," 19, http://www.ohchr.org/EN/HRBodies/HRC/RegularSessions/Session25/Pages/ListReports.aspx. The Special Rapporteur is referencing the commemoration projects undertaken as part of the Settlement Agreement.
231. United Nations Human Rights Council, "Report of the Special Rapporteur," 20–21, http://www.ohchr.org/EN/HRBodies/HRC/RegularSessions/Session25/Pages/ListReports.aspx.
232. United Nations Human Rights Council, "Report of the Special Rapporteur," 21–22, http://www.ohchr.org/EN/HRBodies/HRC/RegularSessions/Session25/Pages/ListReports.aspx.
233. United Nations Human Rights Council, "Report of the Special Rapporteur," 22, http://www.ohchr.org/EN/HRBodies/HRC/RegularSessions/Session25/Pages/ListReports.aspx.
234. The study was based on research conducted by Trina Cooper-Bolam and based in part on her experiences as the Legacy of Hope's former executive director, her work with the Aboriginal Healing Foundation, and her role as a project leader for the Assembly of First Nations and the Aboriginal Healing Foundation's national commemoration project. See: Cooper-Bolam, "Healing Heritage," 8–9, 106–107.
235. Cooper-Bolam, "Healing Heritage," 108–109.
236. Cooper-Bolam, "Healing Heritage," 109.
237. Cooper-Bolam, "Healing Heritage," 61–63.
238. Jeff Corntassel et al., "Indigenous Story-telling, Truth-telling and Community Approaches to Reconciliation," *English Studies in Canada* 35, 1 (2009): 143, cited in Cooper-Bolam, "Healing Heritage," 98.
239. Cooper-Bolam, "Healing Heritage," 97–99.
240. Cooper-Bolam, "Healing Heritage," ii.
241. *Broadcasting Act* (1991), last revised 2014, http://laws-lois.justice.gc.ca/PDF/B-9.01.pdf.
242. David, "Aboriginal Languages Broadcasting in Canada," 14, http://aptn.ca/corporate/PDFs/Aboriginal_Language_and_Broadcasting_2004.pdf.

243. CBC/Radio-Canada, "Going the Distance," 48. The annual report also provides information on CBC's Aboriginal-languages programming and news coverage. See: http://www.cbc.radio-canada.ca/_files/cbcrc/documents/annual-report/2013-2014/cbc-radio-canada-annual-report-2013-2014.pdf. In 2013, Statistics Canada published this data as part of the National Household Survey conducted in 2011. See: Statistics Canada, *Aboriginal Peoples in Canada, 2011*, 4, http://www12.statcan.gc.ca/nhs-enm/2011/as-sa/99-011-x/99-011-x2011001-eng.pdf.
244. Aboriginal Peoples Television Network, Annual Report, 2013, http://aptn.ca/corporate/PDFs/APTN_2013_AnnualReport_ENG.pdf.
245. Aboriginal Peoples Television Network, Corporate Factsheet, http://aptn.ca/corporate/facts.php (accessed 18 March 2015).
246. Canada, Royal Commission on Aboriginal Peoples, *Report*, 5:103–104.
247. Canada, Royal Commission on Aboriginal Peoples, *Report*, 2:614.
248. See, for example: Anderson and Robertson, *Seeing Red*.
249. Journalists for Human Rights is a media development organization that provides education and resources to "help journalists build their capacity to report ethically and effectively on human rights and governance issues in their communities." See: http://www.jhr.ca/en/aboutjhr_learn-about.php (accessed 15 April 2015).
250. Journalists for Human Rights, "Buried Voices," August 2013, 18–19, http://www.documentcloud.org/documents/784473-media-coverage-of-aboriginal-issues.html#document/p1 (accessed 15 April 2015).
251. Journalists for Human Rights, "Buried Voices," 5–6, http://www.documentcloud.org/documents/784473-media-coverage-of-aboriginal-issues.html#document/p1 (accessed 15 April 2015).
252. Journalists for Human Rights, "Buried Voices," 16, http://www.documentcloud.org/documents/784473-media-coverage-of-aboriginal-issues.html#document/p1 (accessed 15 April 2015).
253. Journalists for Human Rights, "Buried Voices," 19, http://www.documentcloud.org/documents/784473-media-coverage-of-aboriginal-issues.html#document/p1.
254. Miller, *Lethal Legacy*, vi.
255. Miller, "Ipperwash and the Media," 11, 14.
256. Miller, "Ipperwash and the Media," 19–20, 22–23.
257. TRC, AVS, Theodore Fontaine, Statement to the Truth and Reconciliation Commission of Canada, Edmonton, Alberta, 28 March 2014, Statement Number: AB202.
258. TRC, AVS, Laura Robinson, Statement to the Truth and Reconciliation Commission of Canada, Edmonton, Alberta, 28 March 2014, Statement Number: ABNE202.
259. "Law Society Throws Support behind Reconciliation Initiatives," *Gazette: Law Society of Upper Canada*, 11 December 2014, http://www.lawsocietygazette.ca/news/law-society-throws-support-behind-reconciliation-initiatives/.
260. Mason and Koehli, "Barriers to Physical Activity," 103–105.
261. *Physical Activity and Sport Act*, http://laws-lois.justice.gc.ca/eng/acts/P-13.4/page-1.html?texthighlight=under-represented#s-5.
262. IndigenACTION, "Roundtable Report," appendix 2, 18–19, http://www.afn.ca/uploads/files/indigenaction/indigenactionroundtablereport.pdf.
263. Te Hiwi, "What Is the Spirit," 3.
264. Sport Canada, Policy Renewal, "Summary Report," July 15, 2011, 4, https://sirc.ca/sites/default/files/content/docs/pdf/aboriginal.pdf.
265. *Canadian Sport Policy*, http://canadiansporttourism.com/sites/default/files/docs/csp2012_en_lr.pdf (acessed 15 April 2015).

266. TRC, AVS, David Courchene Jr., Statement to the Truth and Reconciliation Commission of Canada, Winnipeg, Manitoba, 25 June 2014, Statement Number: SE048.
267. TRC, AVS, Ian Campbell, Statement to the Truth and Reconciliation Commission of Canada, Winnipeg, Manitoba, 25 June 2014, Statement Number: SE048.
268. Jeff Lee, "Tsilhqot'in Nation Strikes Conciliatory Note with Municipalities," *Vancouver Sun,* September 24, 2014, A6.
269. Canada, *Northern Frontier, Northern Homeland,* 1:1, 82–83. Beginning in the 1980s, several land-claims agreements were signed across the North, including the Inuvialuit Final Agreement (1984), the Gwich'in Comprehensive Land Claim Agreement (1992), the Sahtu Dene and Métis Comprehensive Land Claim Agreement (1994), and the Tlicho Agreement (2005) in the Northwest Territories.
Although there have been attempts to revitalize the Mackenzie Valley pipeline project, with the participation of a coalition of Aboriginal partners, as of 2014, it remained unclear as to whether the project would proceed. See: Brent Jang, "Gas Exports from B.C. Seen as Key to Reviving Pipeline," *Globe and Mail,* February 2, 2014, http://www.theglobeandmail.com/report-on-business/industry-news/energy-and-resources/gas-exports-from-bc-said-key-to-reviving-pipeline/article16657138/; Jeff Lewis, "Northwest Territories Eyes Revival of Mackenzie Valley Pipeline Project," *Financial Post,* June 11, 2013, http://business.financialpost.com/2013/06/11/northwest-territories-eyes-revival-of-mackenzie-valley-pipeline-project/?__lsa=c5d4-608a.
270. Canada, Royal Commission on Aboriginal Peoples, *Report,* 1:466–504.
271. See, for example: *Delgamuukw v. British Columbia,* 1997 CanLII 302 (SCC); *Haida Nation v. British Columbia (Minister of Forests),* 2004 SCC 73 (CanLII); *Mikisew Cree First Nation v. Canada (Minister of Canadian Heritage),* 2005 SCC 69 (CanLII); *Rio Tinto Alcan Inc. v. Carrier Sekani Tribal Council,* 2010 SCC 43; *Tsilhqot'in Nation v. British Columbia,* 2014 SCC 44; *Grassy Narrows First Nation v. Ontario (Natural Resources),* 2014 SCC 48.
272. *Delgamuukw v. British Columbia,* 1997 CanLII 302 SCC, para. 165.
273. *Haida Nation v. British Columbia (Minister of Forests),* 2004 SCC 73 (CanLII), para. 53, cited in Newman, *Rule and Role of Law,* 10, http://www.macdonaldlaurier.ca/files/pdf/DutyToConsult-Final.pdf.
274. Newman, *Rule and Role of Law,* 13, http://www.macdonaldlaurier.ca/files/pdf/DutyToConsult-Final.pdf.
275. Public Policy Forum, "Building Authentic Partnerships," 7.
276. Public Policy Forum, "Building Authentic Partnerships," 6.
277. Eyford, "Forging Partnerships," 3, 7, https://www.nrcan.gc.ca/sites/www.nrcan.gc.ca/files/www/pdf/publications/ForgPart-Online-e.pdf.
278. Letter of transmission from Douglas R. Eyford to Prime Minister, 29 November 2013, in Eyford, "Forging Partnerships," np, https://www.nrcan.gc.ca/sites/www.nrcan.gc.ca/files/www/pdf/publications/ForgPart-Online-e.pdf.
279. The Charrette on Energy, Environment and Aboriginal Issues, "Responsible Energy Resource Development," 2.
280. The Charrette on Energy, Environment and Aboriginal Issues, "Responsible Energy Resource Development."
281. The Charrette on Energy, Environment and Aboriginal Issues, "Responsible Energy Resource Development," 8–14.
282. Coates and Newman, *End Is Not Nigh,* 21.
283. United Nations Global Compact, *Business Reference Guide.*

284. TRC, AVS, Wab Kinew, Statement to the Truth and Reconciliation Commission of Canada, Edmonton, Alberta, 28 March 2014, Statement Number: ABNE202.
285. TRC, AVS, Victoria Wells, Statement to the Truth and Reconciliation Commission of Canada, Victoria, British Columbia, 13 April 2012, Statement Number: SP016.
286. TRC, AVS, Lynne Phillips, Statement to the Truth and Reconciliation Commission of Canada, Victoria, British Columbia, 5 December 2010, Statement Number: 01-BC-03DE10-007.
287. TRC, AVS, Roger Epp, Statement to the Truth and Reconciliation Commission of Canada, Hobbema, Alberta, 25 July 2013, Statement Number: SP125.
288. TRC, AVS, Bill Elliot, Statement to the Truth and Reconciliation Commission of Canada, Hobbema, Alberta, 25 July 2013, Statement Number: SP125.
289. TRC, AVS, Bill Elliot, Statement to the Truth and Reconciliation Commission of Canada, Edmonton, Alberta, 29 March 2014, Statement Number: ABNE301.
290. Reconciliation Canada, "City of Vancouver Council Unanimously Support," http://reconciliationcanada.ca/city-of-vancouver-council-unanimously-support-city-of-reconciliation-framework/. See also: Report from City Manager to Vancouver City Council, "Framework for City of Reconciliation," http://former.vancouver.ca/ctyclerk/cclerk/20141028/documents/rr1.pdf.
291. TRC, AVS, Gregor Robertson, Statement to the Truth and Reconciliation Commission of Canada, Vancouver, British Columbia, 18 September 2013, Statement Number: BCNE102.
292. Kim Harvey, *Be the Change: Young People Healing the Past and Building the Future*, Vancouver, British Columbia, 18 September 2013, Statement Number: BCNE105, https://vimeo.com/78638476.
293. Kevin Takahide Lee, *Be the Change: Young People Healing the Past and Building the Future*, Vancouver, British Columbia, 18 September 2013, Statement Number: BCNE105, https://vimeo.com/78638476.
294. Caroline Wong, *Be the Change: Young People Healing the Past and Building the Future*, Vancouver, British Columbia, 18 September 2013, Statement Number: BCNE105, https://vimeo.com/78638476.
295. Danny Richmond, *Be the Change: Young People Healing the Past and Building the Future*, Vancouver, British Columbia, 18 September 2013, Statement Number: BCNE105, https://vimeo.com/78638476.
296. TRC, AVS, Akua Benjamin, Statement to the Truth and Reconciliation Commission of Canada, Toronto, Ontario, 12 November 2013, Statement Number: SE036B.
297. TRC, AVS, Ali Kazimi, Statement to the Truth and Reconciliation Commission of Canada, Toronto, Ontario, 12 November 2013, Statement Number: SE036B.
298. TRC, AVS, Winnie Ng, Statement to the Truth and Reconciliation Commission of Canada, Toronto, Ontario, 12 November 2013, Statement Number: SE036B.
299. Canada, Minister of Citizenship and Immigration Canada, *Discover Canada*, http://www.cic.gc.ca/english/resources/publications/discover/index.asp (accessed 15 April 2015).
300. Canada, Minister of Citizenship and Immigration Canada, *Discover Canada*, http://www.cic.gc.ca/english/resources/publications/discover/index.asp (accessed 15 April 2015).
301. Video recordings of the Walk for Reconciliation are available at: Reconciliation Canada, http://reconciliationcanada.ca/2013/09/ (accessed 15 April 2015).
302. Elders Statement, "A Shared Tomorrow." The statement and video recording of the Elders Circle are available at: Reconciliation Canada, http://reconciliationcanada.ca/explore/elders-statement/ (accessed 15 April 2015).

Appendix 1: The mandate of the Truth and Reconciliation Commission

1. This refers to the Aboriginal principle of "witnessing."
2. The Government of Canada undertakes to provide for wider dissemination of the report pursuant to the recommendations of the Commissioners.
3. The Commission may make recommendations for such further measures as it considers necessary for the fulfillment of the Truth and Reconciliation Mandate and goals.

Appendix 2: Canada's Residential Schools

1. Aboriginal and Northern Affairs Canada, List of Recognized Institutions, https://www.aadnc-aandc.gc.ca/eng/1100100015606/1100100015611 (accessed 3 March 2015).
2. TRC, NRA, Deschatelets Archives, Oblates of Mary Immaculate, Ottawa, HR 6796.C73R 2, Oblates of Mary Immaculate to Indian Affairs, 15 November 1923. [SPR-000436]
3. TRC, NRA, Headquarters, 775/25-1-006, 01/39–08/72, volume 2, HQ., Calgary, L. Beuglet to G. H. Gooderham, 1 February 1951. [AMP-006646]
4. TRC, NRA, INAC - Resolution Sector - IRS Historical Files Collection - Ottawa, 775/6-1-GHC, volume 1, 05/1973–06/1975, RCAP, E. W. Robinson to Don McBride, 27 April 1973. [AMP-010378]
5. TRC, NRA, Library and Archives Canada - Ottawa, RG10, volume 3834, file 65138, part 4, E. M. Legal to Indian Commissioner, Regina, 30 March 1887. [SAC-000211-0001]
6. TRC, NRA, Deschatelets Archives Ottawa, HR 6103.C73R 4, *Report of the Indian Affairs Branch for the Year ended 31 March 1962*, 31. [OMI-030380]
7. Canada, *Annual Report of the Department of Indian Affairs, 1891*, 62.
8. TRC, NRA, Deschatelets Archives Ottawa, HR 6103.C73R 4, *Report of the Indian Affairs Branch for the Year ended 31 March 1962*, 31. [OMI-030380]
9. Canada, *Annual Report of the Department of Indian Affairs, 1908*, xxxiv.
10. TRC, NRA, Deschatelets Archives Ottawa, HR 6103.C73R 4, *Report of the Indian Affairs Branch for the Year ended 31 March 1962*, 31. [OMI-030380]
11. Canada, *Annual Report of the Department of Indian Affairs, 1898*, 444.
12. TRC, NRA, Library and Archives Canada - Edmonton, 4700-10-435, volume 1, 9/87–12/88, NAC, Edmonton, Sheila Carr-Stewart to Jim Twigg, 14 January 1988. [MRY-008208]
13. Canada, *Annual Report of the Department of Indian Affairs, 1890*, 82; Canada, *Annual Report of the Department of Indian Affairs, 1891*, 180.
14. TRC, NRA, INAC - Resolution Sector - IRS Historical Files Collection - Ottawa, 773/6-1-, 04/66–07/75, volume 3, RCAP, E. J. Dosdall to Regional Advisor, Engineering and Architecture, 3 July 1975. [PUL-002529]
15. Canada, *Annual Report of the Department of Indian Affairs, 1900*, 343–344.
16. TRC, NRA, Library and Archives Canada, NAC, file 772/6-1-001, 01/67–10/69, "Cluny Indian School Closing," by Don Peacock [Calgary *Albertan*] , 20 December 1969. [CFT-002237]
17. Indian Residential Schools of the Indian Residential Schools Settlement Agreement 2011, IRS School Chart - INAC 2011, document provided to the TRC by Aboriginal and Northern Affairs Canada, 29 September 2011. Indian Affairs began funding the school in 1902. Canada, *Annual Report of the Department of Indian Affairs, 1903*, 241, 387–388.
18. TRC, NRA, INAC - Resolution Sector - IRS Historical Files Collection - Ottawa, 775/6-1, 03/72–08/76, volume 3, RCAP, E. J. Dosdall to G. K. Gooderham, 26 June 1973. [MAR-001983]

19. Canada, *Annual Report of the Department of Indian Affairs, 1924*, 13.
20. TRC, NRA, INAC – AB Regional Records Office – Edmonton, 774/1-13, volume 2, 07/1968–07/1975, CR – ALB, [Illegible] for W. Evan Armstrong to Churchman, 21 May 1968. [EDM-009699]
21. McCarthy, *From the Great River*, 160; Carney, "Grey Nuns and Children," 291; Duchaussois, *Grey Nuns*, 148.
22. TRC, NRA, INAC – Main Records Office – Ottawa, 701/25-20-1, 1965–1975, volume 1, CR HQ, E. J. Dosdall to Chief, Student Residence Services, Ottawa, 6 March 1974. [RCA-001185]
23. TRC, NRA, Library and Archives Canada – Ottawa, RG10, volume 3952, file 134858, Indian Affairs, Public Archives – Archives Publiques Canada, Indian Affairs, "Minutes," 5 August 1900. [AGL-000570]
24. TRC, NRA, INAC – Main Records Office – Ottawa, 775/6-1-005, Jan/64–Feb/73, volume 5, DIAND, Central Records – HQ, R. F. Davey to Henri Routhier, 23 August 1968. [FTV-006722-0000]
25. Canada, *Annual Report of the Department of Indian Affairs, 1887*, 178.
26. TRC, NRA, INAC – Main Records Office – Ottawa, 772/16-2-002, 1966–1971, volume 2, CR-HQ, H. W. Allen to Mr. D. P. Nigra, 20 April 1971. [OLD-000209]
27. Brandak, "A Study of Missionary Activity," 108.
28. Indian Residential Schools of the Indian Residential Schools Settlement Agreement 2011, IRS School Chart – INAC 2011, document provided to the TRC by Aboriginal and Northern Affairs Canada, 29 September 2011.
29. Canada, *Annual Report of the Department of Indian Affairs, 1884*, 76.
30. TRC, NRA, Provincial Archives of Alberta, PAA 71.220 B92 3866, W. M. Graham to Principal, Ermineskin Roman Catholic Boarding School, 28 October 1922. [OGP-030045]
31. Canada, *Annual Report of the Department of Indian Affairs, 1895*, 131.
32. TRC, NRA, INAC – Resolution Sector – IRS Historical Files Collection – Ottawa, E4974-2021, 1975–1980, volume 2, RCAP, K. W. Johnson to D. W. Simpson, 4 September 1975. [ERM-002507-0000]
33. TRC, NRA, Headquarters, 777/25-1-007, 02/13–03/65, volume 1, HQ., D. C. Scott to Frank Pedley, 9 April 1913. [GRU-002710]
34. Canada, *Annual Report of the Department of Indian Affairs, 1969–1970*, 128.
35. Persson, "Blue Quills," 50.
36. Persson, "Blue Quills," 51.
37. Brandak, "A Study of Missionary Activity," 37.
38. TRC, NRA, Library and Archives Canada, RG10, volume 6380, file 769-1, part 1, A. F. MacKenzie to Dr. T. B. R. Westgate, 8 August 1932. [WFL-000246]
39. TRC, NRA, Library and Archives Canada – Ottawa, 757-1, part 1, volume 6355, 1886–1927, NAC, J. D. McLean to E. H. Yeomans, 28 December 1922. [MOR-004751-0001]
40. Canada, *Annual Report of the Department of Indian Affairs, 1969–1970*, 128.
41. Canada, *Annual Report of the Department of Indian Affairs, 1894*, 91.
42. TRC, NRA, Library and Archives Canada, RG10, volume 6350, file 753-1, part 1, J. F. Woodsworth to James Endicott, 5 June 1919. [EDM-000242]
43. TRC, NRA, Library and Archives Canada, RG10, volume 6345, file 751-5, part 1, 1896–1902, Microfilm reel C-8701, Lumber list for erecting Indian Boarding School Building, 1 August 1898; [BQL-007304] TRC, NRA, Library and Archives Canada, RG10, volume 6345, file 751-5, part 1, 1896–1902, Microfilm reel C-8701, H. Leduc to A. E. Forget, 4 September 1898. [BQL-007314]
44. Indian Residential Schools of the Indian Residential Schools Settlement Agreement 2011, IRS School Chart – INAC 2011, document provided to the TRC by Aboriginal and Northern Affairs Canada, 29 September 2011. In 1987, Indian Affairs informed the Blue Quills administration that it

would not provide funding for the high school program after June 1988. The decision was driven, at least in part, by the desire of other local First Nations to develop their own high school programs. Indian Affairs continued to fund post-secondary programs at Blue Quills. The high school program and associated residence closed in June 1988. That year, seventy-six Grade Twelve students graduated from the school: the largest graduating class in the high school's twelve-year history. TRC, NRA, INAC – Resolution Sector – IRS Historical Files Collection – Ottawa, file E4974-2020, volume 3 (Ctrl #7-7), D. Wattie to G. P. Kerr, 17 March 1988; [NCA-007261-0000] Blue Quills First Nations College, *Pimohteskanaw,* 14.

45. The St. Albert Mission was founded in 1861. Choquette, *The Oblate Assault,* 86. The Grey Nuns arrived in 1853 and established a school in that year. Côté, "St. Albert," 33.
46. TRC, NRA, Library and Archives Canada – Ottawa, RG10, volume 6364, file 760-1, part 2, 1936–1948, Microfilm reel C-8717 PAC, R. A. Hoey to Deputy Minister, 3 September 1948. [SAL-000283]
47. Canada's Historic Places, St. Augustine's Roman Catholic Mission, http://www.historicplaces.ca/en/rep-reg/place-lieu.aspx?id=11611 (accessed 23 February 2015).
48. The Smoky River school is included in the 1908 Indian Affairs annual report list of Alberta boarding schools (Canada, *Annual Report of the Department of Indian Affairs, 1908,* 2:56), but not in the 1909 report (Canada, *Annual Report of the Department of Indian Affairs, 1909,* 2:20).
49. Canada, *Annual Report of the Department of Indian Affairs, 1893*, 292–293.
50. Canada, *Annual Report of the Department of Indian Affairs, 1922,* 18.
51. Brandak, "A Study of Missionary Activity," 37.
52. TRC, NRA, INAC – Main Records Office – Ottawa, 777/16-2-009, 1966–1967, volume 2, CR-HQ, L. E. Wrag for R. F. Davey to Chief Treasury Officer, 15 March 1966. [JON-001035]
53. Brandak, "A Study of Missionary Activity," 83.
54. TRC, NRA, INAC – AB Regional Records Office – Edmonton, 777/6-1-769, 01/05–09/50, CR-AB, [Illegible], Director to L. A. Dixon, 10 June 1950. [WFL-000753]
55. Canada, *Annual Report of the Department of Indian Affairs, 1905*, 249–250.
56. Canada, *Annual Report of the Department of Indian Affairs, 1940*, 186.
57. Canada, *Annual Report of the Department of Indian Affairs, 1894*, 158.
58. TRC, NRA, INAC – Resolution Sector – IRS Historical Files Collection – Ottawa, 978/25-13, volume 1, Student Residence – Gen. 10/05/1973–11/15/1979, Control No. 449-80, IRSRC – Historical Files, Larry Wight to District Supervisor, 2 October 1974. [MIK-008346-0005]
59. Indian Residential Schools of the Indian Residential Schools Settlement Agreement 2011, IRS School Chart – INAC 2011, document provided to the TRC by Aboriginal and Northern Affairs Canada, 29 September 2011.
60. TRC, NRA, Library and Archives Canada – Burnaby, RG10, FA 10-147, V1985-86/476, box 16 [18], file 989/25-8, volume 6, Indian Education – Educational Assist. – Gen., [dates illegible] 1976–77, NAC Burnaby, Smith to Cahoose, 19 July 1977. [JOE-014593]
61. Canada, *Annual Report of the Department of Indian Affairs, 1894*, 203.
62. Canada, *Annual Report of the Department of Indian Affairs, 1941*, 165.
63. Canada, *Annual Report of the Department of Indian Affairs, 1890*, xi.
64. TRC, NRA, Library and Archives Canada – Burnaby, RG10, FA 10-138, volume 13464, file 964/25-1, part 1, Education – General, 05/1969–12/1970, NAC Burnaby, R. M. Hall to G. D. Cromb, 21 May 1970; [EGN-002451] TRC, NRA, Library and Archives Canada – Burnaby, RG10, FA 10-189, Acc. v96-97/816, file 6-1, box 4, 1972 Contract Documents [Kamloops Indian Residential School], NAC – Burnaby, G. D. Cromb to W. L. Fraser, 26 May 1970. [EGN-011708]
65. Canada, *Annual Report of the Department of Indian Affairs, 1922*, 18.

66. TRC, NRA, Library and Archives Canada – Burnaby, file 965/6-1-012, part 22, Lejac Residential School, 1973–1976, FA 10-138, Acc. V1985-86/397, box 2 [502381], National Archives of Canada – Burnaby, Friesen to E. Korchinski, 9 July 1976. [LEJ-009413]
67. Canada, *Annual Report of the Department of Indian Affairs, 1890*, xi.
68. TRC, NRA, Library and Archives Canada – Burnaby, RG10, FA 10-145, Acc. v85-86/496, file 963/25-1, Perm. volume 1, Education 1974–78, NAC – Burnaby, R. G. Lyon to K. W. Manuel, 4 July 1978. [KAM-009590]
69. Canada, *Annual Report of the Department of Indian Affairs, 1906*, 482.
70. TRC, NRA, Library and Archives Canada – Ottawa, file 883-1, part 2, Bella Coola Agency – Kitamaat, Residential School – General Administration, 1933–1950, FA 10-17, Perm. volume 6451, Microfilm reel C-8773, Library and Archives Canada – Ottawa, George Dorey to Harold W. McGill, 21 April 1941. [KMT-095750]
71. Canada, *Annual Report of the Department of Indian Affairs, 1890*, xi.
72. TRC, NRA, Library and Archives Canada, GARDD, V1985-86/397, 901/25-13-1, box 502381, volume 1, 1973–1975, R. Evans to Regional Supervisor, 7 July 1975. [SLT-002387]
73. TRC, NRA, Library and Archives Canada, file 942-5, part 4, 1950–51, volume 6482, Microfilm reel C-8796, A. H. Fleury to B. H. Neary, 22 January 1951. [LOW-000506]
74. TRC, NRA, Library and Archives Canada, RG10, box 66, Acc. 1988-1989/057, General Correspondence Lower Post Students Residence, 1965–1978, G. K. Gooderham to Department Secretariat, 2 May 1975. [LOW-041388]
75. Canada, *Annual Report of the Department of Indian Affairs, 1903*, 437.
76. TRC, NRA, No document location, no document file source, E-4974-2030 V.1, I. R. Shand to J. Epp, 23 August 1979. [GRG-022833]
77. Canada, *Annual Report of the Department of Indian Affairs, 1900*, 281.
78. TRC, NRA, British Columbia Archives – Victoria, Vertical Files – Christie IRS, Microfilm reel 28, frame 1988, B.C. Archives, George Nicholson, "Indian Children Give up Their School in the Forest," *Vancouver Sun*, 15 June 1971. [CST-800006]
79. Gresko, "Paul Durieu," http://www.biographi.ca/en/bio/durieu_paul_12E.html (accessed 31 August 2014). McNally gives the opening as 1862: McNally, *Lord's Distant Vineyard*, 67; TRC, NRA, The British Columbian, 11 May 1865, page 3; [OMS-000291] TRC, NRA, Mission Community Archives, file 660.6, L. Fouquet to J. Douglas, 23 May 1867. [MIS-005038]
80. TRC, NRA, INAC – BC Regional Records Office – Vancouver BC-CR, V87-395, box: 87-09-D40/42-009, E4974-2031, volume 3, 04/83–07/84, C. E. Van Alstyne to Joe Aleck, 25 June 1984. [MIS-000494]
81. Canada, *Annual Report of the Department of Indian Affairs, 1900*, 420.
82. TRC, NRA, Library and Archives Canada – Ottawa, RG10, FA 10-379, 1999-01431-6, box 405, 987/25-1-013, part 1, Indian Education – Fraser District – St. Paul's School, 1959–1968, NAC – Ottawa, W. S. Arneil to R. F. Davey, 16 February 1959. [SQU-000672]
83. Canada, *Annual Report of the Department of Indian Affairs, 1894*, 165.
84. TRC, NRA, INAC – Resolution Sector – IRS Historical Files Collection – Ottawa, 6-1-2032, Alberni Indian Residential School, Control No. 303-13, 11/1970–12/1978, IRSRHF, W. R. Cooke to Regional Director, 9 August 1973. [ABR-021977-0000]
85. Bolt, *Thomas Crosby and the Tsimshian*, 63.
86. TRC, NRA, Library and Archives Canada, file 886-1, part 3, Skeena River Agency – Port Simpson Girls Residential School, 1894–1950, FA 10-17, Perm. volume 6458, Eva Middleton to Superintendent Indian Education, 27 September 1948. [PSM-200706]
87. Canada, *Annual Report of the Department of Indian Affairs, 1905*, 217.

88. TRC, NRA, Library and Archives Canada – Burnaby, RG10, FA 10-137 v86-87/243, volume 4 [501374], 987/25-13-1 School Closures – Sechelt, part 1, 1975–1977, NAC – Burnaby, J. M. Neely to B. Banner, 7 July 1975. [MIS-007429]
89. Canada, *Annual Report of the Department of Indian Affairs, 1890*, 248.
90. TRC, NRA, Agness Jack, "New Use for St. Joseph's Mission: Now Adult Education Centre," *Williams Lake Tribune*, 10 September 1981. [WLM-000627]
91. Canada, *Annual Report of the Department of Indian Affairs, 1888*, xii.
92. TRC, NRA, INAC – Resolution Sector – IRS Historical Files Collection – Ottawa, file 1/25-1-7-3, volume 2 (Ctrl #14-21), J. B. Bergevin to Mrs. Gordon Long, 2 July 1970. [NCA-001847]
93. Canada, *Annual Report of the Department of Indian Affairs, 1895*, 203.
94. TRC, NRA, Library and Archives Canada – Winnipeg, RG10, Acc. 2001-01035-4, box 015, file 501/25-13-082G, volume 1, Soulodre, J. P. to Manitoba Telephone System, 7 June 1972. [BRS-006834]
95. TRC, NRA, Library and Archives Canada, R776-0-5 (RG55), volume 290, T.B. #626127, May 14, 1964, Department of Northern Affairs and National Resources to Treasury Board, "Details of request to the Honourable the Treasury Board," 20 April 1964. [120.10656A]
96. TRC, NRA, Library and Archives Canada, file 380/6-2-007, volume 1, C. L'Heureux to W. J. McGuire, 22 March 1972; [PHQ-005693] INAC – Archival Unit – Ottawa, file 5150/C6-1, volume 1, D. Davidson to the Secretary-Treasurer, "Junior HIgh School – Hearne Hall," 27 March 1973. [CVC-000615-0000]
97. Canada, *Annual Report of the Department of Indian Affairs, 1912*, 351.
98. Canada, *Annual Report of the Department of Indian Affairs, 1969–1970*, 128.
99. TRC, NRA, Library and Archives Canada, RG10, Acc. 88-89/57, file 501/25-2, volume 1, R. D. Ragan to DIAND, 20 June 1957. [DRS-122339-0003]
100. TRC, NRA, INAC – Resolution Sector – IRS Historical Files Collection – Ottawa, file E4974-2012, volume 3, G. R. Maxwell to W. Wright, 25 September 1987. [DRS-000170]
101. Canada, *Annual Report of the Department of Indian Affairs, 1889*, 58.
102. TRC, NRA, Library and Archives Canada, RG10, volume 3925, file 116, 823-1A, Martin Benson to D. C. Scott, 4 March 1918. [ELK-000250]
103. Canada, *Annual Report of the Department of Indian Affairs, 1924*, 13.
104. TRC, NRA, Library and Archives Canada, RG10, volume 6263, file 578-9, part 2, D. M. MacKay to Deputy Minister, 9 August 1949. [ELK-000162]
105. Canada, *Annual Report of the Department of Indian Affairs, 1899*, xxiii.
106. Canada, *Annual Report of the Department of Indian Affairs, 1969–1970*, 128.
107. Canada, *Annual Report of the Department of Indian Affairs, 1890*, 1:94.
108. Canada, *Annual Report of the Department of Indian Affairs, 1969–1970*, 128.
109. Canada, *Annual Report of the Department of Indian Affairs, 1906*, xxxii.
110. TRC, NRA, INAC – Resolution Sector – IRS Historical Files Collection – Ottawa, file 1/25-13, volume 15, R. F. Davey to Assistant Deputy Minister, Indian and Eskimo Affairs, 18 August 1969. [NCA-011279]
111. Canada, *Annual Report of the Department Indian Affairs, 1891*, 99.
112. TRC, NRA, Library and Archives Canada, Winnipeg, RG10, Acc. W86-87/083, box 001, file 501/25-1, volume 2A, J. Malcolm to Friends, 25 May 1975. [PLP-100300]
113. Canada, *Annual Report of the Department of Indian Affairs, 1906*, xxxii.

114. TRC, NRA, INAC – Resolution Sector – IRS Historical Files Collection – Ottawa, file 1/25-13, volume 15, R. F. Davey to Assistant Deputy Minister, Indian and Eskimo Affairs, 18 August 1969. [NCA-011279]
115. Canada, *Annual Report of the Department of Indian Affairs, 1915*, xxvi–xxv.
116. TRC, NRA, Library and Archives Canada, RG10, volume 6267, file 580-1, part. 2, A. F. MacKenzie to Reverend T. B. R. Westgate, 24 April 1933. [DRS-000616]
117. TRC, NRA, Library and Archives Canada, RG10, volume 8638, file 511/6-1-038, part 1, R. S. Davis to Indian Affairs Branch, 15 December 1952. [GUY-000164]
118. TRC, NRA, INAC – Resolution Sector – IRS Historical Files Collection – Ottawa, file E4974-2011, volume 1, Jake Epp to Henry Wilson, 30 August 1979. [GUY-000606]
119. City of Winnipeg, Historical Buildings Committees, "611 Academy – Former Julia Clark School," August 1997, 1–3, 9–10; TRC, NRA, INAC – Resolution Sector – IRS Historical Files Collection – Ottawa, file 6-21-7, volume 1 (Ctrl #25-7), H. M. Jones to Deputy Minister, 4 July 1958. [NCA-011600-0000]
120. TRC, NRA, INAC – Resolution Sector – IRS Historical Files Collection – Ottawa, file 1/25-13, volume 20, D. Hueston to A. Akehurst, 4 July 1973. [PLK-001019]
121. Canada, *Annual Report of the Department of Indian Affairs, 1927*, 14.
122. Canada, *Annual Report of the Department of Indian Affairs, 1958–1959*, 106; Canada, *Annual Report of the Department of Indian Affairs, 1959–1960*, 96.
123. Canada, *Annual Report of the Department of Indian Affairs, 1937*, 208.
124. Canada, *Annual Report of the Department of Indian Affairs, 1958–1959*, 106; Canada, *Annual Report of the Department of Indian Affairs, 1959–1960*, 96.
125. TRC, NRA, Library and Archives Canada – Ottawa, RG85, file 632-108-1, volume 1, box 22, Quarterly Attendance Report/Fort Franklin – NWT, 09/1967–12/1968, "Pupil Residence Quarterly Return, Fort Franklin," 30 September 1967. [FFS-000001-0001]
126. TRC, NRA, Government of Northwest Territories – Education, Culture and Employment, file 73-600-303, volume 2, School Services – Fort Franklin, 01/72–09/73, Transfer No. 0330, box 9, J. A. Coady to N. Macpherson, 22 March 1973. [FFS-000018]
127. Canada, *Annual Report of the Department of Indian Affairs, 1958–1959*, 106.
128. TRC, NRA, Government of Northwest Territories – Education, Culture and Employment, file 73-500-402, volume 2, Fort McPherson Hostel [Anglican] – Quarterly Returns [Fort McPherson], 01/72–12/76, Transfer No. 0330, box 8-21, N. J. Macpherson to Member of the Executive for Education, 21 April 1976. [FHU-002403]
129. McCarthy, *From the Great River,* 159.
130. TRC, NRA, Government of Northwest Territories Archives, file 600-1-1, part 4, School Policy [and Hostels], 1959–1961, Archival box 202-1, Archival Acc. G-1979-003, Department of Northern Affairs and National Resources, "Historic Names for Northern Schools and Residences," news release, 2 March 1961. [RCN-010612-0002]
131. Carney, "Relations in Education," 60.
132. TRC, NRA, INAC – Departmental Library – Ottawa, "Farewell to St. Joseph's School, Fort Resolution, N.W.T.," *Indian Record*, volume XX, number 5, May 1957. [IMR-000160]
133. TRC, NRA, Government of Northwest Territories Archives, file 602, Provincial Schools and Education Systems, 1960–1961, Archival box 211-1, Archival Acc. G-1979-003, Administrator of the Mackenzie to Director, 12 December 1960. [FNU-001695]

134. TRC, NRA, Government of Northwest Territories - Education, Culture and Employment, Miscellaneous Hostel Reports, RIMS ID# 1209, box 9, Student Enrolment in Hostels, 1967–1975. [RCN-007181]
135. TRC, NRA, Government of Northwest Territories Archives, file 602, Provincial Schools and Education Systems, 1960–1961, Archival box 211-1, Archival Acc. G-1979-003, Administrator of the Mackenzie to Director, 12 December 1960. [FNU-001695]
136. TRC, NRA, Government of Northwest Territories - Education, Culture and Employment, Miscellaneous Hostel Reports, RIMS ID #1209, box 9, Student Enrolment in Hostels, 1967–1975. [RCN-007181]
137. TRC, NRA, Government of Northwest Territories Archives, Pupil Residence - General, 1973–1978, Archival box 4-2, Archival Acc. G1995-004, R. L. Julyan to R. W. Halifax, 28 December 1977. [LHU-000685-0001]
138. Roxanna Thompson, "Dehcho Hall to Close its Doors," *Northern News Services* online, 26 January 2009, http://www.nnsl.com/frames/newspapers/2009-01/jan26_09h.html.
139. Canada, *Annual Report of the Department of Indian Affairs, 1958–1959*, 106.
140. TRC, NRA, Government of Northwest Territories - Education, Culture and Employment, Miscellaneous Hostel Reports, RIMS ID #1209, box 9, Student Enrolment in Hostels, 1967–1975. [RCN-007181]
141. TRC, NRA, Government of Northwest Territories Archives, file 600-1-1, part 1A, Education, Schools - General Policy, 1962–1969, Archival box 202-4, Archival Acc. G-1979-003, P. Piché to R. J. Orange, 27 May 1964. [GCU-000178]
142. TRC, NRA, Diocese of Mackenzie - Yellowknife, NWT, Grandin College - Administration Files, Miscellaneous Papers, Letter Sent on Behalf of Bishop P. Piché and his Diocesan Council, 4 June 1985. [GCU-800247]
143. TRC, NRA, Anglican Church of Canada, General Synod Archives, ACC-MSCC-GS 75-103, series 2.15, box 27, file 8, St. Peter's Mission, Hay River, Diocese of Mackenzie River, Parish History, n.d.; [AAC-087477] Hay River Slides, Alf. J. Vale, n.d. [AAC-087480]
144. The Hay River residential school is listed in the 1937–38 Indian Affairs annual report (Canada, *Annual Report of the Department of Indian Affairs, 1938*, 231), but not in the 1938–39 annual report (Canada, *Annual Report of the Department of Indian Affairs, 1939*, 265).
145. Canada, *Annual Report of the Department of Indian Affairs, 1958–1959*, 106; Canada, *Annual Report of the Department of Indian Affairs, 1959–1960*, 96.
146. TRC, NRA, No document location, no document file source, B. Pusharenko, Inuvik, NWT, "Demolition of Former Residential School Called for to Put Bad Memories to Rest," *Edmonton Journal*, 13 August 1998. [GNN-000298-0026]
147. Canada, *Annual Report of the Department of Indian Affairs, 1958–1959*, 106; Canada, *Annual Report of the Department of Indian Affairs, 1959–1960*, 96.
148. TRC, NRA, Government of Northwest Territories - Education, Culture and Employment, ECE [02330-6, 004508], Government of NWT, Yellowknife, NWT, Peter L. McKlusky to Territorial Auditor, 17 December 1975. [SHU-000074-0000]
149. Canada, *Annual Report of the Department of Indian Affairs, 1958–1959*, 106.
150. TRC, NRA, Government of Northwest Territories - Education, Culture and Employment, Misc. Correspondence, 1991–1994, Transfer No. 1531, box 5, C. McLean to J. Stad, 24 June 1994. [AHU-004085]
151. TRC, NRA, Library and Archives Canada, RG10, volume 6054, file 265-1, part 1, Chas Stewart to A. E. MacLean, 22 May 1930. [SRS-000300]

152. TRC, NRA, INAC – Resolution Sector – IRS Historical Files Collection – Ottawa, file 211/6-1-010, volume 6, R. F. Davey to Michael Kearney, 12 June 1967. [SRS-000175]
153. TRC, NRA, Government of Northwest Territories Archives, file A-630/153-11, part 1, Education Facilities – Schools Small Hostels – Eskimo Point, 1961–1966, Archival box 247-12, Archival Acc. G-1979-003, Pupil Residence Quarterly Return, Eskimo Point Student Hostel, 31 March 1962. [EPS-000343]
154. Indian Residential Schools of the Indian Residential Schools Settlement Agreement 2011, IRS School Chart – INAC 2011, document provided to the TRC by Aboriginal and Northern Affairs Canada, 29 September 2011.
155. TRC, NRA, Government of Northwest Territories Archives, file 630-150/12-1,2,3, Cambridge Bay Cottage Hostel General, Reports, 1963–1964, Archival box 247-10, Archival Acc. G-1979-003, Pupil Residence Quarterly Return, Cambridge Bay Federal Hostel, 31 March 1964. [CBS-000002-0001]
156. TRC, NRA, CGS Records Warehouse, Iqaluit, Government of Nunavut, Resid – Correspondence – Kitikmeot, 1991–1992, Kitikmeot Region [Kugluktuk] – box 102, CGS Records Warehouse, Iqaluit, Government of Nunavut, List to Kitikmeot Divisional Education Council, Student Accommodation Information – September 30, 1996, 18 October 1996. [CPU-001700-0002]
157. TRC, NRA, Library and Archives Canada, RG85, volume 711, file 630/158-1, part 5, Government School – Chesterfield Inlet N.W.T., 1956–1957, "Boarding Schools for Eskimos – Chesterfield Inlet," 8 August 1958. [CIU-000485]
158. TRC, NRA, Government of Northwest Territories Archives, CR# 71-602-000, Pupil Residence – General, 04/1968–12/71, Archival box 266, Archival Acc. G1999-046, G. Devitt to Director of Education, 5 December 1969. [CIU-001807]
159. TRC, NRA, Government of Northwest Territories Archives, file 630-145/22-2, Reports and Returns, Coppermine Tent Hostel School, 1954–1956, Archival box 247-3, Archival Acc. G-1979-003, "Report on the Coppermine Experimental Tent Hostel," David S. Wilson, undated report. [CPU-001206-0002]
160. TRC, NRA Library and Archives Canada – Ottawa, RG85, Perm. volume 644, file 630/145-2, part 7, Anglican Schools – Coppermine, N.W.T. [Incl. Tent Hostel] November 1957–December 1959, FA 85-1, Director to Administrator of the Mackenzie, Fort Smith, N.W.T., 26 September 1959. [CPU-000436]
161. TRC, NRA, Government of Northwest Territories Archives, file A-600-1-6-1, part 2, Small Hostel, N.W.T, 1962–1965, Archival box 205-4, Archival Acc. G-1979-003, [Illegible] Director to Administrator of the Arctic, 10 January 1962. [IGS-000239]
162. Indian Residential Schools of the Indian Residential Schools Settlement Agreement 2011, IRS School Chart – INAC 2011, document provided to the TRC by Aboriginal and Northern Affairs Canada, 29 September 2011.
163. TRC, NRA, Government of Northwest Territories – Education, Culture and Employment, Schools Registers and Hostels Forms 1961–1974 [Ukkivik Hostel], Transfer No. 0274, box 4-23, "Student Residence Quarterly Return," September 1971. [FBS-000001]
164. TRC, NRA, No document location, no document file source, B. Pusharenko, Inuvik, NWT, "Demolition of Former Residential School Called for to Put Bad Memories to Rest," *Edmonton Journal*, 13 August 1998. [GNN-000298-0026]
165. Indian Residential Schools of the Indian Residential Schools Settlement Agreement 2011, IRS School Chart – INAC 2011, document provided to the TRC by Aboriginal and Northern Affairs Canada, 29 September 2011.

166. Indian Residential Schools of the Indian Residential Schools Settlement Agreement 2011, IRS School Chart - INAC 2011, document provided to the TRC by Aboriginal and Northern Affairs Canada, 29 September 2011.
167. Indian Residential Schools of the Indian Residential Schools Settlement Agreement 2011, IRS School Chart - INAC 2011, document provided to the TRC by Aboriginal and Northern Affairs Canada, 29 September 2011.
168. Indian Residential Schools of the Indian Residential Schools Settlement Agreement 2011, IRS School Chart - INAC 2011, document provided to the TRC by Aboriginal and Northern Affairs Canada, 29 September 2011.
169. Indian Residential Schools of the Indian Residential Schools Settlement Agreement 2011, IRS School Chart - INAC 2011, document provided to the TRC by Aboriginal and Northern Affairs Canada, 29 September 2011.
170. Indian Residential Schools of the Indian Residential Schools Settlement Agreement 2011, IRS School Chart - INAC 2011, document provided to the TRC by Aboriginal and Northern Affairs Canada, 29 September 2011.
171. TRC, NRA, Government of Northwest Territories Archives, file A-630/170-1, part 1, Education Facilities - Schools Pangnirtung, N.W.T., 1959–1966, Archival box 249-10, Archival Acc. G1979-003, R. L. Kennedy to Regional Administrator, 14 July 1964. [PAS-000083]
172. Indian Residential Schools of the Indian Residential Schools Settlement Agreement 2011, IRS School Chart - INAC 2011, document provided to the TRC by Aboriginal and Northern Affairs Canada, 29 September 2011.
173. TRC, NRA, Government of Northwest Territories Archives, file A-630/159-1, part 1, Education Facilities - School Small Hostels - Baker Lake, 1961–1966, Archival box 248-8, Archival Acc. G-1979-003, M. E. Gordon to Department of Northern Affairs and National Resources, 21 January 1961. [BLS-000320]
174. TRC, NRA, INAC – Resolution Sector – IRS Historical Files Collection – Ottawa, file 600-1-6, volume 10, Hostel Management – N.W.T. [General and Policy], Aug. 1967–Sept. 1968, W. Ivan Mouat, to J. B. Gunn to Regional Administrator to Administrator of the Arctic, 30 January 1968. [RCN-002847]
175. TRC, NRA, Government of Northwest Territories Archives, file A-630/1023-11, volume 1, Small Hostels Broughton Island, 1962–1966, Archival box 251-12, Archival Acc. G-1979-003, Broughton Island Federal School Hostel Quarterly Report, 31 December 1962. [BIS-000001]
176. TRC, NRA, Government of Northwest Territories Archives, file A-630/1023-11, part 1, Small Hostels Broughton Island, 1962–1966, Archival box 251-12, Archival Acc. G-1979-003, Service Agreement of Hostel Mother, Ada Atagoojuk, Broughton Island Hostel, 1 April 1966. [BIS-000097]
177. TRC, NRA, Government of Northwest Territories Archives, file AQR 630/174-11, volume 1, Education Facilities - Small Hostels - Belcher Islands, 1963–1968, Archival box 250-4, Archival Acc. G-1979-003, Peter H. Zacharias to Northern Administration Branch, 31 March 1964. [BES-000002]
178. TRC, NRA, Government of Northwest Territories Archives, file AQR 630/174-1, part 1, Education Facilities - School Belcher Islands, 1960–1969, Archival box 250-3, Archival Acc. G1979-003, H. Helbecque to Northern Administrator, Great Whale River, 24 November 1964. [BES-000036]
179. Graham, *Mush Hole*, 7.
180. TRC, NRA, Library and Archives Canada, RG10, Acc. 1984-85/112, box 47, file 451/25-1, Newspaper article, "Mohawk Institute May Close after 139 Years," no date; [TAY-001133] TRC, NRA, Diocese of Huron Archives, Anglican Church of Canada, Huron University College, London, ON, Luxton Papers, box 27, Indian Reserves, Richard Isaac, Six Nations Council To Whom It May Concern, 13 March 1970; [TAY-001432] TRC, NRA, INAC – Resolution Sector – IRS Historical Files

Collection – Ottawa, file 479/25-13-001, volume 3, G. D. Cromb to Deputy Minister, 20 March 1970. [TAY-003053-0001]

181. Canada, *Annual Report of the Department of Indian Affairs, 1908*, 289.
182. TRC, NRA, Library and Archives Canada, RG10, volume 11091, Shannon File, 1948, Letters to Indian Affairs Branch, J. L. Whitney to Philip Phelan, 31 July 1948. [CRS-002092]
183. TRC, ASAGR, Aboriginal Affairs and Northern Development Canada, letter received 27 July 1976. [AANDC-01471]
184. Auger, *Indian Residential Schools in Ontario*, 193.
185. Taylor, "Northern Algonquians," 350.
186. TRC, NRA, INAC – Resolution Sector – IRS Historical Files Collection – Ottawa, file 486/25-13-1, H. B. Rodine to All Program/Section Heads District Supervisor, 8 April 1976. [FTA-000510-0000]
187. Canada, *Annual Report of the Department of Indian Affairs, 1906*, xxxii.
188. TRC, NRA, INAC – Resolution Sector – IRS Historical Files Collection – Ottawa, file 1/1-8, volume 3 (Ctrl #123-HQ-7), M. Rehaluk to G. K. Gooderham, 11 March 1974. [NCA-016551-0000]
189. TRC, NRA, Library and Archives Canada, RG10, volume 6196, file 464-1, part 1, Report on "Fort William Orphanage," March 1899. [SJS-000153]
190. TRC, NRA, Library and Archives Canada, RG10, volume 11630, file 492/25-2, M. Ouimet to A. F. McWhinnie, 6 August 1968. [SJS-001351]
191. TRC, NRA, Library and Archives Canada – Ottawa, RG10, volume 6468, file 890-1, part 1, Microfilm reel C-8786, A. W. Vowell to Deputy Superintendent General of Indian Affairs, 5 July 1897. [MIS-004738]
192. TRC, NRA, INAC – Resolution Sector – IRS Historical Files Collection – Ottawa, file 487/1-18, volume 1, W. McKim to A. Lacerte, 22, undated. [KNR-000214]
193. Canada, *Annual Report of the Department of Indian Affairs, 1902*, 103.
194. TRC, NRA, INAC – Resolution Sector – IRS Historical Files Collection – Ottawa, file 486/25-13-1, H. B. Rodine to Program/Section Heads, 8 April 1976, [Program/Section Heads]; TRC, NRA, Ontario Regional Service Centre – LAC – Toronto, file 487/25-1, volume 3, Fred Kelly to Erik Weigeldt, 18 November 1976. [CJC-001887]
195. Canada, *Annual Report of the Department of Indian Affairs, 1926*, 17.
196. Canada, *Annual Report of the Department of Indian Affairs, 1969–1970*, 128.
197. General Synod of the Anglican Church of Canada, "Bishop Horden Memorial School."
198. TRC, NRA, INAC – Resolution Sector – IRS Historical Files Collection – Ottawa, file 486/25-13-1, H. B. Rodine to All Program/Section Heads District Supervisor, 8 April 1976. [FTA-000510-0000]
199. *Report of the Special Commissioners 1858*, n.p.
200. TRC, NRA, Library and Archives Canada, RG10, volume 6205, file 468-1, part 3, R. A. Hoey to Dr. McGill, 9 November 1942; [MER-000498] TRC, NRA, Library and Archives Canada, RG10, volume 6205, file 468-1, part 1, M. Benson to Deputy Superintendent General of Indian Affairs, 28 November 1902; [MER-000328] TRC, NRA, Library and Archives Canada, RG10, volume 6205, file 468-1, part 3, R. A. Hoey to Dr. McGill, 9 November 1942; [MER-000498] TRC, NRA, Library and Archives Canada, RG10, volume 6205, file 468-1, part 3, R. A. Hoey to George Dorey, 16 June 1944; [MER-000532] TRC, NRA, Library and Archives Canada, RG10, file 468-1, volume 6205, part 3, R. A. Hoey to George Dorey, 12 June 1943; [IRC-041082] TRC, NRA, Library and Archives Canada, RG10, file 468-1, volume 6205, part 3, George Dorey to R. A. Hoey, 10 June 1943; [MER-000505] TRC, NRA, Library and Archives Canada, RG10, volume 6210, file 468-10, part 5, Samuel Devlin to Indian Affairs, 20 May 1946; [MER-003806-0001] Canada, *Annual Report of the Department of Indian Affairs, 1969–1970*, 128.

201. TRC, NRA, Library and Archives Canada, RG10, volume 11447, file 494/25-2, part 1, Irwin Schantz to D. B. MacBeth, 29 August 1962. [PHD-000451-0000]
202. TRC, NRA, Library and Archives Canada, Margaret Reimer, "Native Mission School Shut Down over Discipline Controversy," *Mennonite Reporter*, volume 19, number 22, 13 November 1989. [PHD-000143]
203. Wilson, *Missionary work,* 129, 130–131.
204. TRC, NRA, Library and Archives Canada, RG10, Acc. 86-87/347, file 411/25-2, volume 1, A. F. McWhinnie to District Superintendent of Education, Sudbury Agency, 8 June 1970. [SWK-007859]
205. Wilson, *Missionary work,* 215.
206. From 1895 onwards, Indian Affairs stopped reporting on the Wawanosh school separately, apparently including the former school's statistics with those for the Shingwauk school. The same principal was responsible for both Anglican schools, which were located in Sault Ste. Marie. Canada, *Annual Report of the Department of Indian Affairs, 1895,* 19, 330.
207. Canada, *Annual Report of the Department of Indian Affairs, 1927,* 18.
208. TRC, NRA, INAC – Resolution Sector – IRS Historical Files Collection – Ottawa, file E-4974-2008, volume 1, V. Gran to J. R. Wright, 29 August 1978. [PLK-000315-0000]
209. Canada, *Annual Report of the Department of Indian Affairs, 1914,* xxii.
210. TRC, NRA, Library and Archives Canada, RG10, volume 11359, file 13/25-2-471, part 3, Reverend Wm. Kearns to Parents and Guardians, 4 July 1958; [NCA-013327] TRC, NRA, The Archives of the Jesuits of Upper Canada, Regis College, Toronto, ON, Jesuit Fathers of Upper Canada Archives, "Parish Announcement," Father E. Dowling, 6 July 1958. [AGA-000812]
211. Canada, *Annual Report of the Department of Indian Affairs, 1914,* xxii.
212. TRC, NRA, Library and Archives Canada, RG10, Acc. 84-85/112, box 51, file 471/25-2, F. L. Hall to Regional Supervisor , 21 June 1962. [AGA-004741] TRC, NRA, United Church of Canada/Victoria University Archives, Acc. No. 83.050C, box 111, file 2, Morley IRS – Correspondence 1961–62, UCC Docs, Toronto, R. F. Davey, Rev. E. E. M. Joblin, 17 August 1962. [UCA-081423]
213. TRC, NRA, Library and Archives Canada, RG10, Acc. 1984-85/112, box 101, file 494/25-1, part 3, I. L. Howes to Assistant Regional Director, 10 January 1973. [PHD-000215]
214. *Fontaine v. Canada (Attorney General),* 2011 CanLII 4938 (ON SC), 6.
215. TRC, NRA, Library and Archives Canada, RG10, volume 7187, file 371/25-1-021, H. M. Jones to Deputy Minister, 22 September 1955. [NCA-005273]
216. TRC, NRA, INAC – Resolution Sector – IRS Historical Files Collection – Ottawa, file 1/25-13, volume 20, D. Hueston to A. Akehurst, 4 July 1973. [PLK-001019]
217. TRC, NRA, Anglican Church of Canada, General Synod Archives, Triennial Report of the Board of Management to the Board of Missions, M.S.C.C. 07/1934, Accession GS 75-2A, Archibald [Fleming], Bishop of the Arctic, "The Arctic," in S. Gould, General Secretary, Board of Management, M.S.C.C., "Triennial Report of the Board of Management, M.S.C.C.," 4 July 1934, 353. [AGS-000185]
218. TRC, NRA, INAC – Resolution Sector – IRS Historical Files Collection – Ottawa, file 371/6-1-019, G. K. Gooderham to E. T. Parker, 27 February 1975. [HFG-000035-0008]
219. TRC, NRA, Anglican Church of Canada, General Synod Archives, ACC-MSCC-GS 75-103, series 3:2, box 55, file 6, S. Gould to D. C. Scott, 18 December 1931. [AAC-090271]
220. TRC, NRA, INAC – Resolution Sector – IRS Historical Files Collection – Ottawa, file 372/25-13-019, volume 1, Laurent Faucher, Director, Financial and Equipment Services, Cree School Board to Jean-Marie St. Jacques, Assistant Director of Finance, Education Department, 2 August 1978. [FTG-000171]

221. Aboriginal and Northern Affairs Canada, List of Recognized Institutions, https://www.aadnc-aandc.gc.ca/eng/1100100015606/1100100015611 (accessed 3 March 2015).
222. Aboriginal and Northern Affairs Canada, List of Recognized Institutions, https://www.aadnc-aandc.gc.ca/eng/1100100015606/1100100015611 (accessed 3 March 2015).
223. TRC, NRA, INAC – Resolution Sector – IRS Historical Files Collection – Ottawa, file 630/304-11, volume 2, T. B. Golding to DIAND, 11 January 1960. [PHQ-005752]
224. TRC, NRA, Library and Archives Canada, file 380/6-2-007, volume 1, C. L'Heureux to W. J. McGuire, 22 March 1970. [PHQ-005693]
225. TRC, NRA, Library and Archives Canada, RG85, Perm. volume 1435, file 600-14, part 1, Seasonal Schools N.W.T.–General, 1959–1964, FA 85-4, Memorandum from Bishop, R. A., A/Chief, Education Division, Northern Administration Branch, Northern Affairs and National Resources, Ottawa to Director, 9 February 1960. [FGR-000012]
226. TRC, NRA, Library and Archives Canada, RG10, 2003-0196-4, box 19, file AQR-630/314-1, "George River Seasonal School Report," November 1960. [FGR-000015-0001]
227. TRC, NRA, Library and Archives Canada, RG10, Acc. 2003-00196-4, file AQR630/313-1, box 19, volume 1, W. G. Devitt to Administrator of the Arctic, Engineering Section, 21 June 1960. [PBH-000107]
228. TRC, NRA, Library and Archives Canada, RG10, Acc. 2003-00196-4, box 19, file AQR630/313-11, volume 1, page 3 of 3, Enrolment form from Meldrum to Regional Superintendent of Schools, Department of Northern Affairs and National Resources, 1 April 1962. [PBH-000121]
229. TRC, NRA, Library and Archives Canada, RG85, volume 1290, file 303/302, part 2, "Great Whale Housing," 21 September 1960. [GWR-000068]
230. TRC, NRA, Library and Archives Canada, RG10, Acc. 2003-00196-4, box 12, file AQR, R. G. Armstrong to Y. Gosselin, 22 December 1970. [GWR-000251]
231. TRC, NRA, INAC – Resolution Sector – IRS Historical Files Collection – Ottawa, file 21/6-1-355, volume 2, Rev. J. E. DeWolf to C. E. Reynolds, 27 March 1963. [LTR-000338-0002]
232. TRC, NRA, Library and Archives Canada, RG55, Acc. 1989-90/143, box 74, file 7878-01, part 1, Status of closed residences as of June 1977. [HFG-000024-0002]
233. *Fontaine v. Canada (Attorney General)*, 2013 CanLII 1293 (QC CS).
234. *Fontaine v. Canada (Attorney General)*, 2013 CanLII 1293 (QC CS).
235. TRC, NRA, INAC – Resolution Sector – IRS Historical Files Collection – Ottawa, file 21/25-1-354, Pointe Bleue Indian Agency, "Confirmation de l'appel téléphonique à Monsieur Jolicoeur du 7 octobre 1960 date de l'ouverture des classes," 12 October 1960. [PTB-000301]
236. TRC, NRA, INAC – Resolution Sector – IRS Historical Files Collection – Ottawa, file E-4974/076, volume NC 3, Rene Carriere to Rejean Perron, 22 April 1991. [BAX-000905-0001]
237. TRC, NRA, INAC – Resolution Sector – IRS Historical Files Collection – Ottawa, file 321/25-1-352 (Ctrl #407-Q-195), Philip Phelan to J. D'Astous, 16 July 1952; [NPC-400716] TRC, NRA, Library and Archives Canada, RG10, Acc. 1999-01431-6, box 125, file 379/16-2-009, part 1, K. A. Cameron to W. Lauchlan, 6 September 1952. [SIR-000504-0000]
238. TRC, NRA, INAC – Resolution Sector – IRS Historical Files Collection – Ottawa, file 379/25-1-009, volume 2 (Ctrl #14-25), G. Cromb to Regional Director, 10 March 1971; [NCA-015502] TRC, NRA, Library and Archives Canada, RG55, Acc. 1989-90/143, box 74, file 7878-01, part 1, Status of closed residences as of June 1977; [HFG-000024-0002] TRC, NRA, INAC – Resolution Sector – IRS Historical Files Collection – Ottawa, file 379/25-1-009, volume 2, A. Gill to G. Cromb, 23 June 1971. [NCA-001483]
239. Canada, *Annual Report of the Department of Indian Affairs, 1889*, 60.

240. TRC, NRA, Library and Archives Canada, RG10, volume 6307, file 653-1, part 2, Director [to Deputy Minister], 22 June 1949. [FHR-000356]
241. Canada, *Annual Report of the Department of Indian Affairs, 1884*, 154.
242. Canada, *Annual Report of the Department of Indian Affairs, 1915*, xxvi.
243. Foran, "'Les Gens de cette place,'" 59.
244. TRC, NRA, INAC – Resolution Sector – IRS Historical Files Collection – Ottawa, file E4965-2013, volume 3, Beauval Residential School, box 1, file 1-5, Memorandum of Understanding and Agreement Re: The Beauval Indian Education Centre, 6 June 1995. [BVL-001306]
245. Canada, *Annual Report of the Department of Indian Affairs, 1901*, xxx.
246. TRC, NRA, Library and Archives Canada, RG10, volume 8756, file 671/25-1-010, "The Fire at the Thunderchild Residential School," J. B. Cabana, January 1948. [THR-000266-0003]
247. Canada, *Annual Report of the Department of Indian Affairs, 1894*, 76.
248. TRC, NRA, INAC – Resolution Sector – IRS Historical Files Collection – Ottawa, file E4974-10474, volume 2, Ray Gamracy to Dana Commercial Credit Canada, 6 June 1996. [SMD-000651-0000]
249. Canada, *Annual Report of the Department of Indian Affairs, 1888*, xii.
250. Gordon's School, Anglican Indian and Eskimo Residential Schools, Anglican Church of Canada, www.anglican.ca/relationships/histories/gordons-school-punnichy, http://www.anglican.ca/relationships/histories/gordons-school-punnichy (accessed 5 May 2014).
251. Canada, *Annual Report of the Department of Indian Affairs, 1899*, 323.
252. TRC, NRA, INAC – Resolution Sector – IRS Historical Files Collection – Ottawa, file E4971-361, volume 3, Myler Savill to Lionel Sparvier, 21 July 1997. [MRS-000002-0001]
253. TRC, NRA, Library and Archives Canada, RG10, volume 6281, file 604-1, part 1, W. McWhinney to E. A. W. R. McKenzie, 10 October 1928. [CTS-000418-0001]
254. TRC, NRA, Library and Archives Canada, RG10, volume 6282, file 604-5, part 7, Philip Phelan to L. J. Bryant, 6 September 1940. [CTS-000474]
255. Canada, *Annual Report for the Department of Indian Affairs, 1889*, 258.
256. TRA, NRA, Library and Archives Canada – Ottawa, RG10, volume 6281, file 604-1, part 1, Rev. W. McWhinney to Secretary, 27 July 1915. [CRW-000208]
257. Canada, *Annual Report of the Department of Indian Affairs, 1928*, 17.
258. Canada, *Annual Report of the Department of Indian Affairs, 1969–1970*, 128.
259. Canada, *Annual Report of the Department of Indian Affairs, 1907, 119.*
260. TRC, NRA, Provincial Archives of Alberta, Anglican Diocese of Athabasca Fonds, Edmonton, AB, Acc. PR1970.0387/1641, box 41, Anglican Diocese of Athabasca Fonds, file A320/572, Indian Schools – General, Official Correspondence of Bishop Sovereign, 1941–1947, Report of Fire at All Saints' School, Lac la Ronge, Sask., 2 February 1947; [PAR-123539] TRC, NRA, Library and Archives Canada, RG10, volume 6317, file 656-5, part 8, R. A. Hoey to C. G. Brault, 29 August 1947. [PAR-003667]
261. Canada, *Annual Report of the Department of Indian Affairs, 1884*, 161.
262. TRC, NRA, INAC – Resolution Sector – IRS Historical Files Collection – Ottawa, file E4974-6-02017, Irvin Starblanket to Roy Bird, 1 October 1997; [PLD-009978-0002] LaRose, "Wrecker's ball Claims White Calf Collegiate"; TRC, NRA, Talking points for the media on the closure of White Calf Collegiate in Lebret, Sask., Andrew Bemister to Media, 26 June 1998; [PLD-014223] TRC, NRA, INAC – Resolution Sector – IRS Historical Files Collection – Ottawa, file E4974-6-02017, volume 1, Huck Andrews to INAC – Resolution Sector – IRS Historical Files Collection – Ottawa, file E4974-6-02017, volume 1, 23 July 1998. [PLD-009201-0001]
263. Canada, *Annual Report of the Department of Indian Affairs, 1889*, 260.

264. TRC, NRA, INAC – Resolution Sector – IRS Historical Files Collection – Ottawa, Muskowekwan Residential School, box 67, file 1, Muskowekwan Education Centre Board of Directors, Minutes 16 July 1997. [MDD-007310-0001]
265. Canada, *Annual Report of the Department of Indian Affairs, 1893*, 75.
266. Canada, *Annual Report of the Department of Indian Affairs, 1944*, 155.
267. Canada, *Annual Report of the Department of Indian Affairs, 1893*, 75.
268. TRC, NRA, National Capital Regional Service Centre – LAC – Ottawa, file 671/6-2-025, volume 4, Onion Lake Band Council Resolution, 31 July 1974. [ORC-008733-0002]
269. TRC, NRA, Library and Archives Canada, RG10, volume 8645, file 651/6-1, part 2, Memorandum to the Deputy Minister, Director [of Indian Affairs], 22 August 1951. [PAR-017615-0000]
270. TRC, NRA, INAC – Resolution Sector – IRS Historical Files Collection – Ottawa, file E4974-1355, volume 8, "Education Centre Set to Re-open," *Prince Albert Herald*, Carrie Hunter, 15 October 1997. [PAR-003103-0001]
271. Canada, *Annual Report of the Department of Indian Affairs, 1944*, 155.
272. TRC, NRA, Library and Archives Canada, RG10, volume 8645, file 651/6-1, part 2, Memorandum to the Deputy Minister, Director [of Indian Affairs], 22 August 1951. [PAR-017615-0000]
273. Canada, *Annual Report of the Department of Indian Affairs, 1890*, xii.
274. Canada, *Annual Report of the Department of Indian Affairs, 1911*, xxvi.
275. Canada, *Annual Report of the Department of Indian Affairs, 1893*, 246.
276. TRC, NRA, Library and Archives Canada, RG10, volume 11539, file 677/25-2, James D. Ormiston to Indian Agent, Kamsack, 31 August 1950. [RLS-001087]
277. Canada, *Annual Report of the Department of Indian Affairs, 1927*, 14.
278. TRC, NRA, Library and Archives Canada, RG10, volume 8638, file 511/6-1-038, part 1, E. S. Jones to J. P. B. Ostrander, 6 September 1952. [GUY-000148]
279. TRC, NRA, Library and Archives Canada – Ottawa, RG10, volume 6479, file 940-1, part 1, "The Chooutla Indian School," *Northern Lights*, volume XV, number 1, February 1927. [CAR-011225]
280. Canada, *Annual Report of the Department of Indian Affairs, 1969–1970*, 128.
281. Peake, *Bishop Who Ate His Boots*, 108; TRC, NRA, Anglican Church of Canada, General Synod Archives Northern Lights, Anglican Church of Canada, Newsletter, "St. Paul's Hostel Dawson," page 8, November 1920. [DYK-201331]
282. TRC, NRA, Library and Archives of Canada, RG10, volume 8762, file 906/25-1-001, R. J. Meek to Indian Affairs Branch, 4 February 1954. [YKS-000750]
283. Johns, "A History of St Peter's Mission," 22; TRC, NRA Anglican Church of Canada, General Synod Archives, Northern Lights, August 1929, "Eskimo Residential School," 16. [DYK-201365]
284. TRC, NRA, Library and Archives Canada – Ottawa, RG85, Perm. volume 1881, file 630/119-2, part 1, Aklavik Area Residential School September 1936–April 1943, FA 85-8, Field Secretary to R. A. Gibson, 11 August 1936. [RCN-004646-0001]
285. TRC, NRA, INAC – Resolution Sector – IRS Historical Files Collection – Ottawa, file 853/25-1, volume 2 (Ctrl #49-5), "Report to the Chief of the Education Division, Indian Affairs Branch, On the Experiment With Integration of Indian Students (R.C.) Into Whitehorse Schools, 1960–1961," E. Cullinane, 1961. [NCA-009389-0001]
286. TRC, NRA, Library and Archives Canada, volume 2, 04/71–02/80, Student Residence, PARC, I. P. Kirkby to G. D. Cromb, 24 November 1971. [YKS-002862, 25-13]
287. TRC, NRA, Library and Archives Canada – Ottawa, file 921-1, part 1, Yukon Agency – Whitehorse Day School – General Admin., 1911–1949, FA 10-17, volume 6477, Microfilm reel C-8793, R. J. Meek

to Unknown, 14 October 1946; [BAP-000307-0001] M. Hackett to P. E. Moore, 24 January 1947. [BAP-000315]

288. TRC, NRA, National Capital Regional Service Centre - LAC - Ottawa, file 1/25-1, volume 15 (locator #H4-77), Yukon, G. R. Cameron to E. A. Côté, 26 May 1966. [NCA-001030]
289. TRC, NRA, INAC - Resolution Sector - IRS Historical Files Collection - Ottawa, 853/25-1, 1956–1968, volume 2, H. M. Jones to Deputy Minister Attention, 18 August 1960. [YHU-090021-0001]
290. Canada, *Annual Report of the Department of Indian Affairs, 1984–1985*, 54; TRC, NRA, INAC - Resolution Sector - IRS Historical Files Collection - Ottawa, E4974-1, volume 1, 10/1979–10/1987, W. F. Lamont to Director, 6 June, 1985. [YKS-005140]

Appendix 3: Persons Found Guilty of Abusing Residential School Students

1. TRC, NRA, No document location, no document file source, Alberta Justice, Clerk of the Provincial Court of Alberta, Conviction, 28 September 1960. [EDM-003354]
2. TRC, ASAGR, R. G. Pooley to R. F. Davey, 23 November 1963; [AANDC-261608] TRC, ASAGR, M. Brodhead to Regional School Superintendent - Alberta, 3 January 1964; [AANDC-261599] "Jail Teacher for One Year," *Winnipeg Free Press*, 26 September 1963.
3. TRC, NRA, Library and Archives Canada, 978/2, volume 1209, 05/1965–06/1971, NAC, V. A. Stephens to H. B. Robinson, 29 May 1970. [ABR-094456]
4. Eva Salinas, "Four-year Hunt Ends in Arrest," *Globe and Mail*, 3 August 2006. http://www.theglobeandmail.com/news/national/four-year-hunt-ends-in-arrest/article713735/.
5. Shea, *Institutional Child Abuse in Canada*, 2.
6. Shea, *Institutional Child Abuse in Canada*, 2.
7. LeBeuf, *Role of the RCMP*, 462.
8. *R. vs. Maczynski*, 1997 CanLII 2491 (BCCA) (appeal of sentence); TRC, NRA, No document location, no document file source, E. Morriset to R. B. Kohls, 28 October 1974. [OBG-002922]
9. "Former Students File Suit Over Sexual, Physical Abuse," Saskatoon *Star-Phoenix*, 26 November 1996; Caroline Murray, "Abuse Victims Recall Atrocities," *Whitehorse Daily Star. 25 November 1996;* Shea, *Institutional Child Abuse in Canada*, 2.
10. Richard Gleeson, "Four Years for Sex Assault," *Northern News Services*, 8 August 1997, http://www.nnsl.com/frames/newspapers/1997-08/aug8_97jail.html; Shea, *Institutional Child Abuse in Canada*, 9.
11. It should be noted that of the eight counts of buggery, five related to offences committed at Lytton and the other three to offences committed at another institution that was not a residential school, the Central City Mission.
12. LeBeuf, *Role of the RCMP*, 462; "School Sex Assaults Bring Jail," *Vancouver Sun*, 4 October 1996; Shea, *Institutional Child Abuse in Canada*, 2.
13. LeBeuf, *Role of the RCMP*, 462; "School Sex Assaults Bring Jail," *Vancouver Sun*, 4 October 1996.
14. Canadian Press, "Former Employee of Residential School Jailed for Sex Abuses," Victoria *Times-Colonist*, January 24, 2004; United Church of Canada Archives, Residential School Archive Project, "The Children Remembered, Alberni Residential School," http://thechildrenremembered.ca/schools-history/alberni/ (accessed 6 November 2013).
15. *R. v. Plint*, [1995] B.C.J. No. 3060 (BCSC); Canadian Press, "Former Employee of Residential School Jailed for Sex Abuses," Victoria *Times-Colonist*, January 24, 2004.

16. *R. v. Plint,* [1995] B.C.J. No. 3060 (BCSC); Canadian Press, "Former Employee of Residential School Jailed for Sex Abuses," Victoria *Times-Colonist,* January 24, 2004.
17. TRC, NRA, Her Majesty the Queen and Harold Daniel McIntee, Reasons for Judgment, Judge C. C. Marnett, Provincial Court of British Columbia, 1 June 1989; [BKM-000204] Ann Rees, "Priest's Victims Admit Sexual Abuse," *The Province* (Vancouver), 19 July 1989; Shea, *Institutional Child Abuse in Canada,* 2–3.
18. *R. v. Constant* (28 September 2005), Court of Queen's Bench (Dauphin Centre), Indictment (5 May 2003), and Disposition (26 September 2005), #03-05-00069, documents obtained from Court of Queen's Bench (Dauphin Centre), Dauphin, Manitoba, 28 January 2014.
19. TRC, NRA, file 630-118/10-1,2,3, part 1A, Fort McPherson Reports, General and Supplies, 1963–1967, Archival box 239-1, Archival Acc. G-1979-003, O. G. Tucker to H. Darkes, 26 March 1963. [FHU-001914]
20. TRC, NRA, Library and Archives Canada – Ottawa, RG22, Perm. volume 1074, file 250-26-17, part 2, Fort McPherson – School, 1959, FA 22-3, David Searle to D. M. Christie, 23 April 1964. [FHU-001380-0001]
21. *R. v. Comeau,* [1998] N.W.T.J. No. 34 (NTSC); Shea, *Institutional Child Abuse in Canada,* 9.
22. Ed Struzik, "Priest's Sordid Past Shocks Parish: Father Houston Was Declared Dangerous Sex Offender, Sent to Prison in 1962," *Edmonton Journal,* 6 June 2002.
23. Andrew Raven, "Grollier Hall Supervisor Sentenced," *Northern News Services,* 20 August 2004, http://www.nnsl.com/frames/newspapers/2004-08/aug20_04crt.html.
24. Justice J. Vertes, "In the Supreme Court of the Northwest Territories, Between Her Majesty the Queen and Paul Leroux," 10 August 1998; Glenn Taylor, "Arrest in Grollier Hall Sex Case: Former Boys Supervisor Faces 32 Counts of Sexual Assault on His Student," *Northern News Services,* 16 June 1997, http://www.nnsl.com/frames/newspapers/1997-06/jun16_97sex.html.
25. Dawn Ostrem, "Back to Court: Paul Leroux Challenges Convictions, Sentence," *Northern News Services,* 26 June 1997, http://www.nnsl.com/frames/newspapers/2000-06/jun26_00back.html.
26. "Ex-residential School Worker Convicted of Abusing Boys," *CBC News,* 5 November 2013, http://www.cbc.ca/news/canada/saskatchewan/ex-residential-school-worker-convicted-of-abusing-boys-1.2415810; "Paul Leroux Gets 3 Years for Residential School Abuse, *CBC News,* 12 December 2013, http://www.cbc.ca/news/canada/saskatoon/paul-leroux-gets-3-years-for-residential-school-abuse-1.2461629.
27. "Nun Guilty in Residential School Assaults," *CBC News,* 28 December 1998, http://www.cbc.ca/news/canada/nun-guilty-in-residential-school-assaults-1.166827.
28. Shea, *Institutional Child Abuse in Canada,* 10. Shea observes only that the sentence did not include jail time.
29. Shea, *Institutional Child Abuse in Canada,* 12.
30. Shea, *Institutional Child Abuse in Canada,* 14–15.
31. "Nun Forced Native Students to Eat Their Own Vomit," *Edmonton Journal,* 25 June 1999.
32. *R. v. Hands,* [1996] O.J. No. 264; LeBeuf, *Role of the RCMP,* 456; Shea, *Institutional Child Abuse in Canada,* 11.
33. TRC, NRA, Library and Archives Canada, RG10, volume 8754, file 654/25-1, volume 1, Henry G. Cook to R. F. Davey, 2 December 1955. [IRC-047015]
34. LeBeuf, *Role of the RCMP,* 457.
35. Ewald Holfeld's last name appears in some records as Schofield and in others as Holdfeld.

36. TRC, NRA, Library and Archives Canada, RG10, volume 6309, file 645-1, part 3, R. S. Davis, extract from Quarterly Report Ending March, 1945, on Touchwood Agency. [IRC-047128]
37. TRC, NRA, Library and Archives Canada, RG10, volume 6309, file 645-1, part 3, Royal Canadian Mounted Police, Constable A. Zimmerman, 28 July 1945. [GDC-010369-0001]
38. TRC, NRA, Library and Archives Canada, RG10, volume 6309, file 645-1, part 3, R. S. Davis to Indian Affairs, 13 February 1947. [GDC-010362-0001]
39. TRC, NRA, Library and Archives Canada, RG10, volume 8754, file 654-1/25-1, volume 1, Henry G. Cook to R. F. Davey, 2 December 1955. [IRC-047015]
40. Mandryk, "Uneasy Neighbours," 210.
41. LeBeuf, *Role of the RCMP*, 458.
42. "Man sentenced to five years for sexually assaulting Native girls," Windspeaker Staff, Prince Albert, Saskatchewan, Windspeaker, Canada's National Aboriginal News Source, Volume 12 Issue 20, 1995, http://www.ammsa.com/publications/windspeaker/man-sentenced-five-years-sexually-assaulting-native-girls, accessed 8 November 2013.
43. *R. v. Frappier*, [1990] Y.J. No.163 (Terr. Ct.) (QuickLaw); Shea, *Institutional Child Abuse in Canada; Criminal Cases*, 17.

Appendix 4: Apologies

1. United Church Social Policy Positions, Apology to Former Students of United Church Indian Residential Schools, and to their Families and Communities (1998) at http://www.united-church.ca/beliefs/policies/1998/a623

Meet the Commissioners

The Honourable Justice Murray Sinclair
Chair

The Honourable Justice Murray Sinclair was appointed Associate Chief Judge of the Provincial Court of Manitoba in March of 1988 and to the Court of Queen's Bench of Manitoba in January 2001. He was Manitoba's first Aboriginal Judge.

Justice Sinclair was born and raised in the Selkirk area north of Winnipeg, graduating from his high school as class valedictorian and athlete of the year in 1968. After serving as Special Assistant to the Attorney General of Manitoba, Justice Sinclair attended the Universities of Winnipeg and Manitoba and, in 1979, graduated from the Faculty of Law at the University of Manitoba.

He was called to the Manitoba Bar in 1980. In the course of his legal practice, Justice Sinclair practiced primarily in the fields of civil and criminal litigation and Aboriginal law. He represented a cross-section of clients but by the time of his appointment, was known for his representation of Aboriginal people and his knowledge of Aboriginal legal issues.

Shortly after his appointment as Associate Chief Judge of the Provincial Court of Manitoba in 1988, Justice Sinclair was appointed Co-Commissioner, along with Court of Queen's Bench Associate Chief Justice A. C. Hamilton, of Manitoba's Aboriginal Justice Inquiry. In November 2000, Justice Sinclair completed the Report of the Pediatric Cardiac Surgery Inquest, a study into the deaths of twelve children in the pediatric cardiac surgery program of Winnipeg's Health Sciences Centre in 1994.

He has been awarded a National Aboriginal Achievement award in addition to many other community service awards, as well as Honourary Degrees from the University of Manitoba, the University of Ottawa, and St. John's College (University of Manitoba). He is an adjunct professor of Law and an adjunct professor in the Faculty of Graduate Studies at the University of Manitoba. Justice Sinclair is married to Katherine Morrisseau-Sinclair (Animiki-quay). They have four children, Manon (Miskodagaginquay) Beaudrie, James (Niigonwedom) (and his partner Lorena Sekwan Fontaine), Déne (Beendighay-geezhigo-quay), Gazheek (Gazhegwenabeek), and one granddaughter Sarah (Nimijiien Niibense) Fontaine-Sinclair.

Dr. Marie Wilson
Commissioner

Marie Wilson has more than 30 years of professional experience as an award-winning journalist, trainer, and senior executive manager. She has also been a university lecturer, a high school teacher in Africa, a senior executive manager in both federal and territorial Crown Corporations, and an independent contractor and consultant in journalism, program evaluation, and project management. She has lived, studied and worked in cross-cultural environments for almost forty years, including Europe, Africa, and various parts of Canada.

As a journalist, Ms Wilson worked in print, radio and television as a regional and national reporter, and later as the Canadian Broadcasting Corporation's senior manager for northern Quebec and the three northern Territories. She was the first television program host of northern Canada's flagship weekly information program, Focus North. Her reports tackled complex issues, from the Quebec sovereignty referendum and national unity debates to the national Constitutional talks of the 1980's; from the settlement of historic aboriginal rights agreements to the state of health in First Nations and Inuit communities; from Papal visits to centennial celebrations of the Riel Rebellion.

As a Regional Director for the Canadian Broadcasting Corporation, Ms Wilson was a pioneer. She launched the first Daily Television News service for northern Canada, against a back-drop of four time zones and ten languages: English, French and eight indigenous. She developed the Arctic Winter Games and True North Concert series, to showcase northern performing artists and traditional indigenous sports for audiences across southern Canada. She fought for the recruitment and development of aboriginal staff and their on-air reflection. She acknowledged staff excellence with the CBC North Awards. She acknowledged the community with program initiatives to support and promote literacy.

A career highlight was to deliver training through the South African Broadcasting Corporation as part of that country's transition to democracy, and coinciding with the start-up of South Africa's own Truth and Reconciliation Commission. For several years she served as an associate board member of what was to become APTN , the Aboriginal Peoples Television Network. Over the years she has worked with various other boards and agencies committed to social justice, journalism and civic engagement, community, spiritual and international development, and the wellbeing of children and youth.

Ms Wilson is the recipient of a CBC North Award for Lifetime Achievement, the Northerner of the Year Award, and various awards and recognitions for journalism, writing excellence, and work-place safety initiatives. In May 2012, she was awarded an honourary Doctor of Laws degree by St. Thomas University of Fredricton, New

Brunswick, in recognition of a professional career "marked by public service and social justice." Ms. Wilson speaks English and French, with some knowledge of Spanish and Sahtu Dene. She and her husband, Stephen Kakfwi, are the proud parents of Kyla, Daylyn and Keenan, and are blessed with four grand-children.

Chief Wilton Littlechild
Commissioner

In 1976, Chief Wilton Littlechild had the distinction of being the first Treaty First Nation person to acquire his law degree from the University of Alberta. He received his Bachelor of Physical Education Degree in 1967 and his Master's Degree in Physical Education in 1975. In June of 2007, the University of Alberta bestowed the Doctor of Laws Degree on Chief Littlechild for his outstanding achievements.

An avid sportsman and athlete, Chief Littlechild has won more than fifty provincial, regional, national and international championships. He has served as a coach and organizer of sports event — being a founder of the North American Indigenous games; and has been inducted into seven Sports Halls of Fame.

Chief Littlechild is a respected lawyer and operates the law firm of J. Wilton Littlechild, Barrister and Solicitor, which is situated in the Ermineskin Reserve. He is a strong advocate for the rights of Indigenous Peoples and promoter of implementation of the treaties between the Indigenous Peoples of Canada and the Crown, now represented by the federal government. Chief Littlechild also served as the Chairperson for the Commission on First Nations and Métis Peoples and Justice Reform, mandated to review the justice system in the province of Saskatchewan.

Chief Littlechild served as a Member of Parliament from 1988 — 1993 for the riding of Wetaskiwin-Rimby. He served on several senior committees in the House of Commons and was a parliamentary delegate to the United Nations. Chief Littlechild organized a coalition of Indigenous Nations that sought and gained consultative status with the Economic and Social Council of the United Nations. He was re-appointed by the E.C.O.S.O.C. President to represent North America and has completed his second and final term as the North American representative to the UN Permanent Forum on Indigenous Issues.

Chief Littlechild was honoured by being appointed the Honourary Chief for the Maskwacis Crees and also honoured by the Chiefs of the Confederacy of Treaty Six First Nations as the International Chief for Treaty No. 6 Confederacy.

Elected by the Chiefs of Treaties 6, 7, 8 (Alberta) as the Regional Chief for the three Treaty territories in October of 2006 to serve a three-year term. He is married to Helen Peacock, and is the father of three children: Teddi, Neil and Megan.

About the Publisher

This edition of the Summary of the Final Report of the Truth and Reconciliation Commission is published by James Lorimer & Company Ltd., Toronto. Lorimer is an independent Canadian book publishing house that has been publishing books that contribute to public knowledge, discussion and debate since 1970.

The company has published other major government reports and documents in book form, to give the public access to this material through bookstores and libraries. These include the final report of the Berger Report on the Mackenzie Valley Pipeline (*Northern Frontier, Northern Homeland - The Report of the Mackenzie Valley Pipeline Inquiry*), 1977, an abridged version of a report by the Combines Investigation Branch (*Canada's Oil Monopoly*, 1981), and *The Supreme Court Decisions on the Canadian Constitution,* the court's historic ruling on repatriation of the Canadian constitution, 1981.

For more information on the publishing house and its books, go to www.lorimer.ca.

Index

MARQUIS
Québec, Canada